TRADITIONS & ENCOUNTERS

TRADITIONS & ENCOUNTERS

A GLOBAL PERSPECTIVE ON THE PAST

JERRY H. BENTLEY

University of Hawai`i

. . .

HERBERT F. ZIEGLER

University of Hawai`i

McGraw-Hill College

Boston   Burr Ridge, IL   Dubuque, IA   Madison, WI   New York   San Francisco   St. Louis
Bangkok   Bagotá   Caracas   Lisbon   London   Madrid
Mexico City   Milan   New Delhi   Seoul   Singapore   Sydney   Taipei   Toronto

McGraw-Hill College

A Division of The McGraw-Hill Companies

TRADITIONS AND ENCOUNTERS: A GLOBAL PERSPECTIVE ON THE PAST

 This book is printed on acid-free paper.

1 2 3 4 5 6 7 8 9 0 VNH/VNH 9 3 2 1 0 9 8

ISBN 0-07-228842-6

Editorial director: *Jane E. Vaicunas*
Senior sponsoring editor: *Lyn Uhl*
Marketing manager: *Annie Mitchell*
Project manager: *Marilyn M. Sulzer*
Senior production supervisor: *Sandra Hahn*
Designer: *Becky Lemna*
Senior photo research coordinator: *Carrie K. Burger*
Photo research: *Deborah Bull/PhotoSearch, Inc.*
Art editor: *Brenda A. Ernzen*
Illustrations: *Magellon Geographix*
Compositor: *Shepherd, Inc.*
Typeface: *10/12 Galliard*
Printer: *Von Hoffmann Press, Inc.*

www.mhhe.com

BRIEF CONTENTS

. . .

v

DETAILED CONTENTS

· · ·

PART I

THE EARLY COMPLEX SOCIETIES, 3500 TO 500 B.C.E.   2

PART II

THE FORMATION OF CLASSICAL SOCIETIES, 500 B.C.E. TO 500 C.E.   126

PART III
THE POST CLASSICAL ERA, 500 TO 1000 C.E.   274

PART IV

AN AGE OF CROSS-CULTURAL INTERACTION, 1000 TO 1500 C.E.   406

LIST OF MAPS

• • •

PREFACE

. . .

During the 1990s the term *globalization* entered the vocabulary of politicians, journalists, scholars, and others who sought to understand the increasingly tight connections linking the world's lands and peoples. By the late twentieth century, the world's transportation, communication, and trade networks had become more intricate than ever before. Meanwhile, pollution, environmental change, and weapons of mass destruction loomed as potential threats to the world's peoples on a scale never before seen. The concept of globalization effectively draws attention to these conditions and problems of the contemporary world. Yet only in the context of past experience is it possible to understand the nature and the problems of the contemporary world. Technological innovation, ethnic tensions, environmental change, and political conflicts all grow from deep roots in world history: there is a long historical context for contemporary globalization.

This book offers an analysis of world history from the emergence of the human species to the present. During an era when peoples from all parts of the earth meet, mingle, interact, and do business with each other, a global perspective has become an essential tool for informed citizenship in the contemporary world. The study of world history involves the application of a global perspective to the human past, and it offers a vision of the past appropriate for an interdependent world.

Given the range of human diversity, the study of world history is a daunting challenge. Economically, for example, human societies have supported themselves in various ways over the millennia. The earliest human groups were foragers who provided for themselves by hunting, fishing, and gathering edible products from the natural environments around them. After 6000 B.C.E. human groups turned increasingly to agriculture and herding, which provided them with larger supplies of food and allowed their populations to expand dramatically. Since the eighteenth century C.E., scientific and technological innovation has underwritten the spread of industrial production, which has transformed societies worldwide and laid a foundation for more rapid population growth than ever before.

Human communities have adopted widely varying forms of political and social as well as economic organization. Foraging peoples have usually lived in small groups led by strong or charismatic individuals. Agricultural peoples have organized themselves in diverse communities, including small villages, bustling city-states, regional kingdoms, and far-flung empires, and within their societies they have recognized classes of rulers, priests, aristocrats, commoners, and sometimes slaves as well. Industrial peoples have lived mostly in national states, but they have devised many and varied ways to organize their public affairs and distribute the economic and social rewards that their communities generate.

To complicate matters further, the cultural traditions elaborated by the world's peoples are even more diverse than the forms of economic, political , and social organization that they have adopted. While most peoples have recognized one or more deities responsible for creating and sustaining the world, they have understood the nature of the gods in profoundly different ways, and they have formulated countless ways to honor the gods and to establish relationships between human and divine beings. Quite apart from their religious beliefs, the world's peoples have devised radically different ways to think about moral and philosophical problems, understand the natural world, and express themselves aesthetically through literature, music, dance, and art.

Given this manifold diversity, it might seem that masses of unrelated detail threaten to swamp any effort to deal with all the world's history. This book seeks to avoid that hazard by focusing on two themes—traditions and encounters—that help to bring order to the study of world history.

From their earliest days on earth, human beings have generated distinctive political, social, economic, and cultural traditions that have guided affairs in their own societies. Some of these traditions arose and disappeared relatively quickly, but others influenced human affairs over the centuries and millennia, sometimes up to the present day. Thus one of the principal purposes of this book is to examine the development of political, social, economic, and cultural traditions that have shaped the lives and experiences of the world's peoples. Emphasis will fall especially on the large, densely populated, complex, city-based societies that have most deeply influenced the course of history for the past 6,000 years, but smaller and less powerful societies will also receive their share of attention.

While elaborating political, social, economic, and cultural traditions to organize their own affairs, the world's peoples have also interacted regularly with each other since the earliest days of human history. By addressing the theme of encounters between peoples of different societies, this book will draw attention to processes of cross-cultural interaction that have been some of the most effective agents of change in all of world history. In the form of mass migrations, campaigns of imperial expansion, long-distance trade, biological exchanges, transfers of technological skills, and the spread of religious and cultural traditions, these cross-cultural interactions have profoundly influenced the experiences of individual societies as well as the development of the world as a whole.

Thus, from beginning to end, this book will focus on the twin themes of traditions and encounters, which in combination go a long way toward accounting for the historical development of the human species on planet earth. By examining humanity's common historical experience in global context, the book seeks to offer a vision of the past that is both meaningful and appropriate for the interdependent world of contemporary times.

A BRIEF NOTE ON USAGE

. . .

This book qualifies dates as B.C.E. ("Before the Common Era") or C.E. ("Common Era"). In practice, B.C.E. refers to the same epoch as B.C. ("Before Christ"), and C.E. refers to the same epoch as A.D. (*Anno Domini,* a Latin term meaning "in the year of the Lord"). As historical study becomes a global, multicultural enterprise, however, scholars increasingly prefer terminology that does not apply the standards of one society to all the others. Thus reference in this book to B.C.E. and C.E. reflects emerging scholarly convention concerning the qualification of historical dates.

Measurements of length and distance appear here according to the metric system, followed by their English-system equivalents in parentheses.

The book transliterates Chinese names and terms into English according to the *pinyin* system, which is increasingly displacing the more cumbersome Wade-Giles system. Transliteration of names and terms from other languages follows contemporary scholarly conventions.

Dear History Student,

This textbook is a preliminary version of Bentley/Ziegler: TRADITIONS AND ENCOUN-
TERS: A GLOBAL PERSPECTIVE ON THE PAST. McGraw-Hill will publish this book
next summer in full color and it will then be available to professors and students across the
country. We would love to have your opinions now in order to make the final version the best
possible book for students of world history.

Background on TRADITIONS AND ENCOUNTERS.

Given the vastness of the topic of world history, this text seeks to order its analysis through a
focus on **traditions and encounters.** From human beings' earliest days, they have generated distinctive political, social, economic, and cultural traditions that have guided affairs in their own societies. One of the principle purposes of this book is to examine the development of these traditions. The world's peoples have also interacted regularly with others since the earliest days of
human history. By addressing these encounters between peoples of different societies, this book
will draw attention to processes of cross-cultural interaction that have been some of the most effective agents of change in all of world history. Please consider the following questions.

In your reading did you see evidence of these twin themes? Please describe.

Each chapter opens with a story (and often it focuses on a cross-cultural encounter). Which is
your favorite story and why?

The large series of maps throughout the text were created especially for this book and with
students in mind. Did you find them clear and well labeled? Can you point to any particular
maps that helped you better understand an event or concept? (The maps will be full color in
the final version of the book).

Would you like to have a study guide or workbook on CD-ROM to accompany this book?
What would you like included?

Do you use the Internet to do research for this course, or for any other courses? Would you
like to be able to visit a website for this book where you could take quizzes and be guided to
other sites of related interest?

Do you have any other comments about this book that we haven't asked about?

In general how would you rate this text overall? Please give it a letter grade (A+, A, B, C...)

What is your name, college, major, address, e-mail address?

May we have permission to quote your remarks in advertising?

Thank you for your time and for your comments on this book. I look forward to reading
about your experiences.

Sincerely,   Please mail, e-mail, or fax your comments to:
Lyn Uhl   McGraw-Hill Higher Education
Senior Sponsoring Editor, History   699 Boylston St., Suite 20
                                        Boston, MA 02116
                                        Fax: (617)375-2285; E-mail: lyn_uhl@mcgraw-hill.com

TRADITIONS & ENCOUNTERS

THE EARLY COMPLEX SOCIETIES, 3500 TO 500 B.C.E.

. . .

For thousands of years after the emergence of the human species, human beings lived in tiny communities with no permanent home. They formed compact, mobile societies, each consisting of a few dozen people, and they traveled regularly in pursuit of game and edible plants. From the vantage point of the fast-moving present, that long first stage of human experience on the earth might seem slow paced and almost changeless. Yet intelligence set human beings apart from the other members of the animal kingdom and enabled human groups to invent tools and techniques that enhanced their ability to exploit the natural environment. Human beings gradually emerged as the most dynamic species of the animal kingdom, and even in remote prehistoric times they altered the face of the earth to suit their needs.

Yet humans' early exploitation of the earth's resources was only a prologue to the extraordinary developments that followed the introduction of agriculture. About twelve thousand years ago human groups began to experiment with agriculture, and it soon became clear that cultivation provided a larger and more reliable food supply than did foraging. Groups that turned to agriculture experienced rapid population growth, and they settled in permanent communities. The world's first cities, which appeared about six

thousand years ago, quickly came to dominate political and economic affairs in their respective regions. Indeed, since the appearance of cities, the earth and its creatures have fallen progressively under the influence of complex societies organized around cities.

The term *complex society* refers to a form of large-scale social organization that emerged in several parts of the ancient world. Early complex societies all depended on robust agricultural economies in which cultivators produced more food than they needed for their own subsistence. This agricultural surplus enabled many individuals to congregate in urban settlements, where they devoted their time and energy to specialized tasks other than food production. Political authorities, government officials, military experts, priests, artisans, craftsmen, and merchants all lived off this surplus agricultural production. Through their organization of political, economic, social, and cultural affairs, complex societies had the capacity to shape the lives of large populations over extensive territories.

During the centuries from 3500 to 500 B.C.E., complex societies arose independently in several widely scattered regions of the world, including Mesopotamia, Egypt, northern India, China, Mesoamerica, and the central Andean region of South America. Most complex societies sprang from small agricultural communities situated either in river valleys or near sources of water that cultivators could tap to irrigate their crops. All established political authorities, built states with formal governmental institutions, collected surplus agricultural production in the form of taxes or tribute, and distributed it to those who worked at tasks other than agriculture. Complex societies traded enthusiastically with peoples who had access to scarce resources, and in an effort to ensure stability and economic productivity in neighboring regions, they often sought to extend their authority to surrounding territories.

Complex societies generated much more wealth than did hunting and gathering groups or small agricultural communities. Because of their high levels of organization, they also were able to preserve wealth and pass it along to their heirs. Some individuals and families accumulated great personal wealth, which enhanced their social status. When bequeathed to heirs and held within particular families, this accumulated wealth became the foundation for social distinctions. These societies developed different kinds of social distinctions, but all recognized several classes of people, including ruling elites, common people, and slaves. Some societies also recognized distinct classes of aristocrats, priests, merchants, artisans, free peasants, and semifree peasants.

All complex societies required cultivators and individuals of lower classes to support the more privileged members of society by paying taxes or tribute (often in the form of surplus agricultural production) and also by providing labor and military service. Cultivators often worked not only their own lands but also those belonging to the privileged classes. Individuals from the lower classes made up the bulk of their societies' armies and contributed the labor for large construction projects such as city walls, irrigation and water control systems, roads, temples, palaces, pyramids, and royal tombs.

The early complex societies also created sophisticated cultural traditions. Most of them either invented or borrowed a system of writing that made it possible to record information and store it for later use. They first used writing to keep political, administrative, and business records, but they soon expanded on these utilitarian applications and used writing to construct traditions of literature, learning, and reflection.

Cultural traditions took different forms in different complex societies. Some societies devoted resources to organized religions that sought to mediate between human communities and the gods, whereas others left religious observances largely in the hands of individual family groups. All of them paid close attention to the heavens, however, since they needed to gear their agricultural labors to the changing seasons.

All the complex societies organized systems of formal education that introduced intellectual elites to skills such as writing and astronomical observation deemed necessary for their societies' survival. In many cases reflective individuals also produced works that explored the nature of humanity and the relationship between human beings, the world, and the gods. Some of these works inspired religious and philosophical traditions for two millennia and more.

Complex society was not the only form of social organization that early human groups constructed, but it was an unusually important and influential type of society. Complex societies produced much more wealth and harnessed human resources on a much larger scale than did bands of hunting and gathering peoples, small agricultural communities, or nomadic groups that herded domesticated animals. As a result, complex societies deployed their power, pursued their interests, and promoted their values over much larger regions than did smaller societies. Indeed, most of the world's peoples have led their lives under the influence of complex societies.

SOUTHWEST ASIA	EAST ASIA	SOUTH ASIA	AFRICA	AMERICAS AND OCEANIA
100,000 B.C.E.	100,000 B.C.E.	100,000 B.C.E.	100,000 B.C.E.	100,000 B.C.E.
Neandertal appearance (100,000) Cro-Magnon appearance (40,000) Venus figurines Cave paintings at Lascaux and Altamira Beginnings of agriculture (10,000) Neolithic age	Paleolithic villages	Paleolithic villages	Paleolithic villages	Human migration to Australia and New Guinea (60,000) Human migration from Siberia to Alaska (40,000) Glaciers melt; Americas isolated again (20,000) Human migration to South America (12,000)
8000 B.C.E.	8000 B.C.E.	8000 B.C.E.	8000 B.C.E.	8000 B.C.E.
Jericho (8000) Çatal Hüyük (7250) Pottery (7000) Copper metallurgy; textile production (6000) Rise of cities (4000)	Domestication of rice (7000) Neolithic villages in Yellow River (Huang He) valley (5000) Yangshao culture (5000–3000) Banpo	Beginnings of agriculture (8000)	Beginnings of agriculture in Nile valley (5000)	Beginnings of agriculture in Mesoamerica (8000) Beginnings of maize cultivation in Mesoamerica (5000) Beginnings of agriculture in New Guinea (5000) First journeys of Austronesians to Bismarck and Solomon Islands (4000)
3500 B.C.E.	3500 B.C.E.	3500 B.C.E.	3500 B.C.E.	3500 B.C.E.
Complex society in Mesopotamia (3500) Cuneiform Epic of Gilgamesh Bronze metallurgy Migration of Hittites into Anatolia (3000) Phoenicians dominate trade in Mediterranean (2500) Mesopotamian unification under Sargon of Akkad (2334) Collapse of Sargon's empire (2100)	Xia dynasty (2200–1766) Erlitou Dikes, dams, flood control projects Metallurgy	Neolithic villages (3500) Rise of cities (3000) Trade with Mesopotamia (3000–1750) Harappan society Harappa and Mohenjo-Daro Written language Sophisticated water and sewage system	Unification under Menes (3100) Archaic period (3100–2660) Hieroglyphics Egyptians sail into Mediterranean Trade with Mesopotamians and Harappans Old Kingdom (2660–2180) Pyramid of Khufu at Giza Middle Kingdom (2080–1640)	Beginnings of agriculture in South America (2500)

SOUTHWEST ASIA	EAST ASIA	SOUTH ASIA	AFRICA	AMERICAS AND OCEANIA
2000 B.C.E.	2000 B.C.E.	2000 B.C.E.	2000 B.C.E.	2000 B.C.E.
Hebrew patriarch Abraham migrates out of Mesopotamia (1800) Early monotheism Hammurabi (1792–1750) Code of Hammurabi Phoenician creation of first alphabet (1500) Rise of Hittites (1400) Iron metallurgy Moses and Ten Commandments (1300) David and Solomon (1000–920)	Shang dynasty (1766–1122) Ao and Yin Written language Bronze metallurgy Oracle bones Zhou dynasty (1122–256) Mandate of Heaven	Decline of Harappan society (2000) Deforestation of Indus valley Mohenjo-Daro and Harappa cease to exist (1700) Collapse of Harappan society (1500) Migration of Aryans (Indo-Europeans) Sanskrit language Caste system *Vedas* (1300)	*The Satire of the Trades* Egyptians sail into Red Sea and western Arabian Sea Migration of Hyksos into Nile delta Bronze metallurgy Nubian expansion New Kingdom (1570–1075) Tuthmosis III (1490–1436) Queen Hatshepsut (1503–1482) Akhenaten (1364–1347) and monotheist worship of Aton	Austronesians reach Vanuatu and New Caledonia (2000), Fiji (1500), Tonga and Samoa (1000) First of South American pottery, temples, pyramids (1800) Olmecs (1200) San Lorenzo (1200–800) Olmec heads Calendar
1000 B.C.E.	1000 B.C.E.	1000 B.C.E.	1000 B.C.E.	1000 B.C.E.
Phoenician colonies in Mediterranean (1200–800) Assyrian empire (744–612) Iron weapons	Iron metallurgy (1000) Trade with societies in the Yangzi River (Chang Jiang) valley (1000) Zhou capital, Hao, sacked (771) Zhou classics *Book of Songs* (600) Period of the Warring States (403–221) Qin unification (221)	Origins of Hinduism *Upanishads* (800–400) *Lawbook of Manu* (100)	Nubians spread iron metallurgy throughout sub-Saharan Africa Nubian kingdom of Kush conquers Egypt (750) Kush driven out of Egypt by Assyrians (664)	Chavín cult in Andes (1000) Later Olmec capitals La Venta (800–400); Tres Zapotes (400–100) Austronesians reach Tahiti and Marquesas Islands (200), Hawai'i and Easter Island (100 C.E.), New Zealand (500 C.E.) Mochica state in Andes (300–700 C.E.) Teotihuacan Pyramid of the Sun Maya (300–900 C.E.) Kaminaljuyú and Tikal Mathematics, concept of zero Calendar and writing

BEFORE HISTORY

. . .

Throughout the evening of 30 November 1974, a tape player in an Ethiopian desert blared the Beatles' song "Lucy in the Sky with Diamonds" at top volume. The site was an archaeological camp at Hadar, a remote spot about 160 kilometers (100 miles) northeast of Addis Ababa. The music helped fuel a spirited celebration: earlier in the day, archaeologists had discovered the skeleton of a woman who died 3.5 million years ago. Scholars refer to this woman's skeleton as AL 288–1, but the woman herself has become by far the world's best-known prehistoric individual under the name Lucy.

At the time of her death, from unknown causes, Lucy was twenty-five to thirty years of age. She stood just over 1 meter (about 3.5 feet) tall and probably weighed about 25 kilograms (55 pounds). After she died, sand and mud covered Lucy's body, hardened gradually into rock, and entombed her remains. By 1974, however, rain waters had eroded the rock and exposed Lucy's fossilized skeleton. The archaeological team working at Hadar eventually found 40 percent of Lucy's bones, which together form the most complete and best-preserved skeleton of any early human ancestor. Later searches at Hadar turned up bones belonging to perhaps as many as sixty-five additional individuals, although no other collection of bones rivals Lucy's skeleton for completeness.

Analysis of Lucy's skeleton and other bones found at Hadar demonstrates that the earliest ancestors of modern human beings walked upright on two feet. Erect walking is crucial for human beings because it frees their arms and hands for other tasks. Lucy and her contemporaries did not possess large or well-developed brains—Lucy's skull was about the size of a small grapefruit—but unlike the neighboring apes, which used their forelimbs for locomotion, Lucy and her companions could carry objects with their arms and manipulate tools with their dexterous hands. These abilities enabled Lucy and her companions to survive better than many other species. As the brains of our human ancestors grew larger and more sophisticated—a process that gradually occurred over several million years—human beings learned to take even better advantage of their arms and hands and established flourishing communities throughout the world.

According to geologists the earth came into being some five billion years ago. The first living organisms made their appearance hundreds of millions of years later. In their wake came increasingly complex creatures such as fish, birds, reptiles, and mammals. About thirty million years ago, short, hairy, monkeylike animals began to populate tropical regions of the world. Humanlike cousins to these animals began to appear only four or five million years ago, and modern human beings only about forty thousand years ago.

Olduvai Gorge in modern Tanzania, where archaeologists have uncovered some of the earliest human remains. • John Reader/Science Photo Library/Photo Researchers, Inc.

Even the most sketchy review of the earth's natural history clearly shows that human society has not developed in a vacuum. The earliest human beings inhabited a world already well stocked with flora and fauna, a world shaped for countless eons by natural rhythms that governed the behavior of all the earth's creatures. Human beings made a place for themselves in this world, and over time they learned to take advantage of the earth's resources more successfully than any other creature. Indeed, it has become clear in recent years that the human animal has exploited the natural environment so thoroughly that the earth has undergone irreversible changes.

A discussion of prehistoric times might seem peripheral to a book that deals with the history of human societies, their origins, development, and interactions. By scholarly convention, *prehistory* refers to the period before the invention of writing, and *history* refers to the period after human communities recorded written information. The availability of written documents vastly enhances the ability of scholars to understand past ages, but human history has followed paths first explored in the earliest days of human existence. Indeed, the historical development of human society is comprehensible only in the light of human experiences in prehistoric times. Long before the invention of writing, prehistoric human beings made a place for their species in the natural world and laid the social, economic, and cultural foundations on which their successors built increasingly complex societies.

 # THE EVOLUTION OF *HOMO SAPIENS*

During the past century or so, archaeologists, evolutionary biologists, and other scholars have vastly increased the understanding of human origins and the lives our distant ancestors led. Their work has done much to clarify the relationship between human beings and other animal species. On one hand, researchers have shown that human beings share some remarkable similarities with the large apes. This point is true not only of external features, such as physical form, but also of the basic elements of genetic makeup and body chemistry—DNA, chromosomal patterns, life-sustaining proteins, and blood types. In the case of some of these elements, scientists have been able to observe only a 1 percent difference between humans and apes. Biologists therefore place human beings in the order of primates, along with monkeys, chimpanzees, gorillas, and the various other large apes.

On the other hand, human beings clearly stand out as the most distinctive of the primate species. Small differences in genetic makeup and body chemistry have led to enormous differences in levels of intelligence and ability to exercise control over the natural world. Human beings developed an extraordinarily high order of intelligence, which enabled them to devise tools, technologies, language skills, and other means of communication and cooperation. Whereas other animal species adapted physically and genetically to their natural environment, human beings altered the natural environment to suit their own needs and desires—a process that began in remote prehistory and continues in the present day. Over the long run, too, intelligence endowed humans with immense potential for social and cultural development.

The Hominids

A series of spectacular discoveries in east Africa has thrown valuable light on the evolution of the human species. In Tanzania, Kenya, Ethiopia, and other places, archaeologists have unearthed bones and tools of human ancestors going back at least five million years. The Olduvai Gorge in Tanzania and Hadar in Ethiopia have yielded especially rich remains of individuals like the famous Lucy. These individuals probably represented several different species belonging to the genus *Australopithecus* ("the southern ape"), which flourished in east Africa during the long period from about four million to one million years ago.

In spite of its name, *Australopithecus* was not an ape but rather a hominid—a creature belonging to the family Hominidae, which includes human and humanlike species. Evolutionary biologists recognize *Australopithecus* as a genus standing alongside *Homo* (the genus in which biologists place prehistoric as well as modern human beings) in the family of hominids. Compared to our own species, *Homo sapiens,* Lucy and other australopithecines would seem short, hairy, and limited in intelligence. They stood something over one meter (three feet) tall, weighed 25 to 55 kilograms (55 to 121 pounds), and had a brain size of about 500 cubic centimeters. (The brain size of modern humans averages about 1,500 cc.)

Australopithecus

Compared to other ape and animal species, however, australopithecines were sophisticated creatures. They walked upright on two legs, which enabled them to use their arms independently for other tasks. They had well-developed hands with opposable thumbs, which enabled them to grasp tools and perform intricate operations. They almost certainly had some ability to communicate verbally, although analysis of their skulls suggests that the portion of the brain responsible for speech was not very large or well developed.

The intelligence of australopithecines was sufficient to allow them to plan complex ventures. They often traveled deliberately—over distances of 15 kilometers (9.3 miles) and more—to obtain the particular kinds of stone that they needed to fashion tools. Chemical analyses show that the stone from which australopithecines made tools was often available only at sites distant from the camps where archaeologists discovered the finished tools. These tools included choppers, scrapers, and other implements for food preparation. The later australopithecines may have also learned to control fire—to build, tend, and extinguish a fire as they wished. With the aid of their tools and intelligence, australopithecines established themselves securely throughout most of eastern and southern Africa.

Fossilized footprints preserved near Olduvai Gorge in modern Tanzania show that hominids walked upright some 3.5 million years ago. • John Reader/Science Photo Library/Photo Researchers, Inc.

MAP [1.1] • Global
spread of hominids and
homo sapiens.

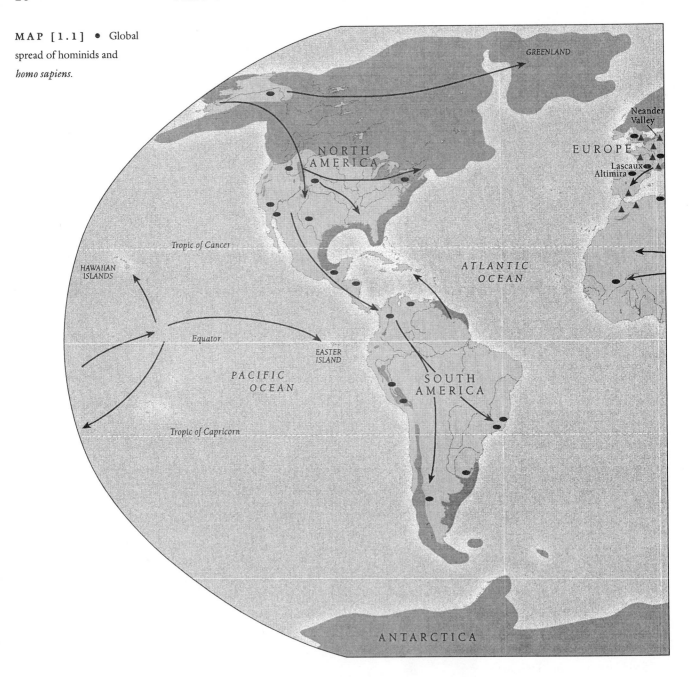

Homo Erectus   Beginning about one million years ago, australopithecines gradually disappeared
as new species of hominids possessing greater intelligence evolved and displaced
their predecessors. The new species belonged to the genus *Homo* and thus represented creatures considerably different from the australopithecines. Most important
of them was *Homo erectus*—"upright-walking human"—who flourished from about
1.5 million to 200,000 years ago. *Homo erectus* possessed a larger brain than the
australopithecines—the average capacity was about 1,000 cc—and fashioned more
sophisticated tools as well. To the australopithecine choppers and scrapers, *Homo*

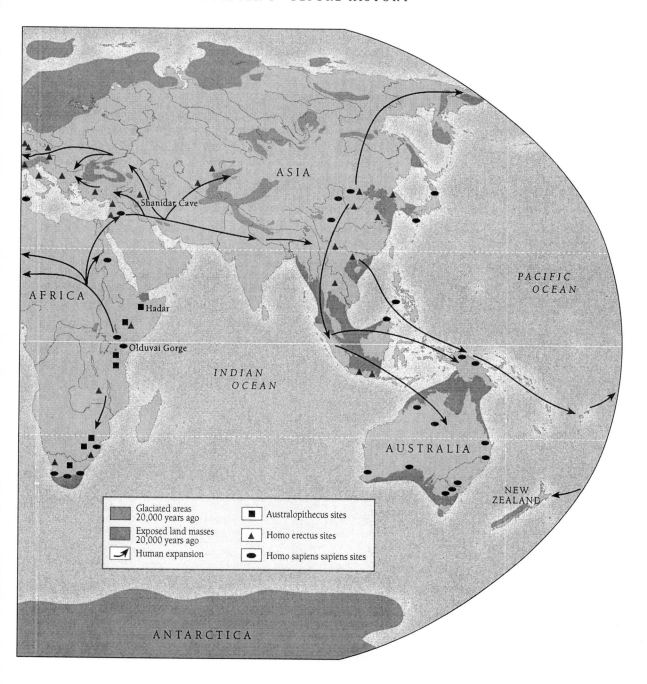

erectus added cleavers and hand axes, which not only were useful in hunting and food preparation but also provided protection against predators. *Homo erectus* definitely knew how to control fire, which furnished the species with a means to cook food, a defense against large animals, and a source of artificial heat.

Even more important than tools and fire were intelligence and language skills, which enabled individuals to communicate complex ideas to each other. Archaeologists have determined, for example, that bands of *Homo erectus* men conducted their hunts in well-coordinated ways that presumed prior communication. Many sites associated with *Homo erectus* served as camps for communities of hunters. The quantities of animal remains found at those sites—particularly bones of large and dangerous animals such as elephant, rhinoceros, and bear—provide evidence that hunters worked in groups and brought their prey back to their camps. Cooperation of this sort presumed both high intelligence and effective language skills.

Migrations of Homo Erectus
With effective tools, fire, intelligence, and language, *Homo erectus* gained increasing control over the natural environment and introduced the human species into widely scattered regions. Whereas australopithecines had not ventured beyond eastern and southern Africa, *Homo erectus* migrated to north Africa and the Eurasian landmass. Beginning about five hundred thousand years ago, *Homo erectus* groups moved to southwest Asia and beyond to Europe, south Asia, east Asia, and southeast Asia. By two hundred thousand years ago they had established themselves throughout the temperate zones of the eastern hemisphere, where archaeologists have unearthed many specimens of their bones and tools.

Homo Sapiens

Like *Australopithecus,* though, *Homo erectus* faded before the advance of more intelligent and successful human species. *Homo sapiens* ("consciously thinking human") evolved perhaps as early as 250,000 years ago and has skillfully adapted to the natural environment ever since. Early *Homo sapiens* already possessed a large brain—one approaching the size of modern human brains. More important than the size of the brain, though, is its structure: the modern human brain is especially well developed in the frontal regions, where conscious and reflective thought takes place. This physical feature provided *Homo sapiens* with an enormous advantage. Although not endowed with great strength and not equipped with natural means of attack and defense—claws, beaks, fangs, shells, venom, and the like—*Homo sapiens* possessed a remarkable intelligence that provided a powerful edge in the contest for survival. It enabled individuals to understand the structure of the world around them, to organize more efficient methods of exploiting natural resources, and to communicate and cooperate on increasingly complex tasks.

Migrations of Homo Sapiens
Intelligence enabled *Homo sapiens* to adapt to widely varying environmental conditions and to establish the species securely throughout the world. Beginning more than one hundred thousand years ago, communities of *Homo sapiens* spread throughout the eastern hemisphere and populated the temperate lands of Africa, Europe, and Asia, where they encountered *Homo erectus* groups that had inhabited those regions for one hundred thousand years or more. *Homo sapiens* soon moved beyond the temperate zones, though, and established communities in progressively colder regions—migrations that were possible because their intelligence allowed *Homo sapiens* to fashion warm clothes from animal skins and to build effective shelters against the cold.

Between 120,000 and 25,000 years ago, *Homo sapiens* extended the range of human population even further. Several ice ages cooled the earth's temperature during that period, resulting in the concentration of water in massive glaciers, the lowering of the world's sea levels, and the exposure of land bridges that linked Asia with regions of the world previously uninhabited by humans. Small bands of individuals crossed those bridges and established communities in the islands of Indonesia and New Guinea, and some of them went further to cross the temporarily narrow straits of water separating southeast Asia from Australia.

RICHARD E. LEAKEY ON THE NATURE OF *HOMO SAPIENS SAPIENS*

• • •

Richard E. Leakey (1944–) has spent much of his life searching for the fossilized remains of early hominids in east Africa. While seeking to explain the evolutionary biology of hominids in a recent book, Leakey offered some reflections on the nature and distinctive characteristics of our own species.

What are we? To the biologist we are members of a sub-species called *Homo sapiens sapiens,* which represents a division of the species known as *Homo sapiens.* Every species is unique and distinct: that is part of the definition of a species. But what is particularly interesting about our species? . . .

Our forelimbs, being freed from helping us to get about, possess a very high degree of manipulative skill. Part of this skill lies in the anatomical structure of the hands, but the crucial element is, of course, the power of the brain. No matter how suitable the limbs are for detailed manipulation, they are useless in the absence of finely tuned instructions delivered through nerve fibres. The most obvious product of our hands and brains is technology. No other animal manipulates the world in the extensive and arbitrary way that humans do. The termites are capable of constructing intricately structured mounds which create their own "air-conditioned" environment inside. But the termites cannot choose to build a cathedral instead. Humans are unique because they have the capacity to *choose* what they do.

Communication is a vital thread of all animal life. Social insects such as termites possess a system of communication that is clearly essential for their complex labours: their language is not verbal but is based upon an exchange of chemicals between individuals and on certain sorts of signalling with the body. In many animal groups, such as birds and mammals, communicating by sound is important, and the posture and movement of the body can also transmit messages. The tilting of the head, the staring or averted eyes, the arched back, the bristled hair or feathers: all are part of an extensive repertoire of animal signals. In animals that live in groups, the need to be able to communicate effectively is paramount.

For humans, body language is still very important but the voice has taken over as the main channel of information-flow. Unlike any other animal, we have a spoken language which is characterized by a huge vocabulary and a complex grammatical structure. Speech is an unparalleled medium for exchanging complex information, and it is also an essential part of social interaction in that most social of all creatures, *Homo sapiens sapiens.*

All the points I have mentioned are characteristics of a very intelligent creature, but humans are more than just intelligent. Our sense of justice, our need for aesthetic pleasure, our imaginative flights, and our penetrating self-awareness, all combine to create an indefinable spirit which I believe is the "soul."

SOURCE: Richard E. Leakey, *The Making of Mankind* (New York: E. P. Dutton, 1981), pp. 18, 20

Homo sapiens arrived in Australia at least 60,000, and perhaps as long as 120,000, years ago. Somewhat later, between about 40,000 and 25,000 years ago, other groups took advantage of land bridges linking Siberia with Alaska and established human communities in North America. From there they migrated throughout the western hemisphere. By about 15,000 years ago, communities of *Homo sapiens* had appeared in almost every habitable region of the world.

Their intellectual abilities enabled members of the *Homo sapiens* species to recognize problems and possibilities in their environment and then to take action that favored their survival. At sites of early settlements, archaeologists have discovered increasingly sophisticated tools that reflect *Homo sapiens'* progressive control over

The Natural Environment

the environment. In addition to the choppers, scrapers, axes, and other tools that earlier species possessed, *Homo sapiens* used knives, spears, bows, and arrows. Individuals made dwellings for themselves in caves and in hutlike shelters fabricated from wood, bones, and animal skins. In cold regions *Homo sapiens* warmed themselves with fire and cloaked themselves in the skins of animals. Mounds of ashes discovered at their campsites show that in especially cold regions, they kept fires burning continuously during the winter months. In all parts of the earth, members of the species learned to use spoken languages to communicate complex ideas and coordinate their efforts in the common interest. *Homo sapiens* used superior intelligence, sophisticated tools, and language to exploit the natural world more efficiently than any other species the earth had seen.

Indeed, intelligent, tool-bearing humans competed so successfully in the natural world that they brought tremendous pressure to bear on other species. As the population of *Homo sapiens* increased, large mammal species in several parts of the world became extinct. Mammoths and the woolly rhinoceros disappeared from Europe, giant kangaroos from Australia, and mammoths, mastodons, and horses from the Americas. Archaeologists believe that changes in the earth's climate might have altered the natural environment enough to harm these species. In most cases, however, human hunting probably helped push them into extinction. Thus from their earliest days on earth, members of the species *Homo sapiens* became effective and efficient competitors in the natural world—to the point that they threatened the very survival of other large but less intelligent species.

PALEOLITHIC SOCIETY

By far the longest portion of the human experience on earth is the period historians and archaeologists call the paleolithic era, the "old stone age." The principal characteristic of the paleolithic era was that human beings foraged for their food: they hunted wild animals or gathered edible products of naturally growing plants. The paleolithic era extended from the evolution of the first hominids until about twelve thousand years ago, when groups of *Homo sapiens* in several parts of the world began to rely on cultivated crops to feed themselves.

Economy and Society of Hunting and Gathering Peoples

In the absence of written records, scholars have drawn inferences about paleolithic economy and society from other kinds of evidence. Archaeologists have excavated many sites that open windows on paleolithic life, and anthropologists have carefully studied hunting and gathering societies that survive in the contemporary world. In the Amazon basin of South America, the tropical forests of Africa and southeast Asia, the deserts of Africa and Australia, and a few other regions as well, small communities of hunters and gatherers continue to follow the ways of our common paleolithic ancestors. Although contemporary hunting and gathering communities reflect the influence of the modern world—they are by no means exact replicas of paleolithic societies—they throw important light on the economic and social dynamics that shaped the experiences of prehistoric foragers. In combination, then, the studies of both archaeologists and anthropologists help to illustrate how the hunting and gathering economy decisively influenced all dimensions of the human experience during the paleolithic era.

A hunting and gathering economy virtually prevents individuals from accumulating private property and basing social distinctions on wealth. In order to survive, hunters and gatherers must follow the animals that they stalk, and they must move with the seasons in search of edible plant life. Given their mobility, it is easy to see that for them, the notion of private, landed property has no meaning at all. Individuals possess only a few small items like weapons and tools that they can carry easily as they move. In the absence of accumulated wealth, hunters and gatherers of paleolithic times, like their contemporary descendants, probably lived an egalitarian existence. Social distinctions no doubt arose, and some individuals became relatively influential because of their age, strength, courage, intelligence, force of personality, or some other trait. But personal or family wealth could not have served as a basis for permanent social differences.

Economic Life

Some scholars believe that paleolithic social equality extended even further, to relations between the sexes. All members of a paleolithic group made important contributions to the survival of the community. Men traveled on sometimes distant hunting expeditions in search of large animals while women and children gathered edible plants, roots, nuts, and fruits from the area near the group's camp. Meat from the hunt was the most highly prized item in the paleolithic diet, but plant foods were essential to survival. Anthropologists calculate that in modern hunting and gathering societies, women contribute more calories to the community's diet than do the men. As a source of protein, meat represents a crucial supplement to the diet. But plant products sustain the men during hunting expeditions and feed the entire community when the hunt does not succeed. Because of the thorough interdependence of the sexes from the viewpoint of food production, paleolithic society probably did not evoke the domination of one sex by the other—certainly not to the extent that became common later.

A hunting and gathering economy has implications not only for social and sexual relations but also for community size and organization. The foraging lifestyle of

Artist's conception of a *Homo erectus* community gathering food about five hundred thousand years ago. • © The Field Museum, Neg #76851c, Chicago

hunters and gatherers dictates that they live in small bands, which today include about thirty to fifty members. Larger groups could not move efficiently or find enough food to survive over a long period. During times of drought or famine, even small bands have trouble providing for themselves. Individual bands certainly have relationships with their neighbors—agreements concerning the territories that the groups exploit, for example, or arrangements to take marriage partners from each others' groups—but the immediate community is the focus of social life.

The survival of hunting and gathering bands depends on a sophisticated understanding of their natural environment. In contemporary studies, anthropologists have found that hunting and gathering peoples do not wander aimlessly about hoping to find a bit of food. Instead, they exploit the environment systematically and efficiently by timing their movements to coincide with the seasonal migrations of the animals they hunt and the life cycles of the plant species they gather.

Big Game Hunting   Paleolithic peoples may or may not have achieved the levels of efficiency displayed by their contemporary descendants, but archaeological remains show that early peoples went about hunting and gathering in a purposeful and intelligent manner. As early as three hundred thousand years ago, for example, *Homo erectus* had learned to hunt big game successfully. Although almost anyone could take a small, young, or wounded animal, the hunting of big game posed difficult problems. Large animals such as elephant, mastodon, rhinoceros, bison, and wild cattle were not only strong and fast but also well equipped to defend themselves and even attack their human hunters. *Homo erectus* and *Homo sapiens* fashioned special tools, such as sharp knives, spears, and bows and arrows, and devised special tactics for hunting these animals. The hunters wore disguises such as animal skins and coordinated their movements so as to attack game simultaneously from several directions. They sometimes even started fires or caused disturbances to stampede herds into swamps or enclosed areas where hunters could kill them more easily. Paleolithic hunting was a complicated venture. It clearly demonstrated the capacity of early human communities to pool their uniquely human traits—high intelligence, ability to make complicated plans, and sophisticated language and communications skills—to exploit the environment.

Paleolithic Culture

Neandertal Peoples   Even in paleolithic times human beings did not limit their creative thinking to strictly practical matters of subsistence and survival. Instead, they reflected on the nature of human existence and the world around them. The earliest evidence of reflective thought comes from sites associated with Neandertal peoples, named after the Neander valley in southwestern Germany where their remains first came to light. Neandertal peoples flourished in Europe and southwest Asia between about one hundred thousand and thirty-five thousand years ago, and Neandertal remains have turned up also in Africa and east Asia.

At several Neandertal sites archaeologists have discovered signs of careful, deliberate burial accompanied by ritual observances. Perhaps the most notable is that of Shanidar cave, located about 400 kilometers (250 miles) north of Baghdad in modern-day Iraq, where survivors laid the deceased to rest on beds of freshly picked wild flowers and then covered the bodies with shrouds and garlands of other flowers. At other Neandertal sites in France, Italy, and central Asia, survivors placed flint tools and animal bones in and around the graves of the deceased. It is impossible to know precisely what Neandertal peoples were thinking when they buried their dead in this fashion. Possibly they simply wanted to honor the memory of the departed, or perhaps they wanted to prepare the dead for a new dimension of existence, a life beyond the grave. Whatever their intentions, Neandertal peoples apparently recognized a significance in the life and death of individuals that none of their ancestors had appreciated. They had developed a capacity for emotions and feelings, and they cared for each other even to the extent of preparing elaborate resting places for the departed.

Another sign of reflective thought occurs in works of art produced by paleolithic peoples. The responsible parties in this case were Cro-Magnon peoples, the first human beings of the fully modern type, who

Statue of a Neandertal man based on the study of recently discovered bones. • Maxwell Museum, University of New Mexico, Photo, Damian Andrus

appeared on the earth about forty thousand years ago. If dressed in modern clothes and groomed in modern fashion, they would be indistinguishable from contemporary human beings. Some archaeologists and evolutionary biologists classify Cro-Magnon peoples as *Homo sapiens sapiens*—our own subspecies—to distinguish them from other *Homo sapiens* subspecies such as the Neandertal. More intelligent than their predecessors, Cro-Magnon peoples gradually displaced their Neandertal neighbors, although they may have absorbed some Neandertal genetic traits through interbreeding.

Cro-Magnon Peoples

Cro-Magnon peoples displayed a noticeable interest in fashion and artistic production. They dressed in animal skins and adorned themselves with jewelry such as necklaces, bracelets, and beads. They also produced decorative pieces for use as furniture in their dwellings.

More important than jewelry and furniture, however, are the Venus figurines and cave paintings found at Cro-Magnon sites. Archaeologists use the term *Venus figurines*—named after the Roman goddess of love—to refer to small sculptures of women, usually depicted with exaggerated sexual features. Hundreds of these statuettes survive, many of them from Cro-Magnon sites in central Europe. Most scholars believe that the figures reflect a deep interest in fertility. The prominent sexual features of the Venus figurines suggest that the sculptors' principal interests were

Venus Figurines

Venus figurine from Austria. The exaggerated sexual features suggest that paleolithic peoples fashioned such figurines out of an interest in fertility. • Erich Lessing/Art Resource, NY

fecundity and the generation of new life—matters of immediate concern to paleolithic societies. Some interpreters even speculate that the figures had a place in ritual observances intended to increase fertility.

Paintings in caves inhabited or frequented by Cro-Magnon peoples are the most dramatic examples of prehistoric art. The known examples of cave art date from about thirty-four thousand to twelve thousand years ago, and most of them come from caves in southern France and northern Spain. In that region alone, archaeologists have discovered more than one hundred caves bearing prehistoric paintings. The best-known are Lascaux in France and Altamira in Spain. There prehistoric peoples left depictions of remarkable sensitivity and power. Most of the subjects were animals, especially large game such as mammoth, bison, and reindeer, although a few human figures also appear.

Cave Paintings

As in the case of the Venus figurines, the explanation for the cave paintings involves a certain amount of educated guesswork. It is conceivable that Cro-Magnon artists sometimes worked for purely aesthetic reasons—to beautify their living quarters. But many examples of cave art occur in places that are almost inaccessible to human beings—deep within remote chambers, for example, or at the end of long and constricted passages. Paintings in such remote locations presumably had some other purpose. Most analysts believe that the prominence of game animals in the paintings reflects the artists' interest in successful hunting expeditions. Thus cave paintings may have represented efforts to exercise "sympathetic magic"—to gain control over subjects (in this case, game animals) by capturing their spirits (by way of accurate representations of their physical forms). Although not universally accepted, this interpretation accounts reasonably well for a great deal of the evidence and has won widespread support among scholars.

Whatever the explanation for prehistoric art, the production of the works themselves represented conscious and purposeful activity of a high order. Cro-Magnon artists compounded their own pigments and manufactured their own tools. They made paints from minerals, plants, blood, saliva, water, animal fat, and other avail-

Cave painting from Lascaux in southern France, perhaps intended to help hunters gain control over the spirits of large game animals. • Francois Ducasse/Photo Researchers, Inc.

able media. They used mortar and pestle for grinding pigments and mixing paints, which they applied with moss, frayed twigs and branches, or primitive brushes fabricated from hair. The simplicity and power of their representations have left deep impressions on modern critics ever since the early twentieth century, when their works became widely known. The display of prehistoric artistic talent clearly reflected once again the remarkable intellectual power of the human species.

THE NEOLITHIC ERA AND THE TRANSITION TO AGRICULTURE

A few hunting and gathering societies still survive in some parts of the world. Demographers estimate the current number of hunters and gatherers to be about thirty thousand, a tiny fraction of the world's human population of more than five billion. The vast majority of the world's peoples, however, have crossed an economic threshold of immense significance. When human beings brought plants under cultivation and animals under domestication, they dramatically altered the natural world and steered human societies in altogether new directions.

The Origins of Agriculture

The term *neolithic era* means "new stone age," as opposed to the old stone age of paleolithic times. Archaeologists first used the term *neolithic* because of refinements in tool-making techniques: they found polished stone tools in neolithic sites, rather than the chipped implements characteristic of paleolithic sites. Gradually, however, archeologists became aware that something more fundamental than tool production distinguished the paleolithic from the neolithic era. Polished stone tools occurred in

Neolithic Era

sites where peoples relied on cultivation, rather than on foraging, for their subsistence. Today the term *neolithic era* refers to the early stages of agricultural society, from about twelve thousand to six thousand years ago.

Because they depended upon the bounty of nature, foraging peoples faced serious risks. Drought, famine, disease, floods, extreme temperatures, and other natural disasters could annihilate entire communities. Even in good times, hunting and gathering peoples had to limit their populations so as not to exceed the capacity of their lands to support them. They most likely resorted routinely to infanticide in order to control their numbers.

Paleolithic peoples recognized their predicament, and they sought workable solutions to their problems. Many scholars today believe, for example, that paleolithic women most likely began the systematic cultivation of plants. As the principal gatherers in their communities, women became familiar with the life cycles of plants and noticed the effects of sunshine, rain, and temperature on vegetation. Hoping perhaps for a larger and more reliable supply of food, paleolithic women began to encourage plants to grow in regular and predictable ways, instead of simply collecting what was available in the wild. Meanwhile, instead of simply stalking wild game, paleolithic men began to domesticate animals—to draw them into dependence upon human keepers. Over a period of hundreds—and even thousands—of years, these practices gradually led to the formation of an agricultural economy.

But by suggesting that agriculture brought about an immediate transformation of human society, the popular term *agricultural revolution* is entirely misleading. The establishment of an agricultural economy was not an event that took place at a given date, but rather a process that unfolded over many centuries, as human beings gradually learned how to cultivate crops and keep animals. It would be more appropriate to speak of an "agricultural transition"—leading from paleolithic experiments with cultivation to early agricultural societies in the neolithic era—rather than an agricultural revolution.

Early Agriculture   The earliest evidence of agricultural activity dates to the period about 10,000 to 8000 B.C.E., but experimentation probably took place even earlier than that. Paleolithic peoples slowly discovered the most efficient methods of cultivating crops and luring wild animals to their communities. Once begun, however, agriculture spread very quickly, partly due to the methods of early cultivators. The earliest technique, known as slash-and-burn cultivation, involved frequent movement on the part of farmers. To prepare a field for cultivation, a community would slash the bark on a stand of trees in a forest and later burn the dead trees to the ground. The resulting patch initially was extremely fertile and produced abundant harvests. After a few years, however, weeds invaded the field, and the soil lost its fertility. The community then turned to another area of forest and repeated the procedure. As communities grew larger and nearby forest land became scarce, some families left the original group and sought cultivable land elsewhere. These periodic migrations helped to spread knowledge of agriculture throughout the temperate zones of Eurasia.

By about 5000 B.C.E. agriculture had become well established in several regions of the world. In southwest Asia wheat and barley were the staple food crops, and sheep and goats were the most common domesticated animals. In southeast Asia neolithic peoples grew yams, peas, and ancestors of modern rice, while domesticating pigs, oxen, and chickens. In the Americas an impressive array of food crops came under cultivation: maize (corn), beans, peppers, squashes, and tomatoes all figured in Mesoamerican diets. At the same time neolithic peoples in the Andean region of

South America cultivated potatoes, maize, and beans. Domesticated animals were far less important in the Americas than they were in Eurasia. Paleolithic peoples had hunted many large species into extinction: mammoths, mastodons, and horses had all disappeared from the Americas by about 7000 B.C.E. (Horses, which have figured so prominently in the modern history of the Americas, were reintroduced to the western hemisphere only five hundred years ago by early Spanish explorers and colonists.) With the exception of the llama and alpaca of the Andean regions, most other American animals were not well suited to domestication.

Wherever it took root, agriculture flourished and eventually displaced the economy of paleolithic hunters and gatherers. From one point of view, the steady spread of agriculture might seem surprising because, compared to foraging, agriculture requires a great deal more work. Anthropologists calculate that modern-day hunters and gatherers spend about four hours per day in providing themselves with food and the other necessities of life. They spend the remainder of their time in games, rest, leisure, and various social activities. Agricultural society by contrast requires long hours of hard physical labor—clearing land, plowing fields, planting seeds, pulling weeds, harvesting crops, and the like—with only a few seasonal breaks during the year.

In the absence of some strong encouragement to change, few hunters and gatherers would have voluntarily chosen to become cultivators. (Of course, from the viewpoint of an individual, the development of an agricultural economy and society was an extremely gradual process, so that few individuals ever made a conscious decision to become cultivators rather than hunters and gatherers.) But there were compelling social reasons for human communities to turn from foraging to agriculture. As humans spread throughout the habitable world, they placed intense pressure on animal populations and on the capacity of the land to support them. As they hunted large game animals into scarcity, and sometimes into extinction, human groups needed to find new supplies of food. Cultivation provided a relatively stable and regular supply of food, and it allowed neolithic peoples to sustain their numbers better than their paleolithic cousins did.

The Spread of Agriculture

Indeed, agriculture actually provided a surplus: for the first time human beings were able to produce more food than they needed to survive. The regularity and relatively large quantities of their food supplies vastly increased the security of human communities. Natural disasters could still cause enormous harm and suffering, but rarely did they threaten the survival of an entire community, since surplus production from previous seasons could help a community to live through difficult times. Even if the community exhausted its own stocks, it could often trade for the surplus production of neighboring peoples.

Early Agricultural Society

Agriculture not only increased the security of neolithic communities but also transformed the lives of their inhabitants. In the wake of agriculture came a series of social and cultural changes that redirected human history. Perhaps the most important change associated with agriculture was a population explosion. Spread thinly across the earth in paleolithic times, the human species multiplied prodigiously after agriculture increased the supply of food. Historians estimate that before agriculture, about 10,000 B.C.E., the earth's human population was about four million. By 5000 B.C.E., when agriculture had appeared in a few regions of the earth, human

MAP [1.2] • Origins and global spread of agriculture.

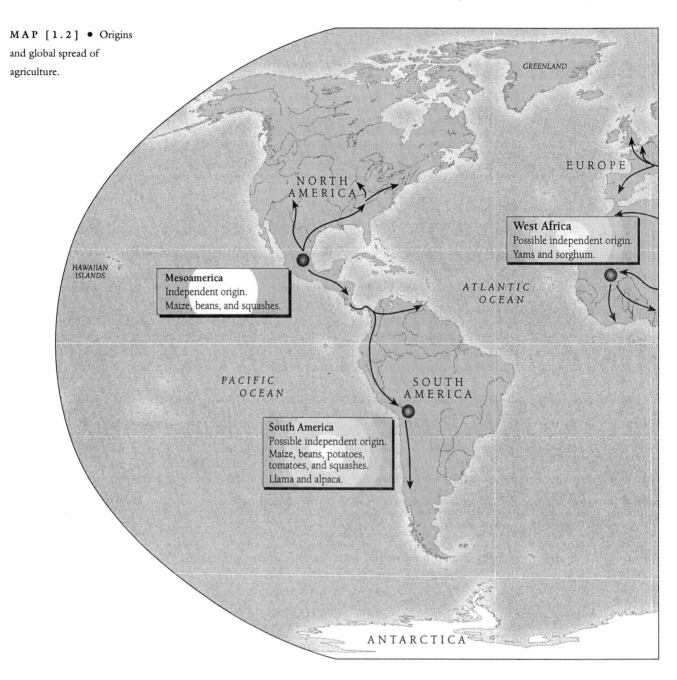

Mesoamerica
Independent origin.
Maize, beans, and squashes.

South America
Possible independent origin.
Maize, beans, potatoes, tomatoes, and squashes.
Llama and alpaca.

West Africa
Possible independent origin.
Yams and sorghum.

population had risen to about five million. Estimates for later dates demonstrate eloquently the speed with which, thanks to agriculture, human numbers increased:

Year	Human Population
3000 B.C.E.	14 million
2000 B.C.E.	27 million
1000 B.C.E.	50 million
500 B.C.E.	100 million

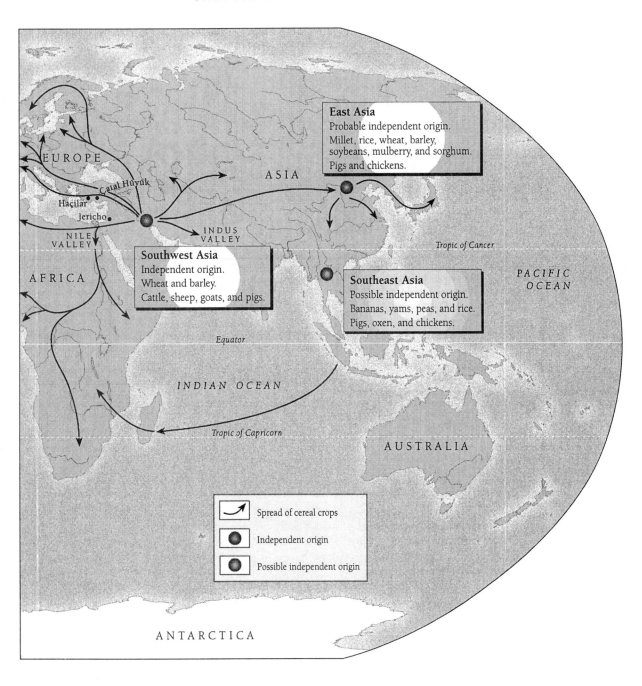

Their agricultural economy and rapidly increasing numbers encouraged neolithic peoples to adopt new forms of social organization. Since they devoted their time to cultivation rather than foraging, neolithic peoples did not continue the migratory life of their paleolithic predecessors, but rather settled near their fields in permanent villages. One of the earliest known neolithic villages was Jericho, site of a fresh water oasis north of the Dead Sea in present-day Israel, which came into existence before 8000 B.C.E. Even in its early days, Jericho may have had two thousand residents—a vast crowd, compared to a paleolithic hunting band. The residents mostly farmed

Emergence of
Villages and Towns

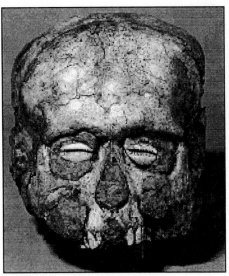

Human skull with facial features modeled in plaster with shells representing the eyes, produced in Jericho in the seventh millennium B.C.E. ● Ashmolean Museum, Oxford

wheat and barley with the aid of water from the oasis. During the earliest days of the settlement, they kept no domesticated animals, but they added meat to their diet by hunting local game animals. They also engaged in a limited amount of trade, particularly in salt and obsidian, a hard, volcanic glass from which ancient peoples fashioned knives and blades. About 7000 B.C.E., the residents surrounded their circular mud huts with a formidable wall and moat—a sign that the wealth concentrated at Jericho had begun to attract the interest of human predators.

The concentration of large numbers of people in villages encouraged specialization of labor. Most people in neolithic villages cultivated crops or kept animals. Many also continued to hunt and forage for wild plants. But a surplus of food enabled some individuals to concentrate their time and talents on

Specialization of Labor

enterprises that had nothing to do with the production of food. The rapid development of specialized labor is apparent from excavations carried out at one of the best-known neolithic settlements, Çatal Hüyük. Located in south-central Anatolia (modern-day Turkey), Çatal Hüyük was occupied continuously from 7250 to 6150 B.C.E., when residents abandoned the site. Originally a small and undistinguished neolithic village, Çatal Hüyük grew into a bustling town, accommodating perhaps as many as eight thousand inhabitants. Archaeologists have uncovered evidence that residents manufactured pots, baskets, textiles, leather, stone and metal tools, wood carvings, carpets, beads, and jewelry, among other products.

Three prehistoric craft industries—pottery, metallurgy, and textile production—illustrate the potential of specialized labor in neolithic times. In all three cases neolithic craftsmen invented new technologies that enabled them to fashion natural products into useful items. In all three cases, too, the enterprises reflected the conditions of early agricultural society: the craft industries either responded to needs for tools and utensils, or they made use of the natural products of cultivators and herders in new ways. Finally, all three enterprises became essential elements of almost all human societies based on agriculture. Thus anonymous prehistoric craftsmen laid some of the crucial economic foundations for a human history that continues into the present day.

Pottery

The earliest of the three craft industries to emerge was pottery. Paleolithic hunters and gatherers had no use for pots. They did not store food for long periods of time, and in any case lugging heavy clay pots around as they moved from one site to another would have been inconvenient. A food-producing society, however, needs containers to store surplus foods. By about 7000 B.C.E. at the latest, neolithic villagers in several parts of the world had discovered processes that transformed malleable clay into permanent, fire-hardened, waterproof pottery capable of storing dry or liquid products. Soon thereafter, neolithic craftsmen discovered that they could etch designs into their clay that fire would harden into permanent decorations and that they could color their products with glazes. As a result, pottery became a medium of artistic expression as well as a source of practical utensils.

Metallurgy soon joined pottery as a neolithic industry. The earliest metal that humans worked with systematically was copper. In many regions of the world, copper occurs naturally in relatively pure and easily malleable form. By simply hammering the cold metal it was possible to turn it into jewelry and simple tools. By 6000 B.C.E., though, neolithic villagers had discov-

Pottery vessel from Haçilar in Anatolia in the shape of a reclining deer, produced about the early sixth millennium B.C.E. • Photo Arlette Mellaart

ered that when heated to high temperatures, copper became much more workable and that they could use heat to extract copper from its ores. By 5000 B.C.E., they had raised temperatures in their furnaces high enough to melt copper and pour it into molds. With the technology of smelting and casting copper, neolithic communities were able to make not only jewelry and decorative items but also tools such as knives, axes, hoes, and weapons. Moreover, copper metallurgy served as a technological foundation on which later neolithic craftsmen developed expertise in the working of gold, bronze, iron, and other metals.

Metal Working

Because natural fibers decay more easily than pottery or copper, the dating of textile production is not certain, but fragments of textiles survive from as early as 6000 B.C.E. As soon as they began to raise crops and keep animals, neolithic peoples experimented with techniques of selective breeding. Before long they had bred strains of plants and animals that provided long, lustrous, easily worked fibers. They then developed technologies for spinning the fibers into threads and for weaving the threads into cloth. The invention of textiles was probably the work of women, who were able to spin thread and weave fabrics at home while nursing and watching over small children. In any case textile production quickly became one of the most important enterprises in agricultural society.

Textile Production

The concentration of people into permanent settlements and the increasing specialization of labor, provided the first opportunity for individuals to accumulate wealth. Individuals could trade surplus food or manufactured products for gems, jewelry, and other valuable items. The institutionalization of privately owned landed property—which occurred at an uncertain date after the introduction of agriculture—enhanced the significance of accumulated wealth. Because land was (and remains) the ultimate source of wealth in any agricultural society, ownership of land carries enormous economic power. When especially successful individuals managed to consolidate wealth in their families' hands and kept it there for several generations, clearly defined social classes emerged. Already at Çatal Hüyük,

Social Distinctions

for example, differences in wealth and social status are clear from the quality of interior decorations in houses and the value of goods buried with individuals from different social classes.

Neolithic Culture

Quite apart from its social effects, agriculture left its mark on the cultural dimension of the human experience. Because their lives and communities depended upon the successful cultivation of crops, neolithic farmers closely observed the natural world around them and noted the conditions that favored successful harvests. In other words, they developed a kind of early applied science. From experience accumulated over the generations, they acquired an impressive working knowledge of the earth and its rhythms. Agricultural peoples had to learn when changes of season would take place: survival depended upon the ability to predict when they could reasonably expect sunshine, rain, warmth, and freezing temperatures. They learned to associate the seasons with the different positions of the sun, moon, and stars. As a result, they accumulated a store of knowledge concerning relationships between the heavens and the earth, and they made the first steps toward the elaboration of a calendar, which would enable them to predict with tolerable accuracy the kind of weather they could expect at various times of the year.

Religious Values   The workings of the natural world also influenced neolithic religion. Paleolithic communities had already honored, and perhaps even worshipped, Venus figurines in hopes of ensuring fertility. Neolithic religion reflected the same interest in fertility, but it celebrated particularly the rhythms that governed agricultural society—birth, growth, death, and regenerated life. Archaeologists have unearthed thousands of neolithic representations of gods and goddesses in the form of clay figurines, drawings on pots and vases, decorations on tools, and ritual objects.

The neolithic gods included not only the life-bearing, Venus-type figures of paleolithic times but also other deities associated with the cycle of life, death, and regeneration. A pregnant goddess of vegetation, for example, represented neolithic hopes for fertility in the fields. Sometimes neolithic worshipers associated these goddesses with animals like frogs or butterflies that dramatically changed form during the course of their lives, just as seeds of grain sprouted, flourished, died, and produced new seed for another agricultural cycle. Meanwhile, young male gods associated with bulls and goats represented the energy and virility that participates in the creation of life.

Some deities were associated with death: many neolithic goddesses possessed the power to bring about decay and destruction. Yet physical death was not an absolute end. The procreative capacities of gods and goddesses resulted in the births of infant deities who represented the regeneration of life—freshly sprouted crops, replenished stocks of domestic animals, and infant human beings to inaugurate a new biological cycle. Thus neolithic religious thought clearly reflected the natural world of early agricultural society.

The Origins of Urban Life

Within four thousand years of its introduction, agriculture had dramatically transformed the face of the earth. Human beings multiplied prodigiously, congregated in

densely populated quarters, placed the surrounding lands under cultivation, and domesticated several species of animals. Besides altering the physical appearance of the
earth, agriculture also transformed the lives of human beings. Even a modest neolithic village dwarfed a paleolithic band of a few dozen hunters and gatherers. In
larger villages and towns, such as Jericho and Çatal Hüyük, with their populations of
several thousand people, their specialized labor, and their craft industries, social relationships became more complex than would have been conceivable during paleolithic times. Gradually, dense populations, specialized labor, and complex social relations gave rise to an altogether new form of social organization—the city.

Like the transition from foraging to agricultural society, the development of   *Emergence of Cities*
cities and complex societies organized around urban centers was a gradual process,
rather than a well-defined event. Because of favorable location, some neolithic villages and towns attracted more people and grew larger than others. Over time, some
of these settlements evolved into cities. What distinguished early cities from their
predecessors, the neolithic villages and towns?

Even in their early days, cities differed from neolithic villages and towns in two
principal ways. In the first place, cities were larger and more complex than neolithic
villages and towns. Çatal Hüyük featured an impressive variety of specialized crafts
and industries. With progressively larger populations, cities fostered more intense
specialization than any of their predecessors among the neolithic villages and
towns. Thus it was in cities that classes of professionals emerged—individuals who
devoted all their time to efforts other than the production of food. Professional
craftsmen refined existing technologies, invented new ones, and raised levels of
quality and production. Professional managers also appeared—governors, administrators, military strategists, tax collectors, and the like—whose services were necessary to the survival of the community. Finally, cities also gave rise to professional
cultural specialists such as priests, who maintained their communities' traditions,
transmitted their values, organized public rituals, and sought to discover meaning
in human existence.

In the second place, whereas neolithic villages and towns served the needs of
their inhabitants and immediate neighbors, cities decisively influenced the political,
economic, and cultural life of large regions. Cities established marketplaces that attracted buyers and sellers from distant parts. Brisk trade, conducted over increasingly
longer distances, promoted economic integration on a much larger scale than was
possible in neolithic times. To ensure adequate food supplies for their large populations, cities also extended their claims to authority to their hinterlands, thus becoming centers of political and military control as well as economic influence. In time,
too, the building of temples and schools in neighboring regions enabled the cities to
extend their cultural traditions and values to surrounding areas.

The earliest known cities grew out of agricultural villages and towns in the valleys of the Tigris and Euphrates Rivers in modern-day Iraq. These communities
crossed the urban threshold during the period about 4000 to 3500 B.C.E. and
soon dominated their regions. During the following centuries cities appeared in
several other parts of the world, including Egypt, northern India, northern China,
central Mexico, and the central Andean region of South America. Cities became
the focal points of public affairs—the sites from which leaders guided human fortunes, supervised neighboring regions, and organized the world's earliest complex
societies.

*I*n many ways the world of prehistoric human beings seems remote and even alien. Yet the evolution of the human species and the development of human society during the paleolithic and neolithic eras have profoundly influenced the lives of all the world's peoples during the past six millennia. Paleolithic peoples enjoyed levels of intelligence that far exceeded those of other animals, and they invented tools and languages that helped them to flourish in all regions of the world. Indeed, they thrived so well that they threatened their sources of food. Their neolithic descendants began to cultivate food in order to sustain their communities, and the agricultural societies that they built transformed the world. Human population rose dramatically, and human groups congregated in villages, towns, and eventually cities. There they engaged in specialized labor and launched industries that produced pottery, metal goods, and textiles as well as tools and decorative items. Thus intelligence, language, reflective thought, agriculture, urban settlements, and craft industries all figure in the legacy that prehistoric human beings left for their descendants.

CHRONOLOGY

4 million–1 million years ago	Era of *Australopithecus*
3.5 million years ago	Era of Lucy
1.5 million–200,000 years ago	Era of *Homo erectus*
250,000 B.C.E.	Early evolution of *Homo sapiens*
100,000–35,000 B.C.E.	Era of Neandertal peoples
40,000 B.C.E.	First appearance of Cro-Magnon people (*Homo sapiens sapiens*)
10,000–8000 B.C.E.	Early experimentation with agriculture
8000 B.C.E.	Appearance of agricultural villages
4000–3500 B.C.E.	Appearance of cities

FOR FURTHER READING

Elizabeth Wayland Barber. *Women's Work: The First 20,000 Years.* New York, 1994. Fascinating study of prehistoric and ancient textiles, which the author argues was a craft industry dominated by women from the earliest times.

V. Gordon Childe. *What Happened in History?* Baltimore, 1964. Survey of human experience from paleolithic times to early urban societies by a distinguished anthropologist.

Mark Nathan Cohen. *The Food Crisis in Prehistory: Overpopulation and the Origins of Agriculture.* New Haven, 1977. Contends that overpopulation and food shortages encouraged human communities to resort to cultivation.

———. *Health and the Rise of Civilization.* New Haven, 1989. Argues that human groups faced new dietary problems and diseases as they relied on agriculture and congregated in urban settings.

Margaret Ehrenberg. *Women in Prehistory.* London, 1989. Brings archaeological discoveries to bear on questions of sex and gender relations in prehistoric times.

Clive Gamble. *Timewalkers: The Prehistory of Global Civilization.* Cambridge, Mass., 1994. Examines the migration of human beings to all parts of the world in the context of human evolution.

Marija Gimbutas. *The Goddesses and Gods of Old Europe.* London, 1982. A provocative examination of the religions of paleolithic Europe.

———. *The Civilization of the Goddess.* San Francisco, 1991. A controversial but often insightful book especially valuable for its analysis of prehistoric art and religion.

John Gowlett. *Ascent to Civilization.* New York, 1984. Well-illustrated work that draws heavily on recent archaeological research.

Donald C. Johanson and Maitland A. Edey. *Lucy: The Beginnings of Humankind*. New York, 1981. Fascinating account of the discovery of Lucy and the scholarly controversies that ensued.

Richard E. Leakey. *The Making of Mankind*. New York, 1981. A richly illustrated volume that outlines the evolutionary history of early hominids for a popular audience.

James Mellaart. *Çatal Hüyük: A Neolithic Town in Anatolia*. New York, 1967. Authoritative analysis of Çatal Hüyük by its excavator.

John E. Pfeiffer. *The Emergence of Man*. 4th ed. New York, 1983. Sound and solid survey of human evolution.

Ian A. Todd. *Çatal Hüyük in Perspective*. Menlo Park, 1976. Examines Çatal Hüyük in the larger context of early neolithic society.

Erik Trinkaus and Pat Shipman. *The Neandertals: Changing the Image of Mankind*. New York, 1993. Insightful account of the discovery, study, and interpretation of Neandertal remains.

Peter J. Ucko and Andrée Rosenfeld. *Paleolithic Cave Art*. New York, 1967. Careful, scholarly study of paleolithic art with reflections on artists and their motives.

Robert J. Wenke. *Patterns in Prehistory: Humankind's First Three Million Years*. 3rd ed. New York, 1990. A well-written, thoughtful, and up-to-date survey of prehistoric societies and the world's earliest complex societies.

EARLY SOCIETIES IN SOUTHWEST ASIA AND NORTH AFRICA

· · ·

For almost three thousand years, Egyptian embalmers preserved the bodies of deceased individuals through a process of mummification. Egyptian records rarely mention the techniques of mummification, but the Greek historian Herodotus traveled in Egypt about 450 B.C.E. and briefly explained the craft. The embalmer first used a metal hook to draw the brain of the deceased out through a nostril, removed the internal organs through an incision made alongside the abdomen, washed them in palm wine, and sealed them with preservatives in stone vessels. The embalmer then washed the body, Herodotus said, filled it with spices and aromatics, and covered it for two months or more with natron, a naturally occuring salt substance. When the natron had extracted all moisture from the body, the embalmer cleansed it again and wrapped it with strips of fine linen covered with resin. Adorned with jewelry, the preserved body then went into a casket bearing a painting or sculpted likeness of the deceased.

Careful preservation of the body was only a part of the funerary ritual for prominent Egyptians. Ruling elites, wealthy individuals, and sometimes common people as well laid their deceased to rest in expensive tombs equipped with furniture, tools, weapons, and ornaments that the departed would need in their next lives. Relatives periodically brought food and wine to nourish the deceased, and archaeologists have discovered soups, beef ribs, pigeons, quail, fish, bread, cakes, and fruits among these offerings. Some tombs featured elaborate paintings of family members and servants who accompanied the departed into a new dimension of existence.

Egyptian funerary customs were expressions of a wealthy agricultural society. Food offerings consisted largely of agricultural products, and scenes painted on tomb walls often depicted workers cultivating their crops. Moreover, bountiful harvests explained the accumulation of wealth that supported expensive funerary practices, and they also enabled some individuals to devote their efforts to specialized tasks like embalming. Agriculture even influenced religious beliefs. Many Egyptians believed fervently in a life beyond the grave, and they associated the human experience of life and death with the agricultural cycle in which crops grow, die, and come to life again in another season.

Excavations surrounding the pyramids as seen from the air. • Will & Deni McIntyre/Tony Stone Images

Productive agricultural economies supported the development of the world's first complex societies, in which sizable numbers of people lived in cities and extended their political, social, economic, and cultural influence over large regions. Urban society emerged during the late fourth millennium B.C.E. in southwest Asia, particularly in Mesopotamia, the land occupied by the modern state of Iraq. Shortly thereafter, a complex society emerged also in Egypt, in the Nile River valley of northeastern Africa.

As people congregated in confined spaces, they needed to find ways to resolve disputes—sometimes between residents of individual settlements, other times between the settlements themselves—that inevitably arose as individual and group interests conflicted. In search of order, settled agricultural peoples recognized political authorities and built states in Mesopotamia and Egypt. The establishment of states led to the creation of empires, as individual states sought to extend their power and enhance their security by expanding their authority to neighboring lands.

Apart from stimulating the establishment of states, urban societies in Mesopotamia and Egypt also encouraged specialization of labor and the emergence of social classes, thus giving rise to increasingly complex social and economic structures. Urban centers fostered specialized labor, and the efficient production of high-quality goods in turn stimulated trade.

Finally, early Mesopotamia and Egypt also developed distinctive cultural traditions. Both societies generated systems of writing, and both supported organized religions. Some of their cultural elements outlasted Mesopotamian and Egyptian societies because other peoples adopted them for their own uses. Indeed, both Mesopotamia and Egypt influenced neighboring peoples: even in their earliest days, while expanding their political boundaries, complex, city-based societies spread their cultural traditions and shaped the lives of peoples around them.

 ## THE QUEST FOR ORDER

During the fourth millennium B.C.E., the number of humans increased rapidly in Mesopotamia and Egypt. Inhabitants of those lands had few precedents to guide them in the construction of an orderly large-scale society. At most they inherited a few techniques for the maintenance of order in the small agricultural villages of neolithic times. By experimentation and adaptation, however, they created states and governmental machinery that brought political and social order to their territories. Moreover, their political and military organization enabled them to extend their authority to neighboring peoples and to build regional empires.

Mesopotamia: "The Land between the Rivers"

The place-name *Mesopotamia* comes from two Greek words meaning "the land between the rivers," and it refers specifically to the valleys of the Tigris and Euphrates Rivers in modern-day Iraq. The Tigris and Euphrates brought large volumes of fresh water to Mesopotamia. Early cultivators realized that by tapping these rivers, building reservoirs, and digging canals, they could irrigate fields of barley, wheat, and peas. Small-scale irrigation began in Mesopotamia soon after 6000 B.C.E.

Sumer   Artificial irrigation led to increased food supplies, which in turn supported a rapidly increasing human population. Human numbers grew especially fast in the land of Sumer in the southern half of Mesopotamia. By about 5000 B.C.E. a people known as the Sumerians had migrated to Sumer from the east and built elaborate irrigation networks. By 3000 B.C.E. the population of Sumer approached one hundred

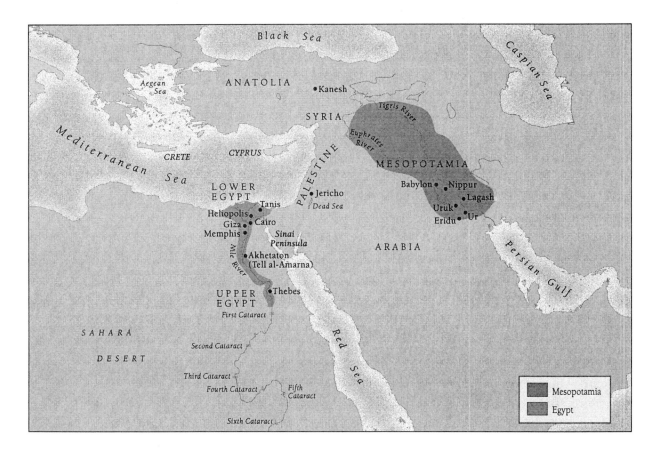

MAP [2.1]
Early Mesopotamia and Egypt.

thousand—an unprecedented concentration of people in ancient times—and the Sumerians were the dominant people of Mesopotamia.

Apart from the Sumerians, the other inhabitants of ancient Mesopotamia were mostly Semites—descendants of nomadic herders who spoke Semitic languages, including Akkadian, Hebrew, Aramaic, and Phoenician. (The most prominent Semitic languages spoken in the world today are Arabic and Hebrew.) The Semitic peoples often intermarried with the Sumerians, and they largely adapted to Sumerian ways.

As more and more people gathered in settlements, the Sumerians built the world's first cities. These cities differed markedly from the neolithic villages and towns that preceded them. Unlike the earlier settlements, the Sumerian cities were centers of political and military authority, and their jurisdiction extended into the surrounding regions. Moreover, the bustling marketplaces that drew buyers and sellers from near and far turned the cities into economic centers as well. Finally, the cities also served as cultural centers where priests maintained organized religions and scribes developed traditions of writing and formal education.

For almost a millennium, from 3200 to 2350 B.C.E., a dozen Sumerian cities— Eridu, Ur, Uruk, Lagash, Nippur, Babylon, Kish, and others—dominated public affairs in Mesopotamia. These cities all experienced internal and external pressures that prompted them to establish states—formal governmental institutions that wielded authority throughout their territories. Internally, the cities needed to maintain order and ensure that inhabitants cooperated on community projects. Moreover, because of their expanding populations, the cities also needed some means to prevent conflicts between urban residents from escalating into serious civic disorder.

Sumerian City-States

The massive temple of the moon god Nanna-Suen (sometimes known as Sin) dominated the Sumerian city of Ur. Constructing temples of this size required a huge investment of resources and thousands of laborers. • George Gerster/Photo Researchers, Inc.

While preserving the peace, government authorities also organized work on projects of value to the entire community. Temples, public buildings, and defensive walls dominated all the Sumerian cities, and all were the work of laborers recruited and coordinated by government authorities. In Uruk, for example, a massive temple complex went up about 3200 B.C.E. or shortly thereafter. Scholars have calculated that its construction required the services of 1,500 laborers working ten hours per day for five years.

Even more important than buildings were the irrigation systems that supported productive agriculture and urban society. As their population grew, the Sumerians expanded their networks of reservoirs and canals. The construction, maintenance, and repair of the irrigation systems required the labor of untold thousands of workers. Only recognized government authorities had the standing to draft workers for this difficult labor and order them to participate in such large-scale projects. Even when the irrigation systems functioned perfectly, recognized authority was still necessary to ensure equitable distribution of water and to resolve disputes.

Alongside internal pressures, the Sumerian cities also faced external problems. The wealth stored in Sumerian cities attracted the interest of peoples outside the cities. Mesopotamia is a mostly flat land with few natural geographical barriers. It was a simple matter for raiders to attack the Sumerian cities and take their wealth. The cities responded to this threat by building defensive walls and organizing military forces. The need to recruit, train, equip, maintain, and deploy military forces created another demand for recognized authority.

The earliest Sumerian governments were probably assemblies of prominent men who made decisions on behalf of the whole community. When crises arose, assemblies yielded their power to individuals who possessed full authority during the period of emergency. These individual rulers gradually usurped the authority of the assemblies and established themselves as monarchs. By about 3000 B.C.E. all Sumerian cities had kings who claimed absolute authority within their realms. In fact, however, the kings generally ruled in cooperation with local nobles, who came mostly from the ranks of military leaders who had displayed special valor in battle.

Sumerian Kings

The Sumerian cities were all city-states; they not only controlled public life within the city walls but also oversaw affairs in surrounding regions. These surrounding regions were crucial to the Sumerian cities, since surplus food produced in the countryside supported urban populations. Thus all the Sumerian cities established military forces, administrators, and tax collectors to ensure the maintenance of order and the delivery of taxes and food supplies from the countryside. By the middle of the third millennium B.C.E., city-states dominated public life in Sumer, and city-states like Assur and Nineveh had also begun to emerge in northern Mesopotamia.

Egypt: "The Gift of the Nile"

While Sumerians organized city-states in southern Mesopotamia, Egyptians built a complex society along the valley of the Nile River in northeastern Africa. During the centuries following 5000 B.C.E., human population concentrated in the Nile valley because the Sahara desert, once much cooler than at present, became increasingly hot, dry, and uninhabitable. This process of desiccation turned rich grasslands into barren desert, and it drove out the large game animals that paleolithic human groups had hunted. Thus humans migrated from the Sahara to more hospitable regions of Africa, such as the valley of the Nile.

Fed by rain and snow in the high mountains of east Africa, the Nile courses more than 6,400 kilometers (3,978 miles) from its source at Lake Victoria to its outlet through the delta to the Mediterranean Sea. Each spring, rain and melting snow swell the river, which surges north through the Sudan and Egypt. Until the completion of the high dam at Aswan in 1974, the Nile's accumulated waters annually flooded the plains downstream. When the waters receded, they left behind a layer of rich, fertile muck, and these alluvial deposits supported a remarkably productive agricultural economy. For that reason, the Greek historian Herodotus proclaimed Egypt "the gift of the Nile."

The Nile River

Egyptians began to experiment with agriculture before 5000 B.C.E. Cultivators simply went into the floodplains in the late summer, after the floods receded, sowed barley and wheat, allowed their crops to mature during the cool months of the year, and harvested them during the winter and early spring. As in Mesopotamia, agriculture led to a rapid increase in population. Demographic pressures forced Egyptians to develop more intense and sophisticated methods of agriculture. Cultivators built dikes to protect fields from floods and catchment basins to store water for irrigation. By 4000 B.C.E. agricultural villages dotted the Nile's shores from the delta to Aswan and beyond.

As in Mesopotamia, dense human population brought a need for formal organization of public affairs. By 4000 B.C.E. agricultural villages along the Nile traded and cooperated in building irrigation networks. Egypt did not face the external dangers that threatened Mesopotamia; the Red Sea, the Mediterranean Sea, and hostile deserts largely protected it from foreign invasion in ancient times. Nevertheless, the

Unification of Egypt

Menes, unifier of Egypt, prepares to sacrifice an enemy. He wears the crown of Upper Egypt, and the falcon representing the god Horus oversees his actions in this relief carving on a votive tablet. Two fallen enemies lie at the bottom of the tablet. • Hirmer Fotoarchiv

Pharaoh

The Pyramids

need to maintain order and organize community projects led Egyptians to create states and recognize official authorities.

Government authority came to Egypt about 3100 B.C.E. in the person of a conqueror named Menes (also known as Narmer). Menes came from southern Egypt (known as Upper Egypt, since the Nile flows north) and extended his authority throughout the Nile valley and into the delta (known as Lower Egypt). According to tradition, Menes founded the city of Memphis, near modern Cairo, which stood at the junction of Upper and Lower Egypt. Memphis served as Menes's capital and eventually became the cultural and political center of ancient Egypt. Other cities also played important roles in Egyptian affairs. Thebes was the administrative center of Upper Egypt, for example, while Heliopolis was center of the sun cult near Memphis and site of an enormous temple to the sun god Re. Tanis was a bustling port and the gateway to the Mediterranean.

Menes and his successors built a centralized state ruled by the pharaoh, the Egyptian king. The early pharaohs claimed to be gods living on the earth in human form, the owners and absolute rulers of all the land. Egyptians associated the pharaohs especially with Horus, the sky god, and they often represented the pharaohs with a hawk, the symbol of Horus. Artistic representations also show pharaohs as enormous figures towering over their human subjects.

The power of the pharaohs was greatest during the first millennium of Egyptian history—the eras known as the Archaic Period (3100–2660 B.C.E.) and the Old Kingdom (2660–2180 B.C.E.). The most enduring symbols of their authority and divine status are the massive pyramids constructed during the Old Kingdom as royal tombs, most of them during the century from 2600 to 2500 B.C.E. These enormous monuments stand today at Giza, near Cairo, as testimony to the pharaohs' ability to marshall Egyptian resources. The largest is the pyramid of Khufu (also known as Cheops), which involved the precise cutting and fitting of 2,300,000 limestone blocks weighing up to 15 tons, with an average weight of 2.5 tons. Scholars estimate that construction of Khufu's pyramid required the services of some eighty-four thousand laborers working eighty days per year (probably during the late fall and winter seasons when the demand for agricultural labor was light) for twenty years. Apart from the laborers, hundreds of architects, engineers, craftsmen, and artists also contributed to the construction of the pyramids.

During Egypt's Middle Kingdom (2080–1640 B.C.E.), local rulers challenged the pharaohs' authority, and Egypt experienced an era of turmoil. Meanwhile, foreign peoples developed powerful new military technologies, most notably horse-drawn chariots, that Egyptians did not possess. As a result of internal instability and external assault, the Middle Kingdom fell to invaders known as the Hyksos. The pharaohs of the New Kingdom (1570–1075 B.C.E.) expelled the Hyksos and undertook impe-

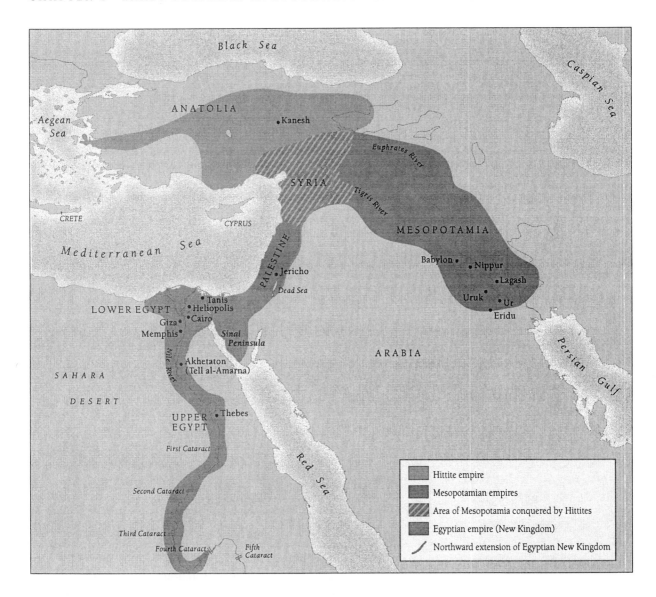

MAP [2.2]

Mesopotamian and
Egyptian empires.

rial campaigns to extend Egyptian control to Palestine, Lebanon, and Syria in hopes
of preventing new invasions. For half a millennium Egypt was an imperial power in
the region embracing north Africa, the Mediterranean basin, and southwest Asia.

The Course of Empire

Once they had organized effective states, both Mesopotamians and Egyptians ventured beyond the boundaries of their own societies. Conflicts between the
Mesopotamian city-states often led to war, as aggrieved or ambitious kings sought
to punish or conquer their neighbors. In hopes of establishing order on a scale
larger than the city-state, conquerors sought to extend their authority and build empires that controlled the affairs of subject cities and peoples. External threats came
later to Egypt than to Mesopotamia, but the invasion of the Hyksos prompted the
pharaohs to seize control of regions that might pose future threats. By 1500 B.C.E.
both Mesopotamians and Egyptians had built powerful regional empires.

Sargon of Akkad

Bronze bust of a Mesopotamian king often thought to represent Sargon of Akkad. The work dates to about 2350 B.C.E. and reflects high levels of expertise in the working of bronze. • Iraq Museum, Baghdad/Hirmer Fotoarchiv

Regional empires emerged as the Semitic peoples of northern Mesopotamia began to overshadow the Sumerians. The creator of empire in Mesopotamia was Sargon of Akkad, a city near Kish and Babylon whose precise location has so far eluded archaeologists. A talented administrator and brilliant warrior, Sargon (2370–2315 B.C.E.) began his career as a minister to the king of Kish. About 2334 B.C.E. he organized a coup against the king, recruited an army, and went on the offensive against the Sumerian city-states. He conquered the cities one by one, destroyed their defensive walls, and placed them under his own governors and administrators. As Sargon's conquests mounted, his armies grew larger and more professional, and no single city-state could withstand his forces. He also seized control of trade routes and supplies of natural resources like silver, tin, and cedar wood. By controlling and taxing trade, Sargon obtained the financial resources he needed to maintain his military juggernaut. At the high point of his reign, his empire embraced all of Mesopotamia, and his armies had ventured as far afield as the Mediterranean and Black Sea.

For several generations Sargon's successors maintained his empire. Gradually, though, it weakened, largely because of chronic rebellion in city-states that resented imperial rule. By about 2100 B.C.E. Sargon's empire had collapsed altogether. Yet the memory of his deeds, recorded in legends and histories, as well as in his own works of propaganda, inspired later conquerors to follow his example.

Hammurabi and the Babylonian Empire

Most prominent of the later conquerors was the Babylonian Hammurabi (reigned 1792–1750 B.C.E.), who styled himself "king of the four quarters of the world." The Babylonian empire dominated Mesopotamia until about 1600 B.C.E. Hammurabi improved on Sargon's administrative techniques by relying on centralized bureaucratic rule and regular taxation. Instead of traveling from city to city with a large and cumbersome army, Hammurabi and his successors ruled from Babylon (located near modern Baghdad) and stationed deputies in the regions they controlled. Instead of confiscating supplies and other wealth in the unfortunate regions their armies visited, Hammurabi and later rulers instituted less ruinous but more regular taxes collected by their officials. By these means Hammurabi developed a more efficient government than that of his predecessors and spread its costs more evenly over the population.

Hammurabi's Laws

Hammurabi also sought to maintain his empire by providing it with a code of law. Earlier Mesopotamian rulers had promulgated laws perhaps as early as 2500 B.C.E., and Hammurabi borrowed liberally from his predecessors in compiling the most extensive and most complete Mesopotamian law code. In the prologue to his laws, Hammurabi proclaimed that the gods had named him "to promote the welfare of the people, . . . to cause justice to prevail in the land, to destroy the wicked and evil, [so] that the strong might not oppress the weak, to rise like the sun over the people, and to light up the land." Hammurabi's laws established high standards of behavior and stern punishments for violators. They prescribed death penalties for murder, theft, fraud, false accusations, sheltering of runaway slaves, failure to obey royal orders, adultery, and incest. Civil laws regulated prices, wages, commercial dealings, marital relationships, and the conditions of slavery.

The code relied heavily on the principle of *lex talionis*—the "law of retaliation," whereby offenders suffered punishments resembling their violations. But the code also took account of social standing when applying this principle. It provided, for example, that a noble who destroyed the eye or broke the bone of another noble would have his own eye destroyed or bone broken, but if a noble destroyed the eye or broke the bone of a commoner, the noble merely paid a fine in silver. Although they were harsh, Hammurabi's laws set common standards designed to hold the Babylonian empire together.

This handsome basalt stele shows Hammurabi receiving his royal authority from the sun god, Shamash. Some four thousand lines of Hammurabi's laws are inscribed below. • © RMN

The Egyptian New Kingdom

Despite Hammurabi's administrative efficiencies and impressive law code, the wealth of the Babylonian empire attracted invaders, particularly the Hittites, who had built a powerful empire in Anatolia (modern-day Turkey), and about 1595 B.C.E. the Babylonian empire crumbled before Hittite assaults. Shortly after its fall, Egyptians also embarked upon imperial ventures. By about 1550 B.C.E. the pharaoh Ahmosis, founder of the New Kingdom, had expelled the Hyksos and reunited Egypt. In an effort to secure his borders, Ahmosis led armies into Palestine and Syria, and his successors continued his policy of intervention in northern lands. Most vigorous of all the New Kingdom pharaohs was Tuthmosis III (reigned 1490–1436 B.C.E.). After seventeen campaigns that he personally led to Palestine and Syria, Tuthmosis dominated the coastal regions of the eastern Mediterranean.

The Assyrian Empire

As Egyptian power waned, imperial rule returned to Mesopotamia with the Assyrians, a hardy people from northern Mesopotamia who extended their authority south after 1000 B.C.E. The Assyrians relied on the administrative techniques pioneered by Hammurabi, but they also organized a powerful and intimidating military machine. They divided their forces into standardized units and placed them under the command of professional officers. They appointed officers because of merit, skill, and bravery, rather than noble birth or family connections. The Assyrians also made effective use of the recently invented horse-drawn chariot, a devastating instrument of war that allowed waves of archers to attack their mostly stationary enemies. The combination of high speed and withering firepower unnerved most of their opponents, who quickly collapsed before an Assyrian assault. At its high point, during the eighth and seventh centuries B.C.E., the Assyrian empire embraced not only Mesopotamia but also Syria, Palestine, much of Anatolia, and most of Egypt.

Nebuchadnezzar and the New Babylonian Empire

Assyrian rulers provoked intermittent rebellion by their subjects, and a combination of internal unrest and external assault brought their empire down in 612 B.C.E. For half a century, from 600 to 550 B.C.E., Babylon once again dominated Mesopotamia during the New Babylonian empire, sometimes called the Chaldean empire. King Nebuchadnezzar (reigned 605–562 B.C.E.) lavished wealth and resources on his capital city. Babylon occupied some 850 hectares (more than 2,100 acres), and the city's defensive walls were reportedly so thick that a four-horse chariot could turn around on top of them. Within the walls there were enormous palaces and 1,179 temples, some of them faced with gold and decorated with thousands of statues. When one of the king's wives longed for flowering shrubs from her mountain homeland, Nebuchadnezzar had them planted in terraces above the city walls, and the hanging gardens of Babylon have symbolized the city's luxuriousness ever since.

By this time, however, peoples beyond Mesopotamia and Egypt had acquired advanced weapons and experimented with techniques of administering large territories. By the mid-sixth century B.C.E. Mesopotamians and Egyptians largely lost control of their affairs, as foreign conquerors absorbed them into their own empires.

 # THE DEVELOPMENT OF COMPLEX SOCIETIES

With the emergence of cities and the congregation of dense populations in urban spaces, specialized labor proliferated. The economies of Mesopotamia and Egypt became increasingly diverse, and trade linked the two lands with other peoples. Meanwhile, clearly defined social classes emerged as small groups of people concentrated wealth and power in their own hands. At the same time, both Mesopotamia and Egypt developed into patriarchal societies that vested authority largely in their adult males.

Economic Specialization and Trade

When large numbers of people began to congregate in cities and work at tasks other than agriculture, they vastly expanded the stock of human skills. Craftsmen refined techniques inherited from earlier generations and experimented with new ways of doing things. Pottery, textile manufacture, woodworking, leather production, brick making, stonecutting, and masonry all became distinct occupations in the world's earliest cities.

Metallurgical innovations ranked among the most important developments that came about because of specialized labor. Neolithic craftsmen had long fashioned copper into tools and jewelry. In pure form, however, copper is too soft for use as an effective weapon or as a tool for heavy work. About 3000 B.C.E. Mesopotamian metalworkers discovered that if they alloyed copper with tin, they could make much harder and stronger implements. Experimentation with copper metallurgy thus led to the invention of bronze. Because both copper and tin were relatively rare and hence expensive, most people could not afford bronze implements. Nevertheless, bronze had an immediate impact on military affairs, as craftsmen turned out swords, spears, axes, shields, and armor made of the newly discovered metal. Over a longer period, bronze also had an impact on agriculture. Mesopotamian farmers began to use bronze knives and bronze-tipped plows instead of tools made of bone, wood, stone, or obsidian.

Bronze Metallurgy

Egyptians did not embrace bronze metallurgy as quickly as Mesopotamians. Use of bronze became widespread in Egypt only after the seventeenth century B.C.E., when the Hyksos relied on bronze weapons to impose their authority on the Nile delta. After the expulsion of the Hyksos, Egyptians began to manufacture bronze implements, and the imperial armies of Tuthmosis and other pharaohs of the New Kingdom carried up-to-date bronze weapons like those used in Mesopotamia and neighboring lands. As in Mesopotamia, the high cost of copper and tin kept bronze out of the hands of most people. Royal workshops closely monitored supplies of the valuable metal: officers weighed the bronze tools issued to workers at royal tombs, for example, to ensure that craftsmen did not divert bronze shavings to personal uses.

After about 1000 B.C.E. Mesopotamian craftsmen began to manufacture effective tools and weapons with iron as well as bronze. Experimentation with iron metallurgy began as early as the fourth millennium B.C.E., but early efforts resulted in products that were too brittle for heavy-duty uses. Between the twelfth and tenth centuries B.C.E., craftsmen learned that by adding carbon to iron they could fashion exceptionally strong tools and weapons. Iron metallurgy rapidly spread throughout Mesopotamia, Anatolia, Egypt, north Africa, and other regions as well. Assyrian conquerors made particularly effective use of iron weapons in building their empire in Mesopotamia, and iron quickly became the metal of choice for weapons and tools.

Iron Metallurgy

While some craftsmen refined the techniques of bronze and iron metallurgy, others worked to devise efficient means of transportation. The precise origin of the wheel is unknown, but Sumerians probably used wheeled carts for several centuries before they began to organize city-states about 3200 B.C.E. Wheeled carts and wagons enabled people to haul heavy loads of bulk goods—such as grain, bricks, or metal ores—over much longer distances than human porters or draft animals could manage. The wheel rapidly diffused from Sumer to neighboring lands, and within a few centuries it had become a standard means of overland transportation.

The Wheel

Both Sumerians and Egyptians experimented with technologies of maritime transportation. By 3500 B.C.E. Sumerians had built watercraft that allowed them to venture into the Persian Gulf and the Arabian Sea. About the same time Egyptians began to navigate the Nile, which was particularly accommodating for travel in river boats. Because the river flows north, boats could ride the currents from Upper to Lower Egypt. Meanwhile, prevailing winds blow almost year-round from the north, so that by raising a sail, boats could easily make their way upriver from Lower to Upper Egypt. Soon after 3000 B.C.E. Egyptians sailed beyond the Nile into the

Shipbuilding

Mediterranean, and by about 2000 B.C.E. they had also thoroughly explored the waters of the Red Sea, the Gulf of Aden, and the western portion of the Arabian Sea.

Long-Distance Trade   Specialized labor and efficient means of transportation encouraged the development of long-distance trade. Mesopotamians and Egyptians traded with each other perhaps as early as 3500 B.C.E., and both peoples also ventured further afield. Trade was especially important for the Sumerians, since southern Mesopotamia was a land with few natural resources. By 2300 B.C.E. Sumerians were trading regularly with merchants of Harappan society in the Indus River valley of northern India (discussed in the next chapter), which they probably reached by sailing the Persian Gulf and the Arabian Sea. Until about 1750 B.C.E. Sumerian merchants shipped woolen textiles, leather goods, sesame oil, and jewelry to India in exchange for copper, ivory, pearls, and semiprecious stones. During the time of the Babylonian empire, Mesopotamians traded extensively with peoples in all directions: they imported silver from Anatolia, cedar wood from Lebanon, copper from Arabia, gold from Egypt, tin from Persia, lapis lazuli from Afghanistan, and semiprecious stones from northern India.

Archaeological excavations have shed bright light on one Mesopotamian trade network in particular. During the early second millennium B.C.E., Assyrian merchants traveled regularly by donkey caravan some 965 kilometers (600 miles) from their home of Assur in northern Mesopotamia to Kanesh (modern Kültepe) in Anatolia. Surviving correspondence shows that during the forty-five years from 1810 to 1765 B.C.E. merchants transported eighty tons of tin and one hundred thousand textiles from Assur and returned from Kanesh with ten tons of silver. The correspondence also shows that the merchants and their families operated a well-organized business. Merchants' wives and children manufactured textiles in Assur and sent them to their menfolk who lived in trading colonies at Kanesh. The merchants responded with orders for textiles in the styles desired at Kanesh.

After 3000 B.C.E. Egyptians traded actively in the Mediterranean. Since Egypt has few trees, all wood came from abroad. Pharaohs especially prized aromatic cedar for their tombs, and Egyptian ships imported huge loads from Lebanon. One record of about 2600 B.C.E. mentions an expedition of forty ships filled with cedar logs. In exchange for cedar Egyptians offered gold, silver, linen textiles, leather goods, and dried foods such as lentils. Egyptians also traded through the Red Sea and the Gulf of Aden with an east African land they called Punt—probably modern-day Somalia and Ethiopia. From Punt they imported gold, ebony, ivory, cattle, slaves, cosmetics, and aromatics. The tomb of Queen Hatshepsut, the first woman to rule Egypt as pharaoh, bears detailed illustrations of a trading expedition Hatshepsut sent to Punt about 1500 B.C.E. Paintings in the tomb show large Egyptian ships bearing jewelry, tools, and weapons to Punt and then loading the exotic products of the southern land, including apes, monkeys, dogs, a live panther, and live myrrh trees with their roots carefully bound in bags. Specialization of labor and increasingly efficient technologies of transportation not only quickened the economies of complex societies but also encouraged interaction between peoples of distant lands.

The Emergence of Stratified Societies

Social Classes   Agriculture enabled human groups to accumulate wealth, and social distinctions between the more and less wealthy appeared in neolithic towns like Jericho and Çatal Hüyük. With specialized labor and long-distance trade, however, cities provided many more opportunities for the accumulation of wealth. Social distinctions in ancient Mesopotamia and Egypt became much more sharply defined than those of neolithic villages and towns.

Queen Hatshepsut's fleet takes on cargo at Punt. Stevedores carry jars of aromatics and trees with carefully wrapped roots onto the Egyptian vessels. In the bottom panel, ships loaded with cargo prepare to depart. • Courtesy of the Trustees of The British Library

Mesopotamian Kings

In early Mesopotamia the ruling classes consisted of kings and nobles who won their positions because of their valor and success as warriors. Community members originally elected their kings, but royal status soon became hereditary, as kings arranged for their sons to succeed them. Nobles were mostly members of royal families and other close supporters of the kings.

The early kings of the Sumerian cities made such a deep impression on their contemporaries that legends portrayed them as offspring of the gods. Gilgamesh, for example, who ruled Uruk and organized the construction of city walls there shortly after 3000 B.C.E., was the hero of a remarkable *Epic of Gilgamesh* that described him as two-thirds human and one-third divine. Later legends recognized him as a full-fledged god. Large-scale construction projects ordered by the kings and the lavish decoration of capital cities also reflected the high status of the Mesopotamian ruling classes. All the Mesopotamian cities boasted massive city walls and imposing public buildings.

Temple Communities

Closely allied with the ruling elites were priests and priestesses, many of whom were younger relatives of the rulers. The principal role of the priestly elites was to intervene with the gods to ensure good fortune for their communities. In exchange for these services, priests and priestesses lived in temple communities and received offerings of food, drink, and clothing from city inhabitants. Temples also generated their own income from vast tracts of land that they owned and large workshops that they maintained. One temple community near the city of Lagash employed six thousand textile workers between 2150 and 2100 B.C.E. Other temple communities cultivated grains, herded sheep and goats, and manufactured leather, wood, metal, and stone goods. Because of their wealth, temples provided comfortable livings for their inhabitants, and they also served the needs of the larger community. Temples functioned as banks where individuals could store wealth and helped underwrite trading ventures to distant lands. They also helped those in need by taking in orphans, supplying grain in times of famine, and providing ransoms for captives taken in battle.

Gypsum carving of an elderly couple from the city of Nippur about 2500 B.C.E. •
Courtesy of the Oriental Institute of the University of Chicago

Apart from the ruling and priestly elites, Mesopotamian society included less privileged classes of free commoners, dependent clients, and slaves. Free commoners mostly worked as peasant cultivators in the countryside on land owned by their families, although some also worked in the cities as builders, craftsmen, or professionals, such as physicians or engineers. Dependent clients had fewer options than free commoners because they possessed no property. Dependent clients usually worked as agricultural laborers on estates owned by others, including the king, nobles, or priestly communities, and they owed a portion of their production to the landowners. Free commoners and dependent clients all paid taxes—usually in the form of surplus agricultural production—that supported the ruling classes, military forces, and temple communities. In addition, when conscripted by ruling authorities, free commoners and dependent clients also provided labor services for large-scale construction projects involving roads, city walls, irrigation systems, temples, and public buildings.

Slaves   Slaves came from three main sources: prisoners of war, convicted criminals, and heavily indebted individuals who sold themselves into slavery in order to satisfy their obligations. Some slaves worked as agricultural laborers on the estates of nobles or temple communities, but most were domestic servants in wealthy households. Many masters granted slaves their freedom, often with a financial bequest, after several years of good service. Slaves with accommodating masters sometimes even engaged in small-scale trade and earned enough money to purchase their own freedom.

Egyptian Society   Like the Mesopotamians, ancient Egyptians also recognized a series of well-defined social classes. Egyptian priests, commoners, and slaves played roles in society similar to those of their Mesopotamian counterparts. The organization of the ruling classes, however, differed considerably between Mesopotamia and Egypt. Instead of a series of urban kings, as in Mesopotamia, Egyptians recognized the pharaoh as a supreme central ruler. Because the pharaoh was theoretically an absolute ruler, Egyptian society had little room for a noble class like that of Mesopotamia. Instead of depending on nobles who owed their positions to their birth, Egypt relied on professional military forces and an elaborate bureaucracy of administrators and tax collectors who served the central government. Thus much more than in Mesopotamia, in Egypt individuals of common birth could attain high positions in society through service to the pharaoh.

The Construction of Patriarchal Societies

Both Mesopotamia and Egypt built patriarchal societies that vested authority over public and private affairs in their men. Within their households men decided the work that family members would perform and made marriage arrangements for their children as well as any others who came under their authority. Men also dominated public life; with rare exceptions men ruled as kings and pharaohs, and decisions about policies and public affairs rested mostly in men's hands.

HAMMURABI'S LAWS ON FAMILY RELATIONSHIPS

• • •

By the time of Hammurabi, Mesopotamian marriages represented important business and economic relationships between families. Hammurabi's laws reflect a desire to ensure the legitimacy of children and to protect the economic interests of both marital partners and their families. While placing women under the authority of their fathers and husbands, the laws also protected women against unreasonable treatment by their husbands or other men.

128: If a seignior acquired a wife, but did not draw up the contracts for her, that woman is no wife.

129: If the wife of a seignior has been caught while lying with another man, they shall bind them and throw them into the water. If the husband of the woman wishes to spare his wife, then the king in turn may spare his subject.

130: If a seignior bound the (betrothed) wife of a(nother) seignior, who had no intercourse with a male and was still living in her father's house, and he has lain in her bosom and they have caught him, that seignior shall be put to death, while that woman shall go free.

131: If a seignior's wife was accused by her husband, but she was not caught while lying with another man, she shall make affirmation by god and return to her house. . . .

138: If a seignior wishes to divorce his wife who did not bear him children, he shall give her money to the full amount of her marriage-price [money or goods that the husband paid to the bride's family in exchange for the right to marry her] and he shall also make good to her the dowry [money or goods that the bride brought to the marriage] which she brought from her father's house and then he may divorce her.

139: If there was no marriage-price, he shall give her one mina of silver as the divorce-settlement.

140: If he is a peasant, he shall give her one-third mina of silver.

141: If a seignior's wife, who was living in the house of the seignior, has made up her mind to leave in order that she may engage in business, thus neglecting her house (and) humiliating her husband, they shall prove it against her; and if her husband has then decided on her divorce, he may divorce her, with nothing to be given her as her divorce-settlement upon her departure. If her husband has not decided on her divorce, her husband may marry another woman, with the former woman living in the house of her husband like a maidservant.

142: If a woman so hated her husband that she has declared, "You may not have me," her record shall be investigated at her city council, and if she was careful and was not at fault, even though her husband has been going out and disparaging her greatly, that woman, without incurring any blame at all, may take her dowry and go off to her father's house.

143: If she was not careful, but was a gadabout, thus neglecting her house (and) humiliating her husband, they shall throw that woman into the water.

SOURCE: James B. Pritchard, ed. *Ancient Near Eastern Texts Relating to the Old Testament.* Princeton: Princeton University Press, 1955, pp. 171–72.

Hammurabi's laws throw considerable light on sex and gender relations in ancient Mesopotamia. The laws recognized men as heads of their households and entrusted all major family decisions to their judgment. Men even had the power to sell their wives and children into slavery to satisfy their debts. In the interests of protecting the reputations of husbands and the legitimacy of offspring, the laws prescribed death by drowning as the punishment for wives caught in adultery, as well as for their partners, but permitted men to engage in consensual sexual relations with concubines, slaves, or prostitutes without penalty.

Women's Roles   In spite of their subordinate legal status, women made their influence felt in both Mesopotamian and Egyptian societies. At ruling courts women influenced kings, pharaohs, and their governments. They sometimes served as regents for young rulers and occasionally took power themselves, as in the case of Queen Hatshepsut (reigned 1503–1482 B.C.E.), who was the first woman to claim the title of pharaoh. A few women wielded great power as high priestesses who managed the enormous estates belonging to their temples. Others obtained a formal education and worked as scribes—literate individuals who prepared administrative and legal documents for governments and private parties. Women also pursued careers as midwives, shopkeepers, brewers, bakers, tavern keepers, and textile manufacturers.

During the second millennium B.C.E., Mesopotamian men progressively tightened their control over the social and sexual behavior of women. To protect family fortunes and guarantee the legitimacy of heirs, Mesopotamians insisted on the virginity of brides at marriage. They prohibited wives from engaging in extramarital sexual relations and even forbade casual socializing between married women and men outside their family. By 1500 B.C.E., and probably even earlier than that, married women in Mesopotamian cities had begun to wear veils when they ventured beyond their own households in order to discourage the attention of men from other families. This concern to control women's social and sexual behavior spread throughout much of southwest Asia and the Mediterranean basin, where it reinforced patriarchal social structures over the long term of history.

WRITING AND THE FORMATION OF SOPHISTICATED CULTURAL TRADITIONS

In both Mesopotamia and Egypt, writing was the foundation of sophisticated cultural traditions. Originally invented for purposes of record keeping, writing quickly became an indispensable tool for government, administration, and trade. Moreover, it became clear that writing had uses that went well beyond purely practical matters of keeping records and storing information. Already in the early third millennium B.C.E., Mesopotamians and Egyptians relied on writing to communicate complex ideas about the world, the gods, human beings, and their relationships with each other. Writing made possible the emergence of distinctive cultural traditions that shaped Mesopotamian and Egyptian values for almost three thousand years.

The Origins of Writing

The world's earliest known writing came from Mesopotamia. Humans who settled in cities and established government institutions needed some means more reliable than human memory to keep track of tax collections and commercial transactions. About the middle of the fourth millennium B.C.E., people began to experiment with pictographs representing animals and produce—such as sheep, oxen, fish, pots, wheat, and barley—that figured prominently in tax and trade records. By 3100 B.C.E. conventional signs representing specific words had spread throughout Mesopotamia.

Cuneiform Writing   A writing system that depends on pictures is useful for purposes such as keeping records, but it is a cumbersome way to communicate abstract ideas. Beginning about 2900 B.C.E. the Sumerians developed a more flexible system of writing that used graphic symbols to represent sounds, syllables, and ideas, as well as physical objects. By combining pictographs and other symbols, the Sumerians created a powerful writing system.

Cuneiform tablet from Ur dating from the period 2900 to 2600 B.C.E. It records deliveries of barley to a temple. • © The British Museum

When writing, a Sumerian scribe used a stylus fashioned from a reed to impress symbols on wet clay. Because the stylus left lines and wedge-shaped marks, Sumerian writing is known as *cuneiform,* a term that comes from two Latin words meaning "wedge-shaped." When dried in the sun or baked in an oven, the clay hardened and preserved a permanent record of the scribe's message; many examples of early Sumerian writing survive to the present day. Babylonians, Assyrians, Hittites, and other peoples later adopted the Sumerians' script to their own languages, and the tradition of cuneiform writing continued for more than three thousand years. Although it entered a period of decline in the fourth century B.C.E. after the arrival of Greek alphabetic script, in which each written symbol represents a distinct, individual sound, scribes produced small numbers of cuneiform documents into the early centuries C.E.

Hieroglyphic Writing

Writing appeared in Egypt about 3100 B.C.E., possibly as a result of Mesopotamian influence. As in Mesopotamia, the earliest Egyptian writing was pictographic, but Egyptians also soon supplemented their pictographs with symbols representing sounds and ideas. Early Greek visitors to Egypt marveled at the large and handsome pictographs that adorned Egyptian monuments and buildings. Since the symbols were particularly prominent on temples, the visitors called them *hieroglyphs,* from two Greek words meaning "holy inscriptions."

In addition to being striking and dramatic, hieroglyphs were also somewhat cumbersome. Egyptians employed hieroglyphs in formal writing and carved them on monuments, but for everyday affairs they relied on the hieratic ("priestly") script, a simplified, cursive form of hieroglyphs. Hieratic appeared in the early centuries of the third millennium B.C.E., and Egyptians made extensive use of the script for more than three thousand years, from 2600 B.C.E. to about 600 C.E. Hieratic largely disappeared after the middle of the first millennium C.E., when Egyptians adapted the Greek alphabet to their own language and developed alphabetic scripts known as the demotic ("popular") and Coptic ("Egyptian") scripts.

Education, Literacy, and Learning

Most education in ancient times was vocational instruction designed to train individuals to work in specific trades and crafts. Yet Mesopotamians and Egyptians also established schools and developed traditions of literature and learning based on writing. Most of those who learned to read and write became scribes or government officials. A few pursued their studies further and became priests, physicians, or professionals such as engineers and architects. Formal education was by no means common; even kings and pharaohs were often illiterate. But education and literacy were essential to the smooth functioning of Mesopotamian and Egyptian societies.

Scribes

Formal education and literacy brought handsome rewards in ancient times. The privileged life of a scribe comes across clearly in a work known as *The Satire of the Trades*. Written by a scribe of Egypt's Middle Kingdom encouraging his son to study diligently, the work detailed all the miseries associated with eighteen different professions: metalsmiths stunk like fish; potters grubbed in the mud like pigs; fishermen ran the risk of sudden death in the jaws of the Nile's ferocious crocodiles. Only the scribe led a comfortable, honorable, and dignified life.

Astronomy and Mathematics

Literacy and education led to a rapid expansion of knowledge. In both Mesopotamia and Egypt, scholars devoted themselves to the study of astronomy and mathematics—both important sciences for agricultural societies. Knowledge of astronomy helped Mesopotamians and Egyptians to prepare accurate calendars, which in turn enabled them to chart the rhythms of the seasons and determine the appropriate times for planting and harvesting crops. They used their mathematical skills to survey agricultural lands and allocate them to the proper owners or tenants. Some Mesopotamian conventions persist to the present day: Mesopotamian scientists divided the year into twelve months, for example, and they divided the hours of the day into sixty minutes, each composed of sixty seconds.

The Epic of Gilgamesh

As their scripts became more flexible and versatile, Mesopotamians and Egyptians used writing to communicate abstract ideas, explore challenging intellectual problems, and reflect on human beings and their place in the world. Best known of the reflective literature from Mesopotamia is the *Epic of Gilgamesh*. Parts of this work came from the earliest Sumerian city-states, but the whole epic, as known today, was the work of compilers who lived after 2000 B.C.E. during the days of the Babylonian empire. In recounting the experiences of Gilgamesh, king of Uruk, the epic explored themes of human friendship, relations between humans and the gods, and especially the meaning of life and death. At the core of the tale stood Gilgamesh and Enkidu, fast friends who roamed the earth searching for adventure. In spite of their heroic deeds, Enkidu offended the gods and fell under a sentence of death. His loss profoundly affected Gilgamesh, who sought for some means to cheat death and gain eternal life. He eventually found a magical plant that had the power to confer immortality, but as Gilgamesh slept, a serpent stole the plant and carried it away. Thus Gilgamesh had to resign himself to the fact that death is the ultimate fate of all human beings.

The Origins of Organized Religion

Community Gods

Mesopotamians and Egyptians believed that deities intervened regularly in human affairs and that proper cultivation of the gods was an important community responsibility. Each Mesopotamian city held one deity in especially high esteem and supported priests and temple communities devoted to the chosen god's cult. Uruk, for example, honored Inanna, the goddess of fertility, while Babylon revered Marduk as patron deity of the city. Temples dedicated to these and other gods were prominent features of urban landscapes in Mesopotamia. Most distinctive were the ziggurats—step pyramids constructed of bricks and topped by altars at which priests carried out ritual observances.

Amon-Re

For much of Egyptian history, priests honored the sun god Re and the air god Amon in the combined cult of Amon-Re. At Heliopolis ("City of the Sun," near Memphis), priests built a massive temple complex where they honored Amon-Re and studied the heavens for astronomical purposes. When Egypt became an imperial power during the New Kingdom, devotees suggested that Amon-Re might even be a universal god who presided over all the earth.

For a brief period Amon-Re faced a monotheistic challenge from the god Aten, also associated with the sun. Aten's champion was Pharaoh Amenhotep IV (reigned 1353–1335 B.C.E.), who changed his name to Akhenaten in honor of his preferred deity. Akhenaten considered Aten the world's "sole god, like whom there is no other." Thus unlike the priests of Amon-Re, who viewed their god as one among many, Akhenaten and other devotees of Aten considered their deity the one and only true god. Their faith might well have represented the world's first monotheism—the belief that a single god rules over all creation.

Akhenaten

Akhenaten built a new capital city called Akhetaten ("Horizon of Aten," located at modern Tell el-Amarna), where broad streets, courtyards, and open temples allowed unobscured vision and constant veneration of the sun. He also dispatched agents to all parts of Egypt with instructions to chisel out the names of Amon-Re and other gods from inscriptions on temples and other public buildings and to encourage the worship of Aten. As long as Akhenaten lived, the cult of Aten flourished. But when the pharaoh died, the priests of Amon-Re mounted a fierce counterattack that restored Amon-Re to privileged status and led to the near annihilation of Aten's cult.

Whereas Mesopotamians believed with Gilgamesh that death brought an end to an individual's existence, many Egyptians believed that death was not an end so much as a transition to a new dimension of existence. The yearning for immortality helps to explain the Egyptian practice of mummifying the dead. During the Old Kingdom, Egyptians believed that only the ruling elites would survive the grave, so they only mummified pharaohs and their close relatives. Later, however, other royal officials and wealthy individuals merited the posthumous honor of mummification. During the Middle and New Kingdoms, Egyptians came to think of eternal life as a condition available to normal mortals as well. Mummification never became general practice in Egypt, but a variety of religious cults promised to lead individuals of all classes to immortality.

The Quest for Immortality

The cult of Osiris, for example, attracted particularly strong popular interest. According to the myths surrounding the cult, Osiris's evil brother Seth murdered him and scattered his dismembered parts throughout Egypt, but the victim's loyal wife, Isis, retrieved his parts and gave her husband a proper burial. Impressed by her devotion, the gods restored Osiris to life—not to physical human life among mortals, however, but to a different kind of existence as god of the underworld, the dwelling place of the departed. Because of his death and resurrection, Egyptians associated Osiris with the Nile (which flooded, retreated, and then flooded again the following year) and with their crops (which similarly grew, died, and then sprouted again.)

Cult of Osiris

Egyptians also associated Osiris with immortality and honored him through a religious cult that demanded observance of high moral standards. As lord of the underworld, Osiris had the power to determine who deserved the blessing of immortality and who did not. Following their deaths, individual souls faced the judgment of Osiris, who had their hearts weighed against a feather symbolizing justice. Those with heavy hearts carrying a burden of evil and guilt did not merit immortality, whereas those of pure heart and honorable deeds gained the gift of eternal life. Thus Osiris's cult held out hope of eternal reward for those who behaved according to high moral standards, and it cast its message in terms understandable to cultivators in early agricultural society.

Isis (standing on the left) and Osiris (seated on the right) watch as an attendant weighs the heart of a recently deceased princess against a feather. This illustration is from a papyrus copy of the *Book of the Dead* that was buried with a royal mummy. • The British Museum/Bridgeman Art Library

  THE BROADER INFLUENCE OF MESOPOTAMIAN AND EGYPTIAN SOCIETIES

Even in the earliest days of their societies, both Mesopotamians and Egyptians influenced peoples living far beyond their own lands. Sometimes their accumulated wealth attracted the attention of neighboring peoples, who then relied on Mesopotamian and Egyptian examples when organizing their own societies. Sometimes Mesoptamians and Egyptians projected their own power into foreign lands and forcibly introduced their own ways. Their experiences show that even in early times, complex agricultural societies organized around cities had a tendency to expand and influence the development of distant human communities.

Mesopotamian Influence on the Hebrews and the Phoenicians

The Hebrews   The earliest Hebrews were pastoral nomads who lived in the regions between Mesopotamia and Egypt during the second millennium B.C.E. According to the Hebrew scriptures (the Old Testament of the Christian Bible), the Hebrew patriarch Abraham was a native of the Sumerian city of Ur, and the Hebrews themselves recognized many of the deities, values, and customs common to Mesopotamian peoples. Hebrew law, for example, borrowed the principle of *lex talionis* from Hammurabi's code. The Hebrews also told the story of a devastating flood that had destroyed all early human society—a variation of a similar flood story related during the earliest days of Sumerian history. The Hebrews altered the story and adapted it to their own interests and purposes, but their familiarity with the story shows that the Hebrews emerged from the larger tradition of Mesopotamian society.

According to their scriptures, some Hebrews migrated to Egypt during the eighteenth century B.C.E. About the year 1300 B.C.E., however, they departed under the leadership of Moses and went to Palestine, where they established a regional kingdom. During the reigns of David and Solomon (1000–930 B.C.E.), the Hebrews dominated the territory between Syria and the Sinai peninsula. They also fashioned a Mesopotamian-style political and social order, abandoning their inherited tribal struc-

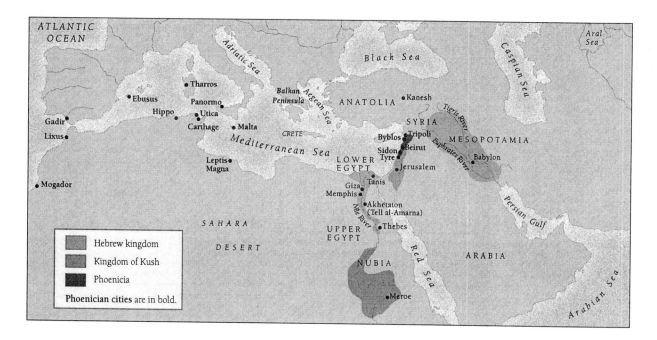

MAP [2.3]
The broader influence of Mesopotamia and Egypt.

ture in favor of a tightly controlled monarchy. They built an elaborate and cosmopolitan capital city at Jerusalem and entered into diplomatic and commercial relations with Mesopotamians and other peoples. The Hebrews also made use of iron technology to strengthen their military forces and produce tough agricultural implements.

Yahweh

After the time of Moses, Hebrew religious beliefs developed along increasingly distinctive lines. Originally, the Hebrews honored many of the same gods as their Mesopotamian neighbors. Moses, however, taught that there was only one supreme god, known as Yahweh, the creator and sustainer of the world and all within it. Yahweh expected his followers to worship him, and he also demanded that they observe high moral and ethical standards. Between the tenth and second centuries B.C.E., the Hebrews compiled their holy scriptures, a body of writings that laid down Yahweh's laws and outlined his role in creating the world and guiding human affairs. Their devotion to Yahweh, their religious texts, and their concern for righteousness provided the Hebrews with a strong sense of identity as a people distinct from Mesopotamians and others. Even after the eighth century B.C.E., when their kingdom fell to the Assyrians, the Hebrews maintained their identity. Over the long term the Hebrews' monotheism, scriptures, and moral concerns also profoundly influenced the development of Christianity and Islam.

The Phoenicians

North of the Hebrew kingdom in Palestine, the Phoenicians occupied a narrow strip of territory between the Mediterranean and the mountains of Lebanon. Their meager lands did not permit development of a large agricultural society, so the Phoenicians turned to industry and trade. They imported food and raw materials from Mesopotamia. In their major cities—Tyre, Sidon, and Byblos—they produced metal goods, textiles, and glass for export, and they also supplied Mesopotamians and Egyptians with cedar logs for construction and shipbuilding. By about 2500 B.C.E. Phoenician merchants and ships already dominated trade in the Mediterranean basin. Between about 1200 and 800 B.C.E., the Phoenicians established colonies in

NORTH SEMITIC			GREEK		EURUSCAN	LATIN	
EARLY PHOENICIAN	EARLY HEBREW	PHOENICIAN	EARLY	CLASSICAL	EARLY	EARLY	CLASSICAL
K	K	X	◁	A	A	A	A
9	9	9	9	B	B		B
1	\	1	1	Γ	ᐃ		C
△	ᑫ	ᐸ	△	△	⋂	ᑫ	D

Phoenician, Greek, Hebrew, and Roman letters. After Ruth Whitehouse and John Wilkins, *The Making of Civilization: History Discovered through Archaeology*. New York Knopf, 1986, p. 136.

Cyprus, Sicily, Spain, and north Africa. Long after the Assyrians and other conquerors overran their home territory in the eighth century B.C.E., Phoenicians continued to dominate Mediterranean trade and shipping from their colonies.

Alphabetic Writing   Like the Hebrews, the Phoenicians largely adapted Mesopotamian cultural traditions to their own needs. They recognized Mesopotamian gods, used Mesopotamian weights and measures, and relied on Mesopotamian astronomy for navigation. In one case, however, a Phoenician adaptation changed history: the Phoenicians invented alphabetic writing. About 1500 B.C.E. Phoenician scribes simplified Mesopotamia's cuneiform writing system by devising twenty-two symbols representing consonants. (The earliest Phoenician alphabet had no vowels.) Learning twenty-two letters and building words with them was much easier than memorizing the hundreds of symbols that mastery of cuneiform writing required. Because alphabetic writing required much less investment in education than did cuneiform writing, more people became literate than ever before.

The Phoenicians not only invented an alphabet but disseminated it as well. As they traveled and traded throughout the Mediterranean, they taught their alphabet to other peoples, who adapted it to their own languages. Greeks, for example, modified the Phoenician alphabet and added symbols representing vowels. Romans later adapted the Greek alphabet to their own needs and passed it along to their cultural heirs in Europe. Meanwhile, Egyptians also turned to simplified, alphabetic writing during the middle centuries of the first millennium B.C.E. as they increasingly used the alphabetic demotic script in place of hieroglyphic and hieratic writing. In later centuries alphabetic writing spread to central Asia, south Asia, southeast Asia, and ultimately throughout most of the world.

Egyptian Influence in Sub-Saharan Africa

Nubia   Like the Mesopotamians, Egyptians interacted with other peoples in the eastern Mediterranean basin, and they left traces of their influence on the Minoan society that arose on the island of Crete during the second millennium B.C.E. and on early Greek society as well. Egyptians also influenced peoples to the south in sub-Saharan Africa. By the second millennium B.C.E., the land that the Egyptians called Nubia (the northern region of the modern state of Sudan) had become the site of an agricultural society. Nubians did not possess such extensive fertile lands as the Egyptians, nor did they build such a powerful state as their northern neighbors. They enjoyed access to gold, ivory, ebony, gems, and aromatics, however, and they traded these items, as well as slaves, for Egyptian cloth and manufactured goods.

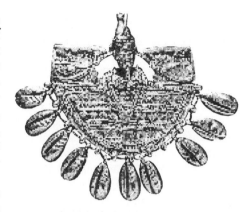

An elaborate gold ring from a tomb at Meroe, dating probably to the third century C.E., depicts a deity named Sebiumeker (sometimes referred to as Sebewyemeker). Although associated with Osiris, Sebiumeker was a Meroitic god with no exact counterpart in Egypt. • Staatliche Museen zu Berlin-Preussischer Kulturbesitz-Aegyptisches Museum/Photo: Margarete Busing

Relations between Egypt and Nubia were not always peaceful. Nubian armies periodically ventured north along the Nile, menacing Thebes in search of the wealth of Egypt. In efforts to secure Upper Egypt, the pharaohs often sent their own forces south into Nubia. During the Middle Kingdom, Egyptians established forts in Nubia, and the militant pharaohs of the New Kingdom imposed direct Egyptian rule on Nubia and sent deputies to administer the land.

Frequent encounters between Egyptians and Nubians led to a great deal of Egyptian influence in the southern land. The sons of Nubian rulers went north to Egypt, where they received an Egyptian education at the pharaohs' courts. Meanwhile, Egyptian cultural traditions went south: Nubians adopted the Egyptians' pyramids, temples, gods, and hieroglyphic writing. At the Nubian capital of Napata, for example, a large temple complex promoted the cult of Amon-Re.

As Egyptian power waned during the first millennium B.C.E., Nubians established the kingdom of Kush, which played a prominent role in the affairs of the Nile valley. About 750 B.C.E. the king of Kush even invaded Egypt and imposed Nubian rule. The fortunes of Egypt and Nubia remained closely intertwined until Assyrian conquerors drove the Kushites from Egypt in 664 B.C.E.

Kush

Thereafter, Kush developed along increasingly independent lines. The kings of Kush moved their capital south from Napata to Meroe, about 500 kilometers (310 miles) upriver, where Egyptian influence was weak, especially during this age of Egyptian decline. From about 530 to 300 B.C.E., the Kushites built a society that reflected Egyptian inspiration but that developed along different lines. They continued to construct pyramids and temples in the Egyptian style and to worship Amon-Re, but they also devoted more attention to their own deities. Meanwhile, Kushite scribes abandoned Egyptian hieroglyphs and devised an alphabetic script for their language.

Nubia exercised a profound influence on African history by spreading the technology of iron metallurgy. Nubians forged iron tools and weapons perhaps as early as the ninth century B.C.E., and slag from the ancient furnaces of Meroe was noticeable into the twentieth century. Ironworking soon spread to other regions of sub-Saharan Africa, where iron ores abound, and iron metallurgy became prominent throughout much of the continent.

Iron Metallurgy

Mesopotamians and Egyptians built on the foundations of neolithic peoples, but they constructed societies that were much more complex and influential than those of their predecessors. Through their city-states, kingdoms, and regional empires, Mesopotamians and Egyptians created formal institutions of government that extended the authority of ruling elites to all corners of their states, and they occasionally mobilized forces that projected their power to lands well beyond their own boundaries. They generated several distinct social classes. Specialized labor fueled productive economies and encouraged the establishment of long-distance trade networks. Both Mesopotamians and Egyptians devised systems of writing, and both relied on writing in developing traditions of literature, learning, and religion. Considering the wealth and power of their societies, it is not surprising that Mesopotamians and Egyptians deeply influenced the development of peoples throughout southwest Asia and the Mediterranean basin.

CHRONOLOGY

MESOPOTAMIA

3200–2350 B.C.E.	Era of Sumerian dominance
2350–1600 B.C.E.	Era of Babylonian dominance
2334–2315 B.C.E.	Reign of Sargon of Akkad
1792–1750 B.C.E.	Reign of Hammurabi
1000–612 B.C.E.	Era of Assyrian dominance
600–550 B.C.E.	New Babylonian empire
605–562 B.C.E.	Reign of Nebuchadnezzar

EGYPT

3100 B.C.E.	Unification of Egypt
3100–2600 B.C.E.	Archaic Period
2660–2180 B.C.E.	Old Kingdom
2080–1640 B.C.E.	Middle Kingdom
1570–1075 B.C.E.	New Kingdom
1490–1436 B.C.E.	Reign of Tuthmosis III
1353–1335 B.C.E.	Reign of Amenhotep IV (Akhenaten)

FOR FURTHER READING

Cyril Aldred. *The Egyptians*. Rev. ed. New York, 1984. A popular, well-illustrated, and reliable survey of ancient Egyptian history.

Maria Eugenia Aubet. *The Phoenicians and the West: Politics, Colonies and Trade*. Trans. by M. Turton. Cambridge, 1993. A scholarly synthesis based on archaeological finds as well as written records.

Elizabeth Wayland Barber. *Women's Work: The First 20,000 Years*. New York, 1994. Fascinating study of ancient textiles, which the author argues was a craft industry dominated by women from the earliest times.

Basil Davidson. *Lost Cities of Africa*. Rev. ed. Boston, 1970. Popular account with discussions of Kush and Meroe.

T. G. H. James. *Pharaoh's People: Scenes from Life in Imperial Egypt*. London, 1984. Draws on recent archaeological and literary scholarship in reconstructing daily life in ancient Egypt.

Miriam Lichtheim, ed. *Ancient Egyptian Literature*. 3 vols. Berkeley, 1973–80. An important collection of primary sources in translation reflecting the results of recent scholarship.

William H. McNeill and Jean Sedlar, eds. *The Ancient Near East*. New York, 1968. A collection of primary sources in translation, concentrating on Mesopotamia and Egypt.

———, eds. *The Origins of Civilization*. New York, 1968. Like its companion volume cited above, a collection of translated sources concentrating on Mesopotamia and Egypt.

Hans J. Nissen. *The Early History of the Ancient Near East, 9000–2000 B.C.* Trans. by E. Lutzeier. Chicago, 1988. A brilliant synthesis of recent scholarship on the development of cities and complex society in Mesopotamia and neighboring regions.

Joan Oates. *Babylon*. London, 1979. Well-illustrated and authoritative examination of ancient Babylonian society.

J. N. Postgate. *Early Mesopotamia: Society and Economy at the Dawn of History*. London, 1992. Outstanding synthesis that draws on both archaeological and textual sources.

James B. Pritchard, ed. *Ancient Near Eastern Texts Relating to the Old Testament*. 2 vols. 3rd ed. Princeton, 1975. Important collection of primary sources in translation, emphasizing parallels between the ancient Hebrews and other peoples.

Michael Roaf. *Cultural Atlas of Mesopotamia and the Ancient Near East*. New York, 1990. Richly illustrated volume with well-informed essays on all dimensions of Mesopotamian history.

Georges Roux. *Ancient Iraq*. 3rd ed. London, 1992. A well-written and engaging survey of Mesopotamian political, social, economic, and cultural history.

N. K. Sandars, trans. *The Epic of Gilgamesh*. Harmondsworth, 1972. Excellent translation of the best-known Mesopotamian literary work.

CHAPTER 3

EARLY SOCIETY IN SOUTH ASIA AND THE INDO-EUROPEAN MIGRATIONS

. . .

For a god, Indra was a very rambunctious fellow. According to the stories told about him by the Aryans, Indra had few if any peers in fighting, feasting, or drinking. The Aryans were a herding people who spoke an Indo-European language and who migrated to south Asia in large numbers after 1500 B.C.E. In the early days of their migrations they took Indra as their chief deity. The Aryans told dozens of stories about Indra and sang hundreds of hymns in his honor.

One story had to do with a war between the gods and the demons. When the gods were flagging, they appointed Indra as their leader, and soon they had turned the tide against their enemies. Another story, a favorite one of the Aryans, had to do with Indra's role in bringing rain to the earth—a crucial concern for any agricultural society. According to this story, Indra did battle with a dragon who lived in the sky and hoarded water in the clouds. Indra first slaked his thirst with generous drafts of *soma*, a hallucinogenic potion consumed by Aryan priests, and then attacked the dragon, which he killed by hurling thunderbolts at it. The dragon's heavy fall caused turmoil both on earth and in the atmosphere, but afterward the rains filled seven rivers that flowed through northern India and brought life-giving waters to inhabitants of the region.

The Aryans took Indra as a leader against earthly as well as heavenly foes. They did not mount a planned invasion of India, but as they migrated in sizable numbers into south Asia, they came into conflict with Dravidian peoples already living there. When they clashed with the Dravidians, the Aryans took the belligerent Indra as their guide. Aryan hymns praised Indra as the military hero who trampled enemy forces and opened the way for the migrants to build a new society.

For all his contributions, Indra did not survive permanently as a prominent deity. As Aryan and Dravidian peoples mixed, mingled, interacted, and intermarried, tensions between them subsided. Memories of the stormy and violent Indra receded into the background, and eventually they faded almost to nothing. For a thousand years and more, however, Aryans looked upon the rowdy, raucous war god as a ready source of inspiration as they sought to build a society in an already occupied land.

Sandstone bust of a distinguished man, perhaps a priest-king, from Mohenjo-daro. • Josephine Powell

Tools excavated by archaeologists show that India was a site of paleolithic communities at least two hundred thousand years ago, long before the Aryans introduced Indra to south Asia. Between 8000 and 5000 B.C.E., cultivators built a neolithic society west of the Indus River, in the region bordering on the Iranian plateau, probably as a result of Mesopotamian influence. By 5000 B.C.E. agriculture had taken root in the Indus River valley. Thereafter agriculture spread rapidly, and by about 3000 B.C.E. Dravidian peoples had established neolithic communities throughout much of the Indian subcontinent. The earliest neolithic settlers cultivated wheat, barley, and cotton, and they also kept herds of cattle, sheep, and goats. Agricultural villages were especially numerous in the valley of the Indus River. As the population of the valley swelled and as people interacted with increasing frequency, some of these villages evolved into bustling cities, which served as the organizational centers of Indian society.

As in Mesopotamia and Egypt, early Indian cities stood at the center of an impressive political, social, and cultural order built by Dravidian peoples on the foundation of an agricultural economy. The earliest urban society in India, known as Harappan society, brought wealth and power to the Indus River valley. Eventually, however, it fell into decline, possibly because of environmental problems, just as large numbers of Indo-European migrants moved into India from central Asia and built a very different society. For half a millennium, from about 1500 to 1000 B.C.E., the Indian subcontinent was a site of turmoil as the migrants struggled with Dravidian peoples for control of the land and its resources. Gradually, however, stability returned with the establishment of numerous agricultural villages and regional states. During the centuries after 1000 B.C.E., Aryan and Dravidian peoples increasingly interacted and intermarried, and their combined legacies led to the development of a distinctive society and a rich cultural tradition.

❦ HARAPPAN SOCIETY

Like Mesopotamia and Egypt, Harappan society—named after Harappa, one of its two chief cities—developed in the valley of a river, the Indus, whose waters were available for irrigation of crops. As agricultural yields increased, the population also grew rapidly, and by about 3000 B.C.E. neolithic villages had evolved into thriving cities.

Unfortunately, it is impossible to follow the development of Harappan society in detail for two reasons. One is that the earliest Harappan physical remains are inaccessible. Silt deposits have raised the level of the land in the Indus valley, and the water table has risen correspondingly. Since the earliest Harappan remains lie below the water table, archaeologists cannot excavate them or study them systematically. The earliest accessible remains date from about 2500 B.C.E., when Harappan society was already well established. As a result, scholars have learned something about Harappa at its high point, but very little about the circumstances that brought it into being or the conditions of life during its earliest days.

A second problem that handicaps scholars who study Harappan society is the lack of deciphered written records. Harappans had a system of writing that used about four hundred symbols to represent sounds and words, and archaeologists have discovered thousands of clay seals, copper tablets, and other artifacts with Harappan inscriptions. Scholars consider the language most likely a Dravidian tongue related to those currently spoken in central and southern India, but they have not yet succeeded in deciphering the script. As a result, the details of Harappan life remain hidden behind the veil of an elaborate pictographic script. The understanding of Harappan society depends entirely on the study of material remains that archaeologists have uncovered since the 1920s.

Foundations of Harappan Society

If the Greek historian Herodotus had known of Harappan society, he might have called it "the gift of the Indus." Like the Nile, the Indus draws its waters from rain and melting snow in towering mountains—in this case, the Hindu Kush and the Himalayas, the world's highest peaks. As the waters charge downhill, they pick up enormous quantities of silt, which they carry for hundreds of kilometers. Like the Nile again, the Indus then deposits its burden of rich soil as it courses through lowlands and loses its force. Today, a series of dams has largely tamed the Indus, but for most of history it spilled its waters annually over a vast floodplain, sometimes with devastating effect. Much less predictable than the Nile, the Indus has many times left its channel altogether and carved a new course to the sea.

The Indus River

Despite its occasional ferocity, the Indus made agricultural society possible in northern India. Early cultivators sowed wheat and barley in September, after the flood receded, and harvested their crops the following spring. Inhabitants of the valley supplemented their harvests of wheat and barley with meat from herds of cattle, sheep, and goats. Their diet also included poultry: cultivators in the Indus valley kept flocks of the world's first domesticated chickens. Indus valley inhabitants cultivated cotton probably before 5000 B.C.E., and fragments of dyed cloth dating to about 2000 B.C.E. testify to the existence of a cotton textile industry.

As in Mesopotamia and Egypt, agricultural surpluses vastly increased the food supply, stimulated population growth, and supported the establishment of cities and specialized labor. Between 3000 and 2500 B.C.E., Dravidian peoples built a complex society that dominated the Indus River valley until its collapse about 1500 B.C.E. The agricultural surplus of the Indus valley fed two large cities, Harappa and Mohenjo-daro, as well as subordinate cities and a vast agricultural hinterland. Archaeologists have excavated about seventy Harappan settlements along the Indus River. Harappan society embraced much of modern-day Pakistan and a large part of northern India as well—a territory about 1.3 million square kilometers (502,000 square miles)—and thus was considerably larger than either Mesopotamian or Egyptian society.

No evidence survives concerning the Harappan political system, but the size of Harappa and Mohenjo-daro have led scholars to speculate that they might have served as twin capitals of the larger society or, alternatively, that they might have stood alongside others in a series of city-dominated regions in the Indus valley. Whatever the precise nature of their relationship, the two cities were very prominent in Harappan society. The population of Mohenjo-daro was about thirty-five thousand to forty thousand, while Harappa was probably slightly smaller. Archaeologists have discovered the sites of about 1,500 Harappan settlements, but none of the others approached the size of Harappa or Mohenjo-daro.

Harappa and Mohenjo-Daro

Both Harappa and Mohenjo-daro had a fortified citadel and a large granary, suggesting that they served as centers of political authority and sites for the collection and redistribution of taxes paid in the form of grain. The two cities represented a considerable investment of human resources: both featured broad streets, marketplaces, temples, public buildings, and extensive residential districts. Mohenjo-daro also had a large pool, perhaps used for religious or ritual purposes, with private dressing rooms for bathers.

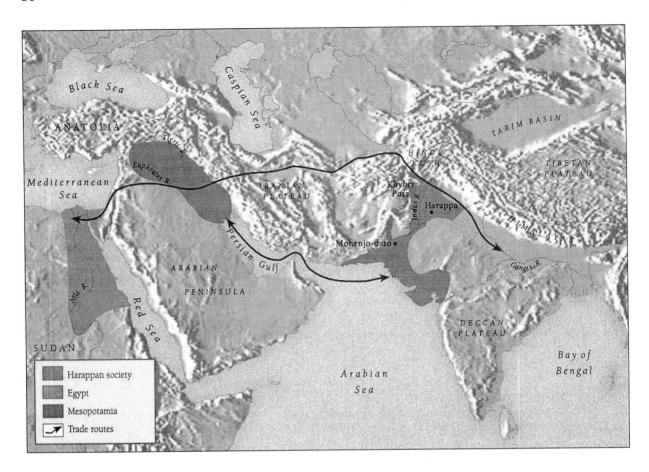

MAP [3.1]

Harappan society and its neighbors.

The two cities clearly established the patterns that shaped the larger society: weights, measures, architectural styles, and even brick sizes were consistent throughout the land, even though the Harappan society stretched almost 1,500 kilometers (932 miles) from one end to the other. This high degree of standardization suggests that Harappa and Mohenjo-daro were powerful central authorities whose influence touched all parts of Harappan society.

Specialized Labor and Trade

Like all complex societies in ancient times, Harappa depended on a successful agricultural economy. But Harappans also engaged in trade, both domestic and foreign. Pottery, tools, and decorative items produced in Harappa and Mohenjo-daro found their way to all corners of the Indus valley. From neighboring peoples in Persia and the Hindu Kush mountains, the Harappans obtained gold, silver, copper, lead, gems, and semiprecious stones. During the period about 2300 to 1750 B.C.E., they also traded with Mesopotamians, exchanging Indian copper, ivory, pearls, and semiprecious stones for Sumerian wool, leather, and olive oil. Some of this trade might have gone by land over the Iranian plateau, but most of it probably traveled by ships that followed the coastline of the Arabian Sea between the mouth of the Indus River and the Persian Gulf.

Harappan Society and Culture

Like Mesopotamia and Egypt, Harappan society generated considerable wealth. Excavations at Mohenjo-daro show that at its high point, from about 2500 to 2000 B.C.E.,

This aerial view of the excavations at Mohenjo-daro illustrates the careful planning and precise layout of the city. • MacQuitty International Collection

the city was a thriving economic center with a population of about forty thousand. Goldsmiths, potters, weavers, masons, and architects, among other professionals, maintained shops that lined Mohenjo-daro's streets. Other cities also housed communities of jewelers, artists, and merchants.

As in Mesopotamia and Egypt, the wealth of Harappan society encouraged the formation of sharp social distinctions. Harappans built no pyramids, palaces, or magnificent tombs, but their rulers wielded great authority from the citadels at Harappa and Mohenjo-daro. It is clear from Harappan dwellings that rich and poor lived in very different styles. In Mohenjo-daro, for example, many people lived in one-room tenements in barrackslike structures, but there were also individual houses of two and three stories with a dozen rooms and an interior courtyard, as well as a few very large houses with several dozen rooms and multiple courtyards. Most of the larger houses had their own wells and built-in brick ovens. Almost all houses had private bathrooms with showers and toilets that drained into city sewage systems. The water and sewage systems of Mohenjo-daro were among the most sophisticated of the ancient world, and they represented a tremendous investment of community resources.

Social Distinctions

In the absence of deciphered writing, Harappan beliefs and values are even more difficult to interpret than its politics and society. Here again, though, material remains shed some tantalizing light. A variety of statues, figurines, and illustrations on carved seals reflect a tradition of representational art. Among the most striking of all the remains is a bronze figurine of a dancing girl discovered at Mohenjo-daro. Provocatively posed and clad only in bracelets and a necklace, the figure expresses a remarkable suppleness and liveliness.

Fertility Cults

Bronze statuette of a dancing girl form Mohenjo-daro. • MacQuitty International Collection

Harappan religion reflected a strong concern for fertility. As in other early agricultural societies, Harappans venerated gods and goddesses whom they associated with creation and procreation. They recognized a mother goddess and a horned fertility god, and they held trees and animals sacred because of their associations with vital forces. For lack of written descriptions, it is impossible to characterize Harappan religious beliefs more specifically. Many scholars believe, however, that some Harappan deities survived the collapse of the larger society and found places later in the Hindu pantheon. Fertility and procreation are prominent concerns in popular Hinduism, and scholars have often noticed similarities between Harappan and Hindu deities associated with these values.

Sometime after 2000 B.C.E., Harappan society entered a period of decline. One cause was ecological degradation: Harappans deforested the Indus valley in order to clear land for cultivation and to obtain firewood. Deforestation led to erosion of topsoil and also to reduced amounts of rainfall. Over hundreds of years—perhaps half a millennium or

Harappan Decline

more—most of the Indus valley became a desert, and agriculture is possible there today only with the aid of artificial irrigation. These climatic and ecological changes reduced agricultural yields, and Harappan society faced a subsistence crisis during the centuries following 2000 B.C.E.

It is also possible that natural catastrophes—periodic flooding of the Indus River or earthquakes—might have weakened Harappan society. Archaeologists found more than thirty unburied human skeletons scattered about the streets and buildings of Mohenjo-daro. No sign of criminal or military violence accounts for their presence, but a sudden flood or earthquake could have trapped some residents who were unable to flee the impending disaster. In any case, by about 1700 B.C.E., the populations of Harappa and Mohenjo-daro had abandoned the cities as mounting difficulties made it impossible to sustain complex urban societies. Some of the smaller, subordinate cities outlived Harappa and Mohenjo-daro, but by about 1500 B.C.E., Harappan society had almost entirely collapsed.

 # THE INDO-EUROPEAN MIGRATIONS AND EARLY ARYAN INDIA

During the second millennium B.C.E., as Harappan society declined, bands of foreigners filtered into the Indian subcontinent and settled throughout the Indus valley and beyond. Most prominent were nomadic and pastoral peoples speaking Indo-European languages who called themselves Aryans ("noble people"). By 1500 B.C.E. or perhaps somewhat earlier, they had begun to file through the passes of the Hindu Kush mountains and establish small herding and agricultural communities throughout northern India.

Their migrations took place over several centuries: by no means did the arrival of the Aryans constitute an invasion or an organized military campaign. It is likely that Indo-European migrants clashed with Dravidians and other peoples already settled in India, but there is no indication that the Aryans conquered or destroyed Harappan society. By the time the Indo-Europeans entered India, internal problems had already brought Harappan society to the point of collapse. During the centuries after 1500 B.C.E., Dravidian and Indo-European peoples intermarried, interacted, and laid social and cultural foundations that would influence Indian society to the present day.

Indo-European Peoples and Their Migrations

The Aryans came from a much larger group of people known as Indo-Europeans. During the late eighteenth and nineteenth centuries, linguists noticed that many languages of Europe, Persia, and India featured remarkable similarities in vocabulary and grammatical structure. Ancient languages displaying these similarities included Sanskrit (the sacred language of Aryan India), Old Persian, Greek, and Latin. Modern descendants of these languages include Hindi and other languages of northern India, Farsi (the language of Iran), and most European languages, excepting only a few, such as Basque, Finnish, and Hungarian. Because of the geographical regions they spread to in ancient times, scholars refer to these tongues as Indo-European languages. Major subgroups of the Indo-European family of languages include Indo-Iranian, Greek, Balto-Slavic, Germanic, Italic, and Celtic. English belongs to the Germanic subgroup of the Indo-European family of languages.

Indo-European Languages

After noticing these linguistic similarities, scholars sought a way to explain the close relationship between the Indo-European languages. It was inconceivable that speakers of all these languages independently adopted similar vocabularies and grammatical structures. The only persuasive explanation for the high degree of linguistic coincidence was that speakers of Indo-European languages were all descendants of ancestors who spoke a common tongue and migrated from their original homeland. As migrants established their own separate communities and lost touch with each other, their languages evolved along different lines, adding new words and expressing ideas in different ways. Yet they retained the basic grammatical structure of their original speech, and they also kept much of their ancestors' vocabulary, even though they often adopted different pronunciations (and consequently different spellings) of these common words.

The original homeland of Indo-European speakers was probably the steppe region of modern-day Ukraine and southern Russia, the region just north of the Black Sea and the Caspian Sea. The earliest community of Indo-European speakers developed here between about 4500 and 2500 B.C.E. Individuals herded cattle, sheep, and goats, and they cultivated barley and millet at least in small quantities. Even more important, the earliest Indo-European speakers also kept herds of horses. In fact, they were probably the first people to domesticate horses and hitch their animals to carts and wagons. It is possible that individuals rode on horseback as early as the fifth millennium B.C.E. In any case horses provided early Indo-Europeans with a means of transportation that enabled them to establish a large zone of communication and interaction in the region north of the Black Sea and the Caspian Sea.

Indo-European Origins

TABLE 3.1

• • •

SIMILARITIES IN VOCABULARY INDICATING CLOSE RELATIONSHIPS BETWEEN SELECT INDO-EUROPEAN LANGUAGES

English	German	Spanish	Greek	Latin	Sanskrit
father	vater	padre	pater	pater	pitar
one	ein	uno	hen	unus	ekam
fire	feuer	fuego	pyr	ignis	agnis
field	feld	campo	agros	ager	ajras
sun	sonne	sol	helios	sol	surya
king	könig	rey	basileus	rex	raja
god	gott	dios	theos	deus	devas

Indo-European Migrations   Horsepower also provided Indo-Europeans with a means of expanding beyond their original homeland. As early as the fourth millennium B.C.E., some Indo-Europeans migrated east to central Asia and ventured as far as the Tarim Basin in what is now western China. Stunning evidence of these migrations recently came to light when archaeologists excavated burials of Caucasian individuals in China's Xinjiang province. Because of the region's extremely dry atmosphere, the fair skin, red hair, and brightly colored garments of some of the deceased individuals are still clearly visible.

About 3000 B.C.E. or soon thereafter, other Indo-Europeans migrated into Anatolia: these were the Hittites, who refined the technology of iron metallurgy and used it to build a powerful state. From Anatolia, Indo-Europeans migrated into eastern and central Europe, and later into western Europe as well. By 2500 B.C.E. Indo-European languages were in use from the Rhine River in central Europe to the Tarim Basin on the border of China.

Later migrations carried Indo-European languages to the west and south. During the second millennium B.C.E. migrants from Anatolia and eastern Europe established new communities throughout central and western Europe, including Italy, France, Spain, and the British Isles. Beginning about 1500 B.C.E. other migrants from central Asia entered India and established an Indo-European presence there. Similar migrations continued for centuries. Among the latest were migrations of Slavic peoples during the period 500 to 1000 C.E.

It is impossible to know the details of the interactions between early Indo-European migrants and the peoples they encountered. Indo-Europeans probably introduced agriculture and herding into some sparsely populated lands, where they most likely absorbed native hunting and gathering peoples into their own society. Elsewhere, Indo-Europeans migrated to lands that already supported settled, agricultural communities. In some cases the migrants might well have blended peacefully with existing populations, but it seems inevitable that their arrival sometimes led to violence. In those cases the Indo-Europeans' horses would have provided them with powerful advantages in conflicts with peoples who were less mobile. It is perhaps significant that many groups of Indo-European migrants considered them-

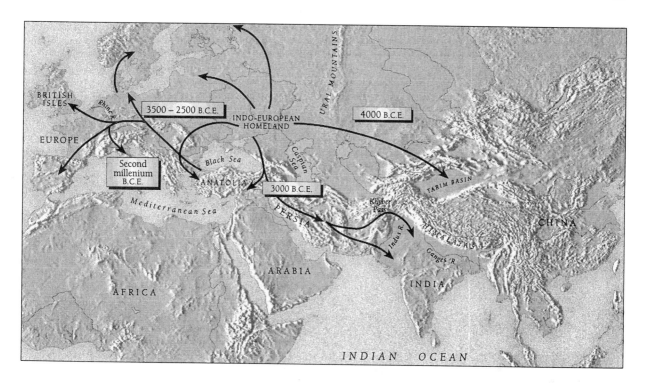

MAP [3.2]

Indo-European migrations, 4000–1000 B.C.E.

selves superior to other peoples: the terms *Aryan, Iran,* and *Eire* (the official name of the Republic of Ireland) all derive from the Indo-European word *aryo,* meaning "nobleman" or "lord."

The Indo-European migrations—reflected in the broad distribution of Indo-European languages throughout much of Eurasia—introduced domesticated horses to lands that had never before seen such animals and brought about interactions between peoples who had never encountered each other before. The arrival of these migrants had an especially deep influence on India.

The Aryans and India

When they entered India, the Aryans practiced a limited amount of agriculture, but they depended much more heavily on a pastoral economy. They kept sheep and goats, but they especially prized their herds of cattle. They consumed both dairy products and beef—cattle did not become sacred, protected animals in India (as they are today among Hindus) until many centuries after the Aryans' arrival. They even calculated wealth and prices in terms of cattle. They also had domesticated horses, which provided the Aryans with an efficient means of transportation when harnessed to wagons and a devastating war machine when hitched to chariots.

The Early Aryans

The Aryans preserved large collections of religious and literary works by memorizing them and transmitting them orally from one generation to another in their sacred language, Sanskrit. (For everyday communication, the Aryans relied on a related but less formal tongue known as Prakrit, which later evolved into Hindi, Bengali, Urdu, and other languages currently spoken in northern India.) The earliest of these orally transmitted works were the Vedas, which were collections of hymns, songs, prayers, and rituals honoring the various gods of the Aryans. There are four Vedas, the earliest

The Vedic Age

This bronze sword manufactured by Aryan craftsmen was a much stronger and more effective weapon than those available to Harappan defenders. • © The British Museum

and most important of which is the *Rig Veda,* a collection of some 1,028 hymns addressed to Aryan gods. Aryan priests compiled the *Rig Veda* between about 1400 and 900 B.C.E., and they committed it to writing, along with the three later Vedas, about 600 B.C.E.

The Vedas represent a priestly perspective on affairs: the word *veda* means "wisdom" or "knowledge" and refers to the knowledge that priests needed to carry out their functions. While transmitting religious knowledge, however, the Vedas also shed considerable light on early Aryan society in India. In view of their importance as historical sources, scholars refer to Indian history during the millennium between 1500 and 500 B.C.E. as the Vedic age.

The Vedas reflect a boisterous society in which the Aryans clashed repeatedly with the Dravidians and other peoples already living in India. The Vedas refer frequently to conflicts between Aryans and indigenous peoples whom the Aryans called *dasas,* meaning "enemies" or "subject peoples." The Vedas identify Indra, the Aryan war god and military hero, as one who ravaged citadels, smashed dams, and destroyed forts the way age consumes cloth garments. These characterizations suggest that the Aryans clashed repeatedly with the Dravidians of the Indus valley, attacking their cities and wrecking the irrigation systems that had supported agriculture in Harappan society.

The Aryans also fought ferociously among themselves. They did not have a state or common government, but rather formed hundreds of chiefdoms organized around herding communities and agricultural villages. Most of the chiefdoms had a leader known as a *raja*—a Sanskrit term related to the Latin word *rex* ("king")—who governed in collaboration with a council of village elders. Given the large number of chiefdoms, there was enormous potential for conflict in Aryan society. The men of one village often raided the herds of their neighbors—an offense of great significance, since the Aryans regarded cattle as the chief form of wealth in their society. Occasionally, too, ambitious chiefs sought to extend their authority by conquering neighbors and dominating the regions surrounding their own communities.

Aryan Migrations in India   During the early centuries of the Vedic age, Aryan groups settled in the Punjab, the upper Indus River valley that straddles the modern-day border between northern India and Pakistan. Later they spread east and south from their base and established communities throughout much of the Indian subcontinent. After 1000 B.C.E. they began to settle in the area between the Himalayan foothills and the Ganges River. About that same time they learned how to make iron tools, and with axes and iron-tipped plows they cleared forests and established agricultural communities in the Ganges valley. Iron implements enabled them to produce more food and support larger populations, which in turn encouraged them to push farther into India. By 500 B.C.E. they had migrated as far south as the northern Deccan, a plateau region in the southern cone of the Indian subcontinent about 1,500 kilometers (950 miles) south of the Punjab.

As they settled into permanent communities and began to rely more on agriculture than herding, the Aryans gradually lost the tribal political organization that they had brought into India and evolved more formal political institutions. In a few places, especially in the isolated hilly and mountainous regions of northern India, councils of elders won recognition as the principal sources of political authority. They directed the affairs of small republics—states governed by representatives of the citizens. In most places, though, chiefdoms developed into regional kingdoms. Between 1000 and 500 B.C.E., tribal chiefs worked increasingly from permanent capitals and depended on the services of professional administrators. They did not build large imperial states: not until the fourth century B.C.E. did an Indian state embrace as much territory as Harappan society. But they established regional kingdoms as the most common form of political organization throughout most of the subcontinent.

VEDIC SOCIETY

Although they did not build a large-scale political structure, the Aryans constructed a well-defined social order. Indeed, in some ways their social hierarchy served to maintain the order and stability that states and political structures guaranteed in other societies, such as Mesopotamia, Egypt, and China. The Aryan social structure rested on sharp hereditary distinctions between individuals and groups, according to their occupations and roles in society. These distinctions became the foundation of the caste system, which largely determined the places that individuals and groups occupied in society. Apart from a social hierarchy reflected in the caste system, the Aryans also constructed a gender hierarchy reflected in a strongly patriarchal social order. Caste distinctions and patriarchal gender relations both emerged as prominent characteristics of Aryan India.

Origins of the Caste System

The term *caste* comes from the Portuguese word *casta,* and it refers to a social class of hereditary and usually unchangeable status. When Portuguese merchants and mariners visited India during the sixteenth century C.E., they noticed the sharp, inherited distinctions between different social groups, which they referred to as castes. Scholars have employed the term *caste* ever since in reference to the Indian social order.

Caste identities developed gradually as the Aryans established settlements throughout India. When the Aryans first entered India, they probably had a fairly simple society consisting of herders and cultivators led by warrior chiefs and priests. As they settled in India, however, growing social complexity and interaction with Dravidian peoples prompted them to refine their social distinctions. The Aryans used the term *varna,* a Sanskrit word meaning "color," to refer to the major social classes.

Caste and Varna

This terminology suggests that social distinctions arose partly from differences in complexion between the Aryans, who referred to themselves as "wheat-colored," and the darker-skinned Dravidians. Over time Aryans and Dravidians mixed, mingled, interacted, and intermarried to the point that distinguishing between them was impossible. Nevertheless, in early Vedic times differences between the two peoples probably prompted Aryans to base social distinctions on Aryan or Dravidian ancestry.

Social Distinctions in the Late Vedic Age

After about 1000 B.C.E. the Aryans increasingly recognized four main *varnas:* priests (*brahmins*); warriors and aristocrats (*kshatriyas*); cultivators, artisans, and merchants (*vaishyas*); and landless peasants and serfs (*shudras*). Some centuries later, probably about the end of the Vedic age, they added the category of the untouchables—people who performed dirty or unpleasant tasks, such as butchering animals or handling dead bodies, and who theoretically became so polluted from their work that their very touch could defile individuals of higher status.

Subcastes and Jati

Until about the sixth century B.C.E., the four *varnas* described Vedic society reasonably well. Because they did not live in cities and did not yet pursue many specialized occupations, the Aryans had little need for a more complicated social order. Over the longer term, however, a much more elaborate scheme of social classification emerged. As Vedic society became more complex and generated increasingly specialized occupations, the caste system served as the umbrella for a complicated hierarchy of subcastes known as *jati.* Occupation largely determined an individual's *jati:* people working at the same or similar tasks in a given area belonged to the same subcaste, and their offspring joined them in both occupation and *jati* membership. By the eighteenth and nineteenth centuries C.E., in its most fully articulated form, the system featured several thousand *jati,* which prescribed individuals' roles in society in minute detail. *Brahmins* alone divided themselves into some 1,800 *jati.* Even untouchables belonged to *jati,* and some of them looked down upon others as far more miserable and polluted than themselves.

Castes and subcastes deeply influenced the lives of individual Indians through much of history. Members of a *jati* ate with one another and intermarried, and they cared for those who became ill or fell on hard times. Elaborate rules dictated forms of address and specific behavior appropriate for communication between members of different castes and subcastes. Violation of *jati* rules could result in expulsion from the larger group. This penalty was serious, since an outcaste individual could not function well and sometimes could not even survive when shunned by all members of the larger society.

Caste and Social Mobility

The caste system never functioned in an absolutely rigid or inflexible manner, but rather operated so as to accommodate social change. Indeed, if the system had entirely lacked the capacity to change and reflect new social conditions, it would have disappeared. Individuals occasionally turned to new lines of work and prospered on the basis of their own initiative, but more often *jati* as groups improved their collective condition. Achieving upward mobility was not an easy matter—it often entailed moving to a new area, or at least taking on a new line of work—but the possibility of improving individual or group status helped to dissipate tensions that otherwise might have severely tested Indian society.

The caste system also enabled foreign peoples to find a place in Indian society. The Aryans were by no means the only foreigners to cross the passes of the Hindu Kush and enter India. Many others followed them over the course of the centuries and, upon arrival, sooner or later organized themselves into well-defined groups and adopted caste identities.

By the end of the Vedic age, caste distinctions had become central institutions in Aryan India. Whereas in other lands states and empires maintained public order, in

THE *RIG VEDA* ON THE ORIGIN OF THE CASTES

• • •

Priests compiled the Rig Veda *over a period of half a millennium, and the work inevitably reflects changing conditions of Aryan India. One of the later hymns of the* Rig Veda *offers a brief account of the world's creation and the origin of the four castes (varnas). The creation came when the gods sacrificed Purusha, a primeval being who existed before the universe, and brought the world with all its creatures and features into being. The late date of this hymn suggests that the Aryans began to recognize the four castes about 1000 B.C.E. The hymn clearly reflects the interests of the* brahmin *priests who composed it.*

A thousand heads hath Purusha, a thousand eyes, a thousand feet.

He covered earth on every side and spread ten fingers' breadth beyond.

This Purusha is all that hath been and all that is to be,

The Lord of Immortality which waxes greater still by food.

So mighty is his greatness; yea, greater than this is Purusha.

All creatures are one-fourth of him, [the other] three-fourths [of him are] eternal life in heaven. . . .

When the gods prepared the sacrifice with Purusha as their offering,

Its oil was spring, the holy gift was autumn; summer was the wood. . . .

From that great general sacrifice the dripping fat was gathered up.

He formed the creatures of the air, and animals both wild and tame.

From that great general sacrifice [sages] and [ritual hymns] were born.

Therefrom were [spells and charms] produced; the Yajas [a book of ritual formulas] had its birth from it.

From it were horses born; from it all creatures with two rows of teeth.

From it were generated [cattle], from it the goats and sheep were born.

When they divided Purusha, how many portions did they make?

What do they call his mouth, his arms? What do they call his thighs and feet?

The *brahmin* was his mouth, of both his arms was the *kshatriya* made.

His thighs became the *vaishya*, from his feet the *shudra* was produced.

The moon was gendered from his mind, and from his eye the sun had birth;

Indra and Agni [the god of fire] from his mouth were born, and Vayu [the wind] from his breath.

Forth from his navel came mid-air; the sky was fashioned from his head;

Earth from his feet, and from his ear the regions. Thus they formed the worlds.

SOURCE: Ralph T. Griffith, trans. *The Hymns of the Rigveda,* 4 vols., 2nd ed. Benares: E. J. Lazarus, 1889–92, 4:289–93. (Translation slightly modified.)

India the caste system served as a principal foundation of social stability. Individuals have often identified more closely with their *jati* than with their cities or states, and castes have played a large role in maintaining social discipline in India.

The Development of Patriarchal Society

Men dominated Aryan society already at the time of the migrations into India. All warriors, priests, and tribal chiefs were men, and the Aryans recognized descent through the male line. Women influenced affairs within their own families but enjoyed no public authority.

This greenish-blue schist carving illustrates the devotion of a mother to her child. • *Mother and Child*. India, Rajasthan, Tanesar-Mahadeva 450–500 A.D. Los Angeles County Museum of Art, From the Nasli and Alice Heeramaneck Collection, Museum Associates Purchase

As the Aryans settled in agricultural communities throughout India, they maintained a thoroughly patriarchal society. Only males could inherit property, unless a family had no male heirs, and only men could preside over family rituals that honored departed ancestors. Since they had no priestly responsibilities, women rarely learned the Vedas, and formal education in Sanskrit remained almost exclusively a male preserve.

The patriarchal spokesmen of Vedic society sought to place women explicitly under the authority of men. During the first century B.C.E. or perhaps somewhat later, an anonymous sage prepared a work and attributed it to Manu, founder of the human race according to Indian mythology. Much of the work, known as the *Lawbook of Manu*, dealt with proper moral behavior and social relationships, including sex and gender relationships. Although com-

The Lawbook of Manu posed after the Vedic age, the *Lawbook of Manu* reflected the society constructed earlier under Aryan influence. The author advised men to treat women with honor and respect, but he insisted that women remain subject to the guidance of the principal men in their lives—first their fathers, then their husbands, and finally, if they survived their husbands, their sons. The *Lawbook* also specified that the most important duties of women were to bear children and maintain wholesome homes for their families.

Sati Thus, like Mesopotamian, Egyptian, and other early agricultural societies, Vedic India constructed and maintained a deeply patriarchal social order. One Indian custom demonstrated in especially dramatic fashion the dependence of women on their men—the practice of *sati* (sometimes spelled *suttee*), by which a widow voluntarily threw herself on the funeral pyre of her deceased husband to join him in death. Although widows occasionally entered the fires during the Vedic age and in later centuries, *sati* never became a popular or widely practiced custom in India. Nevertheless, moralists often recommended *sati* for widows of socially prominent men, since their example would effectively illustrate the devotion of women to their husbands and reinforce the value that Indian society placed on the subordination of women.

RELIGION IN THE VEDIC AGE

As the caste system emerged and helped to organize Indian society, distinctive cultural and religious traditions also took shape. The Aryans entered India with traditions and beliefs that met the needs of a mobile and often violent society. During the early centuries after their arrival in India, these inherited traditions served them well as they fought to establish a place for themselves in the subcontinent. As they spread throughout India and mixed with the Dravidians, however, the Aryans encountered new religious ideas that they considered intriguing and persuasive. The resulting fusion of Aryan traditions with Dravidian beliefs and values laid the foundation for Hinduism, a faith immensely popular in India and parts of southeast Asia for more than two millennia.

Aryan Religion

As in Mesopotamia, Egypt, and other lands, religious values in India reflected the larger society. During the early centuries following their migrations, for example, the Aryans spread through the Punjab and other parts of India, often fighting with the Dravidians and even among themselves. The hymns, songs, and prayers collected in the *Rig Veda* throw considerable light on Aryan values during this period.

Accompanied by an attendant bearing his banner and weapons, Indra rides an elphant that carries him through the clouds, while a king and a crowd of people in the landscape below worship a sacred tree. • Courtesy of the Trustees of The British Library

Aryan Gods

The chief deity of the *Rig Veda* was Indra, the boisterous and often violent character who was partial both to fighting and to strong drink. Indra was primarily a war god. The Aryans portrayed him as the wielder of thunderbolts who led them into battle against their enemies. Indra also had a domestic dimension: the Aryans associated him with the weather and especially with the coming of rain to water the crops and the land. The Aryans also recognized a host of other deities, including gods of the sun, the sky, the moon, fire, health, disease, dawn, and the underworld. The preeminence of Indra, however, reflects the instability and turbulence of early Vedic society.

Although the Aryans accorded high respect to Indra and his military leadership, their religion did not entirely neglect ethics. They believed that the god Varuna presided over the sky from his heavenly palace, where he oversaw the behavior of mortals and preserved the cosmic order. Varuna and his helpers despised lying and evil deeds of all sorts, and they afflicted malefactors with severe punishments, including disease and death. They dispatched the souls of serious evildoers to the subterranean House of Clay, a dreary and miserable realm of punishment, while allowing souls of the virtuous to enter the Aryan heaven known as the World of the Fathers.

Ritual Sacrifices   Yet this ethical concern was a relatively minor aspect of Aryan religion during early Vedic times. Far more important from a practical point of view was the proper performance of ritual sacrifices by which the Aryans hoped to win the favor of the gods. By the time the Aryans entered India, these sacrifices had become complex and elaborate affairs. They involved the slaughter of dozens and sometimes even hundreds of specially prepared animals—cattle, sheep, goats, and horses from the Aryans' herds—as priests spoke the sacred and mysterious chants and worshipers partook of *soma,* a hallucinogenic concoction that produced sensations of power and divine inspiration. The Aryans believed that during the sacrificial event their gods visited the earth and joined the worshipers in ritual eating and drinking. By pleasing the gods with frequent and large sacrifices, the Aryans expected to gain divine support that would ensure military success, large families, long life, and abundant herds of cattle. But these rewards required constant attention to religious ritual: proper honor for the gods called for households to have *brahmins* perform no less than five sacrifices per day—a time-consuming and expensive obligation.

Spirituality   Later in the Vedic age, Aryan religious thought underwent a remarkable evolution. As the centuries passed, many Aryans became dissatisfied with the sacrificial cults of the Vedas, which increasingly seemed like sterile rituals rather than a genuine means of communicating with the gods. Even *brahmins* sometimes became disenchanted with rituals that did not satisfy spiritual longings. Beginning about 800 B.C.E. many thoughtful individuals left their villages and retreated to the forests of the Ganges valley, where they lived as hermits and reflected on the relationships between human beings, the world, and the gods. They contemplated the Vedas and sought mystical understandings of the texts, and they attracted disciples who also thirsted for a spiritually fulfilling faith.

These mystics drew considerable inspiration from the religious beliefs of Dravidian peoples, who often worshiped nature spirits that they associated with fertility and the generation of new life. Dravidians also believed that human souls took on new physical forms after the deaths of their bodily hosts. Sometimes souls returned as plants or animals, sometimes in the bodily shell of newborn humans. The notion that souls could experience transmigration and reincarnation—that an individual soul could depart one body at death and become associated with another body through a new birth—intrigued thoughtful people and encouraged them to try to understand the principles that governed the fate of souls. As a result, a remarkable tradition of religious speculation emerged.

The Blending of Aryan and Dravidian Values

The Upanishads   Traces of this tradition appear in the Vedas, but it achieved its fullest development in a body of works known as the Upanishads, which began to appear late in the Vedic age, about 800 to 400 B.C.E. (Later Upanishads continued to appear until the fifteenth century C.E., but the most important were those composed during the late Vedic age.) The word *upanishad* literally means "a sitting in front of," and it refers to the practice of disciples gathering before a sage for discussion of religious issues. Most of the disciples were men, but not all. Gargi Vakaknavi, for example, was a woman who drove the eminent sage Yajnavalkya to exasperation because he could not answer her persistent questions. The Upanishads often took the form of dialogues that explored the Vedas and the religious issues that they raised.

The Upanishads taught that appearances are deceiving, that individual human beings in fact are not separate and autonomous creatures. Instead, each person participates in a larger cosmic order and forms a small part of a universal soul, known as *Brahman*. Whereas the physical world is a theater of change, instability, and illusion, Brahman is an eternal, unchanging, permanent foundation for all things that exist—hence the only genuine reality. The authors of the Upanishads believed that individual souls were born into the physical world not once, but many times: they believed that souls appeared most often as humans, but sometimes as animals, and possibly even occasionally as plants or other vegetable matter. The highest goal of the individual soul, however, was to escape this cycle of birth and rebirth and enter into permanent union with Brahman.

Brahman, the Universal Soul

The Upanishads developed several specific doctrines that helped to explain this line of thought. One was the doctrine of *samsara*, which held that upon death, individual souls go temporarily to the World of the Fathers and then return to earth in a new incarnation. Another was the doctrine of *karma,* which accounted for the specific incarnations that souls experienced. The *Brhadaranyaka Upanishad* offers a succinct explanation of the workings of karma: "Now as a man is like this or like that, according as he acts and according as he behaves, so will he be: a man of good acts will become good, a man of bad acts, bad. He becomes pure by pure deeds, bad by bad deeds." Thus individuals who lived virtuous lives and fulfilled all their duties could expect rebirth into a purer and more honorable existence—for example, into a higher and more distinguished caste. Those who accumulated a heavy burden of karma, however, would suffer in a future incarnation by being reborn into a difficult existence, or perhaps even into the body of an animal or an insect.

Teachings of the Upanishads

Even under the best of circumstances, the cycle of rebirth involved a certain amount of pain and suffering that inevitably accompany human existence. The authors of the Upanishads sought to escape the cycle altogether and attain the state of *moksha,* which they characterized as a deep, dreamless sleep that came with permanent liberation from physical incarnation. This goal was difficult to reach, since it entailed severing all ties to the physical world and identifying with the ultimate reality of Brahman, the universal soul. The two principal means to the goal were asceticism and meditation. By embarking upon a regime of extreme asceticism—leading extremely simple lives and denying themselves all pleasure—individuals could purge themselves of desire for the comforts of the physical world. By practicing yoga, a form of intense and disciplined meditation, they could concentrate on the nature of Brahman and its relationship to their own souls. Diligent efforts, then, would enable individuals to achieve *moksha* by separating themselves from the physical world of change, illusion, and incarnation; merging their souls with Brahman; and experiencing eternal, peaceful ecstasy.

The religion of the Upanishads dovetailed with the social order of the Vedic age. Indeed, modern commentators have sometimes interpreted the worldview of the Upanishads—particularly the doctrines of samsara and karma—as a cynical ideology designed to justify the social inequalities imposed by the caste system. The doctrines of samsara and karma certainly reinforced the Vedic social order: they explained why individuals were born into their castes—because they had behaved virtuously or badly during a previous incarnation—and they encouraged individuals to observe their caste duties in hopes of enjoying a more comfortable and honorable incarnation in the future.

Religion and Vedic Society

THE *CHANDOGYA UPANISHAD* ON THE NATURE OF REALITY

• • •

One of the earliest and most influential Upanishads was the Chandogya Upanishad. *In one portion of this work, a man named Uddalaka uses a series of analogies to explain to his son, Svetaketu, how the ultimate reality of Brahman pervades the world. Indeed, Uddalaka teaches that Svetaketu himself is not a separate individual, but rather is identical to Brahman and hence is a participant in universal reality.*

"As the bees, my son, make honey by collecting the juices of distant trees, and reduce the juice into one form.

"And as these juices have no discrimination, so that they might say, 'I am the juice of this tree or that,' in the same manner, my son, all these creatures, when they have become merged in the True [i.e., in Brahman] (either in deep sleep or in death), know not that they are emerged in the True.

"Whatever these creatures are here, whether a lion, or a wolf, or a boar, or a worm, or a midge, or a gnat, or a mosquito, that they become again and again.

"Now that which is that subtle essence, in it all that exists has its self. It is the True. It is the Self, and you, Svetaketu, are it."

"Please, sir, inform me still more," said the son.

"Be it so, my child," the father replied. . . .

"Fetch me from thence a fruit of the Nyagrodha tree."

"Here is one, sir."

"Break it."

"It is broken, sir."

"What do you see there?"

"These seeds, almost infinitesimal."

"Break one of them."

"It is broken, sir."

"What do you see there?"

"Not anything, sir."

The father said: "My son, that subtle essence which you do not perceive there, of that very essence this great Nyagrodha tree exists.

"Believe it, my son. That which is the subtle essence, in it all that exists has its self. It is the True. It is the Self, and you, Svetaketu, are it."

"Please sir, inform me still more," said the son.

"Be it so, my child," the father replied.

"Place this salt in water, and then wait on me in the morning."

The son did as he was commanded.

The father said to him: "Bring me the salt, which you placed in the water last night."

The son having looked for it, found it not, for, of course, it was melted.

The father said: "Taste it from the surface of the water. How is it?"

The son replied: "It is salt."

"Taste it from the middle. How is it?"

The son replied: "It is salt."

"Taste it from the bottom. How is it?"

The son replied: "It is salt."

The father said: "Throw it away and then wait on me."

He did so, but salt exists forever.

Then the father said: "Here also, in this body, forsooth, you do not perceive the True, my son; but there indeed it is.

"That which is the subtle essence, in it all that exists has its self. It is the True. It is the Self, and you, Svetaketu, are it."

SOURCE: F. Max Müller, trans. *The Upanishads,* 2 vols. London: Oxford University Press, 1900, 1:101, 104–105. (Translation slightly modified.)

A cave painting from an undetermined age, perhaps several thousand years ago, shows that early inhabitants of India lived in close company with other residents of the natural world.   • V.I. Thayil/DPA/VIT/The Image Works

It would be a mistake, however, to consider these doctrines merely efforts of a hereditary elite to justify its position and maintain its hegemony over other classes of society. The sages who gave voice to these doctrines were conscientiously attempting to deal with genuine spiritual and intellectual problems. To them the material world seemed supremely superficial—a realm of constant change and illusion offering no clear sign as to the nature of ultimate reality. It seemed logical to suppose that a more real and substantial world stood behind the one that they inhabited. Greek philosophers, Christian theologians, and many others have arrived at similar positions during the course of the centuries. It should come as no great surprise, then, that the authors of the Upanishads sought ultimate truth and certain knowledge in an ideal world that transcends our own. Their formulation of concepts like samsara and karma represented efforts to characterize the relationship between the world of physical incarnation and the realm of ultimate truth and reality.

The Upanishads not only influenced Indian thought about the nature of the world but also called for the observance of high ethical standards. They discouraged greed, envy, gluttony, and all manner of vice, since these traits indicated excessive attachment to the material world and insufficient concentration on union with the universal soul. The Upanishads advocated honesty, self-control, charity, and mercy. Most of all, they encouraged the cultivation of personal integrity—a self-knowledge that would incline individuals naturally toward both ethical behavior and union with Brahman. The Upanishads also taught respect for all living things, animal as well as human. Animal bodies, after all, might well hold incarnations of unfortunate souls suffering the effects of a heavy debt of karma. Despite the evil behavior of these souls in their earlier incarnations, devout individuals would not wish to cause them additional suffering or harm. A vegetarian diet thus became a common feature of the ascetic regime.

By the end of the Vedic age, the merging of Aryan and Dravidian traditions had generated a distinctive Indian society. Agriculture and herding had spread with the Aryans to most parts of the Indian subcontinent. Regional states maintained order over substantial territories and established kingship as the most common form of government. The caste system not only endowed social groups with a powerful sense of identity but also helped to maintain public order. Finally, a distinctive set of religious beliefs explained the world and the role of human beings in it, and the use of writing facilitated the further reflection on spiritual and intellectual matters.

CHRONOLOGY

3000(?)–1500 B.C.E.	Harappan society
3000 B.C.E.–1000 C.E.	Indo-European migrations
1500 B.C.E.	Beginning of rapid Aryan migration into India
1500–500 B.C.E.	Vedic age
1400–900 B.C.E.	Compilation of the *Rig Veda*
1000–400 B.C.E.	Formation of regional kingdoms in northern India
800–400 B.C.E.	Composition of the principal Upanishads

FOR FURTHER READING

Bridget and Raymond Allchin. *The Rise of Civilization in India and Pakistan*. Cambridge, 1982. A detailed and authoritative survey of early Indian society based largely on archaeological evidence.

F. R. Allchin. *The Archaeology of Early Historic South Asia: The Emergence of Cities and States*. Cambridge, 1995. A collection of scholarly essays on the roles of cities and states in ancient India.

A. L. Basham. *The Wonder That Was India*. New York, 1954. A popular survey by a leading scholar of ancient India.

Ainslie T. Embree, ed. *Sources of Indian Tradition*. 2nd ed. 2 vols. New York, 1988. An important collection of primary sources in translation.

Walter A. Fairservis. *The Roots of Ancient India*. 2nd ed. Chicago, 1975. A judicious analysis of ancient Indian society, especially Harappan society, based on recent archaeological excavations.

Jonathan Mark Kenoyer. *Ancient Cities of the Indus Valley Civilization*. Oxford, 1998. A well illustrated volume that synthesizes recent archaeological and linguistic scholarship on Harappan society.

William H. McNeill and Jean W. Sedlar, eds. *Classical India*. Oxford, 1969. A useful collection of primary sources in translation.

J. P. Mallory. *In Search of the Indo-Europeans: Language, Archaeology and Myth*. London, 1989. Carefully reviews modern theories about early Indo-European speakers in light of both the linguistic and the archaeological evidence.

Juan Mascaró, trans. *The Upanishads*. London, 1965. A superb English version of selected Upanishads by a gifted translator.

Stuart Piggott. *Prehistoric India*. Harmondsworth, 1950. An older but still useful survey.

Gregory Possehl, ed. *Ancient Cities of the Indus*. New Delhi, 1979. Collection of scholarly essays that bring the results of recent research to bear on Harappan society.

———, ed. *Harappan Civilization: A Recent Perspective*. 2nd ed. New Delhi, 1993. Offers a variety of revisionist interpretations of Harappan society.

Shereen Ratnagar. *Encounters: The Westerly Trade of the Harappan Civilization*. Delhi, 1981. Relies on recent archaeological discoveries in examining commercial relations between Harappan society and Mesopotamia.

Colin Renfrew. *Archaeology and Language: The Puzzle of Indo-European Origins*. Cambridge, 1987. Presents a controversial argument concerning the origins and migrations of Indo-European peoples.

Romila Thapar. *A History of India*. Vol. 1. Harmondsworth, 1966. A sound, reliable, popular survey by a leading scholar of early Indian history.

Mortimer Wheeler. *The Indus Civilization*. Cambridge, 1953. Like Piggot's work, an older but still useful study.

CHAPTER 4

EARLY SOCIETY
IN EAST ASIA

· · ·

Ancient Chinese legends tell the stories of heroic figures who invented agriculture, domesticated animals, taught people to marry and live in families, created music, introduced the calendar, and instructed people in the arts and crafts. Most important of these heroes were three sage-kings—Yao, Shun, and Yu—who laid the foundations of Chinese society. King Yao was a towering figure, sometimes associated with a mountain, who was extraordinarily modest, sincere, and respectful. Yao's virtuous influence brought harmony to his own family, the larger society, and ultimately all the states of China. King Shun succeeded Yao and continued his work by ordering the four seasons of the year and instituting uniform weights, measures, and units of time.

Most dashing of the sage-kings was Yu, a vigorous and tireless worker who rescued China from the raging waters of the flooding Yellow River. Before Yu, according to the legends, experts tried to control the Yellow River's floods by building dikes to contain its waters. The river was much too large and strong for the dikes, however, and when it broke through them it unleashed massive floods. Yu abandoned the effort to dam up the Yellow River and organized two alternative strategies. He dredged the river so as to deepen its channel and minimize the likelihood of overflows, and he dug canals parallel to the river so that flood waters would flow harmlessly to the sea without devastating the countryside.

The legends say that Yu worked on the river for thirteen years without ever returning home. Once he passed by the gate to his home and heard his wife and children crying out of loneliness, but he continued on his way rather than interrupt his flood-control work. Because he tamed the Yellow River, Yu became a popular hero, and poets praised the man who protected fields and villages from deadly and destructive floods. Eventually Yu succeeded King Shun as leader of the Chinese people. Indeed, he founded the Xia dynasty, the first ruling house of ancient China.

The legends of Yao, Shun, and Yu no doubt exaggerated the virtues and deeds of the sage-kings. Agriculture, arts, crafts, marriage, family, government, and means of water control developed over an extended period of time, and no single individual was responsible for introducing them into China. Yet legends about early heroic figures reflected the interest of a people in the practices and customs that defined their society. At the same time, the moral thinkers who transmitted the legends used them to advocate values they considered beneficial for their society. By exalting Yao,

Bronze axe featuring a ferocious human face from the late Shang dynasty. • © The British Museum

Shun, and Yu as exemplars of virtue, Chinese moralists promoted the values of social harmony and selfless, dedicated work that the sage-kings represented.

Human beings appeared in east Asia as early as two hundred thousand years ago. At that early date they used stone tools and relied on a hunting and gathering economy like their counterparts in other regions of the earth. As in Mesopotamia, Egypt, and India, however, population pressures encouraged communities to experiment with agriculture. Peoples of southern China and southeast Asia domesticated rice after about 7000 B.C.E., and by 5000 B.C.E. neolithic villages throughout the valley of the Yangzi River (Chang Jiang) depended on rice as the staple item in their diet. During the same era, millet came under cultivation farther north, in the valley of the Yellow River (Huang He), where neolithic communities flourished by 5000 B.C.E. In later centuries wheat and barley made their way from Mesopotamia to northern China, and by 2000 B.C.E. they supplemented millet as staple foods of the region.

Agricultural surpluses supported numerous neolithic communities throughout east Asia. During the centuries after 3000 B.C.E., residents of the Yangzi River and Yellow River valleys lived in agricultural villages and communicated and traded with others throughout the region. During the second millennium B.C.E., they began to establish cities, build large states, and construct distinctive social and cultural traditions. Three dynastic states based in the Yellow River valley brought much of China under their authority and forged many local communities into a larger Chinese society. Sharp social distinctions emerged in early Chinese society, and patriarchal family heads exercised authority in both public and private affairs. A distinctive form of writing supported the development of sophisticated cultural traditions. As in early Mesopotamia and Egypt, then, and later in India as well, complex society, organized around cities, transformed early China and profoundly influenced the historical development of east Asia in general.

POLITICAL ORGANIZATION IN EARLY CHINA

As agricultural populations expanded, villages and towns flourished throughout the Yellow River and Yangzi River valleys. Originally, these settlements looked after their own affairs and organized local states that maintained order in small territories. By the late years of the third millennium B.C.E., however, much larger regional states began to emerge. Among the most important were those of the Xia, Shang, and Zhou dynasties, which progressively brought much of China under their authority and laid a political foundation for the development of a distinctive Chinese society.

Early Agricultural Society and the Xia Dynasty

The Yellow River Like the Indus, the Yellow River is boisterous and unpredictable. It rises in the mountains bordering the high plateau of Tibet, and it courses almost 4,700 kilometers (2,920 miles) before emptying into the Yellow Sea. It takes its name, Huang He, meaning "Yellow River," from the vast quantities of light-colored loess soil that it picks up along its route. Loess is an extremely fine, powderlike soil deposited on the plains of northern China, as well as in several other parts of the world, after the retreat of the glaciers at the end of the last ice age, about twelve thousand to fifteen thousand years ago. So much loess becomes suspended in the Yellow River that the water turns yellow and the river takes on the consistency of a soup. The soil gradually builds up, raising the river bed and forcing the water out of its established path.

The Yellow River periodically unleashes a tremendous flood that devastates fields, communities, and anything else in its way. The Yellow River has altered its course many times and has caused so much destruction that it has earned the nickname "China's Sorrow."

Yet geographical conditions have also supported the development of complex society in China. During most years, there is enough rainfall for crops, so early cultivators had no need to build complex irrigation systems like those of Mesopotamia. They invested a great deal of labor, however, in dredging the river and building dikes, in a partially successful effort to limit the flood damage. Loess soil is extremely fertile and easy to work, so even before the introduction of metal tools, cultivators using wooden implements could bring in generous harvests.

Yangshao Society and Banpo Village

Abundant harvests in northern China supported the development of several neolithic societies during the centuries after 5000 B.C.E. Each developed its own style of pottery and architecture, and each likely had its own political, social, and cultural traditions. Yangshao society, which flourished from about 5000 to 3000 B.C.E. in the middle region of the Yellow River valley, is especially well known from the discovery in 1952 of an entire neolithic village at Banpo, near modern Xi'an. Excavations at Banpo unearthed a large quantity of fine painted pottery and bone tools used by early cultivators in the sixth and fifth millennia B.C.E.

Pottery bowl from the early Yangshao era excavated at Banpo, near modern Xi'an. The bowl is fine red pottery decorated with masks and fishnets in black. ●
Cultural Relics Publishing House, Beijing

As human population increased, settlements like that at Banpo cropped up throughout much of China, in the valley of the Yangzi River as well as the Yellow River. As in other parts of the world, the concentration of people in small areas brought a need for recognized authorities who could maintain order, resolve disputes, and organize public works projects. Village-level organization sufficed for purely local affairs, but it did little to prevent or resolve conflicts between villages and did not have the authority to organize large-scale projects in the interests of the larger community.

Chinese legends speak of three ancient dynasties—the Xia, Shang, and Zhou—that arose before the Qin and Han dynasties brought China under unified rule in the third century B.C.E. The Xia, Shang, and Zhou dynasties were hereditary states that extended their control over progressively larger regions, although none of them embraced all the territory claimed by later Chinese dynasties. Historians and archaeologists have discovered a variety of materials that shed light on the Shang and Zhou, but the archaeological recovery of the Xia dynasty is still in its early stages.

The Xia Dynasty

Nevertheless, many scholars believe that the Xia dynasty represented the first effort to organize public life in China on a large scale. Most likely the dynasty came into being about 2200 B.C.E. in roughly the same region as the Yangshao society. By extending formal control over this region, the Xia dynasty established a precedent for hereditary monarchical rule in China.

Ancient legends credit the dynasty's founder, the sage-king Yu, with the organization of effective flood-control projects: thus, as in Mesopotamia and Egypt, the need to organize large-scale public works projects helped to establish recognized

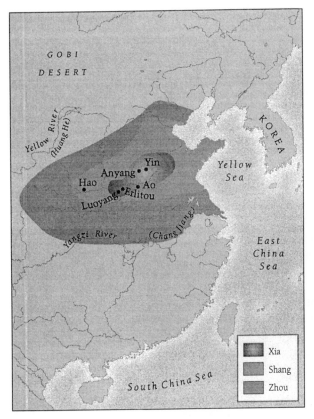

MAP [4.1]

The Xia, Shang, and Zhou
dynasties.

Bronze Metallurgy

authorities and formal political institutions. Although no information survives about the political institutions of the Xia, the dynasty's rulers probably exercised power throughout the middle Yellow River valley by controlling the leaders of individual villages. The dynasty encouraged the founding of cities and the development of metallurgy, since the ruling classes needed administrative centers and bronze weapons to maintain their control. The recently excavated city of Erlitou, near Luoyang, might well have been the capital of the Xia dynasty. Excavations have shown that the city featured a large, palace-type structure as well as more modest houses, pottery workshops, and a bronze foundry.

The Shang Dynasty

According to the legends, the last Xia king was an oppressive despot who lost his realm to the founder of the Shang dynasty. In fact, the Xia state did not entirely collapse and did not disappear so much as it gave way gradually before the Shang, which arose in a region to the south and east of the Xia realm. Tradition assigns the Shang dynasty to the period 1766 to 1122 B.C.E., and archaeological discoveries have largely confirmed these dates. Since the Shang dynasty left written records as well as material remains, the basic features of early Chinese society come into much clearer focus than they did during the Xia.

Technology helps to explain the rise and success of the Shang. Bronze metallurgy transformed Chinese society during Shang times. Because of the high cost of copper and tin, bronze implements were beyond the means of all but wealthy classes. Because bronze made the most effective weapons available and thus had important military and political implications, Shang ruling elites monopolized its production. They controlled access to copper and tin ores, and they employed craftsmen to produce large quantities of bronze axes, spears, knives, and arrowheads. Thus Shang forces possessed arms far superior to those of stone, wood, and bone wielded by their rivals. Shang nobles also used bronze to make fittings for their horse-drawn chariots, which came to China across central Asia from Mesopotamia. With their arsenal of bronze weapons, Shang armies had little difficulty imposing their rule on agricultural villages. Meanwhile, the ruling elites did not allow free production of bronze, so potential competitors had small hope of resisting Shang forces and no possibility of displacing the dynasty.

Shang kings extended their rule to a large portion of northeastern China centered on the modern-day province of Henan. Like state builders in other parts of the world, the kings claimed a generous portion of the surplus agricultural production from the regions they controlled and then used that surplus to support military forces, political allies, and others who could help them maintain their rule. Shang rulers clearly had abundant military force at their disposal. Surviving records mention armies of 3,000, 5,000, 10,000, and even 13,000 troops, and one report mentions the capture of 30,000 enemy troops. Although these numbers are probably somewhat inflated, they still suggest that Shang rulers maintained a powerful military machine.

Like their Xia predecessors, Shang rulers also relied on a large corps of political allies. The Shang state rested on a vast network of walled towns whose local rulers recognized the authority of the Shang kings. During the course of the dynasty, Shang kings may have controlled one thousand or more towns. Apart from local rulers of these towns, others who shared the agricultural surplus of Shang China included advisors, ministers, craftsmen, and metalsmiths, who in their various ways helped Shang rulers shape policy or spread their influence throughout their realm.

Shang Political Organization

Shang society revolved around several large cities. According to tradition, the Shang capital moved six times during the course of the dynasty. Though originally chosen for political and military reasons, in each case the capital also became an important social, economic, and cultural center—the site not only of administration and military command but also of bronze foundries, arts, crafts, trade, and religious observances.

Excavations at two sites have revealed much about the workings of the Shang dynasty. The Shang named one of its earliest capitals Ao, and archaeologists have found its remains near modern Zhengzhou. The most remarkable feature of this site is the city wall, which originally stood at least 10 meters (33 feet) high, with a base some 20 meters (66 feet) thick. The wall consisted of layer upon layer of pounded earth—soil packed firmly between wooden forms and then pounded with mallets until it reached rocklike hardness before the addition of a new layer of soil on top. This building technique, still used in the countryside of northern China, can produce structures of tremendous durability. Even today, for example, parts of the wall of Ao survive to a height of 3 and 4 meters (10 to 13 feet). The investment in labor required to build this wall testifies to Shang power and a high degree of centralized rule: modern estimates suggest that the wall required the services of some ten thousand laborers working almost twenty years.

The Shang Capital at Ao

Even more impressive than Ao is the site of Yin, near modern Anyang, which was the capital during the last two or three centuries of the Shang dynasty. Archaeologists working at Yin have identified a complex of royal palaces, archives with written documents, several residential neighborhoods, two large bronze foundries, several workshops used by potters, bone workers, carvers, and other craftsmen, and scattered burial grounds.

The Shang Capital at Yin

Eleven large and lavish tombs constructed for Shang kings, as well as other more modest tombs, have received particular attention. Like the resting places of the Egyptian pharaohs, most of these tombs attracted grave robbers soon after their construction. Enough remains, however, to show that the later Shang kings continued to command the high respect enjoyed by their predecessors at Ao. The graves included thousands of objects—chariots, weapons, bronze goods, pottery, carvings of jade and ivory, cowrie shells (which served both as money and as exotic ornamentation), and sacrifical victims, including dogs, horses, and scores of human beings intended to serve the deceased royals in another existence. One tomb alone contained skeletons of more than three hundred sacrificial victims—probably wives, servants, friends, and hunting companions—who joined the Shang king in death. The tomb of Fu Hao, a wife or perhaps a consort of King Wu Ding who ruled in the early to middle thirteenth century B.C.E., contained some seven thousand cowrie shells and more than 1,600 manufactured objects, including 440 bronzes, 590 jade pieces, 560 bone carvings, and assorted items made of stone, ivory, pottery, or shells. Also found in Fu Hao's tomb were the sacrificial remains of sixteen human victims and six dogs.

Jade figurines excavted at Anyang from the tomb of Fu Hao, who was one of the wives or consorts of the Shang king Wu Ding. The carvings represent servants who would tend to Fu Hao's needs after death.
● Cultural Relics Publishing House, Beijing/International Division. Photograph courtesy of Michael Sullivan

The Zhou Dynasty

Very little information survives to illustrate the principles of law, justice, and administration by which Shang rulers maintained order. They did not promulgate law codes such as those issued in Mesopotamia, but rather ruled by proclamation or decree, trusting their military forces and political allies to enforce their will. The principles of ancient Chinese politics and statecraft become more clear in the practices of the Zhou dynasty, which succeeded the Shang as the preeminent political authority in northern China. Dwelling in the Wei River valley of northwestern China (modern Shaanxi province), the Zhou were a tough and sinewy people who battled Shang forces in the east and nomadic raiders from the steppes in the west. Eventually the Zhou allied with the Shang and won recognition as kings of the western regions. Since they organized their allies more effectively than the Shang, however, they gradually eclipsed the Shang dynasty and ultimately displaced it altogether.

The Rise of the Zhou

Shang and Zhou ambitions collided in the late twelfth century B.C.E. According to Zhou accounts, the last Shang king was a criminal fool who gave himself over to wine, women, tyranny, and greed. As a result, many of the towns and political districts subject to the Shang transferred their loyalties to the Zhou. After several unsuccessful attempts to discipline the Shang king, Zhou forces toppled his government in 1122 B.C.E. and replaced it with their own state. They allowed Shang heirs to continue governing small districts but reserved for themselves the right to oversee affairs throughout the realm. The new dynasty ruled most of northern and central China, at least nominally, until 256 B.C.E.

The Mandate of Heaven

In justifying the deposition of the Shang, spokesmen for the Zhou dynasty articulated a set of principles that have influenced Chinese thinking about government and political legitimacy over the long term. The Zhou theory of politics rested on the assumption that earthly events were closely related to heavenly affairs. More specifically, heavenly powers granted the right to govern—"the mandate of heaven"—to an especially deserving individual known as the son of heaven. The ruler then served as a link between heaven and earth. He had the duty to govern conscientiously, observe high standards of honor and justice, and maintain order and harmony within his realm. As long as he did so, the heavenly powers would approve of his work, the cosmos would enjoy a harmonious and well-balanced stability, and the ruling dynasty would retain its mandate to govern. If a ruler failed in his duties, however, chaos and suffering would afflict his realm, the cosmos would fall out of balance, and the displeased heavenly powers would withdraw the mandate to rule and transfer it to a more deserving candidate. On the basis of this reasoning, spokesmen for the new dynasty explained the fall of the Shang and the transfer of the mandate of heaven to the Zhou. Until the twentieth century, Chinese ruling houses emulated the Zhou dynasty by claiming the mandate of heaven for their rule, and emperors took the title "son of heaven."

The Zhou state was much larger than the Shang. In fact, it was so extensive that a single central court could not rule the entire land effectively, at least not with the transportation and communication technologies available during the second and first millennia B.C.E. As a result, Zhou rulers relied on a decentralized administration: they entrusted power, authority, and responsibility to subordinates who in return owed allegiance, tribute, and military support to the central government.

Political Organization

During the early days of the dynasty, this system worked reasonably well. The conquerors themselves continued to rule the Zhou ancestral homeland from their capital at Hao, near modern Xi'an, but they allotted possessions in conquered territories to relatives and other allies. The subordinates ruled their territories with limited supervision from the central government. In return for their political rights, they visited the Zhou royal court on specified occasions to demonstrate their continued loyalty to the dynasty, they delivered taxes and tribute that accounted for the major part of Zhou finances, and they provided military forces that the kings deployed in the interests of the Zhou state as a whole. When not already related to their subordinates, the Zhou rulers sought to arrange marriages that would strengthen their ties to their political allies.

Despite their best efforts, however, the Zhou kings could not maintain control indefinitely over this decentralized political system. Subordinates gradually established their own bases of power: they ruled their territories not only as allies of the Zhou kings but also as long-established and traditional governors. They set up regional bureaucracies, armies, and tax systems, which allowed them to consolidate their rule and to exercise their authority. They promulgated law codes and enforced them with their own forces. As they became more secure in their rule, they also became more independent of the Zhou dynasty itself. Subordinates sometimes ignored their obligations to appear at the royal court or to deliver tax proceeds. Occasionally, they refused to provide military support or even turned their forces against the dynasty in an effort to build up their own regional states.

Weakening of the Zhou

Technological developments also worked in favor of subordinate rulers. The Zhou kings were not able to control the production of bronze as closely as their Shang predecessors had, and subordinates built up their own stockpiles of weapons. Moreover, during the first millennium B.C.E., the technology of iron metallurgy spread to China, and the production of iron expanded rapidly. Because iron ores are both cheaper and more abundant than copper and tin, the Zhou kings simply could not monopolize iron production. As a result, subordinates outfitted their forces with iron weapons that enabled them to resist the central government and pursue their own interests.

Iron Metallurgy

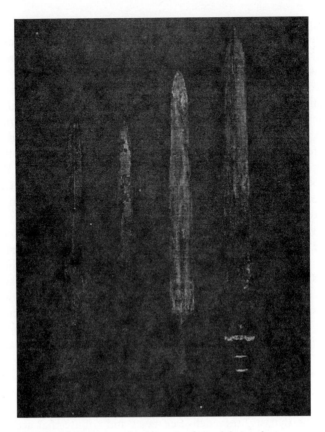

The Zhou dynasty saw a development of sword design that resulted in longer, stronger, and more lethal weapons. The iron swords depicted here reflect the political instability and chronic warfare of the late Zhou dynasty. • © The British Museum

In the early eighth century B.C.E., the Zhou rulers faced severe problems that brought the dynasty to the point of collapse. In 771 B.C.E. nomadic peoples invaded China from the west. They came during the rule of a particularly ineffective king who did not enjoy the respect of his political allies. When subordinates refused to support the king, the invaders overwhelmed the Zhou capital at Hao. Following this disaster, the royal court moved east to Luoyang in the Yellow River valley, which served as the Zhou capital until the end of the dynasty.

In fact, the political initiative had passed from the Zhou kings to their subordinates, and the royal court never regained its authority. By the fifth century B.C.E., territorial princes ignored the central government and used their resources to build, strengthen, and expand their own states. They fought ferociously with one another in hopes of establishing themselves as leaders of a new political order. So violent were the last centuries of the Zhou dynasty that they are known as the Period of the Warring States (403–221 B.C.E.). In 256 B.C.E. the Zhou dynasty ended when the last king abdicated his position under pressure from his ambitious subordinate the king of Qin. Only with the establishment of the Qin dynasty in 221 B.C.E. did effective central government return to China.

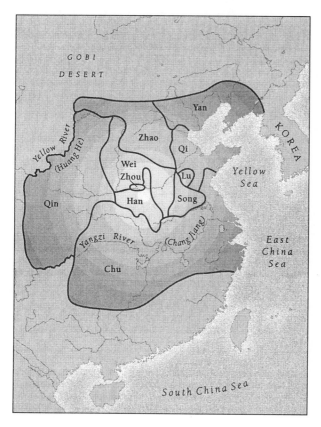

MAP [4.2]

China during the Period of the Warring States.

SOCIETY AND FAMILY IN ANCIENT CHINA

In China as in other parts of the ancient world, the introduction of agriculture enabled individuals to accumulate wealth and preserve it within their families. Social distinctions began to appear during neolithic times, and after the establishment of the Xia, Shang, and Zhou dynasties the distinctions became even sharper. Throughout China the patriarchal family emerged as the institution that most directly influenced individuals' lives and their roles in the larger society.

The Social Order

Already during the Xia dynasty, but especially under the Shang and early Zhou, the royal family and allied noble families occupied the most honored positions in Chinese society. They resided in large, palatial compounds made of pounded earth, and they lived on the agricultural surplus and taxes delivered by their subjects. Their conspicuous consumption of bronze clearly set them apart from the less privileged classes of society. They possessed much of the bronze weaponry that ensured military strength and political negemony, and through their subordinates and retainers they controlled most of the remaining bronze weapons available in northern China.

Ruling Elites

The delicate design of this bronze wine vessel displays the high level of craftsmanship during the late Shang dynasty. • Courtesy of the Freer Gallery of Art, Smithsonian Institution, Washington, D.C. 23.1

They also supplied their households with cast-bronze utensils—pots, jars, wine cups, plates, serving dishes, mirrors, bells, drums, and vessels used in ritual ceremonies—which were beyond the means of less privileged people. These utensils often featured elaborate, detailed decorations that indicated remarkable skill on the part of the artisans who built the molds and cast the metal. Expensive bronze utensils bore steamed rice and rich dishes of fish, pheasant, poultry, pork, mutton, and rabbit to royal and aristocratic tables, whereas less privileged classes relied on clay pots and consumed much simpler fare, such as vegetables and porridges made of millet, wheat, or rice.

A privileged class of hereditary aristocrats rose from the military allies of Shang and Zhou rulers. Aristocrats possessed extensive land holdings, and they worked at administrative and military tasks. By Zhou times many of them lived in cities where they obtained at least an elementary education, and their standard of living was much more refined than that of the commoners and slaves who worked their fields and served their needs. Manuals of etiquette from Zhou times instructed the privileged classes in decorous behavior and outlined the proper way to carry out rituals. When dining in polite company, for example, the cultivated aristocrat should show honor to the host and refrain from gulping down food, swilling wine, making unpleasant noises, picking teeth at the table, and playing with food by rolling it into a ball.

Specialized Labor   A small class of free artisans and craftsmen plied their trades in the cities of ancient China. Some, who worked almost exclusively for the privileged classes, enjoyed a reasonably comfortable existence. During the Shang dynasty, for example, bronzesmiths often lived in houses built of pounded earth. Although their dwellings were modest, they were also sturdy and relatively expensive to build because of the amount of labor required for pounded-earth construction. Jewelers, jade workers, embroiderers, and manufacturers of silk textiles also benefitted socially because of their importance to the ruling elites.

Merchants and Trade   There is very little information about merchants and trade in ancient China until the latter part of the Zhou dynasty, but archaeological discoveries show that long-

PEASANTS' PROTEST

. . .

Peasants in ancient China mostly did not own their own land. Instead, they worked as tenants on plots allotted to them by royal or aristocratic owners, who took sizable portions of the harvest for their own uses. In the following poem from the Book of Songs, a collection of verses dating from Zhou times, peasants liken their lords to rodents, protest the bite they take from the peasants' agricultural production, and threaten to abandon the lords' lands for a neighboring state where conditions were better.

Large rats! Large rats!
Do not eat our millet.
Three years have we had to do with you.
And you have not been willing to show any regard for us.
We will leave you,
And go to that happy land.
Happpy land! Happy land!
There shall we find our place.

Large rats! Large rats!
Do not eat our wheat.
Three years have we had to do with you.
And you have not been willing to show any kindness to us.

We will leave you,
And go to that happy state.
Happy state! Happy state!
There shall we find ourselves aright.

Large rats! Large rats!
Do not eat our springing grain!
Three years have we had to do with you,
And you have not been willing to think of our toil.
We will leave you,
And go to those happy borders.
Happy borders! Happy borders!
Who will there make us always to groan?

SOURCE: James Legge, trans. *The Chinese Classics,* 5 vols. London: Henry Frowde, 1893, 4:171–72.

distance trade routes reached China during Shang and probably Xia times as well. Despite the high mountain ranges and forbidding deserts that stood between China and complex societies in India and southwest Asia, trade networks linked China with lands to the west and south early in the third millennium B.C.E. Jade in Shang tombs came from central Asia, and military technology involving horse-drawn chariots came through central Asia from Mesopotamia. Shang bronzesmiths worked with tin that came from the Malay peninsula in southeast Asia, and cowrie shells came through southeast Asia from Burma and the Maldive Islands in the Indian Ocean. The identity of the most important trade items that went from China to other lands is not clear, but archaeologists have unearthed a few pieces of Shang pottery from Mohenjo-daro and other Harappan sites.

Peasants

A large class of semiservile peasants populated the Chinese countryside. They owned no land but provided agricultural, military, and labor services for their lords in exchange for plots to cultivate, security, and a portion of the harvest. They lived like their neolithic predecessors in small subterranean houses excavated to a depth of about one meter (three feet) and protected from the elements by thatched walls and roofs. Women's duties included mostly indoor activities such as wine making, weaving, and cultivation of silkworms, whereas men spent most of their time outside working in the fields, hunting, and fishing.

A wooden digging stick with two prongs was the agricultural tool most commonly used for cultivation of loess soils in the Yellow River valley. • Wang-go Weng, Inc.

Few effective tools were available to cultivators until the late Zhou dynasty. They mostly relied on wooden digging sticks and spades with bone or stone tips, which were strong enough to cultivate the powdery loess soil of northern China, since bronze tools were too expensive for peasant cultivators. Beginning about the sixth century B.C.E., however, iron production increased dramatically in China, and iron plows, picks, spades, hoes, sickles, knives, and rakes all came into daily use in the countryside.

Slaves   Finally, there was a sizable class of slaves, most of whom were enemy warriors captured during battles between the local states allied with the Xia, Shang, and Zhou kings. Slaves performed hard labor, such as the clearing of new fields or the building of city walls, that required a large work force. During the Shang dynasty, but rarely thereafter, hundreds of slaves also figured among the victims sacrificed during funerary, religious, and other ritual observances.

Family and Patriarchy

Throughout human history the family has served as the principal institution for the socialization of children and the preservation of cultural traditions. In China the extended family emerged as a particularly influential institution during neolithic times, and it continued to play a prominent role in the shaping of both private and public affairs after the appearance of the Xia, Shang, and Zhou states. Indeed, the early dynasties ruled their territories largely through family and kinship groups.

Veneration of Ancestors   One reason for the pronounced influence of the Chinese family is the veneration of ancestors, a practice with roots in neolithic times. In those early days agricultural peoples in China diligently tended the graves and memories of their departed ancestors. They believed that spirits of their ancestors passed into another realm of existence from which they had the power to support and protect their surviving families if the descendants displayed proper respect and ministered to the spirits' needs. Survivors buried tools, weapons, jewelry, and other material goods along with their dead. They also offered sacrifices of food and drink at the graves of departed relatives. The strong sense of ancestors' presence and continuing influence in the world led to an equally strong ethic of family solidarity. A family could expect to prosper only if all of its members—the dead as well as the living—worked cooperatively toward common interests. The family became an institution linking departed generations to the living and even to those yet unborn—an institution that wielded enormous influence over both the private and the public lives of its members.

FAMILY SOLIDARITY IN ANCIENT CHINA

• • •

A poem from the Book of Songs illustrates clearly the importance of family connections in ancient China.

The flowers of the cherry tree—
Are they not gorgeously displayed?
Of all the men in the world
There are none equal to brothers.

On the dreaded occasions of death and burial,
It is brothers who greatly sympathize.
When fugitives are collected on the heights and low grounds,
They are brothers who will seek one another out.

There is the wagtail on the level height—
When brothers are in urgent difficulties,
Friends, though they may be good
Will only heave long sighs.

Brothers may quarrel inside the walls [of their own home],
But they will oppose insult from without,
When friends, however good they may be,
Will not afford help.

When death and disorder are past,
And there are tranquillity and rest,
Although they have brothers,
Some reckon them not equal to friends.

Your dishes may be set in array,
And you may drink to satiety.
But it is when your brothers are all present
That you are harmonious and happy, with child-like joy.

Loving union with wife and children
Is like the music of lutes.
But it is the accord of brothers
That makes the harmony and happiness lasting.

For the ordering of your family,
For the joy in your wife and children,
Examine this and study it—
Will you not find that it is truly so?

SOURCE: James Legge, trans. *The Chinese Classics,* 5 vols. London: Henry Frowde, 1893, 4:250–53. (Translation slightly modified.)

In the absence of organized religion or official priesthood in ancient China, the patriarchal head of the family presided at rites and ceremonies honoring ancestors' spirits. As mediator between the family's living members and its departed relatives, the family patriarch possessed tremendous authority. He officiated not only at ceremonies honoring ancestors of his own household but also at memorials for collateral and subordinate family branches that might include hundreds of individuals.

Patriarchal Society

Chinese society vested authority principally in elderly males who headed their households. Like its counterparts in other regions, Chinese society took on a strongly patriarchal character—one that intensified with the emergence of large states. During neolithic times Chinese men wielded public authority, but they won their rights to it by virtue of the female line of their descent. Even if it did not vest power and authority in women, this system provided solid reasons for a family to honor its female members. As late as Shang times, two queens posthumously received the high honor of having temples dedicated to their memories.

When burying their departed kin, survivors placed bronze ritual vessels with food and drink in their tombs. In the tombs of wealthy individuals, these vessels sometimes took elaborate shapes. • Cultural Relics Bureau, Beijing

With the establishment of the Shang and Zhou states, however, and perhaps even the Xia, women lived increasingly in the shadow of men. Large states brought the military and political contributions of men into sharp focus. The ruling classes performed elaborate ceremonies publicly honoring the spirits of departed ancestors, particularly males who had guided their families and led especially notable lives. Gradually, the emphasis on men became so intense that Chinese society lost its matrilineal character. After the Shang dynasty, not even queens and empresses merited temples dedicated exclusively to their memories: at most, they had the honor of being remembered in association with their illustrious husbands.

EARLY CHINESE WRITING AND CULTURAL DEVELOPMENT

Organized religion did not play as important a role in ancient China as it did in other early societies. Early Chinese myths and legends explained the origins of the world, the human race, agriculture, and the various arts and crafts. But Chinese thinkers saw no need to organize these ideas into systematic religious traditions. They often spoke of an impersonal heavenly power—*tian* ("heaven"), the agent responsible for bestowing and removing the mandate of heaven on rulers—but they did not recognize a personal supreme deity who intervened in human affairs or took special interest in human behavior. Nor did ancient China support a large class of priests like those of Mesopotamia, Egypt, and India who mediated between human beings and the gods. A few priests conducted ritual observances in honor of royal ancestors at royal courts, but for the most part family patriarchs represented the interests of living generations to the spirits of departed ancestors.

In this environment, then, writing served as the foundation for a distinctive secular cultural tradition in ancient China. Chinese scribes may have used written symbols to keep simple records during Xia times, but surviving evidence suggests that writing came into extensive use only during the Shang dynasty. As in other lands, writing quickly became an indispensable tool of government as well as a means of expressing ideas and offering reflections on human beings and their world.

Oracle Bones and Early Chinese Writing

In Mesopotamia and India merchants pioneered the use of writing. In China, however, the earliest known writing served the interests of rulers rather than traders. Writing in China goes back at least to the early part of the second millennium B.C.E. Surviving records indicate that scribes at the Shang royal court kept written accounts of important events on strips of bamboo or pieces of silk. Unfortunately, almost all of these materials have perished, along with their messages. Yet one medium employed by ancient Chinese scribes has survived the ravages of time to prove beyond doubt that writing figured prominently in the political life of the Shang dynasty. Recognized just over a century ago, inscriptions on so-called oracle bones have thrown tremendous light both on the Shang dynasty and on the early stages of Chinese writing.

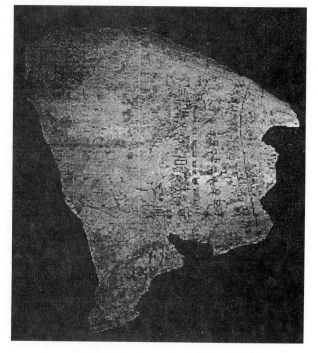

Oracle bone from Shang times with an inscribed question and cracks caused by exposure of the bone to heat. • Werner Forman/Art Resource, NY

Oracle Bones

Oracle bones were the principal instruments used by fortune-tellers in ancient China. In other early societies specialists forecast the future by examining the entrails of sacrificed animals, divining the meaning of omens or celestial events such as eclipses, studying the flight of birds, or interpreting weather patterns. In China, diviners used specially prepared broad bones, such as the shoulder blades of sheep or turtle shells. They inscribed a question on the bone and then subjected it to heat, either by placing it into a fire or by scorching it with an extremely hot tool. When heated, the bone developed networks of splits and cracks. The fortune-teller then studied the patterns and determined the answer to the question inscribed on the bone. Often the diviner recorded the answer on the bone, and later scribes occasionally added further information about the events that actually came to pass.

During the nineteenth century, peasants working in the fields around Anyang discovered many oracle bones bearing inscriptions in archaic Chinese writing. They did not recognize the writing, but they knew they had found an unusual and valuable commodity. They called their finds "dragon bones" and sold them to druggists, who ground them into powder that they resold as an especially potent medicine. Thus an untold number of oracle bones went to the relief of aches, pains, and ills before scholars recognized their true nature. During the late 1890s dragon bones came to the attention of historians and literary scholars, who soon determined that the inscriptions represented an early and previously unknown form of Chinese writing. Since then, more than one hundred thousand oracle bones have come to light.

Most of the oracle bones have come from royal archives, and the questions posed on them clearly reveal the day-to-day concerns of the Shang royal court. Will the season's harvest be abundant or poor? Should the king attack his enemy or not? Will the queen bear a son or a daughter? Would it please the royal ancestors to receive a sacrifice of animals—or perhaps of human slaves? Taken together, bits of information preserved on the oracle bones have allowed historians to piece together an understanding of the political and social order of Shang times.

Early Chinese Writing

Even more important, the oracle bones offer the earliest glimpse into the tradition of Chinese writing. As in Sumer and Egypt, the earliest form of Chinese writing was the pictograph—a conventional or stylized representation of an object. To represent complex or abstract notions, the written language often combined various pictographs into an ideograph. Thus, for example, the combined pictographs of a mother and child mean "good" in written Chinese. Unlike most other languages, written Chinese did not include an alphabetic or phonetic component.

The characters used in contemporary Chinese writing are direct descendants of those used in Shang times. Scholars have identified more than two thousand characters inscribed on oracle bones, most of which have a modern counterpart. (Contemporary Chinese writing regularly uses about five thousand characters, although thousands of additional characters are also used for technical and specialized purposes.) Over the centuries written Chinese characters have undergone considerable modification: generally speaking, they have become more stylized, conventional, and abstract. Yet the affinities between Shang and later Chinese written characters are apparent at a glance.

Thought and Literature in Ancient China

The political interests of the Shang kings may have accounted for the origin of Chinese writing, but once established, the technology was available for other uses. Since Shang writing survives only on oracle bones and a small number of bronze inscriptions—all products that reflected the interests of the ruling elite that commissioned them—evidence for the expanded uses of writing comes only from the Zhou dynasty and later times.

Turtle   Horse

Oracle-bone script
of the Shang dynasty
(16th century–11th century B.C.E.)

Zhou dynasty script
(11th century–3rd century B.C.E.)

Qin dynasty script
(221–207 B.C.E.)

Han dynasty script
(207 B.C.E.–220 C.E.)

Modern script
(3rd century C.E.–present)

Contemporary script,
People's Republic of China
(1950–the present)

The Evolution of Chinese Characters from the Shang Dynasty to the Present

A few oracle bones survive from Zhou times, along with a large number of inscriptions on bronze ceremonial utensils that the ruling classes used during rituals venerating their ancestors. Apart from these texts, the Zhou dynasty also produced books of poetry and history, manuals of divination and ritual, and essays dealing with moral, religious, philosophical, and political themes. Best known of these works are the reflections of Confucius and other late Zhou thinkers (discussed in chapter 7), which served as the intellectual foundation of classical Chinese society. But many other less famous works show that Zhou writers, mostly anonymous, were keen observers of the world and subtle commentators on human affairs.

Several writings of the Zhou dynasty won recognition as works of high authority, and they exercised deep influence because they served as textbooks in Chinese schools. Among the most popular of these works in ancient times was the *Book of Changes,* which was a manual instructing diviners in the art of foretelling the future. Zhou ruling elites also placed great emphasis on the *Book of History,* a collection of documents that justified the Zhou state and called for subjects to obey their overlords. Zhou aristocrats learned the art of polite behavior and the proper way to conduct rituals from the *Book of Etiquette,* also known as the *Book of Rites.*

Zhou Literature

Most notable of the classic works, however, was the *Book of Songs,* also known as the *Book of Poetry* and the *Book of Odes,* a collection of verses on themes both light and serious. Though compiled and edited after 600 B.C.E., many of the 311 poems in the collection date from a much earlier period and reflect conditions of the early Zhou dynasty. Some of the poems had political implications because they recorded the illustrious deeds of heroic figures and ancient sage-kings, and others were hymns sung at ritual observances. Yet many of them are charming verses about life, love, family, friendship, eating, drinking, work, play, nature, and daily life that offer reflections on human affairs without particular concern for political or social conditions. One poem, for example, described a bride about to join the household of her husband:

The Book of Songs

> The peach tree is young and elegant;
> Brilliant are its flowers.
> This young lady is going to her future home,
> And will order well her chamber and house.
>
> The peach tree is young and elegant;
> Abundant will be its fruit.
> This young lady is going to her future home,
> And will order well her house and chamber.
>
> The peach tree is young and elegant;
> Luxuriant are its leaves.
> This young lady is going to her future home,
> And will order well her family.

The *Book of Songs* and other writings of the Zhou dynasty offer only a small sample of China's earliest literary tradition, for most Zhou writings have perished. Those written on delicate bamboo strips and silk fabrics have deteriorated: records indicate that the tomb of one Zhou king contained hundreds of books written on bamboo strips, but none of them survive. Other books fell victim to human enemies. When the imperial house of Qin ended the chaos of the Period of the Warring States and brought all of China under tightly centralized rule in 221 B.C.E., the victorious emperor ordered the destruction of all writings that did not have some immediate utilitarian value. He spared works on divination, agriculture, and medicine, but he condemned those on poetry, history, and philosophy, which he

Destruction of Early Chinese Literature

feared might inspire doubts about his government or encourage an independence of mind. Only a few items escaped, hidden away for a decade and more until scholars and writers could once again work without fear of persecution. These few survivors represent the earliest development of Chinese literature and moral thought.

 ## THE BROADER INFLUENCE OF ANCIENT CHINESE SOCIETY

High mountain ranges, forbidding deserts, and turbulent seas stood between China and early societies in India, Mesopotamia, and Egypt. These geographical features did not entirely prevent communication between China and other lands, but they hindered the establishment of direct long-distance trade relations such as those linking Mesopotamia with Harappan India or those between the Phoenicians and other peoples of the Mediterranean basin. Nevertheless, like early societies in other parts of the world, ancient China exhibited a tendency to expand and to influence the lives of neighboring peoples. The influence of early Chinese society was particularly strong in the west and the south.

Chinese Cultivators and Nomadic Peoples of Central Asia

From the valley of the Yellow River, Chinese agriculture spread to the north and west. The dry environment of the steppes limited expansion in these directions, however, since harvests progressively diminished to the point that agriculture became impractical. During the Zhou dynasty, the zone of agriculture extended about 300 kilometers (186 miles) west of Xi'an, to the eastern region of modern Gansu province.

Steppelands   But the influence of Chinese society extended well beyond the zone of agriculture. As Chinese communities brought new lands under cultivation and expanded the boundaries of agricultural society, they encountered hunting and gathering societies. Some of these foragers became cultivators and joined Chinese society. Others remained apart and sought to move beyond the range of Chinese agricultural society. As they migrated to the north and west, however, they entered the grassy steppelands of central Asia that were inhospitable to foragers as well as cultivators. These peoples gradually devised their own distinctive societies and economies based on the herding of domesticated animals that could consume grass. The steppes north and west of the fields cultivated by Chinese farmers thus became the home of nomadic peoples—ancestors of the Turks and Mongols— who herded horses, sheep, goats, and yaks in the thinly populated grasslands of central Asia.

Nomadic Society   Nomadic peoples did very little farming, since the arid steppe did not reward efforts at cultivation. Instead, the nomads concentrated on herding their animals, driving them to regions where they could find food and water. The herds provided meat and milk, as well as skins and bones from which they fashioned clothes and tools. Nomadic peoples depended upon the agricultural society of China for grains and finished products, such as textiles and metal goods, which they could not produce for themselves. In exchange for these products, they offered horses, which they could raise easily on the steppes.

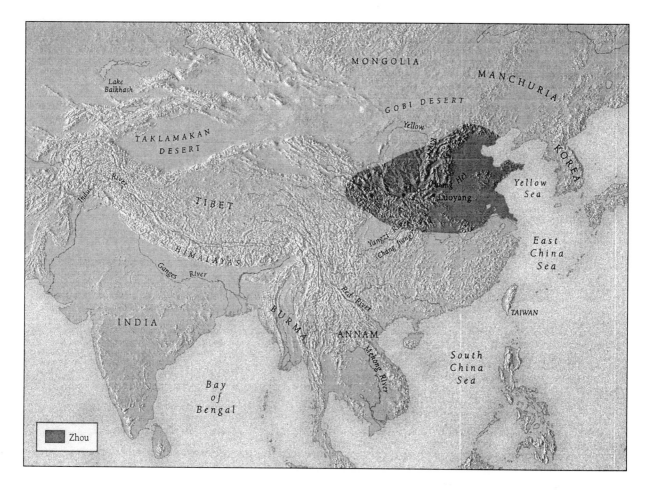

MAP [4.3]

Asia during the late Zhou dynasty.

Despite this somewhat symbiotic arrangement, Chinese and nomadic peoples always had tense relations. Indeed, they often engaged in bitter wars, since the relatively poor but hardy nomads frequently fell upon the rich agricultural society at their doorstep and sought to seize its wealth. At least from the time of the Shang dynasty, and probably from the Xia as well, nomadic raids posed a constant threat to the northern and western regions of China. The Zhou state grew strong enough to overcome the Shang partly because Zhou military forces honed their skills waging campaigns against nomadic peoples to the west. Later, however, the Zhou state almost crumbled under the pressure of nomadic incursions compounded by disaffection among Zhou allies and subordinates.

Nomadic peoples did not imitate Chinese ways. The environment of the steppe prevented them from cultivating crops, and the need to herd their animals made it impossible for them to settle permanently in towns or to build cities. Nomadic peoples did not adopt Chinese political or social traditions, but rather organized themselves into clans under the leadership of charismatic warrior chiefs. Nor did they use writing until about the seventh century C.E. Yet pastoral nomadism was an economic and social adaptation to agricultural society: the grains and manufactured goods available from agricultural lands enabled nomadic peoples to take advantage of the steppe environment by herding animals.

Extensive paddies in the Yangzi River valley of southern China have long produced abundant harvests of rice. • Robert Harding Picture Library

The Southern Expansion of Chinese Society

The Yangzi Valley   Chinese influence spread to the south as well as to the north and west. There was no immediate barrier to cultivation in the south: indeed, the valley of the Yangzi River supports even more intensive agriculture than is possible in the Yellow River basin. Known in China as the Chang Jiang ("Long River"), the Yangzi carries enormous volumes of water some 6,300 kilometers (3,915 miles) from its headwaters in the lofty Qinghai mountains of Tibet to its mouth near the modern Chinese cities of Nanjing and Shanghai, where it empties into the East China Sea. The moist, sub-tropical climate of southern China lent itself readily to the cultivation of rice: ancient cultivators sometimes raised two crops of rice per year.

There was no need for a King Yu to tame the Yangzi River, which does not bring devastating floods like those of the Yellow River. But intensive cultivation of rice depended upon the construction and maintenance of an elaborate irrigation system that allowed cultivators to flood their paddies and release the waters at the appropriate time. The Shang and Zhou states provided sources of authority that could supervise a complex irrigation system, and harvests in southern China burgeoned during the second and first millennia B.C.E. The populations of cultivators' communities surged along with their harvests.

As their counterparts did in lands to the north and west of the Yellow River valley, the indigenous peoples of southern China responded in two ways to the increasing prominence of agriculture in the Yangzi River valley. Many became cultivators themselves and joined Chinese agricultural society. Others continued to live by hunting and gathering: some moved into the hills and mountains, where conditions did not favor agriculture, and others migrated to Taiwan or southeast Asian lands like Vietnam and Thailand, where agriculture was more limited.

Agricultural surpluses and growing populations led to the emergence of cities, *The State of Chu*
states, and complex societies in the Yangzi as well as the Yellow River valley. During
the late Zhou dynasty, the powerful state of Chu, situated in the central region of
the Yangzi, governed its affairs autonomously and challenged the Zhou for supremacy. By the end of the Zhou dynasty, Chu and other states in southern China
were in regular communication with their counterparts in the Yellow River valley.
They adopted Chinese political and social traditions as well as Chinese writing, and
they built societies closely resembling those of the Yellow River valley. Although
only the northern portions of the Yangzi River valley fell under the authority of the
Shang and Zhou states, by the end of the Zhou dynasty all of southern China
formed part of a larger Chinese society.

Early societies in east Asia had little direct contact with peoples to the west. Metallurgical technologies, wheat cultivation, and wheeled vehicles diffused to east Asia
from Mesopotamia, but geographical barriers prevented the establishment of extensive trade, travel, and communication networks linking the distant regions of the
eastern hemisphere. Yet agricultural peoples in east Asia built complex societies that
in broad outline were much like those to the west. Particularly in the valley of the
Yellow River, early Chinese cultivators organized powerful states, developed social
distinctions, and established sophisticated cultural traditions. Their language, writing, beliefs, and values differed considerably from those of other peoples, and these
cultural elements lent a distinctiveness to Chinese society. But the emergence of
powerful states and complex societies in east Asia demonstrated once again the potential of agriculture to serve as a foundation for large-scale social organization.

CHRONOLOGY

2500–2200 B.C.E.	Yangshao society
2200–1766 B.C.E.	Xia dynasty
1766–1122 B.C.E.	Shang dynasty
1122–256 B.C.E.	Zhou dynasty
403–221 B.C.E.	Period of the Warring States

FOR FURTHER READING

Cyril Birch, ed. *Anthology of Chinese Literature.* 2 vols. New York, 1965. Collection of primary sources in
    translation.
Kwang-chih Chang. *The Archaeology of Ancient China.* 4th ed. New Haven, 1986. Brings the results of
    recent excavations to bear on ancient Chinese history.
————. *Early Chinese Civilization: Anthropological Perspectives.* Cambridge, Mass., 1976. Essays by a dis-
    tinguished archaeologist.
————. *Shang Civilization.* New Haven, 1980. Based on the most recent archaeological research.
H. G. Creel. *The Birth of China: A Study of the Formative Period of Chinese Civilization.* New York, 1954.
    An older popular account, well written though somewhat dated, by a leading scholar.
Jacques Gernet. *Ancient China from the Beginnings to the Empire.* Trans. by R. Rudorff. London, 1968.
    A brief popular survey of early Chinese society.
Cho-yun Hsu. *Ancient China in Transition: An Analysis of Social Mobility, 722–222 B.C.* Stanford, 1965.
    A scholarly examination of social change during the later Zhou dynasty.

Cho-yun Hsu and Katheryn M. Linduff. *Western Chou Civilization*. New Haven, 1988. Draws on both literary sources and archaeological discoveries in offering a comprehensive study of the early Zhou dynasty.

David N. Keightley, ed. *The Origins of Chinese Civilization*. Berkeley, 1983. An important collection of scholarly articles dealing with all aspects of early Chinese society.

Owen Lattimore. *Inner Asian Frontiers of China*. 2nd ed. New York, 1951. Fascinating analysis of the relationship between Chinese and nomadic peoples of central Asia by a geographer who traveled through much of central Asia.

Jessica Rawson. *Ancient China: Art and Archaeology*. New York, 1980. An outstanding and well-illustrated volume with especially strong treatment of archaeological discoveries.

William Watson. *Early Civilization in China*. New York, 1966. Well-illustrated popular account dealing with the period from prehistoric times to the Zhou dynasty.

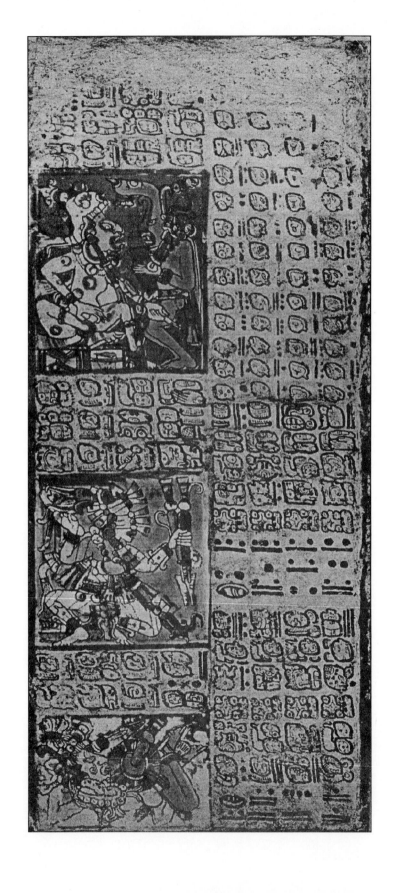

EARLY SOCIETIES IN THE AMERICAS AND OCEANIA

. . .

In early September of the year 683 C.E., a Maya man named Chan Bahlum grasped a sharp obsidian knife and cut three deep slits into the skin of his penis. He inserted into each slit a strip of paper made from beaten tree bark so as to encourage a continuing flow of blood. His younger brother Kan Xul performed a similar rite, while other members of his family also drew blood from their own bodies.

The bloodletting observances of September 683 were political and religious rituals, acts of deep piety performed as Chan Bahlum presided over funeral services for his recently deceased father, Pacal, king of the Maya city of Palenque in the Yucatan peninsula. The Maya believed that the shedding of royal blood was essential to the world's survival. Thus as Chan Bahlum prepared to succeed his father as king of Palenque, he let his blood flow copiously.

Throughout Mesoamerica, Maya and other peoples performed similar rituals for a millennium and more. Maya rulers and their family members regularly spilled their own blood by opening wounds with obsidian knives, stingray spines, or sharpened bones. Men commonly drew blood from the penis, like Chan Bahlum, while women often drew from the tongue. Both sexes occasionally drew blood also from the earlobes, lips, or cheeks, and they sometimes increased the flow by pulling long, thick cords through their wounds.

This shedding of blood was so crucial to Maya rituals because of its association with rain and agriculture. According to Maya priests, the gods had shed their own blood to water the earth and nourish crops of maize, and they expected human beings to honor them by imitating their sacrifice. By spilling human blood the Maya hoped to please the gods and ensure that life-giving waters would bring bountiful harvests to their fields. By inflicting painful wounds not just on their enemies, but on their own bodies as well, the Maya demonstrated their conviction that bloodletting rituals were essential to the coming of rain and the survival of their agricultural society.

This agricultural society was the product of a distinctive tradition. Human groups migrated to the Americas and Oceania long after they had established communities throughout most of the eastern hemisphere, but long before any people

Maya deities from a book on calendrical matters. • Courtesy Dept. of Library Services, American Museum of Natural History, #1909

began to experiment with agriculture. Their migrations took place during ice ages when glaciers locked up much of the earth's water, causing sea levels all over the world to decline precipitously—sometimes by as much as 300 meters (984 feet). For thousands of years, temporary land bridges joined regions that both before and after the ice ages were separated by the seas. One land bridge linked Siberia with Alaska. Another joined the continent of Australia to the island of New Guinea. Low sea levels also exposed large stretches of land that connected Sumatra, Java, and other Indonesian islands to the peninsula of southeast Asia. Human groups took advantage of these bridges by migrating to new lands.

When the earth's temperature rose and the glaciers melted, beginning about twenty thousand years ago, the waters returned and flooded low-lying lands around the world. Once again, the seas divided Asia from America by the body of water known as the Bering Straits, and they also separated Australia, New Guinea, and the islands of Indonesia. By that time, however, human communities had become well established in the Americas, the islands of southeast Asia, and Australia, where they independently built distinctive societies.

The return of high waters did not put an end to human migrations. Human groups fanned out from Alaska and ventured to all corners of North America, Central America, and South America. Beginning about 3000 B.C.E. coastal peoples of southeast Asia built large sailing canoes and established human settlements in the previously uninhabited islands of the Pacific Ocean. By about 700 C.E. human beings had established communities in almost every habitable part of the world.

Despite their different origins and their distinctive political, social, and cultural traditions, peoples of the Americas and Oceania built societies that in some ways resembled those of the eastern hemisphere. Human communities independently discovered agriculture in several regions of North America and South America, and migrants introduced cultivation to the inhabited Pacific islands as well. With agriculture came increasing populations, settlement in towns, specialized labor, formal political authorities, hierarchical social orders, long-distance trade, and organized religious traditions. The Americas also generated large, densely populated societies featuring cities, monumental public works, imperial states, and sometimes traditions of writing as well. Thus like their counterparts in the eastern hemisphere, the earliest societies of the Americas and Oceania reflected a common human tendency toward the development of increasingly complex social forms.

 ## EARLY SOCIETIES OF MESOAMERICA

Humans first trekked from Siberia to Alaska perhaps as early as forty thousand years ago, and in any case no later than twenty-five thousand years ago. They traveled in small groups in search of big game such as mastodons, mammoths, bison, and horses that had also made their way across land bridges to North America. After venturing to lands that human beings had not yet visited, they did not return to Siberia, but pushed farther and established communities in all parts of the Americas. By 7000 B.C.E. at the latest, and perhaps several thousand years earlier than that, humans had reached the southern-most part of South America, more than 17,000 kilometers (10,566 miles) from the land bridge that led their ancestors from Siberia.

The earliest human inhabitants of the Americas lived exclusively by hunting and gathering. Beginning about 10,000 B.C.E., however, it became increasingly difficult for them to survive by foraging. Large game animals became scarce, partly because they did not adapt well to the rapidly warming climate and partly because of over-hunting by expanding human communities. By 7500 B.C.E. many species of large animals in the Americas were well on the road to extinction. Some human communities relied on fish and small game to supplement foods that they gathered. Others turned to agriculture, and they gave rise to the first complex societies in the Americas.

The Olmecs

By 8000 to 7000 B.C.E., the peoples of Mesoamerica—the region from the central portion of modern Mexico to Honduras and El Salvador—had begun to experiment with the cultivation of beans, chili peppers, avocados, squashes, and gourds. By 5000 B.C.E. they had discovered the agricultural potential of maize, which soon became the staple food of the region. Later they added tomatoes to the crops they cultivated. Agricultural villages appeared soon after 3000 B.C.E., and by 2000 B.C.E. agriculture had spread throughout Mesoamerica.

Early Agriculture in Mesoamerica

Early Mesoamerican peoples had a diet rich in cultivated foods, but they did not keep as many animals as their counterparts in the eastern hemisphere. Their domesticated animals included turkeys and small, barkless dogs, both of which they consumed as food. But most large animals of the western hemisphere were not susceptible to domestication, so Mesoamericans were unable to harness animal energy. Human laborers prepared fields for cultivation, and human porters carried trade goods on their backs. Mesoamericans had no need for wheeled vehicles, which would have been useful only if draft animals were available to pull them.

Toward the end of the second millennium B.C.E., the tempo of Mesoamerican life quickened as elaborate ceremonial centers with monumental pyramids, temples, and palaces arose alongside the agricultural villages. The first of these centers were not cities like those of early societies in the eastern hemisphere. Permanent residents of the ceremonial centers included members of the ruling elite, priests, and a few artisans and craftsmen who tended to the needs of the ruling and priestly classes. Large numbers of people gathered in the ceremonial centers on special occasions to observe rituals or on market days to exchange goods, but most people then returned to their homes in neighboring villages and hamlets.

Ceremonial Centers

The earliest known ceremonial centers of the ancient Americas appeared on the coast of the Gulf of Mexico, near the modern Mexican city of Veracruz, and they served as the nerve center of the first complex society of the Americas, that of the Olmecs. Historians and archaeologists have systematically studied Olmec society only since the 1940s, and many questions about them remain unanswered. Even their proper name is unknown: the term *Olmec* (meaning "rubber people") did not come from the ancient people themselves, but derives instead from the rubber trees that flourish in the region they inhabited. Nevertheless, some of the basic features of Olmec society have become reasonably clear, and it is certain that Olmec cultural traditions influenced all complex societies of Mesoamerica until the arrival of European peoples in the sixteenth century C.E.

Olmecs: The "Rubber People"

The first Olmec ceremonial center arose about 1200 B.C.E. on the site of the modern town of San Lorenzo, and it served as their capital for some four hundred years. When the influence of San Lorenzo waned, leadership passed to new ceremonial centers at La Venta (800–400 B.C.E.) and Tres Zapotes (400–100 B.C.E.). These sites defined the heartland of Olmec society, where agriculture produced rich harvests. The entire region receives abundant rainfall, so there was no need to build extensive systems of irrigation. Like the Harappans, however, the Olmecs constructed

MAP [5.1]

Early Mesoamerican
societies.

elaborate drainage systems to divert waters that otherwise might have flooded their fields or destroyed their settlements. Some Olmec drainage construction remains visible and effective today.

Olmec Society

Olmec society was probably authoritarian in nature. Untold thousands of laborers participated in the construction of the ceremonial centers at San Lorenzo, La Venta, and Tres Zapotes. Each of the principal Olmec sites featured an elaborate complex of temples, pyramids, altars, stone sculptures, and tombs for rulers. Common subjects delivered a portion of their harvests for the maintenance of the elite classes living in the ceremonial centers and provided labor for the various large-scale construction projects.

Indeed, common subjects labored regularly on behalf of the Olmec elite—not only in building drainage systems and ceremonial centers but also in providing appropriate artistic adornment for the capitals. The most distinctive artistic creations of the Olmecs were colossal human heads—possibly likenesses of rulers—sculpted from basalt rock. The largest of these sculptures stands three meters (almost ten feet) tall and weighs some twenty tons. In the absence of draft animals and wheels, human laborers dragged enormous boulders from quarries, floated them on rafts to points near their destinations, dragged them to their intended sites, and then positioned them for the sculptors. The largest sculptures required the services of about one thousand laborers. Apart from the colossal heads, the Olmec capitals featured many other large stone sculptures and monumental buildings that required the services of laborers by the hundreds and thousands. Construction of the huge pyramid at La Venta, for example, required some eight hundred thousand man-days of labor.

Trade in Jade and Obsidian

Olmec influence extended to much of the central and southern regions of modern Mexico and beyond that to modern Guatemala and El Salvador. The Olmecs spread their influence partly by military force, but trade was a prominent link between the Olmec heartland and the other regions of Mesoamerica. The Olmecs produced large numbers of decorative objects from jade, which they had to import. In the absence of any metal technology, they also made extensive use of obsidian from which they fashioned knives and axes with wickedly sharp cutting edges. Like jade, obsidian came to the Gulf coast from distant regions in the interior of Mesoamerica. In exchange for the imports, the Olmecs traded small works of art fashioned from jade, basalt, or ceramics and perhaps also local products such as animal skins.

Colossal Olmec head carved from basalt rock between 1000 and 600 B.C.E. and discovered at La Venta. Olmecs carved similar heads for their ceremonial centers at San Lorenzo and Tres Zapotes. ● Andrew Rakaczy/Photo Researchers, Inc.

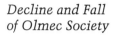

Decline and Fall of Olmec Society

Among the many mysteries surrounding the Olmecs, one of the most perplexing concerns the decline and fall of their society. The Olmecs systematically destroyed their ceremonial centers at both San Lorenzo and La Venta and then deserted the sites. Archaeologists studying these sites found statues broken and buried, monuments defaced, and the capitals themselves burned. Although intruders may have ravaged the ceremonial centers, many scholars believe that the Olmecs deliberately destroyed their capitals, perhaps because of civil conflicts or doubts about the effectiveness and legitimacy of the ruling classes. In any case, by about 400 B.C.E. Olmec society had fallen on hard times, and soon thereafter societies in other parts of Mesoamerica eclipsed it altogether.

Yet later Mesoamerican societies adopted several Olmec traditions. They cultivated maize, built ceremonial centers with temple pyramids, and maintained a calendar based on one inherited from Olmec priests.

Olmec ceremonial axe head carved from jade about 800 to 400 B.C.E. Jaguar features, such as those depicted here, are prominent in Olmec art. ● Courtesy Dept. of Library Services, American Museum of Natural History, #1298(3). Photo, Denis Finnin

Influence of Olmec Traditions

They also borrowed Olmec ballgames and rituals involving human sacrifice. However, the Olmecs left no written records beyond calendrical inscriptions, so the exact roles that ballgames and human sacrifices played in their society are not clear.

Heirs of the Olmecs: The Maya

During the thousand years following the Olmecs' disappearance about 100 B.C.E., complex societies arose in several Mesoamerican regions. Human population grew dramatically, and ceremonial centers cropped up at sites far removed from the Olmec heartland. Some of them evolved into genuine cities: they attracted large populations of permanent residents, embarked on ambitious programs of construction, maintained large markets, and encouraged increasing specialization of labor. Networks of long-distance trade linked the new urban centers and extended their influence to all parts of Mesoamerica. Within the cities themselves, priests devised written languages and compiled a body of astronomical knowledge. In short, Mesoamerican societies developed in a manner roughly parallel to their counterparts in the eastern hemisphere.

The Maya   The earliest heirs of the Olmecs were the Maya, who created a remarkable society in the region now occupied by southern Mexico, Guatemala, Belize, Honduras, and El Salvador. The highlands of Guatemala offer fertile soil and excellent conditions for agriculture. Permanent villages began to appear there during the third century B.C.E. The most prominent of them was Kaminaljuyú, located on the site of modern Guatemala City. Like the Olmec capitals, Kaminaljuyú was a ceremonial center rather than a true city, but it dominated the life of other communities in the region. Some twelve thousand to fifteen thousand laborers worked to build its temples, and its products traveled the trade routes as far as central Mexico. During the fourth century C.E., Kaminaljuyú fell under the economic and perhaps also the political dominance of the much larger city of Teotihuacan in central Mexico and lost much of its influence in Maya society.

After the fourth century Maya society flourished mostly in the poorly drained Mesoamerican lowlands, where thin, tropical soils quickly lost their fertility. To enhance the agricultural potential of the region, the Maya built terraces designed to trap silt carried by the numerous rivers passing through the lowlands. By artificially retaining rich earth, they dramatically increased the agricultural productivity of their lands. They harvested maize in abundance, and they also cultivated cotton from which they wove fine textiles highly prized both in their own society and by trading partners in other parts of Mesoamerica. Maya cultivators also raised cacao, the large bean that is the source of chocolate. Cacao was a precious commodity consumed mostly by nobles in Maya society. They whisked powdered cacao into water to create a stimulating beverage, and they sometimes even ate the bitter cacao beans as snacks. The product was so valuable that Maya used cacao beans as money.

Tikal   From about 300 to 900 C.E., the Maya built more than eighty large ceremonial centers in the lowlands, all with pyramids, palaces, and temples, as well as numerous smaller settlements. Some of the larger centers attracted dense populations and evolved into genuine cities. Foremost among them was Tikal, the most important Maya political center between the fourth and the ninth centuries C.E. At its height, roughly 600 to 800 C.E., Tikal was a wealthy and bustling city with a population approaching forty thousand. It boasted enormous paved plazas and scores of temples, pyramids, palaces, and public buildings. The Temple of the Giant Jaguar, a stepped pyramid rising sharply to a height of 47 meters (154 feet), dominated the skyline and represented Tikal's control over the surrounding region with a population of about five hundred thousand.

The Maya organized themselves politically into scores of small city-kingdoms. Tikal was probably the largest, but Palenque and Chichén Itzá also were sizable states. The smaller kingdoms had populations between ten thousand and thirty thousand people. Maya kings often bore menacing names like Curl Snout, Smoking Frog, and Stormy Sky. Especially popular were names associated with the jaguar, the most dangerous predator of the Mesoamerican forests. Prominent Maya kings included Great Jaguar Paw, Shield Jaguar, Bird Jaguar, and Jaguar Penis (meaning the progenitor of other jaguar-kings).

The Maya kingdoms fought constantly with each other. Victors generally destroyed the peoples they de-

Temple of the Giant Jaguar at Tikal, which served as funerary pyramid for Lord Cacao, a prominent Maya ruler of the late sixth and early seventh centuries C.E. ● Richard Steedman/ Stock Market

feated and took over their ceremonial centers, but the purpose of Maya warfare was not so much to kill enemies as to capture them in hand-to-hand combat on the battlefield. Warriors won enormous prestige when they brought back important captives from neighboring kingdoms. They stripped captives of their fine dress and symbols of rank, and sometimes they kept high-ranking captives alive for years, displaying them as trophies. Ultimately, most captives ended their lives either as slaves or as sacrificial victims to Maya gods. High-ranking captives in particular often underwent ritual torture and sacrifice in public ceremonies on important occasions.

Maya Warfare

Bitter conflicts between small kingdoms were sources of constant tension in Maya society. Only about the ninth century C.E. did the state of Chichén Itzá in the northern Yucatan peninsula seek to dampen hostile instincts and establish a larger political framework for Maya society. The rulers of Chichén Itzá preferred to absorb captives and integrate them into their own society rather than annihilate them or offer them up as sacrificial victims. Some captives refused the opportunity and went to their deaths as proud warriors, but many agreed to recognize the authority of Chichén Itzá and participate in the construction of a larger society. Between the ninth and eleventh centuries C.E., Chichén Itzá organized a loose empire that brought a measure of political stability to the northern Yucatan.

Chichén Itzá

Maya Decline

By about 800 C.E., however, most Maya populations had begun to desert their cities. Within a century Maya society was in full decline everywhere except the northern Yucatan, where Chichén Itzá continued to flourish. Historians have suggested many possible causes of the decline, including invasion by foreigners from Mexico, internal dissension and civil war, failure of the system of water control leading to diminished harvests and demographic collapse, ecological problems caused by destruction of the forests, the spread of epidemic diseases like yellow fever, and natural catastrophes such as earthquakes. Possibly several problems combined to destroy Maya society. In any case the population declined, the people abandoned their cities, and long-distance trade with Mexico came to a halt. Meanwhile, the tropical jungles of the lowlands encroached upon human settlements and gradually smothered the cities, temples, pyramids, and monuments of a once-vibrant society.

Maya Society and Religion

Apart from the kings and ruling families, Maya society included a large class of priests who maintained an elaborate calendar and transmitted knowledge of writing, astronomy, and mathematics. A hereditary nobility owned most land and cooperated with the kings and priests by organizing military forces and participating in religious rituals. Maya merchants came from the ruling and noble classes. Their travels had strong political overtones, since they served not only as traders but also as ambassadors to neighboring lands and allied peoples. Moreover, they traded mostly in exotic and luxury goods, such as rare animal skins, cacao beans, and finely crafted works of art, which rulers coveted as signs of special status. Apart from the ruling and priestly elites, Maya society generated several other distinct social classes. Professional architects and sculptors oversaw construction of large monuments and public buildings. Artisans specialized in the production of pottery, tools, and cotton textiles. Finally, large classes of peasants and slaves fed the entire society and provided physical labor for the construction of cities and monuments.

The Maya built upon the cultural achievements of their Olmec predecessors. Maya priests studied astronomy and mathematics, and they devised both a sophisticated calendar and an elaborate system of writing. They understood the movements of heavenly bodies well enough to plot planetary cycles and predict eclipses of the sun and moon. They invented the concept of zero and used a symbol to represent zero mathematically, which facilitated their manipulation of large numbers. By combining their astronomical observations and mathematical reasoning, Maya priests calculated the length of the solar year at 365.242 days—about seventeen seconds shorter than the figure reached by modern astronomers.

The Maya Calendar

Maya priests constructed the most elaborate calendar of the ancient Americas. Its complexity reflected a powerful urge to identify meaningful cycles of time and to understand human events in the context of those cycles. The Maya calendar interwove two kinds of year: a solar year of 365 days governed the agricultural cycle, and a ritual year of 260 days governed daily affairs by organizing time into twenty "months" of thirteen days apiece. The Maya believed that each day derived certain specific characteristics from its position in both the solar and the ritual calendar and that the combined attributes of each day would determine the fortune of activities undertaken on that day. It took fifty-two years for the two calendars to work through all possible combinations of days and return simultaneously to their respective starting points, so 18,980 different combinations of characteristics could influence the prospects of an individual day. Maya priests carefully studied the various

In this extraordinarily well-preserved mural, musicians celebrate the designation of an heir to the Maya king at Bonampak (located in the southern part of modern Mexico) ● Mural Room 1 Bonampak, Chiapas, Mexico. Mayan. Classic Period c790-800 A.D. Watercolor copy by Antonio Tejeda, Peabody Museum, Harvard University. Photo: Hillel Burger

opportunities and dangers that would come together on a given day in hopes that they could determine which activities were safe to initiate. Apart from calculating the prospects of individual days, the Maya attributed especially great significance to the fifty-two-year periods in which the two calendars ran. They believed that the end of a cycle would bring monumental changes and that ultimately the world would end after one such cycle.

While building on the calendrical calculations of the Olmecs, the Maya also ex- *Maya Writing* panded upon their predecessors' tradition of written inscriptions. In doing so they created the most flexible and sophisticated of all the early American systems of writing. The Maya script contained both ideographic elements (like Chinese characters) and symbols for syllables. Scholars have begun to decipher this script only since the 1960s, and it has become clear that writing was just as important to the Maya as it was to early complex societies in the eastern hemisphere. Maya scribes wrote works of history, poetry, and myth, and they also kept genealogical, administrative, and astronomical records. Most Maya writing survives today in the form of inscriptions on temples and monuments, but scribes produced untold numbers of books written on paper made from beaten tree bark or on vellum made from deerskin. When Spanish conquerors and missionaries arrived in Maya lands in the sixteenth century

Maya Religious Thought

Bloodletting Rituals

Best preserved of the ancient Maya books is the Dresden Codex, which deals with astronomical matters, written probably in the late thirteenth or early fourteenth century. The page depicted here features illustrations of Maya deities (top) and a warrior (bottom). • Courtesy Dept. of Library Services, American Museum of Natural History, #1909

C.E., however, they destroyed all the books they could find in hopes of undermining native religious beliefs. Today only four books of the ancient Maya survive, all dealing with astronomical and calendrical matters.

Surviving inscriptions and other writings shed considerable light on Maya religious and cultural traditions. The *Popol Vuh,* a Maya creation myth, taught that the gods had created human beings out of maize and water, the ingredients that became human flesh and blood. Thus, as in early complex societies of the eastern hemisphere, Maya religious thought reflected the fundamental role of agriculture in their society. Maya priests also taught that the gods kept the world going and maintained the agricultural cycle in exchange for honors and sacrifices performed for them by human beings.

The most important of these sacrifices involved the shedding of human blood, which the Maya believed would prompt the gods to send rain to water their crops of maize. Some bloodletting rituals centered on war captives. Before sacrificing the victims by decapitation, their captors cut off the ends of their fingers or lacerated their bodies so as to cause a copious flow of blood in honor of the gods. Yet the Maya did not look upon these rituals simply as opportunities to torture their enemies. The frequent and voluntary shedding of royal blood, as in the case of Chan Bahlum's self-sacrifice at Palenque, testifies to the depth of Maya convictions that they inhabited a world created and sustained by deities who expected honor and reverence from their human subjects.

Apart from the calendar and sacrificial rituals, the Maya also inherited a distinc-

The Maya Ball Game

tive ballgame from the Olmecs. The game sometimes pitted two men against each other, but it often involved teams of two to four members apiece. (There is no evidence that women played the game.) The object of the game was for players to score points by propelling a rubber ball through a ring or onto a marker without using their hands. The Maya used a ball about twenty centimeters (eight inches) in diameter. Made of solid baked rubber, the ball was both heavy and hard—a blow to the

THE *POPOL VUH* ON THE CREATION OF HUMAN BEINGS

• • •

The Popol Vuh outlines traditional Maya views on the creation of the world and human beings. The version of the work that survives today dates from the mid-sixteenth century, but it reflects beliefs of a much earlier era. According to the Popol Vuh, the gods wanted to create intelligent beings that would recognize and praise them. Three times they tried to fashion such beings out of animals, mud, and wood, but without success. Then they decided to use maize and water as their ingredients.

And here is the beginning of the conception of humans, and of the search for the ingredients of the human body. So they spoke, the [gods] Bearer, Begetter, the Makers, Modelers named Sovereign Plumed Serpent:

"The dawn has approached, preparations have been made, and morning has come for the provider, nurturer, born in the light, begotten in the light. Morning has come for humankind, for the people of the face of the earth," they said. It all came together as they went on thinking in the darkness, in the night, as they searched and they sifted, they thought and they wondered.

And here their thoughts came out in clear light. They sought and discovered what was needed for human flesh. . . . Broken Place, Bitter Water Place is the name: the yellow corn, white corn came from there. . . .

And these were the ingredients for the flesh of the human work, the human design, and the water was for the blood. It became human blood, and corn was also used by the Bearer, Begetter. . . .

And then the yellow corn and white corn were ground, and Xmucane did the grinding nine times. Corn was used, along with the water she rinsed her hands with, for the creation of grease; it became human fat when it was worked by the Bearer, Begetter, Sovereign Plumed Serpent, as they are called. . . .

It was staples alone that made up their flesh.

These are the names of the first people who were made and modeled.

This is the first person: Jaguar Quitze.

And now the second: Jaguar Night.

And now the third: Mahucutah.

And the fourth: True Jaguar.

And these are the names of our first mother-fathers. They were simply made and modeled, it is said; they had no mother and no father. We have named the men by themselves. No woman gave birth to them, nor were they begotten by the builder, sculptor, Bearer, Begetter. By sacrifice alone, by genius alone they were made, they were modeled by the Maker, Modeler, Bearer, Begetter, Sovereign Plumed Serpent. And when they came to fruition, they came out human:

They talked and they made words.

They looked and they listened.

They walked, they worked. . . .

And then their wives and women came into being. Again, the same gods thought of it. It was as if they were asleep when they received them, truly beautiful women were there with Jaguar Quitze, Jaguar Night, Mahucutah, and True Jaguar. With their women there they became wider awake. Right away they were happy at heart again, because of their wives.

Celebrated Seahouse is the name of the wife of Jaguar Quitze.

Prawn House is the name of the wife of Jaguar Night.

Hummingbird House is the name of the wife of Mahucutah.

Macaw House is the name of the wife of True Jaguar.

So these are the names of their wives, who became ladies of rank, giving birth to the people of the tribes, small and great.

SOURCE: Dennis Tedlock, trans. *Popol Vuh: The Definitive Edition of the Mayan Book of the Dawn of Life and the Glories of Gods and Kings.* New York: Simon and Schuster, 1985, pp. 163–65, 167.

This painted pottery vase produced between 550 and 900 C.E. depicts figures playing the Mesoamerican ball game. The padded gear enabled players to propel the hard rubber ball without injuring themselves. • Bowers Museum of Cultural Art. Foundation Acquisition Fund Purchase BMCA F74.9.2

head could easily cause a concussion—and players needed great dexterity and skill to maneuver it accurately using only their feet, legs, hips, torso, shoulders, or elbows. The game was extremely popular: almost all Maya ceremonial centers, towns, and cities had stone-paved courts on which players performed publicly.

The Maya played the ball game for several reasons. Sometimes individuals competed for sporting purposes, and sometimes players or spectators laid bets on the outcome of contests between professionals. The ball game figured also in Maya political and religious rituals. High-ranking captives often engaged in forced public competition in which the stakes were their very lives: losers became sacrificial victims and faced torture and execution immediately following the match. Alongside some ball courts were skull racks that bore the decapitated heads of losing players. Thus Maya concerns to please the gods by shedding human blood extended even to the realm of sport.

Heirs of the Olmecs: Teotihuacan

While the Maya flourished in the Mesoamerican lowlands, a different society arose to the north in the highlands of Mexico. For most of human history, the valley of central Mexico, situated some two kilometers (more than a mile) above sea level, was the site of several large lakes fed by the waters coming off the surrounding mountains. Most of the lakes have disappeared during the past two or three centuries as a result of environmental changes and deliberate draining of their waters. In earlier times, however, their abundant supplies of fish and waterfowl attracted human settlers. The lakes also served as sources of fresh water and as transportation routes linking communities situated on their shores.

The earliest settlers in the valley of Mexico did not build extensive irrigation systems, but they channeled some of the waters from the mountain streams into their fields and established a productive agricultural society. Expanding human population led to the congregation of people in cities and the emergence of a complex society in the Mesoamerican highlands. The earliest center of this society was the large and bustling city of Teotihuacan, located about fifty kilometers (thirty-one miles) northeast of modern Mexico City.

The City of Teotihuacan — Teotihuacan was probably a large agricultural village by 500 B.C.E. It expanded rapidly after about 200 B.C.E., and by the end of the millennium its population approached fifty thousand. By the year 100 C.E., the city's two most prominent monuments, the colossal pyramids of the sun and the moon, dominated the skyline. The Pyramid of the Sun is the largest single structure in Mesoamerica. It occupies nearly as much space as the pyramid of Khufu in Egypt, though it stands only half as tall. At its high point, about 400 to 600 C.E., Teotihuacan was home to almost two hun-

Aerial view of Teotihuacan, looking toward the Pyramid of the Moon (top center) from the Pyramid of the Sun (bottom left). Shops and residences occupied the spaces surrounding the main street and the pyramids. • Robert Frerck/Odyssey/Chicago

dred thousand inhabitants, a thriving metropolis with scores of temples, several palatial residences, neighborhoods with small apartments for the masses, busy markets, and hundreds of workshops for artisans and craftsmen.

The organization of a large urban population, along with the hinterland that supported it, required a recognized source of authority. Although Teotihuacan generated large numbers of books and records that perhaps would have shed light on the character of this authority, they unfortunately perished when the city itself declined. Paintings and murals suggest that Teotihuacan was a theocracy of sorts. Priests figure prominently in the works of art, and scholars interpret many figures as representations of deities. Priests were crucial to the survival of the society, since they kept the calendar and ensured that planting and harvesting took place at the appropriate seasons. Thus it would not have been unusual for them to govern Teotihuacan in the name of the gods, or at least to cooperate closely with a secular ruling class.

Apart from rulers and priests, Teotihuacan's population included cultivators, artisans, and merchants. Perhaps as many as two-thirds of the city's inhabitants worked during the day in fields surrounding Teotihuacan and returned to their small apartments in the city at night. Artisans of Teotihuacan were especially famous for their obsidian tools and fine orange pottery, and scholars have identified numerous workshops and stores where toolmakers and potters produced and marketed their goods within the city itself. The residents of Teotihuacan also participated in extensive trade and exchange networks. Professional merchants traded their products throughout Mesoamerica. Archaeologists have found numerous samples of the distinctive obsidian tools and orange pottery at sites far distant from Teotihuacan, from the region of modern Guatemala City in the south to Durango and beyond in the north.

The Society of Teotihuacan

Until about 500 C.E. there was little sign of military organization in Teotihuacan. The city did not have defensive walls, and works of art rarely depicted warriors. Yet the influence of Teotihuacan extended to much of modern Mexico and beyond. The Maya capital of Kaminaljuyú, for example, fell under the influence of Teotihuacan during the fourth century C.E. Although the rulers of Teotihuacan may have established colonies to protect their sources of obsidian and undertaken military expeditions to back up their authority throughout central Mexico, the city's influence apparently derived less from military might than from its ability to produce fine manufactured goods that appealed to consumers in distant markets.

Cultural Traditions

Like the Maya, the residents of Teotihuacan built on cultural foundations established by the Olmecs. They played the ball game, adapted the Olmec calendar to their own uses, and expanded the Olmecs' graphic symbols into a complete system of writing. Unfortunately, only a few samples of their writing survive in stone carvings. Because their books have all perished, it is impossible to know exactly how they viewed the world and their place in it. Works of art suggest that they recognized an earth god and a rain god, and it is certain that they carried out human sacrifices during their religious rituals.

Decline of Teotihuacan

Teotihuacan began to experience increasing military pressure from other peoples around 500 C.E. Works of art from this period frequently depicted eagles, jaguars, and coyotes—animals that Mesoamericans associated with fighting and military conquest. After about 650 C.E. Teotihuacan entered a period of decline. About the middle of the eighth century invaders sacked and burned the city, destroying its books and monuments. After that catastrophe most residents deserted Teotihuacan, and the city slowly fell into ruin.

 # EARLY SOCIETIES OF SOUTH AMERICA

By about 12,000 B.C.E. hunting and gathering peoples had made their way across the narrow isthmus of Central America and into South America. Those who migrated into the region of the northern and central Andes mountains hunted deer, llama, alpaca, and other large animals. Both the mountainous highlands and the coastal regions below benefited from a cool and moist climate that provided natural harvests of squashes, gourds, and wild potatoes. Beginning about 8000 B.C.E., however, the climate of this whole region became increasingly warm and dry, and the changes placed pressure on natural food supplies. To maintain their numbers, the human communities of the region began to experiment with agriculture. As elsewhere, agriculture encouraged population growth, the establishment of villages and cities, the building of states, and the elaboration of organized cultural traditions. During the centuries after 1000 B.C.E., the central Andean region generated complex societies parallel to those of Mesoamerica.

Early Andean Society and the Chavín Cult

Although they were exact contemporaries, early Mesoamerican and Andean societies developed largely in isolation. The heartland of early Andean society was the region now occupied by the states of Peru and Bolivia. In the absence of abundant pack animals or a technology to facilitate long-distance transportation, geography discouraged the establishment of communications between the Andean region and Mesoamerica. Neither the Andes mountains nor the lowlands of modern Panama and

Nicaragua offered an attractive highway linking the two regions. Several agricultural products and technologies diffused slowly from one area to the other: cultivation of maize and squashes spread from its Mesoamerican home to the central Andean region while Andean gold, silver, and copper metallurgy traveled north to Mesoamerica.

Geography even conspired against the establishment of communications within the central Andean region. Deep valleys crease the western flank of the Andes mountains, as rivers drain waters from the highlands to the Pacific Ocean, so transportation and communication between the valleys has always been very difficult. Nevertheless, powerful Andean states sometimes overcame the difficulties and influenced human affairs as far away as modern Ecuador and Colombia to the north and northern Chile to the south.

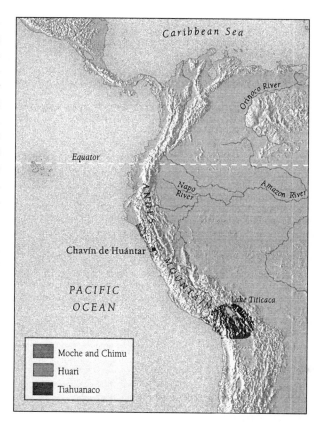

MAP [5.2]

Early societies of Andean South America.

Most of the early Andean heartland came under cultivation between 2500 and 2000 B.C.E., and permanent settlements dotted the coastal regions in particular. The earliest cultivators of the region relied on beans, peanuts, and sweet potatoes as their main food crops. They also cultivated cotton, which they used to make fish nets and textiles. The rich marine life of the Pacific Ocean supplemented agricultural harvests, enabling coastal peoples to build an increasingly complex society. Settlements probably appeared later in the Andean highlands than in the coastal regions, but many varieties of potato supported agricultural communities in the highlands after about 2000 B.C.E. By 1800 B.C.E. peoples in all the Andean regions had begun to fashion distinctive styles of pottery and to build temples and pyramids in large ceremonial centers.

Early Agriculture in South America

Shortly after the year 1000 B.C.E., a new religion appeared suddenly in the central Andes. The Chavín cult, which enjoyed enormous popularity during the period 900 to 800 B.C.E., spread through most of the territory occupied by modern Peru and then vanished about 300 B.C.E. Unfortunately, no information survives to indicate the precise significance of the cult, nor even its proper name: scholars have named it after the modern town of Chavín de Huántar, one of the cult's most prominent sites. One theory suggests that the cult arose when maize became an important crop in South America. The capacity of maize to support large populations

The Chavín Cult

might well have served as the stimulus for the emergence of a cult designed to promote fertility and abundant harvests. In any case the large temple complexes and elaborate works of art that accompanied the cult demonstrate its importance to those who honored it. Devotees produced intricate stone carvings representing their deities with the features of humans and wild animals such as jaguars, hawks, eagles, and snakes. The extensive distribution of the temples and carvings shows that the Chavín cult seized the imagination of agricultural peoples throughout the central Andean region.

During the era of the Chavín cult, Andean society became increasingly complex. Weavers devised techniques of producing elaborate cotton textiles, some with intricate patterns and designs. Artisans manufactured large, light, and strong fishing nets from cotton string. Craftsmen experimented with minerals and discovered techniques of gold, silver, and copper metallurgy. They mostly fashioned metals into pieces of jewelry or other decorative items but also made small tools out of copper.

Early Cities   There is no evidence to suggest that Chavín cultural and religious beliefs led to the establishment of a state or any organized political order. Indeed, they probably inspired the building of ceremonial centers, rather than the making of true cities. As the population increased and society became more complex, however, cities began to appear shortly after the disappearance of the Chavín cult. Beginning about 200 B.C.E. large cities emerged at the modern-day sites of Huari, Pucara, and Tiahuanaco. Each of these early Andean cities had a population exceeding ten thousand, and each also featured large public buildings, ceremonial plazas, and extensive residential districts.

Early Andean States: Mochica

Along with cities there also appeared regional states. The earliest Andean states arose in the many valleys on the western side of the mountains. These states emerged when conquerors unified the individual valleys and organized them into integrated societies. They coordinated the building of irrigation systems so that the lower valleys could support intensive agriculture, and they established trade and exchange networks that tied the highlands, central valleys, and coastal regions together. Each region contributed its own products to the larger economy of the valley: from the highlands came potatoes, llama meat, and alpaca wool; the central valleys supplied maize, beans, and squashes, and the coasts provided sweet potatoes, fish, and cotton.

This organization of the Andean valleys into integrated economic zones did not come about by accident. Builders of early Andean states worked deliberately and did not hesitate to use force to consolidate their domains. Surviving stone fortifications and warriors depicted in works of art testify that the early Andean states relied heavily on arms to introduce order and maintain stability in their small realms.

The Mochica State   Since early Andean societies did not make use of writing, their beliefs, values, and ways of life remain largely hidden behind veils of time. One of the early Andean states, however, left a remarkable artistic legacy that allows a glimpse into the life of a society otherwise almost entirely lost. The Mochica state had its base in the valley of the Moche River, and it dominated the coasts and valleys of northern Peru during the period about 300 to 700 C.E. Mochica painting survives largely on pottery vessels, and it offers a detailed and expressive depiction of early Andean society in all its variety.

Many Mochica ceramics take the form of portraits of individuals' heads. Others represent the major gods and the various subordinate deities and demons. Some of the most interesting depict scenes in the everyday life of the Mochica people: aristocrats embarking on a hunting party, warriors leading captives bound by ropes, women working in a textile factory under the careful eye of a supervisor, rulers receiving messengers or ambassadors from neighboring states, and beggars looking for handouts on a busy street. Even in the absence of writing, Mochica artists left abundant evidence of a complex society with considerable specialization of labor.

The Mochica was only one of several large states that dominated the central Andean region during the first millennium C.E. Although they integrated the regional economies of the various Andean valleys,

Mochica Ceramics

Many Mochica pots portray human figures, often depicting distinctive characteristics of individuals or typical scenes from daily life. This pot represents two women helping a man who consumed a little bit too much maize beer. ● Bildarchivn Preussischer Kulturbesitz/Museum für Völkerkunde, Berlin

none of these early states was able to impose order on the entire region or even to dominate a portion of it for very long. The exceedingly difficult geographical barriers posed by the Andes mountains presented challenges that ancient technology and social organization simply could not meet. As a result, at the end of the first millennium C.E., Andean society exhibited regional differences much sharper than those of Mesoamerica and early complex societies in the eastern hemisphere.

EARLY SOCIETIES OF OCEANIA

Human migrants entered Australia and New Guinea at least by 60,000 years before the present, and possibly as early as 120,000 years ago. They arrived in watercraft—probably canoes fitted with sails—but because of the low sea levels of that era, the migrants did not have to cross large stretches of open ocean. These earliest inhabitants of Oceania also migrated—perhaps over land when sea levels were still low—to the Bismarcks, Solomons, and other small island groups near New Guinea. Beginning

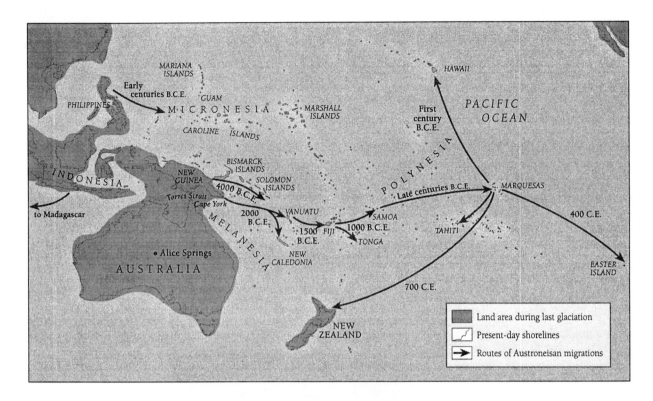

MAP [5.3]

Early societies of Oceania.

about 5,000 years ago, seafaring peoples from southeast Asia visited the northern coast of New Guinea for purposes of trade. Some of them settled there, but many others ventured farther and established communities in the island groups of the western Pacific Ocean. During the centuries that followed, their descendants sailed large, ocean-going canoes throughout the Pacific basin, and by the middle centuries of the first millennium C.E., they had established human communities in all the habitable islands of the Pacific Ocean.

Early Societies in Australia and New Guinea

Human migrants reached Australia and New Guinea long before any people had begun to cultivate crops or keep herds of domesticated animals. Inevitably, then, the earliest inhabitants of Australia and New Guinea lived by hunting and gathering their food. For thousands of years, foraging peoples probably traveled back and forth between Australia and New Guinea. These migrations ceased about ten thousand years ago when rising seas separated the two lands. After that time human societies in Australia and New Guinea followed radically different paths. The aboriginal peoples of Australia maintained hunting and gathering societies until large numbers of European migrants established settler communities there in the nineteenth and twentieth centuries C.E. In New Guinea, however, human communities turned to agriculture: beginning about 3000 B.C.E. the cultivation of root crops like yams and taro and the keeping of pigs and chickens spread rapidly throughout the island.

Early Hunting and Gathering Societies in Australia
    Like hunting and gathering peoples elsewhere, the aboriginal Australians lived in small, mobile communities that undertook seasonal migrations in search of food. Over the centuries, they learned to exploit the resources of the various ecological re-

Austronesian mariners sailed double-hulled voyaging canoes much like this one from Ra'iatea in the Society Islands drawn in 1769 by an artist who accompanied Captain James Cook on his first voyage in the Pacific Ocean. • © The British Library

gions of Australia. Plant foods, including fruits, berries, roots, nuts, seeds, shoots, and green leaves, constituted the bulk of their diet. In the tropical region of Cape York in northern Australia, they consumed no fewer than 141 different species of plants. Aboriginal peoples found abundant plant life even in the harsh desert regions of interior Australia. In the vicinity of modern Alice Springs in central Australia, for example, they included about twenty species of greens and forty-five kinds of seeds and nuts in their diet. They also used at least 124 plants as medicines, ointments, and drugs. To supplement their plant-based diet, they used axes, spears, clubs, nets, lassoes, snares, and boomerangs to bring down animals ranging in size from rats to giant kangaroos, which grew to a height of three meters (almost ten feet), and to catch fish, waterfowl, and small birds.

The earliest inhabitants of New Guinea foraged for food, like their neighbors to the south. About five thousand years ago, however, a process of social and economic change began to unfold in New Guinea. The agents of change were seafaring peoples from southeast Asia speaking Austronesian languages, whose modern linguistic relatives include Malayan, Indonesian, Filipino, Polynesian, and other Oceanic languages, as well as the Malagasy language of Madagascar and the tongues spoken by the indigenous peoples of Taiwan and southern China. Austronesian-speaking peoples possessed remarkable seafaring skills. They sailed the open ocean in large canoes equipped with outriggers, which stabilized their craft and reduced the risks of long voyages. By paying close attention to winds, currents, stars, cloud formations, and other natural indicators, they learned how to find distant lands reliably and return home safely. Beginning about 3000 B.C.E. these mariners visited the northern coast of New Guinea, where they traded with the indigenous peoples and established their own communities.

Austronesian Peoples

Early Agriculture in New Guinea   Austronesian seafarers came from societies that depended on the cultivation of root crops and the herding of animals. When they settled in New Guinea, they introduced yams, taro, pigs, and chickens to the island, and the indigenous peoples themselves soon began to cultivate crops and keep animals. Within a few centuries agriculture and herding had spread to all parts of New Guinea. As in other lands, agriculture brought population growth and specialization of labor: after the change to agriculture, permanent settlements, pottery, and carefully crafted tools appeared throughout the island.

Separated from New Guinea only by the narrow Torres Strait, the aboriginal peoples of northern Australia knew about the cultivation of foodstuffs, since they had occasional dealings with traders from New Guinea. Agriculture even spread to the islands of the Torres Strait, but it did not take root in Australia until the arrival of European peoples in the eighteenth century C.E. Meanwhile, Austronesian-speaking peoples who introduced agriculture and herding to New Guinea sailed their outrigger canoes farther and established the first human settlements in the islands of the Pacific Ocean.

The Peopling of the Pacific Islands

The hunting and gathering peoples who first inhabited Australia and New Guinea also established a few settlements in the Bismarck and Solomon island groups east of New Guinea. They ventured to these islands during the era when the seas were low and sailing distances from New Guinea were consequently very short. They did not have the maritime technology, however, to sail far beyond the Solomons to the more distant islands in the Pacific Ocean. Even if they had, the small Pacific islands, with limited supplies of edible plants and animals, would not have supported communities of foragers.

Austronesian Migrations to Polynesia   Austronesian-speaking peoples possessed a sophisticated maritime technology as well as agricultural expertise, and they established human settlements in the islands of the Pacific Ocean. Their outrigger canoes enabled them to sail safely over long distances of open ocean, and their food crops and domesticated animals enabled them to establish agricultural societies in the islands. Once they had established coastal settlements in New Guinea, Austronesian seafarers sailed easily to the Bismarck and Solomon islands, perhaps in the interests of trade. From there they undertook exploratory voyages that led them to previously unpopulated islands.

By about 2000 B.C.E. Austronesian mariners had arrived at Vanuatu (formerly called New Hebrides) and New Caledonia, by 1500 B.C.E. at Fiji, and by 1000 B.C.E. at Tonga and Samoa. During the late centuries of the first millennium B.C.E., they established settlements in Tahiti and the Marquesas. From there they launched ventures that took them to the most remote outposts of Polynesia—the territory falling in the triangle with Hawai`i, Easter Island, and New Zealand at the points—which required them to sail over thousands of nautical miles of blue water. They reached the islands of Hawai`i by about the first century B.C.E., Easter Island by 400 C.E., and the large islands of New Zealand by 700 C.E.

Austronesian Migrations to Micronesia and Madagascar   While one branch of the Austronesian-speaking peoples populated the islands of Polynesia, other branches sailed in different directions. From the Philippines some ventured to the region of Micronesia, which includes small islands and atolls such as the Mariana, Caroline, and Marshall islands of the western Pacific. Yet others looked west from their homelands in Indonesia, sailed clear across the Indian Ocean, and became the first human settlers of the large island of Madagascar off the east African coast. Malagasy, the principal language of modern-day Madagascar, is clearly identifiable as an Austronesian tongue.

As in New Guinea, Austronesian peoples built agricultural societies everywhere they settled. The Pacific islands offered little edible plant life, and the settlers soon killed off most of the large animals and birds (some of which, in the absence of natural predators, had evolved into flightless species) that were suitable for human consumption. Long-term survival required the settlers to introduce food crops to the Pacific islands. They took cuttings, seedlings, and domesticated animals on their voyages, and they introduced yams, taro, breadfruit, bananas, dogs, pigs, and chickens into the Pacific islands. Apart from cultivated crops and meat from domestic animals, the settlers also ate fish and seaweed from nearby waters.

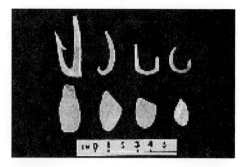

Pacific islanders fashioned fishhooks out of shell, as here, and also out of bone or wood. • Bishop Museum, Honolulu. Photograph courtesy of Dr. Yoshiko Sinoto

Early Agriculture in the Pacific Islands

Austronesian peoples established hierarchical chiefdoms in the Pacific islands. Leadership passed from a chief to his eldest son, and near relatives constituted a local aristocracy. Contests for power and influence between ambitious subordinates frequently caused tension and turmoil, but the possibility of migration offered an alternative to conflict. Dissatisfied or aggrieved parties often built voyaging canoes, recruited followers, and set sail with the intention of establishing new settlements in uninhabited or lightly populated islands. Indeed, the spread of Austronesian peoples throughout the Pacific islands came about partly because of population pressures and conflicts that encouraged small parties to seek fresh opportunities in more hospitable lands.

Chiefly Political Organization

Over the longer term Austronesian peoples built strong, chiefly societies, particularly on large islands with relatively dense populations like those of the Tongan, Samoan, and Hawaiian groups. In Hawai`i, for example, militarily skilled chiefs cooperated closely with priests, administrators, soldiers, and servants in ruling their districts, which might include a portion of an island, an entire island, or even several islands. Chiefs and their retinues claimed a portion of the agricultural surplus produced by their subjects, and they sometimes required subjects to deliver additional products, such as fish, birds, or timber. Apart from organizing public life in their own districts, chiefs and their administrators vied with the ruling classes of neighboring districts, led public ritual observances, and oversaw irrigation systems that watered the taro plants that were crucial to the survival of Hawaiian society. Eventually, the chiefly and aristocratic classes became so entrenched and powerful that they regarded themselves as divine or semidivine, and the law of the land prohibited common subjects from even gazing directly at them.

Very little writing survives to illuminate the historical development of early societies in the Americas and Oceania. Thus it is impossible to offer the sort of richly detailed account of their political organization, social structures, and cultural traditions that historians commonly provide for societies of the eastern hemisphere. Nevertheless, the earliest inhabitants of the Americas and Oceania built productive and vibrant societies whose development roughly paralleled that of their counterparts in the eastern hemisphere. Many communities depended on an agricultural economy, and on the foundation of their surplus production they supported dense populations, engaged in specialized labor, established formal political authorities, constructed hierarchical social orders, carried on long-distance trade, and formed distinctive cultural traditions. The early historical development of the Americas and Oceania demonstrates once again the tendency of agriculture to encourage human communities to construct ever more elaborate and complex forms of social organization.

CHRONOLOGY

AMERICAS

40,000–10,000 B.C.E.	Human migration to North America from Siberia
8000–7000 B.C.E.	Origins of agriculture in Mesoamerica
5000 B.C.E.	Origins of maize cultivation in Mesoamerica
2500–2000 B.C.E.	Origins of agriculture in South America
1200–100 B.C.E.	Olmec society
1000–300 B.C.E.	Chavín cult
200 B.C.E.–750 C.E.	Teotihuacan society
300–1100 C.E.	Maya society
300–700 C.E.	Mochica society

OCEANIA

120,000–60,000 B.C.E.	Human migration to Australia and New Guinea
3000 B.C.E.	Origins of agriculture in New Guinea
3000 B.C.E.	Austronesian migrations to New Guinea
2000 B.C.E.–700 C.E.	Austronesian migrations to Pacific islands

FOR FURTHER READING

Robert McC. Adams. *The Evolution of Urban Society.* Chicago, 1966. Provocative analysis comparing the development of Mesopotamian and Mesoamerican societies by a leading archaeologist.

Peter Bellwood. *The Polynesians: Prehistory of an Island People.* Rev. ed. London, 1987. Well-illustrated popular account emphasizing the origins and early development of Polynesian societies.

Ignacio Bernal. *Mexico before Cortez: Art, History, and Legend.* Trans. by W. Barnstone. Garden City, 1963. Judicious survey by a leading student of ancient Mesoamerica.

———. *The Olmec World.* Trans. by D. Heyden and F. Horcasitas. Berkeley, 1969. The best general study of the Olmecs.

Geoffrey Blainey. *Triumph of the Nomads: A History of Aboriginal Australia.* Melbourne, 1975. A sympathetic account of Australia before European arrival, well informed by recent archaeological discoveries.

Michael D. Coe. *The Maya.* 4th ed. London, 1987. Well-illustrated popular account by one of the world's leading scholars of the Maya.

Nigel Davies. *The Ancient Kingdoms of Mexico.* Harmondsworth, 1983. Popular account that reflects recent research.

David Freidel, Linda Schele, and Joy Parker. *Maya Cosmos: Three Thousand Years on the Shaman's Path.* New York, 1993. Fascinating investigation of Maya conceptions of the world and their continuing influence in the present day.

Jesse D. Jennings, ed. *The Prehistory of Polynesia.* Cambridge, Mass., 1979. Brings together essays by prominent scholars on Polynesia before the arrival of Europeans in the Pacific Ocean.

Friedrich Katz. *The Ancient American Civilizations.* Trans. by K.M.L. Simpson. New York, 1972. Detailed survey that compares the experiences of Mesoamerica and Andean South America.

Patrick V. Kirch. *The Evolution of the Polynesian Chiefdoms.* Cambridge, 1984. Careful examination of the development of Polynesian societies in light of recent archaeological discoveries.

Edward P. Lanning. *Peru before the Incas.* Englewood Cliffs, 1967. Summarizes the results of recent archaeological research that has transformed scholars' understanding of ancient Andean societies.

David Lewis. *We, the Navigators: The Ancient Art of Landfinding in the Pacific.* Honolulu, 1973. Fascinating reconstruction of traditional methods of noninstrumental navigation used by seafaring peoples
of the Pacific islands.

Linda Schele and David Freidel. *A Forest of Kings: The Untold Story of the Ancient Maya.* New York,
1990. Draws heavily on recently deciphered inscriptions in reconstructing the history of the ancient
Maya.

Linda Schele and Mary Ellen Miller. *The Blood of Kings: Dynasty and Ritual in Maya Art.* New York,
1986. A richly illustrated volume that explores Maya society through works of art and architecture as
well as writing.

Dennis Tedlock, trans. *Popol Vuh: The Definitive Edition of the Mayan Book of the Dawn of Life and the
Glories of Gods and Kings.* New York, 1985. The best translation of the *Popol Vuh;* with an excellent
introduction.

Muriel Porter Weaver. *The Aztecs, Maya, and Their Predecessors: Archaeology of Mesoamerica.* 3rd ed. San
Diego, 1993. An up-to-date survey based on recent historical and archaeological research.

PART II

THE FORMATION
OF CLASSICAL SOCIETIES,
500 B.C.E. TO 500 C.E.

. . .

Shortly after *Homo sapiens sapiens* turned to agriculture, human communities began to experiment with methods of social organization. In several cases this experimentation encouraged the development of complex societies that integrated the lives and livelihoods of peoples over large regions. These early complex societies launched human history on a trajectory that it continues to follow today. States, social classes, technological innovation, specialization of labor, trade, and sophisticated cultural traditions rank among the most important legacies of these societies.

Toward the end of the first millennium B.C.E., several early societies achieved particularly high degrees of internal organization, extended their authority over extremely large regions, and elaborated especially influential cultural traditions. The most prominent of these societies developed in Persia, China, India, and the Mediterranean basin. Because their legacies have endured so long and have influenced the ways that literally billions of people have led their lives, historians often refer to them as classical societies.

The classical societies of Persia, China, India, and the Mediterranean basin differed from one another in many ways. They raised different food crops, constructed buildings out of different materials, lived by different legal and moral codes, and recognized different gods. Classical China and India depended on the cultivation of rice, millet, and wheat, while in Persia and the Mediterranean wheat was the staple food crop. In China packed earth and wood served as the principal construction material even for large public buildings; in India wood alone was the most common building material, and in Persia and the Mediterranean, architects designed buildings of brick and stone. The classical societies differed even more strikingly when it came to beliefs and values. They generated a wide variety of ideas about the organization of family and society, the understanding of what constituted proper public and private behavior, the nature of the gods or other powers thought to influence human affairs, and proper relationships between human beings, the natural world, and the gods.

Despite these differences, however, these societies faced several common problems. They all confronted the challenge, for example, of administering vast territories without advanced technologies of transportation and communication. Rulers built centralized imperial states on a scale much larger than had

126

their predecessors in earlier complex societies. They constructed elaborate systems of bureaucracy, and they experimented with administrative organization in an effort to secure as much influence as possible for central governments and to extend imperial authority to the far reaches of their realms. To encourage political and economic integration of their lands, classical rulers also built roads and supported networks of trade and communication that linked the sometimes far-flung regions under their authority.

The classical societies all faced military challenges, and they raised powerful armies for both defensive and offensive purposes. Military challenges frequently arose from within classical societies themselves in the form of rebellion, civil war, or conflict between powerful factions. External threats came from nomadic and migratory peoples who sought to share in the wealth generated by the productive agricultural economies of classical societies. Sometimes mounted nomadic warriors charged into settlements, seized what they wished, and departed before the victims could mount a defense. In other cases, migratory peoples moved into classical societies in such large numbers that they disrupted the established political and social order. In hopes of securing their borders and enhancing the welfare of their lands, rulers of most classical societies launched campaigns of expansion that ultimately produced massive imperial states.

The bureaucracies and armies that enabled classical societies to address some problems effectively created difficulties as well. One particularly pressing problem revolved around the maintenance of the bureaucracies and armies. To finance expensive administrative and military machinery, rulers of the classical societies all claimed some portion of the agricultural and industrial surplus of their lands in the form of taxes or tribute. Most of them also required their subjects to provide compulsory, uncompensated labor services for large-scale public projects involving the building and maintenance of structures such as defensive walls, highways, bridges, and irrigation systems.

The classical societies also faced the challenge of trying to maintain an equitable distribution of land and wealth. As some individuals flourished and accumulated land and wealth, they enjoyed economic advantages over their neighbors. Increasingly sharp economic distinctions gave rise to tensions that fueled bitter class conflict. In some cases conflicts escalated into rebellions and civil wars that threatened the very survival of the classical societies.

All the classical societies engaged in long-distance trade. This trade encouraged economic integration within the societies, since their various regions came to depend on one another for agricultural products and manufactured items. Long-distance trade led also to the establishment of regular commerce between peoples of different societies and cultural regions. The volume of trade increased dramatically when classical empires pacified large stretches of the Eurasian landmass. Long-distance trade became common enough that a well-established network of land and sea routes, known collectively as the silk roads, linked lands as distant as China and Europe.

Finally, all the classical societies generated sophisticated cultural and religious traditions. Different societies held widely varying beliefs and values, but their cultural and religious traditions offered guidance on moral, religious, political, and social issues. These traditions often served as foundations for educational systems that prepared individuals for careers in government. As a result, they shaped the values of people who made law and implemented policy. Several cultural and religious traditions also attracted large popular followings and created institutional structures that enabled them to survive over a long term and extend their influence through time.

Over the centuries specific political, social, economic, and cultural features of the classical societies have disappeared. Yet their legacies deeply influenced future societies and in many ways continue to influence the lives of the world's peoples. Appreciation of the legacies of classical societies in Persia, China, India, and the Mediterranean basin is crucial for the effort to understand the world's historical development.

EAST ASIA	SOUTH ASIA	SOUTHWEST ASIA	MEDITERRANEAN BASIN
600 B.C.E.	600 B.C.E.	600 B.C.E.	600 B.C.E.
Confucius (Kong Fuzi) (551–479)—*Analects* Laozi (6th century)— *Daodejing*	Siddharta Gautama the Buddha (563–483) Vardhamana Mahavira (540–468) Charvaka sect (6th century) Cyrus of Persia conquers Gandhara Persian influence	Zarathustra and origins of Zoroastrianiam Magi preserve *Gathas* Achaemenid dynasty (558–330) Cyrus the Achaemenid (558–530) Conquest of Babylonia by Cyrus (539) Cambyses (530–522) Darius (521–486) Persian Wars (500–479) Xerxes (486–465)	Sappho (600) Solon's reforms and rise of democracy (500s) Establishment of Roman republic (509) Battles of Marathon (490) and Salamis (480) Golden Age of Athens (400's) Pericles, Socrates, Plato, Aristotle Aeschylus, Sophocles, Euripides Peloponnesian War (430–404)
400 B.C.E.	400 B.C.E.	400 B.C.E.	400 B.C.E.
Shang Yang (390–338)— *The Book of Lord Shang* Mencius (372–289) Zhuangzi (369–286)— *Zhuangzi* Xunzi (298–238) Han Feizi (280–233) Qin unification of China (221) Qin Shihuangdi (221–210) Former Han Dynasty (206 B.C.E.–9 C.E.) Liu Bang (206)	Alexander of Macedon enters India (327) Unification under Chandragupta Maurya (321) *Arthashastra* Ashoka (268–232) Spread of Buddhism	Alexander invades Persia (334) Battle of Gaugamela (331) Alexander crowned Persian king (330) Seleucid dynasty (323) Parthian dynasty (247)	Greek conquest by Philip II of Macedon (359–336) Conquests of Alexander of Macedon (336–323) Antigonid, Ptolemaic, and Seleucid dynasties Hellenistic age Epicurianism, Skepticism, Stoicism Punic Wars (264–146)
200 B.C.E.	200 B.C.E.	200 B.C.E.	200 B.C.E.
Spread of Buddhism to Central Asia Han Wudi (141–87) Imperial university (124) Defeat of Xiongnu Opening of silk roads Sima Qian (99) Spread of Buddhism to China	Mauryan dynasty ends (185)	Mithradates (171–155) Seleucids defeated by Rome (83)	Reforms and assassinations of Gracchi brothers (133–121) Marius and Sulla (87–78) Julius Caesar (100–44) Battle of Actium (31) Octavian receives title of Augustus (27) Pax Romana

EAST ASIA	SOUTH ASIA	SOUTHWEST ASIA	MEDITERRANEAN BASIN
0 C.E.	0 C.E.	0 C.E.	0 C.E.
Wang Mang (9–23) Later Han dynasty (23–220) Invention of paper (100) Epidemic disease Yellow Turban rebellion (189)	*Mahabharata* and *Ramayana* in written form	Parthian dynasty falls to Sasanids Sasanid dynasty (224) Shapur I (239–272)	Jesus of Nazareth (4 B.C.E.–29 C.E.) Paul of Tarsus and spread of Christianity (55) Epidemic disease (165–180) Mani and spread of Manichaeism (216–272) Diocletian (284–305)
300 C.E.	300 C.E.	300 C.E.	300 C.E.
	Gupta dynasty (320–550) Samudra Gupta (335–375) Chandra Gupta II (375–415) Final form of *Bhagavad Gita* (400) Nalanda Buddhist monastery founded Invasion of White Huns		Constantine (313) Edict of Milan Theodosius—Christianity as official religion (380) St. Augustine (354–430) Rome falls to Odovacer (476)
600 C.E.	600 C.E.	600 C.E.	600 C.E.
		Sasanid dynasty ends (651)	

THE EMPIRES OF PERSIA

· · ·

The Greek historian Herodotus relished a good story, and he related many a tale about the Persian empire and its conflicts with other peoples, including Greeks. One story had to do with a struggle between Cyrus, leader of the expanding Persian realm, and Croesus, ruler of the powerful and wealthy kingdom of Lydia in southwestern Anatolia. Croesus noted the growth of Persian influence with concern and asked the Greek oracle at Delphi whether to go to war against Cyrus. The oracle responded that an attack on Cyrus would destroy a great kingdom.

Overjoyed, Croesus lined up his allies and prepared for war. In 546 B.C.E. he launched an invasion and seized a small town, provoking Cyrus to engage the formidable Lydian cavalry. The resulting battle was hard fought but inconclusive. Because winter was approaching, Croesus disbanded his troops and returned to his capital at Sardis, expecting Cyrus to retreat as well. But Cyrus was a vigorous and unpredictable warrior, and he pursued Croesus to Sardis. When he learned of the pursuit, Croesus hastily assembled an army to confront the invaders. Cyrus threw it into disarray, however, by advancing a group of warriors mounted on camels, which spooked the Lydian horses and sent them into headlong flight. Cyrus's army then surrounded Sardis and took the city after a seige of only two weeks. Croesus narrowly escaped death in the battle, but he was taken captive and afterward became an advisor to Cyrus. Herodotus could not resist pointing out that events proved the Delphic oracle right: Croesus's attack on Cyrus did indeed lead to the destruction of a great kingdom—his own.

The victory over Lydia was a major turning point in the development of the Persian empire. Lydia had a reputation as a kingdom of fabulous wealth, partly because it was the first land to use standardized coins with values guaranteed by the state. Taking advantage of its coins and its geographical location on the Mediterranean, Lydia conducted maritime trade with Greece, Egypt, and Phoenicia, as well as overland trade with Mesopotamia and Persia. Lydian wealth and resources gave Cyrus tremendous momentum as he extended Persian authority to new lands and built the earliest of the vast imperial states of classical times.

Classical Persian society began to take shape during the sixth century B.C.E. when warriors conquered the region from the Indus River to Egypt and southeastern Europe. Their conquests yielded an enormous realm much larger than the earlier Babylonian or Assyrian empires. The very size of the Persian empire created political and administrative problems for its rulers. Once they solved those problems, however, a series of Persian-based empires governed much of the territory between India and the Mediterranean Sea for more than a millennium—from the mid-sixth century

Gold plaque depicting a figure who was perhaps a priest in Achaemenid times. • © The British Museum

B.C.E. until the early seventh century C.E.—and brought centralized political organization to many distinct peoples living over vast geographical spaces.

In organizing their realm, Persian rulers relied heavily on Mesopotamian techniques of administration, which they adapted to their own needs. Yet they did not hesitate to create new institutions or adopt new administrative procedures. In the interest of improved communications and military mobility, they also invested resources in the construction of roads and highways linking the regions of the empire. As a result of these efforts, central administrators were able to send instructions throughout the empire, dispatch armies in times of turmoil, and ensure that local officials would carry out imperial policies.

The organization of the vast territories embraced by the classical Persian empires had important social, economic, and cultural implications. High agricultural productivity enabled many people to work at tasks other than cultivation: classes of bureaucrats, administrators, priests, craftsmen, and merchants increased in number as the production and distribution of food became more efficient. Meanwhile, social extremes became more pronounced: a few individuals and families amassed enormous wealth, many led simple lives, and some fell into slavery. Good roads fostered trade within imperial borders, and Persian society itself served as a commercial and cultural bridge between Indian and Mediterranean societies. As a crossroads, Persia served not only as a link in long-distance trade networks but also as a conduit for the exchange of philosophical and religious ideas. Persian religious traditions did not attract many adherents beyond the imperial boundaries, but they inspired religious thinkers subject to Persian rule and deeply influenced Judaism, Christianity, and Islam.

 ## THE RISE AND FALL OF THE PERSIAN EMPIRES

The empires of Persia arose in the arid land of Iran. For centuries Iran had developed under the shadow of the wealthier and more productive Mesopotamia to the west while absorbing intermittent migrations and invasions of nomadic peoples coming out of central Asia to the northeast. During the sixth century B.C.E., rulers of the province of Persia in southwestern Iran embarked on a series of conquests that resulted in the formation of an enormous empire. For more than a millennium, four ruling dynasties—the Achaemenids (558–330 B.C.E.), Seleucids (323–83 B.C.E.), Parthians (247 B.C.E.–224 C.E.), and Sasanids (224–651 C.E.)—maintained a continuous tradition of imperial rule in much of southwest Asia.

The Achaemenid Empire

The Medes and the Persians

The origins of classical Persian society trace back to the late stages of Mesopotamian society. During the centuries before 1000 B.C.E., two closely related peoples known as the Medes and the Persians migrated from central Asia to Persia (the southwestern portion of the modern-day state of Iran), where they lived in loose subjection to the Babylonian and Assyrian empires. The Medes and Persians spoke Indo-European languages, and their movements were part of the larger Indo-European migrations. They shared many cultural traits with their distant cousins, the Aryans, who migrated into India. They were mostly pastoralists, although they also practiced a limited amount of agriculture. They organized themselves by clans, rather than by states or formal political institutions, but they recognized leaders who collected taxes and delivered tribute to their Mesopotamian overlords.

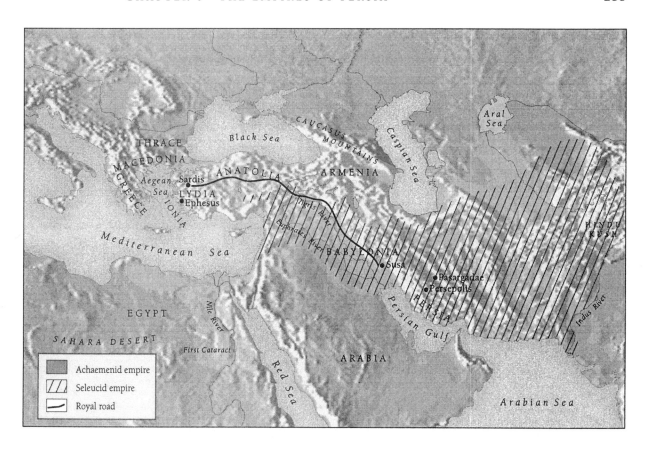

MAP [6.1]

The Achaemenid and Seleucid empires.

Though not tightly organized politically, the Medes and Persians were peoples of considerable military power. As descendants of nomadic peoples from central Asia, they possessed the equestrian skills common to many steppe peoples. They were expert archers, even when mounted on their horses, and they frequently raided the wealthy lands of Mesopotamia. When the Assyrian and Babylonian empires weakened in the sixth century B.C.E., the Medes and Persians embarked on a vastly successful imperial venture of their own.

Cyrus

Cyrus the Achaemenid (reigned 558–530 B.C.E.) launched the Persians' imperial venture. In some ways Cyrus was an unlikely candidate for this role. He came from a mountainous region of southwestern Iran, and in reference to the region's economy, his contemporaries often called him Cyrus the Shepherd. Yet Cyrus proved to be a tough, wily leader and an outstanding military strategist. His conquests laid the foundation of the first Persian empire, also known as the Achaemenid empire, since its rulers claimed descent from Cyrus's Achaemenid clan.

Cyrus's Conquests

In 558 B.C.E. Cyrus became king of the Persian tribes, which he ruled from his mountain fortress at Pasargadae. In 553 he initiated a rebellion against his Median overlord, whom he crushed within three years. By 548 he had brought all of Iran under his control, and he began to look for opportunities to expand his influence. In 546 he conquered the powerful kingdom of Lydia in Anatolia (modern-day Turkey). Between 545 and 539 he campaigned in central Asia and Bactria (modern Afghanistan). In a swift campaign of 539, he seized Babylonia, whose vassal states immediately recognized him as their lord. Within twenty years Cyrus went from minor regional king to ruler of an empire that stretched from India to the borders of Egypt.

The tomb of Cyrus at Pasargadae—one of very few Achaemenid monuments that have survived to the present. ● Courtesy of The Oriental Institute Museum, The University of Chicago

Cyrus no doubt would have mounted a campaign against Egypt, the largest and wealthiest neighboring state outside his control, had he lived long enough. But in 530 he fell, mortally wounded, while protecting his northeastern frontier from nomadic raiders. His troops recovered his body and placed it in a simple tomb, which still stands, that Cyrus had prepared for himself at his palace in Pasargadae.

Darius   Cyrus's empire survived and expanded during the reigns of his successors. His son Cambyses (reigned 530–522 B.C.E.) conquered Egypt in 525 and brought its wealth into Persian hands. The greatest of the Achaemenid emperors, Darius (reigned 521–486 B.C.E.), a younger kinsman of Cyrus, extended the empire both east and west. His armies pushed into northwestern India as far as the Indus River, absorbing the northern Indian kingdom of Gandhara, while also capturing Thrace, Macedonia, and the western coast of the Black Sea in southeastern Europe. By the late sixth century, Darius presided over the largest empire the world had yet seen with boundaries extending from the Indus River in the east to the Aegean Sea in the west, and from the Armenian hills in the north to the first cataract of the Nile in the south.

Carving from Persepolis showing an enthroned Darius (with his son Xerxes standing behind him) receiving a high court official, as incense burners perfume the air. ● Courtesy of The Oriental Institute Museum, The University of Chicago

Ruins of Persepolis, showing the imperial reception hall and palaces.   •   Fred J. Maroon/Photo
Researchers, Inc.

Yet Darius was more important as an administrator than as a conqueror. Governing a far-flung empire was a much more difficult challenge than conquering it. The
Achaemenid rulers presided over more than seventy distinct ethnic groups, including
peoples who lived in widely scattered regions, spoke many different languages, and
observed a profusion of religious and cultural traditions. To maintain their empire,
the Achaemenids needed to establish lines of communication with all parts of their
realm and design institutions that would enable them to tax and administer their territories. In doing so, they not only made it possible for the Achaemenid empire to
survive but also pioneered administrative techniques that would outlast their own
dynasty and influence political life in southwestern Asia for centuries to come.

Soon after his rise to power, Darius began to centralize his administration. About   *Persepolis*
520 B.C.E. he started to build a new capital of astonishing magnificence at Persepolis,
near Pasargadae. Darius intended Persepolis to serve not only as an administrative
center but also as a monument to the Achaemenid dynasty. Structures at Persepolis
included vast reception halls, lavish royal residences, and a well-protected treasury.
From the time of Darius to the end of the Achaemenid dynasty in 330 B.C.E., Persepolis served as the nerve center of the Persian empire—a resplendent capital bustling
with advisors, ministers, diplomats, scribes, accountants, translators, and bureaucratic
officers of all descriptions. Even today, massive columns and other ruins bespeak the
grandeur of Darius's capital.

The government of the Achaemenid empire depended on a finely tuned balance   *Achaemenid*
between central initiative and local administration. The Achaemenid rulers made   *Administration:*
great claims to authority in their official title—"The Great King, King of Kings,   *The Satrapies*
King in Persia, King of Countries." Like their Mesopotamian predecessors, the
Achaemenids appointed governors to serve as agents of the central administration

and oversee affairs in the various regions. Darius divided his realm into twenty-three satrapies—administrative and taxation districts governed by satraps. Yet the Achaemenids did not try to push direct rule on their subjects: most of the satraps were Persians, but the Achaemenids recruited local officials to fill almost all administrative posts below the level of the satrap.

Since the satraps often held posts distant from Persepolis, there was always a possibility that they might ally with local groups and become independent of Achaemenid authority, or even threaten the empire itself. The Achaemenid rulers relied on two measures to discourage this possibility. First, each satrapy had a contingent of military officers and tax collectors who served as checks on the satraps' power and independence. Second, the rulers created a new category of officials—essentially imperial spies—known as "the eyes and ears of the king." These agents traveled throughout the empire with their own military forces conducting surprise audits of accounts and procedures in the provinces and collecting intelligence reports. The division of provincial responsibilities and the institution of the eyes and ears of the king helped the Achaemenid rulers maintain control over a vast empire that otherwise might easily have split into a series of independent regional kingdoms.

Taxes, Coins, and Laws

Darius also sought to improve administrative efficiency by regularizing tax levies and standardizing laws. Cyrus and Cambyses had accepted periodic "gifts" of tribute from subject lands and cities. Though often lavish, the gifts did not provide a consistent and reliable source of income for rulers who needed to finance a large bureaucracy and army. Darius replaced irregular tribute payments with formal tax levies. He required each satrapy to pay a set quantity of silver—and in some cases a levy of horses or slaves as well—deliverable annually to the imperial court. To expedite the payment of taxes, Darius followed the example of the Lydian rulers and issued standardized coins—a move that also fostered trade throughout his empire. In an equally important initiative begun in the year 520 B.C.E., he sought to bring the many legal systems of his empire closer to a single standard. He did not abolish the existing laws of individual lands or peoples, nor did he impose a uniform law code on his entire empire. But he directed legal experts to study and codify the laws of his subject peoples, modifying them when necessary to harmonize them with the legal principles observed in the empire as a whole.

Roads and Communications

Alongside their administrative and legal policies, the Achaemenid rulers took other measures to knit their far-flung realm into a coherent whole. They built good roads across their realm, notably the so-called Persian Royal Road—parts of it paved with stone—that stretched some 2,575 kilometers (1,600 miles) from the Aegean port of Ephesus to Sardis in Anatolia, through Mesopotamia along the Tigris River, to Susa in Iran, with an extension to Pasargadae and Persepolis. Caravans took some ninety days to travel this road, lodging at inns along the well-policed route.

The imperial government also organized a courier service and built 111 postal stations at intervals of 25 to 30 kilometers (40 to 48 miles) along the Royal Road. Each station kept a supply of fresh horses, enabling couriers to speed from one end of the Royal Road to the other in a week's time. The Greek historian Herodotus spoke highly of these imperial servants, and even today the United States Postal Service takes his description of their efforts as a standard for its own employees: "Neither snow nor rain nor heat nor gloom of night stays these couriers from the swift completion of their appointed rounds." The Achaemenids also improved existing routes between Mesopotamia and Egypt, and they built a new road between Persia and the Indus River to link the imperial center with the satrapy of Gandhara in northwestern India. In addition to improving communications, these roads facilitated trade, which helped to integrate the empire's various regions into a larger economy.

Decline and Fall of the Achaemenid Empire

The Achaemenids' administrative machinery enabled them to govern a vast empire, but difficulties between the rulers and their subject peoples eventually undermined its integrity. Cyrus and Darius both consciously pursued a policy of toleration in administering their vast multicultural empire: they took great care to respect the values and cultural traditions of the peoples they ruled. In Mesopotamia, for example, they did not portray themselves as Persian conquerors, but rather as legitimate Babylonian rulers and representatives of Marduk, the patron deity of Babylon. Darius also won high praise from Jews in the Achaemenid empire, since he allowed them to return to Jerusalem and rebuild the temple that Babylonian conquerors had destroyed in 587 B.C.E.

Darius's successor, Xerxes (reigned 486–465 B.C.E.), retreated from this policy of toleration, however, flaunted his Persian identity, and sought to impose his own values on conquered lands. This policy caused enormous ill will, especially in Mesopotamia and Egypt where peoples with their own cultural traditions resented Xerxes's pretensions. Xerxes successfully repressed rebellions against his rule in Mesopotamia and Egypt. Yet resentment of Persian conquerors continued to fester, and it caused serious problems for the later Achaemenids as they tried to hold their empire together.

The Achaemenids had an especially difficult time with their ethnic Greek subjects, and efforts to control the Greeks helped to bring about the collapse of the Achaemenid empire. Ethnic Greeks inhabited many of the cities in Anatolia—particularly in Ionia on the Aegean coast of western Anatolia—and they maintained close economic and commercial ties with their cousins in the peninsula of Greece itself. The Ionian Greeks fell under Persian domination during the reign of Cyrus. They became restive under Darius's Persian governors—"tyrants," the Greeks called them—who oversaw their affairs. In 500 B.C.E. the Ionian cities rebelled, expelled or executed their governors, and asserted their independence. Their rebellion launched a series of conflicts known as the Persian Wars (500–479 B.C.E.).

The Persian Wars

The conflict between the Ionian Greeks and the Persians expanded considerably when the cities of peninsular Greece sent fleets to aid their kinsmen in Ionia. Darius managed to put down the rebellion and reassert Achaemenid authority, but he and his successors became entangled in a difficult and ultimately destructive effort to extend their authority to the Greek peninsula. In 490 B.C.E. Darius attempted to forestall future problems by mounting an expedition to conquer the wealthy Greek cities and absorb them into his empire. Though larger and much more powerful than the forces of the disunited Greek city-states, the Persian army had to contend with long and fragile lines of supply as well as a hostile environment. After some initial successes the Persians suffered a rout at the battle of Marathon (490 B.C.E.), and they returned home without achieving their goals. Xerxes sent another expedition ten years later, but within eighteen months, it too had suffered defeat both on land and at sea and had returned to Persia.

For almost 150 years the Persian empire continued to spar intermittently with the Greek cities. The adversaries mounted small expeditions against each other, attacking individual cities or fleets, but they did not engage in large-scale campaigns. The Greek cities were too small and disunited to pose a serious challenge to the enormous Persian empire. Meanwhile, for their part, the later Achaemenids had to concentrate on the other restive and sometimes rebellious regions of their own empire and could not embark on new rounds of expansion.

Alexander of Macedon

The standoff ended with the rise of Alexander of Macedon, often called Alexander the Great (discussed more fully in chapter 9). In 334 B.C.E. Alexander invaded Persia with an army of tough, battle-hardened Macedonians. Though far smaller than the Persian army in numbers, the well-disciplined Macedonians carried heavier arms and employed more sophisticated military tactics than their opponents. As a result, they sliced through the Persian empire, advancing almost at will and dealing their adversaries a series of devastating defeats. In 331 B.C.E. Alexander shattered Achaemenid forces at the battle of Gaugamela, and within a year the empire founded by Cyrus the Shepherd had dissolved.

Alexander led his forces into Persepolis, confiscated the wealth stored in the imperial treasury there, paid his respects at the tomb of Cyrus in Pasargadae, and proclaimed himself heir to the Achaemenid rulers. After a brief season of celebration, Alexander and his forces ignited a blaze—perhaps intentionally—that destroyed Persepolis. The conflagration was so great that when archaeologists first began to explore the ruins of Persepolis in the eighteenth century, they found layers of ash and charcoal up to one meter (three feet) deep.

The Achaemenid empire had crumbled, but its legacy was by no means exhausted. Alexander portrayed himself in Persia and Egypt as a legitimate successor of the Achaemenids who observed their precedents and deserved their honors. He retained the Achaemenid administrative structure, and he even confirmed the appointments of many satraps and other officials. As it happened, Alexander had little time to enjoy his conquests, since he died in 323 B.C.E. after a brief effort to extend his empire to India. But the states that succeeded him—the Seleucid, Parthian, and Sasanid empires—continued to employ a basically Achaemenid structure of imperial administration.

A coin issued by Alexander with an image of the conqueror. • Courtesy, Museum of Fine Arts, Boston

The Seleucid, Parthian, and Sasanid Empires

The Seleucids

After Alexander died, his chief generals carved his empire into three large realms, which they divided among themselves. The choicest realm, which included most of the former Achaemenid empire, went to Seleucus (reigned 305–281 B.C.E.), formerly commander of an elite corps of guards in Alexander's army. Like Alexander, Seleucus and his successors retained the Achaemenid systems of administration and taxation, as well as the imperial roads and postal service. The Seleucids also founded new cities throughout the realm and attracted Greek colonists to occupy them. The migrants, who represented only a fraction of the whole population of the empire, largely adapted to their new environment. Nonetheless, the establishment of cities greatly stimulated trade and economic development both within the Seleucid empire and beyond.

As foreigners, the Seleucids faced opposition from native Persians and especially their ruling classes. Satraps often revolted against Seleucid rule, or at least worked to build power bases that would enable them to establish their independence. The Seleucids soon lost their holdings in northern India, and the seminomadic Parthians progressively took over Iran during the third century B.C.E. The Seleucids continued to rule a truncated empire until 83 B.C.E., when Roman conquerors put an end to their empire.

The Parthians

Meanwhile, the Parthians established themselves as lords of a powerful empire based in Iran that they extended to wealthy Mesopotamia. The Parthians had occupied the region of eastern Iran around Khurasan since Achaemenid times. They retained many of the customs and traditions of nomadic peoples from the steppes of central Asia. They did not have a centralized government, for example, but organized themselves politically through a federation of leaders who met in councils and jointly determined policy for all allied groups. They were skillful warriors, accustomed to defending themselves against constant threats from nomadic peoples farther east.

As they settled and turned increasingly to agriculture, the Parthians also devised an effective means to resist nomadic invasions. Since they had no access to feed grains, nomadic peoples allowed their horses to forage for food on the steppes during the winter. The Parthians discovered that if they fed their horses on alfalfa during the winter, their animals would grow much larger and stronger than the small horses and ponies of the steppes. Their larger ani-

Gold sculpture of a nomadic horseman discharging an arrow. This figurine dates from the fifth or fourth century B.C.E. and might well represent a Parthian. • The State Hermitage Museum, St. Petersburg

mals could then support heavily armed warriors outfitted with metal armor, which served as an effective shield against the arrows of the steppe nomads. Well-trained forces of heavily armed cavalry could usually put nomadic raiding parties to flight. Indeed, few existing forces could stand up to Parthian heavy cavalry.

As early as the third century B.C.E., the Parthians began to wrest their independence from the Seleucids. The Parthian satrap revolted against his Seleucid overlord in 238 B.C.E., and during the following decades his successors gradually enlarged their holdings. Mithradates I, the Parthians' greatest conqueror, came to the throne about 171 B.C.E. and transformed his state into a mighty empire. By about 155 B.C.E. he had consolidated his hold on Iran and had also extended Parthian rule to Mesopotamia.

Parthian Conquests

The Parthians portrayed themselves as enemies of the foreign Seleucids, as restorers of rule in the Persian tradition. To some extent this characterization was accurate. The Parthians largely followed the example of the Achaemenids in structuring their empire: they governed through satraps, employed Achaemenid techniques of administration and taxation, and built a capital city at Ctesiphon on the Euphrates River near modern Baghdad. But the Parthians also retained elements of their own steppe traditions. They did not develop nearly so centralized a regime as the Achaemenids or Seleucids, but rather vested a great deal of authority and responsibility in their clan leaders. These men often served as satraps, and they regularly worked to build independent bases of power in their regions. They frequently mounted rebellions against the imperial government, though without much success.

Parthian Government

For about three centuries the Parthians presided over a powerful empire between India and the Mediterranean. Beginning in the first century C.E., they faced pressure in the west from the expanding Roman empire. The Parthian empire as a whole never stood in danger of falling to the Romans, but on three occasions in the second century C.E. Roman armies captured the Parthian capital at Ctesiphon. Combined with internal difficulties caused by the rebellious satraps, Roman pressure contributed to the weakening of the Parthian state. During the early third century C.E., internal rebellion brought it down.

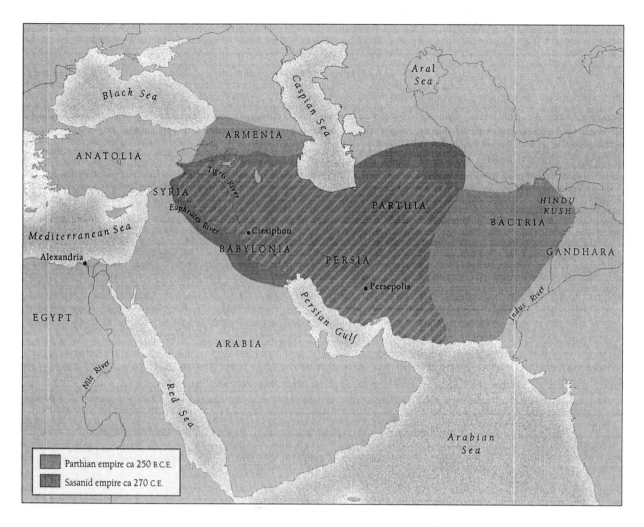

MAP [6.2]

The Parthian and Sasanid empires.

The Sasanids

Once again, though, the tradition of imperial rule continued, this time under the Sasanids, who came from Persia and claimed direct descent from the Achaemenids. The Sasanids toppled the Parthians in 224 C.E. and ruled until the year 651, recreating much of the splendor of the Achaemenid empire. From their cosmopolitan capital at Ctesiphon, the Sasanid "king of kings" provided strong rule from Parthia to Mesopotamia while also rebuilding an elaborate system of administration and founding or refurbishing numerous cities. Sasanid merchants traded actively with peoples to both east and west, and they introduced into Iran the cultivation of crops like rice, sugarcane, citrus fruits, eggplant, and cotton that came west over the trade routes from India and China.

During the reign of Shapur I (239–272 C.E.), the Sasanids stabilized their western frontier and created a series of buffer states between themselves and the Roman empire. Shapur even defeated several Roman armies and settled the prisoners in Iran, where they devoted their famous engineering skills to the construction of roads and dams. After Shapur, the Sasanids did not expand militarily, but entered into a standoff relationship with the Kushan empire in the east and the Roman and Byzantine empires in the west. None of these large empires was strong enough to overcome the others, but they contested border areas and buffer states, sometimes engaging in lengthy and bitter disputes that sapped the energies of all involved.

These continual conflicts seriously weakened the Sasanid empire in particular. The empire came to an end in 651 C.E. when Arab warriors killed the last Sasanid ruler, overran his realm, and incorporated it into their rapidly expanding Islamic empire. Yet even conquest by external invaders did not end the legacy of classical Persia, since Persian administrative techniques and cultural traditions were so powerful that the Arab conquerors adopted them for their own use in building a new Islamic society.

IMPERIAL SOCIETY AND ECONOMY

Throughout Eurasia during the classical era, public life and social structure became much more complicated than they had been during the days of the early complex societies. Centralized imperial governments needed large numbers of administrative officials, which led to the emergence of educated classes of bureaucrats. Stable empires enabled many individuals to engage in trade or other specialized labor as artisans, craftsmen, or professionals of various kinds. Some of them accumulated vast wealth, which led to increased distance and tensions between rich and poor. Meanwhile, slavery became more common than in earlier times. The prominence of slavery had to do partly with the expansion of imperial states, which often enslaved conquered foes, but it also reflected the increasing gulf between rich and poor, which placed such great economic pressure on some individuals that they had to give up their freedom in order to survive. All these developments had implications for the social structures of classical societies in Persia as well as China, India, and the Mediterranean basin.

Social Development in Classical Persia

During the early days of the Achaemenid empire, Persian society reflected its origins on the steppes of central Asia. When they migrated to Iran, the social structure of the Medes and Persians was very similar to that of the Aryans in India, consisting primarily of warriors, priests, and peasants. For centuries when they lived on the periphery and in the shadow of the Mesopotamian empires, the Medes and Persians maintained steppe traditions. Even after the establishment of the Achaemenid empire, some of them followed a seminomadic lifestyle and maintained ties with their cousins on the steppes. Family and clan relationships were extremely important in the organization of Persian political and social affairs. Male warriors headed the clans, which retained much of their influence long after the establishment of the Achaemenid empire.

The development of a cosmopolitan empire, however, brought considerable complexity to Persian society. The requirements of imperial administration, for example, called for a new class of educated bureaucrats who to a large extent undermined the position of the old warrior elite. The bureaucrats did not directly challenge the patriarchal warriors and certainly did not seek to displace them from their privileged position in society. Nevertheless, their crucial role in running the day-to-day affairs of the empire guaranteed them a prominent and comfortable place in Persian society. By the time of the later Achaemenids and the Seleucids, Persian cities were home to masses of administrators, tax collectors, and record keepers. The bureaucracy even included a substantial corps of translators, who facilitated communications among the empire's many linguistic groups. Imperial survival depended on these literate professionals, and high-ranking bureaucrats came to share power and influence with warriors and clan leaders.

Imperial Bureaucrats

In this sculpture from Persepolis, Persian nobles dressed in fine cloaks and hats ascend the staircase leading to the imperial reception hall. • Fred Maroon/Photo Researchers, Inc.

Free Classes   The bulk of Persian society consisted of individuals who were free but did not enjoy the privileges of clan leaders and important bureaucrats. In the cities the free classes included artisans, craftsmen, merchants, and low-ranking civil servants. Priests and priestesses were also prominent urban residents, along with servants who maintained the temple communities in which they lived. As in earlier Mesopotamian societies, members of the free classes participated in religious observances conducted at local temples, and they had the right to share in the income that temples generated from their agricultural operations and from craft industries such as textile production that the temples organized. The weaving of textiles was mostly the work of women, who received rations of grain, wine, beer, and sometimes meat from the imperial and temple workshops that employed them.

In the countryside the free classes included peasants who owned their own land as well as landless cultivators who worked as laborers or tenants on properties owned by the state, temple communities, or other individuals. Free residents of rural areas had the right to marry and move as they wished, and they could seek better opportunities in the cities or in military service. Because the Persian empires embraced a great deal of parched land that received little rainfall, work in the countryside involved not only cultivation but also the building and maintenance of irrigation systems.

The most remarkable of these systems were underground canals known as *qanat,* which allowed cultivators to distribute water to fields without losing large quantities to evaporation through exposure to the sun and open air. Numerous *qanat* criss-crossed the Iranian plateau, in the heartland of the Persian empire, where extreme scarcity of water justified the enormous investment of human labor required to build them. Although they had help from slaves, free residents of the countryside contributed much of the labor that went into the excavation and maintenance of the *qanat.*

Slaves

A large class of slaves also worked in both the cities and the countryside. Individuals passed into slavery by two main routes. Most were prisoners of war who became slaves as the price of survival. These prisoners usually came from military units, but the Persians also enslaved civilians who resisted their advance or who rebelled against imperial authorities. Other slaves came from the ranks of free subjects who accumulated debts that they could not satisfy. In the cities, for example, merchants, artisans, and craftsmen borrowed funds to purchase goods or open shops, while in the countryside small farmers facing competition from large-scale cultivators borrowed against their property and liberty to purchase tools, seed, or food. Failure to repay these debts in timely fashion often forced the borrowers not only to forfeit their property but also to sell their children, their spouses, or themselves into slavery.

Slave status deprived individuals of their personal freedom. Slaves became the property of an individual, the state, or an institution such as a temple community: they worked at tasks set by their owners, and they could not move or marry at will, although existing family units usually stayed together. Most slaves probably worked as domestic servants or skilled laborers in the households of the wealthy, but at least some slaves cultivated their owners' fields in the countryside. State-owned slaves provided much of the manual labor for large-scale construction projects such as roads, irrigation systems, city walls, and palaces.

In Mesopotamia temple communities owned many slaves who worked at agricultural tasks and performed administrative chores for their priestly masters. During the mid- to late sixth century B.C.E., a slave named Gimillu served the temple community of Eanna in Uruk, and his career is relatively well-known because records of his various misadventures survive in archives. Gimillu appeared in numerous legal cases because he habitually defrauded his masters, pocketed bribes, and embezzled temple funds. Yet he held a high position in the temple community and always managed to escape serious punishment. His career reveals that slaves sometimes had administrative talents and took on tasks involving considerable responsibility. Gimillu's case clearly shows that slaves sometimes enjoyed close relationships with powerful individuals who could protect them from potential enemies.

Economic Foundations of Classical Persia

Agriculture was the economic foundation of classical Persian society. Like other classical societies, Persia needed large agricultural surpluses to support military forces and administrative specialists, as well as residents of cities who were artisans, craftsmen, and merchants rather than cultivators. The Persian empires embraced several regions of exceptional fertility—notably Mesopotamia, Egypt, Anatolia, and northern India—and it prospered by mobilizing the agricultural surpluses of these lands.

Agricultural Production

Barley and wheat were the grains cultivated most commonly in the Persian empires. Peas, lentils, mustard, garlic, onions, cucumbers, dates, apples, pomegranates, pears, and apricots supplemented the cereals in diets throughout Persian society, and beer and wine were the most common beverages. In most years agricultural production far exceeded the needs of cultivators, making sizable surpluses available for sale in the cities or for distribution to state servants through the imperial bureaucracy. Vast quantities of produce flowed into the imperial court from state-owned lands cultivated by slaves or leased out to tenants in exchange for a portion of the annual harvest. Even though they are incomplete, surviving records show that, for example, in 500 B.C.E., during the middle period of Darius's reign, the imperial court received almost eight hundred thousand liters of grain, quite apart from vegetables, fruits,

Tribute bearers from lands subject to Achaemenid rule bring rams, horses, and fabrics to the imperial court at Persepolis.   •   Courtesy of The Oriental Institute Museum, The University of Chicago

meat, poultry, fish, oil, beer, wine, and textiles. Officials distributed some of this produce to the imperial staff as wages in kind, but much of it also found its way into the enormous banquets that Darius organized for as many as ten thousand guests. Satraps and other high officials lived on a less lavish scale than the Persian emperors but also benefited from agricultural surpluses delivered to their courts from their own lands.

Trade   Agriculture was the foundation of the Persian economy, but long-distance trade grew rapidly during the course of the Persian empires and linked lands from India to Egypt in a vast commercial zone. Several conditions promoted the growth of trade: the relative political stability maintained by the Persian empires, the general prosperity of the realm, the use of standardized coins, and the availability of good trade routes, including long-established routes, newly constructed highways such as the Persian Royal Road, and sea routes through the Red Sea, Persian Gulf, and Arabian Sea. Markets operated regularly in all the larger cities of the Persian empires, and the largest cities, such as Babylon, also were home to banks and companies that invested in commercial ventures.

As trade grew, the regions of the Persian empires all contributed particular products to the larger imperial economy. India supplied gold, ivory, and aromatics. Iran and central Asia provided lapis lazuli, turquoise, and other semiprecious stones. Mesopotamia and Iran were sources of finished products like textiles, mirrors, and jewelry. Anatolia supplied gold, silver, iron, copper, and tin. Phoenicia contributed glass, cedar, timber, and richly dyed woolen fabrics. Spices and aromatics came from Arabia. Egypt provided grain, linen textiles, and writing materials made from papyrus, as well as gold, ebony, and ivory obtained from Ethiopia. Greek oil, wine, and ceramics also made their way throughout the empire and even beyond its borders.

Long-distance trade of this sort became especially prominent during the reigns of Alexander of Macedon and his Seleucid successors. The cities they established and the colonists they attracted stimulated trade throughout the whole region from the Mediterranean to northern India. Indeed, Greek migrants facilitated cultural as well as commercial exchanges by encouraging the mixing and mingling of religious faiths, art styles, and philosophical speculation throughout the Persian realm.

RELIGIONS OF SALVATION IN CLASSICAL PERSIAN SOCIETY

Cross-cultural influences were especially noticeable in the development of Persian religion. Persians came from the family of peoples who spoke Indo-European languages, and their earliest religion closely resembled that of the Aryans of India. During the classical era, however, the new faith of Zoroastrianism emerged and became widely popular in Iran and to a lesser extent also in the larger Persian empires. Zoroastrianism reflected the cosmopolitan society of the empires, and it profoundly influenced the beliefs and values of Judaism, Christianity, and Islam. During the late centuries of the classical era, from about 100 to 500 c.e., three missionary religions—Buddhism, Christianity, and Manichaeism—also found numerous converts in the Persian empire.

Zarathustra and His Faith

The earliest Persian religion centered on cults that celebrated outstanding natural elements and geographical features such as the sun, the moon, water, and especially fire. Persians recognized many of the same gods as the ancient Aryans, and their priests performed sacrifices similar to those conducted by the *brahmins* in India. The priests even made ceremonial use of a hallucinogenic agent called *haoma* in the same way that the Aryans used *soma*, and indeed the two concoctions were probably the same substance. Like the Aryans, the ancient Persians glorified strength and martial virtues, and the cults of both peoples sought principally to bring about a comfortable material existence for their practitioners.

During the classical era Persian religion underwent considerable change, as moral and religious thinkers sought to adapt their messages to the circumstances of a complex, cosmopolitan society. One result was the emergence of Zoroastrianism, which emerged from the teachings of Zarathustra. Though he was undoubtedly a historical person and the subject of many early stories, little certain information survives about Zarathustra's life and career. It is not even clear when he lived, though most scholars date his life to the late seventh and early sixth centuries B.C.E. He came from an aristocratic family, and he probably was a priest who became disenchanted with the traditional religion and its concentration on sacrifices and mechanical rituals. In any case, when he was about twenty years old, Zarathustra left his family and home in search of wisdom. After about ten years of travel, he experienced a series of visions and became convinced that the supreme god, Ahura Mazda ("the wise lord"), had chosen him to serve as his prophet and spread his message.

Zarathustra

Like his life, Zarathustra's doctrine has also proven to be somewhat elusive for modern analysts. Many of the earliest Zoroastrian teachings have perished, since the priests, known as *magi*, at first transmitted them orally. Only during the Seleucid dynasty did *magi* begin to preserve religious texts in writing, and only under the

The Gathas

Sasanids did they compile their scriptures in a holy book known as the Avesta. Nevertheless, many of Zarathustra's own compositions survive, since *magi* preserved them with special diligence through oral transmission. Known as the *Gathas,* Zarathustra's works were hymns that he composed in honor of the various deities that he recognized. Apart from the *Gathas,* ancient Zoroastrian literature included a wide variety of hymns, liturgical works, and treatises on moral and theological themes. Though some of these works survive, the arrival of Islam in the seventh century C.E. and the subsequent decline of Zoroastrianism resulted in the loss of most of the Avesta and later Zoroastrian works.

Zoroastrian Teachings

Zarathustra and his followers were not strict monotheists. They recognized Ahura Mazda as a supreme deity, an eternal and beneficent spirit, and the creator of all good things. But Zarathustra also spoke of six lesser deities, whom he praised in the *Gathas.* Furthermore, he believed that Ahura Mazda engaged in a cosmic conflict with an independent adversary, an evil and malign spirit known as Angra Mainyu ("the destructive spirit" or "the hostile spirit"). Following a struggle of some twelve thousand years, Zarathustra believed, Ahura Mazda and the forces of good would ultimately prevail, and Angra Mainyu and the principle of evil would disappear forever. At that time individual human souls would undergo judgment and would experience rewards or punishments according to the holiness of their thoughts, words, and deeds. Honest and moral individuals would enter into a heavenly paradise, whereas demons would fling their evil brethren into a hellish realm of pain and suffering.

A gold clasp or button of the fifth century B.C.E. with the symbol of Ahura Mazda as a winged god.

• The State Hermitage Museum, St. Petersburg

Zarathustra did not call for ascetic renunciation of the world in favor of a future heavenly existence. To the contrary, he considered the material world a blessing that reflected the benevolent nature of Ahura Mazda. His moral teachings allowed human beings to enjoy the world and its fruits—including wealth, sexual pleasure, and social prestige—as long as they did so in moderation and behaved honestly toward others. Zoroastrians have often summarized their moral teachings in the simple formula "good words, good thoughts, good deeds."

Popularity of Zoroastrianism

Zarathustra's teachings began to attract large numbers of followers during the sixth century B.C.E., particularly among Persian aristocrats and ruling elites. Wealthy patrons donated land and established endowments for the support of Zoroastrian temples. The Achaemenid era saw the emergence of a sizable priesthood, whose members conducted religious rituals, maintained a calendar, taught Zoroastrian values, and preserved Zoroastrian doctrine through oral transmission.

Cyrus and Cambyses probably observed Zoroastrian rites, although little evidence survives to illustrate their religious preferences. Beginning with Darius, however, the Achaemenid emperors closely associated themselves with Ahura Mazda and claimed divine sanction for their rule. Darius ordered stone inscriptions celebrating his achievements, and in these monuments he clearly revealed his devotion

ZARATHUSTRA ON GOOD AND EVIL

• • •

Like many other religious faiths of classical times, Zoroastrianism encouraged the faithful to observe high moral and ethical standards. In this hymn from the Gathas, *Zarathustra relates how Ahura Mazda and Angra Mainyu—representatives of good and evil, respectively—made choices about how to behave based on their fundamental natures. Human beings did likewise, according to Zarathustra, and ultimately all would experience the rewards and punishments that their choices merited.*

In the beginning, there were two Primal Spirits, Twins spontaneously active;
These are the Good and the Evil, in thought, and in word, and in deed:
Between these two, let the wise choose aright;
Be good, not base.

And when these Twin Spirits came together at first,
They established Life and Non-Life,
And so shall it be as long as the world shall last;
The worst existence shall be the lot of the followers of evil,
And the Good Mind shall be the reward of the followers of good.

Of these Twin Spirits, the Evil One chose to do the worst;
While the bountiful Holy Spirit of Goodness,
Clothing itself with the mossy heavens for a garment,
chose the Truth;
And so will those who [seek to] please Ahura Mazda with righteous deeds, performed with faith in Truth. . . .

And when there cometh Divine Retribution for the Evil One,
Then at Thy command shall the Good Mind establish the Kingdom of Heaven, O Mazda,
For those who will deliver Untruth into the hands of Righteousness and Truth.

Then truly cometh the blow of destruction on Untruth,
And all those of good fame are garnered up in the Fair Abode,
The Fair Abode of the Good Mind, the Wise Lord, and of Truth!

O ye mortals, mark these commandments—
The commandments which the Wise Lord has given, for Happiness and for Pain;
Long punishment for the evil-doer, and bliss for the follower of Truth,
The joy of salvation for the Righteous ever afterwards!

SOURCE: D. J. Irani, *The Divine Songs of Zarathustra.* London: George Allen & Unwin, 1924; also New York: Macmillan, 1924.

to Ahura Mazda and his opposition to the principle of evil. He did not attempt to suppress other gods or religions, but tolerated the established faiths of the various peoples in his empire. Yet he personally regarded Ahura Mazda as a deity superior to all others.

In one of his inscriptions, Darius praised Ahura Mazda as the great god who created the earth, the sky, and humanity, and who moreover elevated Darius himself to the imperial honor. With the aid of imperial sponsorship, Zoroastrian temples cropped up throughout the Achaemenid realm. The faith was most popular in Iran, but it attracted sizable followings also in Mesopotamia, Anatolia, Egypt, and other parts of the Achaemenid empire, even though there was no organized effort to spread it beyond its original homeland.

Darius faces Ahura Mazda, to whom he attributed his authority, as the various kings he had conquered acknowledge him as their lord. • Deutsches Archaeologisches Institut, Berlin

Officially Sponsored Zoroastrianism

Religions of Salvation in a Cosmopolitan Society

The arrival of Alexander of Macedon inaugurated a difficult era for the Zoroastrian community. During his Persian campaign, Alexander's forces burned many temples and killed numerous *magi*. Since at that time the *magi* still transmitted Zoroastrian doctrines orally, an untold number of hymns and holy verses disappeared. The Zoroastrian faith survived, however, and the Parthians cultivated it in order to rally support against the Seleucids. Once established in power, the Parthians observed Zoroastrian rituals, though they did not support the faith as enthusiastically as their predecessors did.

During the Sasanid dynasty, however, Zoroastrianism experienced a revival. As self-proclaimed heirs to the Achaemenids, the Sasanids identified closely with Zoroastrianism and supported it zealously. Indeed, the Sasanids often persecuted other faiths if they seemed likely to become popular enough to challenge the supremacy of Zoroastrianism. With generous imperial backing, the Zoroastrian faith and the *magi* flourished as never before. Theologians prepared written versions of the holy texts and collected them in the Avesta. They also explored points of doctrine and addressed difficult questions of morality and theology. Most people probably did not understand the theologians' reflections, but they flocked to Zoroastrian temples where they prayed to Ahura Mazda and participated in rituals.

The Zoroastrian faith faced severe difficulties in the seventh century C.E. when Islamic conquerors toppled the Sasanid empire. The conquerors did not outlaw the religion altogether, but they placed political and financial pressure on the *magi* and Zoroastrian temples. Some Zoroastrians fled their homeland and found refuge in India, where their descendants, known as Parsis ("Persians"), continue even today to observe Zoroastrian traditions. But most Zoroastrians remained in Iran and eventually converted to Islam. As a result, Zoroastrian numbers progressively dwindled. Only a few thousand faithful maintain a Zoroastrian community in modern-day Iran.

Other Faiths

Meanwhile, even though Zoroastrianism ultimately declined in its homeland, the cosmopolitan character of the Persian realm offered it opportunities to influence other religious faiths. Numerous Jewish communities had become established in Mesopotamia, Anatolia, and Persia after the Hebrew kingdom of David and Solomon fell in 930 B.C.E. During the Seleucid, Parthian, and Sasanid eras, the Persian empire attracted merchants, emissaries, and missionaries from the whole region between the Mediterranean and India. Three religions of salvation—Buddhism, Christianity, and Manichaeism, all discussed in later chapters—found a footing alongside Judaism and attracted converts. Indeed, Christianity and Manichaeism became extremely popular faiths, in spite of intermittent rounds of persecution organized by Sasanid authorities.

Influence of Zoroastrianism

While foreign faiths influenced religious developments in classical Persian society, Zoroastrianism also left its mark on the other religions of salvation. Jews living in Persia during Achaemenid times adopted several central teachings of Zoroastrianism. These included the encouragement of high moral standards, the belief in supernatural forces promoting good and evil, the doctrine that individuals will undergo judgment, the belief in a system of future rewards and punishments, and the conviction that the forces of good will ultimately prevail over those of evil. The Book of Daniel in particular reflects the influence of the Zoroastrian belief that in a future existence human beings will experience rewards or punishments for their behavior during their lives on earth. This doctrine became prominent in the moral thought of several Jewish sects. Early Christians developed it further, and their teachings about heaven and hell became central elements of their faith. In later centuries Islam also made a place for these doctrines, which derived ultimately from Zoroastrian teachings.

Just as Persian administrative techniques broadly influenced political development during the classical era, so Persian religious beliefs influenced cultural developments in southwest Asia and the Mediterranean basin. Already during the classical era, peoples from different societies mingled regularly. In doing so, they often borrowed the beliefs, values, and practices of their neighbors and adapted them for their own purposes. By sponsoring cross-cultural interactions on a relatively systematic basis, the classical Persian empires facilitated the spread of cultural and religious traditions across cultural boundary lines.

CHRONOLOGY

7th–6th centuries B.C.E.(?)	Life of Zarathustra
558–330 B.C.E.	Achaemenid dynasty
558–530 B.C.E.	Reign of Cyrus the Achaemenid
521–486 B.C.E.	Reign of Darius
334–330 B.C.E.	Invasion and conquest of the Achaemenid empire by Alexander of Macedon
323–83 B.C.E.	Seleucid dynasty
247 B.C.E.–224 C.E.	Parthian dynasty
224–651 C.E.	Sasanid dynasty

FOR FURTHER READING

Mary Boyce, ed. *Textual Sources for the Study of Zoroastrianism.* Totowa, N.J., 1984. Sources in translation with numerous explanatory comments by the author.

———. *Zoroastrians: Their Religious Beliefs and Practices.* London, 1979. A survey of Zoroastrian history by a leading revisionist scholar.

Maria Brosius. *Women in Ancient Persia, 559–331 B.C.* Oxford, 1996. Carefully examines both Persian and Greek sources for information about women and their role in Achaemenid society.

J. M. Cook. *The Persian Empire.* New York, 1983. A popular account of the Achaemenid empire that draws usefully on recent scholarship.

William Culican. *The Medes and the Persians.* New York, 1965. Well-illustrated survey with generous attention to art and architecture.

Muhammad A. Dandamaev and Vladimir G. Lukonin. *The Culture and Social Institutions of Ancient Iran.* Ed. by P. L. Kohl. Cambridge, 1989. Scholarly account that brings the results of recent Russian research to bear on the Achaemenid empire.

Jacques Duchesne-Guillemin. *The Hymns of Zarathustra.* London, 1952. A translation and commentary of Zarathustra's most important *Gathas.*

Richard N. Frye. *The Heritage of Persia.* Cleveland, 1963. A solid survey of Persia up to the Islamic conquest by a leading scholar.

R. Ghirshman. *Iran.* Harmondsworth, 1954. An older work but still valuable for the archaeological information it provides.

William W. Malandra. *An Introduction to Ancient Iranian Religion.* Minneapolis, 1983. Careful study of Zoroastrian textual sources.

A. T. Olmstead. *History of the Persian Empire (Achaemenid Period).* Chicago, 1948. An older study concentrating on political history, exceptionally well written and still valuable.

Susan Sherwin-White and Amélie Kuhrt. *From Samarkhand to Sardis: A New Approach to the Seleucid Empire.* Berkeley, 1993. Detailed scholarly analysis of the Seleucid empire concentrating on political and economic matters.

Mortimer Wheeler. *Flames over Persepolis.* New York, 1968. Deals with Alexander's conquest of the Achaemenid empire and especially the spread of Greek art styles throughout the Persian empire.

Robert C. Zaehner. *The Dawn and Twilight of Zoroastrianism.* London, 1961. An important interpretation of Zoroastrianism that concentrates on the Achaemenid and Sasanid periods.

———, ed. *The Teachings of the Magi: A Compendium of Zoroastrian Beliefs.* London, 1956. Translations of texts by later Zoroastrian theologians.

CHAPTER 7

THE UNIFICATION
OF CHINA

· · ·

In the year 99 B.C.E., Chinese imperial officials sentenced the historian Sima Qian to punishment by castration. For just over a decade Sima Qian had worked on a project that he had inherited from his father, a history of China from earliest times to his own day. This project brought Sima Qian high prominence at the imperial court. When he spoke in defense of a dishonored general, his views attracted widespread attention. The emperor reacted furiously when he learned that Sima Qian had publicly expressed opinions that contradicted the ruler's judgment and ordered the historian to undergo his humiliating punishment.

Human castration was by no means uncommon in premodern times. Thousands of boys and young men of undistinguished birth underwent voluntary castration in China and many other lands as well in order to pursue careers as eunuchs. Ruling elites often appointed eunuchs, rather than nobles, to sensitive posts because eunuchs did not sire families and so could not build power bases to challenge established authorities. As personal servants of ruling elites, eunuchs sometimes came to wield enormous power because of their influence with rulers and their families.

Exemplary punishment was not an appealing alternative, however, to educated elites and other prominent individuals: when sentenced to punitive castration, Chinese men of honor normally avoided the penalty by taking their own lives. Yet Sima Qian chose to endure his punishment. In a letter to a friend he explained that an early death by suicide would mean that a work that only he was capable of producing would go forever unwritten. To transmit his understanding of the Chinese past, then, Sima Qian opted to live and work in disgrace until his death about 90 B.C.E.

During his last years Sima Qian completed a massive work consisting of 130 chapters, most of which survive. He consulted court documents and the historical works of his predecessors, and when writing about his own age he supplemented these sources with personal observations and information gleaned from political and military figures who played leading roles in Chinese society. He composed historical accounts of the emperors' reigns and biographical sketches of notable figures, including ministers, statesmen, generals, empresses, aristocrats, scholars, officials, merchants, and rebels. He even described the societies of neighboring peoples with whom Chinese sometimes conducted trade and sometimes made war. The work of the disgraced but conscientious scholar Sima Qian provides the best information available about the development of early imperial China.

Tomb figurine: a servant holds a light for her mistress in Han China. • Cultural Relics Bureau, Beijing

A rich body of political and social thought prepared the way for the unification of China under the Qin and Han dynasties. Confucians, Daoists, Legalists, and others formed schools of thought and worked to bring political and social stability to China during the chaotic years of the late Zhou dynasty and the Warring States Period. Legalist ideas contributed directly to unification by outlining means by which rulers could strengthen their states. The works of the Confucians and Daoists did not lend themselves so readily to the unification process, but both schools of thought survived over the long term and profoundly influenced Chinese political and cultural traditions.

Rulers of the Qin and Han dynasties adopted Legalist principles and imposed centralized imperial rule on all of China. Like the Achaemenids of Persia, the Qin and Han emperors ruled through an elaborate bureaucracy, and they built roads that linked the various regions of China. They went further than the Persian emperors in their efforts to foster cultural unity in their realm. They imposed a common written language throughout China and established an educational system based on Confucian thought and values. For almost 450 years the Qin and Han dynasties guided the fortunes of China and established a strong precedent for centralized imperial rule.

Especially during the Han dynasty, political stability was the foundation of economic prosperity. High agricultural productivity supported the development of iron and silk industries, and Chinese goods found markets in central Asia, India, the Persian empire, and even the Mediterranean basin. In spite of economic prosperity, however, later Han society experienced deep divisions between the small class of extremely wealthy landowners and the masses of landless poor. These divisions eventually led to civil disorder and the emergence of political factions, which ultimately brought the Han dynasty to an end.

❧ IN SEARCH OF POLITICAL AND SOCIAL ORDER

The late centuries of the Zhou dynasty brought political confusion to China and led eventually to the chaos associated with the Period of the Warring States (403–221 B.C.E.). During those same centuries, however, there also took place a remarkable cultural flowering that left a permanent mark on Chinese history. In a way political turmoil helps to explain the cultural creativity of the late Zhou dynasty and the Period of the Warring States because it forced thoughtful people to reflect on the nature of society and the proper roles of human beings in society. Some sought to identify principles that would restore political and social order. Others concerned themselves with a search for individual tranquillity apart from society. Three schools of thought that emerged during those centuries of confusion and chaos—Confucianism, Daoism, and Legalism—exercised a particularly deep influence on Chinese political and cultural traditions.

Confucius and His School

Confucius   The first Chinese thinker who addressed the problem of political and social order in a straightforward and self-conscious way was Kong Fuzi (551–479 B.C.E.)—"Master Philosopher Kong," as his disciples called him, or Confucius, as he is known in English. He came from an aristocratic family in the state of Lu in northern China, and for many years he sought an influential post at the Lu court. But Confucius was a strong-willed man who often did not get along well with others. He refused to compromise his beliefs in the interest of political expediency, and he insisted on observing principles that frequently clashed with state policy. When he realized that he would never obtain anything more than a minor post in Lu, Confucius left in search of a more prestigious appointment elsewhere. For about ten years he traveled to courts throughout northern China, but he found none willing to accept his services. In 484 B.C.E., bitterly disappointed, he returned to Lu, where he died five years later.

Confucius never realized his ambition to become a powerful minister. Throughout his career, however, he served as an educator as well as a political advisor, and in this capacity he left an enduring mark on Chinese society. He attracted numerous disciples who aspired to political careers. Some of his pupils compiled the master's sayings and teachings in a book known as the *Analects,* a work that has profoundly influenced Chinese political and cultural traditions.

No contemporary portrait of Confucius survives, but artists have used their imaginations and depicted him in many ways over the years. This portrait of 1735 identifies Confucius as "the Sage and Teacher" and represents him in the distinctive dress of an eighteenth-century Confucian scholar-bureaucrat. • AKG London

Confucian Ideas

Confucius's thought was fundamentally moral, ethical, and political in character. It was also thoroughly practical: Confucius did not address abstruse philosophical questions, because he thought they would not help to solve the political and social problems of his day. Nor did he deal with religious questions, because he thought they went beyond the capacity of mortal human intelligence. He did not even concern himself much with the structure of the state, because he thought political and social harmony arose from the proper ordering of human relationships rather than the establishment of state offices. In an age when bureaucratic institutions were not yet well developed, Confucius believed that the best way to promote good government was to fill official positions with individuals who were both well educated and extraordinarily conscientious. Thus Confucius concentrated on the formation of what he called *junzi*—"superior individuals"—who took a broad view of public affairs and did not allow personal interests to influence their judgments.

In the absence of an established educational system and a formal curriculum, Confucius had his disciples study works of poetry and history produced during the Zhou dynasty, since he believed that they provided excellent insight into human nature. He carefully examined the *Book of Songs*, the *Book of History*, the *Book of Rites*, and other works with his students, concentrating especially on their practical value for prospective administrators. As a result of Confucius's influence, literary works of the Zhou dynasty became the core texts of the traditional Chinese education. For more than two thousand years, until the early twentieth century C.E., talented Chinese seeking government posts proceeded through a cycle of studies deriving from the one developed by Confucius in the fifth century B.C.E.

For Confucius, though, an advanced education represented only a part of the preparation needed by the ideal government official. More important than formal learning was the possession of a strong sense of moral integrity and a capacity to deliver wise and fair judgments. Thus Confucius encouraged his students to cultivate high ethical standards and to hone their faculties of analysis and judgment.

Confucian Values   Confucius emphasized several qualities in particular. One of them he called *ren*, by which he meant an attitude of kindness and benevolence or a sense of humanity. Confucius explained that individuals possessing *ren* were courteous, respectful, diligent, and loyal, and he considered *ren* a characteristic desperately needed in government officials. Another quality of central importance was *li*, a sense of propriety, which called for individuals to behave in conventionally appropriate fashion: they should treat all other human beings with courtesy, while showing special respect and deference to elders or superiors. Yet another quality that Confucius emphasized was *xiao*, filial piety, which reflected the high significance of the family in Chinese society. The demands of filial piety obliged children to respect their parents and other family elders, look after their welfare, support them in old age, and remember them along with other ancestors after their deaths.

Confucius emphasized personal qualities like *ren, li,* and *xiao* because he believed that individuals who possessed these traits would gain influence in the larger society. Those who disciplined themselves and properly molded their own characters would not only possess personal self-control but also have the power of leading others by example. Only through enlightened leadership by morally strong individuals, Confucius believed, was there any hope for the restoration of political and social order in China. Thus his goal was not simply the cultivation of personal morality for its own sake, but rather the creation of *junzi* who could bring order and stability to China.

Because Confucius expressed his thought in general terms, later disciples could adapt it to the particular problems of their times. Indeed, the flexibility of Confucian thought helps to account for its remarkable longevity and influence in China. Two later disciples of Confucius—Mencius and Xunzi—illustrate especially well the ways in which Confucian thought lent itself to elaboration and adaptation.

Mencius   Mencius (372–289 B.C.E.) was the most learned man of his age and the principal spokesman for the Confucian school. During the Period of the Warring States, he traveled widely throughout China, consulting with rulers and offering advice on political issues. Mencius firmly believed that human nature was basically good, and he argued for policies that would allow it to influence society as a whole. Thus he placed special emphasis on the Confucian virtue of *ren* and advocated government by benevolence and humanity. This principle implied that rulers would levy light taxes, avoid wars, support education, and encourage harmony and cooperation. Critics charged that Mencius held a naively optimistic view of human nature, arguing that his policies would rarely succeed in the real world where human interests,

CONFUCIUS ON GOOD GOVERNMENT
• • •

Confucius never composed formal writings, but his disciples collected his often pithy remarks into a work known as the Analects *("sayings"). Referred to as "the Master" in the following excerpts from the* Analects, *Confucius consistently argued that only good men possessing moral authority could rule effectively.*

The Master said, "He who exercises government by means of his virtue may be compared to the north polar star, which keeps its place, while all the stars turn toward it. . . ."

The Master said, "If the people be led by laws, and uniformity be imposed on them by punishments, they will try to avoid the punishment, but will have no sense of shame.

"If they be led by virtue, and uniformity be provided for them by the rules of propriety, they will have the sense of shame, and moreover will become good. . . ."

The duke Ai asked, saying, "What should be done in order to secure the submission of the people?" Confucius replied, "Advance the upright and set aside the crooked, and then the people will submit. Advance the crooked and set aside the upright, and then the people will not submit."

Ji Kang asked how to cause the people to reverence their ruler, to be faithful to him, and to go on to seek virtue. The Master said, "Let him preside over them with gravity; then they will reverence him. Let him be filial and kind to all; then they will be faithful to him. Let him advance the good and teach the incompetent; then they will eagerly seek to be virtuous. . . ."

Zigong asked about government. The Master said, "The requisites of government are that there be suffi-ciency of food, sufficiency of military equipment, and the confidence of the people in their ruler."

Zigong said, "If it cannot be helped, and one of these must be dispensed with, which of the three should be foregone first?" "The military equipment," said the Master.

Zigong again asked, "If it cannot be helped, and one of the remaining two must be dispensed with, which of them should be foregone?" The Master answered, "Part with the food. From olden times, death has been the lot of all men; but if the people have no faith in their rulers, there is no standing for the state. . . ."

Ji Kang asked Confucius about government, saying, "What do you say to killing the unprincipled for the good of the principled?" Confucius replied, "Sir, in carrying on your government, why should you use killing at all? Let your evinced desires be for what is good, and the people will be good. The relation between superiors and inferiors is like that between the wind and the grass. The grass must bend when the wind blows across it. . . ."

The Master said, "When a prince's personal conduct is correct, his government is effective without the issuing of orders. If his personal conduct is not correct, he may issue orders, but they will not be followed."

SOURCE: James Legge, trans. *The Chinese Classics*, 7 vols. Oxford: Clarendon Press, 1893, 1:145, 146, 152, 254, 258–59, 266. (Translations slightly modified.)

wills, and ambitions constantly clash. Indeed, Mencius's advice had little practical effect during his lifetime. Over the long term, however, his ideas deeply influenced the Confucian tradition. Since about the tenth century C.E., many Chinese scholars have considered Mencius the most authoritative of Confucius's early expositors.

Like Confucius and Mencius, Xunzi (298–238 B.C.E.) was a man of immense learning, but unlike his predecessors, he also served for many years as a government administrator. His practical experience encouraged him to develop a view of human nature that was less rosy than Mencius's view. Xunzi believed that human beings selfishly pursued their own interests, no matter what effects their actions had on others,

Xunzi

and resisted making any contribution voluntarily to the larger society. He considered strong social discipline the best means to bring order to society. Thus whereas Mencius emphasized the Confucian quality of *ren,* Xunzi emphasized *li.* He advocated the establishment of clear, well-publicized standards of conduct that would set limits on the pursuit of individual interests and punish those who neglected their obligations to the larger society. Xunzi once likened human beings to pieces of warped lumber: just as it was possible to straighten out bad wood, so too it was possible to turn selfish and recalcitrant individuals into useful, contributing members of society. But the process involved harsh social discipline similar to the steam treatments, heat applications, hammering, bending, and forcible wrenching that turned warped wood into useful lumber.

Like Confucius and Mencius, however, Xunzi also believed that it was possible to improve human beings and restore order to society. This fundamental optimism was a basic characteristic of Confucian thought. It explains the high value that Confucian thinkers placed on education and public behavior, and it accounts also for their activist approach to public affairs. Confucians involved themselves in society: they sought government positions and made conscientious efforts to solve political and social problems and to promote harmony in public life. By no means, however, did the Confucians win universal praise for their efforts: to some of their contemporaries, Confucian activism represented little more than misspent energy.

Daoism

The Daoists were the most prominent critics of Confucian activism. Like Confucianism, Daoist thought developed in response to the turbulence of the late Zhou dynasty and the Period of the Warring States. But unlike the Confucians, the Daoists considered it pointless to waste time and energy on problems that defied solution. Instead of Confucian social activism, the Daoists devoted their energies to reflection and introspection, in hopes that they could understand the natural principles that governed the world and could learn how to live in harmony with them. The Daoists believed that over a long term, this approach would bring harmony to society as a whole, as people ceased to meddle in affairs that they could not understand or control.

Laozi and the Daodejing   According to Chinese tradition, the founder of Daoism was a sage named Laozi who lived during the sixth century B.C.E. Although there probably was a historical Laozi, it is almost certain that several hands contributed to the *Daodejing* (*Classic of the Way and of Virtue*), the basic exposition of Daoist beliefs traditionally ascribed to Laozi, and that the book acquired its definitive form over several centuries. After the *Daodejing,* the most important Daoist work was the *Zhuangzi,* named after its author, the philosopher Zhuangzi (369–286 B.C.E.), who provided a well-reasoned compendium of Daoist views.

The Dao   Daoism represented an effort to understand the fundamental character of the world and nature. The central concept of Daoism is *dao,* meaning "the way," more specifically "the way of nature" or "the way of the cosmos." *Dao* is an elusive concept, and the Daoists themselves did not generally characterize it in positive and forthright terms. In the *Daodejing,* for example, *dao* figures as the original force of the cosmos, an eternal and unchanging principle that governs all the workings of the world. Yet the *Daodejing* envisioned *dao* as a supremely passive force and spoke of it mostly in negative terms: *dao* does nothing, and yet it accomplishes everything. *Dao* resembles water, which is soft and yielding, yet is also so powerful that it eventually erodes even the hardest rock placed in its path. *Dao* also resembles the cavity of a pot or the hub of a wheel: although they are nothing more than empty spaces, they make the pot and the wheel useful tools.

If the principles of *dao* governed the world, it followed that human beings should tailor their behavior to its passive and yielding nature. To the Daoists, living in harmony with *dao* meant retreating from engagement in the world of politics and administration. Ambition and activism had not solved political and social problems. Far from it: human striving had brought the world to a state of chaos. The proper response to this situation was to cease striving and live in as simple a manner as possible.

Thus early Daoists recognized as the chief moral virtue the trait of *wuwei*—disengagement from the affairs of the world. *Wuwei* required that individuals refrain from advanced education (which concentrated on abstruse trivialities) and from personal striving (which indicated excessive concern with the tedious affairs of the world). *Wuwei* called instead for individuals to live simply, unpretentiously, and in harmony with nature.

Wuwei also had implications for state and society: the less government, the better. Instead of expansive kingdoms and empires, the *Daodejing* envisioned a world of tiny, self-sufficient communities where people had no desire to conquer their neighbors or to trade with them. Indeed, even when people lived so close to the next community that they could hear the dogs barking and cocks crowing, they would be so content with their existence that they would not even have the desire to visit their neighbors!

The Doctrine of Wuwei

Daoist interest in the natural world inspired a long tradition of Chinese painting that represents human figures and human creations as tiny parts of a much larger landscape. In this painting by Fan Kuan, who was active in the late tenth and early eleventh centuries C.E., mountains, forests, and gorges dwarf human travelers and their animals. • National Palace Museum, Taipei, Taiwan, Republic of China

Political Implications of Daoism

By encouraging the development of a reflective and introspective consciousness, Daoism served as a counterbalance to the activism and extroversion of the Confucian tradition. Indeed, Daoism encouraged the cultivation of self-knowledge in a way that appealed strongly to Confucians as well as to Daoists. Because neither Confucianism nor Daoism was an exclusive faith that precluded observance of the other, it has been possible through the centuries for individuals to study the Confucian

LAOZI ON LIVING IN HARMONY WITH DAO

• • •

Committed Daoists mostly rejected opportunities to play active roles in government. Yet like the Confucians, the Daoists held strong views on virtuous behavior, and their understanding of dao *had deep political implications, as exemplified by the following excerpts from the* Daodejing.

The highest goodness is like water, for water is excellent in benefitting all things, and it does not strive. It occupies the lowest place, which men abhor. And therefore it is near akin to the *dao*. . . .

In governing men and in serving heaven, there is nothing like moderation. For only by moderation can there be an early return to the normal state of humankind. This early return is the same as a great storage of virtue. With a great storage of virtue there is nothing that may not be achieved. If there is nothing that may not be achieved, then no one will know to what extent this power reaches. And if no one knows to what extent a man's power reaches, that man is fit to be the ruler of a state. Having the secret of rule, his rule shall endure. Setting the tap-root deep, and making the spreading roots firm: this is the way to ensure long life to the tree. . . .

Use uprightness in ruling a state; employ indirect methods in waging war; practice non-interference in order to win the empire. . . .

The greater the number of laws and enactments, the more thieves and robbers there will be. Therefore the Sage [Laozi] says: "So long as I do nothing, the people will work out their own reformation. So long as I love calm, the people will right themselves. If only I keep from meddling, the people will grow rich. If only I am free from desire, the people will come naturally back to simplicity. . . ."

There is nothing in the world more soft and weak than water, yet for attacking things that are hard and strong, there is nothing that surpasses it, nothing that can take its place.

The soft overcomes the hard; the weak overcomes the strong. There is no one in the world but knows this truth, and no one who can put it into practice.

SOURCE: Lionel Giles, trans. *The Sayings of Lao Tzu.* London: John Murray, 1905, pp. 26, 29–30, 41, 50. (Translations slightly modified.)

curriculum and take administrative posts in the government while devoting their private hours to reflection on human nature and the place of humans in the larger world—to live as Confucians by day, as it were, and Daoists by night.

Legalism

Ultimately, neither Confucian activism nor Daoist retreat was able to solve the problems of the Period of the Warring States. Order returned to China only after the emergence of a third school of thought—that of the Legalists—which promoted a practical and ruthlessly efficient approach to statecraft. Unlike the Confucians, the Legalists did not concern themselves with ethics, morality, or propriety. Unlike the Daoists, the Legalists cared nothing about principles governing the world or the place of human beings in nature. Instead, they devoted their attention exclusively to the state, which they sought to strengthen and expand at all costs.

Shang Yang   Legalist doctrine emerged from the insights of men who participated actively in Chinese political affairs during the late fourth century B.C.E. Most notable of them was Shang Yang (ca. 390–338 B.C.E.), who served as chief minister to the duke of the Qin state in western China. His policies survive in a work entitled *The Book of Lord Shang,* which most likely includes contributions from other ministers as well as from Shang Yang himself. Though a clever and efficient administrator, Shang Yang also was despised and feared because of his power and ruthlessness. Upon the death of his patron, the duke of Qin, Shang Yang quickly fell: his enemies at court executed him, mutilated his body, and annihilated his family.

The most systematic of the Legalist theorists was Han Feizi (ca. 280–233 B.C.E.), a student of the Confucian scholar Xunzi. Han Feizi carefully reviewed Legalist ideas from political thinkers in all parts of China and synthesized them in a collection of powerful and well argued essays on statecraft. Like Shang Yang, Han Feizi served as an advisor at the Qin court, and he too fell afoul of other ambitious men, who forced him to end his life by taking poison. The Legalist state itself consumed the two foremost exponents of Legalist doctrine.

Han Feizi

Shang Yang, Han Feizi, and other Legalists reasoned that the foundations of a state's strength were agriculture and armed forces. Thus Legalists sought to channel as many individuals as possible into cultivation or military service, while discouraging them from pursuing careers as merchants, entrepreneurs, scholars, educators, philosophers, poets, or artists, since those lines of work did not directly advance the interests of the state.

Legalist Doctrine

The Legalists expected to harness subjects' energy by means of clear and strict laws—hence the name "Legalist." Their faith in laws distinguished the Legalists clearly from the Confucians, who relied upon ritual, custom, education, a sense of propriety, and the humane example of benevolent *junzi* administrators to induce individuals to behave appropriately. The Legalists believed that these influences were not powerful enough to persuade subjects to subordinate their self-interest to the needs of the state. They imposed a strict legal regimen that clearly outlined expectations and provided severe punishment, swiftly administered, for violators. They believed that if people feared to commit small crimes, they would hesitate all the more before committing great crimes. Thus Legalists imposed harsh penalties even for minor infractions: individuals could suffer amputation of their hands or feet, for example, for disposing of ashes or trash in the street. The Legalists also established the principle of collective responsibility before the law. They expected all members of a family or community to observe the others closely, forestall any illegal activity, and report any infractions. Failing these obligations, all members of a family or community were liable to punishment along with the actual violator.

The Legalist's principles of government did not win them much popularity. Over the course of the centuries, Chinese moral and political philosophers have had little praise for the Legalists, and few have openly associated themselves with the Legalist school. Yet Legalist doctrine lent itself readily to practical application, and Legalist principles of government quickly produced remarkable results for rulers who adopted them. In fact, Legalist methods put an end to the Period of the Warring States and brought about the unification of China.

THE UNIFICATION OF CHINA

During the Period of the Warring States, rulers of several regional states adopted elements of the Legalist program. Legalist doctrines met the most enthusiastic response in the state of Qin, in western China, where Shang Yang and Han Feizi oversaw the

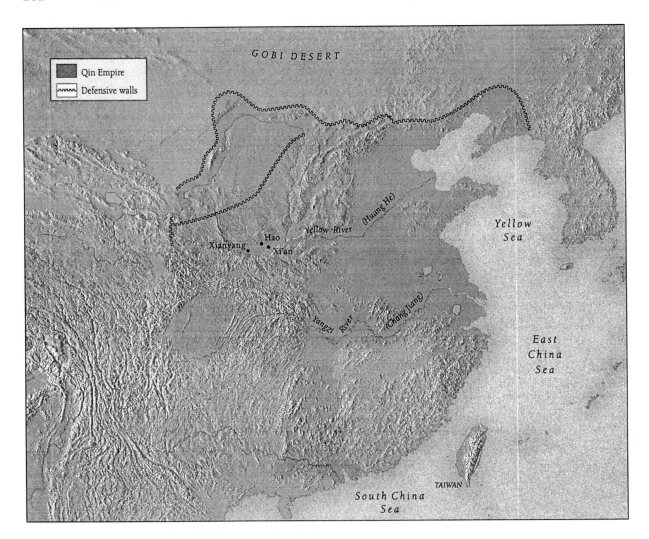

MAP [7.1]
China under the Qin
dynasty.

implementation of Legalist policies. The Qin state soon dominated its neighbors and imposed centralized imperial rule throughout China. Qin rule survived only for a few years, but the succeeding Han dynasty followed the Qin example by governing China through a centralized imperial administration.

The Qin Dynasty

The Kingdom of Qin

During the fourth and third centuries B.C.E., the Qin state underwent a remarkable round of economic, political, and military development. Shang Yang encouraged peasant cultivators to migrate to the sparsely populated state. By granting them private plots and allowing them to enjoy generous profits, his policy dramatically boosted agricultural production. By granting land rights to individual cultivators, his policy also weakened the economic position of the hereditary aristocratic classes. This approach allowed Qin rulers to establish centralized, bureaucratic rule throughout their state. Meanwhile, they devoted the new-found wealth of their state to the organization of a powerful army equipped with the most effective iron weapons available. During the third century B.C.E., the kingdom of Qin gradually but consistently grew at the expense of the other Chinese states. Qin rulers attacked one state after another, absorbing each new conquest into their centralized structure, until finally they had brought China for the first time under the sway of a single state.

In the year 221 B.C.E., the king of Qin proclaimed himself the First Emperor and decreed that his descendants would follow him and reign for thousands of generations. The First Emperor, Qin Shihuangdi (reigned 221–210 B.C.E.), could not know that his dynasty would last only fourteen years and in 207 B.C.E. would dissolve because of civil insurrections. Yet the Qin dynasty had a significance out of proportion to its short life. Like the Achaemenid empire in Persia, the Qin dynasty established a tradition of centralized imperial rule that provided large-scale political organization over the long term of Chinese history.

The First Emperor

A life-size model of an infantryman suggests the discipline that drove the armies of Qin Shihuangdi. • O. Louis Mazzatenta/ © National Geographic Society

Like his ancestors in the kingdom of Qin, the First Emperor of China ignored the nobility and ruled his empire through a centralized bureaucracy. He governed from his capital at Xianyang, near the early Zhou capital of Hao and the modern city of Xi'an. The remainder of China he divided into administrative provinces and districts, and he entrusted the communication and implementation of his policies to officers of the central government who served at the pleasure of the emperor himself. He disarmed regional military forces and destroyed fortresses that might serve as points of rebellion or resistance. He built roads to facilitate communications and the movement of armies. He also drafted laborers by the hundreds of thousands to build defensive walls. Regional kings in northern and western regions of China had already constructed many walls in their own realms in an effort to discourage raids by nomadic peoples. Qin Shihuangdi ordered workers to link the existing sections into a massive defensive barrier that was a precursor to the Great Wall of China.

*Resistance
to Qin Policies*

It is likely that many Chinese welcomed the political stability introduced by the Qin dynasty, but by no means did the new regime win universal acceptance. Confucians, Daoists, and others launched a vigorous campaign of criticism. In an effort to reassert his authority, Qin Shihuangdi ordered execution for those who criticized his regime, and he demanded the burning of all books of philosophy, ethics, history, and literature. His decree exempted works on medicine, fortune-telling, and agriculture, on the grounds that they had some utilitarian value. The emperor also spared the official history of the Qin state. Other works, however, largely went into the flames during the next few years.

*The Burning
of the Books*

The First Emperor took his policy seriously and enforced it earnestly. In the year following his decree, Qin Shihuangdi sentenced some 460 scholars residing in the capital to be buried alive for their criticism of his regime, and he forced many other critics from the provinces into the army and dispatched them to dangerous frontier posts. For the better part of a generation, there was no open discussion of classical literary or philosophical works. When it became safe again to speak openly, scholars began a long and painstaking task of reconstructing the suppressed texts. In some cases scholars had managed, at great personal risk, to hide copies of the forbidden books, which they retrieved and recirculated. In other cases they reassembled texts that they had committed to memory. In many cases, however, works suppressed by Qin Shihuangdi simply disappeared.

Qin Centralization

The First Emperor launched several initiatives that enhanced the unity of China. In keeping with his policy of centralization, he standardized the laws, currencies, weights, and measures of the various regions of China. Previously, regional states had organized their own legal and economic systems, which often conflicted with one another and hampered commerce and communications across state boundaries. Uniform coinage and legal standards encouraged the integration of China's various regions into a more tightly knit society than had ever been conceivable before. As in other classical societies, the roads and bridges that Qin Shihuangdi built throughout his realm also encouraged economic integration: though constructed largely with military uses in mind, they served as fine highways for interregional commerce.

Standardized Script

Perhaps even more important than his legal and economic policies was the First Emperor's standardization of Chinese script. Before the Qin dynasty, all regions of China used scripts derived from the one employed at the Shang court, but they had developed along different lines and had become mutually unrecognizable. In hopes of ensuring better understanding and uniform application of his policies, Qin Shihuangdi mandated the use of a common script throughout his empire. The regions of China continued to use different spoken languages, as they do even today, but they wrote these languages with a common script—just as if Europeans spoke English, French, German, Italian, Russian, Spanish, and other languages but wrote them all down in Latin. In China, speakers of different languages use the same written symbols, but pronounce them and process them mentally in different ways. Nevertheless, the common script enables them to communicate in writing across linguistic boundaries.

In spite of his ruthlessness, Qin Shihuangdi ranks as one of the most important figures in Chinese history. The First Emperor established a precedent for centralized imperial rule, which remained the norm in China until the early twentieth century. He also pointed China in the direction of political and cultural unity, and with some periods of interruption, China has remained politically and culturally unified to the present day.

One detachment of the formidable, life-size, terra cotta army buried in the vicinity of Qin Shihuangdi's tomb to protect the emperor after his death. • O. Louis Mazzatenta/© National Geographic Society

Tomb of the First Emperor

Qin Shihuangdi died in 210 B.C.E. His final resting place was a lavish tomb constructed by some seven hundred thousand drafted laborers as a permanent monument to the First Emperor. Rare and expensive grave goods accompanied the emperor in burial, along with sacrificed slaves, concubines, and many of the craftsmen who designed and built the tomb. Qin Shihuangdi was laid to rest in an elaborate underground palace lined with bronze and protected by traps and crossbows rigged to fire at intruders. The ceiling of the palace featured paintings of the stars and planets, and a vast map of the First Emperor's realm, with flowing mercury representing its rivers and seas, decorated the floor. Buried in the vicinity of the tomb itself was an entire army of life-sized pottery figures to guard the emperor in death. Since 1974, when scholars began to excavate the area around Qin Shihuangdi's tomb, more than fifteen thousand terra cotta sculptures have come to light, including magnificently detailed soldiers, horses, and weapons.

The terra cotta army of Qin Shihuangdi protected his tomb until recent times, but it could not save his successors or his empire. The First Emperor had conscripted millions of laborers from all parts of China to work on massive public works projects such as palaces, roads, bridges, irrigation systems, defensive walls, and his own tomb. While they increased productivity and promoted the integration of China's various regions, these projects also generated tremendous ill will among laborers compelled to leave their families and their lands. Revolts began in the year after Qin Shihuangdi's death, and in 207 B.C.E. waves of rebels overwhelmed the Qin court, slaughtering government officials and burning state buildings. The Qin dynasty quickly dissolved in chaos.

The Early Han Dynasty

Liu Bang The bloody end of the Qin dynasty might well have ended the experiment with centralized imperial rule in China. Although ambitious governors and generals could have carved China into regions and contested one another for hegemony in a reprise of the Period of the Warring States, centralized rule returned almost immediately, largely because of a determined commander named Liu Bang. Judging from the historian Sima Qian's account, Liu Bang was not a colorful or charismatic figure, but he was a persistent man and a methodical planner. He surrounded himself with brilliant advisors and enjoyed the unwavering loyalty of his troops. By 206 B.C.E. he had restored order throughout China and established himself at the head of a new dynasty.

Liu Bang called the new dynasty the Han, in honor of his native land. The Han dynasty turned out to be one of the longest and most influential in all of Chinese history. It lasted for more than four hundred years, from 206 B.C.E. to 220 C.E., although for a brief period (9–23 C.E.) a usurper temporarily displaced Han rule. Thus historians conventionally divide the dynasty into the Former Han (206 B.C.E.–9 C.E.) and the Later Han (25–220 C.E.).

The Han dynasty consolidated the tradition of centralized imperial rule that the Qin dynasty had pioneered. During the Former Han, emperors ruled from Chang'an, a cosmopolitan city near modern Xi'an that became the cultural capital of China. They mostly used wood as a building material, and later dynasties built over their city, so nothing of Han-era Chang'an survives. Contemporaries described Chang'an as a thriving metropolis with a fine imperial palace, busy markets, and expansive parks. During the Later Han, the emperors moved their capital east to Luoyang, also a cosmopolitan city second in importance only to Chang'an throughout much of Chinese history.

Early Han Policies During the early days of the Han dynasty, Liu Bang attempted to follow a middle path between the decentralized network of political alliances of the Zhou dynasty and the tightly centralized state of the Qin. Zhou decentralization encouraged political chaos, he thought, because regional governors were powerful enough to resist the emperor and pursue their own ambitions. Liu Bang thought that Qin centralization created a new set of problems, however, because it provided little incentive for imperial family members to support the dynasty.

Liu Bang tried to save the advantages and avoid the excesses of both Zhou and Qin dynasties. On the one hand, he allotted large landholdings to members of the imperial family, in the expectation that they would provide a reliable network of support for his rule. On the other hand, he divided the empire into administrative districts governed by officials who served at the emperor's pleasure in the expectation that he could exercise effective control over the development and implementation of his policies.

Liu Bang learned quickly that reliance on his family did not guarantee support for the emperor. In 200 B.C.E. an army of nomadic Xiongnu warriors besieged Liu Bang and almost captured him. He managed to escape—but without receiving the support he had expected from his family members. From that point forward, Liu Bang and his successors followed a policy of centralization. They reclaimed lands from family members, absorbed those lands into the imperial domain, and entrusted political responsibilities to an administrative bureaucracy. Thus despite a brief flirtation with a decentralized government, the Han dynasty left as its principal political legacy a tradition of centralized imperial rule.

Much of the reason for the Han dynasty's success was the long reign of the dynasty's greatest and most energetic emperor, Han Wudi, the "Martial Emperor," who occupied the imperial throne for fifty-four years, from 141 to 87 B.C.E. Han Wudi ruled his empire with vision and vigor. He pursued two policies in particular: administrative centralization and imperial expansion.

The Martial Emperor

Domestically, Han Wudi worked strenuously to increase the authority and prestige of the central government. He built an enormous bureaucracy to administer his empire, and he relied upon Legalist principles of government. Like Qin Shihuangdi, Han Wudi sent imperial officers to implement his policies and maintain order in administrative provinces and districts. He also continued the Qin policy of building roads and canals to facilitate trade and communication between China's regions. To finance the vast machinery of his government, he levied taxes on agriculture, trade, and craft industries, and he established imperial monopolies on the production of essential goods such as iron and salt while placing the lucrative liquor industry under state supervision.

Han Centralization

In building such an enormous governmental structure, Han Wudi faced a serious problem of recruitment. He needed thousands of reliable, intelligent, educated individuals to run his bureaucracy, but education in China took place largely on an individual, ad hoc basis. Men such as Confucius, Mencius, and

Clay model of an aristocratic house of the sort inhabited by a powerful clan during the Han dynasty. This model came from a tomb near the city of Guangzhou in southern China. ● The Nelson-Atkins Museum of Art, Kansas City, Missouri, Purchase: Nelson Trust

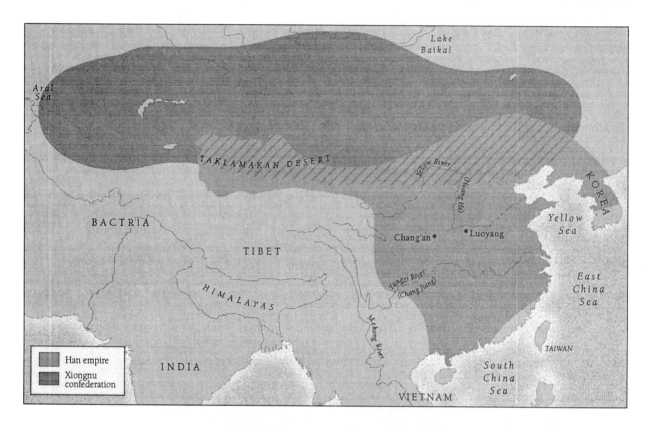

MAP [7.2]

East Asia and central Asia at the time of Han Wudi.

The Confucian Educational System

Han Imperial Expansion

Xunzi accepted students and tutored them, but there was no system to provide a continuous supply of educated candidates for office.

Han Wudi addressed this problem in 124 B.C.E. by establishing an imperial university that prepared young men for government service. Personally, the Martial Emperor was a practical man of affairs who cared little for learning. In this respect he resembled all the other early Han emperors: Liu Bang once emptied his bladder in the distinctive cap worn by Confucian scholars in order to demonstrate his contempt for academic pursuits! Yet Han Wudi recognized that the success of his efforts at bureaucratic centralization would depend on a corps of educated officeholders. The imperial university took Confucianism—the only Chinese cultural tradition developed enough to provide rigorous intellectual discipline—as the basis for its curriculum. Ironically, then, while he relied on Legalist principles of government, Han Wudi ensured the long-term survival of the Confucian tradition. By the end of the Former Han dynasty, the imperial university enrolled more than three thousand students, and by the end of the Later Han, the student population had risen to more than thirty thousand.

While he moved aggressively to centralize power and authority at home, Han Wudi pursued an equally vigorous foreign policy of imperial expansion. He invaded northern Vietnam and Korea, subjected them to Han rule, and brought them into the orbit of Chinese society. He ruled both lands through a Chinese-style government, and Confucian values followed the Han armies into the new colonies. Over the course of the centuries, the educational systems of both northern Vietnam and Korea drew their inspiration almost entirely from Confucianism.

The greatest foreign challenge that Han Wudi faced came from the Xiongnu, a *The Xiongnu*
nomadic people from the steppes of central Asia who spoke a Turkish language. Like
most of the other nomadic peoples of central Asia, the Xiongnu were superb horsemen. Xiongnu boys learned to ride sheep and shoot rodents at an early age, and as
they grew older they graduated to larger animals and aimed their bows and arrows
at larger prey. Their weaponry was not as sophisticated as that of the Chinese: their
bows and arrows were not nearly as lethal as the ingenious and powerful crossbows
wielded by Chinese warriors. But their mobility offered the Xiongnu a distinct advantage. When they could not satisfy their needs and desires through peaceful trade,
they mounted sudden raids into villages or trading areas, where they commandeered
food supplies or manufactured goods and then rapidly departed. Because they had
no cities or settled places to defend, the Xiongnu could quickly disperse when confronted by a superior force.

During the reign of Maodun (210–174 B.C.E.), their most successful leader, the
Xiongnu ruled a vast federation of nomadic peoples that stretched from the Aral Sea
to the Yellow Sea. Maodun brought strict military discipline to the Xiongnu. According to Sima Qian, Maodun once instructed his forces to shoot their arrows at
whatever target he himself selected. He aimed in succession at his favorite horse, one
of his wives, and his father's best horse, and he summarily executed those who failed
to discharge their arrows. When his forces reliably followed his orders, Maodun tar-
geted his father, who immediately fell under a hail of arrows, leaving Maodun as the
Xiongnu chief.

With its highly disciplined army, the Xiongnu empire was a source of concern to
the Han emperors. During the early days of the dynasty, they attempted to pacify
the Xiongnu by paying them tribute—providing them with food and finished goods
in hopes that they would refrain from mounting raids in China—or by arranging
marriages between the ruling houses of the two peoples in hopes of establishing
peaceful diplomatic relations. Neither method succeeded for long.

Ultimately, Han Wudi decided to go on the offensive against the Xiongnu. He *Han Expansion*
invaded central Asia with vast armies—sometimes composed of as many as one hun- *into Central Asia*
dred thousand troops—and brought much of the Xiongnu empire under Chinese
military control. He pacified a long central Asian corridor extending almost to Bactria, which prevented the Xiongnu from maintaining the integrity of their empire
and which served also as the lifeline of a trade network that linked much of the
Eurasian landmass. He even planted colonies of Chinese cultivators in the oasis communities of central Asia. As a result of these efforts, the Xiongnu empire soon fell
into disarray. For the moment, the Han state enjoyed uncontested hegemony in
both east Asia and central Asia. Before long, however, economic and social problems
within China brought serious problems for the Han dynasty itself.

FROM ECONOMIC PROSPERITY
TO SOCIAL DISORDER

Already during the Xia, Shang, and Zhou dynasties, a productive agricultural economy supported the emergence of complex society in China. High agricultural productivity continued during the Qin and Han dynasties, and it supported the development of craft industries such as the forging of iron tools and the weaving of silk
textiles. During the Han dynasty, however, China experienced serious social and

A painted brick depicts a peasant working in the fields with a team of oxen and a wooden harrow. By the Han dynasty many plows of this type had iron teeth. Produced in the third or fourth century C.E., this brick painting came from a tomb in Gansu Province in western China. • Wang-go Weng, Inc.

economic problems as land became concentrated in the hands of a small, wealthy elite class. Social tensions generated banditry, rebellion, and even the temporary deposition of the Han state itself. Although Han rulers regained the throne, they presided over a much-weakened realm. By the early third century C.E., social and political problems had brought the Han dynasty to an end.

Productivity and Prosperity during the Former Han

The structure of Chinese society during the Qin and Han dynasties was very similar to that of the Zhou era. Patriarchal households averaged five inhabitants, although several generations of aristocratic families sometimes lived together in large compounds. During the Han dynasty, moralists sought to enhance the authority of patriarchal family heads by emphasizing the importance of filial piety and women's subordination to their menfolk. The anonymous Confucian *Classic of Filial Piety*, composed probably in the early Han dynasty, taught that children should obey and honor their parents as well as other superiors and political authorities. Similarly, Ban Zhao, a well-educated woman from a prominent Han family, wrote a widely read treatise entitled *Admonitions for Women* that emphasized humility, obedience, subservience, and devotion to their husbands as the virtues most appropriate for women. To Confucian moralists and government authorities alike, orderly, patriarchal families were the foundations of a stable society.

The vast majority of the Chinese population worked in the countryside cultivating grains and vegetables, which they harvested in larger quantities than ever before. In late Zhou times cultivators often strengthened their plows with iron tips, but metalworkers did not produce enough iron to provide all-metal tools. During the Han dynasty the iron industry entered a period of rapid growth—partly because Han rulers favored the industry and encouraged its expansion—and cultivators soon used not only plows but also shovels, picks, hoes, sickles, and spades with iron parts. The tougher implements enabled cultivators to produce more food and support larger populations than ever before. The agricultural surplus allowed many Chinese to produce fine manufactured goods and to engage in trade.

The significance of the iron industry went far beyond agriculture. Han artisans *Iron Metallurgy*
experimented with production techniques and learned to craft fine utensils for both
domestic and military uses. Iron pots, stoves, knives, needles, axes, hammers, saws,
and other tools became standard fixtures in households that could not have afforded
more expensive bronze utensils. The ready availability of iron also had important
military implications. Craftsmen designed suits of iron armor to protect soldiers
against arrows and blows, and the strength and sharpness of Han swords, spears, and
arrowheads help to explain the success of Chinese armies against the Xiongnu and
other nomadic peoples.

Textile production—particularly sericulture, the manufacture of silk—became an *Silk Textiles*
especially important industry. The origins of sericulture predate the ancient Xia dynasty, but only in Han times did sericulture expand from its original home in the
Yellow River valley to most parts of China. It developed especially rapidly in the
southern regions known today as Sichuan and Guangdong provinces, and the industry thrived after the establishment of long-distance trade relations with western lands
in the second century B.C.E.

Although silkworms inhabited much of Eurasia, Chinese silk was especially fine
because of advanced sericulture techniques. Chinese producers bred their silkworms,
fed them on finely chopped mulberry leaves, and carefully unraveled their cocoons so
as to obtain long fibers of raw silk that they wove into light, strong, lustrous fabrics.
(In other lands producers relied on wild silkworms that ate a variety of leaves and
chewed through their cocoons, leaving only short fibers that yielded lower-quality
fabrics.) Chinese silk became a prized commodity in India, Persia, Mesopotamia, and
even the distant Roman empire. Commerce in silk and other products led to the establishment of an intricate network of trade routes known collectively as the silk
roads (discussed in chapter 11).

While expanding the iron and silk industries, Han craftsmen also invented paper. *Paper*
In earlier times Chinese scribes had written mostly on bamboo strips and silk fabrics
but also inscribed messages on oracle bones and bronze wares. Probably before 100
C.E. Chinese craftsmen began to fashion hemp, bark, and textile fibers into sheets of
paper, which was less expensive than silk and easier to write on than bamboo. Although wealthy elites continued to read books written on silk rolls, paper soon became the preferred medium for most writing.

High agricultural productivity supported rapid demographic growth and general *Population Growth*
prosperity during the early part of the Han dynasty. About 220 B.C.E., just after the
founding of the Qin dynasty, historians estimate the Chinese population at about
twenty million. By the year 9 C.E., at the end of the Former Han dynasty, it had
tripled to sixty million. Meanwhile, taxes claimed only a small portion of production, yet state granaries bulged so much that their contents sometimes spoiled before they could be consumed.

Economic and Social Difficulties

In spite of general prosperity, China began to experience economic and social difficulties in the Former Han period. The military adventures and the central Asian policy of Han Wudi caused severe economic strain. Expeditions against the Xiongnu
and the establishment of agricultural colonies in central Asia were extremely expensive undertakings, and they rapidly consumed the empire's surplus wealth. To finance his ventures, Han Wudi raised taxes and confiscated land and personal property from wealthy individuals, sometimes on the pretext that they had violated
imperial laws. These measures did not kill industry and commerce in China, but they

In Han times the wealthiest classes enjoyed the privilege of being buried in suits of jade plaques sewn together with gold threads, like the burial dress of Liu Sheng, who died in 113 B.C.E. at Manzheng in Hebei Province. Legend held that jade prevented decomposition of the deceased's body. Scholars have estimated that a jade burial suit like this one required ten years' worth of labor. • Erich Lessing/Art Resource, NY

discouraged investment in manufacturing and trading enterprises, which in turn had a dampening effect on the larger economy.

Social Tensions   Distinctions between rich and poor hardened during the course of the Han dynasty. Wealthy individuals wore fine silk garments, leather shoes, and jewelry of jade and gold, whereas the poor classes made do with rough hemp clothing and sandals. Tables in wealthy households held pork, fish, fowl, and fine aged wines, but the diet of the poor consisted mostly of grain or rice supplemented by small quantities of vegetables or meat. By the first century B.C.E., social and economic differences had generated serious tensions, and peasants in hard-pressed regions began to organize rebellions in hopes of gaining a larger share of Han society's resources.

Land Distribution   A particularly difficult problem concerned the distribution of land. Individual economic problems brought on by poor harvests, high taxes, or crushing burdens of debt forced many small landowners to sell their property under unfavorable conditions, or even to forfeit it in exchange for cancellation of their debts. In extreme cases individuals had to sell themselves and their families into slavery to satisfy their creditors. Owners of large estates not only increased the size of their holdings by absorbing the property of their less fortunate neighbors but also increased the efficiency of their operations by employing cheap labor. Sometimes cheap laborers came in the form of slaves, other times in the form of tenant farmers who had to deliver as much as half of their produce to the landowner for the right to till his property. In either case the laborers worked on terms that favored the landlords.

By the end of the first century B.C.E., land had accumulated in the hands of a relatively small number of individuals who owned vast estates, while ever-increasing numbers of peasant cultivators led difficult lives with few prospects for improvement. Landless peasants became restive, and Chinese society faced growing problems of banditry and sporadic rebellion. Since the Han emperors depended heavily on the political cooperation of large landowners, however, they did not attempt any serious reform of the landholding system.

The Reign   Tensions came to a head during the early first century C.E. when a powerful and
of Wang Mang   respected Han minister named Wang Mang undertook a thoroughgoing program of reform. In 6 C.E. a two-year-old boy inherited the Han imperial throne. Since he was

unable to govern, Wang Mang served as his regent. Many officials regarded Wang as more capable than members of the Han family and urged him to claim the imperial honor for himself. In 9 C.E. he did just that: announcing that the mandate of heaven had passed from the Han to his own family, he seized the throne. Wang Mang then introduced a series of wide-ranging reforms that have prompted historians to refer to him as the "socialist emperor."

The most important reforms concerned landed property: Wang Mang limited the amount of land that a family could hold and ordered officials to break up large estates, redistribute them, and provide landless individuals with property to cultivate. Despite his good intentions, the socialist emperor attempted to impose his policy without adequate preparation and communication. The result was confusion: landlords resisted a policy that threatened their holdings, and even peasants found its application inconsistent and unsatisfactory. After several years of chaos, Wang Mang faced the additional misfortune of poor harvests and famine, which sparked widespread revolts against his rule. In 23 C.E. a coalition of disgruntled landlords and desperate peasants ended both his dynasty and his life.

The Later Han Dynasty

Within two years a recovered Han dynasty returned to power, but it ruled over a weakened realm. The Later Han emperors even decided to abandon Chang'an, which had suffered grave damage during the years of chaos and rebellion, and establish a new capital at Luoyang. Nevertheless, during the early years of the Later Han, emperors ruled vigorously in the manner of Liu Bang and Han Wudi. They regained control of the centralized administration and reorganized the state bureaucracy. They also maintained the Chinese presence in central Asia, continued to keep the Xiongnu in submission, and exercised firm control over the silk roads.

The Yellow Turban Uprising

The Later Han emperors did not seriously address the problem of land distribution that had helped to bring down the Former Han dynasty. The wealthy classes still lived in relative luxury while peasants worked under difficult conditions. The empire continued to suffer the effects of banditry and rebellions organized by desperate peasants with few opportunities to improve their lot. The Yellow Turban uprising—so named because of the distinctive headgear worn by the rebels—was a particularly serious revolt that raged throughout China and tested the resilience of the Han state during the late second century C.E. Although the Later Han dynasty possessed the military power required to keep civil disorder under reasonable control, rebellions by the Yellow Turbans and others weakened the Han state during the second and third centuries C.E.

Collapse of the Han Dynasty

The Later Han emperors were unable, however, to prevent the development of factions at court that paralyzed the central government. Factions of imperial family members, Confucian scholar bureaucrats, and court eunuchs sought to increase their influence, protect their own interests, and destroy their rivals. On several occasions relations between the various factions became so strained that they made war against each other. In 189 C.E., for example, a faction led by an imperial relative descended on the Han palace and slaughtered more than two thousand beardless men in an effort to destroy the eunuchs as a political force. In this respect the attack succeeded. From the unmeasured violence of the operation, however, it is clear that the Later Han dynasty had reached a point of internal weakness from which it could not easily recover. Indeed, early in the next century, the central government disintegrated, and for almost four centuries China remained divided into several large regional kingdoms.

Han gentleman sport luxurious silk gowns as they engage in sophisticated conversation. Wealthy individuals and ruling elites commonly dressed in silk, but peasants and others of the lower classes rarely if ever donned silk garments. • Courtesy, Museum of Fine Arts, Boston. Denman Waldo Ross Collection. 25.10–13

*T*he Qin state lasted for a short fourteen years, but it opened a new era in Chinese history. Qin conquerors imposed unified rule on a series of politically independent kingdoms and launched an ambitious program to forge culturally distinct regions into a larger Chinese society. The Han dynasty endured for more than four centuries and largely completed the project of unifying China. Han rulers built a centralized bureaucracy that administered a unified empire, thus establishing a precedent for centralized imperial rule in China. They also entered into a close alliance with Confucian moralists who organized a system of advanced education that provided recruits for the imperial bureaucracy. Moreover, on the basis of a highly productive economy stimulated by technological innovations, Han rulers projected Chinese influence abroad to Korea, Vietnam, and central Asia. Thus as in the cases of other classical societies in Persia, India, and the Mediterranean basin, Han China produced a set of distinctive political and cultural traditions that shaped Chinese and neighboring societies over the long term.

CHRONOLOGY

6th century B.C.E. (?)	Laozi
551–479 B.C.E.	Confucius
403–221 B.C.E.	Period of the Warring States
390–338 B.C.E.	Shang Yang
372–289 B.C.E.	Mencius
298–238 B.C.E.	Xunzi
280–233 B.C.E.	Han Feizi
221–207 B.C.E.	Qin dynasty
206 B.C.E.–9 C.E.	Former Han dynasty
141–87 b.c.e.	Reign of Han Wudi
9–23 C.E.	Reign of Wang Mang
25–220 C.E.	Later Han dynasty

FOR FURTHER READING

Thomas J. Barfield. *The Perilous Frontier: Nomadic Empires and China*. Cambridge, Mass., 1989. A provocative analysis of the relations between Chinese and central Asian peoples.

Derk Bodde. *China's First Unifier: A Study of the Ch'in Dynasty as Seen in the Life of Li Ssu*. Leiden, 1938. Important study of the minister responsible for much of the Qin dynasty's policy.

H. G. Creel. *The Birth of China*. New York, 1937. An older work offering a lively and well-written popular account.

Sebastian De Grazia, ed. *Masters of Chinese Political Thought from the Beginnings to the Han Dynasty*. New York, 1973. A valuable collection of primary sources in translation, all of them bearing on political themes.

Mark Elvin. *The Pattern of the Chinese Past*. Stanford, 1973. A remarkable analysis of Chinese history by an economic historian who brings a comparative perspective to his work.

Cho-yun Hsu. *Han Agriculture: The Formation of Early Chinese Agrarian Economy (206 B.C.–A.D. 220)*. Seattle, 1980. Studies the development of intensive agriculture in Han China and provides English translations of more than two hundred documents illustrating the conditions of rural life.

Michael Loewe. *Everyday Life in Early Imperial China*. London, 1968. Deals with the social, economic, and cultural history of China during the Han dynasty.

Victor H. Mair, trans. *Tao Te Ching: The Classic Book of Integrity and the Way*. New York, 1990. A fresh and lively translation of the Daoist classic *Daodejing,* based on recently discovered manuscripts.

Frederick W. Mote. *Intellectual Foundations of China*. 2nd ed. New York, 1989. A compact and concise introduction to the cultural history of classical China, based on recent research.

Michele Pirazzoli-t'Serstevens. *The Han Dynasty*. Trans. by J. Seligman. New York, 1982. An excellent and well-illustrated survey of Han China that draws on recent scholarship and archaeological discoveries.

Benjamin I. Schwartz. *The World of Thought in Ancient China*. Cambridge, Mass., 1985. A synthesis of classical Chinese thought by a leading scholar.

Arthur Waldron. *The Great Wall of China: From History to Myth*. Cambridge, 1989. Places the modern Great Wall in the tradition of Chinese wall building from Qin times forward.

Arthur Waley, trans. *The Analects of Confucius*. New York, 1938. An English version of Confucius's sayings by a gifted translator.

———, trans. *Three Ways of Thought in Ancient China*. New York, 1940. Translations and comments on works from Confucian, Daoist, and Legalist traditions.

Wang Zhongshu. *Han Civilization*. Trans. by K. C. Chang. New Haven, 1982. A scholarly work that reviews the results of recent archaeological research.

Burton Watson, trans. *Basic Writings of Mo Tzu, Hsün Tzu, and Han Fei Tzu*. New York, 1967. Translations of important political and social treatises from classical China.

———, trans. *Records of the Grand Historian*. Rev. ed. 2 vols. New York, 1993. Excellent translation of Sima Qian's history, the most important narrative source for Han China.

CHAPTER 8

STATE, SOCIETY, AND THE QUEST FOR SALVATION IN INDIA

• • •

The earliest description of India by a foreigner came from the pen of a Greek ambassador named Megasthenes. As the diplomatic representative of the Seleucid emperor, Megasthenes lived in India for many years during the late fourth and early third centuries B.C.E., and he traveled throughout much of northern India. Although Megasthenes's book, the *Indika,* has long been lost, many quotations from it survive in Greek and Latin literature. These fragments clearly show that Megasthenes had great respect for the Indian land, people, and society.

Like travel writers of all times, Megasthenes included a certain amount of spurious information in his account of India. He wrote, for example, of ants the size of foxes that mined gold from the earth and fiercely defended their hoards from any humans who tried to steal them. Only by distracting them with slabs of meat, Megasthenes said, could humans safely make away with their treasure. He also reported races of monstrous human beings: some with no mouth who survived by breathing in the odors of fruits, flowers, and roots, others with feet pointing backwards and eight toes per foot, and yet others with the heads of dogs who communicated by barking.

Beyond the tall tales, Megasthenes offered a great deal of reliable information. He portrayed India as a fertile land that supported two harvests of grain per year. He described the capital of Pataliputra as a rectangle-shaped city situated along the Ganges River and surrounded by a moat and a massive timber wall with 570 towers and sixty-four gates. He mentioned large armies that used elephants as war animals. He pointed out the strongly hierarchical character of Indian society (although he incorrectly held that there were seven instead of four main castes). He noted that two main schools of "philosophers" (Hindus and Buddhists) enjoyed special prominence, as well as exemption from taxes, and he described the ascetic lifestyles and vegetarian diets followed by particularly devout individuals. In short, Megasthenes portrayed India as a wealthy land that supported a distinctive society with well-established cultural traditions.

Head of the Buddha carved in limestone. • The James W. and Marilynn Alsdorf Collection AL.166. Photograph by Michael Trope, Chicago. Photograph © 1998, The Art Institute of Chicago. All rights reserved.

In India as in Persia and China, the centuries after 500 B.C.E. witnessed the development of a classical society whose influence has persisted over the centuries. Its most prominent features were a well-defined social structure, which left individuals with few doubts about their position and role in society, and several popular religious traditions that helped to shape Indian beliefs and values. Two religions, Buddhism and Hinduism, also appealed strongly to peoples beyond the subcontinent.

Efforts to maintain an imperial government did not succeed nearly as well in India as they did in Persia and China. For the most part, classical India fell under the sway of regional kingdoms rather than centralized empires. Imperial regimes were crucial for the consolidation of Indian cultural traditions, however, because they sponsored cultural leaders and promoted their ideals throughout the subcontinent and beyond. The spread of Buddhism is a case in point: imperial support helped the faith secure its position in India and attract converts in other lands. Thus even in the absence of a strong and continuing imperial tradition like that of Persia or China, the social and cultural traditions of classical India not only shaped the lives and experiences of the subcontinent's inhabitants but also influenced peoples in distant lands.

THE FORTUNES OF EMPIRE IN CLASSICAL INDIA

Following their migrations to India after 1500 B.C.E., the Aryans established a series of small kingdoms throughout the subcontinent. For centuries the rulers of these kingdoms fought constantly among themselves and sought to expand their states by absorbing others. By the sixth century B.C.E., wars of expansion had resulted in the consolidation of several large regional kingdoms that dominated much of the subcontinent. Despite strenuous efforts, none of these kingdoms was able to establish hegemony over the others. During the classical era, the Mauryan and the Gupta dynasties founded centralized, imperial states that embraced much of India, but neither empire survived long enough to establish centralized rule as a lasting feature of Indian political life.

The Mauryan Dynasty and the Temporary Unification of India

The unification of India came about partly as a result of intrusion from beyond the subcontinent. About 520 B.C.E. Cyrus, the emperor of Persia, crossed the Hindu Kush mountains, conquered parts of northwestern India, and made the kingdom of Gandhara in the northern Punjab a province of the Achaemenid empire. The establishment of Achaemenid authority in India introduced local rulers to Persian techniques of administration. Almost two centuries later, in 327 B.C.E., after overrunning the Persian empire, Alexander of Macedon crossed the Indus River and crushed the states he found there. Alexander remained in India only for a short time, and he did not make a deep impression on the Punjabi people: he departed after his forces mutinied in the year 325 B.C.E., and contemporary Indian sources did not even mention his name. Yet his campaign had an important effect on Indian politics and history, since he created a political vacuum in northwestern India by destroying the existing states and then withdrawing his own forces.

Kingdom of Magadha   Poised to fill the vacuum was the dynamic kingdom of Magadha, located in the central portion of the Ganges plain. Several regional kingdoms in the valley of the Ganges had become wealthy as workers turned forests into fields and trade became

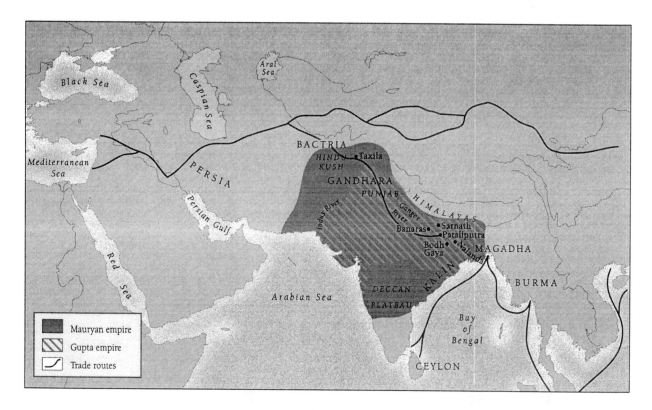

MAP [8.1]
The Mauryan and Gupta empires.

an increasingly prominent feature of the local economy. By about 500 B.C.E. Magadha had emerged as the most important state in northeastern India. During the next two centuries, the kings of Magadha conquered the neighboring states and gained control of Indian commerce passing through the Ganges valley, as well as overseas trade between India and Burma passing across the Bay of Bengal. The withdrawal of Alexander from the Punjab presented Magadha with a rare opportunity to expand.

Chandragupta Maurya

During the late 320s B.C.E., an ambitious adventurer named Chandragupta Maurya exploited that opportunity and laid the foundation for the Mauryan empire, the first state to bring a centralized and unified government to most of the Indian subcontinent. Chandragupta began by seizing control of small, remote regions of Magadha and then worked his way gradually toward the center. By 321 B.C.E. he had overthrown the ruling dynasty and consolidated his hold on the kingdom. He then moved into the Punjab and brought northwestern India under his control. Next he ventured beyond the Indus River and conquered the Greek state in Bactria—a large region straddling the border between modern Pakistan and Afghanistan, where Alexander of Macedon's Greek successors maintained a kingdom during the Seleucid era. By the end of the fourth century B.C.E., Chandragupta's empire embraced all of northern India from the Indus to the Ganges.

Chandragupta's Government

A careful and systematic advisor named Kautalya devised procedures for the governance of Chandragupta's realm. Some of Kautalya's advice survives in the ancient Indian political handbook known as the *Arthashastra*, a manual offering detailed instructions on the uses of power and the principles of government. The *Arthashastra* outlined methods of administering the empire, overseeing trade and agriculture, collecting taxes, maintaining order, conducting foreign relations, and waging war. Kautalya also advised Chandragupta to make abundant use of spies, and he even included prostitutes in his stable of informants. Like the emperors of Persia and China, Chandragupta and Kautalya built a bureaucratic administrative system that enabled them to implement policies throughout the state.

Ashoka Maurya   Tradition holds that Chandragupta abdicated his throne for an existence so ascetic that he starved himself to death. Whether this report is true or not, it is certain that his son succeeded him in 297 B.C.E. and added most of southern India to the growing empire. The high point of the Mauryan empire, however, came during the reign of Chandragupta's grandson Ashoka.

As a symbol of his rule, Ashoka had this sculpture of four lions mounted atop a column about twenty meters (sixty-six feet) tall. The lion capital is the official symbol of the modern Republic of India. • Robert Harding Picture Library

Ashoka began his reign (268–232 B.C.E.) as a conqueror. When he came to power, the only major region that remained independent of the Mauryan empire was the kingdom of Kalinga (modern Orissa) in the east-central part of the subcontinent. In fact, Kalinga was not only independent of Mauryan rule but also actively hostile to its spread. The kingdom's resistance created difficulties for Ashoka because it controlled the principal trade routes, both by land and by sea, between the Ganges plain and southern India. Thus Ashoka's first major undertaking as emperor was to conquer Kalinga and bring it under Mauryan control, which he did in a bloody campaign in 260 B.C.E. By Ashoka's estimate 100,000 Kalingans died in the fighting, 150,000 were driven from their homes, and untold numbers of others perished in the ruined land.

In spite of this campaign, Ashoka is much better known as a governor than as a conqueror. With Kalinga subdued Ashoka ruled almost the entire subcontinent—only the southernmost region escaped his control—and he turned his attention to the responsible government of his realm. As heir to the administrative structure that Chandragupta and Kautalya had instituted, Ashoka ruled through a tightly organized bureaucracy. He established his capital at the fortified city of Pataliputra (near modern Patna), where a central administration developed policies for the whole empire. Pataliputra

Archaeological excavations have unearthed parts of the defensive palisade, constructed of timbers almost five meters (sixteen feet) tall, that surrounded Pataliputra during Mauryan times. • British Library/ Oriental and India Office Archaeological Survey of India

was a thriving and cosmopolitan city: Megasthenes reported that a local committee looked after the interests of foreigners in the city—and also carefully observed their movements. Ashoka went to great pains to ensure that his local subordinates implemented his policies. A central treasury oversaw the efficient collection of taxes—a hallmark of Kautalya's influence—which supported legions of officials, accountants, clerks, soldiers, and other imperial employees.

As a result of Ashoka's policies, the various regions of India became well integrated, and the subcontinent benefitted from both an expanding economy and stable government. Ashoka encouraged the expansion of agriculture—the foundation of the empire's wealth—by building irrigation systems. He encouraged trade by building roads, most notably a highway of more than 1,600 kilometers (1,000 miles) linking Pataliputra with Taxila, the chief political and commercial center of northern India, which offered access to Bactria, Persia, and other points west. Ashoka also provided comforts for administrators, merchants, and other travelers by planting banyan trees to offer shade, digging wells, and establishing inns along the roads.

Decline of the Mauryan Empire

Ashoka's policies did not long survive his rule, nor did his empire. Ashoka died in 232 B.C.E., and decline set in almost immediately. During its later years the Mauryan empire suffered from acute financial and economic difficulties. The empire depended on a strong army and a large corps of officials to administer imperial policy. Salaries for soldiers and bureaucrats were very expensive: Megasthenes said that in times of peace, military forces spent their time in idleness and drinking bouts while continuing to draw their pay. Eventually, these administrative costs outstripped the revenues that flowed into the central treasury. The later Mauryan emperors often resorted to the tactic of debasing their currency—reducing the amount of precious metal in a coin without reducing its nominal value. Because of their financial difficulties, they were unable to hold the realm together. They maintained control of the Ganges valley for some fifty years after Ashoka's death, but eventually they lost their grip even on this heartland of the Mauryan empire. By about 185 B.C.E. northwestern India had fallen into the hands of Greek-speaking rulers of Bactria, and the Mauryan empire had disappeared.

The Revival of Empire under the Guptas

The end of the Mauryan empire did not mean that India crumbled into anarchy. The northwestern part of the subcontinent was unstable, as local Indian rulers and Bactrian Greeks jockeyed for power. The region also experienced periodic invasions by nomadic peoples from central Asia. Meanwhile, however, the remainder of the subcontinent fell under the sway of large regional kingdoms. Although they waged intermittent war against their neighbors, generally speaking the regional kingdoms provided good order and stability within their realms, and they enabled merchants to conduct business safely throughout the subcontinent. A high volume of trade provided sources of revenue for these kingdoms, which controlled and taxed the commerce that passed through their territories. On several occasions ambitious kings sought to expand their realms and imitate the Mauryas by building a subcontinental empire. Only the Guptas, however, were able to realize these imperial ambitions.

The Gupta Dynasty

Like the Mauryas, the Guptas based their state in Magadha, a crucial region because of its wealth, its dominance of the Ganges valley, and its role as intermediary between the various regions of the subcontinent. The new empire arose on foundations laid by Chandra Gupta (not related to Chandragupta Maurya), who forged alliances with powerful families in the Ganges region and established a dynamic kingdom about the year 320 C.E. His successors, Samudra Gupta (reigned 335–375 C.E.) and Chandra Gupta II (reigned 375–415 C.E.), made the Magadhan capital of Pataliputra once again the center of a large empire. Between the two of them, Samudra Gupta and Chandra Gupta II conquered many of the regional kingdoms of India, and they established tributary alliances with others that elected not to fight. Only the Deccan and the southern-most part of the subcontinent remained outside the orbit of Gupta influence.

The Gupta empire rivaled the Mauryan in size, but it differed considerably in organization. Ashoka had insisted on knowing the details of regional affairs, which he closely monitored from his court at Pataliputra. The Guptas left local government and administration, and even the making of basic policy, in the hands of their allies in the various regions of their empire. When nomadic invaders threatened the empire during the later fifth century C.E., it split easily along the fault lines of the administrative regions. But during the late fourth and early fifth centuries C.E., the Gupta dynasty brought stability and prosperity to the subcontinent. A Chinese Buddhist monk named Faxian traveled widely in India searching for texts of the Buddhist scriptures during the reign of Chandra Gupta II. In an account of his travels, Faxian reported that India was a prosperous land with little crime. It was possible to travel throughout the country, he said, without fear of molestation and even without official travel documents.

Gupta administrative talents were not a match, however, for the invasions of the White Huns, a nomadic people from central Asia who occupied Bactria during the fourth century C.E., and then prepared to cross the Hindu Kush mountains into India. For the first half of the fifth century, the Guptas repelled the Huns, but the defense cost them dearly in resources and eventually weakened their state. By the end of the fifth century, the Huns moved across the Hindu Kush almost at will and established several kingdoms in northern and western India.

Gupta Decline

The Gupta dynasty continued in name only: regional governors progressively usurped imperial rights and powers, and contemporary documents do not even record the names of all the later Gupta emperors. Once again, imperial government survived only for a short term in India. Not until the establishment of the Mughal dynasty in the sixteenth century C.E. did any state rule as much of India as the Mauryan and Gupta empires ruled. Memories of empire remained, to be sure, and there were periodic efforts to bring all of the subcontinent again under the control of a unified regime. But for the most part, large regional kingdoms dominated political life in India during the millennium between the Gupta and the Mughal dynasties.

Erected about 400 C.E., this iron pillar commemorates a mighty king of the Gupta dynasty, probably Chandra Gupta II. The pillar is 7.5 meters (25 feet) tall and still stands, barely rusted, near Delhi. • Underwood & Underwood/Corbis-Bettmann

ECONOMIC DEVELOPMENT AND SOCIAL DISTINCTIONS

After spreading through the subcontinent, Aryan migrants turned increasingly from herding to agriculture. After about 1000 B.C.E., when they learned the techniques of iron metallurgy, they used iron axes and tools to advance into regions previously inaccessible to them, notably the jungle-covered valley of the Ganges River. The Aryans dispatched *shudras*, semifree serfs, to work in recently cleared fields, and from fertile lands they reaped large harvests. Agricultural surpluses supported the large-scale states such as the regional kingdoms and the Mauryan and Gupta empires

Jewel-bedecked flying goddesses drop flowers on the earth from their perch in the heavens. Their gems and personal adornments reflect the tastes of upper-class women during the Gupta dynasty. This painting on a rock wall, produced about the sixth century C.E., survives in modern Sri Lanka. • E-T Archive

that organized Indian public life. Agricultural surpluses also encouraged the emergence of towns, the growth of trade, and further development of the caste system.

Towns and Trade

Towns and Manufacturing   After about 600 B.C.E. towns dotted the Indian countryside, especially in the northwestern corner of the subcontinent. These towns served the needs of a stable agricultural society by providing manufactured products for local consumption—pots, textiles, iron tools, and other metal utensils—as well as luxury goods such as jewelry destined for the wealthy and elite classes. Demand for manufactured products was very high, and some entrepreneurs organized businesses on a large scale. During Mauryan times, for example, a pottery manufacturer named Saddalaputta owned about five hundred workshops, whose products he distributed throughout the Ganges valley in his own fleet of boats.

Flourishing towns maintained marketplaces and encouraged the development of trade. Within the subcontinent itself trade was most active along the Ganges River, although trade routes also passed through the Ganges delta east to Burma and down the east Indian coast to the Deccan and southern India. Roads built by Ashoka also facilitated overland commerce within the subcontinent.

Meanwhile, the volume of long-distance trade also grew as large imperial states in China, southwest Asia, and the Mediterranean basin provided a political foundation enabling merchants to deal with their counterparts in distant lands. Direct political and military links with foreign peoples drew Indians into long-distance commercial relations. Beginning with Cyrus, the Achaemenid rulers of Persia coveted the wealth of India and included the northern kingdom of Gandhara as a province of their empire. The presence of Persian administrators in India and the building of roads between Persia and India facilitated commerce between the two lands. Alexander of Macedon's conquests helped to establish even more extensive trade networks by forging links between India and the Mediterranean basin by way of Bactria, Persia, and Anatolia.

Long-Distance Trade

From India, long-distance trade passed overland in two directions: through the Hindu Kush mountains and the Gandharan capital of Taxila to Persia and the Mediterranean basin, and across the silk roads of central Asia to markets in China. Cotton, aromatics, black pepper, pearls, and gems were the principal Indian exports, in exchange for which Indian merchants imported horses and bullion from western lands and silk from China.

During the Mauryan era merchants continued to use land routes, but they increasingly turned to the sea to transport their goods. Seaborne trade benefitted especially from the rhythms of the monsoon winds that

Many surviving gold coins reflect the commercial vitality of northern India in the late first and early second centuries C.E. This one depicts the Buddha gesturing to his followers. • Courtesy, Museum of Fine Arts, Boston. Seth K. Sweetser Fund

govern weather and the seasons in the Indian Ocean basin. During the spring and summer the winds blow from the southwest, and during the fall and winter they come from the northeast. Once they recognized these rhythms, mariners could sail easily and safely before the wind to any part of the Indian Ocean basin.

Trade in the Indian Ocean Basin

As early as the fifth century B.C.E., Indian merchants had traveled to the islands of Indonesia and the southeast Asian mainland, where they exchanged pearls, cotton, black pepper, and Indian manufactured goods for spices and exotic local products. Many of these goods did not remain in India, but instead traveled west through the Arabian Sea to the lands bordering the Persian Gulf and the Red Sea. Indian products also found markets in the Mediterranean basin. Indian pepper became so popular there that the Romans established direct commercial relations and built several trading settlements in southern India. Archaeologists working in southern India have unearthed hoards of Roman coins that testify to the large volume of trade between classical India and Mediterranean lands.

Family Life and the Caste System

Social and Gender Relations

In the midst of urban growth and economic development, Indian moralists sought to promote stability by encouraging respect for strong patriarchal families and the maintenance of a social order in which all members played well-defined roles. Most people lived with members of their nuclear family. Particularly among higher castes, however, several generations of a family often lived in large compounds ruled by powerful patriarchs. Literary works suggest that women were largely subordinate to men. The two great Indian epics, the *Mahabharata* and the *Ramayana,* commonly portrayed women as weak-willed and emotional creatures and exalted wives who devoted themselves to their husbands. In the *Ramayana,* for example, the beautiful Sita loyally followed her husband Rama into undeserved exile in a wild forest and remained faithful to him even during a long separation.

During the early centuries C.E., patriarchal dominance became more pronounced in India. By the Gupta era child marriage was common: when girls were eight or nine years of age, their parents betrothed them to men in their twenties. Formal marriage took place just after the girls reached puberty. Wives often came to dominate domestic affairs in their households, but the practice of child marriage placed them under the control of older men and encouraged them to devote themselves to family matters, rather than to public affairs in the larger society.

After their arrival in India, the Aryans recognized four main castes or classes of people: priests (*brahmins*); warriors and aristocrats (*kshatriyas*); peasants and merchants (*vaishyas*), and serfs (*shudras*). *Brahmins* in particular endorsed this social order, which brought them honor, prestige, and sometimes considerable wealth as well. The growth of trade and the proliferation of industries, however, had deep implications for the larger structure of Indian society, since they encouraged further development of the caste system.

Castes and Guilds

As trade and industrial activity expanded, new groups of artisans, craftsmen, and merchants appeared, many of whom who did not fit easily in the established structure. Individuals working in the same craft or trade usually joined together to form a guild, a corporate body that supervised prices and wages in a given industry and provided for the welfare of members and their families. Guild members lived in the same quarter of town, socialized with each other, intermarried, and cared for the group's widows, orphans, and needy.

In effect, the guilds functioned as subcastes, known as *jati,* based on occupation. In fact, *jati* assumed much of the responsibility for maintaining social order in India. *Jati* regularly organized their own courts, through which they disciplined guild members, resolved differences, and regulated community affairs. Individuals who did not abide by group rules were liable to expulsion from the community. These outcastes then had to make their way through life—often by working as butchers, leather tanners, or undertakers or in other occupations deemed low and unclean—without the networks of support provided by *jati.* Thus Indian guilds and *jati* performed services that central governments provided in other lands. The tendency for individuals and their families to associate closely with others of the same occupation remained a prominent feature of Indian society well into modern times.

Wealth and the Social Order

Beyond encouraging further development of the caste system, economic development in the subcontinent also generated tremendous wealth, which posed a serious challenge to the social order that arose in India following the Aryan migrations. Traditional social theory accorded special honor to the *brahmins* and *kshatriyas* because of the worthy lives they had led during previous incarnations and the heavy responsibilities they assumed as priests, warriors, and rulers during their current incarnations. Members of the *vaishya* and *shudra* castes, on the other hand, merited no special respect, but rather had the obligation to work as directed by the higher castes. During the centuries after 600 B.C.E., however, trade and industry brought prosperity to many *vaishyas* and even *shudras,* who sometimes became wealthier and more influential in society than their *brahmin* and *kshatriya* contemporaries.

Economic development and social change in classical India had profound implications for the established cultural as well as the social order. The beliefs, values, and rituals that were meaningful in early Aryan society seemed increasingly irrelevant during the centuries after 600 B.C.E. Along with emerging towns, growing trade, increasing wealth, and a developing social structure, classical India also saw the appearance of new religions that addressed the needs of the changing times.

RELIGIONS OF SALVATION IN CLASSICAL INDIA

Ancient Indian religion revolved around ritual sacrifices offered by *brahmin* priests in hopes that the gods would reward their loyal human servants with large harvests and abundant herds. Since they performed services deemed crucial for the survival of society, the *brahmins* enjoyed exemption from taxation. They also received hefty fees and generous gifts in return for their services. As the Indian economy developed, however, these services seemed less meaningful than they had before, especially to the newly wealthy classes of merchants and artisans. Many of these individuals came from the lower castes, and they resented the *brahmins'* pretensions to superiority.

During the sixth and fifth centuries B.C.E., a rash of new religions and philosophies rejected the *brahmins'* cults and appealed to the interests of new social classes. Some of them tended toward atheistic materialism: members of the Charvaka sect, for example, believed that the gods were figments of the imagination, that *brahmins* were charlatans who enriched themselves by hoodwinking others, and that human beings came from dust and returned to dust like any other animal in the natural world. The Charvakas' beliefs clearly reflected the increasingly materialistic character of Indian society and economy. Others, like the Jains, Buddhists, and Hindus, turned to intense spirituality as an alternative to the mechanical rituals of the *brahmins.*

Jainism and the Challenge to the Established Cultural Order

Among the most influential of the new religions was Jainism. Although Jainist doctrines first appeared during the seventh century B.C.E., they became popular only when the great teacher Vardhamana Mahavira turned to Jainism in the late sixth century B.C.E. Mahavira ("the great hero") was born in northern India about 540 B.C.E. to a prominent *kshatriya* family. According to the semilegendary accounts of his life, he left home at the age of thirty to seek salvation by escaping from the cycle of incarnation. For twelve years he led an ascetic life wandering throughout the Ganges valley, after which he gained enlightenment. He abandoned all his worldly goods, even his clothes, and taught an ascetic doctrine of detachment from the world. For the next thirty years, until his death about 468 B.C.E., he expounded his thought to a group of dedicated disciples who formed a monastic order to perpetuate and spread his message. These disciples referred to Mahavira as *Jina* ("the conqueror"), and borrowing from this title his followers referred to themselves as *Jains.*

Vardhamana Mahavira

Mahavira with one of his disciples. Representations of the early Jains often depict them in the nude because of their ascetic lifestyle. • © The British Museum

Much of the inspiration for Jainist doctrine came from the Upanishads. Jains believed that everything in the universe—humans, animals, plants, the air, bodies of water, and even inanimate physical objects such as rocks—possessed a soul. As long as they remained trapped in terrestrial bodies, these souls experienced both physical and psychological suffering. Only by purification from selfish behavior could souls gain release from their imprisonment, shed the burdens of karma that they had accumulated during their various incarnations, and attain a state of bliss.

Individuals underwent purification by observing the principle of *ahimsa,* or nonviolence to other living things or their souls. Devout Jain monks went to extremes to avoid harming the millions of souls they

Jainist Ethics   encountered each day. They swept the ground before them as they walked to avoid causing harm to invisible insects; they strained their drinking water through cloth filters to remove tiny animals they might unwittingly consume; they followed an abstemious and strictly vegetarian diet; they even wore masks and avoided making sudden movements so that they would not bruise or otherwise disturb the tiny souls inhabiting the surrounding air.

Jainist ethics were so demanding that few people other than devout monks could hope to observe them closely. The Jains believed that almost all occupations inevitably entailed violence of some kind: farming involved the killing of pests and the harvesting of living plants, for example, while crafts like leather tanning depended on the slaughter of animals. Thus for most people Jainism was not a practical alternative to the religion of the *brahmins.*

Appeal of Jainism   For certain groups, however, Jainism represented an attractive alternative to the traditional cults. Jainist values and ethics had significant social implications. If all creatures possessed souls and participated in the ultimate reality of the world, it made little sense to draw sharp distinctions between different classes of human beings. As a result, the Jains did not recognize social hierarchies based on caste or *jati.* It is not surprising, then, that their faith became popular especially among members of lower castes who did not command much respect in the traditional social order, including merchants, scholars, and literary figures. In a typical day, individuals in these classes did little overt violence to other creatures or their souls, and they appreciated the spiritual sensitivity and the high moral standards that Jainism encouraged. They provided substantial lay support for the Jainist monks and helped to maintain the ideal of *ahimsa* as a prominent concern of Indian ethics. Their ascetic tradition continues even in the present day: some two million Indians currently identify themselves as Jains.

In spite of the moral respect it has commanded and the influence it has wielded through the centuries, however, Jainism has always been the faith of a small minority. It has simply been too difficult—or even impossible—for most people to observe. A more popular and practical alternative to the *brahmins'* cults came in the form of Buddhism.

Early Buddhism

Like Mahavira, the founder of Buddhism came from a *kshatriya* family, but he gave up his position and inheritance in order to seek salvation. His name was Siddhartha Gautama, born about 563 B.C.E. in a small tribal state governed by his father in the foothills of the Himalayas. According to early accounts, Gautama lived a pampered and sheltered life in palaces and parks, because his father had determined that Gautama would experience only happiness and would never know misery. He married his cousin and excelled in the program of studies that would prepare him to succeed his father as governor.

Siddhartha Gautama

Eventually, however, Gautama became dissatisfied with his comfortable life. One day, according to an early legend, while riding toward a park in his chariot, Gautama saw a man made miserable by age and infirmity. When he asked for an explanation of this unsettling sight, Gautama learned from his chariot driver that human beings grow old and weak. On later outings Gautama saw a sick man and a corpse, from whose fates he learned that disease and death were also inevitable features of the human condition. Finally Gautama noticed a monk traveling by foot in his distinctive dress, and he learned that some individuals withdraw from the active life of the world to lead holy lives and to perfect their spiritual qualities. In light of the misery he had previously witnessed, Gautama considered the monk a noble character and determined to take up an ascetic, wandering life for himself in the hope that it would help him to understand the phenomenon of suffering. Though not a strictly historical account, this story conveys well the Buddhist concern with suffering.

About 534 B.C.E. Gautama left his wife, family, and the comforts of home to lead the existence of a holy man. He wandered throughout the Ganges valley searching for spiritual enlightenment and an explanation for suffering. He survived for awhile by begging for his food but then abandoned society altogether to live as a hermit. He sought enlightenment first by means of intense meditation and later through the rigors of extreme asceticism. None of these tactics satisfied him. Then, according to Buddhist legends, as he sat one day beneath a large bo tree in Bodh Gaya, southwest of Pataliputra, Gautama decided that he would remain exactly where he was until he understood the problem of suffering. For forty-nine days he sat in meditation as various demons tempted him with pleasures and threatened him with terrors in efforts to shake his resolution. Eventually the demons withdrew, and Gautama prevailed. After forty-nine days under the bo tree, he received enlightenment: he understood both the problem of suffering and the means by which humans could eliminate it from the world. At that point, Gautama became the Buddha—"the enlightened one."

Gautama's Search for Enlightenment

The Buddha and his
Followers

A confident and serene Buddha preaches his first
sermon at the Deer Park of Sarnath.   ● The
British Library/Oriental and India Office

Buddhist Doctrine:
The Dharma

Appeal of Buddhism

The Buddha publicly announced his doctrine for the first time about 528 B.C.E. at the Deer Park of Sarnath, near the Buddhist holy city of Banaras (modern Varanasi), in a sermon delivered to friends who had formerly been his companions in asceticism. Buddhists refer to this sermon as the "Turning of the Wheel of the Law" because it represented the beginning of the Buddha's quest to promulgate the law of righteousness. His teachings quickly attracted attention, and disciples came from all parts of the Ganges valley. He organized them into a community of monks who owned only their yellow robes and their begging bowls. They traveled on foot, preaching the Buddha's doctrine and seeking handouts for their meals. For more than forty years, the Buddha himself led his disciples throughout much of northern India in hopes of bringing spiritual enlightenment to others. About 483 B.C.E., at an age of some eighty years, he died after leaving his companions with a final message: "Decay is inherent in all component things! Work out your salvation with diligence!"

The fundamental doctrine of Buddhism, known as the Four Noble Truths, teaches that all life involves suffering; that desire is the cause of suffering; that elimination of desire brings an end to suffering; and that a disciplined life conducted in accordance with the Noble Eightfold Path brings the elimination of desire. The Noble Eightfold Path calls for individuals to lead balanced and moderate lives, rejecting both the devotion to luxury often found in human society and the regimes of extreme asceticism favored by hermits and Jains. Specifically, the Noble Eightfold Path demands right belief, right resolve, right speech, right behavior, right occupation, right effort, right contemplation, and right meditation.

A moderate lifestyle characterized by quiet contemplation, thoughtful reflection, and disciplined self-control would enable Buddhists to reduce their desires for material goods and other worldly attractions, resulting eventually in detachment from the world itself. Ultimately, they believed that this lifestyle would lead them to personal salvation, which for Buddhists meant an escape from the cycle of incarnation and attainment of *nirvana,* a state of perfect spiritual independence. Taken together, the teachings of the Four Noble Truths and the Noble Eightfold Path constitute the *dharma*—the basic doctrine shared by Buddhists of all sects.

Like the Jains, the Buddhists sought to escape the cycle of incarnation without depending on the services of the *brahmins.* Like the Jains, too, they did not recognize social distinctions based on caste or *jati.* As a result, their message appealed strongly to members of lower castes. Because it did not demand the rigorous asceticism of Jainism, Buddhism became far more popular. Merchants were especially prominent in the ranks of the early Buddhists, and they often used Buddhist monasteries as inns when they traveled through northern India.

Apart from the social implications of the doctrine, there were several other reasons for the immense popularity of early Buddhism in India. One has to do with language. Following the example of the Buddha himself, early Buddhist monks and preachers avoided the use of Sanskrit, the literary language of the Vedas that the *brahmins* employed in their rituals, in favor of vernacular tongues that reached a much larger popular audience. Furthermore, early Buddhists recognized holy sites that served as focal points for devotion. Even in the early days of Buddhism, pilgrims flocked to Bodh Gaya, where Gautama received enlightenment, and the Deer Park of Sarnath, where as the Buddha he preached his first sermon. Also popular with the faithful were stupas—shrines housing relics of the Buddha and his first disciples that pilgrims venerated while meditating on Buddhist values.

Yet another reason for the early popularity of Buddhism was the organization of the Buddhist movement. From the days of the Buddha himself, the most enthusiastic and highly motivated converts joined monastic communities where they dedicated their lives to the search for enlightenment and salvation. Gifts and grants from pious lay supporters provided for the land, buildings, finances, and material needs of the monasteries. The monks themselves spent much of their time preaching, explaining the *dharma* to lay audiences, and encouraging their listeners to follow the Noble Eightfold Path in their daily lives. During the centuries following the Buddha's death, this monastic organization proved to be extremely efficient at spreading the Buddhist message and winning converts to the faith.

Ashoka's Support

The early Buddhist movement also benefitted from the official patronage and support of the Mauryan dynasty. The emperor Ashoka became a devout Buddhist about 260 B.C.E. after his war against Kalinga. The violence of the campaign and the suffering of the Kalingans deeply saddened him, and he decided that in the future he would pursue his aims by means of virtue, benevolence, and humanity rather than by arms. In honor of *ahimsa*, the doctrine of nonviolence, he banned animal sacrifices in Pataliputra, gave up his beloved hunting expeditions, and eliminated most meat dishes from the tables of his court. Ashoka rewarded Buddhists with grants of land, and he encouraged them to spread their faith throughout India. He built monasteries and stupas and made pilgrimages to the holy sites of Buddhism. Ashoka also sent missionaries to Bactria and Ceylon (modern Sri Lanka), thus inaugurating a process by which Buddhism attracted large followings in central Asia, east Asia, and southeast Asia.

Mahayana Buddhism

From its earliest days Buddhism attracted merchants, artisans, and others of low rank in the traditional Indian social order. Its appeal was due both to its disregard for social classes and to its concern for ethical behavior instead of complicated ceremonies that seemed increasingly irrelevant to the lives and experiences of most people. Yet even though it vastly simplified religious observances, early Buddhism made heavy demands on individuals seeking to escape from the cycle of incarnation. A truly righteous existence involved considerable sacrifice: giving up personal property, forsaking the search for social standing, and resolutely detaching oneself from the

The famous Buddhist stupa at Sanchi, originally built by Ashoka and enlarged in later times. • Foto Features

charms of family and the world. The earliest Buddhists thought that numerous physical incarnations, stretching over thousands of years, might be necessary before an individual soul would become pure enough to achieve salvation and pass into nirvana. While perhaps more attractive than the religion of the *brahmins*, Buddhism did not promise to make life easy for its adherents.

Development of Buddhism

Between the third century B.C.E. and the first century C.E., however, three new developments in Buddhist thought and practice reduced obligations of believers, opened new avenues to salvation, and brought explosive popularity to the faith. In the first place, whereas the Buddha had not considered himself divine, some of his later followers began to worship him as a god. Thus Buddhism acquired a devotional focus that helped converts channel their spiritual energies and identify more closely with their faith. In the second place, theologians articulated the notion of the *boddhisatva* ("an enlightened being"). *Boddhisatvas* were individuals who had reached spiritual perfection and merited the reward of nirvana, but who intentionally delayed their entry into nirvana in order to help others who were still struggling. Some theologians taught that *boddhisatvas* could even perform good deeds on behalf of their less spiritually inclined brethren. Like Christian saints, *boddhisatvas* served as examples of spiritual excellence, and they provided a source of inspiration. Finally, Buddhist monasteries began to accept gifts from wealthy individuals and to regard the bequests as acts of generosity that merited salvation. Thus wealthy individuals could enjoy the comforts of the world, avoid the sacrifices demanded by early Buddhist teachings, and still ensure their salvation.

Since these innovations opened the road to salvation for large numbers of people, their proponents called their faith the *Mahayana* ("the greater vehicle," which could carry more people to salvation), as opposed to the *Hinayana* ("the lesser vehicle"), a pejorative term for the earlier and stricter doctrine known also as Theravada Buddhism. During the early centuries C.E., Mahayana Buddhism spread rapidly throughout India and attracted many converts from lay and wealthy classes. In later centuries Mahayana Buddhism became established also in central Asia, China, Japan, and Korea. The stricter Theravada faith did not disappear: it remained the dominant school of Buddhism in Ceylon, and in later centuries it spread also to Burma, Thailand, and other parts of southeast Asia. Since the first century C.E., however, most of the world's Buddhists have sought to ride the greater vehicle to salvation.

Mahayana Buddhism flourished because of its popularity and partly also because of educational institutions that efficiently promoted the faith. During the Vedic era Indian education was mostly an informal affair involving a sage and his students. When Jains and Buddhists organized monasteries, however, they

The Spread of Mahayana Buddhism

Carving of a boddhisatva from the second or third century C.E. This carving perhaps represents Avalokitesvara, also known as the Lord of Compassion. Almost as perfect as the Buddha, Avalokitesvara had a reputation for protecting merchants and sailors, helping women conceive, and turning enemies into kind-hearted friends. • The James W. and Marilynn Alsdorf Collection, AL.110 Photograph by Michael Tropea. Photograph © 1998 The Art Institute of Chicago. All rights reserved.

began to offer regular instruction and established educational institutions. Most monasteries provided basic education, and larger communities offered advanced instruction as well. Best known of all was the Buddhist monastery at Nalanda, founded during the Gupta dynasty in the Ganges River valley near Pataliputra. At Nalanda it was possible to study not only Buddhism but also the Vedas, Hindu philosophy, logic, and medicine. Nalanda soon became so famous as an educational center that pilgrims and students from foreign lands traveled there to study with the most renowned masters of Buddhist doctrine. By the end of the Gupta dynasty, several thousand students may have been in residence there.

Nalanda

The Emergence of Popular Hinduism

As Buddhism generated new ideas and increased its popularity, Hinduism underwent a similar evolution that transformed it into a popular religion of salvation. While drawing inspiration from the Vedas and Upanishads, popular Hinduism increasingly departed from the older traditions of the *brahmins*. As in the case of Mahayana Buddhism, changes in doctrine and observances resulted in a faith that addressed the interests and met the needs of ordinary people.

The Epics   The great epic poems, the *Mahabharata* and the *Ramayana,* illustrate the development of Hindu values. Both works originated as secular tales transmitted orally during the late years of the Vedic age (1500–500 B.C.E.). *Brahmin* scholars revised them and committed them to writing probably during the early centuries C.E. The *Mahabharata* dealt with a massive war for the control of northern India between two groups of cousins. Though originally a purely secular work, the *brahmins* made a prominent place in the poem for the god Vishnu, the preserver of the world who intervened frequently on behalf of virtuous individuals.

The *Ramayana* too was originally a love and adventure story involving the trials faced by the legendary Prince Rama and his loyal wife Sita. Rama went to great lengths to rescue Sita after the demon king of Ceylon kidnapped her, and his alliance with Hanuman, general of the monkeys, led to exciting clashes with his enemies. Later *brahmin* editors made Rama an incarnation of Vishnu, and they portrayed Rama and Sita as the ideal Hindu husband and wife, devoted and loyal to each other even in times of immense difficulty.

The Bhagavad Gita   A short poetic work known as the *Bhagavad Gita* ("song of the lord") best illustrates both the expectations that Hinduism made of individuals and the promise of salvation that it held out to them. The *Gita* was the work of many hands, and the date of its composition is uncertain. Scholars have placed it at various points between 300 B.C.E. and 300 C.E., and it most likely underwent several rounds of revision before taking on its final form about 400 C.E. Yet it eloquently evokes the cultural climate of India between the Mauryan and the Gupta dynasties.

The work is a self-contained episode of the *Mahabharata*. It presents a dialogue between Arjuna, a *kshatriya* warrior about to enter battle, and his charioteer Krishna, who was in fact a human incarnation of the god Vishnu. The immediate problem addressed in the work was Arjuna's reluctance to fight: the enemy included many of his friends and relatives, and even though he recognized the justice of his cause, he shrank from the conflict. In an effort to persuade the warrior to fight, Krishna presented Arjuna with several lines of argument. In the first place, he said, Arjuna must not worry about harming his friends and relatives, because the soul does not die with the human body. Arjuna's weapons did not have the power to touch the soul, so he could never harm or kill another person in any meaningful way.

Krishna also held that Arjuna's caste imposed specific moral duties and social responsibilities upon him. The duty of *shudras* was to serve, of *vaishyas* to work, of *brahmins* to learn the scriptures and seek wisdom. Similarly, Krishna argued, the duty of *kshatriyas* was to govern and fight. Indeed, Krishna went further and held that an individual's social responsibilities had spiritual significance. He told Arjuna that failure to fulfill caste duties was a grievous sin, whereas their observance brought spiritual benefits.

Hindu Ethics   Hindu ethics thus differed considerably from those of earlier Indian moralists. The Upanishads had taught that only through renunciation and detachment from the world could individuals escape the cycle of incarnation. As represented in the *Bhagavad Gita,* however, Hindu ethical teachings made life much easier for the lay classes by holding out the promise of salvation precisely to those who participated actively in the world and met their caste responsibilities. To be sure, Krishna taught that individuals should meet their responsibilities in detached fashion: they should not become personally or emotionally involved in their actions, and they especially should not strive for material reward or recognition. Rather, they should perform their duties faithfully, concentrating on their actions alone, with no thought as to their consequences.

CASTE DUTIES ACCORDING TO THE *BHAGAVAD GITA*

· · ·

In urging Arjuna to enter battle, Krishna pointed out that Arjuna could not harm the immortal souls of his family and friends on the other side. Beyond that, however, Krishna emphasized the duty to fight that Arjuna inherited as a member of the kshatriya caste. Yet Krishna also counseled Arjuna to perform his duty in a spirit of detachment, not caring for victory or defeat.

As a man, casting off old clothes, puts on others and new ones, so the embodied self, casting off old bodies, goes to others and new ones. Weapons do not divide the self into pieces; fire does not burn it; waters do not moisten it; the wind does not dry it up. It is not divisible; it is not combustible; it is not to be moistened; it is not to be dried up. It is everlasting, all-pervading, stable, firm, and eternal. It is said to be unperceived, to be unthinkable, to be unchangeable. Therefore knowing it to be such, you ought not to grieve. But even if you think that the self is constantly born, and constantly dies, still, O you of mighty arms, you ought not to grieve thus. For to one that is born, death is certain; and to one that dies, birth is certain. Therefore about this unavoidable thing, you ought not to grieve. . . .

Having regard to your own duty, you ought not to falter, for there is nothing better for a *kshatriya* than a righteous battle. Happy those *kshatriyas* who can find such a battle—an open door to heaven! But if you will not fight this righteous battle, then you will have abandoned your own duty and your fame, and you will incur sin. All beings, too, will tell of your everlasting infamy; and to one who has been honored, infamy is a greater evil than death. Warriors who are masters of great chariots will think that you have abstained from the battle

through fear, and having been highly thought of by them, you will fall down to littleness. Your enemies, too, decrying your power, will speak much about you that should not be spoken. And what, indeed, could be more lamentable than that? Killed, you will obtain heaven; victorious, you will enjoy the earth. Therefore arise, resolved to engage in battle. Looking on pleasure and pain, on gain and loss, on victory and defeat as the same, prepare for battle, and thus you will not incur sin. . . .

The state of mind that consists in firm understanding regarding steady contemplation does not belong to those who are strongly attached to worldly pleasures and power, and whose minds are drawn away by that flowery talk that is full of specific acts for the attainment of pleasures and power, and that promises birth as the fruit of actions—that flowery talk uttered by unwise ones who are enamored of Vedic words, who say there is nothing else, who are full of desires, and whose goal is heaven. . . .

Your business is with action alone, not by any means with the fruit of the action. Let not the fruit of action be your motive to action. Let not your attachment be fixed on inaction. Having recourse to devotion, perform actions, casting off all attachment, and being equable in success or ill success.

SOURCE: *the Bhagavad Gita*. trans. by Kashinath Trimbak Telang in F. Max Müller, ed. *The Sacred Books of the East*, vol. 8. Oxford: Clarendon Press, 1908, pp. 45–48. (Translation slightly modified.)

In other works early Hindu moralists acknowledged even more openly than did the *Bhagavad Gita* that individuals could lead honorable lives in the world. Indeed, Hindu ethics commonly recognized four principal aims of human life: obedience to religious and moral laws (*dharma*), the pursuit of economic well-being and honest prosperity (*artha*), the enjoyment of social, physical, and sexual pleasure (*kama*), and the salvation of the soul (*moksha*). According to Hindu moral precepts, a proper balance of *dharma, artha,* and *kama* would help an individual to attain *moksha*.

As devotional Hinduism evolved and became increasingly distinct from the teachings of the Upanishads and the older traditions of the *brahmins,* it also enhanced its appeal to all segments of Indian society. Hinduism offered salvation to masses of people who, as a matter of practical necessity, had to lead active lives in the world and thus could not even hope to achieve the detachment envisioned in the Upanishads.

Popularity of Hinduism

Hinduism gradually displaced Buddhism as the most popular religion in India. Buddhism remained strong through much of the first millennium C.E., and until about the eighth century pilgrims traveled to India from as far away as China to visit the holy sites of Buddhism and learn about the faith in its original homeland. Within India itself, however, Buddhism grew remote from the popular masses. Later Buddhist monks did not seek to communicate their message to the larger society in the zealous way of their predecessors, but increasingly confined themselves to the comforts of monasteries richly endowed by wealthy patrons.

Meanwhile, devotional Hinduism also attracted political support and patronage, most notably from the Gupta emperors. The Guptas and their successors bestowed grants of land on Hindu *brahmins* and supported an educational system that promoted Hindu values. Just as Ashoka Maurya had advanced the cause of Buddhism, the Guptas and their successors later helped Hinduism become the dominant religious and cultural tradition in India. By about 1000 C.E., Buddhism had entered a noticeable decline in India while Hinduism grew in popularity. Within a few centuries devotional Hinduism and the more recently introduced faith of Islam almost completely eclipsed Buddhism in its homeland.

As in classical Persia and China, a robust agricultural economy supported the creation of large-scale states and interregional trade in India. Although an imperial state did not become a permanent feature of Indian political life, the peoples of the subcontinent maintained an orderly society based on the caste system. Indian cultural and religious traditions reflected the conditions of the larger society in which they developed. Mahayana Buddhism and devotional Hinduism in particular addressed the needs of the increasingly prominent lay classes, and the two faiths profoundly influenced the religious life of Asian peoples over the long term of history.

CHRONOLOGY

563–483 B.C.E.	Life of Siddartha Gautama, the Buddha
540–468 B.C.E.	Life of Vardhamana Mahavira
520 B.C.E.	Invasion of India by Cyrus of Persia
327 B.C.E.	Invasion of India by Alexander of Macedon
321–185 B.C.E.	Mauryan dynasty
321–297 B.C.E.	Reign of Chandragupta Maurya
268–232 B.C.E.	Reign of Ashoka Maurya
320–550 C.E.	Gupta dynasty

FOR FURTHER READING

Roy C. Amore and Larry D. Shinn. *Lustful Maidens and Ascetic Kings.* New York, 1981. Translations of stories and moral tales from Hindu and Buddhist writings.

Jeannine Auboyer. *Daily Life in Ancient India.* Trans. by S. W. Taylor. New York, 1965. An excellent and well-researched, though somewhat dated, introduction to Indian social history during the classical era.

A. L. Basham. *The Wonder That Was India.* New York, 1954. Popular survey by a leading scholar of early Indian history.

Edward Conze. *Buddhism: Its Essence and Development.* New York, 1959. Systematic account of Buddhism from a theological point of view.

William Theodore De Bary, ed. *Sources of Indian Tradition.* 2 vols. 2nd ed. New York, 1988. Important collection of sources in translation.

Kautalya. *The Kautilya Arthashastra.* 3 vols. 2nd ed. Ed. by R. P. Kangle. Bombay, 1960–69. Translation of the most important political treatise of classical India.

Juan Mascaró, trans. *The Bhagavad Gita.* Harmondsworth, 1962. Brilliant and evocative English version by a gifted translator.

William H. McNeill and Jean W. Sedlar, eds. *Classical India.* New York, 1969. Collection of primary sources in translation.

Jean W. Sedlar. *India and the Greek World: A Study in the Transmission of Culture.* Totowa, N.J., 1980. Important study of relations between India and Greece, based on solid research.

Romila Thapar. *A History of India,* vol. 1. Harmondsworth, 1966. Popular account by one of the leading scholars of early Indian history.

Mortimer Wheeler. *Flames over Persepolis.* New York, 1968. Examines the influence of Greek and Persian traditions in northern India after the time of Alexander of Macedon.

CHAPTER 9

MEDITERRANEAN SOCIETY: THE GREEK PHASE

· · ·

For a man who perhaps never existed, Homer has been a profoundly influential figure. According to tradition, Homer composed the two great epic poems of ancient Greece, the *Iliad* and the *Odyssey*. In fact, scholars now know that bards recited both poems for generations before Homer lived—the mid-eighth century B.C.E., if he was indeed a historical figure. Some experts believe that Homer was not a real man so much as a convenient name for several otherwise anonymous scribes who committed the *Iliad* and the *Odyssey* to writing. Others believe that a man named Homer had a part in preparing a written version of the epics, but that others also contributed significantly to his work.

Whether Homer ever really lived or not, the epics attributed to him profoundly influenced the development of classical Greek thought and literature. The *Iliad* offered a Greek perspective on a war waged by a band of Greek warriors against the city of Troy in Anatolia during the twelfth century B.C.E. The *Odyssey* recounted the experiences of the Greek hero Odysseus as he sailed home after the Trojan war. The two works described scores of difficulties faced by Greek warriors—not only battles with Trojans, but also challenges posed by deities and monsters, conflicts among themselves, and even psychological barriers that individuals had to surmount. Between them, the two epics preserved a rich collection of stories that literary figures mined for more than a millennium, reworking Homer's material and exploring his themes from fresh perspectives.

Quite apart from their significance as literary masterpieces, the *Iliad* and the *Odyssey* also testify to the frequency and normality of travel, communication, and interaction in the Mediterranean basin during the second and first millennia B.C.E. Both works portray Greeks as expert and fearless seamen, almost as comfortable aboard their ships as on land, who did not hesitate to venture into the waters of what Homer called the "wine-dark sea" in pursuit of their goals. Homer lovingly described the sleek galleys in which Greek warriors raced across the waters, sometimes to plunder the slower but heavily laden cargo vessels that plied the Mediterranean sea lanes, more often to launch strikes at enemy targets. He even had Odysseus construct a sailing ship singlehandedly when he found himself shipwrecked on an island inhabited only by a goddess. The *Iliad* and the *Odyssey* make it clear that maritime links touched peoples throughout the Mediterranean basin in Homer's time, and further that Greeks were among the most prominent seafarers of the age.

The theater at Delphi. • Jose Fuste Raga/The Stock Market

Already during the second millennium B.C.E., Phoenician merchants had established links between lands and peoples at the far ends of the Mediterranean Sea. During the classical era, however, the Mediterranean basin became much more tightly integrated than before as Greeks, and later Romans, organized commercial exchange and sponsored interaction throughout the region. Under Greek and Roman supervision, the Mediterranean served not as a barrier, but rather as a highway linking Anatolia, Egypt, Greece, Italy, France, Spain, north Africa, and even southern Russia (by way of routes through the Black Sea).

Ancient Greece differed from classical societies in other lands. For most of the classical era, the Greeks lived in independent, autonomous city-states. Only after the late third century B.C.E. did they play prominent roles in the large, centralized empire established by their neighbors to the north in Macedon. Yet from the seventh through the second centuries B.C.E., the Greeks integrated the societies and economies of distant lands through energetic commercial activity over the Mediterranean sea lanes. They also generated a remarkable body of moral thought and philosophical reflection. Just as the traditions of classical Persia, China, and India shaped the cultural experiences of those lands, the traditions of the Greeks profoundly influenced the long-term cultural development of the Mediterranean basin, Europe, and southwest Asia as well.

EARLY DEVELOPMENT OF GREEK SOCIETY

Humans inhabited the Balkan region and the Greek peninsula from an early but indeterminate date. During the third millennium B.C.E., they increasingly met and mingled with peoples from different societies who traveled and traded in the Mediterranean basin. As a result, early inhabitants of the Greek peninsula built their societies under the influence of Mesopotamians, Egyptians, Phoenicians, and others active in the region. Beginning in the ninth century B.C.E., the Greeks organized a series of city-states, which served as the political context for the development of classical Greek society.

Minoan and Mycenaean Societies

Knossos During the late third millennium B.C.E., a sophisticated society arose on the island of Crete. Scholars refer to it as Minoan society, after Minos, a legendary king of ancient Crete. Between 2000 and 1700 B.C.E., the inhabitants of Crete built a series of lavish palaces throughout the island, most notably the enormous complex at Knossos decorated with vivid frescos depicting Minoans at work and play. These palaces were the nerve centers of Minoan society: they were residences of rulers, and they also served as storehouses where officials collected taxes in kind from local cultivators. Palace officials devised a script known as Linear A, in which written symbols stood for syllables rather than words, ideas, vowels, or consonants. Although linguists have not yet been able to decipher Linear A, it is clear that Cretan administrators used the script to keep detailed records of economic and commercial matters.

Between 2200 and 1450 B.C.E., Crete was a principal center of Mediterranean commerce. Due to its geographical location in the east-central Mediterranean, Crete received early influences from Phoenicia and Egypt. By 2200 B.C.E. Cretans were

In this wall painting from Knossos known as the *toreador* fresco, Minoan athletes leap over the horns of a bull. The individual at the right will catch his companion who is bounding over the bull. ● Erich Lessing/Art Resource, NY

traveling aboard advanced sailing craft of Phoenician design. Minoan ships sailed to Greece, Anatolia, Phoenicia, and Egypt, where they exchanged Cretan wine, olive oil, and wool for grains, textiles, and manufactured goods. Archaeologists have discovered pottery vessels used as storage containers for Minoan wine and olive oil as far away as Sicily. After 1600 B.C.E. Cretans established colonies on Cyprus and many islands in the Aegean Sea, probably to mine local copper ores and gain better access to markets where tin was available.

Decline of Minoan Society

After 1700 B.C.E. Minoan society experienced a series of earthquakes, volcanic eruptions, and tidal waves. Most destructive was a massive volcanic eruption about 1628 B.C.E. on the island of Thera (Santorini) north of Crete. Between 1600 and 1450 B.C.E., Cretans embarked on a new round of palace building to replace structures destroyed by these natural catastrophes: they built luxurious complexes with indoor plumbing and drainage systems and even furnished some of them with flush toilets. After 1450 B.C.E., however, the wealth of Minoan society attracted a series of invaders, and by 1100 B.C.E. Crete had fallen under foreign domination. Yet the Minoan traditions of maritime trade, writing, and construction deeply influenced the inhabitants of nearby Greece.

Mycenaean Society

Beginning about 2000 B.C.E. migratory Indo-European peoples filtered over the Balkans and into the Greek peninsula. By 1600 B.C.E. they had begun to trade with Minoan merchants and visit Crete, where they learned about writing and large-scale construction. They adapted Minoan Linear A to their own language, which was an

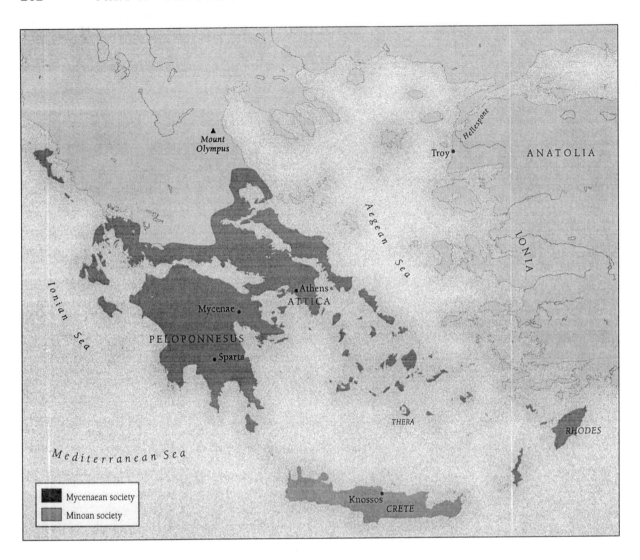

MAP [9.1]

Early Greece.

early form of Greek, and devised a syllabic script known as Linear B. After 1450 B.C.E. they also built massive stone fortresses and palaces throughout the southern part of the Greek peninsula, known as the Peloponnesus. Because the fortified sites offered protection, they soon attracted settlers who built small agricultural communities. Their society is known as Mycenaean, after Mycenae, one of their most important settlements.

From 1500 to 1100 B.C.E., the Mycenaeans expanded their influence beyond peninsular Greece. They largely overpowered Minoan society, and they took over the Cretan palaces, where they established craft workshops. Archaeologists have unearthed thousands of clay tablets in Linear B that came from the archives of Mycenaean rulers in Crete as well as peninsular Greece. The Mycenaeans also established settlements in Anatolia, Sicily, and southern Italy.

Chaos in the
Eastern
Mediterranean

About 1200 B.C.E. the Mycenaeans engaged in a conflict with the city of Troy in Anatolia. This Trojan war, which Homer recalled from a Greek perspective in his *Iliad*, coincided with invasions of foreign mariners in the Mycenaean homeland. Indeed, from

1100 to 800 B.C.E. chaos reigned throughout the eastern Mediterranean region. Invasions and civil disturbances made it impossible to maintain stable governments or even productive agricultural societies. Mycenaean palaces fell into ruin, the population sharply declined, and people abandoned most settlements. Many inhabitants of the Greek peninsula fled to the islands of the Aegean Sea, Anatolia, or Cyprus. Writing in both Linear A and Linear B disappeared. The boisterous character of the era comes across clearly in Homer's works. Though set in an earlier era, both the *Iliad* and the *Odyssey* reflect the tumultuous centuries after 1100 B.C.E. They portray a society riven with conflict, and they recount innumerable episodes of aggression, treachery, and violence alongside heroic bravery and courage.

The Lion Gate at Mycenae illustrates the heavy fortifications built by Myceneans to protect their settlements. • Walter S. Clark/ Photo Researchers, Inc.

The World of the Polis

In the absence of a centralized state or empire, local institutions took the lead in restoring political order in Greece. The most important institution was the city-state or polis. The term *polis* originally referred to a citadel or fortified site that offered refuge for local communities during times of war or other emergencies. These sites attracted increasing populations, and many of them gradually became lively commercial centers. They took on an increasingly urban character and extended their authority over surrounding regions. They levied taxes on their hinterlands and appropriated a portion of the agricultural surplus to support the urban population. By about 800 B.C.E. many poleis (the plural of polis) had become bustling city-states that functioned as the principal centers of Greek society.

The Polis

The poleis took various political forms. Some differences reflected the fact that poleis emerged independently and elaborated their traditions with little outside influence. Others arose from different rates of economic development. A few developed as small monarchies, but most were under the collective rule of local notables.

Many fell into the hands of generals or ambitious politicians—called "tyrants" by the Greeks—who gained power by irregular means. (The tyrants were not necessarily oppressive despots: indeed, many of them were extremely popular leaders. The term *tyrant* referred to their routes to power rather than their policies.) The most important of the poleis were Sparta and Athens, whose contrasting constitutions help to illustrate the variety of political styles in classical Greece.

Sparta

Sparta was situated in a fertile region of the Peloponnesus. As their population and economy expanded during the eighth and seventh centuries B.C.E., the Spartans progressively extended their control over the Peloponnesus. In doing so, they reduced neighboring peoples to the status of *helots,* servants of the Spartan state. Although they were not slaves, the helots also were not free. They could form families, but they could not leave the land. Their role in society was to provide agricultural labor and keep Sparta supplied with food. By the sixth century B.C.E., the helots probably outnumbered the Spartan citizens themselves by more than ten to one. With their large subject population, the Spartans were able to cultivate the Peloponnesus efficiently, but they also faced the constant threat of rebellion. As a result, the Spartans devoted most of their resources to maintaining a powerful and disciplined military machine.

Spartan Society

In theory, all Spartan citizens were equal in status. To discourage the development of economic and social distinctions, Spartans observed an extraordinarily austere lifestyle as a matter of policy. They did not wear jewelry or elaborate clothes, nor did they pamper themselves with luxuries or accumulate private wealth on a large scale. They generally did not even circulate coins made of precious metals, but instead used iron bars for money. It is for good reason, then, that our adjective *spartan* refers to a lifestyle characterized by simplicity, frugality, and austerity.

A painted cup produced in Sparta about 550 B.C.E. depicts hunters attacking a boar. Spartans regarded hunting as an exercise that helped to sharpen fighting skills and aggressive instincts. ●
Louvre/©Photo RMN-H. Lewandowski

Distinction among the ancient Spartans came not by wealth or social status, but by prowess, discipline, and military talent, which the Spartan educational system cultivated from an early age. All boys from families of Spartan citizens left their homes at age seven and went to live in military barracks, where they underwent a rigorous regime of physical training. At age twenty they began active military service, which they continued until retirement. Spartan authorities also prescribed vigorous physical exercise for girls in hopes that they would bear strong children. When they reached eighteen to twenty years of age, young women married and had occasional sexual relations, but did not live with their husbands. Only at about age thirty did men leave the barracks and set up a household with their wives and children.

By the fourth century B.C.E., Spartan society had lost much of its ascetic rigor. Aristocratic families had accumulated great wealth, and Spartans had developed a taste for luxury in food and dress. Nevertheless, Spartan society stood basically on the foundation of military discipline, and its institutions both reflected and reinforced the larger society's commitment to military values. In effect, Sparta sought to maintain public order—and discourage rebellion by the helots—by creating a military state that could crush any threat.

In Athens as in Sparta, population growth and economic development caused political and social strain, but the Athenians relieved tensions by establishing a government based on democratic principles. Whereas Sparta sought to impose order by military means, Athens sought to negotiate order by considering the interests of the polis's various constituencies. Citizenship was by no means open to all residents: only free adult males from Athens played a role in public affairs, leaving foreigners, slaves, and women with no direct voice in government. In seeking to resolve social problems, Athenians opened government offices to all citizens and broadened the base of political participation in classical Greece.

Athens

During the seventh century B.C.E., an increasing volume of maritime trade brought prosperity to Attica, the region around Athens. The principal beneficiaries of this prosperity were aristocratic landowners, who also controlled the Athenian government. As their wealth grew, the aristocrats increased their landholdings and cultivated them with greater efficiency. Owners of small plots could not compete and fell heavily into debt. Competitive pressures often forced them to sell their holdings to aristocrats, and debt burdens sometimes overwhelmed them and pushed them into slavery.

Athenian Society

By the early sixth century B.C.E., Attica had a large and growing class of people extremely unhappy with the structure of their society and poised to engage in war against their wealthy neighbors. Many poleis that experienced similar economic conditions suffered decades of brutal civil war between aristocrats and less privileged classes. In Athens, however, an aristocrat named Solon served as a mediator between classes, and he devised a solution to class conflict in Attica.

Solon forged a compromise between the classes. He allowed aristocrats to keep their lands—rather than confiscate them and redistribute them to landless individuals, as many preferred—but he cancelled debts, forbade debt slavery, and liberated those already enslaved for debt. To ensure that aristocrats would not undermine his reforms, Solon also provided representation for the common classes in the Athenian government by opening the councils of the polis to any citizen wealthy enough to devote time to public affairs, regardless of his lineage. Later reformers went even further. During the late sixth and fifth centuries B.C.E., Athenian leaders increased opportunities for commoners to participate in government, and they paid salaries to officeholders so financial hardship would not exclude anyone from service.

Solon and Athenian Democracy

These reforms gradually transformed Athens into a democratic state. The high tide of Athenian democracy came under the leadership of the statesman Pericles. Though he was of aristocratic birth, Pericles was the most popular Athenian leader from 443 B.C.E. until his death in 429 B.C.E. He wielded enormous personal influence in a government with hundreds of officeholders from the common classes, and he supported building programs that provided employment for thousands of construction workers and laborers. Under the leadership of Pericles, Athens became the most sophisticated of the poleis, with a vibrant community of scientists,

Pericles

The image of Pericles, wearing a helmet that symbolizes his post as Athenian leader, survives in a Roman copy of a Greek statue. •
Scala/Art Resource, NY

philosophers, poets, dramatists, artists, and architects. Little wonder, then, that in a moment of civic pride, Pericles boasted that Athens was "the education of Greece."

GREECE AND THE LARGER WORLD

As the poleis prospered, Greeks became increasingly prominent in the larger world of the Mediterranean basin. They established colonies throughout the Mediterranean and the Black Sea, and they traded throughout the region. Eventually, their political and economic interests brought them into conflict with the expanding Persian empire. During the fifth century B.C.E., a round of intermittent war between the Greeks and Persians ended in stalemate, but in the next century Alexander of Macedon toppled the Achaemenid empire. Indeed, Alexander built an empire stretching from India to Egypt and Greece. His conquests created a vast zone of trade and communication that encouraged commercial and cultural exchange on an unprecedented scale.

Greek Colonization

By about 800 B.C.E. the poleis were emerging as centers of political organization in Greece. During the next century increasing population strained the resources available in the rocky and mountainous Greek peninsula. To relieve population pressures, the Greeks began to establish colonies in other parts of the Mediterranean basin. Between the mid-eighth and the late sixth centuries B.C.E., they founded more than four hundred colonies along the shores of the Mediterranean and the Black Sea.

Greek Colonies   The Greeks established their first colonies in the central Mediterranean during the early eighth century B.C.E. The most popular sites were Sicily and southern Italy, particularly the region around modern Naples, which was itself originally a Greek colony called Neapolis ("new polis"). Apart from fertile fields that yielded large agricultural surpluses, these colonies provided merchants with convenient access to the

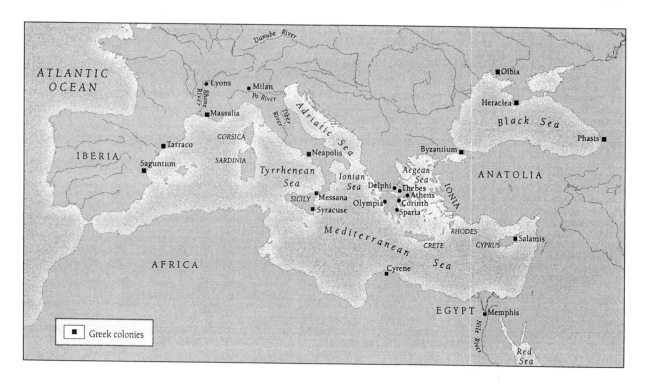

MAP [9.2]

Classical Greece and the Mediterranean basin.

copper, zinc, tin, and iron ores of central Italy. By the sixth century B.C.E., Greek colonies dotted the shores of Sicily and southern Italy, and more Greeks lived in these colonies than in the Greek peninsula itself. By 600 B.C.E. the Greeks had ventured even further west and established the important colony of Massalia (modern Marseilles) in what is now southern France.

Greek colonies arose also in the eastern Mediterranean and the Black Sea. Hundreds of islands in the Aegean Sea beckoned to a maritime people such as the Greeks. Colonists also settled in Anatolia, where their Greek cousins had established communities during the centuries of political turmoil after 1100 B.C.E. During the eighth and seventh centuries B.C.E., they ventured into the Black Sea in large numbers and established colonies all along its shores. These settlements offered merchants access to rich supplies of grain, fish, furs, timber, honey, wax, gold, and amber, as well as slaves captured in southern Russia and transported to markets in the Mediterranean.

Unlike their counterparts in classical Persia, China, and India, the Greeks did not build a centralized imperial state. Greek colonization was not a process controlled by a central government so much as an ad hoc response of individual poleis to population pressures. Colonies often did not take guidance from the poleis from which their settlers came, but rather relied on their own resources and charted their own courses.

Nevertheless, Greek colonization sponsored more communication, interaction, and exchange than ever before among Mediterranean lands and peoples. From the early eighth century B.C.E., colonies facilitated trade between their own regions and the poleis in peninsular Greece and Anatolia. At the same time, colonization spread Greek language and cultural traditions throughout the Mediterranean basin. Moreover, the Greek presence quickened the tempo of social life, especially in the western Mediterranean and the Black Sea. Except for a few urban districts surrounding

Effects of Greek Colonization

Two Greek ships under sail, a merchant vessel (left) and a galley (right) powered by oars as well as sails. • © The British Museum

Phoenician colonies in the western Mediterranean, these regions were home mostly to small-scale agricultural societies organized by clans. As Greek merchants brought wealth into these societies, local clan leaders built small states in areas like Sicily, southern Italy, southern France, the Crimean peninsula, and southern Russia where trade was especially strong. Thus Greek colonization had important political and social effects throughout the Mediterranean basin.

Conflict with Persia and Its Results

During the fifth century B.C.E., their links abroad brought the poleis of the Greek peninsula into direct conflict with the Persian empire in a long struggle known as the Persian Wars (500–479 B.C.E.). As the Persian emperors Cyrus and Darius tightened their grip on Anatolia, the Greek cities on the Ionian coast became increasingly restless. In 500 B.C.E. they revolted against Persian rule and expelled the Achaemenid administrators. In support of their fellow Greeks and commercial partners, the Athenians sent a fleet of ships to aid the Ionian effort. Despite this gesture, Darius repressed the Ionian rebellion by 493 B.C.E.

The Persian Wars   To punish the Athenians and forestall future interference in Persian affairs, Darius then mounted a campaign against peninsular Greece. In 490 B.C.E. he sent an army and a fleet of ships to attack Athens. Although greatly outnumbered, the Athenians routed the Persian army at the battle of Marathon and then marched back to Athens in time to fight off the Persian fleet.

Ten years later Darius's successor Xerxes decided to avenge the Persian losses. In 480 B.C.E. he dispatched a massive force consisting of perhaps one hundred thousand troops and a fleet of one thousand ships to subdue the Greeks. The Persian army succeeded in capturing and burning Athens, but a Greek fleet led by Athenians shattered the Persian navy at the battle of Salamis. Xerxes himself viewed the conflict from a temporary throne set up on a hillside overlooking the narrow strait of water between Athens and the island of Salamis. The following year a Greek force at Plataea routed the Persian army, whose survivors retreated to Anatolia.

Greeks and Persians continued to skirmish intermittently for more than a century, although their conflict did not expand into full-scale war. The Persian rulers were unwilling to invest resources in the effort to conquer small and distant Greece, and after Xerxes' reign, they faced domestic problems that prevented them from undertaking foreign adventures. For their part, the Greeks had neither the resources nor the desire to challenge the Persian empire, and they remained content with maintaining their independence.

Pericles organized the construction of numerous marble buildings, partly with funds collected from poleis belonging to the Delian League. Most notable of his projects was the Parthenon, a temple dedicated to the goddess Athena, which symbolizes the prosperity and grandeur of classical Athens. • G. Anderson/The Stock Market

The Delian League

Once the Persian threat subsided, however, serious conflict arose among the Greek poleis themselves. After the Persian Wars the poleis created an alliance known as the Delian League to discourage further Persian actions in Greece. Because of its superior fleet, Athens became the leader of the alliance. In effect, Athens supplied the league's military force, and the other poleis contributed financial support, which went largely to the Athenian treasury. Indeed, these contributions financed much of the Athenian bureaucracy and the vast construction projects that employed Athenian workers during the era of Pericles' leadership. In the absence of a continuing Persian threat, however, the other poleis resented having to make contributions that seemed to benefit only the Athenians.

The Peloponnesian War

Ultimately, the tensions resulted in a bitter and destructive civil conflict known as the Peloponnesian War (431–404 B.C.E.). Both in peninsular Greece and throughout the larger Greek world, poleis divided into two armed camps under the leadership of Athens and Sparta, the most powerful of the poleis and the principal contenders for hegemony in the Greek world. The fortunes of war favored first one side, then the other, but by 404 B.C.E. the Spartans and their allies had forced the Athenians to unconditional surrender. Sparta's victory soon generated new jealousies, however, and conflicts broke out again. During the decades following Athenian surrender, hegemony in the Greek world passed to Sparta, Thebes, Corinth, and other poleis. As internal struggles weakened the world of the poleis, a formidable power took shape in the north.

The Macedonians and the Coming of Empire

The Kingdom of Macedon

Until the fourth century B.C.E., the kingdom of Macedon was a frontier state north of peninsular Greece. The Macedonian population consisted partly of cultivators and partly of sheepherders who migrated seasonally between the mountains and valleys. Although the Macedonians recognized a king, semiautonomous clans controlled political affairs.

Proximity to the wealthy poleis of Greece brought change to Macedon. From the seventh century B.C.E., the Greek cities traded with Macedon. They imported grain, timber, and other natural resources in exchange for olive oil, wine, and finished products. Macedonian political and social elites, who controlled trade from their side of the border, became well acquainted with Greek merchants and their society.

Philip of Macedon

During the reign of King Philip II (359–336 B.C.E.), Macedon underwent a thorough transformation. Philip built a powerful military machine that enabled him to overcome the traditional clans and make himself the ruler of Macedon. His military force featured an infantry composed of small landowners and a cavalry staffed by aristocrats holding large estates. During the fourth century B.C.E., both elements proved to be hardy, well trained, and nearly invincible.

When Philip had consolidated his hold on Macedon, he turned his attention to two larger prizes: Greece and the Persian empire. During the years following 350 B.C.E., Philip moved into northern Greece, annexing poleis and their surrounding territories. The poleis recognized the Macedonian threat, but the Peloponnesian War had poisoned the atmosphere so much that the poleis could not agree to form an alliance against Philip. Thus as he moved into Greece, Philip faced nothing more than small forces patched together by shifting and temporary alliances. By 338 B.C.E. he had overcome all organized resistance and brought Greece under his control.

Philip intended to use his conquest of Greece as a launching pad for an invasion of Persia. He did not have the opportunity to carry out his plans, however, because an assassin brought him down in 336 B.C.E. The invasion of Persia thus fell to his son, the young Alexander of Macedon, often called Alexander the Great.

At the age of twenty, Alexander succeeded Philip as ruler of an expanding empire. He soon began to assemble an army of about thirty-seven thousand men to invade the Persian empire. Alexander was a brilliant strategist and an inspired leader, and he inherited a well-equipped, well-disciplined, highly spirited veteran force from his

Alexander of Macedon

This head of Alexander, probably sculpted during the 330s B.C.E., presents an idealized image of a vigorous, youthful conqueror. •
Hirmer Verlag

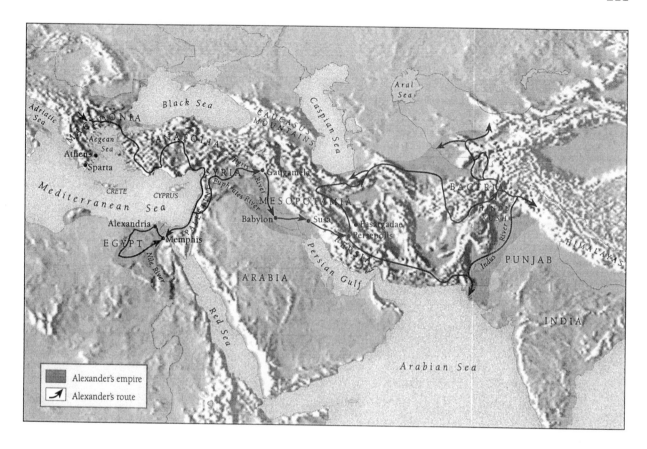

MAP [9.3]

Alexander's empire.

father. By 333 B.C.E. Alexander had subjected Ionia and Anatolia to his control; within another year he held Syria, Palestine, and Egypt; by 331 B.C.E. he controlled Mesopotamia and prepared to invade the Persian homeland. He took Pasargadae and burned the Achaemenid palace at Persepolis late in 331 B.C.E., and he pursued the dispirited Persian army for another year until the last Achaemenid ruler fell to an assassin. Alexander established himself as the new emperor of Persia in 330 B.C.E.

By 327 B.C.E. Alexander had larger ambitions: he took his army into India and crossed the Indus River, entering the Punjab. He subjected local rulers and probably would have continued to campaign in India except that his troops refused to proceed any further from home. By 324 B.C.E. Alexander and his army had returned to Susa in Mesopotamia, where they celebrated their exploits in almost continuous feasting. Alexander busied himself with plans for governing his empire and for conducting further explorations. In June of 323 B.C.E., however, after an extended round of feasting and drinking, he suddenly fell ill and died at the age of thirty-three.

During the course of a meteoric career, Alexander proved to be a brilliant conqueror, but he did not live long enough to construct a genuine state for his vast realm or to develop a system of administration. He established cities throughout the lands he conquered and reportedly named about seventy of them Alexandria in his own honor. Alexander also toyed with some intriguing ideas about governing his empire, notably a scheme to marry his officers to Persian women and create a new ruling class of Greek, Macedonian, and Persian ancestry, but his early death prevented him from turning this plan into a coherent policy. So long as he lived, he relied on established institutions such as the Persian satrapies to administer the lands he conquered.

Alexander's Conquests

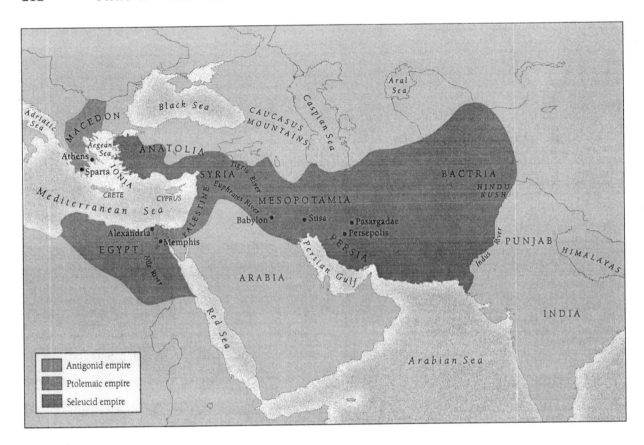

MAP [9.4]

The Hellenistic empires.

The Hellenistic Empires

When Alexander died, his generals jockeyed for position in hopes of taking over choice parts of his realm, and by 275 B.C.E. they had divided the empire into three large states. Antigonus took Greece and Macedon, which his Antigonid successors ruled until the Romans established their authority in the eastern Mediterranean during the second century B.C.E. Ptolemy took Egypt, which the Ptolemaic dynasty ruled until the Roman conquest of Egypt in 31 B.C.E. Seleucus took the largest portion, the former Achaemenid empire stretching from Bactria to Anatolia, which his Seleucid successors ruled until the Parthians displaced them during the second century B.C.E.

The Hellenistic Era   Historians refer to the age of Alexander and his successors as the Hellenistic age—an era when Greek cultural traditions expanded their influence beyond Greece itself (*Hellas*) to a much larger world. During the centuries between Alexander's death and the expansion of the Roman empire in the eastern Mediterranean, the Hellenistic empires governed cosmopolitan societies and sponsored interactions between peoples from Greece to India. Like imperial states in classical Persia, China, and India, the Hellenistic empires helped to integrate the economies and societies of distant regions. They facilitated trade, and they made it possible for beliefs, values, and religions to spread over larger distances than ever before.

The Antigonid   Although the Antigonid realm of Greece and Macedon was the smallest of the
Empire   Hellenistic empires, it benefitted handsomely from the new order. There was continual tension between the Antigonid rulers and the Greek cities, which sought to retain their independence by forming defensive leagues that stoutly resisted Antigonid

efforts to control the Greek peninsula. The poleis often struck bargains with the Antigonids, offering to recognize their rule in exchange for tax relief and local autonomy. Internal social tensions also flared, as Greeks wrestled with the perennial problem of land and its equitable distribution. Yet cities like Athens and Corinth flourished during the Hellenistic era as enormous volumes of trade passed through their ports. Moreover, the overpopulated Greek peninsula sent large numbers of colonists to newly founded cities, especially in the Seleucid empire.

The Ptolemaic Empire

Perhaps the wealthiest of the Hellenistic empires was Ptolemaic Egypt. Greek and Macedonian overlords did not interfere in Egyptian society, but contented themselves with the efficient organization of agriculture, industry, and tax collection. They maintained the irrigation networks and monitored the cultivation of crops and the payment of taxes. They also established royal monopolies over the most lucrative industries, such as textiles, salt making, and the brewing of beer.

Alexandria

Much of Egypt's wealth flowed to the Ptolemaic capital of Alexandria. Founded by Alexander at the mouth of the Nile, Alexandria served as the Ptolemies' administrative headquarters, but it became much more than a bureaucratic center. Alexandria's enormous harbor was able to accommodate 1,200 ships simultaneously, and the city soon became the most important port in the Mediterranean. Its wealth attracted migrants from all parts of the Mediterranean basin and beyond. Alongside Greeks, Macedonians, and Egyptians lived sizable communities of Phoenicians, Jews, Arabs, and Babylonians. The city was indeed an early megalopolis, where peoples of different ethnic, religious, and cultural traditions conducted their affairs. Under the Ptolemies, Alexandria also became the cultural capital of the Hellenistic world. It was the site of the famous Alexandrian Museum—a state-financed institute of higher learning where philosophical, literary, and scientific scholars carried on advanced research—and of the equally famous Alexandrian Library, which supported the scholarship sponsored by the museum and which, by the first century B.C.E., boasted a collection of more than seven hundred thousand works.

The Seleucid Empire

It was in the Seleucid realm, however, that Greek influence reached its greatest extent. The principal channels of this influence were the numerous cities that Alexander and his successors founded in the former Persian empire. Most of them were small settlements intended to serve as fortified sites or administrative centers, though some developed into thriving commercial centers. Greek and Macedonian colonists flocked to these cities, where they joined the ranks of imperial bureaucrats and administrators. Though few in number compared to the native populations, the colonists created a Mediterranean-style urban society that left its mark on lands as distant as Bactria and India. Recent archaeological expeditions have uncovered Greek shrines and inscriptions from Bactria, and Emperor Ashoka of India himself had his edicts promulgated in Greek and Aramaic, the two most commonly used languages of the Hellenistic empires.

Local customs survived in the rural districts of Egypt, Mesopotamia, Persia, Bactria, and other lands embraced by the Hellenistic empires. In the Hellenistic cities, however, many individuals spoke Greek, dressed according to Greek fashions, and adopted Greek ways. Art and sculpture reflected the influence of Greek style as far away as Bactria and northern India. Like the Achaemenids before them, the Hellenistic ruling classes constituted a thin, supervisory veneer over long-established societies that largely continued to observe their own inherited customs. Nevertheless, like classical states in Persia, China, and India, the Hellenistic empires brought distant lands into interaction by way of trade and cultural exchange.

THE FRUITS OF TRADE: GREEK ECONOMY AND SOCIETY

The geography of the Greek peninsula posed difficult challenges for its inhabitants: its mountainous terrain and rocky soil yielded only small harvests of grain, and the southern Balkan mountains hindered travel and communication. Indeed, until the construction of modern roads, much of Greece was more accessible by sea than by land. As a result, early Greek society depended heavily upon maritime trade.

Trade and the Integration of the Mediterranean Basin

Although it produced little grain, much of Greece is ideally suited to the cultivation of olives and grapes. After the establishment of the poleis, the Greeks discovered that they could profitably concentrate their efforts on the production of olive oil

Trade   and wine. Greek merchants traded these products around the Mediterranean, returning with abundant supplies of grain and other items as well.

By the early eighth century B.C.E., trade had generated considerable prosperity in the Greek world. Merchants and mariners linked Greek communities throughout the Mediterranean world—not only those in the Greek peninsula but also those in Anatolia, the Mediterranean islands, and the Black Sea. The populations of all these communities grew dramatically, encouraging further colonization. In the colonies merchants offered Greek olive oil and wine for local products. Grain came from Egypt, Sicily, and southern Russia, salted fish from Spain and Black Sea lands, timber and pitch from Macedon, tin from Anatolia, and slaves from Egypt and Russia. Merchant ships with a capacity of four hundred tons were common in the classical Mediterranean, and a few vessels had a capacity of

Harvesting olives. In this painting on a vase two men knock fruit off the branches while a third climbs the tree to shake the limbs, and another gathers olives from the ground. • © The British Museum

one thousand tons. Some cities, such as Athens and Corinth, relied more on commerce than on agriculture for their livelihood and prosperity.

Large volumes of trade promoted commercial and economic organization in the Mediterranean basin. In Greece, for example, shipowners, merchants, and money-lenders routinely formed partnerships to spread the risks of commercial ventures. Usually, a merchant borrowed money from a banker or an individual to purchase cargo and rented space from a shipowner, who transported the goods and returned the profits to the merchant. In the event of a shipwreck, the contract became void, leaving both the merchant and the lender to absorb their losses.

Commercial and Economic Organization

The production of cultivators and manufacturers filled the holds of Mediterranean merchant vessels. Manufacturers usually operated on a small scale, but there are records of pottery workshops with upwards of sixty employees. One factory in fourth-century Athens employed 120 slaves in the manufacture of shields. Throughout the trading world of the Mediterranean basin, entrepreneurs established small businesses and offered their wares in the larger market.

Trade links between the Greek cities and their colonies contributed to a sense of a larger Greek community. Colonists recognized the same gods as their cousins in the Greek peninsula. They spoke Greek dialects, and they maintained commercial relationships with their native communities. Greeks from all parts gathered periodically to participate in panhellenic festivals that reinforced their common bonds. Many of these festivals featured athletic, literary, or musical contests in which individuals sought to win glory for their polis.

Panhellenic Festivals

Best known of the panhellenic festivals were the Olympic games. According to tradition, in 776 B.C.E. Greek communities from all parts of the Mediterranean sent their best athletes to the polis of Olympia to engage in contests of speed, strength, and skill. Events included footracing, long jump, boxing, wrestling, javelin tossing, and discus throwing. Winners of events received olive wreaths, and they became celebrated heroes in their home polis. The ancient Olympic games took place every four years for more than a millennium before quietly disappearing from Greek life. So although they were not united politically, by the sixth century B.C.E. Greek communities had nevertheless established a sense of collective identity.

The Olympic Games

During the Hellenistic era trade drew the Greeks into an even larger world of commerce and communication; colonists and traders expanded the range of their operations throughout Alexander's empire and the realms that succeeded him. Caravan trade linked Persia and Bactria to the western regions of the Hellenistic world. Dependent on horses and donkeys, caravans could not transport heavy or bulky goods, but rather carried luxury products such as gems, jewelry, perfumes, and aromatic oils. These goods all had high value relative to weight, so that traders could feed themselves and their animals, pay the high costs of overland transport, and still turn a profit. Traffic in bulkier goods traveled the sea-lanes of the Mediterranean, Red Sea, Persian Gulf, and Arabian Sea.

Family and Society

Homer's works portrayed a society composed of heroic warriors and their outspoken wives. Strong-willed human beings clashed constantly with each other and sometimes even defied the gods in pursuing their interests. These aggressive and assertive characters depended on less flamboyant individuals to provide them with food and other necessities, but Homer had no interest in discussing the humdrum lives of farmers and their families.

Patriarchal Society

With the establishment of poleis in the eighth century B.C.E., the nature of Greek family and society came into clearer focus. Like urban societies in southwest Asia and Anatolia, the Greek poleis adopted strictly patriarchal family structures. Male family heads ruled their households, and fathers even had the right to decide whether or not to keep infants born to their wives. They could not legally kill infants, but they could abandon newborns in the mountains or the countryside where they would soon die of exposure unless found and rescued by others.

Greek women fell under the authority of their fathers, husbands, or sons. Upper-class women living in poleis spent most of their time in the family home, and they ventured outside in the company of servants or chaperones and often wore veils to discourage the attention of men from other families. In most of the poleis, women could not own landed property, but they sometimes operated small businesses such as shops and food stalls. The only public position open to Greek women was that of priestess of a religious cult. Sparta was something of a special case when it came to gender relations: there women participated in athletic contests, went about town by themselves, joined in public festivals, and sometimes even took up arms to defend the polis. Even in Sparta, however, men were family authorities, and men alone determined state policies.

Sappho

Literacy was common among upper-class Greek women, and a few women earned reputations for literary talent. Most famous of them was the poet Sappho, who was active during the years around 600 B.C.E. Sappho, probably a widow from an aristocratic family, invited young women into her home for instruction in music and literature. Critics charged her with homosexual activity, and her surviving verse speaks of her strong physical attraction to young women. Greek society readily tolerated sexual relationships between men but frowned on female homosexuality. As a result, Sappho fell under a moral cloud, and only fragments of her poetry survive.

Aristocratic families with extensive landholdings could afford to provide girls with a formal education, but in less privileged families all hands contributed to the welfare of the household. In rural families men performed most of the outside work while women took care of domestic chores and wove wool textiles. In artisan families living in the poleis, both men and women often participated in businesses and maintained stands or booths in the marketplace.

Slavery

As in other classical societies, slavery was a prominent means of mobilizing labor throughout the Greek world. Slaves came from several different backgrounds. Some were formerly free Greeks who entered slavery because they could not pay their debts. Many came from the ranks of soldiers captured in war. A large number came from the peoples with whom the Greeks traded: slave markets at Black Sea ports sold seminomadic Scythians captured in Russia, while Egyptians provided African slaves from Nubia and other southern regions.

Greek law regarded all slaves as the private chattel property of their owners, and the conditions of slaves' lives depended on the needs and the temperament of their owners. Physically powerful slaves with no special skills most often provided heavy labor on the estates of large landholders. Other unskilled slaves worked at lighter tasks as domestic servants or caretakers of their owners' children. Educated slaves and those skilled at some craft or trade had special opportunities. Their owners often regarded them as economic investments, provided them with shops, and allowed them to keep a portion of their earnings as an incentive and a reward for efficient work. In some cases slaves with entrepreneurial talent succeeded well enough in their businesses to win their freedom. A slave named Pasion, for example, worked first as a porter and then as a clerk at a prominent Athenian bank during the late fifth and early fourth centuries B.C.E. Pasion's owners entrusted him with larger responsibilities and rewarded him for his efforts. Ultimately, Pasion gained his freedom, took over management of the bank, outfitted five warships from his own pocket, and won a grant of Athenian citizenship.

THE CULTURAL LIFE OF CLASSICAL GREECE

During the eighth and seventh centuries B.C.E., as Greek merchants ventured throughout the Mediterranean basin, they became acquainted with the sophisticated cultural traditions of Mesopotamia and Egypt. They learned astronomy, science, mathematics, medicine, and magic from the Babylonians, as well as geometry, medicine, and divination from the Egyptians. They also drew inspiration from the myths, religious beliefs, art motifs, and architectural styles of Mesopotamia and Egypt. About 800 B.C.E. they adapted the Phoenician alphabet to their own language. To the Phoenicians' consonants they added symbols for vowels and thus created an exceptionally flexible system for representing human speech in written form.

During the fifth and fourth centuries B.C.E., the Greeks combined these borrowed cultural elements with their own intellectual interests to elaborate a rich cultural tradition. The most distinctive feature of classical Greek culture was the effort to construct a consistent system of philosophy based purely on human reason. Greek cultural figures also exercised enormous influence over art, literature, and moral thought in the Mediterranean basin and western Europe.

A slave carrying a lantern guides his drunken master home following a party. • © The British Museum

Rational Thought and Philosophy

The pivotal figure in the development of philosopy was Socrates (470–399 B.C.E.), a thoughtful and reflective Athenian driven by a powerful urge to understand human beings and human affairs in all their complexity. During his youth Socrates studied the ideas of Greek scientists who pursued the interests of their Mesopotamian and Egyptian predecessors. Gradually, however, he became disenchanted with their efforts to understand the natural world, which he regarded as less important than human affairs.

Socrates

Socrates did not commit his thought to writing, but his disciple Plato later composed dialogues that represented Socrates' views. Nor did he expound his views assertively: rather he posed questions that encouraged reflection on human issues, particularly on matters of ethics and morality. He suggested that human beings could lead honest lives and that honor was far more important than wealth, fame, or other

Tradition holds that Socrates was not a physically attractive man, but this statue emphasizes his sincerity and simplicity. • © The British Museum

superficial attributes. He scorned those who preferred public accolades to personal integrity, and he insisted on the need to reflect on the purposes and goals of life. "The unexamined life is not worth living," he held, implying that human beings had an obligation to strive for personal integrity, behave honorably toward others, and work toward the construction of a just society.

In elaborating these views, Socrates often played the role of a gadfly who subjected traditional ethical teachings to critical scrutiny. This tactic outraged some of his fellow citizens, who brought him to trial on charges that he encouraged immorality and corrupted the Athenian youths who joined him in the marketplace to discuss moral and ethical issues. A jury of Athenian citizens decided that Socrates had indeed passed the bounds of propriety and condemned him to death. In 399 B.C.E. Socrates drank a potion of hemlock sap and died in the company of his friends.

Socrates' influence survived in the work of his most zealous disciple, Plato (430–347 B.C.E.), and in Plato's disciple, Aristotle (384–322 B.C.E.). Inspired by his mentor's reflections, Plato elaborated a systematic philosophy of great sub-

Plato   tlety. He presented his thought in a series of dialogues in which Socrates figured as the principal speaker. In the earliest dialogues, written shortly after Socrates' death, Plato largely represented his mentor's views. As time passed, Plato gradually formulated his thought into a systematic vision of the world and human society.

The cornerstone of Plato's thought was his theory of Forms or Ideas. It disturbed Plato that he could not gain satisfactory intellectual control over the world. The quality of virtue, for example, meant different things in different situations, as did honesty, courage, truth, and beauty. Generally speaking, for example, virtue required individuals to honor and obey their parents. But if a parent engaged in illegal behavior, virtue required offspring to denounce the offense and seek punishment. How was it possible, then, to understand virtue as an abstract quality? In seeking an answer to this question, Plato developed his belief that the world in which we live was not the only world—indeed, was not the world of genuine reality, but only a pale and imperfect reflection of the world of Forms or Ideas. Displays of virtue or other qualities in the world imperfectly reflected the ideal qualities. Only by entering the world of Forms or Ideas was it possible to understand the true nature of virtue and other qualities. The secrets of this world were available only to philosophers—those who applied their rational faculties to the pursuit of wisdom.

Though abstract, Plato's thought had important political and social implications. In his dialogue *The Republic*, for example, Plato sketched an ideal state that reflected

SOCRATES' VIEW OF DEATH

• • •

In one of his earliest dialogues, The Apology, Plato offered an account of Socrates' defense of himself during his trial before a jury of Athenian citizens. After the jury had convicted him and condemned him to death, Socrates reflected on the nature of death and reemphasized his commitment to virtue rather than to wealth or fame.

And if we reflect in another way we shall see that we may well hope that death is a good thing. For the state of death is one of two things: either the dead man wholly ceases to be and loses all sensation; or, according to the common belief, it is a change and a migration of the soul unto another place. And if death is the absence of all sensation, like the sleep of one whose slumbers are unbroken by any dreams, it will be a wonderful gain. For if a man had to select that night in which he slept so soundly that he did not even see any dreams, and had to compare with it all the other nights and days of his life, and then had to say how many days and nights in his life he had slept better and more pleasantly than this night, I think that a private person, nay, even the great king of Persia himself, would find them easy to count, compared with the others. If that is the nature of death, I for one count it a gain. For then it appears that eternity is nothing more than a single night.

But if death is a journey to another place, and the common belief be true, that all who have died dwell there, what good could be greater than this, my judges? Would a journey not be worth taking if at the end of it, in the other world, we should be released from the self-styled judges of this world, and should find the true judges who are said to sit in judgment below? . . . It would be an infinite happiness to converse with them, and to live with them, and to examine them. Assuredly there they do not put men to death for doing that. For

besides the other ways in which they are happier than we are, they are immortal, at least if the common belief be true.

And you too, judges, must face death with a good courage, and believe this as a truth, that no evil can happen to a good man, either in life, or after death. His fortunes are not neglected by the gods, and what has come to me today has not come by chance. I am persuaded that it is better for me to die now, and to be released from trouble. . . . And so I am hardly angry with my accusers, or with those who have condemned me to die. Yet it was not with this mind that they accused me and condemned me, but rather they meant to do me an injury. Only to that extent do I find fault with them.

Yet I have one request to make of them. When my sons grow up, visit them with punishment, my friends, and vex them in the same way that I have vexed you if they seem to you to care for riches or for anything other than virtue: and if they think that they are something when they are nothing at all, reproach them as I have reproached you for not caring for what they should and for thinking that they are great men when in fact they are worthless. And if you will do this, I myself and my sons will have received our deserts at your hands.

But now the time has come, and we must go hence: I to die, and you to live. Whether life or death is better is known to God, and to God only.

SOURCE: F. J. Church, trans. *The Trial and Death of Socrates*, 2nd ed. London: Macmillan, 1886, pp. 76–78. (Translation slightly modified.)

his philosophical views. Since philosophers were in the best position to understand ultimate reality, and hence to design policies in accordance with the Form or Idea of justice, he held that the best state was one where either philosophers ruled as kings or else kings were themselves philosophers. In effect, then, Plato advocated an intellectual aristocracy: the philosophical elite would rule, and other, less intelligent classes would work at functions for which their talents best suited them.

Aristotle   During the generation after Plato, Aristotle also elaborated a systematic philosophy that equaled Plato's work in its long-term influence. Though originally a disciple of Plato, Aristotle came to distrust the theory of Forms or Ideas, which he considered artificial intellectual constructs unnecessary for understanding the world. Unlike Plato, Aristotle believed that philosophers could rely on their senses to provide accurate information about the world and then depend on reason to sort out its mysteries. Like Plato, Aristotle explored the nature of reality in subtle metaphysical works, and he devised rigorous rules of logic in an effort to construct powerful and compelling arguments. But he also wrote on biology, physics, astronomy, psychology, politics, ethics, and literature. His work provided such a coherent and comprehensive vision of the world that his later disciples, the Christian Scholastic philosophers of medieval Europe, called him "the master of those who know."

The Greek philosophers deeply influenced the development of European and Islamic cultural traditions. Until the seventeenth century C.E., most European philosophers regarded the Greeks as intellectual authorities. Christian and Islamic theologians alike went to great lengths to harmonize their religious convictions with the philosophical views of Plato and Aristotle. Thus like philosophical and religious figures in other classical societies, Plato and Aristotle provided a powerful intellectual framework that shaped thought about the world and human affairs for two millennia and more.

Popular Religion and Greek Drama

Because most Greeks of the classical era did not have an advanced education and did not chat regularly with the philosophers, they did not rely on systems of formal logic when seeking to understand their place in the larger world. Instead, they turned to traditions of popular culture and popular religion that shed light on human nature and offered guidance for human behavior.

Greek Deities   The Greeks did not recognize a single, exclusive, all-powerful god. Their Indo-European ancestors had attributed supernatural powers to natural elements such as sun, wind, and rain. Over the course of the centuries, the Greeks personified these powers and came to think of them as gods. They constructed myths that related the stories of the gods, their relations with one another, and their roles in bringing the world to its present state.

In the beginning, they believed, there was the formless void of chaos out of which emerged the earth, the mother and creator of all things. The earth then generated the sky, and together they produced night, day, sun, moon, and other natural phenomena. Struggles between the deities led to bitter heavenly battles, and ultimately Zeus, grandson of the earth and sky gods, emerged as paramount ruler of the divine realm. Zeus's heavenly court included scores of subordinate deities who had various responsibilities: the god Apollo promoted wisdom and justice, for example, while the goddess Fortune brought unexpected opportunities and difficulties, and the Furies wreaked vengeance on those who violated divine law.

Religious Cults   Like religious traditions in other lands, Greek myths sought to explain the world and the forces that shape it. They served also as foundations for religious cults that contributed to a powerful sense of community in classical Greece. Many of the cults conducted ritual observances that were open only to initiates. One especially popular cult known as the Eleusinian mysteries, for example, sponsored a ritual community meal and encouraged initiates to observe high moral standards.

Some cults admitted only women. Because women could not participate in legal and political life, the cults provided opportunities for them to play roles in society outside the home. The fertility cult of Demeter, goddess of grain, excluded men. In honor of Demeter women gathered on a hill for three days, offered sacrifices to the goddess, and took part in a celebratory feast. This event occurred in October or November before the planting of grain and sought to ensure bountiful harvests.

Women were also the most prominent devotees of Dionysus, the god of wine, also known as Bacchus, although men sometimes joined in his celebration. During the spring of the year, when the vines produced their fruit, devotees retreated into the hills to celebrate Dionysus with song and dance. The dramatist Euripides offered an account of one such Dionysian season in his play *The Bacchae*. Euripides described the preparations for the festival and the celebrants' joyful march to the mountains. Spirited music and dance brought the devotees to such a state of frenzy that they fell upon a sacrificial goat—and also a man hiding in the brush in an unwise effort to observe the proceedings—ripped the victims apart, and presented them as offerings to Dionysus. Though he was a skeptic who regarded much of Greek religion as sham and hypocrisy, Euripides nonetheless recognized that powerful emotional bonds held together the Dionysian community.

During the fifth century B.C.E., as the poleis strengthened their grip on public and political life, the religious cults became progressively more tame. The cult of Dionysus, originally one of the most unrestrained, became one of the most thoroughly domesticated. The venue of the rituals shifted from the mountains to the polis, and the nature of the observances changed dramatically. Instead of emotional festivals, the Dionysian season saw the presentation of plays that honored the traditions of the polis, examined relations between human beings and the gods, or reflected on problems of ethics and morality.

This transformation of Dionysus's cult set the stage for the emergence of Greek dramatic literature as dramatists composed plays for presentation at annual theatrical festivals. Of the thousands of plays written in classical Greece, only a few survive: thirty-two tragedies and a dozen comedies have come down to the present in substantially complete form. Yet this small sample shows that the dramatists engaged audiences in subtle reflection on complicated themes. The great tragedians—Aeschylus, Sophocles, and Euripides—whose lives spanned the fifth century B.C.E., explored the possibilities and limitations of human action. To what extent could human beings act as responsible agents in society? What was their proper role when they confronted the limits that the gods or other humans placed on their activity? How should they proceed when the gods and human authorities presented them with conflicting demands?

Tragic Drama

Comic dramatists such as Aristophanes also dealt with serious issues of human striving and responsible behavior. They took savage delight in lampooning the public and political figures of their time. The comedians aimed to influence popular attitudes by ridiculing the foibles of prominent public figures and calling attention to the absurd consequences of ill-considered action.

Hellenistic Philosophy and Religion

As the Hellenistic empires seized the political initiative in the Mediterranean basin and eclipsed the poleis, Greek philosophy and religion lost their civic character. Since the poleis no longer controlled their own destinies, but rather figured as small elements in a large administrative machine, residents ceased to regard their polis as the focus of individual loyalties. Instead, they inclined toward cultural and religious alternatives that ministered to the needs and interests of individuals living in a large, cosmopolitan society.

The Hellenistic Philosophers

The most popular Hellenistic philosophers—the Epicureans, Skeptics, and Stoics—addressed individual needs by searching for personal tranquility and serenity. Epicureans, for example, identified pleasure as the greatest good. By *pleasure* they did not mean unbridled hedonism, but rather a state of quiet satisfaction that would shield them from the pressures of the Hellenistic world. Skeptics refused to take strong positions on political, moral, and social issues because they doubted the possibility of certain knowledge. Rather than engage in fruitless disputes, they sought equanimity and left contentious issues to others.

The most respected and influential of the Hellenistic philosophers were the Stoics, who considered all human beings members of a single, universal family. Unlike the Epicureans and Skeptics, the Stoics did not seek to withdraw from the pressures of the world, but rather taught that individuals had the duty to aid others and lead virtuous lives. The Stoics believed that individuals could avoid anxieties caused by the pressures of Hellenistic society by concentrating their attention strictly on the duties that reason and nature demanded of them. Thus like the Epicureans and Skeptics, the Stoics sought ways to bring individuals to a state of inner peace and tranquility.

Religions of Salvation

While the philosophers' doctrines appealed to educated elites, religions of salvation enjoyed surging popularity in Hellenistic society. Mystery religions promised eternal bliss for initiates who observed their rites and lived in accordance with their doctrines. Some of these faiths spread across the trade routes and found followers far from their homelands. The Egyptian cult of Osiris, for example, became extraordinarily popular because it promised salvation for those who led honorable lives. Cults from Persia, Mesopotamia, Anatolia, and Greece also attracted disciples throughout the Hellenistic world.

Many of the mystery religions involved the worship of a savior whose death and resurrection would lead the way to eternal salvation for devoted followers. Some philosophers and religious thinkers speculated that a single, universal god might rule the entire universe—just as Alexander and his successors governed enormous empires on earth—and that this god had a plan for the salvation of all humankind. Like the Hellenistic philosophies, then, religions of salvation addressed the interests of individuals searching for security in a complex world.

Greek travelers linked the regions of the Mediterranean basin in classical times. Although they did not build a centralized empire, the Greeks dotted the Mediterranean and Black Sea shorelines with their colonies, and their merchant fleets stimulated both commercial and cultural interactions between peoples of distant lands. Greek merchants, soldiers, and administrators also played prominent roles in the massive empires of Alexander and the Hellenistic rulers. Quite apart from their political and economic significance, the Greeks also left a remarkably rich cultural legacy. Greek philosophy, literature, and science profoundly influenced the intellectual and cultural development of peoples from southwest Asia to western Europe. The Greek poleis and the Hellenistic cities provided nurturing environments for rational thought and academic pursuits, and the frequent travels of the Greeks promoted the spread of popular religious faiths throughout the Mediterranean basin and beyond. Like classical Persia, China, and India, the Mediterranean basin became an integrated world.

CHRONOLOGY

2200–1100 B.C.E.	Minoan society
1600–1100 B.C.E.	Mycenaean society
800–338 B.C.E.	Era of the classical Greek polis
around 600 B.C.E.	Life of Sappho
500–479 B.C.E.	Persian Wars
490 B.C.E.	Darius's invasion of Greece
490 B.C.E.	Battle of Marathon
480 B.C.E.	Xerxes' invasion of Greece
480 B.C.E.	Battle of Salamis
479 B.C.E.	Battle of Plataea
470–399 B.C.E.	Life of Socrates
443–429 B.C.E.	Pericles' leadership in Athens
431–404 B.C.E.	Peloponnesian War
430–347 B.C.E.	Life of Plato
384–322 B.C.E.	Life of Aristotle
359–336 B.C.E.	Reign of Philip II of Macedon
336–323 B.C.E.	Reign of Alexander of Macedon

FOR FURTHER READING

Martin Bernal. *Black Athena: The Afroasiatic Roots of Classical Civilization.* 2 vols. to date. New Brunswick, 1987–. Provocative and controversial study arguing for Egyptian and Semitic influences on early Greek society.

Sue Blundell. *Women in Ancient Greece.* Cambridge, Mass., 1995. A comprehensive survey of women and their roles in ancient Greek society, solidly based on recent scholarship.

Walter Burkert. *The Orientalizing Revolution: Near Eastern Influence on Greek Culture in the Early Archaic Age.* Trans. by M. E. Pinder and W. Burkert. Cambridge, Mass., 1992. An important scholarly work tracing Mesopotamian influence in early Greece.

Lionel Casson. *The Ancient Mariners: Seafarers and Sea Fighters of the Mediterranean in Ancient Times.* 2nd ed. Princeton, 1991. Draws heavily on recent discoveries of underwater archaeologists in reconstructing the maritime history of the ancient Mediterranean.

F. M. Cornford. *Before and after Socrates.* Cambridge, 1965. A short but brilliant synthesis of classical Greek philosophy.

C. R. Dodds. *The Greeks and the Irrational.* Berkeley, 1968. An influential study of Greek religion in light of modern psychological and anthropological theories.

Kenneth Dover. *The Greeks.* Austin, 1980. An engaging personal interpretation of classical Greece.

M. I. Finley. *Ancient Slavery and Modern Ideology.* New York, 1980. Presents a thoughtful analysis of Greek and Roman slavery in light of modern slavery and contemporary debates.

Frank J. Frost. *Greek Society.* 2nd ed. Lexington, 1980. Concentrates on economic and social history from Myceanean to Hellenistic times.

Frederick C. Grant, ed. *Hellenistic Religions: The Age of Syncretism.* Indianapolis, 1953. Fascinating collection of translated documents and texts that throw light on religious and philosophical beliefs of the Hellenistic era.

J. R. Hamilton. *Alexander the Great.* London, 1973. The best recent work on Alexander of Macedon.

William H. McNeill and Jean W. Sedlar, eds. *The Classical Mediterranean World.* New York, 1969. Primary sources from classical Greece and the Hellenistic world in English translation.

Sarah B. Pomeroy. *Goddesses, Whores, Wives, and Slaves: Women in Classical Antiquity.* New York, 1995. Outstanding study analyzing the status and role of women in classical Greece and Rome.

Susan Sherwin-White and Amélie Kuhrt. *From Samarkhand to Sardis: A New Approach to the Seleucid Empire.* Berkeley, 1993. Detailed scholarly analysis of the Seleucid empire concentrating on political and economic matters.

F. W. Wallbank. *The Hellenistic World.* Sussex, 1981. Takes account of recent discoveries by archaeologists.

Mortimer Wheeler. *Flames over Persepolis.* New York, 1968. Examines the influence of Hellenistic artists in Persia, Bactria, and India.

CHAPTER 10

MEDITERRANEAN SOCIETY: THE ROMAN PHASE

· · ·

About 55 C.E. Roman guards transported a prisoner named Paul of Tarsus from the port of Caesarea in Palestine to the city of Rome. The journey turned out to be more eventful than the travelers had planned. The party boarded a sailing ship loaded with grain and carrying 276 passengers as well. The ship departed in the fall—after the main sailing season, which ran from May through September—and soon encountered a violent storm. For two frightening weeks crew and passengers alike worked furiously to keep the ship afloat, jettisoning baggage, tackle, and cargo to lighten the load as wind and rain battered the vessel. Eventually, the ship ran aground on the island of Malta, where storm-driven waves destroyed the craft. Yet most of the passengers and crew survived, including Paul and his guards, who spent three months on Malta before catching another ship to Rome.

Paul had become embroiled in a dispute between Jews and early proponents of the fledgling Christian religion. Though born a Jew, Paul was an enthusiastic Christian missionary. He sought to attract converts not only from the ranks of Jews but also from outside the Jewish community, where the new faith had originated. A crowd of his enemies attacked him in Jerusalem, and the resulting disturbance became so severe that authorities of the Roman imperial government intervened to restore order. Under normal circumstances Roman authorities would deliver an individual like Paul to the leaders of his own ethnic community, and the laws and customs of that community would determine the person's fate.

Paul's case, however, was different. Knowing that Jewish leaders would condemn him and probably execute him, Paul asserted his rights as a Roman citizen. Although he had never traveled west of Greece, Paul had inherited Roman citizenship from his father. As a result, he had the right to appeal his case to Rome, and he did so. His appeal did not succeed. No record of his case survives, but tradition holds that imperial authorities executed him out of concern that Christianity threatened the peace and stability of the Roman state.

Paul's experience reflects the cosmopolitan character of the early Roman empire, which by the first century C.E. dominated the entire Mediterranean basin. Roman administrators oversaw affairs from Anatolia and Palestine in the east to Spain and Morocco in the west. Roman military forces maintained order in an empire with scores of different and sometimes conflicting ethnic and religious groups. Like many

Music from the cithara, an ancestor of the guitar, in a wealthy Roman home. • Erich Lessing/Art Resource, NY others, Paul of Tarsus traveled freely through much of the Roman empire in an effort to attract converts to Christianity. Indeed, except for the integration of the Mediterranean basin by the Roman empire, Paul's message and his faith might never have expanded beyond the small community of early Christians in Jerusalem.

Like the Phoenicians and Greeks before them, the Romans established close links between the various Mediterranean regions. As they conquered new lands, pacified them, and brought them into their empire, the Romans enabled merchants, missionaries, and others to travel readily throughout the Mediterranean basin. The Romans differed from their predecessors, however, by building an extensive land empire and centralizing the administration of their realm. At its high point the Roman empire dominated the entire Mediterranean basin and parts of southwest Asia, including Anatolia, Mesopotamia, Syria, Egypt, and north Africa, besides much of continental Europe, and even parts of Britain as well.

The Roman empire also served as a vehicle for the spread of Christianity. The early Christians encountered harsh opposition and persecution from Roman officials. Yet the new faith took advantage of the Romans' well-organized imperial holdings and spread rapidly throughout the Mediterranean basin and beyond. Eventually, Christianity became the official religion of the Roman empire, and imperial sponsorship enabled Christianity to spread more effectively than before.

 # FROM KINGDOM TO REPUBLIC

Founded in the eighth century B.C.E., the city of Rome was originally a small city-state ruled by a single king. Late in the sixth century B.C.E., the city's aristocrats deposed the king, ended the monarchy, and instituted a republic—a form of government in which delegates represented the interests of various constituencies. The Roman republic survived for more than five hundred years, and it was under the republican constitution that Rome established itself as the dominant power in the Mediterranean basin.

The Etruscans and Rome

Romulus and Remus The city of Rome arose from origins both obscure and humble. According to the ancient legends, the city owed its existence to the flight of Aeneas, a refugee from Troy who migrated to Italy when Greek invaders destroyed his native land. Two of his descendants, the twins Romulus and Remus, almost did not survive infancy because an evil uncle abandoned them by the flooded Tiber River, fully expecting them to drown or die of exposure. But a kindly she-wolf found them and nursed them to health. The boys grew strong and courageous, and in 753 B.C.E. Romulus founded the city of Rome and established himself as its first king.

Modern scholars do not tell so colorful a tale, but they agree that Rome grew from humble beginnings. Beginning about 2000 B.C.E., bands of Indo-European migrants crossed the Alps and settled throughout the Italian peninsula. Like their distant cousins in India, Greece, and northern Europe, these migrants blended with the neolithic inhabitants of the region, adopted agriculture, and established tribal federations. Sheepherders and small farmers occupied much of the Italian peninsula, including the future site of Rome itself. Bronze metallurgy appeared about 1800 B.C.E. and iron about 900 B.C.E.

Paintings in Etruscan tombs often represent scenes from daily life. Illustrations in the Tomb of the Leopards in Tarquinia depict musicians playing pipes and lyre during a banquet. • Hirmer Verlag

The Etruscans

During the middle centuries of the first millennium B.C.E., Italy underwent rapid political and economic development. The agents of this development were the Etruscans, a dynamic people who dominated much of Italy between the eighth and fifth centuries B.C.E. The Etruscans probably migrated to Italy from Anatolia. They settled first in Tuscany, the region around modern Florence, but they soon controlled much of the territory from the Po River valley in northern Italy to the region around modern Naples in the south. They built thriving cities and established political and economic alliances between their settlements. They manufactured high-quality bronze and iron goods, and they worked gold and silver into jewelry. They built a fleet and traded actively in the western Mediterranean. During the late sixth century B.C.E., however, the Etruscans encountered a series of challenges from other peoples, and their society began to decline. Greek fleets defeated the Etruscans at sea while Celtic peoples attacked them from Gaul (modern France).

The Kingdom of Rome

The Etruscans deeply influenced the early development of Rome. Like the Etruscan cities, Rome was a monarchy during the early days after its foundation, and several Roman kings were Etruscans. The kings ruled Rome through the seventh and sixth centuries B.C.E., and they provided the city with paved streets, public buildings, defensive walls, and large temples.

Etruscan merchants drew a large volume of traffic to Rome, thanks partly to the city's geographical advantages. Rome enjoyed easy access to the Mediterranean by way of the Tiber River, but since it was not on the coast, it did not run the risk of invasion or attack from the sea. Already during the period of Etruscan dominance, trade routes from all parts of Italy converged on Rome. When Etruscan society declined, Rome was in a strong position to play a more prominent role both in Italy and in the larger Mediterranean world.

The Roman Republic and Its Constitution

Establishment of the Republic

In 509 B.C.E. the Roman nobility deposed the last Etruscan king and replaced the monarchy with an aristocratic republic. At the heart of the city, they built the Roman forum, a political and civic center filled with temples and public buildings where leading citizens tended to government business. They also instituted a republican constitution that entrusted executive responsibilties to two consuls who wielded civil and military power. Consuls were elected by an assembly dominated by hereditary aristocrats and wealthy classes, known in Rome as the patricians, and they served one-year terms. The powerful Senate, whose members were mostly aristocrats with extensive political experience, advised the consuls and ratified all major decisions. Senators included Rome's most prominent political and military leaders. Together with the consuls, the Senate largely controlled public affairs in Rome. Because the consuls and Senate both represented the interests of the patricians, there was constant tension between the wealthy classes and the common people, known as the plebeians.

Conflicts between Patricians and Plebeians

During the early fifth century B.C.E., relations between the classes became so strained that the plebeians threatened to secede from Rome and establish a rival settlement. In order to maintain the integrity of the Roman state, the patricians granted plebeians the right to elect officials, known as tribunes, who represented their interests in the Roman government. Originally plebeians chose two tribunes, but the number eventually rose to ten. Tribunes had the power to intervene in all political matters, and they possessed the right to veto measures that they judged unfair.

Ruins of the Roman forum, where political leaders conducted public affairs during the era of the republic, still stand today. • Comstock

Although the tribunes provided a voice in government for the plebeians, the patricians continued to dominate Rome. Tensions between the classes persisted for as long as the republic survived. During the fourth century B.C.E., plebeians became eligible to hold almost all state offices and gained the right to have one of the consuls come from their ranks. By the early third century, plebeian-dominated assemblies won the power to make decisions binding on all of Rome. Thus like fifth-century Athens, republican Rome gradually broadened the base of political participation.

Constitutional compromises eased class tensions, but they did not solve all political problems confronted by the republic. When faced with civil or military crises, the Romans appointed an official, known as a dictator, who wielded absolute power for a term of six months. By providing for strong leadership during times of extraordinary difficulty, the republican constitution enabled Rome to maintain a reasonably stable society throughout most of the republic's history. Meanwhile, however, by allowing various constituencies a voice in government, the constitution also helped to prevent crippling class tensions.

The Expansion of the Republic

While the Romans dealt constructively with internal problems, external challenges mounted. During the fifth century B.C.E., for example, Rome faced threats not only from peoples living in the neighboring hills but also from the Etruscans. Beyond Italy itself were the Gauls, a powerful Celtic people who on several occasions invaded Italy. Between the fourth and second centuries B.C.E., however, a remarkable expansion of power and influence transformed Rome from a small and vulnerable city-state to the center of an enormous empire.

First the Romans consolidated their position in central Italy. During the fifth and early fourth centuries B.C.E., the Romans founded a large regional state in central Italy at the expense of the declining Etruscans and other neighboring peoples. Their conquests gave them access to the iron industry built by the Etruscans and greatly expanded the amount of land under Roman control.

MAP [10.1]

Expansion of the Roman republic.

During the later fourth century, the Romans built on their early conquests and emerged as the predominant power in the Italian peninsula. The Romans secured control of the peninsula partly because they established military colonies in regions they overcame and partly because of a generous policy toward the peoples they conquered. Instead of ruling them as vanquished subjects, the Romans often exempted them from taxation and allowed them to govern their own internal affairs. Conquered peoples in Italy enjoyed the right to trade in Rome and take Roman spouses. Some gained Roman citizenship and rose to high positions in Roman society. The Romans forbade conquered peoples from making military or political alliances except with Rome itself and required them to provide soldiers and military support. These policies provided the political, military, and diplomatic support Rome needed to put down occasional rebellions and to dominate affairs throughout the Italian peninsula.

Expansion in the Mediterranean

With Italy under its control, Rome began to play a major role in the affairs of the larger Mediterranean basin and to experience conflicts with other Mediterranean powers. The principal power in the western Mediterranean during the fourth and third centuries B.C.E. was the city-state of Carthage, located near modern Tunis. Originally established as a Phoenician colony, Carthage enjoyed a strategic location that enabled it to trade actively throughout the Mediterranean. From the wealth generated by this commerce, Carthage became the dominant political power in north Africa (excluding Egypt), the southern part of the Iberian peninsula, and the western region of grain-rich Sicily as well. Meanwhile, the three Hellenistic empires that succeeded Alexander of Macedon continued to dominate the eastern Mediterranean: the Antigonids ruled Macedon, the Ptolemies ruled Egypt, and the Seleucids included wealthy Syria and Anatolia among their many possessions. The prosperity of the Hellenistic realms supported a thriving network of maritime commerce in the eastern Mediterranean, and as in the case of Carthage, commercial wealth enabled rulers to maintain powerful states and armies.

The Punic Wars

The Romans clashed first with Carthage. Between 264 and 146 B.C.E., they fought three devastating conflicts known as the Punic Wars with the Carthaginians. Friction first arose from economic competition, particularly over Sicily, the most important source of grain in the western Mediterranean. Later on, Romans and Carthaginians struggled for supremacy in the region. The rivalry ended after Roman forces razed the city of Carthage, salted the surrounding earth to render it unfit for agriculture and settlement, and forced many of the survivors into slavery. The Romans then annexed Carthaginian possessions in north Africa and Iberia—rich in grain, oil, wine, silver, and gold—and used these resources to finance continued imperial expansion.

Shortly after the beginning of the Carthaginian conflict, Rome became embroiled in disputes in the eastern Mediterranean. Conflict arose partly because pirates and ambitious local lords ignored the weakening Hellenistic rulers and threatened regional stability. On several occasions Roman leaders dispatched armies to protect the interests of Roman citizens and merchants, and these expeditions brought them into conflict with the Antigonids and Seleucids. Between 215 and 148 B.C.E., Rome fought five major wars, mostly in Macedon and Anatolia, against Antigonid and Seleucid opponents. The Romans did not immediately annex lands in the eastern Mediterranean, but rather entrusted them to allies in the region. Nevertheless, by the middle of the second century B.C.E., Rome clearly ranked as the preeminent power in the eastern as well as the western Mediterranean.

Roman expansion depended upon well-equipped and highly disciplined military forces. In this detail from Trajan's column, troops assume the siege formation known as the *testudo* (literally, the "tortoise") by surrounding themselves with their shields to avoid defenders' missiles while approaching city walls.

• C. M. Dixon

FROM REPUBLIC TO EMPIRE

Imperial expansion brought wealth and power to Rome, but wealth and power brought problems as well as benefits. Unequal distribution of wealth aggravated class tensions and gave rise to conflict over political and social policies. Meanwhile, the need to administer conquered lands efficiently strained the capacities of the republican constitution. During the first century B.C.E. and the first century C.E., Roman civil and military leaders gradually dismantled the republican constitution and imposed a centralized imperial form of government on the city of Rome and its empire.

Imperial Expansion and Domestic Problems

As in classical China and Greece, patterns of land distribution caused serious political and social tensions in Rome. Conquered lands fell largely into the hands of wealthy elites, who organized enormous plantations known as *latifundia*. Because they enjoyed economies of scale and often employed slave labor, owners of *latifundia* operated at lower costs than did owners of smaller holdings, who often had to mortgage their lands or sell out to their wealthier neighbors.

During the second and first centuries B.C.E., severely strained class relations led to violent social conflict and civil war. In 133 B.C.E. Tiberius Gracchus served as one of the tribunes representing the interests of Rome's lower classes. Gracchus believed that the rural economy faced ruin if a small number of individuals continued

The Gracchi Brothers

to accumulate land because immense, slave-operated *latifundia* would eventually drive small farmers out of business. Disruption of the rural economy in turn would have adverse consequences for the state because small farmers constituted the core of the Roman army.

In hopes of avoiding an economic and military crisis, Gracchus sponsored a law limiting the amount of conquered land that any individual could hold. Those whose lands exceeded the limit would lose some of their holdings, which would then become available to small farmers. The effort at land redistribution had little success, however, because most members of the wealthy and ruling classes considered Gracchus a dangerous radical and found ways to circumvent the laws that he sponsored. Indeed, fearing that he might seek higher office and exercise more influence over Roman affairs, a group of his enemies assassinated Tiberius Gracchus in 132 B.C.E.

During the following decade Gaius Gracchus, younger brother of Tiberius, served as leader of the social reformers in Rome. Like Tiberius, Gaius zealously promoted land reform. He also advocated the establishment of state subsidies that would make inexpensive grain available to the lower-class residents of Rome. Finally, he proposed to extend full Roman citizenship to peoples in most of the Italian peninsula—a move that would have diluted the influence of the powerful classes within Rome. Roman elites came to regard Gaius Gracchus as a radical in the mold of his brother and worked strenuously to defeat his proposals. Ultimately, they rid themselves of Gaius altogether: in 121 B.C.E., in the aftermath of a violent scuffle, they branded him an outlaw and sent a squad of foreign mercenaries to kill him.

The experiences of the Gracchi brothers clearly showed that the constitution of the Roman republic, originally designed for a small city-state, was not suitable for a large and growing empire. Formal political power remained in the hands of a small, privileged class of people in Rome, and their policies often reflected the interests of their class rather than the concerns of the empire as a whole. For the century following Tiberius Gracchus's term as tribune, Roman politicians and generals jockeyed for power and position as they sought to mobilize support and design a political structure that could maintain the empire.

Marius and Sulla   The contest for power sometimes took exceedingly violent forms. During the late second century B.C.E., for example, a prominent general named Gaius Marius recruited an army not from the ranks of small farmers—traditionally the core of the Roman army—but from landless rural residents and urban workers. Because his troops had no economic cushion to fall back on, they were intensely loyal to their general and placed the interests of the army before those of the state. Marius was himself of common birth, and he sympathized with social reformers such as the Gracchi. With the support of his private army, Marius became the most prominent political leader in Rome during the late second century B.C.E. He advocated distribution of land to small holders, especially to discharged veterans of his army, and he provided cheap grain supplies for the urban poor.

The conservative and aristocratic classes of Rome responded by organizing military support for their own interests. Their general was Lucius Cornelius Sulla, a respected veteran of several foreign conflicts. Like Marius, Sulla formed an army composed mostly of lower-class recruits intensely loyal to their commander.

Civil War   During the early first century B.C.E., Rome fell into civil war. In 87 B.C.E. Marius marched on Rome, placed the city under military occupation, and hunted down his political enemies. After Marius died the following year, Sulla made plans to take his place. In 83 B.C.E. he seized Rome and initiated a grisly slaughter of his enemies. Sulla posted lists naming "proscribed" individuals whom he labeled enemies of the state, and he encouraged the Roman populace to kill these individuals on sight and confiscate their properties. During a reign of terror that lasted almost five years, Sulla brought about the murder or execution of some ten thousand individuals. By the time Sulla died in 78 B.C.E., he had imposed an extremely conservative legislative program that weakened the influence of the lower classes and strengthened the hand of the wealthy in Roman politics.

Since Sulla's program did not address Rome's most serious social problems, however, it had no chance to succeed over a long term. *Latifundia* continued to pressure small farmers, who increasingly left the countryside and swelled the ranks of the urban lower classes. Poverty in the cities, especially Rome, led to periodic social eruptions when the price of grain rose or the supply fell. Meanwhile, the urban poor increasingly joined the personal armies of ambitious generals, who themselves posed threats to social and political stability. In this chaotic context Gaius Julius Caesar inaugurated the process by which Rome replaced its republican constitution with a centralized imperial form of government.

The Foundation of Empire

A nephew of the general Marius, Julius Caesar favored liberal policies and social reform. In spite of these well-known political sympathies, he escaped danger during the reign of Sulla and the conservatives who followed him. Caesar's survival was due in some measure to his youth—Sulla and his supporters simply did not consider Caesar *Julius Caesar*

to be a serious threat—but partly also to a well-timed excursion to Greece and the eastern Mediterranean. During the decade of the 60s B.C.E., Caesar played an active role in Roman politics. He spent enormous sums of money sponsoring public spectacles—such as battles between gladiators and wild animals—which helped him build a reputation and win election to posts in the republican government. This activity kept him in the public eye and helped to publicize his interest in social reform. During the next decade Caesar led a Roman army to Gaul, which he conquered and brought into the still-growing Roman empire.

The conquest of Gaul helped to precipitate a political crisis. As a result of his military victories, Caesar had become extremely popular in Rome. Conservative leaders sought to maneuver him out of power and regain the initiative for their own programs. Caesar refused to stand aside, and in 49 B.C.E. he turned his army toward Rome. By early 46 B.C.E. he had made himself master of the Roman state and named himself dictator—an office that he claimed for life rather than

A bust of Julius Caesar depicts a trim conqueror and a canny political leader. • Vatican Museum/ Robert Harding Picture Library

for the constitutional six-month term. Caesar then centralized military and political functions and brought them under his own control. He confiscated property from conservatives and distributed it to veterans of his armies and other supporters. He launched large-scale building projects in Rome as a way to provide employment for the urban poor. He also extended Roman citizenship to peoples in the imperial provinces, and he even appointed Gauls to the Roman Senate.

Caesar's policies pointed the way toward a centralized, imperial form of government for Rome and its possessions, but the consolidation of that government had to wait for a new generation of leaders. Caesar's rule alienated many members of the Roman elite classes, who considered him a tyrant. In 44 B.C.E. they organized a plot to assassinate Caesar and restore the republic. They attacked Caesar and stabbed him to death in the Roman forum, but the restoration of an outmoded form of government was beyond their powers. Instead, they plunged Rome into a fresh round of civil conflict that persisted for another thirteen years.

Augustus   When the struggles ended, power belonged to Octavian, a nephew and protégé of Julius Caesar and the dictator's adopted son. In a naval battle at Actium in Greece (31 B.C.E.), Octavian defeated his principal rival, Mark Antony, who had joined forces with Cleopatra, last of the Ptolemaic rulers of Egypt. He then moved quickly and efficiently to consolidate his rule. In 27 B.C.E. the Senate bestowed upon him the title Augustus, a term with strong religious connotations suggesting the divine or semidivine nature of its holder. During his forty-five years of virtually unopposed rule, Augustus fashioned an imperial government that guided Roman affairs for the next three centuries.

Augustus's Administration

In this statue, which emphasizes his civil and military leadership in Rome, Augustus wears the uniform of a Roman general. • Erich Lessing/Art Resource, NY

Augustus's government was a monarchy disguised as a republic. Like Julius Caesar, Augustus ruled by centralizing political and military power. Yet he proceeded more cautiously than had his patron: Augustus preserved traditional republican offices and forms of government and included members of the Roman elite in his government. At the same time, though, he fundamentally altered the nature of that government. He accumulated vast powers for himself and ultimately took responsibility for all important governmental functions. He reorganized the military system, creating a new standing army with commanders who owed allegiance directly to the emperor—a reform that eliminated problems

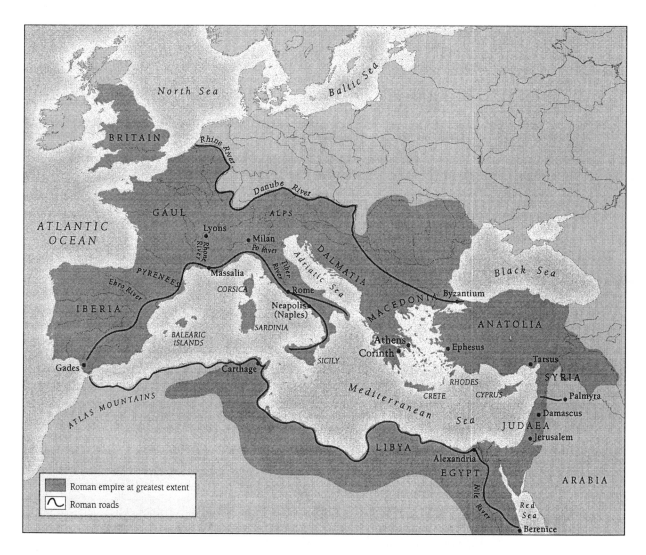

MAP [10.2]

Expansion of the Roman empire.

caused during the late republic by generals with personal armies. He also was careful to place individuals loyal to him in all important positions. Augustus served as emperor until his death in the year 14 C.E. During his long reign he stabilized a land racked by civil war and enabled the institutions of empire to take root.

Continuing Expansion and Integration of the Empire

During the two centuries following Augustus's rule, Roman armies conquered distant lands and integrated them into a larger economy and society. During republican times Rome already held Italy, Greece, Syria, Gaul, and most of the Iberian peninsula, with small outposts in north Africa and Anatolia. By Augustus's reign imperial holdings included much of southeastern Europe, most of north Africa, including Egypt, and sizable territories in Anatolia and southwest Asia. At its high point, during the late second century C.E., the Roman empire embraced much of Britain as well as a continuous belt of possessions surrounding the Mediterranean and extending to rich agricultural regions inland, including Mesopotamia.

Roman expansion had especially dramatic effects in European lands embraced by the empire. Egypt, Anatolia, Syria, and Mesopotamia had long been sites of complex city-based societies, but Gaul, Germany, Britain, and Spain were sparsely populated lands occupied by cultivators who lived in small villages. When Roman soldiers, diplomats, governors, and merchants began to arrive in large numbers, they stimulated the development of local economies and states. They sought access to resources like tin, and they encouraged local inhabitants to cultivate wheat, olives, and grapes. Local ruling elites allied with Roman representatives and used the wealth that came into their communities to control natural resources and build states on a much larger scale than ever before. Cities emerged where administrators and merchants conducted their business, and the tempo of European society noticeably quickened: Paris, Lyons, Cologne, Mainz, London, Toledo, and Segovia all trace their origins to Roman times.

The Pax Romana

Within the boundaries of the Roman empire itself, a long era of peace facilitated economic and political integration from the first to the middle of the third century C.E. Augustus brought peace not only to Rome, by ending the civil disturbances that had plagued the city for more than a century, but also to the empire. His reign inaugurated the era known as the *pax romana* ("Roman peace") that persisted for two and a half centuries. In spite of occasional flareups, especially among conquered peoples who resented Roman rule, the *pax romana* facilitated trade and communication throughout the region from Mesopotamia to the Atlantic Ocean.

Roman Roads

Like their Persian, Chinese, Indian, and Hellenistic counterparts, the Romans integrated their empire by building networks of transportation and communication. Since ancient times, Roman engineers have enjoyed a reputation as outstanding road builders. Roman engineers prepared a deep bed for their roads, edged them with curbs, provided for drainage, and then topped them off with large, flat paving stones. Their main roads were 6 to 8 meters wide (20 to 26 feet)—large enough to accommodate two-way traffic—while even roads winding through mountains were 2 to 3 meters wide (6 to 10 feet). Builders placed milestones along the roads, and the imperial postal system maintained stations for couriers. The roads and postal system permitted urgent travel and messages to proceed with remarkable speed: Tiberius, successor of Augustus as Roman emperor, once traveled 290 kilometers (180 miles) in a single day over Roman roads.

Roads linked all parts of the Roman empire. One notable highway of more than 2,500 kilometers (1,554 miles) stretched along the northeast imperial frontier from the Black Sea to the North Sea, parallel to the Danube and Rhine Rivers. Another road linked Rome to the city of Gades (modern Cadiz) in southern Spain. A road of 4,800 kilometers (2,983 miles) ran parallel to the coast of north Africa, and numerous spurs reached south, enabling merchants and soldiers to range deep into the Sahara desert. Romans also built new roads that facilitated travel and trade in the eastern Mediterranean region. One route linked the port of Berenice on the Red Sea to Alexandria, while others linked the towns and ports of the eastern Mediterranean seaboard to Palmyra, a principal way station of caravan traffic coming west from central Asia.

Roman Law

Under conditions of political stability and the *pax romana,* jurists constructed an elaborate system of law. Romans began a tradition of written law about 450 B.C.E., when they promulgated the Twelve Tables as a basic law code for citizens of the early republic. As armies spread Roman influence throughout the Mediterranean, jurists worked to construct a rational body of law that would apply to all peoples under Roman rule. During the late republic and especially during the empire, the jurists articulated standards of justice and gradually applied them throughout Roman territory. They established the principle that defendants were innocent until proven guilty, and they ensured that defendants had a right to challenge their accusers before a judge in a court of law. They also permitted judges to set aside laws that were inequitable or unfair. Like transportation and communication networks, Roman law helped to integrate the diverse lands that made up the empire, and the principles of Roman law continued to shape Mediterranean and European society long after the empire had disappeared.

Even in distant Britain, Roman engineers built paved roads with drainage ditches. This stretch survives near modern Manchester.
• © Mick Sharp

ECONOMY AND SOCIETY IN THE ROMAN MEDITERRANEAN

The rapid expansion of Roman influence and the imposition of Roman imperial rule brought economic and social changes to peoples throughout the Mediterranean basin. Good roads and the *pax romana* encouraged trade between regions. Existing cities benefitted handsomely from the wealth generated by trade, and in the lands they conquered, the Romans founded new cities to serve as links between local regions and the larger Mediterranean economy. Meanwhile, like most other peoples of classical times, the Romans built a strictly patriarchal society and made extensive use of slave labor.

Trade and Urbanization

Like other classical societies, the Roman Mediterranean experienced economic development and social change as the state expanded and brought new regions into its network of trade and communication. Agricultural production, the economic foundation of the Roman empire, also underwent transformation with the expansion of empire and the growth of trade. Instead of planting crops for immediate local use, owners of *latifundia* concentrated on production for export. Grain from *latifundia*

Commercial Agriculture

in north Africa, Egypt, and Sicily routinely found its way to the large cities of the empire. The ship that Paul of Tarsus boarded at Caesarea, for example, carried several hundred tons of wheat destined for consumers in Rome.

Commercial agriculture played an important role in the economic specialization and integration of the empire. Because it was possible to import grain at favorable prices from lands that routinely produced large surpluses, other regions could concentrate on the cultivation of fruits and vegetables or on the production of manufactured items. Greece, for example, concentrated on olives and vines. Syria and Palestine produced fruits, nuts, and wool fabrics. Gaul produced grain, supplied copper, and began to experiment with the cultivation of vines. Spain produced high-quality olive oil as well as wine, horses, and most of the precious metal used in the Roman empire. Italy became a center for the production of pottery, glassware, and bronze goods. Archaeologists have uncovered one pottery factory north of Rome that might have employed hundreds of workers and that had a mixing vat capable of holding more than 40,000 liters (10,568 gallons) of clay.

Mediterranean Trade

Specialized production of agricultural commodities and manufactured goods set the stage for vigorous trade. Sea-lanes linked ports from Syria and Palestine to Spain and north Africa. Roman military and naval power kept the seas largely free of pirates so that sizable cargoes could move safely over long distances, barring foul weather. Indeed, the Mediterranean became essentially a Roman lake, which the Romans called *mare nostrum* ("our sea"). As Roman military forces, administrators, tax collectors, and other officials traveled throughout the empire carrying out their duties, they joined the merchants in linking the Mediterranean's regions into a well-integrated network of communication and exchange.

The City of Rome

Cities benefitted handsomely from Mediterranean integration and played a prominent role in promoting economic and social change. Along with taxes, tributes, booty, and other wealth generated by military expansion, much of the profit from Mediterranean trade flowed to Rome, where it fueled remarkable urban development. In the first century C.E., some ten thousand statues decorated the city, along with seven hundred pools, five hundred fountains, and thirty-six monumental marble arches celebrating military victories and other achievements. The Roman state financed the construction of temples, bath houses, public buildings, stadiums, and perhaps most important of all, aqueducts that brought fresh water into the city from the neighboring mountains. Construction projects benefitted from the use of concrete, invented by Roman engineers during the republican era, which strengthened structures and allowed builders to meet high standards of precision required for plumbing and water control.

Construction provided employment for hundreds of thousands of workers. As a result, the population of Rome surged, and the city's economy experienced rapid growth. Shopkeepers, artisans, merchants, and bankers proliferated in the imperial capital. Economic development attracted large numbers of migrants from the countryside and from foreign lands. Most received low wages as laborers, construction workers, or servants, but those with skills sometimes found good employment as craftsmen. Some who went to Rome with a bit of money established successful businesses, and by hard work or good fortune, a few entrepreneurs became wealthy and respected businessmen.

Urban growth and development also took place beyond the capital. Some parts of the empire, such as Greece and Syria, had long-standing urban traditions. There trade and economic development brought additional prosperity. Elsewhere the

A wall painting from Stabiae (a small community near Pompeii destroyed by the eruption of Vesuvius in
79 C.E.) depicts an Italian harbor with ships, wharves, warehouses, markets, and decorative columns
topped by statues. • Erich Lessing/Art Resource, NY

Romans founded cities at strategic sites for purposes of government and administration, especially in Spain, Gaul, and Britain, which encouraged economic and social
development at the far reaches of the empire.

As wealth concentrated in the cities, urban residents came to expect a variety of
comforts not available in rural areas. Roman cities enjoyed abundant supplies of
fresh water, sometimes brought from distant mountains by aqueducts, and elaborate
sewage and plumbing systems. All sizable cities and even many smaller towns had
public baths featuring hot and cold rooms, and often swimming pools and gymnasia
as well. Underground sewers carried away waste waters.

Enormous circuses, stadiums, and amphitheaters provided sites for the entertainment of the urban masses. Circuses were oval structures with tracks for chariot races,
which were wildly popular in the Roman empire. The Circus Maximus at Rome accommodated about 250,000 spectators. Entertainment in stadiums often took forms

*Roman Cities and
Their Attractions*

Many Roman aqueducts survive to the present day. This one carried water to the city of Nemausus in Gaul (modern Nîmes in France). The water flowed through a trough supported by the top layer of arches. • Michael Holford

now considered coarse and cruel—battles to the death between gladiators or between humans and wild animals—but urban populations flocked to such events, which they looked upon as exciting diversions from daily routine. The Roman Colosseum, a magnificent marble stadium and sports arena opened in 80 C.E., provided seating for about 50,000 spectators. The structure had a multicolored awning that protected viewers from sun and rain, and its construction was so precise that it was possible to flood the arena with water and stage mock naval battles within its walls.

Family and Society in Roman Times

The Pater Familias   Roman law vested immense authority in male heads of families. The Roman family consisted of an entire household, including slaves, free servants, and close relatives who lived together. Usually the eldest male ruled the household as *pater familias*— "father of the family." Roman law gave the *pater familias* the authority to arrange marriages for his children, determine the work or duties they would perform, and punish them for offenses as he saw fit. He had rights also to sell them into slavery and even to execute them.

Although legally endowed with extraordinary powers, the Roman *pater familias* rarely ruled tyrannically over his charges. In fact, women usually supervised domestic affairs in Roman households, and by the time they reached middle age, women generally wielded considerable influence within their families. They helped select marriage partners for their offspring, and they sometimes played large roles in managing their families' financial affairs. Although Roman law placed strict limits on the ability of women to receive inheritances, enforcement was inconsistent, and clever individuals found ways to evade the law or take advantage of its loopholes. During the third and second centuries B.C.E., as Roman expansion in the Mediterranean brought wealth to the capital, women came to possess a great deal of property. By the first century B.C.E., in spite of the authority legally vested in the *pater familias,* many women supervised the financial affairs of family businesses and wealthy estates.

Wealth and Social Change

Increasing wealth had important consequences for Roman society. New classes of merchants, landowners, and construction contractors accumulated enormous private wealth and rivaled the old nobility for prominence. The newly rich classes built palatial houses with formal gardens and threw lavish banquets with rare and exotic foods such as boiled ostrich, tree fungus served in a sauce of fish fat, jellyfish, and eggs, and parrot-tongue pie. While wealthy classes probed culinary frontiers, cultivators and urban masses subsisted largely on porridge and vegetables occasionally supplemented by eggs, fish, sausage, or meat.

By the first century B.C.E., the poor classes had become a considerable problem in Rome and other large cities of the empire. Often unemployed, the urban masses sometimes rioted to express their dissatisfaction and seek improved conditions, and they readily provided recruits for private armies of ambitious generals like Marius and Sulla. Imperial authorities never developed a true urban policy, but rather sought to keep the masses contented with "bread and circuses"—subsidized grain and spectacular public entertainments.

Slavery

Roman society made extensive use of slave labor: by the second century C.E., slaves may have represented as much as one-third of the population of the Roman empire. In the countryside they worked mostly on *latifundia,* though many labored in state quarries and mines. Rural slaves worked under extremely harsh conditions, often chained together in teams. Discontent among rural slaves led to several massive revolts, especially during the second and first centuries B.C.E. During the most serious uprising, in 73 B.C.E., the escaped slave Spartacus assembled an army of seventy thousand rebellious slaves. The Roman army dispatched eight legions, comprising more than forty thousand well-equipped, veteran troops, to quell the revolt.

In the cities conditions were much less difficult than in the countryside. Female slaves commonly worked as domestic servants while males toiled as servants, laborers, craftsmen, shopkeepers, or business agents for their owners. Slaves who had an education or possessed some particular talent had the potential to lead comfortable lives. The first-century Anatolian slave Epictetus even became a prominent Stoic philosopher. He spent much of his life studying with Rome's leading intellectuals, and he lectured to large audiences that included high Roman officials and perhaps even emperors.

More than their counterparts in rural areas, urban slaves could hope for manumission as a reward for a long term of loyal service: it was common, though not mandatory, for masters to free urban slaves about the time they reached thirty years of age. Until freed, however, slaves remained under the strict authority of their masters, who had the right to sell them, arrange their family affairs, punish them, and even execute them for serious offenses.

THE COSMOPOLITAN MEDITERRANEAN

The integration of the Mediterranean basin had important effects not only for the trade and economy of the Roman empire but also for its cultural and religious traditions. As travelers ventured throughout the Mediterranean basin, they became acquainted with other cultural and religious traditions. When migrants moved to

Built between 118 and 125 C.E., the Pantheon in Rome was a temple honoring all gods, and it survives as one of the outstanding examples of Roman architecture. With a diameter of 43 meters (141 feet), the building's dome was the largest constructed until the twentieth century. • Robert Frerck/The Stock Market

Rome and other large cities, they often continued to observe their inherited traditions and thus contributed to the cosmopolitan cultural atmosphere of the empire. Roads and communication networks favored the spread of new popular religions. Most important of these was Christianity, which originated as a small and persecuted Jewish sect. Within three centuries, however, Christianity had become the official religion of the Roman empire and the predominant faith of the Mediterranean basin.

Greek Philosophy and Religions of Salvation

During the early days of their history, the Romans recognized many gods and goddesses, who they believed intervened directly in human affairs. Jupiter was the principal god, lord of the heavens, while Mars was the god of war, Ceres the goddess of grain, Janus the

Roman Deities   god who watched the threshold of individual houses, and Vesta the goddess of the hearth. In addition to these major deities, most Roman households also honored tutelary deities, gods who looked after the welfare of individual families.

As the Romans expanded their political influence and built an empire, they encountered the religious and cultural traditions of other peoples. Often they adopted the deities or the cultural traditions of other peoples and used them for their own purposes. From the Etruscans, for example, they learned of Juno, the moon goddess, and Minerva, the goddess of wisdom, as well as certain religious practices, such as divination of the future through examination of the internal organs of ritually sacrificed animals.

Greek Influence   The Romans also drew inspiration from the Greek tradition of rational thought and philosophy. When the Romans established political hegemony in the eastern Mediterranean in the third and second centuries B.C.E., the most prominent school of thought in Hellenistic Greece was Stoicism. Recognizing that they lived in a large and interdependent world, the Stoics sought to identify a set of universal moral standards based on nature and reason that would transcend local ethical codes.

This approach to moral thought appealed strongly to Roman intellectuals, and thinkers such as Marcus Tullius Cicero (106–43 B.C.E.) readily adopted Stoic values. Cicero studied in Greece and became thoroughly acquainted with both classical and Hellenistic schools of thought. He was a persuasive orator, and he wrote clear, elegant, polished Latin prose. In adapting Hellenistic thought to Roman needs, Cicero drew heavily from the Stoics' moral and ethical teachings. His letters and treatises emphasized the individual's duty to live in accordance with nature and reason. He argued that the pursuit of justice was the individual's highest public duty, and he scorned those who sought to accumulate wealth or to become powerful through immoral, illegal, or unjust means. Through his speeches and especially his writings, Cicero helped to establish Stoicism as the most prominent school of moral philosophy in Rome.

Cicero and Stoicism

While educated thinkers drew inspiration from the Greeks, the masses found comfort in religions of salvation that established their presence throughout the Mediterranean basin and beyond. Like Stoicism, these religions clearly reflected the political and social conditions of the Hellenistic period: in an imperial era, when close-knit city-states no longer served as a focus for individual loyalties, religions of salvation appealed to the popular masses by providing a sense of purpose and the promise of a glorious future existence.

Religions of Salvation

These religions became prominent features of Mediterranean society during Hellenistic times and became increasingly noticeable in Rome during the late republic as migrants settled in the capital and brought their faiths with them. Under the Roman empire religions of salvation flourished both in Rome and throughout the Mediterranean basin. Merchants, soldiers, and administrators carried their cults as they conducted their business, and missionaries traveled alongside them in search of converts. The roads of the empire and the sea-lanes of the Mediterranean thus served not only as trade routes and lines of official communication but also as highways for religions of salvation, which traveled to all the ports and large cities of the empire.

Among the most popular of these religions of salvation was the cult dedicated to Mithras. In Zoroastrian mythology Mithras was a god closely identified with the sun and light. Roman soldiers serving in the Hellenistic world, particularly Anatolia, encountered the cult of Mithras and adapted it to their interests. They associated Mithras less with the sun than with military virtues such as strength, courage, and discipline, and the cult of Mithras quickly became exceptionally popular among the Roman armed forces.

Mithraism

The Mithraic religion provided divine sanction for human life and especially for purposeful moral behavior. It brought together a community that welcomed and nurtured like-minded individuals. Finally, it offered hope for individuals who conscientiously observed the cult's teachings by promising them ecstatic and mysterious union with Mithras himself. During the late republic Mithraic altars and temples appeared in military garrisons throughout the empire. During the early centuries C.E., administrators and merchants also became enchanted with Mithras, and his cult attracted followers among the male populations of all sizable communities and commercial centers in the Roman empire.

The cult of Mithras did not admit women, but cults dedicated to the Anatolian mother goddess Cybele, the Egyptian goddess Isis, and other deities made a place for both men and women. As in the case of the Mithraic religion, these cults attracted followers in Rome and other cities throughout the Mediterranean basin. The immense popularity of these religions of salvation provides a context that helps to explain the remarkable success of Christianity in the Roman empire.

This mithraeum—a shrine to the god Mithras—survives beneath the church of San Clemente in Rome. Benches accommodated worshipers. The sculpture on the altar depicts Mithras sacrificing a bull to the god Apollo. • Alinari/Art Resource. Photo: G. Tatge

Judaism and Early Christianity

The Jews and the Empire   After the dissolution of the Jewish kingdom of David and Solomon in the early tenth century B.C.E., the Jewish people maintained their faith and their communities under various imperial regimes: Babylonian, Achaemenid, Alexandrian, Seleucid, and Roman. All these empires embraced many different ethnic and religious groups and mostly tolerated the cultural preferences of their subjects, providing that communities paid their taxes and refrained from rebellious activities. In an effort to encourage political loyalty, these empires often created state cults that honored their emperors as gods, and they sometimes called for subjects to participate in the cults and revere the emperor-gods. This requirement created a serious problem for the strictly monotheistic Jews, who recognized only their own god, Yahweh, as divine. Jews considered the pretensions of the state cults to be blasphemy, and many of them refused to pay homage to a mortal being who laid claim to divinity. Sometimes they even declined to pay taxes to regimes that required subjects to revere their emperors. Relations between Jews and imperial authorities became especially tense as the Romans extended their empire in the eastern Mediterranean region. Between the third century B.C.E. and the first century C.E., Jews in Palestine mounted several rebellions against their Seleucid and Roman overlords. Ultimately the resistance failed, and Roman forces decisively defeated the rebels during the Jewish War of 66 to 70 C.E.

The Essenes   While some Jews actively fought the Romans, others founded new sects that looked for saviors to deliver them from subjection. The Essenes formed one such sect. In 1947 shepherds accidentally discovered some Essene writings known as the Dead Sea scrolls, which have shed a great deal of light on the sect and its beliefs. The Essenes formed their community in Palestine during the first century B.C.E. They observed a strict moral code and participated in rituals designed to reinforce a sense of community: they admitted new members after a rite of baptism in water, and they took part in ritual community meals. They also looked for a savior who would deliver them from Roman rule and lead them in the establishment of a community in which they could practice their faith without interference.

The early Christians probably had little contact with the Essenes, but they shared many of the same concerns. The Christians formed their community around Jesus of Nazareth, a charismatic Jewish teacher whom they recognized as their savior. Born about the year 4 B.C.E., Jesus grew up at a time of high tension between Roman overlords and their Jewish subjects. He was a peaceful man who taught devotion to God and love for fellow human beings. He attracted large crowds because of a reputation for wisdom and miraculous powers, especially the ability to heal the sick.

Jesus of Nazareth

Yet Jesus alarmed the Romans because he also taught that "the kingdom of God is at hand." To Jesus, the kingdom of God was a spiritual realm in which God would gather those faithful to him. To Roman administrators, however, his message carried political overtones: an impending kingdom of God sounded like a threat to Roman rule in Palestine, especially since enthusiastic crowds routinely accompanied Jesus. In an effort to forestall a new round of rebellion, Roman administrators executed Jesus by fixing him to a cross in the early 30s C.E.

Jesus' crucifixion did not put an end to his movement. Even after his execution Jesus' close followers strongly felt his presence and proclaimed that he had triumphed over death by rising from his grave. They called him "Christ," meaning "the anointed one," the savior who would bring individuals into the kingdom of God. They taught that he was the son of God and that his sacrifice served to offset the sins of those who had faith in him. They taught further that like Jesus, the faithful would survive death and would experience eternal life in the spiritual kingdom of God. Following Jesus' teachings, the early Christians observed a demanding moral code and devoted themselves uncompromisingly to God. They also compiled a body of writings—accounts of Jesus' life, reports of his followers' works, and letters outlining Christian teachings—that gained recognition as the New Testament. Together with the Jews' Hebrew scriptures, which Christians referred to as the Old Testament, the New Testament became the holy book of Christianity.

Jesus and his earliest followers were all Jews. Beginning about the middle of the first century C.E., however, some Christians avidly sought converts from non-Jewish communities in the Hellenistic world and the Roman empire. The principal figure in the expansion of Christianity beyond Judaism was Paul of Tarsus, a Jew from Anatolia who zealously preached his faith, especially in the Greek-speaking eastern region of the Roman empire. Paul taught a Christianity that attracted the urban masses in the same way as other religions of salvation that spread widely in the Roman empire. His doctrine called for individuals to observe high moral standards and to place their faith ahead of personal and family interests. His teaching also explained the world and human history as the results of God's purposeful activity so that it provided a framework of meaning for individuals' lives. Furthermore, Paul's doctrine promised a glorious future existence for those who conscientiously observed the faith.

Paul of Tarsus

Like missionaries of other faiths, Paul was no stranger to Roman roads and Mediterranean sea-lanes. He traveled widely in search of converts and made several journeys through Greece, Anatolia, Syria, and Palestine to visit fledgling Christian communities and offer them guidance. His last journey took him by ship from Palestine to Rome, where he sought converts for about two years before losing his appeal to the emperor and suffering execution.

JESUS' MORAL AND ETHICAL TEACHINGS

• • •

Several accounts of Jesus' life record the Sermon on the Mount in which Jesus challenged his followers to honor God and observe a demanding code of ethics. Here Jesus explicitly instructed his listeners to reject moral and legal principles that southwest Asian peoples had followed since the third millennium B.C.E. and that the Babylonian emperor Hammurabi had enshrined in his famous code of laws about 1750 B.C.E. Jesus enjoined them to refrain from revenge against those who had caused them harm, for example, and instead to repay harm with kindness.

Blessed are the poor in spirit: for theirs is the kingdom of heaven. Blessed are they that mourn: for they shall be comforted. Blessed are the meek: for they shall inherit the earth. Blessed are they which do hunger and thirst after righteousness: for they shall be filled. Blessed are the merciful: for they shall obtain mercy. Blessed are the pure in heart: for they shall see God. Blessed are the peacemakers: for they shall be called the children of God. Blessed are they which are persecuted for righteousness's sake: for theirs is the kingdom of heaven. Blessed are ye when men shall revile you and persecute you and shall say all manner of evil against you falsely for my sake. Rejoice, and be exceeding glad: for great is your reward in heaven. . . .

Ye have heard that it hath been said, "An eye for an eye, and a tooth for a tooth." But I say unto you that ye resist not evil: but whosoever shall smite thee on thy right cheek, turn to him the other also. And if any man will sue thee at the law, and take away thy coat, let him have thy cloak also. And whosoever shall compel thee to go a mile, go with him two. Give to him that asketh thee, and from him that would borrow of thee turn not thou away.

Ye have heard that it hath been said, "Thou shalt love thy neighbour, and hate thine enemy." But I say unto you, love your enemies, bless them that curse you, do good to them that hate you, and pray for them which despitefully use you and persecute you, that ye may be the children of your Father which is in heaven: for he maketh his sun to rise on the evil and on the good, and sendeth rain on the just and on the unjust. . . .

Ask, and it shall be given you; seek, and ye shall find; knock, and it shall be opened unto you. For every one that asketh receiveth; and he that seeketh findeth; and to him that knocketh it shall be opened. What man is there of you, whom if his son ask bread, will he give him a stone? Or if he ask a fish, will he give him a serpent? If ye then, being evil, know how to give good gifts unto your children, how much more shall your Father which is in heaven give good things to them that ask him? Therefore all things whatsoever ye would that men should do to you, do ye even so to them.

SOURCE: Matthew 5:3–13, 5:38–45, 6:7–12 (Authorized Version). (Translation slightly modified.)

The Growth of Early Christianity   Like the Jews from whose ranks they had sprung, the early Christians refused to honor the Roman state cults or revere the emperor as a god. As a result, Roman imperial authorities launched sporadic campaigns of persecution designed to eliminate Christianity as a threat to the empire. In spite of this repression, Christian numbers grew rapidly. During the first three centuries of the faith's existence, Christianity found its way to almost all parts of the Roman empire, and Christians established thriving communities throughout the Mediterranean basin and further east in Mesopotamia and Iran. Rome itself had a sizable Christian population by 300 C.E.

The remarkable growth of Christianity reflected the new faith's appeal particularly to the lower classes, urban populations, and women. Christianity accorded honor and dignity to individuals who did not enjoy high standing in Roman society, and it endowed them with a sense of spiritual freedom more meaningful than wealth, power, or social prominence. Unlike the popular cult of Mithras, which admitted only men, Christianity taught the spiritual equality of the sexes and welcomed the contributions of both men and women. Like Mithraism and other religions of salvation, Christianity provided a sense of purpose and a promise of future glory for those who placed their faith in Jesus. Thus although Christianity originated as a minor sect of Judaism, urban populations in the Roman empire embraced the new faith with such enthusiasm that by the third century C.E. it had become the most dynamic and influential religious faith in the Mediterranean basin.

Under Roman influence Mediterranean lands became a tightly integrated society. The Roman empire provided a political structure that administered lands as distant as Mesopotamia and Britain. Highly organized trade networks enabled peoples throughout the empire to concentrate on specialized agricultural or industrial production and import foods and other goods that they did not produce themselves. Popular religions spread widely and attracted enthusiastic converts. Like Confucianism and Buddhism in classical China and India, rational philosophy and Christianity became prominent sources of intellectual and religious authority in the classical Mediterranean and continued to influence cultural development in the Mediterranean, Europe, and southwest Asia over the long term.

CHRONOLOGY

753 B.C.E.	Founding of Rome, according to tradition
509 B.C.E.	Establishment of the Roman republic
264–146 B.C.E.	Roman expansion in the Mediterranean basin
106–43 B.C.E.	Life of Marcus Tullius Cicero
first century B.C.E.	Civil war in Rome
46–44 B.C.E.	Rule of Gaius Julius Caesar as dictator
31 B.C.E.–14 C.E.	Rule of Augustus
4 B.C.E.–early 30s C.E.	Life of Jesus of Nazareth
first century C.E.	Life of Paul of Tarsus
66–70 C.E.	Jewish War

FOR FURTHER READING

Henry C. Boren. *Roman Society.* 2nd ed. Lexington, 1992. An authoritative synthesis that places social and economic history in its political context.

Keith R. Bradley. *Discovering the Roman Family: Studies in Roman Social History.* New York, 1991. A provocative analysis of Roman family life with illustrations from individual experiences.

———. *Slavery and Society at Rome.* Cambridge, 1994. An engaging and readable essay on slavery and its role in Roman society, with special attention to individual experiences.

Barry Cunliffe. *Greeks, Romans and Barbarians: Spheres of Interaction*. New York, 1988. Draws on archaeological evidence in assessing the effects of the Roman presence in Gaul, Britain, and Germany.

M. I. Finley. *Ancient Slavery and Modern Ideology*. New York, 1980. A thoughtful analysis of Greek and Roman slavery in light of modern slavery and contemporary debates.

Michael Grant. *Cities of Vesuvius: Pompeii and Herculaneum*. London, 1971. Fascinating glimpse of Roman society as reconstructed by archaeologists working at sites destroyed by the eruption of Vesuvius in 79 C.E.

A.H.M. Jones. *Augustus*. New York, 1970. A distinguished historian of ancient Rome provides the best study of Augustus and his career.

Naphtali Lewis and Meyer Reinhold, eds. *Roman Civilization: Selected Readings*. 2 vols. 3rd ed. New York, 1990. A rich collection of translated texts and documents that illuminate Roman history and society.

Paul MacKendrick. *The Mute Stones Speak: The Story of Archaeology in Italy*. New York, 1960. An older but engaging work with still valuable information on Roman architecture and construction techniques.

Ramsay MacMullen. *Christianizing the Roman Empire*. New Haven, 1984. Scholarly study of the processes by which Christianity became established in the Roman empire.

Harold Mattingly. *The Man in the Roman Street*. New York, 1966. An engaging study of popular culture and religion in the Roman empire.

Elaine Pagels. *Adam, Eve, and the Serpent*. New York, 1988. Provocative and fascinating analysis of early Christianity and its relationship with the Roman state.

Sarah B. Pomeroy. *Goddesses, Whores, Wives, and Slaves: Women in Classical Antiquity*. New York, 1975. Outstanding study analyzing the status and role of women in classical Greece and Rome.

CHAPTER 11

CROSS-CULTURAL EXCHANGES ON THE SILK ROADS

• • •

In the year 139 B.C.E., the Chinese emperor Han Wudi sent an envoy named Zhang Qian on a mission to lands west of China. The emperor's purpose was to find allies who could help combat the nomadic Xiongnu, who menaced the northern and western borders of the Han empire. From captives he had learned that other nomadic peoples in far western lands bore grudges against the Xiongnu, and he reasoned that they might ally with Han forces to pressure their common enemy.

The problem for Zhang Qian was that to communicate with potential allies against the Xiongnu, he had to pass directly through lands they controlled. Soon after Zhang Qian left Han territory, Xiongnu forces captured him. For ten years the Xiongnu held him in comfortable captivity: they allowed him to keep his personal servant, and they provided him with a Xiongnu wife, with whom he had a son. When suspicions about him subsided, however, Zhang Qian escaped with his family and servant. He even had the presence of mind to keep with him the yak tail that Han Wudi had given him as a sign of his ambassadorial status. He fled to the west and traveled as far as Bactria, but he did not succeed in lining up allies against the Xiongnu. While returning to China, Zhang Qian again fell into Xiongnu hands but managed to escape after one year's detention when the death of the Xiongnu leader led to a period of turmoil. In 126 B.C.E. Zhang Qian and his party returned to China and a warm welcome from Han Wudi.

Although his diplomatic efforts did not succeed, Zhang Qian's mission had far-reaching consequences. Apart from political and military intelligence about western lands and their peoples, Zhang Qian also brought back information of immense commercial value. While in Bactria about 128 B.C.E., he noticed Chinese goods—textiles and bamboo articles—offered for sale in local markets. Upon inquiry he learned that they had come from southwest China by way of Bengal. From this information he deduced the possibility of establishing trade relations between China and Bactria through India.

Han Wudi responded enthusiastically to this idea and dreamed of trading with peoples inhabiting lands west of China. From 102 to 98 B.C.E., he mounted a massive campaign that broke the power of the Xiongnu and pacified central Asia. His conquests simplified trade relations, since it became unnecessary to route commerce

Ruins of an ancient fort at Jiaohe, near Turpan, on the silk road. • © 1993 Pamela Logan through India. The intelligence that Zhang Qian gathered during his travels thus contributed to the opening of the silk roads—the network of trade routes that linked lands as distant as China and the Roman empire—and more generally to the establishment of relations between China and lands to the west.

China and other classical societies imposed political and military control over vast territories. They promoted trade and communication within their own empires, bringing regions that had previously been self-sufficient into a larger economy and society. They also fostered the spread of cultural and religious traditions to distant regions, and they encouraged the construction of institutional frameworks that promoted the long-term survival of those traditions.

The influence of the classical societies did not stop at the imperial boundaries. Nearby peoples regarded their powerful neighbors with a mixture of envy and suspicion, and they sought to share the wealth they generated. They pursued this goal by various means, both peaceful and violent, and relations with neighboring peoples, particularly nomadic peoples, became a major preoccupation of all the classical societies.

Beyond their relations with neighboring peoples, the classical societies established a broad zone of communication and exchange throughout much of the earth's eastern hemisphere. Trade networks crossed the deserts of central Asia and the depths of the Indian Ocean. Long-distance trade passed through much of Eurasia and north Africa, from China to the Mediterranean basin, and to parts of sub-Saharan Africa as well.

This long-distance trade profoundly influenced the experiences of peoples and the development of societies throughout the eastern hemisphere. It brought wealth and access to foreign products, and it enabled peoples to concentrate their efforts on economic activities best suited to their regions. It facilitated the spread of religious traditions beyond their original homelands, since merchants carried their beliefs and sometimes attracted converts in the lands they visited. It also facilitated the transmission of disease: pathogens traveled the trade routes alongside commercial wares and religious faiths. Indeed, the transmission of disease over the silk roads helped bring an end to the classical societies, since infectious and contagious diseases sparked devastating epidemics that caused political, social, and economic havoc. Long-distance trade thus had deep political, social, and cultural as well as economic and commercial implications for classical societies.

 ## LONG-DISTANCE TRADE AND THE SILK ROADS NETWORK

Ever since the earliest days of history, human communities have traded with one another, sometimes over long distances. Before classical times, however, long-distance trade was a risky venture. Ancient societies often policed their own realms effectively, but since they were relatively small and compact, extensive regions lay beyond their control. Trade passing between societies was therefore liable to interception by bandits or pirates. This risk increased the costs of long-distance transactions in ancient times.

During the classical era two developments reduced the risks associated with travel and stimulated long-distance trade. In the first place, rulers invested heavily in the construction of roads and bridges. They undertook these expensive projects primarily for military and administrative reasons, but roads also had the effect of encouraging trade within individual societies and facilitating exchanges between different societies. In the second place, classical societies built large imperial states that

Parthian merchants and other travelers like the soldiers depicted here followed in the footsteps of their Achaemenid and Seleucid predecessors and became regular visitors to northern India. This gray schist carving from Gandhara dates from the second century B.C.E. • Photograph courtesy of the Royal Ontario Museum. © ROM

sometimes expanded to the point that they bordered on one another: the campaigns of Alexander of Macedon, for example, brought Hellenistic and Indian societies into direct contact, and only small buffer states separated the Roman and Parthian empires. Even when they did not encounter each other so directly, classical empires pacified large stretches of Eurasia and north Africa. As a result, merchants did not face such great risk as in previous eras, the costs of long-distance trade dropped, and its volume rose dramatically.

Trade Networks of the Hellenistic Era

The tempo of long-distance trade increased noticeably during the Hellenistic era, partly because of the many colonies established by Alexander of Macedon and the Seleucid rulers in Persia and Bactria. Though originally populated by military forces and administrators, these settlements soon attracted Greek merchants and bankers who linked the recently conquered lands to the Mediterranean basin. The Seleucid rulers worked diligently to promote trade. They controlled land routes linking Bactria, which offered access to Indian markets, to Mediterranean ports in Syria and Palestine. Archaeologists have unearthed hundreds of coins, pieces of jewelry, and other physical remains, including Greek-style sculptures and buildings, that testify to the presence of Greek communities in Persia and Bactria during the Hellenistic era.

Like the Seleucids, the Ptolemies maintained land routes—in their case, routes going south from Egypt to the kingdoms of Nubia and Meroe in east Africa—but they also paid close attention to sea-lanes and maritime trade. They ousted pirates from sea-lanes linking the Red Sea to the Arabian Sea and the Indian Ocean. They also built several new ports, the most important being Berenice on the Red Sea, while Alexandria served as their principal window on the Mediterranean.

The Monsoon System   Even more important, perhaps, mariners from Ptolemaic Egypt learned about the monsoon winds that governed sailing and shipping in the Indian Ocean. During the summer the winds blow regularly from the southwest, while in the winter they come from the northeast. Knowledge of these winds enabled mariners to sail safely and reliably to all parts of the Indian Ocean basin. During the second century B.C.E., Hellenistic mariners learned the rhythm of these winds from Arab and Indian seamen whose ancestors had sailed before the monsoons for centuries. Merchant seamen then established regular links by way of the Red Sea between India and Arabia in the east and Egypt and the Mediterranean basin in the west.

Establishment and maintenance of these trade routes was an expensive affair calling for substantial investment in military forces, construction, and bureaucracies to administer the commerce that passed over the routes. But the investment paid handsome dividends. Long-distance trade stimulated economic development within the Hellenistic realms themselves, bringing benefits to local economies throughout the empires. Moreover, Hellenistic rulers closely supervised foreign trade and levied taxes on it, thereby deriving income even from foreign products.

Trade in the Hellenistic World   With official encouragement, a substantial trade developed throughout the Hellenistic world, from Bactria and India in the east to the Mediterranean basin in the west. Spices, pepper, cosmetics, gems, and pearls from India traveled by caravan and ship to Hellenistic cities and ports. Grain from Persia and Egypt fed urban populations in distant lands. Mediterranean wine, olive oil, jewelry, and works of art made their way to Persia and Bactria. And throughout the region from India to the Mediterranean, merchants conducted a brisk trade in slaves recruited largely from the ranks of kidnapping victims or prisoners of war.

The Silk Roads

The establishment of classical empires greatly expanded the scope of long-distance trade, as much of Eurasia and north Africa fell under the sway of one classical society or another. The Han empire maintained order in China and pacified much of central Asia, including a sizable corridor offering access to Bactria and western markets. The Parthian empire displaced the Seleucids in Persia and extended its authority to Mesopotamia. The Roman empire brought order to the Mediterranean basin. With the decline of the Mauryan dynasty, India lacked a strong imperial state, but regional states provided stability and security, particularly in northern India, that favored long-distance trade.

Overland Trade Routes   As the classical empires expanded, merchants and travelers created an extensive network of trade routes that linked much of Eurasia and north Africa. Historians refer to these routes collectively as the silk roads, since high-quality silk from China was one of the principal commodities exchanged over the roads. The overland silk roads took caravan trade from China to the Roman empire, thus linking the extreme ends of the Eurasian landmass. From the Han capital of Chang'an, the main silk road went west through Mongolia and Turkestan (modern-day Xinjiang Autonomous Region in China) until it arrived at the Taklamakan desert, also known as the Tarim Basin. This desert is one of the most dangerous and inhospitable regions of the earth: its very name, Taklamakan, warns that "he who enters does not come back out." The silk road then split into two branches that skirted the desert proper and passed through oasis towns that ringed it to the north and south. The branches came together at Kashgar (now known as Kashi, located in the western-most corner of modern China). From there the reunited road went west to Bactria, where a

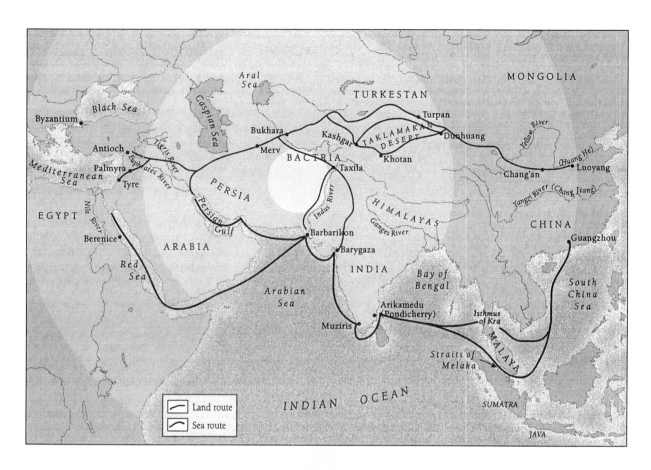

MAP [11.1]

The silk roads

branch forked off to offer access to Taxila and northern India, while the principal route continued across northern Iran. There it joined with roads to ports on the Caspian Sea and the Persian Gulf and proceeded to Palmyra (in modern Syria), where it met roads coming from Arabia and ports on the Red Sea. Continuing west, it terminated at the Mediterranean ports of Antioch (in modern Turkey) and Tyre (in modern Lebanon).

Sea-Lanes and Maritime Trade

The silk roads also included a network of sea-lanes that sustained maritime commerce throughout much of the eastern hemisphere. From Guangzhou in southern China, sea-lanes through the South China Sea linked the east Asian seaboard to the mainland and the islands of southeast Asia. Routes linking southeast Asia with Ceylon (modern Sri Lanka) and India were especially busy during classical times. From India sea-lanes passed through the Arabian Sea to Persia and Arabia, and through the Persian Gulf and the Red Sea they offered access to land routes and the Mediterranean basin, which already possessed a well-developed network of trade routes.

Trade Goods

A wide variety of manufactured products and agricultural commodities traveled over the silk roads. Generally speaking, silk and spices traveled west from producers in southeast Asia, China, and India to consumers in central Asia, Iran, Arabia, and the Roman empire (including Egypt and north Africa as well as the European regions of the empire). Silk came mostly from China, the only land in classical times where cultivators and weavers had developed techniques for producing high-quality silk fabrics. The fine spices—cloves, nutmeg, mace, and cardamom—all came from southeast Asia. Ginger came from China, cinnamon from China and southeast Asia,

During the first century B.C.E., Romans developed advanced glass-blowing techniques that enabled them to produce wares like this jar that were popular with wealthy consumers. • © The British Museum

A roman coin dated 189 C.E. depicts a merchant ship near the lighthouse at Alexandria. Ships like this one regularly picked up pepper and cinnamon from India along with other cargoes. • Photograph courtesy of the Royal Ontario Museum. © ROM

pepper from India, and sesame oil from India, Arabia, and southwest Asia. Spices were extremely important commodities in classical times because they had many more uses than they do in the modern world. They served not only as condiments and flavoring agents but also as drugs, anesthetics, aphrodisiacs, perfumes, aromatics, and magical potions. Apart from spices, India also exported cotton textiles and valuable exotic items such as pearls, coral, and ivory.

The more western lands exchanged a variety of manufactured goods and other commodities for the silks and spices that they imported. Central Asia produced large, strong horses and high-quality jade, much prized in China by stone carvers. From the Roman empire came glassware, jewelry, works of art, decorative items, perfumes, bronze goods, wool and linen textiles, pottery, iron tools, olive oil, wine, and gold and silver bullion. Mediterranean merchants and manufacturers often imported raw materials such as uncut gemstones, which they exported as finished products in the form of expensive jewelry and decorative items.

Some individuals made very long journeys during classical times: Zhang Qian ventured from China as far west as Bactria; Chinese merchants traveled regularly to central Asia and Persia; several Indian embassies called on Roman emperors; Roman merchants traveled by sea at least as far east as southern India; and Malay merchant-mariners sailed from the islands of southeast Asia to India and east Africa. On a few occasions individuals even traveled across much or all of the eastern hemisphere between China and the Roman empire. A Chinese ambassador named Gang Ying embarked on a mission to distant western lands in 97 C.E. and proceeded as far as Mesopotamia before reports of the long and dangerous journey ahead persuaded him to return home. And Chinese sources reported the arrival in 166 C.E. of a delegation claiming to represent the Roman emperor Marcus Aurelius. No information survives to throw light on the experiences of this party—or even to confirm its identity—but Roman subjects from Egypt or Syria might well have traveled as far as China in search of trading opportunities.

Individual merchants did not usually travel from one end of Eurasia to the other. Instead, they handled long-distance trade in stages. On the caravan routes between China and Bactria, for example, Chinese and central Asian nomadic peoples dominated trade. Rarely if ever did they go farther west, however, because the Parthians took advantage of their power and geographical position to control overland trade within their boundaries and to reserve it for their own subjects. Once it reached Palmyra, merchandise passed mostly into the hands of Roman subjects such as Greeks, Jews, and Armenians, who were especially active in the commercial life of the Mediterranean basin.

Meanwhile, on the seas, other peoples became involved in long-distance trade. From south China through southeast Asia to Ceylon and India, the principal figures were Malay and Indian mariners. In the Arabian Sea, Persians joined Egyptian and Greek subjects of the Roman empire as the most prominent trading peoples. The Parthian empire largely controlled trade in the Persian Gulf, whereas the Ptolemaic dynasty and later the Roman empire dominated affairs in the Red Sea. After Roman emperors absorbed Egypt in the first century C.E., their subjects carried on an especially brisk trade between India and the Mediterranean. The Greek geographer Strabo reported in the early first century C.E. that as many as 120 ships departed annually from the Red Sea for India. Archaeologists have unearthed the remains of a Roman trading outpost at Arikamedu, near modern Pondicherry in southern India, and literary sources report that merchants subject to Roman rule established Indian colonies also at Muziris (near modern Cranganore), Barygaza (near modern Broach), Barbarikon (near modern Karachi), and other sites as well. Meanwhile, since the mid-first century C.E., the Romans also had dominated both the eastern and western regions of *mare nostrum,* the Mediterranean.

It is impossible to determine the quantity or value of trade that passed over the silk roads in classical times, but it clearly made a deep impression on contemporaries. By the first century C.E., silk garments had become items of high

Early Buddhist sculpture in Bactria reflected the influence of Mediterranean and Greek artistic styles. This seated Buddha from the first or second century C.E. bears Caucasian features and wears Mediterranean-style dress. • Photograph courtesy of the Royal Ontario Museum. © ROM

fashion in Rome, where pepper, cinnamon, and other spices graced the tables of the wealthy classes. Some Romans worried that hefty expenditures for luxury items would weaken or even bankrupt the empire—an anxiety that revealed indirectly the powerful attraction that imported silks and spices had for consumers in classical Rome.

As it happened, long-distance trade did not cause serious economic problems for the Roman empire or any other state in classical times. Indeed, it more likely stimulated rather than threatened local economies. Yet long-distance trade did not occur in a vacuum. Commercial exchanges encouraged cultural and biological exchanges, some of which had large implications for classical societies.

CULTURAL AND BIOLOGICAL EXCHANGES ALONG THE SILK ROADS

The silk roads served as magnificent highways for merchants and their commodities, but others also took advantage of the opportunities they offered to travel in relative safety over long distances. Merchants, missionaries, and other travelers carried their beliefs, values, and religious convictions to distant lands: Buddhism, Hinduism, and Christianity all traveled the silk roads and attracted converts far from their original homelands. Meanwhile, invisible travelers such as disease pathogens also crossed the silk roads and touched off devastating epidemics when they found fresh populations to infect. Toward the end of the classical era, epidemic disease spread over the silk roads caused dramatic demographic decline especially in China and the Mediterranean basin and to a lesser extent in other parts of Eurasia as well.

The Spread of Buddhism and Hinduism

By the third century B.C.E., Buddhism had become well established in northern India, and with the sponsorship of the emperor Ashoka the faith spread to Bactria and Ceylon. Buddhism was particularly successful in attracting merchants as converts. When they traveled, Buddhist merchants observed their faith among themselves and explained it to others. Gradually, Buddhism made its way along the silk roads to Iran, central Asia, China, and southeast Asia.

Buddhism in Central Asia   Buddhism first established a presence in the oasis towns along the silk roads—notably Merv, Bukhara, Samarkand, Kashgar, Khotan, Kuqa, Turpan, and Dunhuang—where merchants and their caravans found food, rest, lodging, and markets. The oases depended heavily on trade for their prosperity, and they allowed merchants to build monasteries and invite monks and copyists into their communities. Perhaps as early as the second century B.C.E., the oasis towns themselves had largely adopted Buddhism.

From the oasis communities Buddhism spread to the steppelands of central Asia and to China. Nomadic peoples from the steppes visited the oases regularly to trade animal products from their herds for grains and manufactured items. They often found Buddhism intriguing, and in the early centuries C.E. they increasingly responded to its appeal. By the fourth century C.E., they had sponsored the spread of Buddhism throughout much of central Asia.

Buddhism in China   By the first century B.C.E., Buddhism had also established a foothold in China. The earliest Buddhists in China were foreign merchants—Indians, Parthians, and central Asian peoples—who observed their faith in the enclaves that Han dynasty of-

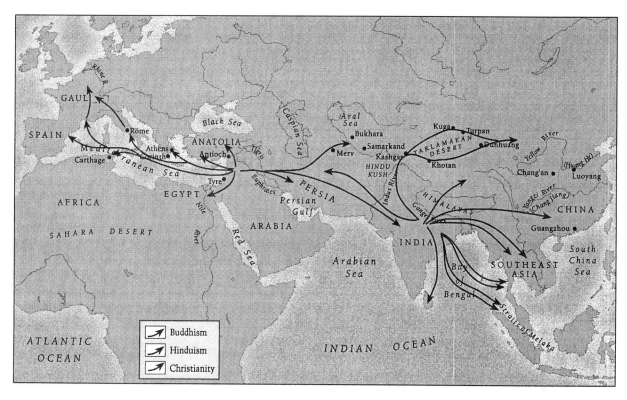

MAP [11.2]

The spread of Buddhism, Hinduism, and Christianity.

ficials allowed them to inhabit in Chang'an and other major cities. For several centuries Buddhism remained the faith largely of these expatriate merchants, and it did not appeal very strongly to native Chinese. Yet the presence of monasteries and missionaries offered Buddhism the potential to attract Chinese converts. Beginning about the fifth century C.E., Chinese began to respond enthusiastically to Buddhism, which during the post-classical era became the most popular religious faith throughout all of east Asia, including Japan and Korea as well as China.

As Buddhism spread north from India into central Asia and China, both Buddhism and Hinduism also began to attract a following in southeast Asia. Once again, merchants traveling the silk roads—in this case the sea-lanes through the Indian Ocean—played prominent roles in spreading these faiths. Merchant mariners regularly plied the waters between India and southeast Asia during the late centuries B.C.E. By the first century C.E., clear signs of Indian cultural influence had appeared in southeast Asia. In Java, Sumatra, and other islands, as well as in the Malay peninsula and territories embraced by modern Vietnam and Cambodia, rulers of southeast Asian states called themselves *rajas* ("kings"), in the manner of Indian rulers, and they adopted Sanskrit as a means of written communication. Many rulers converted to Buddhism, while others promoted the Hindu cults of Shiva and Vishnu. They built walled cities around lavish temples constructed in the Indian style. They appointed Buddhist or Hindu advisors, and they sought to enhance their authority by associating themselves with honored religious traditions.

Buddhism and Hinduism in Southeast Asia

Chinese military leaders placed high value on the large, strong horses bred in central Asia and imported as many of the animals as possible. The fortunate owners of these horses often commissioned artists to prepare representations of their animals, as in this wall tile from an aristocratic tomb in central China dating to the second or first century B.C.E. • Photograph courtesy of the Royal Ontario Museum. © ROM

The Spread of Christianity

Early Christians faced intermittent persecution from Roman officials. During the early centuries C.E., Roman authorities launched a series of campaigns to stamp out Christianity, since most Christians refused to observe the state cults that honored emperors as divine beings. Paradoxically, imperial officials viewed Christians as irreligious because they declined to participate in state-approved religious ceremonies. They also considered Christianity a menace to society because zealous missionaries attacked other religions and generated sometimes violent conflict. Nevertheless, Christian missionaries took full advantage of the Romans' magnificent network of roads and sea-lanes, which enabled them to carry their message throughout the Roman empire and the Mediterranean basin.

Christianity in the Mediterranean Basin

During the second and third centuries C.E., countless missionaries took Paul of Tarsus as their example and worked zealously to attract converts. One of the more famous was Gregory the Wonderworker, a tireless missionary with a reputation for performing miracles, who popularized Christianity in central Anatolia during the mid-third century C.E. Contemporaries reported that Gregory not only preached Christian doctrine but also expelled demons, moved boulders, diverted a river in flood, and persuaded observers that he had access to impressive supernatural powers. Gregory and his fellow missionaries helped to make Christianity the most popular religion of salvation in the Roman empire. By the late third century C.E., in spite of continuing imperial opposition, devout Christian communities flourished throughout the Mediterranean basin in Anatolia, Syria, Palestine, Egypt, and north Africa, as well as in Greece, Italy, Spain, and Gaul.

Christianity in Southwest Asia

As Christianity became the principal source of religious inspiration within the Roman empire, the young faith also traveled the trade routes and found followers beyond the Mediterranean basin. By the second century C.E., sizable Christian communities flourished throughout Mesopotamia and Iran, and a few Christian churches had appeared as far away as India. Christians did not dominate eastern lands as they did the Roman empire, but they attracted large numbers of converts in southwest Asia. Indeed, alongside Jews and Zoroastrians, Christians constituted one of the major religious communities in the region, and they remained so even after the seventh century C.E., when the Islamic faith of Arab Muslim conquerors began to displace the older religious communities.

Christian communities in Mesopotamia and Iran deeply influenced Christian practices in the Roman empire. To demonstrate utter loyalty to their faith, Christians in southwest Asia often followed strict ascetic regimes: inspired by Indian traditions, they abstained from sexual contact, refused fine foods and other comforts, and sometimes even withdrew from family life and society. These practices impressed devout Christians in the Roman empire. By the third century C.E., some Mediterranean Christians had begun to abandon society altogether and live as hermits in the deserts of Egypt, the mountains of Greece, and other isolated locations. Others withdrew from lay society but lived in communities of like-minded individuals who devoted their efforts to prayer and praise of God. Thus ascetic practices of Christians living in lands east of the Roman empire helped to inspire the formation of Christian monastic communities in the Mediterranean basin.

After the fifth century C.E., Christian communities in southwest Asia and the Mediterranean basin increasingly went separate ways. Most of the faithful in southwest Asia became Nestorians—followers of the Greek theologian Nestorius, who lived during the early fifth century and emphasized the human as opposed to the divine nature of Jesus. Mediterranean church authorities rejected Nestorius's views, and many of his disciples departed for Mesopotamia and Iran. They soon became prominent in local Christian communities, and they introduced a strong organizational framework to the church in southwest Asia. Although they had limited dealings with Mediterranean Christians, the Nestorians spread their faith east across the silk roads. Nestorian merchants took their faith with them on trade missions, and by the early seventh century they had established communities in central Asia, India, and China.

The Spread of Manichaeism

The explosive spread of Manichaeism dramatically illustrated how missionary religions made effective use of the silk roads trading network. Manichaeism was the faith derived from the prophet Mani (216–272 C.E.), a devout Zoroastrian from Babylon in Mesopotamia. Apart from Zoroastrianism, Mani drew deep influence from Christianity and Buddhism. He regarded Zarathustra as the prophet of Persia, Buddha as the prophet of India, and Jesus as the prophet of the Mediterranean world. Because of the intense interaction between peoples of different societies, Mani saw a need for a prophet for all humanity, and he promoted a syncretic blend of Zoroastrian, Christian, and Buddhist elements as a religious faith that would serve the needs of a cosmopolitan world.

Mani and Manichaeism

Mani viewed the world as the site of a cosmic struggle between the forces of light and darkness, good and evil. He associated light with spiritual awareness and darkness with the material world. He urged his followers to reject worldly pleasures, which entangled the spirit in matter, and rise toward the light. His doctrine had strong appeal because it offered a rational explanation for the presence of good and evil in the world while also providing a means for individuals to achieve personal salvation and contribute to the triumph of good over evil.

Mani promoted an ascetic lifestyle and insisted that disciples observe high ethical standards. Devout Manichaeans, known as "the elect," abstained from marriage, sexual relations, fine clothing, meat, rich foods, and other personal comforts, dedicating themselves instead to prayer, fasting, and ritual observances. Less zealous Manichaeans, known as "hearers," led more conventional lives, but they followed a strict moral code and provided food and gifts to sustain the elect. All Manichaeans looked forward to individual salvation and eternal association with the forces of light and good.

Mani was a fervent missionary: he traveled widely to promote his faith, corresponded tirelessly with Manichaean adherents, and dispatched disciples to lands that he could not visit himself. He also created a Manichaean church with its own services, rituals, hymns, and liturgies. His doctrine attracted converts first in Mesopotamia, and before Mani's death it had spread throughout the Sasanid empire and into the eastern Mediterranean region. In spite of its asceticism, Manichaeism appealed especially strongly to merchants, who adopted the faith as hearers and supported the Manichaean church. By the end of the third century C.E., Manichaean communities had appeared in all the large cities and trading centers of the Roman empire.

Decline of Manichaeism

Manichaeism soon came under tremendous pressure. Zoroastrian leaders urged the Sasanid rulers to suppress Mani's movement as a threat to public order. Mani himself died in chains as a prisoner of the Sasanid emperor, who sought to use Zoroastrianism as a cultural foundation for the unification of his realm. Authorities in the Roman empire also persecuted Manichaeans, whom they suspected because of the religion's origins in the rival Sasanid empire. Indeed, during the fifth and sixth centuries, political authorities largely exterminated Manichaeism in the Mediterranean basin. Yet Manichaeism survived in central Asia, where it attracted converts among nomadic Turkish peoples who traded with merchants from China, India, and southwest Asia. Like Buddhism, Hinduism, and Christianity, then, Manichaeism relied on the trade routes of classical times to extend its influence to new lands and peoples.

The Spread of Epidemic Disease

Like religious faiths, infectious and contagious diseases also spread along the trade routes of the classical world. Aided by long-distance travelers, pathogens had opportunities to spread beyond their original environments and attack populations with no inherited or acquired immunities to the diseases they caused. The resulting epidemics took a ferocious toll in human lives.

Information about human populations in classical times is scanty and full of gaps. Scholars often do not have records to work with and must draw inferences about population size from the area enclosed by city walls, the number of houses discovered in a settlement, the agricultural potential of a region, and similar considerations. As a result, population estimates for premodern societies are rough approximations, rather than precise figures. Moreover, within a single society, individual regions often had very different demographic experiences. Nevertheless, even for classical times, the general outlines of population history are reasonably clear.

Epidemic Diseases

During the second and third centuries C.E., the Han and Roman empires suffered large-scale outbreaks of epidemic disease. The most destructive of these diseases were probably smallpox and measles, and epidemics of bubonic plague may also have erupted. All three diseases are devastating when they break out in populations without resistance, immunities, or medicines to combat them. As disease ravaged the two empires, Chinese and Roman populations declined sharply.

ST. CYPRIAN ON EPIDEMIC DISEASE IN THE ROMAN EMPIRE

• • •

St. Cyprian, bishop of Carthage, was an outspoken proponent of Christianity during the early and middle decades of the third century C.E. When epidemic disease struck the Roman empire in 251 C.E., imperial authorities blamed the outbreak on Christians who refused to honor pagan gods. Cyprian refuted this charge in his treatise On Mortality, *which described the symptoms of epidemic disease and reflected on its significance for the Christian community.*

It serves as validation of the [Christian] faith when the bowels loosen and drain the body's strength, when fever generated in bone marrow causes sores to break out in the throat, when continuous vomiting roils the intestines, when blood-shot eyes burn, when the feet or other bodily parts are amputated because of infection by putrefying disease, when through weakness caused by injuries to the body either mobility is impeded, or hearing is impaired, or sight is obscured. It requires enormous greatness of heart to struggle with resolute mind against so many onslaughts of destruction and death. It requires great loftiness to stand firm amidst the ruins of the human race, not to concede defeat with those who have no hope in God, but rather to rejoice and embrace the gift of the times. With Christ as our judge, we should receive this gift as the reward of his faith, as we vigorously affirm our faith and, having suffered, advance toward Christ by Christ's narrow path. . . .

Many of us [Christians] are dying in this epidemic—that is, many of us are being liberated from the world. The epidemic is a pestilence for the Jews and the pagans and the enemies of Christ, but for the servants of God it is a welcome event. True, without any discrimination, the just are dying alongside the unjust, but you should not imagine that the evil and the good face a common destruction. The just are called to refreshment, while the unjust are herded off to punishment: the faithful receive protection, while the faithless receive retribution. We are unseeing and ungrateful for divine favors, beloved brethren, and we do not recognize what is granted to us. . . .

How suitable and essential it is that this plague and pestilence, which seems so terrible and ferocious, probes the justice of every individual and examines the minds of the human race to determine whether the healthy care for the ill, whether relatives diligently love their kin, whether masters show mercy to their languishing slaves, whether physicians do not abandon those seeking their aid, whether the ferocious diminish their violence, whether the greedy in the fear of death extinguish the raging flames of their insatiable avarice, whether the proud bend their necks, whether the shameless mitigate their audacity, whether the rich will loosen their purse strings and give something to others as their loved ones perish all around them and as they are about to die without heirs.

SOURCE: Wilhelm von Hartel, ed. *S. Thasci Caecili Cypriani opera omnia* in *Corpus scriptorum ecclesiasticorum latinorum*, Vienna: 1868, vol. 3, pp. 305–306. (Translation by Jerry H. Bentley.)

During the reign of Augustus, the population of the Roman empire stood at about sixty million people. During the second century C.E., epidemics reduced Roman population by about one-quarter to forty-five million. Most devastating was an outbreak of smallpox that spread throughout the Mediterranean basin during the years 165 to 180 C.E. The epidemic was especially virulent in cities, and it even claimed the life of the Roman emperor Marcus Aurelius (180 C.E.). In combination with war and invasions, continuing outbreaks caused a significant population decline during the third and fourth centuries: by 400 C.E. the number of Romans had fallen to perhaps forty million. By the sixth century C.E., population had probably stabilized or perhaps even begun to expand in the eastern Mediterranean, but western Mediterranean lands experienced demographic stagnation until the tenth century.

Epidemics appeared slightly later in China than in the Mediterranean region. From fifty million people at the beginning of the millennium, Chinese population rose to sixty million in 200 C.E. As diseases found their way east, however, Chinese numbers fell back to fifty million by 400 C.E. and to forty-five million by 600 C.E. Thus by 600 C.E. both Mediterranean and Chinese populations had fallen by a quarter to a third from their high points during classical times.

Effects of Epidemic Diseases

Demographic decline in turn brought economic and social change. Trade within the empires declined, and both the Chinese and Roman economies contracted. Both economies also moved toward regional self-sufficiency: whereas previously the Chinese and Roman states had integrated the various regions of their empires into a larger network of trade and exchange, after about 200 C.E. they increasingly embraced several smaller regional economies that concentrated on their own needs instead of the larger imperial market. In the Roman empire, for example, the eastern Mediterranean regions of Anatolia, Egypt, and Greece continued to form a larger, integrated society, but regional economies increasingly emerged in western Mediterranean lands, including Italy, Gaul, Spain, and northwest Africa.

The demographic histories of classical India, Persia, and other lands are not as clear as they are for China and the Roman empire. Persia most likely experienced demographic, economic, and social problems similar to those that afflicted China and the Mediterranean basin, but India seems largely to have escaped epidemic outbreaks and steep population losses. In China and the Mediterranean, however, epidemic disease seriously weakened the Han and Roman empires, thus contributing to their decline and fall.

THE FALL OF THE HAN DYNASTY

By the time epidemic diseases struck China, internal political problems had already begun to weaken the Han dynasty. By the late second century C.E., Han authorities had largely lost their ability to maintain order. Early in the third century C.E., the central government dissolved, and a series of autonomous regional kingdoms took the place of the Han state. With the disappearance of the Han dynasty, China experienced significant cultural change, most notably increasing interest in Buddhism.

Internal Decay of the Han State

The Han dynasty collapsed largely because of internal problems that its rulers could not solve. One problem involved the development of factions within the ranks of the ruling elites. Marriage alliances between imperial and aristocratic families led to the formation of many factions whose members sought to advance their own prospects in the imperial government and exclude others from important positions. This atmosphere led to constant infighting and back stabbing among the ruling elites, which in turn reduced the effectiveness of the central government.

An even more difficult problem had to do with the perennial issue of land and its equitable distribution. At the turn of the millennium, the usurper Wang Mang had attempted to redistribute land in China, but his program did not survive his own brief reign (9–23 C.E.). During the last two centuries of the Han dynasty, large landowners gained new influence in the government. They managed to reduce their share of taxes and shift the burden onto peasants. They even formed private armies to advance the interests of their class.

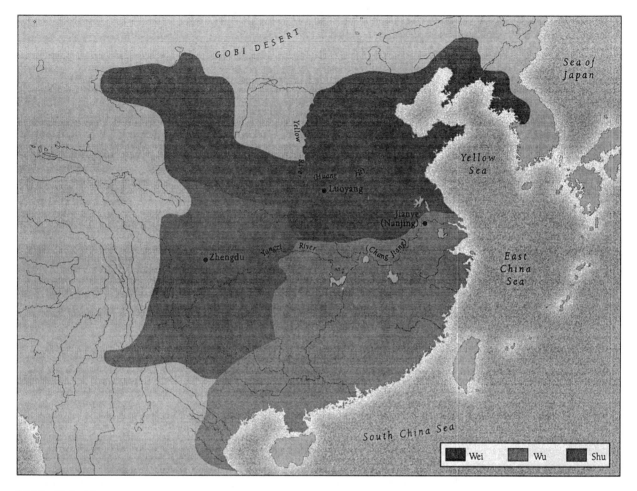

MAP [11.3]

Dissolution of the Han empire.

Peasant Rebellion

These developments provoked widespread unrest, particularly among peasants, who found themselves under increasing economic pressure with no means to influence the government. Pressures became particularly acute during the late second and third centuries when epidemics began to take their toll. In 184 C.E. peasant discontent fueled a massive uprising known as the Yellow Turban rebellion, so called because the rebels wore yellow headbands that represented the color of the Chinese earth and symbolized their peasant origins. Although quickly suppressed, the rebellion proved to be only the first in a series of insurrections that plagued the late Han dynasty.

Collapse of the Han Dynasty

Meanwhile, Han generals increasingly usurped political authority. By 190 C.E. the Han emperor had become a mere puppet, and the generals effectively ruled the regions controlled by their armies. They allied with wealthy landowners of their regions and established themselves as warlords who maintained a kind of rough order based on force of arms. The generals continued to recognize an emperor for a short time, but in 220 C.E. they formally abolished the Han dynasty and divided the empire into three large kingdoms.

Once the dynasty had disappeared, large numbers of nomadic peoples migrated into China, especially the northern regions, and they helped to keep China disunited for more than 350 years. Between the fourth and sixth centuries C.E., nomadic peoples established large kingdoms that dominated much of northern China as well as the steppelands.

Cultural Change in Post-Han China

In some ways the centuries following the fall of the Han dynasty present a spectacle of chaos and disorder. One kingdom toppled another, only to fall in its turn to a temporary successor. War and nomadic invasions led to population decline in much of northern China. By the mid-fifth century, the region around Chang'an and Luoyang—the heartland of classical China—had experienced almost complete devastation because of armies that ravaged the region in search of food and plunder. Contemporaries reported that the Former Han capital of Chang'an had no more than one hundred households and that the Later Han capital of Luoyang resembled a trash heap more than a city.

Sinicization of Nomadic Peoples

Beneath the disorderly surface of political events, however, several important social and cultural changes were taking place. In the first place, nomadic peoples increasingly adapted to the Chinese environment. They took up agriculture and built permanent settlements. They married Chinese spouses and took Chinese names. They wore the clothes, ate the food, and adopted the customs of China. Some sought a formal Chinese education and became well versed in Chinese philosophy and literature. In short, nomadic peoples became increasingly sinicized, and as the generations passed, distinctions between peoples of nomadic and Chinese ancestry became less and less obvious. Partly because of this development, a new imperial dynasty was eventually able to reconstitute a centralized imperial state in north China.

In the second place, with the disintegration of political order, the Confucian tradition lost much of its credibility. The original goal of Confucius and his early followers was to find some means to move from chaos to stability during the Period of the Warring States. As long as Confucian methods and principles helped to maintain order, ruling elites and intellectual classes honored the Confucian tradition. When the Han dynasty collapsed, Confucianism became irrelevant.

Individuals who in earlier centuries might have committed themselves to Confucian values turned instead to Daoism and Buddhism. As in the Period of the Warring States, Daoism offered a way to find peace in a turbulent world. Originally, Daoism was a school of speculative philosophical thought that appealed mostly to an educated elite. After the fall of the Han, however, it became more a religious than a philosophical doctrine. Daoist sages not only promised salvation to those who observed their doctrines and rituals but also experimented with spices, herbs, and drugs to concoct elixirs or potions that conferred health and immortality. Daoism attracted widespread interest among a population afflicted by war and disease and became much more popular than before, especially because it faced less competition from the Confucian tradition.

Popularity of Buddhism

Even more important than Daoism for Chinese cultural history was Buddhism. Until about the fourth century C.E., Buddhism was largely the faith of foreign merchants in China and attracted little interest on the part of native Chinese. After the fall of the Han empire, however, Buddhism received strong support from nomadic peoples who migrated into northern China and who in many cases had long been familiar with Buddhism in central Asia. Meanwhile, as a result of missionary efforts, the Indian faith began to attract a following among native Chinese as well. Indeed, between the fourth and sixth centuries C.E., Buddhism became well established in China. When a centralized imperial state took shape in the late sixth century C.E., Buddhism provided an important cultural foundation for the restoration of a unified political order.

THE FALL OF THE ROMAN EMPIRE

Moralists have often interpreted the fall of the Roman empire as a symbol of the transitory nature of human creations. Fascination with imperial Rome has encouraged the proliferation of theories—many of them quite silly—seeking to explain the fall of the empire as the result of some single, simple cause. By various accounts, the Roman empire declined and fell because of lead poisoning, radiation given off by bricks, immorality of the upper classes, or the rise of Christianity. Notwithstanding the zeal with which proponents have promoted pet theories, there was no single cause for the decline and fall of the Roman empire. Instead, a combination of internal problems and external pressures weakened the empire and brought an end to Roman authority in the western portion of the empire, whereas in the eastern Mediterranean imperial rule continued until the fifteenth century C.E. In the Mediterranean basin as in China, imperial weakness and collapse coincided with significant cultural change, notably the increasing popularity of Christianity.

Internal Decay in the Roman Empire

As in the case of the Han dynasty, internal political problems go a long way toward explaining the fall of the Roman empire. Like their Han counterparts, the Roman emperors faced internal opposition. During the half century from 235 to 284 C.E., there were no fewer than twenty-six claimants to the imperial throne. Known as the "barracks emperors," most of them were generals who seized power, held it briefly, and then suddenly lost it when they were displaced by rivals or their own mutinous troops. Not surprisingly, most of the barracks emperors died violently: only one is known for sure to have succumbed to natural causes. *The Barracks Emperors*

Apart from divisions and factions, the Roman empire also faced problems because of its sheer size. Even during the best of times, when the emperors could count on abundant revenues and disciplined armed forces, the sprawling empire posed a challenge for central governors. After the third century, as epidemics spread throughout the empire and its various regions moved toward local, self-sufficient economies, the empire as a whole became increasingly unmanageable.

The emperor Diocletian (284–305 C.E.) attempted to deal with this problem by dividing the empire into two administrative districts. The eastern district included the wealthy lands of Anatolia, Syria, Egypt, and Greece, and the western district embraced Italy, Gaul, Spain, Britain, and north Africa. A coemperor ruled each district with the aid of a powerful lieutenant, and the four officials, known as the tetrarchs, were able to administer the vast empire more effectively than an individual emperor could. As long as Diocletian ruled as coemperor, his administrative structure enabled officials to maintain domestic order and respond quickly to military threats. *Diocletian*

Sculpture of the tetrarchs, or four corulers of the Roman empire, during the late third century C.E.; from left, Galerius, Constantius, Diocletian, and Maximian. • Michael Holford

Only the colossal head of Constantine survives from a statue that originally stood about fourteen meters (forty-six feet) tall. • Erich Lessing/Art Resource, NY

Yet Diocletian's reform also encouraged ambition among the four top corulers and their generals, and his retirement from the imperial office in 305 C.E. set off a round of internal struggles and bitter civil war. Already in 306 C.E. Constantine, son of Diocletian's coruler Constantius, moved to stake his claim as sole emperor. By 313 C.E. he had defeated most of his enemies, although he overcame his last rivals only in 324 C.E. Once he had consolidated his grip on power, Constantine ordered the construction of a new capital city, Constantinople, at a strategic site overlooking the Bosporus, the strait linking the Black Sea to the Sea of Marmara and beyond to the wealthy eastern Mediterranean. After 340 C.E. Constantinople became the capital of a united Roman empire.

Constantine   Constantine himself was an able emperor. With the reunion of the eastern and western districts of the empire, however, he and his successors faced the same sort of administrative difficulties that Diocletian had attempted to solve by dividing the empire. As population declined and the economy contracted, emperors found it increasingly difficult to marshall the resources needed to govern and protect the vast Roman empire. The need for protection against external threats became especially acute during the late fourth and early fifth centuries C.E.

Germanic Invasions and the Fall of the Western Roman Empire

Apart from internal problems, the Roman empire also faced a formidable military threat from migratory Germanic peoples. Indeed, during the fifth century C.E., Germanic invasions brought an end to Roman authority in the western half of the empire, although imperial rule survived for an additional millennium in the eastern Mediterranean.

Germanic peoples had migrated from their homelands in northern Europe and lived on the eastern and northern borders of the Roman empire since the second century C.E. Most notable were the Visigoths, who came originally from Scandinavia and Russia. Like the nomadic peoples who moved into northern China after the fall of the Han dynasty, the Visigoths settled, adopted agriculture, and drew deep inspiration from Roman society. They adapted Roman law to the needs of their own society, for example, converted to Christianity, and translated the Bible into the Visigothic language. They also contributed large numbers of soldiers to the Roman armies. In the interests of social order, however, the Romans discouraged settlement of the Visigoths and other Germanic peoples within the empire, preferring that they constitute buffer societies outside imperial borders.

Germanic Migrations

During the late fourth century, the relationship between Visigoths and Romans changed dramatically when the nomadic Huns began an aggressive westward migration from their homeland in central Asia. During the mid-fifth century C.E., the warrior-king Attila organized the Huns into a virtually unstoppable military juggernaut. Under Attila, the Huns invaded Hungary, probed Roman frontiers in the Balkan region, menaced Gaul and northern Italy, and attacked Germanic peoples living on the borders of the Roman empire.

The Huns

Attila did not create a set of political institutions or a state structure, and the Huns disappeared as a political and military force soon after his death in 453 C.E. By that time, however, the Huns had placed such pressure on Visigoths, Ostrogoths, Vandals, Franks, and other Germanic peoples that they streamed en masse into the Roman empire in search of refuge. Once inside imperial boundaries, they encountered little effective resistance and moved around almost at will. They established settlements throughout the western half of the empire—Italy, Gaul, Spain, Britain, and north Africa—where populations were less dense than in the eastern Mediterranean. Under the command of Alaric, the Visigoths even stormed and sacked Rome in 410 C.E. By the middle of the fifth century, the western part of the Roman empire was in shambles. In 476 C.E. imperial authority came to an ignominious end when the Germanic general Odovacer deposed Romulus Augustulus, the last of the Roman emperors in the western half of the empire.

Collapse of the Western Roman Empire

Unlike the Han dynasty, the Roman empire did not entirely disintegrate: imperial authority survived for another millennium in the eastern half of the empire, known after the fifth century C.E. as the Byzantine empire. In the western half, however, Roman authority dissolved, and nomadic peoples built successor states in regions formerly subject to Rome. Vandals and then Visigoths governed Spain, Franks ruled Gaul, Angles and Saxons invaded Britain, and Italy fell under the sway of a variety of peoples, including Visigoths, Vandals, and Lombards.

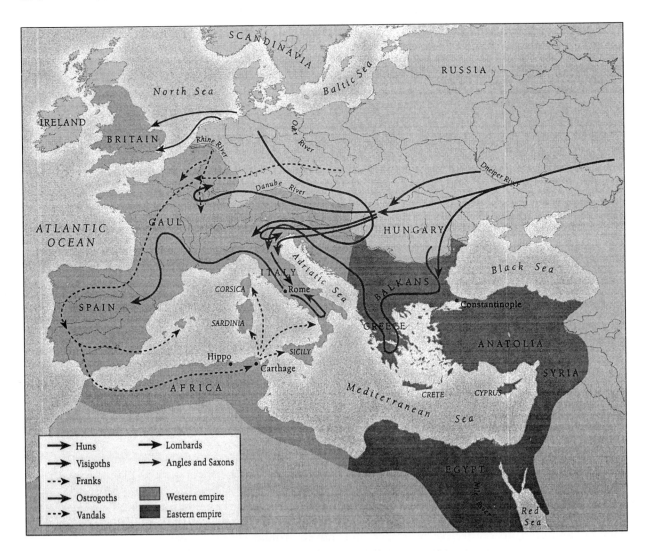

MAP [11.4]

Germanic invasions and the fall of the western Roman empire.

Cultural Change in the Late Roman Empire

As in China, the collapse of the imperial state coincided with important social and cultural changes. The Germanic peoples who toppled the empire looked to their own traditions for purposes of organizing society and government. When they settled in the regions of the former empire, however, they absorbed a good deal of Roman influence. They adapted Roman law to their own needs, for example, thus preserving one of the most important features of Roman society. Over time, the mingling of Roman and Germanic traditions led to the emergence of an altogether new society—medieval Europe.

Prominence of Christianity

Christianity was perhaps the most prominent survivor of the western Roman empire. During the fourth century C.E., several developments enhanced its influence throughout the Mediterranean basin. In the first place, Christianity won recognition as a legitimate religion in the Roman empire. In 313 C.E., while seeking to establish himself as sole Roman emperor, Constantine experienced a vision that impressed upon him the power of the Christian God. He believed that the Christian God helped him to prevail over his rivals, and he promulgated the Edict of Milan, which allowed Christians to practice their faith openly in the Roman empire. At some point during his reign, perhaps after his edict, Constantine himself converted to Christianity, and in 380 C.E. the emperor Theodosius proclaimed Christianity the official religion of the empire. By the mid-fourth century, Christians held important political and military positions, and imperial sponsorship helped their faith to attract more converts than ever before.

Christianity also began to attract thoughtful and talented converts who articulated a Christian message for the intellectual elites of the Roman empire. The earliest Christians had come largely from the ranks of ordinary working people, and their doctrine struck philosophers and the educated elites as unsophisticated and unbelievable. During its first three centuries, the new faith grew as a popular religion of salvation favored by the masses, rather than as a reasoned doctrine of intellectual substance. During the fourth century, however, intellectual elites began to take more interest in Christianity. Among the most notable was St. Augustine (354–430 C.E.), bishop of Hippo in north Africa. Well educated in philosophy, Augustine explained the Christian message in terms

Portrait of St. Augustine holding a copy of his most famous work, *The City of God,* which sought to explain the meaning of history and the world from a Christian point of view. • The Ancient Art and Architecture Collection Ltd.

that educated classes could appreciate by harmonizing it with Platonic thought.

Besides winning the right to practice their faith openly and attracting intellectual talent, Christian leaders constructed an institutional apparatus that transformed a popular religion of salvation into a powerful church. In the absence of recognized leadership, the earliest Christians generated a range of conflicting and sometimes contradictory doctrines. Some taught that Jesus was a mortal human being, others that he was a god, and yet others that he was both human and divine. Some allowed women to serve as priests and attributed great powers to Jesus' mother Mary, while others restricted church offices to men and conceived of Christian deities as males.

To standardize their faith, Christian leaders instituted a hierarchy of church officials. At the top were five religious authorities—the bishop of Rome and the patriarchs of Jerusalem, Antioch, Alexandria, and Constantinople—who resided in the most important spiritual and political centers of the Roman empire. These five authorities wielded roughly equal influence in the larger Christian community, although the bishop of Rome enjoyed somewhat greater prestige than the others. (His enhanced status derived both from his claim to be the spiritual descendant of Jesus' chief disciple, St. Peter, and from the fact that he had his seat at Rome, the original imperial capital.)

The Institutional Church

Subordinate to the five principal authorities were bishops, who presided over religious affairs in their districts, known as dioceses, which included all the prominent cities of the Roman empire. When theological disputes arose, the patriarchs and bishops assembled in church councils to determine which views would prevail as official doctrine. The councils of Nicaea (325 C.E.) and Chalcedon (451 C.E.), for example, took up the contentious issue of Jesus' nature and decided against the Nestorians and others that he simultaneously possessed both human and divine natures.

As Roman imperial authority crumbled, the bishop of Rome, known as the pope (from the Latin *papa,* meaning "father"), emerged as spiritual leader of Christian communities in the western regions of the empire. As the only sources of established and recognized authority, the popes and the bishops of other important cities organized local government and defensive measures for their communities. They also mounted missionary campaigns to convert Germanic peoples to Christianity. Although Roman imperial authority disappeared, Roman Christianity survived and served as a foundation for cultural unity in lands that had formerly made up the western half of the Roman empire.

By 500 C.E. classical societies in Persia, China, India, and the Mediterranean basin had either collapsed or fallen into decline. Yet all the classical societies left rich legacies that shaped political institutions, social orders, and cultural traditions for centuries to come. Moreover, by sponsoring commercial and cultural relations between different peoples, the classical societies laid a foundation for intensive and systematic cross-cultural interaction in later times. After the third century C.E., the decline of the Han and Roman empires resulted in less activity over the silk roads than in the preceding three hundred years. But the trade routes survived, and when a new series of imperial states reestablished order throughout much of Eurasia and north Africa in the sixth century C.E., the peoples of the eastern hemisphere avidly resumed their crossing of cultural boundary lines in the interests of trade and communication.

CHRONOLOGY

third century B.C.E.	Spread of Buddhism and Hinduism to southeast Asia
second century B.C.E.	Introduction of Buddhism to central Asia
139–126 B.C.E.	Travels of Zhang Qian in central Asia
first century B.C.E.	Introduction of Buddhism to China
second century C.E.	Spread of Christianity in the Mediterranean basin and southwest Asia
184 C.E.	Yellow Turban rebellion
216–272 C.E.	Life of Mani
220 C.E.	Collapse of the Han dynasty
284–305 C.E.	Reign of Diocletian
313–337 C.E.	Reign of Constantine
313 C.E.	Edict of Milan and the legalization of Christianity in the Roman empire
325 C.E.	Council of Nicaea
451 C.E.	Council of Chalcedon
476 C.E.	Collapse of the western Roman empire

FOR FURTHER READING

Thomas J. Barfield. *The Perilous Frontier: Nomadic Empires and China.* Cambridge, Mass., 1989. Provocative study of the Xiongnu and other central Asian peoples.

Jerry H. Bentley. *Old World Encounters: Cross-Cultural Contacts and Exchanges in Pre-Modern Times.* New York, 1993. Studies the spread of cultural and religious traditions before 1500 C.E.

Luce Boulnois. *The Silk Road.* Trans. by D. Chamberlain. New York, 1966. Popular account of trade and travel over the silk roads.

Peter Brown. *The Making of Late Antiquity.* Cambridge, Mass., 1978. Brilliant and evocative analysis of the cultural and religious history of the late Roman empire.

———. *The World of Late Antiquity, A.D. 150–750.* London, 1971. Well-illustrated essay concentrating on social and cultural themes.

Averil Cameron. *The Later Roman Empire, A.D. 284–430.* Cambridge, Mass., 1993. Short and lively synthesis that takes account of recent scholarship.

———. *The Mediterranean World in Late Antiquity, A.D. 395–600.* London, 1993. Like its companion volume cited above, a well-informed synthesis.

Philip D. Curtin. *Cross-Cultural Trade in World History.* New York, 1984. A synthetic work that concentrates on merchant communities in distant lands and their roles in facilitating cross-cultural trade.

Edward Gibbon. *The Decline and Fall of the Roman Empire.* Many editions available. A classic account, still well worth reading, by a masterful historical stylist of the eighteenth century.

C. D. Gordon, ed. *The Age of Attila: Fifth-Century Byzantium and the Barbarians.* Ann Arbor, 1972. Translations of primary sources on the society and history of nomadic and migratory peoples.

A. H. M. Jones. *The Decline of the Ancient World.* New York, 1966. Synthetic study of the Roman empire in decline by a foremost scholar of the subject.

J. Innes Miller. *The Spice Trade of the Roman Empire, 29 B.C. to A.D. 641.* Oxford, 1969. Scholarly study of long-distance trade during classical times.

Samuel Hugh Moffett. *A History of Christianity in Asia,* vol. 1. San Francisco, 1992. Draws on recent scholarship in surveying the spread of early Christianity east of the Roman empire.

C. G. F. Simkin. *The Traditional Trade of Asia.* London, 1968. Survey of Eurasian trade with a chapter on the classical era.

Joseph A. Tainter. *The Collapse of Complex Societies.* Cambridge, 1988. Scholarly review of theories and evidence bearing on the fall of empires and societies.

Mortimer Wheeler. *Flames over Persepolis.* New York, 1968. Well-illustrated volume dealing with the interactions of Greek, Persian, and Indian peoples during the Hellenistic era.

PART III

THE POSTCLASSICAL ERA, 500 TO 1000 C.E.

. . .

The postclassical era was a period of major readjustment for societies throughout the eastern hemisphere. The early centuries C.E. brought turbulence and instability to classical societies in China, India, southwest Asia, and the Mediterranean basin. Most of the classical empires collapsed under the strain of internal power struggles, external invasions, or a combination of the two. During the postclassical era the settled societies of the eastern hemisphere underwent political, social, economic, and cultural change that would shape their experiences over the long term. Indeed, the influence of the postclassical era continues to the present day.

The first task that settled societies faced in the postclassical era was the need to restore political and social order. They went about this task in very different ways. In the eastern Mediterranean the eastern half of the Roman empire survived as the Byzantine empire—the only empire that outlasted the difficulties of the late classical era—but underwent political and social reorganization in order to deal with external pressures. In southwest Asia, Arab conquerors inspired by the recently founded Islamic faith overcame the Sasanid empire of Persia. In China the Sui and Tang dynasties restored centralized imperial authority after almost four centuries of rule by competing regional kingdoms and nomadic

conquerors. In India, by contrast, centralized imperial rule did not return: authority devolved instead to a series of regional kingdoms, some of them quite large. In western Europe centralized imperial rule returned only for a brief moment during the eighth and ninth centuries under the Carolingian empire. Economic difficulties and new rounds of invasions, however, brought down the empire and encouraged devolution of authority to local rulers: the result was the development of feudalism and a decentralized political order in western Europe. In different ways, then, all the settled societies of the eastern hemisphere embarked upon a quest for political and social order during the centuries after the collapse of the classical empires.

The reestablishment of political and social order enabled postclassical societies to revive networks of long-distance trade and participate more actively in processes of cross-cultural communication and exchange. As a result, the postclassical era was a time of rapid economic growth in most of the eastern hemisphere. The volume of long-distance trade increased dramatically, and manufacturers began to produce goods explicitly for export rather than local consumption. Meanwhile, increased trade facilitated biological and technological as well as commercial exchanges: agricultural crops migrated far beyond the lands of their origin, and improved techniques of irrigation and cultivation spread through much of Eurasia. New crops and improved agricultural techniques led to enlarged harvests and enriched diets particularly in China, India, and southwest Asia.

As agricultural production increased, so did human population. Growing numbers of people devoted their efforts to trade and manufacturing rather than cultivation. China, India, and the eastern Mediterranean region were especially prominent sites for the production of textiles, ceramics, and metal goods. Increased trade and manufacturing activity encouraged a remarkable round of technological invention and innovation. The magnetic compass, printing technologies, and gunpowder, for example, first appeared in postclassical China and then diffused to other lands. These inventions and others of the era have profoundly influenced the course of human history since their first appearance.

The postclassical era was also crucially important for the formation and development of cultural and religious traditions. Islam first appeared during the postclassical era, and it soon became the cultural and religious foundation of an expansive empire stretching from north Africa to northern India. Buddhism expanded beyond the Indian subcontinent and central Asia, attracting converts in China, Korea, Japan, and southeast Asia. Christianity was the official faith of the Byzantine empire, where the Eastern Orthodox church emerged and gave shape to a distinctive form of Christianity. Orthodox missionaries also spread their faith to formerly pagan lands throughout much of eastern Europe and Russia. Further west, Christianity spread from the Mediterranean basin to western and northern Europe, where papal leadership guided the emergence of the Roman Catholic church. For a millennium and more, Roman Catholic Christianity served as the foundation for cultural unity in the politically disunited world of western and northern Europe. Meanwhile, quite apart from the expansion of religious faiths, the postclassical era also witnessed the spread of literacy and formal education throughout much of the eastern hemisphere.

The empires and regional states of the postclassical era disappeared long ago, but the social, economic, and cultural legacies of the age are noticeable even today. Long-distance trade surged in postclassical times and helped to structure economic and social development throughout much of the eastern hemisphere. Even more notable, perhaps, religious and cultural traditions continue to flourish in lands where they first attracted converts in postclassical times. In some ways, then, the postclassical age survives even in the modern world.

EAST ASIA	SOUTH AND SOUTHEAST ASIA	SOUTHWEST ASIA	EUROPE AND MEDITERRANEAN BASIN
400	400	400	400
Sui dynasty (589–618) Yang Jian (589–604)	Invasion of White Huns (451) Harsha (606–648)	Justinian (527–565) Hagia Sophia *Corpus iuris civilis*	Germanic general Odoacer deposes last Roman emperor (476) Migration and conquests of Visigoths, Ostrogoths, Franks, Lombards Conversion of Clovis (481–511) St. Benedict of Nursia (480–547) Benedict's Rule St. Scholastica (482–543) Invention of heavy plow (6th century) Pope Gregory I (590–604)
600	600	600	600
Sui Yangdi (604–618) Grand Canal Tang dynasty (618–907) Tang Taizong (627–649) Xuanzang's journey to India (629–645) Silla dynasty in Korea (7th century) An Lushan rebellion (755–757) Nara period in Japan (710–794) Heian period in Japan (794–1185)	Arab forces enter India (mid-17th century) Kingdom of Srivijaya on Sumatra (670–1025) Sind falls to Umayyad conquerors (711)	Muhammad (570–632) Hijra (622) Compilation of Quran (650s) Ali (565–661) Split between Sunni and Shia Unmayyad dynasty (661–750) Abbasid dynasty (750–1258) Harun al-Rashid (786–809)	Emperor Leo III (717–741) Charles Martel (700s) Charlemagne (768–814)
800	800	800	800
Huang Chao rebellion (875–884) Song dynasty (960–1279) Song Taizu (960–976) Invention of magnetic compass	Hindu philosopher Shau Kara (9th century) Chola kingdom (850–1267) Angkor kingdom of Cambodia (889–1431) *Book of the Wonders of India* by Buzurg ibn Shahriyar	Hajj of Jamila bint Nasir al-Dawla (976–977)	Louis the Pious (814–840) Division of Charlemagne's empire (843) Saints Cyril and Methodius (mid-19th century) King Alfred of England (871–899) Vikings raid Russia, Germany, England, Ireland, France, Spain King Otto of Saxony (936–973) Foundation of Holy Roman Empire (962) Conversion of Prince Vladimir of Kiev (989) Saint Basil II (976–1025)

EAST ASIA	SOUTH AND SOUTHEAST ASIA	SOUTHWEST ASIA	EUROPE AND MEDITERRANEAN BASIN
1000	1000	1000	1000
The Tale of Genji by Murasaki Shikibu Song movable type and paper money Jurchen overrun northern China (12th century) Kamakura shogunate	Mahmud of Ghazni invades India (1001–1027) Hindu philosopher Ramanuja (early 11th century) Bhakti movement (early 12th century) Buddhist city of Nalanda overrun by Islamic forces (1196)	Philosophers al Ghazali and Ibn Rushd	Vikings reach Newfoundland (1000) Split between Eastern Orthodox and Roman Catholic churches (1054) Battle of Manzikert (1071)
1200	1200	1200	1200
Yuan dynasty (1279–1368) Muromachi shogunate (1336–1573)	Delhi sultanate (1206–1526) Singosari kingdom of Java (1222–1292) Majapahit kingdom on Java (1293–1520) Vijayanagar kingdom	Fourth Crusade (1202–1204) Byzantine forces recapture Constantinople (1261) *Rubaiyat* of Omar Kyayyam	
1400	1400	1400	1400
	Bhakti teacher Guru Kabir (1440–1518) Rise of Islamic state of Melaka (mid-15th century)		Constantinople falls to Ottoman Turks (1453)

CHAPTER 12

A SURVIVOR SOCIETY:
BYZANTIUM

· · ·

According to the Byzantine historian Procopius, two Christian monks from Persia set out on a momentous journey about the middle of the sixth century C.E. The result of their travels was the introduction of high-quality silk production to the eastern Mediterranean. Although local craftsmen had long produced coarse fabrics from the cocoons of wild silkworms, fine silks had come to the Mediterranean only from China, where manufacturers closely guarded both their carefully bred strains of silkworms and the complex technology that yielded high-quality textiles. Mediterranean consumers did not obtain silk directly from Chinese producers, but rather through middlemen subject to the Sasanid empire of Persia.

According to Procopius's account, the two Christian monks observed the techniques of silk production during the course of a mission to China. Upon departure they hollowed out their walking staffs and filled them with silkworm eggs, which they smuggled out of China, through their native land of Persia, and into the Byzantine empire. The monks' motives are unknown. Perhaps they resented Sasanid religious policies favoring Zoroastrians and sought to aid Christians in the Byzantine empire. Perhaps they hoped to receive a handsome reward for their efforts. Whatever their motives might have been, it is likely that the techniques of fine silk production reached the Byzantine empire by several routes and that Procopius simplified a complex story by focusing attention on the monks.

In any case Byzantine craftsmen soon learned how to breed silkworms, feed them mulberry leaves, unravel their cocoons, and produce high-quality silk fabrics. By the late sixth century, Byzantine silks matched the quality of Chinese products. Mediterranean consumers no longer relied on Chinese producers and Persian middlemen, and local production of high-quality silk greatly strengthened the Byzantine economy. Thus Procopius's anonymous monks participated in a momentous transfer of technology between distant lands. Their efforts contributed to the vibrance of Byzantine society, and their story highlights the significance of cross-cultural interactions during the postclassical era.

During the centuries after 200 C.E., most of the classical societies faced a series of problems—epidemic disease, declining population, economic contraction, political turmoil, social unrest, and military threats from outside—that brought about their collapse. Only in the eastern Mediterranean did a classical empire survive. The eastern

A sixth-century icon depicting an enthroned Virgin Mary and infant Jesus attended by angels and saints.

• Erich Lessing/Art Resource, NY

half of the Roman empire, known as the Byzantine empire, withstood the various problems that brought down other classical societies and survived for almost a millennium after the collapse of the western Roman empire in the fifth century C.E.

The Byzantine empire did not reconstitute the larger Mediterranean society of classical times. The Roman empire had dominated an integrated Mediterranean basin; the Byzantine empire mostly faced a politically and culturally fragmented Mediterranean region. After the seventh century C.E., Islamic states controlled lands to the east and south of the Mediterranean, Slavic peoples dominated lands to the north, and western Europeans organized increasingly powerful states in lands to the west.

Although it was more compact than the Roman empire, the Byzantine empire was a political and economic powerhouse of the postclassical era. Until the twelfth century Byzantine authority dominated the wealthy and productive eastern Mediterranean region. Manufactured goods from the Byzantine empire enjoyed a reputation for high quality in markets from the Mediterranean basin to India. The Byzantine empire also deeply influenced the historical development of the Slavic peoples of eastern Europe and Russia. Byzantine missionaries and diplomats introduced writing, codified law, sophisticated political organization, and Christianity into lands settled by Slavic peoples. As a result, even though the Byzantine empire itself disappeared during the fifteenth century, its legacy survives to the present day.

 ## THE EARLY BYZANTINE EMPIRE

The Byzantine empire takes its name from Byzantion—latinized as Byzantium—a modest market town and fishing village that occupied a site of enormous strategic significance. Situated on a defensible peninsula and blessed with a magnificent natural harbor known as the Golden Horn, Byzantion had the potential to control the Bosporus, the strait of water leading from the Black Sea to the Sea of Marmara and beyond to the Dardanelles, the Aegean Sea, and the Mediterranean. Apart from its maritime significance, Byzantion also offered convenient access to the rich lands of Anatolia, southwestern Asia, and southeastern Europe. Trade routes linked Byzantion to ports throughout the Mediterranean basin.

Because of its strategic value, the Roman emperor Constantine designated Byzantion as the site of a new imperial capital, which he named Constantinople ("city of Constantine"). He built the new capital partly because the eastern Mediterranean was the wealthier and more productive part of the Roman empire and partly because relocation enabled the imperial court to maintain close watch over both the Sasanid empire in Persia and the Germanic peoples who lived along the lower stretches of the Danube River. The imperial government moved to Constantinople in 340 C.E., and the new capital rapidly reached metropolitan dimensions. By the late fourth century, it was the most important political and military center of the eastern Roman empire, and it soon became the dominant economic and commercial center in the eastern Mediterranean basin. The city kept the name Constantinople until 1453 C.E., when it fell to the Ottoman Turks, who renamed it Istanbul. By convention, however, historians refer to the realm governed from Constantinople between the fifth and fifteenth centuries C.E. as the Byzantine empire, or simply as Byzantium, in honor of the original settlement.

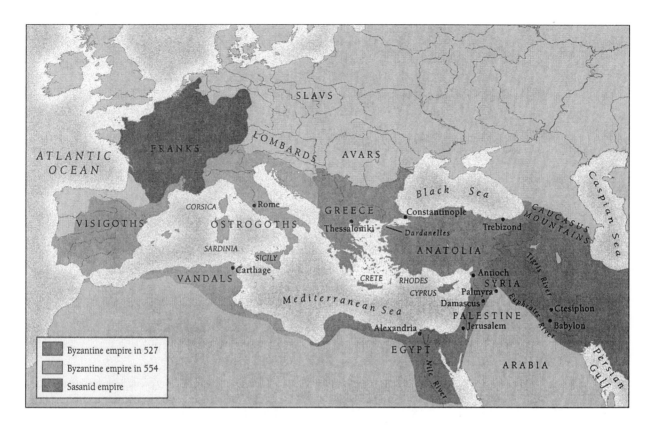

The Later Roman Empire and Byzantium

MAP [12.1]
The Byzantine empire and its neighbors.

The Byzantine empire originated as the eastern half of the classical Roman empire, which survived the collapse of the western Roman empire in the fifth century C.E. In its early days the Byzantine empire embraced Greece, the Balkan region, Anatolia, Syria, Palestine, Egypt, and northeast Africa. Byzantine rulers occasionally expanded their boundaries, and neighboring peoples sometimes seized portions of the Byzantine empire for themselves. During the seventh and eighth centuries C.E., for example, the southern regions of the empire fell into the hands of Arab Muslim conquerors. Generally speaking, however, Byzantium figured as a major power of the eastern Mediterranean basin until the thirteenth century C.E.

As the western Roman empire crumbled in the fifth century C.E., the eastern half of the empire remained intact, complete with roads, communications, lines of authority, and a set of functioning imperial institutions, all inherited from Roman predecessors. Yet the early Byzantine emperors faced challenges different from those of their predecessors, and they built a state significantly different from the classical Roman empire.

The Later Roman Empire

The principal challenges that confronted the late Roman and early Byzantine empires were the consolidation of the dynamic Sasanid dynasty (226–641 C.E.) in Persia and the invasions of migratory peoples from the north and east. The Sasanid emperors sought to rebuild the Achaemenid empire of classical Persia, a goal that brought them into conflict with Roman forces in Mesopotamia and Syria. By the late third century, Roman armies had largely stabilized their eastern borders, but until their fall in the seventh century, the Sasanids remained the principal foreign threat to the eastern

In 260 C.E. the Sasanid emperor Shapur I (right) captured the Roman emperor Valerian, as depicted in this cameo medallion of the fourth century. • Cabinet des Medailles, Bibliothèque Nationale de France

Roman empire. Germanic invasions also menaced the late Roman empire. Because they did not have adequate resources to respond strongly to the threat on all fronts, Roman authorities concentrated on maintaining the integrity of the wealthy eastern portion of the empire. As a result, migratory peoples were rarely a serious threat to Constantinople or the other heavily defended cities of the eastern empire.

The Early Byzantine State   Having secured their realm against Sasanids and migratory invaders, the Byzantine emperors built a distinctive tradition of statecraft. The most important feature of the Byzantine state was tightly centralized rule that concentrated power in the hands of a highly exalted emperor. This characteristic was noticeable already in the time of Constantine, who built his new capital to lavish standards. He filled it with libraries, museums, and artistic treasures, and he constructed magnificent marble palaces, churches, baths, and public buildings—all in an effort to create a new Rome fit for the ruler of a mighty empire.

Caesaropapism   Constantine also set a precedent by hedging his rule with an aura of divinity. As protector of the Christians and a baptized Christian himself, Constantine could not claim the divine status that some of his imperial predecessors had sought to appropriate. As the first Christian emperor, however, Constantine claimed divine favor and sanction for his rule. He intervened in theological disputes and used his political position to support views that he considered orthodox and condemn those that he regarded as heretical. Constantine initiated a policy that historians call "caesaropapism," whereby the emperor not only ruled as secular lord but also played an active and prominent role in ecclesiastical affairs.

Particularly after the sixth century, Byzantine emperors became exalted, absolute rulers. According to Roman law, emperors stood above the law: theoretically, they wielded absolute authority in political, military, judicial, financial, and religious matters. They also enjoyed the services of a large and complex bureaucracy. Indeed, its intricacy gave rise to the adjective *byzantine,* which suggests unnecessary complexity and convolution. In combination, law and bureaucracy produced an exceptionally centralized state.

Even dress and court etiquette drew attention to the lofty status of Byzantine rulers. The emperors wore heavily bejeweled crowns and dressed in magnificent silk robes dyed a dark, rich purple—a color reserved for imperial use and strictly forbidden to those not associated with the ruling house. High officials announced themselves to the emperor as slaves, not subjects. When approaching him, they prostrated themselves three times and then ceremoniously kissed the imperial hands and feet before taking up matters of business. By the tenth century engineers had contrived a series of mechanical devices that worked dazzling effects and impressed foreign envoys at the Byzantine court: imitation birds sang as ambassadors approached the emperor while mechanical lions roared and swished their tails. During an audience the imperial throne itself sometimes moved up and down to emphasize the awesome splendor of the emperor.

The Byzantine Court

Justinian and His Legacy

The most important of the early Byzantine emperors was Justinian (527–565 C.E.), an energetic and tireless worker known to his subjects as "the sleepless emperor," who profoundly influenced the development of the Byzantine empire with the aid of his ambitious wife Theodora. The imperial couple came from obscure origins: Justinian was born into a Macedonian peasant family, and Theodora, the daughter of a bear keeper in the circus, worked as a striptease artist before meeting the future emperor. Yet both Justinian and Theodora were intelligent, strong willed, and disciplined. Thanks to these qualities, Justinian received an excellent education, found a position in the imperial bureaucracy, and soon mastered the intricacies of Byzantine finance. Theodora proved to be a sagacious advisor: she offered Justinian advice on sensitive political, diplomatic, and theological issues, and she contributed to the formation of a grand imperial court.

Justinian and Theodora

Like Constantine, Justinian lavished resources on the imperial capital. During the early years of his rule, riots against high taxes had destroyed much of Constantinople. After Theodora persuaded him to deploy the imperial army and quash the disturbances, Justinian embarked on an ambitious construction program that thoroughly remade the city. The most notable building erected during this campaign was the church of Hagia Sophia, a magnificent domed structure that later became a mosque and a museum and that ranks as one of the world's most important examples of Christian architecture. Visitors marveled at the church's enormous dome, which they likened to the heavens encircling the earth, and they expressed awe at the gold, silver, gems, precious stones, and thousands of lamps that decorated and illuminated Hagia Sophia. Over time, the church even acquired a reputation for working miraculous cures: its columns and doors reportedly healed the illnesses of people who stood beside them or rubbed against them.

Justinian's most significant political contribution was his codification of Roman law. The origins of Roman law go back to the time of the kings of Rome, and legal scholars worked to systematize Roman law during the Roman republic and the early empire. Almost immediately upon taking the throne, Justinian ordered a systematic review of Roman law that was more thorough than any that had taken place before. On the basis of this work, he issued the *Corpus iuris civilis (Body of the Civil Law),* which immediately won recognition as the definitive codification of Roman law. Later emperors updated Roman law by adding new provisions, but Justinian's code continued to serve as a source of legal inspiration. Through Justinian's code, for example, Roman law influenced civil law codes throughout much of western Europe.

Justinian's Code

Justinian wears imperial purple robes in this mosaic from the church of San Vitale in Ravenna, which depicts him in the company of ecclesiastical, military, and court officials. • Scala/Art Resource, NY

Belisarius and Byzantine Conquests
Justinian's most ambitious venture was his effort to reconquer the western Roman empire from Germanic peoples and reestablish Roman authority throughout the Mediterranean basin. Beginning in 533 he sent his brilliant general Belisarius on military campaigns that returned Italy, Sicily, northwestern Africa, and southern Spain to imperial hands. By the end of his reign in 565, Justinian had reconstituted a good portion of the classical Roman empire.

Justinian's accomplishment, however, did not long survive his own rule. Byzantium simply did not possess the resources to sustain Belisarius's conquests. Reconstitution of the Roman empire would have required a long-term occupation of reconquered regions and a costly reassertion of imperial authority. Yet Byzantine forces were unable to hold Rome itself for very long, and the city of Ravenna on Italy's Adriatic coast became the headquarters of Byzantine authority in the western Mediterranean. As a result, Ravenna possesses magnificent Byzantine art and architecture. But Justinian's dream of restoring Roman authority throughout the Mediterranean basin soon faded.

Indeed, Justinian's efforts clearly showed that the classical Roman empire was beyond recovery. While Justinian devoted his attention to the western Mediterranean, the Sasanids threatened Byzantium from the east and Slavic peoples approached from the north. Justinian's successors had no choice but to withdraw their resources from the western Mediterranean and redeploy them in the east. Even though Belisarius's reconquest of the western Roman empire was a spectacular military accomplishment, it was also something of an anachronism, since the lands of the eastern and western

Mediterranean had already begun to follow different historical trajectories.

Islamic Conquests and Byzantine Revival

After the seventh century C.E., the emergence of Islam and the development of a powerful and expansive Islamic state (topics discussed in chapter 13) posed a serious challenge to Byzantium. Inspired by their Islamic faith, Arab peoples conquered the Sasanid empire and overran large portions of the Byzantine empire as well. By the mid-seventh century Byzantine Syria, Palestine, Egypt, and north Africa had fallen under Islamic rule. During the late

The interior of the church of Hagia Sophia ("Holy Wisdom"), built by Justinian and transformed into a mosque in the fifteenth century. The dome rises almost 60 meters (197 feet) above the floor, and its windows allow abundant light to enter the massive structure. • Robert Frerck/The Stock Market

seventh and early eighth centuries, Islamic forces threatened the heart of the empire and subjected Constantinople itself to prolonged siege (in 674–678 and again in 717–718). Byzantium resisted this northern thrust of Islam partly because of military technology. Byzantine forces used a weapon known as "Greek fire"—a devastating incendiary weapon compounded of sulphur, lime, and petroleum—which they launched at both the fleets and the ground forces of the invaders. Greek fire burned even when floating on water and thus created a serious hazard when deployed around wooden ships. On land it caused panic among enemy forces, since it was very difficult to extinguish and often burned troops to death. As a result of this defensive effort, the Byzantine empire retained its hold on Anatolia, Greece, and the Balkan region.

Though much reduced by the Islamic conquests, the Byzantine empire was more compact and manageable after the eighth century than was the far-flung realm of Justinian. Byzantine rulers responded to the challenge of Islam with political and social adjustments that strengthened the empire that remained in their hands. The most important innovation was the reorganization of Byzantine society under the *theme* system, which Byzantine rulers had tentatively experimented with during earlier periods of hostility with Sasanid Persia. The *theme* system placed an imperial province (*theme*) under the jurisdiction of a general, who assumed responsibility for both its military defense and its civil administration. Generals received their appointments from the imperial government, which closely supervised their activities to prevent decentralization of power and authority. Generals recruited armies from the ranks of free peasants, who received allotments of land in exchange for military service. The armies proved to be effective military forces, and the system as a whole strengthened the class of free peasants, which in turn solidified Byzantium's agricultural economy. The *theme* system enabled Byzantine forces to mobilize quickly and resist further Islamic advances and also undergirded the political order and social organization of the empire from the eighth through the twelfth century.

Imperial Organization

Illustration in a manuscript depicts Byzantine naval forces turning Greek fire on their Arab enemies.

• The Granger Collection

Indeed, strengthened by the *theme* system, Byzantium vastly expanded its influence between the late ninth and the late eleventh century. During the tenth century Byzantine forces shored up defenses in Anatolia and reconquered Syria from Arab Muslims. During the reign of Basil II (976–1025 C.E.) known as "Basil the Bulgar-Slayer," Byzantine armies turned west and crushed the neighboring Bulgars, who had built a large and expansive kingdom in the Balkans. After his victory at the battle of Kleidion in 1014 C.E., Basil reportedly commanded his forces to blind fourteen thousand Bulgarian survivors, though he spared one eye in a few who then guided the others home. By the mid-eleventh century the Byzantine empire embraced lands from Syria and Armenia in the east to southern Italy in the west, from the Danube River in the north to Cyprus and Crete in the south. Byzantine expansion brought in so much wealth that Basil was able to waive the collection of taxes for two years. Once again, Byzantium dominated the eastern Mediterranean.

Byzantium and Western Europe

Tensions between Byzantium and Western European States

While they went to war with their Arab Muslim and pagan Slavic neighbors, Byzantines also experienced tense ecclesiastical and political relations with their Christian counterparts in the western Mediterranean. The Christian church of Constantinople conducted its affairs in Greek and bowed to the will of the caesaropapist emperors, whereas the Christian church of Rome conducted its affairs in Latin and rejected imperial claims to oversee ecclesiastical matters. Ecclesiastical authorities in Byzantium regarded Roman Christians as poorly educated and uncouth. Church leaders in Rome considered their Byzantine counterparts subtle and learned but insincere and insufficiently wary of heresy.

Political grievances also strained relations between Byzantium and western European lands. During the fifth and sixth centuries, imperial authorities could do little more than watch as Germanic peoples established successor states to the western Roman empire. Visigoths, Vandals, Franks, and others imposed their rule on lands that Byzantine emperors regarded as their rightful inheritance. Worse yet, some of the upstart powers claimed imperial authority for themselves. In 800, for example, the Frankish ruler Charlemagne received an imperial crown from the pope in Rome, thereby directly challenging Byzantine claims to imperial authority over western lands. Charlemagne's empire soon dissolved, but in 962 Otto of Saxony lodged his own claim to rule as emperor over the western lands of the former Roman empire.

Adding injury to insult, Otto then attacked lands in southern Italy that had been in Byzantine possession since the days of Justinian.

Liudprand of Cremona

The tenor of relations between Byzantium and western European lands emerges clearly from the report of an ambassador named Liudprand of Cremona, whom Otto sent on a diplomatic mission to Constantinople in 968. Liudprand described the Byzantine emperor as "a monstrosity of a man, a dwarf, fat-headed and with tiny mole's eyes; disfigured by a short, broad, thick beard half going gray; disgraced by a neck scarcely an inch long; piglike by reason of the big close bristles on his head." Liudprand despised Byzantine food, drink, dress, and shelter, and he denounced his diplomatic counterparts as slippery, scheming liars. He described Constantinople it-self as a formerly prosperous and illustrious city that had become shabby, sleazy, and pretentious. Given these attitudes, it is hardly surprising that Byzantium and western European lands experienced almost continuously strained relations until the fall of the Byzantine empire.

BYZANTINE ECONOMY AND SOCIETY

Byzantium dominated the political and military affairs of the eastern Mediterranean largely because of its strong economy. Ever since classical times, the territories em-braced by the Byzantine empire had produced abundant agricultural surpluses, sup-ported large numbers of craftsmen, and participated in trade with lands throughout the Mediterranean. The economic and social assets of the eastern Mediterranean did not disappear with the classical Roman empire. Instead, they continued to provide a solid material foundation for Byzantium, and they helped to make the Byzantine empire an economic powerhouse of the postclassical era.

The Agricultural Economy

Until its conquest by Arab forces, Egypt was the major source of grain for Byzantium. Afterwards, Anatolia and the lower Danube region served as the imperial breadbasket. All these lands produced abundant harvests of wheat, which supported large popula-tions in Constantinople, Thessaloniki, Antioch, Trebizond, and other major cities. Throughout most of Byzantium's existence, Constantinople was the largest city in Europe: between the fifth and the early thirteenth century, its population approached or exceeded one million people. Only on the basis of a reliable and productive agricul-tural economy was it possible for a city of this size to survive and flourish.

The Peasantry

Byzantine economy and society were strongest when the empire supported a large class of free peasants who owned small plots of land. Besides serving as the backbone of the Byzantine military system, free peasants cultivated their land intensively in hope of improving their families' fortunes. As in other societies, however, wealthy individu-als and families sought to accumulate land, the principal source of wealth in Byzan-tium as elsewhere. Especially in the early centuries of the Byzantine empire, wealthy cultivators ran large estates and supervised the peasantry as a dependent class. Peasants did not become slaves, but neither did they remain entirely free. Sometimes they were bound to the land, forbidden to depart without permission of their lords. Other times they worked under sharecropping arrangements, whereby landlords contracted land-less peasants to cultivate their lands in exchange for a large portion of the yield. Rarely did sharecroppers accumulate enough wealth to gain their independence: often they worked the same holdings for years—or for life—on terms set by the landlords.

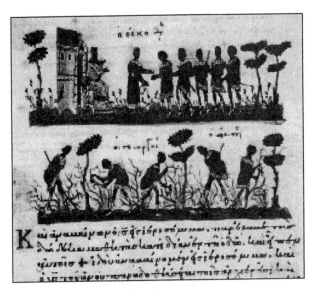

Peasants—probably sharecroppers—receive seeds and tend to vineyards in this painting from a Byzantine manuscript.

• Bibliothèque Nationale de France

The invasions of the sixth and seventh centuries broke up many large estates and afforded peasants an opportunity to rebuild small holdings. The *theme* system strengthened the free peasantry by making land available to those who performed military service. The imperial government also made periodic efforts to support free peasants and prevent wealthy landowners from gaining control over their lands. During the sixth, eighth, and tenth centuries in particular, Byzantine authorities limited the accumulation of land by wealthy classes and thereby strengthened the peasantry.

Over the long term, however, wealthy landowners built ever larger estates. From the eleventh century onward, they transformed the peasants into an increasingly dependent class, and by the thirteenth century free peasants accounted for only a small portion of the rural population.

Quite apart from its social effects, the accumulation of landholdings had important implications for financial and military affairs. Large estates did not contribute to imperial tax coffers at the rate of small peasants' holdings, since wealthy landowners had the influence to obtain concessions and exemptions. Moreover, the decline of the free peasantry diminished the pool of recruits available for service in military forces organized under the *theme* system. Large landowners raised forces from their estates, but they often deployed them to advance their own interests rather than those of the imperial government. Concentration of land and rural resources worked against the financial interests of the central government, and it caused political, military, and economic difficulties for the Byzantine state during the last three centuries of its existence.

Industry and Trade

In spite of social and economic problems, Byzantium remained a wealthy land. Byzantine prosperity derived both from the empire's productive capacity and from the importance of Constantinople as a center of trade.

Manufacturing Enterprises   Constantinople was already a major site of crafts and industry in classical times, and it became even more important as capital of the Byzantine empire. The city was home to many artisans and craftsmen, not to mention thousands of imperial officials and bureaucrats. Byzantine craftsmen enjoyed a reputation especially for their glassware, linen and woolen textiles, gems, jewelry, and fine work in gold and silver.

By the late sixth century, after the arrival of silkworms in monks' walking staffs and probably by other routes as well, craftsmen had added high-quality silk textiles to the list of products manufactured in the Byzantine empire. Silk was a most important addition to the economy, and Byzantium became the principal supplier of this fashionable fabric to lands in the Mediterranean basin. The silk industry was so important to the Byzantine economy that the government closely supervised every step in its production and sale. Regulations allowed individuals to participate in only one activity—such as weaving, dyeing, or sales—to prevent the creation of a monopoly in the industry by a few wealthy or powerful entrepreneurs.

Trade also helped to sustain the Byzantine economy. Situated astride routes going east and west as well as north and south, Constantinople served as the main clearinghouse for trade in the western part of Eurasia. The merchants of Constantinople maintained direct commercial links with manufacturers and merchants in central Asia, Russia, Scandinavia, northern Europe, and

After the sixth century Constantinople became a major center of silk production. The remains of this eighth-century silk fabric depict two horsemen hunting lions. • Giraudon/Art Resource, NY

Trade

the lands of the Black Sea and the Mediterranean basin. Even after the early Islamic conquests, Byzantine merchants dealt regularly with their Muslim counterparts in Persia, Syria, Palestine, and Egypt except during periods of outright war between Byzantium and Islamic states. Byzantium dominated trade to such an extent that trading peoples recognized the Byzantine gold coin, the *bezant,* as the standard currency of the Mediterranean basin for more than half a millennium, from the sixth through the twelfth centuries.

Byzantium drew enormous wealth simply from the control of trade and the levying of customs duties on merchandise that passed through its lands. More important, Byzantium served as the western anchor of a Eurasian trading network that revived the silk roads of classical times. Silk and porcelain came to Constantinople from China, spices from India and southeast Asia. Carpets arrived from Persia, woolen textiles from western Europe, and timber, furs, honey, amber, and slaves came from Russia and Scandinavia. Byzantine subjects consumed some commodities from distant parts, but they redistributed most merchandise, often after adding to its value by further processing—by fashioning jewelry out of gems imported from India, for example, or by dyeing raw woolen cloth imported from western Europe.

Banks and business partnerships helped to fuel Byzantine trade. Banks advanced loans to individuals seeking to launch business ventures and thus made trade possible even when merchants did not personally possess large supplies of liquid wealth. Byzantine merchants often formed partnerships, which allowed them to pool their resources and limit their risks. Neither banking nor partnership was an altogether new technique: both had origins in classical Mediterranean business practices. Yet Byzantine businessmen made much more extensive use than their predecessors had of banking and cooperative partnerships, which provided both support and stimulus for a dynamic commercial economy.

The Organization of Trade

Urban Life

Constantinople had no rival among Byzantine cities. Subjects of the Byzantine empire referred to it simply as "the City." The heart of the City was the imperial palace, which employed twenty thousand workers as palace staff. Peacocks strutted through gardens filled with sculptures and fountains. Most famous was a gold fountain in the shape of a pineapple that spouted wine for imperial guests.

Housing in Constantinople Aristocrats maintained enormous palaces that included courtyards, reception halls, libraries, chapels, and quarters for members of the extended family as well as servants and slaves. Women lived in separate apartments and did not receive male visitors from outside the household. Indeed, women often did not participate in banquets and parties, especially if wine flowed freely or when the affairs were likely to become so festive that they could compromise a woman's honor.

The less privileged classes of Constantinople occupied less splendid dwellings. Artisans and craftsmen usually lived in rooms above their shops, while clerks and government officials lived in multistory apartment buildings. Workers and the poor occupied dangerous and rickety tenements, sharing kitchens and sanitary facilities with their neighbors.

Attractions of Constantinople Even for the poor, though, the City had its attractions. As the heir to Rome, Constantinople was a city of baths, which were sites of relaxation and exercise as well as hygenic bathing. Taverns and restaurants offered settings for social gatherings—checkers, chess, and dice games were especially popular activities at taverns—and theaters provided entertainment in the form of song, dance, and striptease. Mass entertainment took place in the Hippodrome, a large stadium adjacent to the imperial palace. There Byzantine subjects watched athletic matches, contests between wild animals, and circuses featuring clowns, jugglers, acrobats, and dwarfs.

Greens and Blues Most popular of the City's pastimes were the chariot races that took place in the Hippodrome. Spectators' passions for chariot teams ran high, and until the seventh century they often contributed to public disturbances. Racing fans formed two factions—the Greens and the Blues—that pursued their rivalry well beyond the Hippodrome. Greens and Blues frequently fought in the streets and constantly sought to influence imperial officials to favor one group over the other. On one occasion Greens and Blues united and mounted a serious popular uprising against the high taxes imposed by Justinian. In 532 they seized the Hippodrome and proclaimed a new emperor. Belisarius's army quelled the disturbance, but only after killing thousands of rioters. The rebellion left Constantinople in shambles, and Justinian took the opportunity to rebuild the city on a lavish scale. By the late seventh century, the rivalry between Greens and Blues had faded. The parties remained, but they increasingly took on the character of civic societies, and leaders of the two groups became respected officials at the imperial court.

CLASSICAL HERITAGE AND ORTHODOX CHRISTIANITY

The first Christian emperor of the Roman empire gave both his name and his faith to Constantinople. Like the Byzantine state, however, Byzantine Christianity developed along distinctive lines, and it became a faith different from the early Christianity of the Roman empire. The philosophy and literature of classical Greece had a much deeper influence in Byzantium than in western Europe, and the classical

THE WEALTH AND COMMERCE OF CONSTANTINOPLE

• • •

The Spanish rabbi Benjamin of Tudela traveled throughout Europe, north Africa, and southwest Asia between 1165 and 1173 C.E. He may have ventured as far as India, and he mentioned both India and China in his travel account. His main purpose was to record the conditions of Jewish communities, but he also described the many lands and about three hundred cities that he visited. His travels took place during an era of political decline for the Byzantine empire, yet he still found Constantinople a flourishing and prosperous city.

The circumference of the city of Constantinople is eighteen miles; half of it is surrounded by the sea, and half by land, and it is situated upon two arms of the sea, one coming from the sea of Russia [the Black Sea], and one from the sea of Sepharad [the Mediterranean].

All sorts of merchants come here from the land of Babylon, from the land of Shinar [Mesopotamia], from Persia, Media [western Iran], and all the sovereignty of the land of Egypt, from the land of Canaan [Palestine], and the empire of Russia, from Hungary, Patzinakia [Ukraine], Khazaria [southern Russia], and the land of Lombardy [northern Italy] and Sepharad [Spain].

Constantinople is a busy city, and merchants come to it from every country by sea or land, and there is none like it in the world except Baghdad, the great city of Islam. In Constantinople is the church of Hagia Sophia, and the seat of the pope of the Greeks, since Greeks do not obey the pope of Rome. There are also as many churches as there are days of the year. . . . And in this church [Hagia Sophia] there are pillars of gold and silver, and lamps of silver and gold more than a man can count.

Close to the walls of the palace is also a place of amusement belonging to the emperor, which is called the Hippodrome, and every year on the anniversary of

the birth of Jesus the emperor gives a great entertainment there. And in that place men from all the races of the world come before the emperor and empress with jugglery and without jugglery, and they introduce lions, leopards, bears, and wild asses, and they engage them in combat with one another; and the same thing is done with birds. No entertainment like this is to be found in any other land. . . .

From every part of the Byzantine empire tribute is brought here every year, and they fill strongholds with garments of silk, purple, and gold. Like unto these storehouses and this wealth there is nothing in the whole world to be found. It is said that the tribute of the city amounts every year to 20,000 gold pieces, derived both from the rents of shops and markets and from the tribute of merchants who enter by sea or land.

The Greek inhabitants are very rich in gold and precious stones, and they go clothed in garments of silk and gold embroidery, and they ride horses and look like princes. Indeed, the land is very rich in all cloth stuffs and in bread, meat, and wine.

Wealth like that of Constantinople is not to be found in the whole world. Here also are men learned in all the books of the Greeks, and they eat and drink, every man under his vine and his fig-tree.

SOURCE: Benjamin of Tudela. *The Itinerary of Benjamin of Tudela*. Trans. by M. N. Adler. London: H. Frowde, 1907. (Translation slightly modified.)

legacy helped to shape Byzantine education and cultural development as well as Orthodox Christianity. Byzantine church leaders disagreed with their western counterparts on matters of doctrine, ritual, and church authority. By the mid-eleventh century differences between the eastern and western churches had become so great that their leaders formally divided Mediterranean Christianity into the Eastern Orthodox and Roman Catholic churches.

The Legacy of Classical Greece

Although local inhabitants spoke Greek, the official language of early Constantinople was Latin, the language of Rome. The connection between Byzantium and Rome was apparent in Justinian's code of laws, which appeared in Latin. After the sixth century, however, Greek replaced Latin as the language of government in the Byzantine empire. Byzantine scholars often did not learn to read Latin, and they drew intellectual inspiration from the New Testament (originally composed in Greek) and the philosophy and literature of classical Greece rather than classical Rome.

Byzantine Education   The legacy of classical Greece was especially noticeable in Byzantine education. An educational system was necessary because of the large bureaucracy that administered the empire: government machinery called for large numbers of literate and intelligent individuals. Byzantine aristocrats often hired tutors to provide private instruction for their children, girls as well as boys. But the bureaucratic workforce emerged mostly from a state-organized school system that offered a primary education in reading, writing, and grammar, followed by studies of classical Greek literature, philosophy, and science.

Although most peasants and many urban workers had no formal education, basic literacy was widespread in Byzantine society. Alongside the bureaucrats, Byzantine merchants, manufacturers, clergy, and military personnel usually had at least a primary education. At the pinnacle of the state educational system was a school of higher learning in Constantinople that offered advanced instruction in law, medicine, and philosophy. This school functioned almost continuously from its founding in 425 C.E. until the end of the Byzantine empire more than one thousand years later in 1453.

Byzantine Scholarship   Like the educational system, Byzantine scholarship also reflected the cultural legacy of classical Greece. Byzantine scholars concentrated on the humanities—literature, history, and philosophy—rather than on the natural sciences or medicine. They produced commentaries on Homer, Plato, Aristotle, and other prominent figures, and their works served as textbooks studied in schools alongside writings from classical times. Byzantines with a literary education considered themselves the direct heirs of classical Greece, and they went to great lengths to preserve and transmit the classical legacy. Indeed, almost all literary and philosophical works of classical Greece that survive have come down to the present in copies made between the tenth and twelfth centuries in the Byzantine empire.

The Byzantine Church

Church and State   The most distinctive feature of Byzantine Christianity was its close relationship with the imperial government. From the time of Constantine on, caesaropapist emperors participated actively in religious and theological matters. Constantine himself intervened in theological debates, even when the issues at stake had little or no direct political implication. In 325 C.E., for example, Constantine organized the Council of Nicaea, which brought together bishops, spokesmen, and leaders from all the important Christian churches in order to consider the views of the Arians. Followers of a priest from Alexandria named Arius (250–336 C.E.), the Arians taught that Jesus had been a mortal human being and that he was a creation of God rather than a divine being coeternal with God. Yet many Christian theologians held to the contrary: that in a unique and mysterious way Jesus was both a mortal human being and a manifestation of God himself, that he simultaneously possessed fully human and fully divine natures. Although he originally favored Arian views, Constantine came

to accept the alternative and personally attended sessions of the Council of Nicaea in order to support it. His presence encouraged the council to endorse his preferred view as orthodox and condemn Arianism as heresy.

Throughout Byzantine history the emperors treated the church as a department of state. They appointed individuals to serve as patriarch of Constantinople—the highest ecclesiastical official in the Byzantine church, counterpart of the pope in Rome—and they instructed patriarchs, bishops, and priests to deliver sermons that supported imperial policy and encouraged obedience to imperial authorities. This caesaropapism was a source of constant conflict between imperial and ecclesiastical authorities, and it also had the potential to generate large-scale dissent and protest when imperial views clashed with those of the larger society.

The most divisive ecclesiastical policy implemented by Byzantine emperors was iconoclasm, inaugurated by Emperor Leo III (reigned 717–741 C.E.). By the time of Leo's rule, Byzantium had a long tradition of producing icons—paintings of Jesus, saints, and other figures of religious significance—many of which were splendid works of art. For most theologians these icons served a useful purpose in that they inspired the popular imagination and encouraged reverence for holy personages. Leo, however, became convinced that the veneration of religious images was sinful, tantamount to the worship of physical idols. In 726 C.E. he embarked on the policy of iconoclasm (which literally means "the breaking of icons"), destroying religious images and prohibiting their use in churches. The policy immediately sparked protests and riots throughout the empire, since icons were extremely popular among the laity. Debates about iconoclasm raged in Byzantium for more than a century.

This illustration from a psalter prepared about 900 C.E. depicts an iconoclast whitewashing an image of Jesus painted on a wall. • Historical Museum, Moscow

Iconoclasm

Only in 843 did the iconoclasts abandon their efforts. In spite of its resolution, the controversy demonstrated once again the willingness of Byzantine emperors to involve themselves directly in religious and theological matters.

In its theology Byzantine Christianity reflected the continuing influence of classical Greek philosophy. Christianity had originally emerged from Jewish sources. As it attracted adherents in the Roman empire, theologians sought ways to harmonize Christianity with other, long-established cultural traditions, notably Greek philosophy. A faith embracing both Christian revelation and Greek reason, they recognized, would have a powerful appeal.

Greek Philosophy and Byzantine Theology

The influence of Greek philosophy in Christian theology was especially prominent in Greek-speaking Byzantium. Theologians invested a great deal of time and intellectual energy in the examination of religious questions from a philosophical point of view. They looked to classical philosophy, for example, when seeking to understand the nature of Jesus and the extent to which he possessed both human and divine characteristics. Although these debates often became extremely technical, they illustrate the continuing influence of classical Greek philosophy. Debates about Jesus' nature represented an effort to understand Christian doctrine in light of the terms and concepts that classical philosophers had employed in their analysis of the world. A school maintained by the patriarch of Constantinople provided instruction for clergy and church officials in advanced theology of this sort. Though it differed in many ways from Mediterranean society of classical times, Byzantium built its own cultural and religious traditions on a solid classical foundation.

Monasticism and Popular Piety

Caesaropapist emperors, powerful patriarchs, and other high church officials concerned themselves with theological and ritual matters and rarely dealt directly with the lay population of the Byzantine church. For their part the Byzantine laity had little interest in fine points of theology or high-level church administration, and they positively resented policies like iconoclasm that infringed on cherished patterns of worship. For religious inspiration, the laity looked less to the church hierarchy than to the local monasteries.

Asceticism

Byzantine monasticism grew out of the efforts of devout individuals to lead especially holy lives. Drawing inspiration from early Christian ascetics in Egypt, Mesopotamia, and Persia, they observed regimes of extreme asceticism and self-denial. Some abandoned society altogether and went to live in the desert or in caves as hermits. Others dedicated themselves to celibacy, fasting, and prayer. During the fifth century a few men and at least two women demonstrated their ascetic commitments by perching for years at a time atop tall pillars. St. Simeon Stylite, the first and most famous of these "pillar saints," attracted the attention of admirers from as far away as Gaul.

Byzantine Monasticism and St. Basil

Because of the extreme dedication of hermits and ascetics, disciples often gathered around them and established communities of men and women determined to follow their example. These communities became the earliest monasteries of the Byzantine church. They had few rules until St. Basil of Caesarea (329–379 C.E.), the patriarch of Constantinople during the mid-fourth century, urged them to adopt reforms that enhanced their effectiveness. In Basilian monasteries monks and nuns gave up their personal possessions and lived communally. They obeyed the rule of elected superiors, and all community members devoted themselves to work and prayer. After the fourth century Basilian monasticism spread rapidly throughout the Byzantine empire.

The piety and devotion of monks and nuns endeared them to the Byzantine laity. They went to great lengths in search of mystical union with God through meditation and prayer. Sometimes they employed special techniques such as controlled breathing and intensely focused gazing to bring divine illumination. Because of their own devotion, they inspired piety among the laity. Monks and nuns represented a religious faith more immediate and meaningful than that of the theologians and ecclesiastical bureaucrats of Constantinople.

Monks and nuns also provided social services to their communities. They provided spiritual counsel to local laity, and they organized relief efforts by bringing food and medical attention to communities struck by disasters. They won the support of the Byzantine populace, too, when they vigorously opposed the policy of iconoclasm and fought to restore icons to churches and monasteries. Unlike their counterparts in western Europe and other lands, Byzantine monasteries for the most part did not become centers of thought and learning. Nevertheless, by setting examples of devotion and by tending to the needs and interests of the laity, monks helped to maintain support for their faith in the Byzantine empire.

Tensions between Eastern and Western Christianity

Byzantine Christianity developed in tension particularly with the Christian faith of western Europe. During the centuries following Constantine's legalization of Christianity, church leaders in Jerusalem, Alexandria, Antioch, Constantinople, and Rome exercised great influence in the larger Christian community. After Arab peoples conquered most of southwest Asia and introduced Islam there in the seventh century, the influence of the patriarchs in Jerusalem, Alexandria, and Antioch declined, leaving only Constantinople and Rome as the principal centers of Christian authority.

Constantinople and Rome

The tensions that developed between Constantinople and Rome mirrored political strains between Byzantine and western European societies. The specific issues that divided the two Christian communities, however, were religious and theological. One of them was the iconoclastic movement of the eighth and ninth centuries. Western theologians regarded religious images as perfectly appropriate aids to devotion and resented Byzantine claims to the contrary, whereas the iconoclasts took offense at the efforts of their Roman counterparts to have images restored in Byzantium.

In later centuries Christian churches based in Constantinople and Rome disagreed on many other points. Some ritual and doctrinal differences concerned forms of worship and the precise wording of theological teachings—relatively minor issues that by themselves need not have caused deep division in the larger Christian community. Byzantine theologians objected, for example, to the fact that western priests shaved their beards and used unleavened instead of leavened bread when saying Mass. Other differences concerned substantive theological matters such as the precise relationship between God, Jesus, and the Holy Spirit—all regarded as manifestations of God by most Christian theologians.

Schism

Alongside these ritual and doctrinal differences, the Byzantine patriarchs and Roman popes disputed their respective rights and powers. Patriarchs argued for the autonomy of all major Christian jurisdictions, including that of Constantinople, while popes asserted the primacy of Rome as the sole seat of authority for all Christendom. Ultimately, relations became so strained that the eastern and western churches went separate ways. In 1054 C.E. the patriarch and pope mutually excommunicated each other, each refusing to recognize the other's church as properly Christian. Despite efforts at reconciliation, the resulting schism between eastern and western churches persists to the present day. In recognition of the split, historians refer to the eastern Christian church after 1054 as the Eastern Orthodox church and its western counterpart as the Roman Catholic church.

THE INFLUENCE OF BYZANTIUM IN EASTERN EUROPE

Byzantines called themselves *Romaioi* ("Romans"), and aristocrats sometimes traced their lineage back to ancestors who went to Constantinople with Constantine himself. Yet by about 1000 C.E., Byzantium differed profoundly from Mediterranean society of classical times. Under Roman rule the Mediterranean basin had formed a coherent political and economic unit, as trade and cultural exchanges linked all lands and peoples of the region. By the second millennium C.E., however, a dynamic society founded on the Islamic faith had seized control of the lands on the Mediterranean's southern and eastern rim, and Byzantines and western Europeans contested the northern rim. Hemmed in and increasingly pressured by Islamic and western European societies, Byzantium entered a period of decline beginning about the late eleventh century.

As its Mediterranean influence waned, however, Byzantium turned its attention to eastern Europe and Russia. Through political, commercial, and cultural relations, Byzantium decisively influenced the history of Slavic peoples. Although the Byzantine state came to an end in the fifteenth century C.E., the legacy of Byzantium survives and continues to shape the lives of millions of people in Russia and eastern Europe.

Domestic Problems and Foreign Pressures

When Basil II "the Bulgar-Slayer" died in 1025 C.E., the Byzantine empire was a political, military, and economic dynamo. Within fifty years, however, the empire was suffering from serious internal weaknesses and had endured a series of military reverses. In fact, it had entered a long period of gradual but sustained decline from which it never fully recovered. Both domestic and foreign problems help to explain this decline.

Social Problems   Domestic problems arose, ironically, from the success of the *theme* system. Generals who governed the *themes* were natural allies of local aristocrats who held large tracts of land. Generals and their offspring intermarried with the local aristocracies, creating an elite class with tremendous military, political, social, and economic power. Some of these powerful families resisted the policies of the imperial government and even mounted rebellions against central authorities. The rebels never managed to defeat the imperial forces, but their revolts seriously disrupted local economies. Moreover, the elite class accumulated vast estates that placed the free peasantry under increasing pressure. Formerly the backbone of Byzantium's military system and its agricultural economy, by the mid-eleventh century the free peasantry was declining both in numbers and in prosperity. As a result, Byzantine military forces had fewer recruits available for service, and declining tax receipts from free peasants caused fiscal problems for the imperial government.

Challenges   As domestic problems mounted, Byzantium also faced fresh foreign challenges.
from the West   From the west came representatives of a dynamic and expanding western European society. Beginning in the eleventh century, vigorous economic development in west-

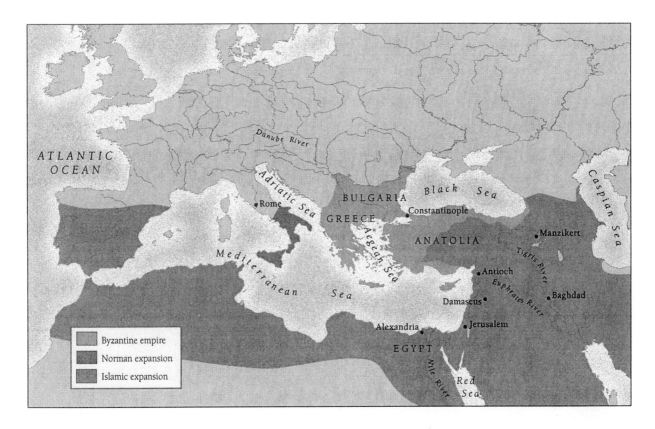

Decline of the Byzantine empire.

ern Europe supported a remarkable round of military and political expansion. During the early eleventh century, the Normans—a Scandinavian people who had seized Normandy (in northern France) and settled there—established themselves as an independent power in southern Italy. By midcentury Norman adventurers led by Robert Guiscard had taken control of southern Italy and expelled Byzantine authorities there.

During the twelfth and thirteenth centuries, the Normans and other western European peoples mounted a series of crusades—vast military campaigns intended to recapture Jerusalem and other sites holy to Christians from Muslims—and took the opportunity to carve out states in the heart of the Byzantine empire. Venetian merchants even managed to divert the fourth crusade (1202–1204) from its original mission in the eastern Mediterranean to Constantinople. Venetians had become prominent in the commercial life of the eastern Mediterranean, and they viewed the fourth crusade as an opportunity to strengthen their position against Byzantine competition. As it happened, the expedition never got beyond Constantinople, which crusaders conquered and sacked in 1204. Byzantine forces recaptured the capital in 1261, but the destruction of Constantinople dealt the Byzantine empire a blow from which it never completely recovered.

As Europeans expanded into Byzantine territory from the west, nomadic Turkish peoples invaded from the east. Most important among them were the Muslim Saljuqs, who beginning in the eleventh century sent waves of invaders into Anatolia. Given the military and financial problems of the Byzantine empire, the Saljuqs found Anatolia ripe for plunder. In 1071 they subjected the Byzantine army to a demoralizing defeat

Challenges from the East

During the sack of Constantinople in 1204, crusading forces seized and carted away Byzantine treasures of all sorts—including the great bronze horses that now stand over the entrance to St. Mark's basilica in Venice. • Erich Lessing/Art Resource, NY

at the battle of Manzikert. Byzantine factions then turned on each other in civil war, allowing the Saljuqs almost free rein in Anatolia. By the late twelfth century, the Saljuqs had seized much of Anatolia, and crusaders held most of the remainder.

The loss of Anatolia—the principal source of Byzantine grain, wealth, and military forces—sealed the fate of the Byzantine empire. A territorially truncated Byzantium survived until the mid-fifteenth century, but the late Byzantine empire enjoyed little autonomy and continually faced fresh challenges from Italian merchants, western European adventurers, and Turkish nomads. In 1453, after a long era of decline, the Byzantine empire came to an end when Ottoman Turks captured Constantinople and absorbed its territories into their own expanding realm.

Early Relations between Byzantium and Slavic Peoples

By the time Constantinople fell, Byzantine traditions had deeply influenced the political and cultural development of Slavic peoples in eastern Europe and Russia. Close relations between Byzantium and Slavic peoples date from the sixth century. When Justinian deployed Byzantium's military resources in the western Mediterranean, Slavic peoples from the north took advantage of the opportunity to move into Byzantine territory. Serbs and Croats moved into the Balkan peninsula, and

Bulgars established a powerful kingdom in the lower Danube region.

Relations between Byzantium and Bulgaria were especially tense. By the eighth century, however, as a result of its wealth and sophisticated diplomacy, Byzantium had begun to influence Bulgarian politics and society. Byzantine emperors recognized Bulgarian rulers, enhancing their status as legitimate sovereigns. Byzantium and Bulgaria entered into political, commercial, and cultural relations. Members of Bulgarian ruling families often went to Constantinople for a formal education in Greek language and literature and followed Byzantine examples in organizing their court and capital.

Byzantium also sent missionaries to Balkan lands, and Bulgars and other Slavic peoples began to convert to Orthodox Christianity. The most famous of the missionaries to the Slavs were Saints

This illustration from a twelfth-century manuscript depicts ninth-century incursions of Bulgarians into Byzantine territory, culminating in a lecture by the Bulgarian king to the Byzantine emperor, shown here with bound hands.   •   Biblioteca Apostolica, Vatican Library/Index s.a.s.

Missions to the Slavs

Cyril and Methodius, two brothers from Thessaloniki in Greece. During the mid-ninth century Cyril and Methodius conducted missions in Bulgaria and Moravia (which included much of the modern Czech, Slovakian, and Hungarian territories). While there, they devised an alphabet, known as the Cyrillic alphabet, for the previously illiterate Slavic peoples. Though adapted from written Greek, the Cyrillic alphabet represented the sounds of Slavic languages more precisely than did the Greek, and it remained in use in much of eastern Europe until supplanted by the Roman alphabet in the twentieth century. In Russia and most other parts of the former Soviet Union, the Cyrillic alphabet survives to the present day.

The creation of a written Slavic language enabled Slavic peoples to organize complex political structures and develop sophisticated traditions of thought and literature. More immediately, the Cyrillic alphabet stimulated conversion to Orthodox Christianity. Missionaries translated the Christian scriptures and church rituals into Slavonic, and Cyrillic writing helped them explain Christian values and ideas in Slavic terms. Meanwhile, schools organized by missionaries ensured that Slavs would receive religious instruction alongside their introduction to basic literacy. As a result, Orthodox Christianity deeply influenced the cultural traditions of many Slavic peoples.

Byzantium and Russia

North of Bulgaria another Slavic people began to organize large states: the Russians. About the mid-ninth century Russians created several principalities governed from thriving trading centers, notably Kiev. Strategically situated on the Dnieper River along the main trade route linking Scandinavia and Byzantium, Kiev became a wealthy and powerful center, and it dominated much of the territory between the Volga and the Dnieper from the tenth to the thirteenth century. Russian merchants visited Constantinople in large numbers and became well acquainted with Byzantine society. Russian princes sought alliances with Byzantine rulers and began to express an interest in Orthodox Christianity.

The Conversion of Prince Vladimir

About 989 Prince Vladimir of Kiev converted to Orthodox Christianity and ordered his subjects to follow his example. Vladimir was no paragon of virtue: he lauded drunkenness and reportedly maintained a harem of eight hundred girls. After his conversion, however, Byzantine influences flowed rapidly into Russia. Cyrillic writing, literacy, and Orthodox missions all spread quickly throughout Russia. Byzantine teachers traveled north to establish schools, and Byzantine priests conducted services for Russian converts. For two centuries Kiev served as a conduit for the spread of Byzantine cultural and religious influence in Russia.

Byzantine art and architecture dominated Kiev and other Russian cities. Icons in the Byzantine style encouraged popular piety, and religious images became a principal form of Russian artistic expression. The onion domes that are a distinctive feature of early Russian churches were the result of architects' efforts to imitate the domed structures of Constantinople using wood as their principal building material.

The Growth of Kiev

The princes of Kiev established firm, caesaropapist control over the Russian Orthodox church—so called to distinguish it from the Eastern Orthodox church of the Byzantine empire. They also drew inspiration from Byzantine legal tradition and compiled a written law code for their lands. By controlling trade with Byzantium and other lands, they gained financial resources to build a flourishing society. In the eleventh century Kiev reportedly had four hundred churches and eight large marketplaces. By the early twelfth century its population approached thirty thousand, and a fire in 1124 consumed six hundred churches.

Eventually, Russians even claimed to inherit the imperial mantle of Byzantium. According to a popular theory of the sixteenth century, Moscow was the world's third Rome: the first Rome had fallen to Germanic invaders in the fifth century, whereas the second Rome, Constantinople, had fallen to the Turks a thousand years later. Moscow survived as the third Rome, the cultural and religious beacon that would guide the world to Orthodox Christian righteousness. Inspired by this theory, missionaries took their Russian Orthodox faith to distant lands. During the sixteenth and later centuries, they brought Siberia into the fold of the Orthodox church, crossed the Bering Strait, and dispatched missions to Alaska and even northern California. Thus long after the collapse of the eastern Roman empire, the Byzantine legacy continued to work its influence through the outward reach of the Russian Orthodox church.

The Byzantine empire originated as a survivor of the classical era. Byzantium inherited a hardy economy, a set of governing institutions, an imperial bureaucracy, an official religion, an established church, and a rich cultural tradition from classical Mediterranean society and the Roman empire. Byzantine leaders drew heavily on this legacy as they dealt with new challenges. Throughout Byzantine history classical inspiration was especially noticeable in the imperial office, the bureaucracy, the church, and the educational system. Yet in many ways Byzantium changed profoundly over the course of its thousand-year history. After the seventh century the Byzantine empire shrank dramatically in size, and after the eleventh century it faced relentless foreign pressure from western Europeans and nomadic Turkish peoples. Changing times also brought transformations in Byzantine social and economic organization. Yet from the fifth to the twelfth century and beyond, Byzantium brought political stability and economic prosperity to the eastern Mediterranean basin, and Byzantine society served as a principal anchor supporting commercial and cultural exchanges in the postclassical world.

CHRONOLOGY

313–337	Reign of Constantine
325	Council of Nicaea
329–379	Life of St. Basil of Caesarea
340	Transfer of Roman government to Constantinople
527–565	Reign of Justinian
976–1025	Reign of Basil II, "the Bulgar Slayer"
717–741	Reign of Leo III
726–843	Iconoclastic controversy
ninth century	Missions of St. Cyril and St. Methodius to the Slavs
989	Conversion of Prince Vladimir of Kiev to Orthodox Christianity
1054	Beginning of the schism between the eastern and western Christian churches
1071	Battle of Manzikert
1202–1204	Fourth crusade
1453	Fall of Constantinople

FOR FURTHER READING

Peter Arnott. *The Byzantines and Their World.* New York, 1973. A lively, popular, personal vision of Byzantine history.

Louis Bréhier. *The Life and Death of Byzantium.* Trans. by M. Vaughan. Amsterdam, 1977. A detailed political history of the Byzantine empire.

Averil Cameron. *The Mediterranean World in Late Antiquity,* A.D. 395–600. London, 1993. A thoughtful synthesis that draws on recent scholarship in placing Byzantium in the context of the late Roman empire.

Charles Diehl. *Byzantium: Greatness and Decline.* Trans. by N. Walford. New Brunswick, 1957. Well-written analysis concentrating on the institutional strengths and weaknesses of Byzantium.

Francis Dvornik. *Byzantine Missions among the Slavs: SS. Constantine-Cyril and Methodius.* New Brunswick, 1970. Deals with the spread of Orthodox Christianity to eastern Europe.

J. M. Hussey. *The Byzantine World.* London, 1982. A brief and reliable survey.

Liudprand of Cremona. *The Works of Liudprand of Cremona.* Trans. by F. A. Wright. London, 1930. Translations that include accounts of tenth-century Byzantium and of Liudprand's diplomatic mission to Constantinople.

Dimitri Obolensky. *The Byzantine Commonwealth: Eastern Europe, 500–1453.* New York, 1971. A well-informed overview of early Slavic history and relations between Byzantine and Slavic peoples.

George Ostrogorsky. *History of the Byzantine State.* Rev. ed. Trans. by J. Hussey. New Brunswick, 1969. Comprehensive and detailed survey emphasizing political developments.

Procopius. *History of the Wars, Secret History, and Buildings.* Trans. by A. Cameron. New York, 1967. Translations of writings by the most important historian in the time of Justinian.

Michael Psellus. *Fourteen Byzantine Rulers.* Trans. by E. R. A. Sewter. Harmondsworth, 1966. Memoirs of eleventh-century Byzantium by a highly placed adviser to several emperors.

Steven Runciman. *Byzantine Civilization.* Cleveland, 1965. An authoritative overview concentrating on Byzantine institutions by a distinguished scholar.

———. *The Byzantine Theocracy.* Cambridge, 1977. Set of engaging lectures on the Orthodox church.

A. A. Vasiliev. *History of the Byzantine Empire.* 2 vols. Madison, 1958. A detailed survey that devotes attention to cultural as well as political matters.

Speros Vryonis Jr. *Byzantium and Europe.* London, 1967. Well-illustrated and well-written perusal of Byzantine history and Byzantine relations with western Europe.

———. *The Decline of Medieval Hellenism in Asia Minor and the Process of Islamization from the Eleventh through the Fifteenth Century.* Berkeley, 1971. Authoritative analysis of the Turkish conquest of the Byzantine empire.

Serge A. Zenkovsky, ed. *Medieval Russia's Epics, Chronicles, and Tales.* New York, 1963. A rich collection of literary and historical sources in English translation.

A NEW SOCIETY: THE REALM OF ISLAM

· · ·

In 632 C.E. the prophet Muhammad visited his native city of Mecca from his home in exile at Medina, and in doing so he set an example that devout Muslims have sought to emulate ever since. The *hajj*—the holy pilgrimage to Mecca—draws Muslims by the hundreds of thousands from all parts of the world to Saudi Arabia. Each year Muslims travel to Mecca by land, sea, and air to make the pilgrimage and visit the holy sites of Islam.

In centuries past the numbers of pilgrims were smaller, but their observance of the hajj was no less conscientious. By the ninth century pilgrimage had become so popular that Muslim rulers went to some lengths to meet the needs of travelers passing through their lands. With the approach of the pilgrimage season—the last month of the Islamic lunar calendar—crowds gathered at major trading centers like Baghdad, Damascus, and Cairo. There they lived in tent cities, surviving on food and water provided by government officials, until they could join caravans bound for Mecca. Muslim rulers invested considerable sums in the maintenance of roads, wells, cisterns, and lodgings that accommodated pilgrims—as well as castles and police forces that protected travelers—on their journeys to Mecca and back.

The hajj was not only solemn observance but also an occasion for joy and celebration. Muslim rulers and wealthy pilgrims often made lavish gifts to caravan companions and others they met en route to Mecca. During her famous hajj of 976–977, for example, the Mesopotamian princess Jamila bint Nasir al-Dawla provided food and fresh green vegetables for her fellow pilgrims and furnished five hundred camels for handicapped travelers. She also purchased freedom for five hundred slaves and distributed fifty thousand fine robes among the common people of Mecca.

Most pilgrims did not have the resources to match Jamila's generosity, but for common travelers, too, the hajj became a special occasion. Merchants and craftsmen made acquaintances and arranged business deals with pilgrims from other lands. Students and scholars exchanged ideas during their weeks of traveling together. For all pilgrims participation in ritual activities lent new meaning and significance to their faith.

The word *Islam* means "submission," signifying obedience to the rule and will of Allah, the only god recognized in the strictly monotheistic Islamic religion. An individual who accepts the Islamic faith is a *Muslim,* meaning "one who has submitted."

A fifteenth-century Persian manuscript depicts pilgrims praying at Mecca in the mosque surrounding the Ka'ba. • © The British Library

Though it began as one man's expression of unqualified faith in Allah, Islam quickly attracted followers and took on political and social as well as religious significance. During the first century of the new faith's existence, Islam reached far beyond its Arabian homeland, bringing Sasanid Persia and parts of the Byzantine empire into its orbit. By the eighth century the realm of Islam stood alongside the Byzantine empire as a political and economic anchor of the postclassical world.

Islamic society originally reflected the nomadic and mercantile Arabian society from which Islam arose. Yet over time, Muslims drew deep inspiration from other societies as well. After toppling the Sasanid dynasty, Muslim conquerors adopted Persian techniques of government and finance to administer their lands. Persian literature, science, and religious values also found a place in Islamic society. During later centuries Muslims drew inspiration from Greek and Indian traditions as well. Thus Muslims did not invent a new Islamic society, but rather fashioned it by blending elements from Arab, Persian, Greek, and Indian societies.

While drawing influence from other societies, however, the Islamic faith thoroughly transformed the cultural traditions that it absorbed. The expansive realm of Islam eventually provided a political framework for trade and diplomacy over a vast portion of the eastern hemisphere, from west Africa to the islands of southeast Asia. Many lands of varied cultural background thus became part of a larger society often called the *dar al-Islam*—an Arabic term that means the "house of Islam" and that refers to lands under Islamic rule.

A PROPHET AND HIS WORLD

Islam arose in the Arabian peninsula, and the new religion faithfully reflected the social and cultural conditions of its homeland. Desert covers most of the peninsula, and agriculture is possible only in the well-watered area of Yemen in the south and in a few other places, such as the city of Medina, where oases provide water. Yet human communities have occupied Arabia for millennia. Nomadic peoples known as Bedouin kept herds of sheep, goats, and camels, migrating through the deserts to find grass and water for their animals. The Bedouin organized themselves in family and clan groups. Individuals and their immediate families depended heavily on their larger kinship networks for support in times of need. In an environment as harsh and unforgiving as the Arabian desert, cooperation with kinsmen often made the difference between death and survival. Bedouin peoples developed a strong sense of loyalty to their clans and guarded their common interests with determination. Clan identities and loyalties survived for centuries after the appearance of Islam.

Arabia also figured prominently in the long-distance trade networks of the postclassical era. Commodities arrived at ports on the Persian Gulf (near modern Bahrain), the Arabian Sea (near modern Aden), and the Red Sea (near Mecca), and then traveled overland by camel caravan to Palmyra or Damascus, which offered access to the Mediterranean basin. After the third century c.e., Arabia became an increasingly important link in trade between China and India in the east and Persia and Byzantium in the west. With the weakening of classical empires, trade routes across central Asia had become insecure. Merchants abandoned the overland routes in favor of sea-lanes connecting with land routes in the Arabian peninsula. Trade passing across the peninsula was especially important for the city of Mecca, which became an important site of fairs and a stopping point for caravan traffic.

Muhammad and His Message

The prophet Muhammad came into this world of nomadic Bedouin herders and merchants. Born about 570 C.E. into a reputable family of merchants in Mecca, Muhammad ibn Abdullah lost both his parents by the time he was six years old. His grandfather and uncle cared for him and provided him with an education, but Muhammad's early life was difficult. As a young man, he worked for a woman named Khadija, a wealthy widow whom he married about the year 595. Through this marriage he gained a position of some prominence in Meccan society, although he did not by any means enter the ranks of the elite.

Muhammad's Early Life

By age thirty Muhammad had established himself as a merchant. He made a comfortable life for himself in Arabian society, where peoples of different religious and cultural traditions regularly dealt with each other. Most Arabs recognized many gods, goddesses, demons, and nature spirits whose favor they sought through prayers and sacrifices. Large communities of Jewish merchants also worked throughout Arabia, and especially in the north, many Arabs had converted to Christianity by Muhammad's time. Although he was not deeply knowledgeable about Judaism or Christianity, Muhammad had a basic understanding of both faiths. He may even have traveled by caravan to Syria, where he would certainly have dealt with Jewish and Christian merchants.

About 610 C.E., as he approached age forty, Muhammad underwent a profound spiritual experience that transformed his life and left a deep mark on world history. His experience left him with the convictions that in all the world there was only one true god, Allah ("the god"), that he ruled the universe, that idolatry and the recognition of other gods amounted to wickedness, and that Allah would soon bring his judgment on the world, rewarding the righteous and punishing the wicked. Muhammad experienced visions, which he understood as messages or revelations

Muhammad's Spiritual Transformation

Ruins of a temple, which probably honored the moon deity, at Tayma in northern Arabia. The temple dates to about the mid-sixth century B.C.E. Altars with round basins are visible in the foreground.
• © 1997 Wayne Eastep

Current Islamic doctrine forbids artistic representations of Muhammad and Allah to prevent the worship of their images as idols. Although artists of previous centuries occasionally produced paintings of Muhammad, Islamic art has emphasized geometric design and calligraphy. This handsome page from a Quran written on vellum dates from the ninth or early tenth century. • Reproduced by kind permission of the Trustees of the Chester Beatty Library, Dublin.

from Allah, delivered through the archangel Gabriel, instructing him to explain his faith to others. (Jews and Christians also recognized Gabriel as an archangel, a special messenger of God.) Muhammad did not intend to found a new religion, but in accordance with the instructions transmitted to him, he began to expound his faith to his family and close friends. Gradually, others became interested in his message, and by about 620 c.e. a zealous and expanding minority of Mecca's citizenry had joined Muhammad's circle.

The Quran   Muhammad originally presented oral recitations of the revelations he received during his visions. As the Islamic community grew, his followers prepared written texts of his teachings. During the early 650s devout Muslims compiled these written versions of Muhammad's revelations and issued them as the Quran ("recitation"), the holy book of Islam. A work of magnificent poetry, the Quran communicates in powerful and moving terms Muhammad's understanding of Allah and his relation to the world, and it serves as the definitive authority for Islamic religious doctrine and social organization.

Muhammad's Migration to Medina

Conflict at Mecca   The growing popularity of Muhammad's preaching brought him into conflict with the ruling elites at Mecca. Conflict centered on religious issues. Muhammad's insistence that Allah was the only divine power in the universe struck many Arabs as offensive and dangerous as well, since it disparaged long-recognized deities and spirits thought to wield influence over human affairs. The tensions also had a personal dimension. Mecca's ruling elites, who were also the city's wealthiest merchants, took it as a personal affront and a threat to their position when Muhammad denounced greed as moral wickedness that Allah would punish.

THE QURAN ON ALLAH AND HIS JUDGMENT OF HUMANKIND

• • •

The foundation of the Islamic faith is the understanding of Allah, his nature, and his plan for the world as outlined in the Quran. Through his visions Muhammad came to understand Allah as the one and only god, the creator and sustainer of the world in the manner of the Jews' Yahweh and the Christians' God. Those who rejected Allah and his message would suffer eternal punishment, while those who recognized and obeyed him would receive his mercy and secure his blessings.

Say "Allah is God alone!
God the eternal!
He begets not and is not begotten!
Nor is there like unto Him anyone!". . . .

Celebrated be the name of thy Lord most high, who created and fashioned, and who decreed and guided, and who brings forth the pasture, and then makes it dusky stubble!

We will make thee recite, and thou shalt not forget, save what Allah pleases. Verily He knows what is open and what is concealed. . . .

Prosperous is he who purifies himself and remembers the name of his Lord and prays!

But ye prefer the life of this world, although the hereafter is better and more lasting.

Verily this was in the books of old—the books of [the Hebrew patriarchs] Abraham and Moses.

Woe to every slanderous backbiter who collects wealth and counts it.

He thinks that his wealth can immortalize him. Not so! He shall be hurled into hell!

And what shall make thee understand what hell is? It is the fire of Allah kindled, which rises above the hearts. Verily it is an archway [of fire] over them on long-drawn columns. . . .

Allah promises those who believe and do right that He will give them the succession in the earth as He gave the succession to those [who believed and did right] before them, and He will establish for them their religion which He has chosen for them, and He promises to give them safety in exchange for their fear. They shall worship me, they shall not associate any other god with me, but whoever disbelieves, those are sinners.

And be steadfast in prayer and give alms and obey the Prophet [Muhammad], that ye may obtain mercy.

Do not imagine that those who disbelieve can frustrate Allah in the earth, for their destination is the fire, and an ill journey it shall be.

SOURCE: *The Qur'an.* 2 vols. Trans. by E.H. Palmer. Oxford: Clarendon Press, 1880, 2: 344, 2:328–29, 2: 341, 2:80–81. (Translation slightly modified.)

Muhammad's attack on idolatry also represented an economic threat to those who owned and profited from the many shrines to deities that attracted merchants and pilgrims to Mecca. The best known of these shrines was a large and magnificent black rock long considered to be the dwelling of a powerful deity. Housed in a cube-shaped building known as the Ka'ba, it drew worshipers from all over Arabia and brought considerable wealth to Mecca. As Muhammad relentlessly condemned the idolatry officially promoted at the Ka'ba and other shrines, the ruling elites of Mecca began to persecute the prophet and his followers.

The pressure became so great that some of Muhammad's followers fled to Abyssinia (modern Ethiopia). Muhammad himself remained in Mecca until 622 C.E., when he too fled and joined a group of his followers in Yathrib, a rival trading city 345 kilometers (214 miles) north of Mecca. Muslims called their new home Medina ("the city," meaning "the city of the prophet"). Known as the *hijra* ("migration"), Muhammad's move to Medina serves as the starting point of the official Islamic calendar.

The Hijra

The Umma   In Mecca Muhammad had lived within the established political framework and concentrated on the moral and religious dimensions of his faith. In Medina he found himself at the head of a small but growing society in exile that needed guidance in practical as well as spiritual affairs. He organized his followers into a cohesive community called the *umma* ("community of the faithful") and provided it with a comprehensive legal and social code. He led this community both in daily prayers to Allah and in battle with enemies at Medina, Mecca, and other places. He looked after the economic welfare of the *umma*—sometimes by organizing commercial ventures and sometimes by launching raids against caravans from Mecca. Remembering the difficult days of his own youth, he provided relief for widows, orphans, and the poor, and he made almsgiving a prime moral virtue.

The "Seal *of the Prophets"*   Muhammad's understanding of his religious mission expanded during his years at Medina. He began to refer to himself as a prophet, indeed as the "seal of the prophets"—the final prophet through whom Allah would reveal his message to humankind. Muhammad accepted the authority of earlier Jewish and Christian prophets, including Abraham, Moses, and Jesus, and he held the Hebrew scriptures and the Christian New Testament in high esteem. He also accepted his predecessors' monotheism: Allah was the same omnipotent, omniscient, omnipresent, and exclusive deity as the Jews' Yahweh and the Christians' God. Muhammad taught, however, that the message entrusted to him offered a more complete revelation of Allah and his will than Jewish and Christian faiths had made available. Thus while at Medina, Muhammad came to see himself consciously as Allah's final prophet: not simply as a devout man who explained his spiritual insights to a small circle of family and friends, but as the messenger who communicated Allah's wishes and his plan for the world to all humankind.

The Establishment of Islam in Arabia

Muhammad's *Return to Mecca*   Throughout their sojourn at Medina, Muhammad and his followers planned ultimately to return to Mecca, which was both their home and the leading city of Arabia. In 629 C.E. they arranged with the authorities to participate in the annual pilgrimage to the Ka'ba, but they were not content with a short visit. In 630 they attacked Mecca and conquered the city. They forced the elites to adopt Muhammad's faith, and they imposed a government dedicated to Allah. They also destroyed the pagan shrines and replaced them with mosques, buildings that sought to instill a sense of sacredness and community where Muslims gathered for prayers. Only the Ka'ba escaped their efforts to cleanse Mecca of pagan monuments.

Muhammad and his followers denied that the Ka'ba was the home of a deity, but they preserved the black rock and its housing as a symbol of Mecca's greatness. They allowed only the faithful to approach the shrine, and in 632 Muhammad himself led the first Islamic pilgrimage to the Ka'ba, thus establishing the hajj as an example for all devout Muslims. Building on the conquest of Mecca, Muhammad and his followers launched campaigns against other towns and Bedouin clans, and by the time of the prophet's death in 632, shortly after his hajj, they had brought most of Arabia under their control.

The Five Pillars *of Islam*   Muhammad's faith and his personal leadership decisively shaped the values and the development of the Islamic community. The foundation of the Islamic faith as elaborated by Muhammad consists of obligations known as the Five Pillars of Islam: (1) Muslims must acknowledge Allah as the only god and Muhammad as his prophet. (2) They must pray to Allah daily while facing Mecca. (3) They must observe a fast during the daylight hours of the month of Ramadan. (4) They must contribute alms for the relief of the weak and poor. (5) Finally, in honor of Muhammad's visit to Mecca in 629, those who are physically and financially able must undertake the hajj and make at least one pilgrimage to Mecca. During the centuries since its appearance, Islam has generated many schools and sects, each with its own particular legal, social, and doctrinal features. The Five Pillars of Islam, however, constitute a simple but powerful framework that has bound the *umma* as a whole into a cohesive community of faith.

Beyond the general obligations prescribed by the Five Pillars, Islamic holy law, known as the *sharia,* emerged during the centuries after Muhammad and offered detailed guidance on proper behavior in almost every aspect of life. Elaborated by jurists and legal scholars, the *sharia* drew its inspiration especially from the Quran and the early historical accounts of Muhammad's life and teachings. It offered precise guidance on matters as diverse as marriage and family life, inheritance, slavery, business and commercial relationships, political authority in the *dar al-Islam,* and crime. Through the *sharia,* Islam became more than a religious doctrine: it developed into a way of life complete with social and ethical values derived from Islamic religious principles.

Islamic Law: The Sharia

THE EXPANSION OF ISLAM

After Muhammad's death the Islamic community might well have unraveled and disappeared. Muhammad had made no provision for a successor, and there was serious division within the *umma* concerning the selection of a new leader. Many of the towns and Bedouin clans that had recently accepted Islam took the opportunity of Muhammad's death to renounce the faith, reassert their independence, and break free from Mecca's control. Within a short time, however, the Islamic community had embarked on a stunningly successful round of military expansion that extended its political and cultural influence far beyond the boundaries of Arabia. These conquests laid the foundation for the rapid growth of Islamic society.

The Early Caliphs and the Umayyad Dynasty

Because Muhammad was the "seal of the prophets," it was inconceivable that another prophet should succeed him. Shortly after Muhammad's death his advisors selected Abu Bakr, a genial man who was one of the prophet's closest friends and most devoted disciples, to serve as *caliph* ("deputy"). Thus Abu Bakr and later caliphs led the *umma* not as prophets, but as lieutenants or substitutes for Muhammad. Abu Bakr became head of state for the Islamic community as well as chief judge, religious leader, and military commander. Under the new caliph's leadership, the *umma* went on the offensive against the towns and Bedouin clans that had renounced Islam after Muhammad's death, and within a year it had compelled them to recognize the faith of Islam and the rule of the caliph.

The Caliph

Indeed, during the century after Muhammad's death, Islamic armies ranged well beyond the boundaries of Arabia, carrying their religion and their authority to Byzantine and Sasanid territories and beyond. Between 633 and 637 C.E., they seized Byzantine Syria and Palestine and took most of Mesopotamia from the Sasanids. During the 640s they conquered Byzantine Egypt and north Africa. In 651 they toppled the Sasanid dynasty and incorporated Persia into their expanding

The Expansion of Islam

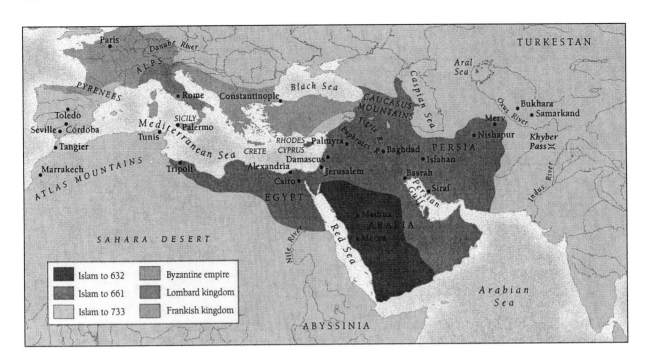

MAP [13.1]

The expansion of Islam.

empire. In 711 they conquered the Hindu kingdom of Sind in northwestern India. Between 711 and 718 they extended their authority to northwest Africa and crossed the Strait of Gibraltar, conquering most of the Iberian peninsula and threatening the Frankish kingdom in Gaul. By the mid-eighth century an immense Islamic empire ruled lands from India and the central Asian steppelands in the east to northwest Africa and Iberia in the west.

During this rapid expansion the empire's rulers encountered difficult problems of governance and administration. One problem had to do with the selection of caliphs. During the early decades after Muhammad's death, leaders of the most powerful Arab clans negotiated among themselves and appointed the first four caliphs. Political ambitions, personal differences, and clan loyalties complicated their deliberations, however, and disputes soon led to the rise of factions and parties within the Islamic community.

The Shia   Disagreements over succession led to the emergence of the Shia sect, the most important and enduring of all the alternatives to the faith observed by the majority of Muslims, known as Sunni Islam. The Shia sect originated as a party supporting the appointment of Ali and his descendants as caliphs. A cousin and son-in-law of Muhammad, Ali was a candidate for caliph when the prophet died, but support for Abu Bakr was stronger. Ali served briefly as the fourth caliph (656–661 C.E.), but his enemies assassinated him, killed many of his relatives, and imposed their own candidate as caliph. Partisans of Ali then organized the Shia ("party"), furiously resisted the victorious faction, and struggled to return the caliphate to the line of Ali. Although persecuted, the Shia survived and strengthened its identity by adopting doctrines and rituals distinct from those of the Sunnis ("traditionalists"), who accepted the legitimacy of the early caliphs. During later centuries the Shia sect served as both a refuge and a source of support for opponents of the policies of Sunni leaders.

The Umayyad   After the assassination of Ali, the establishment of the Umayyad dynasty
Dynasty   (661–750 C.E.) solved the problem of succession, at least temporarily. The

Interior courtyard of the Great Mosque of Damascus, built by the Umayyad caliphs between 706 and 715. Beyond the covered portico stands the minaret, the tower from which the official crier (muezzin) summons the faithful to prayer. • Photo: Barbara Brend

Umayyads ranked among the most prominent of the Meccan merchant clans, and their reputation and network of alliances helped them bring stability to the Islamic community. Despite their association with Mecca, the Umayyads established their capital at Damascus, a thriving commercial city in Syria, whose central location enabled them to maintain better communication with the vast and still-expanding Islamic empire.

Although the Umayyads' dynasty solved the problem of succession, their tightly centralized rule and the favor they showed to their fellow Arabs generated an administrative problem. The Umayyads ruled the *dar al-Islam* as conquerors, and their policies reflected the interests of the Arab military aristocracy. The Umayyads appointed members of this elite as governors and administrators of conquered lands, and they distributed the wealth that they extracted among this privileged class.

This policy contributed to high morale among Arab conquerors, but it caused severe discontent among the scores of ethnic and religious groups embraced by the Umayyad empire. Apart from Muslims the empire included Christians, Jews, Zoroastrians, and Buddhists. Apart from Arabs and Bedouin, it included Indians, Persians, Mesopotamians, Greeks, Egyptians, and nomadic Berbers in north Africa. The Arabs mostly allowed conquered peoples to observe their own religions—particularly Christians and Jews—but they levied a special head tax, called the *jizya,* on those who did not convert to Islam. Even those who converted did not enjoy access to wealth and positions of authority, which the Umayyads reserved almost exclusively for members of the Arab military aristocracy. These policies caused deep resentment among conquered peoples and led to restiveness against Umayyad rule.

Policy toward Conquered Peoples

Beginning in the early eighth century, the Umayyad caliphs became alienated even from other Arabs. They devoted themselves increasingly to luxurious living

Umayyad Decline

rather than to zealous leadership of the *umma,* and they scandalized devout Muslims by their casual attitudes toward Islamic doctrine and morality. By midcentury the Umayyad caliphs faced not only the resistance of the Shia faction, whose members continued to promote descendants of Ali for caliph, but also the discontent of conquered peoples throughout their empire and even the disillusionment of Muslim Arab military leaders.

The Abbasid Dynasty

Abu al-Abbas

Rebellion in Persia brought the Umayyad dynasty to an end. The chief leader of the rebellion was Abu al-Abbas, a descendant of Muhammad's uncle. Although he was a Sunni Arab, Abu al-Abbas allied readily with Shias and with Muslims who were not Arabs, such as converts to Islam from southwest Asia. Particularly prominent among his supporters were Persian converts who resented the preference shown by the Umayyads to Arab Muslims. During the 740s Abu al-Abbas's party rejected Umayyad authority and seized control of Persia and Mesopotamia. In 750 his army shattered Umayyad forces in a massive battle. Afterward Abu al-Abbas invited the remaining members of the Umayyad clan to a banquet under the pretext of reconciling their differences. During the festivities his troops arrested the Umayyads and slaughtered them, effectively annihilating the clan. Abu al-Abbas then founded the Abbasid dynasty, which was the principal source of authority in the *dar al-Islam* until the Mongols toppled it in 1258 C.E.

The Abbasid Dynasty

The Abbasid dynasty differed considerably from the Umayyad. For one thing the Abbasid state was far more cosmopolitan than its predecessor. Even though they sprang from the ranks of conquering Arabs, Abbasid rulers did not show special favor to the Arab military aristocracy. Arabs continued to play a large role in government, but Persians, Egyptians, Mesopotamians, and others also rose to positions of wealth and power.

The Abbasid dynasty differed from the Umayyad also in that it was not a conquering dynasty. The Abbasids sparred intermittently with the Byzantine empire, they clashed frequently with nomadic peoples from central Asia, and in 751 they defeated a Chinese army at Talas River near Samarkand. Only marginally, however, did they increase the size of their empire by conquest. The *dar al-Islam* as a whole continued to grow during the Abbasid era, but the caliphs had little to do with the expansion. During the ninth and early tenth centuries, for example, largely autonomous Islamic forces from distant Tunisia mounted naval expeditions throughout the Mediterranean, conquering Crete, Sicily, and the Balearic Islands while occasionally seizing territories also in Cyprus, Rhodes, Sardinia, Corsica, southern Italy, and southern France.

Abbasid Administration

Instead of conquering new lands, the Abbasids largely contented themselves with administering the empire they inherited. Fashioning a government that could administer a sprawling realm with scores of linguistic, ethnic, and cultural groups was a considerable challenge. In designing their administration, the Abbasids relied heavily on Persian techniques of statecraft. Central authority came from the court at Baghdad (capital of modern Iraq), the magnificent new city that the early Abbasid caliphs built near the Sasanid capital of Ctesiphon. Baghdad was a round city protected by three round walls. At the heart of the city was the caliph's green-domed palace from which instructions flowed to the distant reaches of the Abbasid realm. In the provinces governors represented the caliph and implemented his political and financial policies.

Learned officials known as *ulama* ("people with religious knowledge") and *qadis* ("judges") set moral standards in local communities and resolved disputes. *Ulama* and *qadis* were not priests—Islam does not recognize priests as a distinct class of religious specialists—but they had a formal education that emphasized study of the Quran and the *sharia*. *Ulama* were pious scholars who sought to develop public policy in accordance with the Quran and *sharia*. *Qadis* heard cases at law and rendered decisions based on the Quran and *sharia*. Because of their moral authority, *ulama* and *qadis* became extremely influential officials who helped to ensure widespread observance of Islamic values. Apart from provincial governors, *ulama,* and *qadis,* the Abbasid caliphs kept a standing army, and they established bureaucratic ministries in charge of taxation, finance, coinage, and postal services. They also maintained the magnificent network of roads that the Islamic empire inherited from the Sasanids.

In this manuscript illustration a Muslim teacher (the figure with the open book) instructs students in the fine points of Islamic law in a library near Baghdad. • Bibliothèque Nationale de France

Harun al-Rashid

The high point of the Abbasid dynasty came during the reign of the caliph Harun al-Rashid (786–809 C.E.). By the late eighth century, Abbasid authority had lost some of its force in provinces distant from Baghdad, but it remained strong enough to bring reliable tax revenues from most parts of the empire. Flush with wealth, Baghdad became a center of banking, commerce, crafts, and industrial production, a metropolis with a population of several hundred thousand people. According to stories from his own time, Harun al-Rashid provided liberal support for artists and writers, bestowed lavish and luxurious gifts on his favorites, and distributed money to the poor and the common classes by tossing coins into the streets of Baghdad. Once he sent an elephant and a collection of rich presents as gifts to his contemporary Charlemagne, who ruled the Carolingian empire of western Europe.

Abbasid Decline

Soon after Harun al-Rashid's reign, the Abbasid empire entered a period of decline. Civil war between Harun's sons seriously damaged Abbasid authority, and disputes over succession rights became a recurring problem for the dynasty. Provincial governors took advantage of disorder in the ruling house by acting independently of the caliphs: instead of implementing imperial policies and delivering taxes to Baghdad, they built up local bases of power and in some cases actually seceded from the

BENJAMIN OF TUDELA ON THE CALIPH'S COURT AT BAGHDAD

• • •

Like Constantinople, Baghdad was in a period of deline when the Spanish rabbi Benjamin of Tudela visited in the later twelfth century. Nevertheless, again like the Byzantine capital, Baghdad remained an immensely prosperous city. Benjamin's report on Baghdad concentrated largely on the court and palace of the Abbasid caliph.

The caliph is the head of the Muslim religion, and all the kings of Islam obey him; he occupies a similar position to that held by the pope over the Christians. He has a palace in Baghdad three miles in extent, wherein there is a great park with all varieties of trees, fruit-bearing and otherwise, and all manner of animals. The whole is surrounded by a wall, and in the park there is a lake whose waters are fed by the river Hiddekel. Whenever the king desires to indulge in recreation and to re-joice and feast, his servants catch all manner of birds, game, and fish, and he goes to his palace with his counsellors and princes. . . .

Each of his brothers and the members of his family has an abode in his palace, but they are all fettered in chains of iron, and guards are placed over each of their houses so that they may not rise against the great caliph. For once it happened to a predecessor that his brothers rose up against him and proclaimed one of themselves as caliph; then it was decreed that all the members of his family should be bound, that they might not rise up against the ruling caliph. Each one of them resides in his palace in great splendor, and they own villages and towns, and their stewards bring them the tribute thereof, and they eat and drink and rejoice all the days of their life.

Within the domains of the palace of the caliph there are great buildings of marble and columns of silver and gold, and carvings upon rare stones are fixed in the walls. In the caliph's palace are great riches and towers filled with gold, silken garments, and all precious stones. . . .

The caliph is a benevolent man. On the other side of the river, on the banks of an arm of the Euphrates which there borders the city, he built a hospital consisting of blocks of houses and hospices for the sick poor who come to be healed. Here there are about sixty physicians' stores which are provided from the caliph's house with drugs and whatever else may be required. Every sick man who comes is maintained at the caliph's expense and is medically treated. Here is a building which is called Dar-al-Maristan, where they keep charge of the demented people who have become insane in the towns through the great heat in the summer, and they chain each of them in iron chains until their reason becomes restored to them in the winter. While they abide there, they are provided with food from the house of the caliph, and when their reason is restored they are dismissed and each one of them goes to his house and his home. Money is given to those that have stayed in the hospices on their return to their homes. Every month the officers of the caliph inquire and investigate whether they have regained their reason, in which case they are discharged. All this the caliph does out of charity to those that come to the city of Baghdad, whether they be sick or insane. The caliph is a righteous man, and all his actions are for good. . . .

The city of Baghdad is twenty miles in circumference, situated in a land of palms, gardens, and plantations, the like of which is not to be found in the whole land of Mesopotamia. People come thither with merchandise from all lands. Wise men live there, philosophers who know all manner of wisdom, and magicians expert in all manner of witchcraft.

SOURCE: Benjamin of Tudela. *The Itinerary of Benjamin of Tudela*. Trans. by M. N. Adler. London: H. Frowde, 1907, pp. 35–42. (Translation slightly modified.)

Abbasid state. Meanwhile, popular uprisings and peasant rebellions, which often enjoyed the support of dissenting sects and heretical movements, further weakened the empire.

As a result of these difficulties, the Abbasid caliphs became mere figureheads long before the Mongols extinguished the dynasty in 1258. In 945 members of a Persian noble family seized control of Baghdad and established their clan as the power behind the Abbasid throne. Later, imperial authorities in Baghdad fell under the control of the Saljuq Turks, a nomadic people from central Asia who also invaded the Byzantine empire. In response to rebellions mounted by peasants and provincial governors, authorities in Baghdad allied with the Saljuqs, who began to enter the Abbasid realm and convert to Islam about the mid-tenth century. By the mid-eleventh century the Saljuqs effectively controlled the Abbasid empire. During the 1050s they took possession of Baghdad, and during the following decades they extended their authority to Syria, Palestine, and Anatolia. They retained Abbasid caliphs as nominal sovereigns, but for two centuries, until the arrival of the Mongols, the Saljuq *sultan* ("ruler") was the true source of power in the Abbasid empire.

ECONOMY AND SOCIETY OF THE EARLY ISLAMIC WORLD

In the *dar al-Islam,* as in other agricultural societies, peasants tilled the land as their ancestors had done for centuries before them while manufacturers and merchants supported a thriving urban economy. As in other lands, the creation of large empires had dramatic economic implications. The Umayyad and Abbasid empires created a zone of trade, exchange, and communication stretching from India to Iberia. Commerce throughout this zone served as a vigorous economic stimulus for both the countryside and the cities of the early Islamic world.

New Crops, Agricultural Experimentation, and Urban Growth

As soldiers, administrators, diplomats, and merchants traveled throughout the *dar al-Islam,* they encountered plants, animals, and agricultural techniques peculiar to the empire's various regions. They often introduced particularly useful crops to new regions. The most important of the transplants traveled west from India to Persia, southwest Asia, Arabia, Egypt, north Africa, Spain, and the Mediterranean islands of Cyprus, Crete, Sicily, and Sardinia. They included staple crops such as sugarcane, rice, and new varieties of sorghum and wheat; vegetables such as spinach, artichokes, and eggplants; fruits such as oranges, lemons, limes, bananas, coconuts, watermelons, and mangoes; and industrial crops such as cotton, indigo, and henna.

The Spread of Food and Industrial Crops

The introduction of these crops into the western regions of the Islamic world had wide-ranging effects. New food crops led to a richer and more varied diet. They also increased quantities of food available because they enabled cultivators to extend the growing season. In much of the Islamic world, summers are so hot and dry that cultivators traditionally left their fields fallow during that season. Most of the transplanted crops grew well in high heat, however, so cultivators in southwest Asia, north Africa, and other hot zones could till their lands year-round. The result was a dramatic increase in food supplies.

Effects of New Crops

*Agricultural
Experimentation*

In a thirteenth-century manuscript illustration, a fictional Muslim traveler passes a lively agricultural village. On the left a woman spins cotton thread. Sheep, goats, chickens, and date palms figure prominently in the local economy. • Bibliothèque Nationale de France

Some new crops had industrial uses. The most important of these was cotton, which became the basis for a thriving textile industry throughout much of the Islamic world. Indigo and henna yielded dyes that textile manufacturers used in large quantities.

Travel and communication in the *dar al-Islam* also encouraged experimentation with agricultural methods. Cultivators paid close attention to methods of irrigation, fertilization, crop rotation, and the like, and they outlined their findings in hundreds of agricultural manuals. Copies of these works survive in numerous manuscripts that circulated widely throughout the Islamic world. The combined effect of new crops and improved techniques was a far more productive agricultural economy, which in turn supported vigorous economic growth throughout the *dar al-Islam*.

Urban Growth   Increased agricultural production contributed to the rapid growth of cities in all parts of the Islamic world from India to Spain. Delhi, Samarkand, Bukhara, Merv, Nishapur, Isfahan, Basra, Baghdad, Damascus, Jerusalem, Cairo, Alexandria, Palermo, Tunis, Tangier, Córdoba, and Toledo were all bustling cities, some with populations of several hundred thousand people. All these cities had flourishing markets supporting thousands of artisans, craftsmen, and merchants. Most of them were also important centers of industrial production, particularly of textiles, pottery, glassware, leather, iron, and steel.

One new industry appeared in Islamic cities during the Abbasid era: paper manufacture. Chinese craftsmen had made paper since the first century C.E., but their technology did not spread far beyond China until Arab forces defeated a Chinese army at the battle of Talas River in 751 and took prisoners skilled in paper production. Paper was cheaper and easier to use than writing materials such as vellum sheets made from calfskin and soon became popular throughout the Islamic world. Paper facilitated the keeping of administrative and commercial records, and it made possible the dissemination of books and treatises in larger quantities than ever before. By the tenth century mills produced paper in Persia, Mesopotamia, Arabia, Egypt, and Spain, and the industry soon spread further to western Europe.

The Formation of a Hemispheric Trading Zone

From its earliest days Islamic society drew much of its prosperity from commerce. Muhammad himself was a merchant, and he held merchants in high esteem. According to early accounts of his life, Muhammad once said that honest merchants would stand alongside martyrs to the faith on the day of judgment. By the time of the Abbasid caliphate, elaborate trade networks linked all the regions of the Islamic world and joined it to a larger hemispheric economy.

Overland trade traveled mostly by camel caravan. Although they are unpleasant and often uncooperative beasts, camels endure the rigors of desert travel much better than horses or donkeys. Moreover, when fitted with a well-designed saddle, camels can carry heavy loads. During the early centuries C.E., the manufacture

Caravanserais offered splendid facilities for caravan merchants, but they sometimes harbored dangers. In this illustration from a thirteenth-century manuscript, drugged merchants sleep soundly while burglars relieve them of their valuables. • Bibliothèque Nationale de France

Camels and Caravans

of camel saddles spread throughout Arabia, north Africa, southwest Asia, and central Asia, and camels became the favored beasts of burden in deserts and other dry regions. As camel transport became more common, the major cities of the Islamic world and central Asia built and maintained caravanserais—inns offering lodging for caravan merchants, as well as food, water, and care for their animals.

Maritime Trade

Meanwhile, innovations in nautical technology contributed to a steadily increasing volume of maritime trade in the Red Sea, Persian Gulf, Arabian Sea, and Indian Ocean. Arab and Persian mariners borrowed the compass from its Chinese inventors and used it to guide them on the high seas. From southeast Asian and Indian mariners, they borrowed the lateen sail, a triangular sail that increased a ship's maneuverability. From the Hellenistic Mediterranean they borrowed the astrolabe, an instrument that enabled them to calculate latitude.

Thus equipped, Arab and Persian mariners ventured throughout the Indian Ocean basin, calling at ports from southern China to southeast Asia, Ceylon, India, Persia, Arabia, and the eastern coast of Africa. The twelfth-century Persian merchant Ramisht of Siraf (a flourishing port city on the Persian Gulf) amassed a huge fortune from long-distance trading ventures. One of Ramisht's clerks once returned to Siraf

Arab dhows fitted with lateen sails skim across the Indian Ocean much like their ancestors of the Abbasid era. • George Hulton/Photo Researchers, Inc.

from a commercial voyage to China with a cargo worth half a million dinars—gold coins that were the standard currency in the Islamic world. Ramisht himself was one of the wealthiest men of his age, and he spent much of his fortune on pious causes. He outfitted the Ka'ba with a Chinese silk cover that reportedly cost him eighteen thousand dinars, and he also founded a hospital and a religious sanctuary in Mecca.

Banks   Banking also stimulated the commercial economy of the Islamic world. Banks had operated since classical antiquity, but Islamic banks of the Abbasid period conducted business on a much larger scale and provided a more extensive range of services than their predecessors. They not only lent money to entrepreneurs, but also served as brokers for investments and exchanged different currencies. They established multiple branches that honored letters of credit known as *sakk*—the root of the modern word for "check"—drawn on the parent bank. Thus merchants could draw letters of credit in one city and cash them in another, and they could settle accounts with distant business partners without having to deal in cash.

The Organization   Trade benefitted also from techniques of business organization. As in the case of
of Trade   banking, there were precedents for these techniques in classical Mediterranean society, but increasing volumes of trade enabled entrepreneurs to refine their methods of organization. Furthermore, Islamic law provided security for entrepreneurs by explicitly recognizing certain forms of business organization. Usually Islamic businessmen preferred not to embark on solo ventures, since an individual could face financial ruin if an entire cargo of commodities fell prey to pirates or went down with a ship that sank in a storm. Instead, like their counterparts in other postclassical societies, Abbasid entrepreneurs often pooled their resources in group investments. If several individuals invested in several cargos, they could distribute their risks and more easily absorb losses. Furthermore, if several groups of investors rented cargo space on several different

ships, they spread their risks even more. Entrepreneurs entered into several different kinds of joint endeavors during the Abbasid caliphate. Some involved simply the investment of money in an enterprise, whereas others called for some or all of the partners to play active roles in their business ventures.

As a result of improved transportation, expanded banking services, and refined techniques of business organization, long-distance trade surged in the early Islamic world. Muslim merchants dealt in silk and ceramics from China, spices and aromatics from India and southeast Asia, and jewelry and fine textiles from the Byzantine empire. Merchants also ventured beyond settled societies in China, India, and the Mediterranean basin to distant lands that previously had not engaged systematically in long-distance trade. They crossed the Sahara desert by camel caravan to

In this thirteenth-century illuminated manuscript, merchants at a slave market in southern Arabia deal in black slaves captured in sub-Saharan Africa. Slaves traded in Islamic markets also came from Russia and eastern Europe. • Bibliothèque Nationale de France

trade salt, steel, copper, and glass for gold and slaves from the kingdoms of west Africa. They visited the coastal regions of east Africa, where they obtained slaves and exotic local commodities such as animal skins. They engaged in trade with Russia and Scandinavia by way of the Dnieper and Volga Rivers and obtained high-value commodities such as animal skins, furs, honey, amber, and slaves, as well as bulk goods such as timber and livestock. The vigorous economy of the Abbasid empire thus helped to establish networks of communication and exchange throughout much of the eastern hemisphere.

The prosperity of Islamic Spain, known as al-Andalus, illustrates the far-reaching *Al-Andalus* effects of long-distance trade during the Abbasid era. Most of the Iberian peninsula had fallen into the hands of Muslim Berber conquerors from north Africa during the early eighth century. As allies of the Umayyads, the governors of al-Andalus refused to recognize the Abbasid dynasty, and beginning in the tenth century they styled themselves caliphs in their own right rather than governors subject to Abbasid authority. Despite political and diplomatic tensions, al-Andalus participated actively in the commercial life of the larger Islamic world. The merchant-scholar al-Marwani of Córdoba, for example, made his hajj in 908 and then traveled to Iraq and India on commercial ventures. His profits amounted to thirty thousand dinars—all of which he lost in a shipwreck during his return home.

Imported crops increased the supply of food and enriched the diet of al-Andalus, enabling merchants and manufacturers to conduct thriving businesses in cities like Córdoba, Toledo, and Seville. Ceramics, painted tiles, lead crystal, and gold jewelry from al-Andalus enjoyed a reputation for excellence and helped pay for imported goods and the building of a magnificent capital city at Córdoba. During the tenth century Córdoba had more than sixteen kilometers (ten miles) of publicly lighted roads, as well as free Islamic schools, a gargantuan mosque, and a splendid library with four hundred thousand volumes.

The Changing Status of Women

A patriarchal society had emerged in Arabia long before Muhammad's time, but Arab women enjoyed rights not accorded to women in many other lands. They could legally inherit property, divorce husbands on their own initiative, and engage in business ventures. Khadija, the first of Muhammad's four wives, managed a successful commercial business.

The Quran and Women

In some respects the Quran enhanced the security of women in Arabian society. It outlawed female infanticide, and it provided that dowries went directly to brides rather than to their husbands and male guardians. It portrayed women not as the property of their menfolk, but as honorable individuals, equal to men before Allah, with their own rights and needs. Muhammad's own kindness and generosity toward his wives, as related in early accounts of the prophet's life, also served as an example that may have improved the lives of Muslim women.

For the most part, however, the Quran—and later the *sharia* as well—reinforced male dominance. The Quran and Islamic holy law recognized descent through the male line, and to guarantee proper inheritance, they placed a high premium on genealogical purity. To ensure the legitimacy of heirs, they subjected the social and sexual lives of women to the strict control of male guardians—fathers, brothers, and husbands. While teaching that men should treat women with sensitivity and respect, the

Interior of the mosque at Córdoba, originally built in the late eight century and enlarged during the ninth and tenth centuries. One of the largest structures in the *dar al-Islam,* the mosque rests on 850 columns and features nineteen aisles. • Benjamin Rondel/ The Stock Market

Quran and the *sharia* permitted men to follow Muhammad's example and take up to four wives, whereas women could have only one husband. The Quran and the *sharia* thus provided a religious and legal foundation for a decisively patriarchal society.

Veiling of Women

When Islam expanded into the Byzantine and Sasanid empires, it encountered strong patriarchal traditions, and Muslims readily adopted long-standing customs such as the veiling of women. Social and family pressures had induced upper-class urban women to veil themselves in Mesopotamia as early as the thirteenth century B.C.E., and long before Muhammad the practice of veiling had spread to Persia and the eastern Mediterranean. As a sign of modesty, upper-class urban women covered their faces and ventured outside their homes only in the company of servants or chaperones so as to discourage the attention of men from other families. When Muslim Arabs conquered Mesopotamia, Persia, and eastern Mediterranean lands, they adopted the practice. A conspicuous symbol of male authority thus found a prominent place in the early Islamic community.

The Quran served as the preeminent source of authority in the world of Islam, and it provided specific rights for Muslim women. Over the centuries, however, jurists and legal scholars interpreted the Quran in ways that progressively limited those rights and placed women increasingly under the control of male guardians. To a large extent the increased emphasis on male authority in Islamic law reflected the influence of the strongly hierarchical and patriarchal societies of Mesopotamia, Persia, and eastern Mediterranean lands as Islam developed from a local faith to a large-scale complex society.

ISLAMIC VALUES AND CULTURAL EXCHANGES

Since the seventh century C.E., the Quran has served as the cornerstone of Islamic society. Arising from a rich tradition of Bedouin poetry and song, the Quran established Arabic as a flexible and powerful medium of communication. Even today Muslims regard the Arabic text of the Quran as the only definitive and reliable scripture: translations do not carry the power and authority of the original. When carrying their faith to new lands during the era of Islamic expansion, Muslim missionaries spread the message of Allah and provided instruction in the Quran's teachings, although usually they also permitted continued observance of pre-Islamic traditions. Muslim intellectuals drew freely from the long-established cultural traditions of Persia, India, and Greece, which they became acquainted with during the Umayyad and Abbasid eras.

The Formation of an Islamic Cultural Tradition

Muslim theologians and jurists looked to the Quran, stories about Muhammad's life, and other sources of Islamic doctrine in their efforts to formulate moral guidelines appropriate for their society. The body of civil and criminal law embodied in the *sharia* provided a measure of cultural unity for the vastly different lands of the Islamic world. Islamic law did not by any means erase the differences, but it established a common cultural foundation that facilitated dealings between peoples of various Islamic lands and that lent substance to the concept of the *dar al-Islam*.

Promotion of Islamic Values

On a more popular level, *ulama, qadis,* and missionaries helped to bridge differences in cultural traditions and to spread Islamic values throughout the *dar al-Islam*. *Ulama* and *qadis* held positions at all Islamic courts, and they were prominent in the public life of all cities in the Islamic world. By resolving disputes according to Islamic law and ordering public observance of Islamic social and moral standards, they helped to bring the values of the Quran and the *sharia* into the lives of peoples living far from the birthplace of Islam.

Formal educational institutions also helped promote Islamic values. Many mosques maintained schools that provided an elementary education and religious instruction, and wealthy Muslims sometimes established schools and provided endowments for their support. By the tenth century institutions of higher education known as *madrasas* had begun to appear, and by the twelfth century they had become established in the major cities of the Islamic world. Muslim rulers often supported the *madrasas* in the interests of recruiting literate and learned students with an advanced education in Islamic theology and law for administrative positions. Inexpensive paper enhanced scholars' ability to instruct students and disseminate their views.

Sufis   Among the most effective Islamic missionaries were mystics known as Sufis. The term *Sufi* probably came from the patched woolen garments favored by the mystics. Sufis sometimes had an advanced education in Islamic law and theology, but they sought an emotional and mystical union with Allah rather than an intellectual understanding of Islam. They often relied on rousing sermons, passionate singing, or spirited dancing to encourage devotion to Allah.

Most important of the early Sufis was the Persian theologian al-Ghazali (1058–1111) who argued that human reason was too frail to understand the nature of Allah and hence could not explain the mysteries of the world. Only through devotion and guidance from the Quran could human beings begin to appreciate the uniqueness and power of Allah. Indeed, al-Ghazali held that philosophy and human reasoning were vain pursuits that would inevitably lead to confusion rather than understanding.

Sufis were especially effective as missionaries because they emphasized devotion to Allah above mastery of doctrine. They sometimes encouraged individuals to revere Allah in their own ways, even if their methods did not have a basis in the Quran. They tolerated the continued observance of pre-Islamic customs, for example, as well as the association of Allah with deities recognized and revered in other faiths. The Sufis themselves led ascetic and holy lives, which won them the respect of the peoples to whom they preached. Because of their kindness, holiness, tolerance, and charismatic appeal, Sufis attracted numerous converts particularly in lands like Persia and India, where long-established religious faiths such as Zoroastrianism, Christianity, Buddhism, and Hinduism had enjoyed a mass following for centuries.

The Hajj   The symbol of Islamic cultural unity was the Ka'ba at Mecca, which from an early date attracted pilgrims from all parts of the Islamic world. The Abbasid caliphs especially encouraged observance of the hajj: they saw themselves as supreme leaders of a cohesive Islamic community, and as a matter of policy they sought to enhance the cultural unity of their realm. They built inns along the main roads to Mecca for the convenience of travelers, policed the routes to ensure the safety of pilgrims, and made lavish gifts to shrines and sites of pilgrimage. Individuals from far-flung regions of the Abbasid empire made their way to Mecca, visited the holy sites, and learned at first hand the traditions of Islam. Over of the centuries these pilgrims helped to spread Islamic beliefs and values to all parts of the Islamic world, and alongside the work of *ulama, qadis,* and Sufi missionaries, their efforts helped to make the *dar al-Islam* not just a name, but a reality.

Through song, dance, and ecstatic experiences, sometimes enhanced by wine, Persian sufis expressed their devotion to Allah, as in this sixteenth-century painting. • *Heavenly and Earthly Drunkenness from a "Divan" of Hafiz*, Sultan-Muhammad. 1526–7. Iranian, Tabriz, Safavid. Courtesy of the Arthur M. Sackler Museum, Harvard University Art Museums. Gift of Mr. And Mrs. Stuart Cary Welch, Jr., in honor of the students.

Islam and the Cultural Traditions of Persia, India, and Greece

As the Islamic community expanded, Muslims of Arab ancestry interacted regularly with peoples from other cultural traditions, especially those of Persia, India, and Greece. In some cases, particularly in lands ruled by the Umayyad and Abbasid dynasties, large numbers of conquered peoples converted to Islam, and they brought elements of their inherited cultural traditions into Islamic society. In other cases, particularly in lands beyond the authority of Islamic rulers, Muslims became acquainted with the literary, artistic, philosophical, and scientific traditions of peoples who chose not to convert. Nevertheless, their traditions often held considerable interest for Muslims, who adapted them for their own purposes.

Persian Influences on Islam

Persian traditions quickly found a place in Islamic society, since the culturally rich land of Persia fell under Islamic rule at an early date. Especially after the establishment of the Abbasid dynasty and the founding of its capital at Baghdad, Persian traditions deeply influenced Islamic political and cultural leaders. Persian influence is most noticeable in literary works from the Abbasid dynasty. While Arabic served as the language of religion, theology, philosophy, and law, Persian was the principal language of literature, poetry, history, and political reflection. The verses of Omar Khayyam entitled the *Rubaiyat* ("quatrains") are widely known, thanks to a popular English translation by the Victorian poet Edward Fitzgerald, but many other writers composed works that in Persian display even greater literary elegance and originality. The marvelous collection of stories known as *The Arabian Nights* or *The Thousand and One Nights,* for example, presented popular tales of adventure and romance set in the Abbasid empire and the court of Harun al-Rashid.

Indian Influences on Islam

Indian mathematics intrigued Arab and Persian Muslims who established Islamic states in northern India. During the Gupta dynasty Indian scholars had elaborated a sophisticated tradition of mathematics, which Muslims found attractive both as a field of scholarship and for the practical purposes of reckoning and keeping accounts. They readily adopted what they called "Hindi numerals," which European peoples later called "Arabic numerals," since they learned of them through Arab Muslims. Indian numerals included a symbol for zero, and because of the flexibility they afford for purposes of calculations they have come into almost universal use in modern times. It is much simpler to multiply 11×99, for example, than to multiply $XI \times XCIX$. Using Hindi numerals, Muslims developed an impressive tradition of mathematical thought, concentrating on algebra—an Arabic word—as well as trigonometry and geometry. Meanwhile, from a more practical point of view, Indian numerals vastly simplified bookkeeping for Muslim merchants working in the lively commercial economy of the Abbasid dynasty.

Greek Influences on Islam

Muslims also admired the philosophical, scientific, and medical writings of classical Greece. They became especially interested in Plato and Aristotle, whose works they translated and interpreted in commentaries. During the tenth and eleventh centuries, some Muslim philosophers sought to synthesize Greek and Muslim thought by harmonizing Plato with the teachings of Islam. They encountered resistance among conservative theologians like the Sufi al-Ghazali, who considered Greek philosophy a completely unreliable guide to ultimate truth, since it relied on frail human reason rather than the revelation of the Quran.

Partly in response to al-Ghazali's attacks, twelfth-century Muslim philosophers turned their attention more to Aristotle than Plato. The most notable figure in this development was Ibn Rushd (1126–1198), *qadi* of Seville in the caliphate of Córdoba, who followed Aristotle in seeking to articulate a purely rational understanding of the world. Ibn Rushd's work not only helped to shape Islamic philosophy but also found its way to the schools and universities of western Europe, where Christian scholars knew Ibn Rushd as Averroes. During the thirteenth century his work profoundly influenced the development of scholasticism, the effort of medieval European philosophers to harmonize Christianity with Aristotelian thought.

Ibn Rushd's reliance on natural reason went too far for many Muslims, who placed more value on the revelations of the Quran than on the fruits of human logic. After the thirteenth century Muslim philosophers and theologians who dominated the *madrasas* drew inspiration more from Islamic sources than from Greek philosophy. Platonic and Aristotelian influences did not disappear, but they lost favor in official seats of learning and fell increasingly under the shadow of teachings from the Quran and Sufi mystics. As with political and cultural traditions from Persia and India, Muslim thinkers absorbed Greek philosophy, reconsidered it, and used it to advance the interests of their own society.

The prophet Muhammad did not intend to found a new religion. Instead, his intention was to express his faith in Allah and perfect the teachings of earlier Jewish and Christian prophets by announcing a revelation more comprehensive than those Allah had entrusted to his predecessors. His message soon attracted a circle of devout and committed disciples, and by the time of his death most of Arabia had accepted Islam, the faith founded on the individual's submission to Allah and his will. During the two centuries following the prophet's death, Arab conquerors spread Islam throughout southwest Asia and north Africa and introduced their faith to central Asia, India, the Mediterranean islands, and Iberia. This rapid expansion of Islam encouraged the development of a massive trade and communication network: merchants, diplomats, and other travelers moved easily throughout the Islamic world exchanging goods and introducing agricultural crops to new lands. Rapid expansion also led to encounters between Islam and long-established religious and cultural traditions such as Hinduism, Judaism, Zoroastrianism, Christianity, Persian literature and political thought, and classical Greek philosophy and science. Muslim rulers built a society that made a place for those of different faiths, and Muslim thinkers readily adapted earlier traditions to their own needs. As a result of its expansion, its extensive trade and communication networks, and its engagement with other religious and cultural traditions, the *dar al-Islam* became probably the most prosperous and cosmopolitan society of the postclassical world.

CHRONOLOGY

570–632	Life of Muhammad
622	The *hijra*
632	Muhammad's *hajj*
650s	Compilation of the Quran
661–750	Umayyad dynasty
750–1258	Abbasid dynasty
786–809	Reign of Harun al-Rashid
1050s	Establishment of Saljuq control over the Abbasid dynasty
1058–1111	Life of al-Ghazali
1126–1198	Life of Ibn Rushd

FOR FURTHER READING

Muhammad Manazir Ahsan. *Social Life under the Abbasids*. New York, 1979. Draws on a wide range of sources in discussing dress, food, drink, housing, and daily life during the Abbasid era.

Richard W. Bulliet. *The Camel and the Wheel*. New York, 1990. Fascinating study of the domestication of camels and transportation technologies based on camels.

Abu Hamid Muhammad al-Ghazzali. *The Alchemy of Happiness*. Trans. by Claude Field. Rev. by Elton L. Daniel. New York, 1991. Translation of one of the classic works of early Islamic religious and moral thought.

H. A. R. Gibb. *Mohammedanism*. 2nd ed. London, 1953. A short, analytical overview of the Islamic faith and its history by a prominent scholar.

Mahmood Ibrahim. *Merchant Capital and Islam*. Austin, 1990. Examines the role of trade in Arabia during Muhammad's time and in early Islamic society.

Ira M. Lapidus. *A History of Islamic Societies*. Cambridge, 1988. Authoritative survey of Islamic history, concentrating on social and cultural issues.

Bernard Lewis. *The Arabs in History*. Rev. ed. New York, 1967. A short but incisive survey of Islamic history.

Ilse Lichtenstadter. *Introduction to Classical Arabic Literature*. New York, 1974. A brief overview, accompanied by an extensive selection of texts in English translation.

M. Lombard. *The Golden Age of Islam*. Amsterdam, 1975. Concentrates on the social and economic history of the Abbasid period.

William H. McNeill and Marilyn R. Waldman, eds. *The Islamic World*. New York, 1973. An excellent collection of primary sources in translation.

F. E. Peters. *The Hajj: The Muslim Pilgrimage to Mecca and the Holy Places*. Princeton, 1994. Draws on scores of travelers reports in studying the Muslim practice of making a pilgrimage to Mecca through the ages.

———. *Muhammad and the Origins of Islam*. Albany, 1994. Excellent introduction to Muhammad's life and thought and the early days of his movement.

Al Qur'an: A Contemporary Translation. Trans. by Ahmed Ali. Princeton, 1984. A recent and sensitive translation of the holy book of Islam.

Maxime Rodinson. *Islam and Capitalism*. Trans. by B. Pearce. New York, 1973. An influential volume that examines Islamic teachings on economic matters as well as economic practice in the Muslim world.

———. *Mohammed*. Trans. by Anne Carter. New York, 1971. Places Muhammad in his social and economic context.

Andrew M. Watson. *Agricultural Innovation in the Early Islamic World: The Diffusion of Crops and Farming Techniques, 700–1100*. Cambridge, 1983. Important scholarly study of the diffusion of food and industrial crops throughout the early Islamic world.

W. Montgomery Watt. *Muhammad: Prophet and Statesman*. London, 1961. An older but still valuable study of Muhammad's life and thought.

CHAPTER 14

THE RESURGENCE
OF EMPIRE IN EAST ASIA

. . .

Early in the seventh century C.E., the emperor of China issued an order forbidding his subjects to travel beyond Chinese borders into central Asia. In 629, however, in defiance of the emperor, a young Buddhist monk slipped past imperial watchtowers under cover of darkness and made his way west. His name was Xuanzang, and his destination was India, homeland of Buddhism. Although educated in Confucian texts as a youth, Xuanzang had followed his older brother into a monastery where he became devoted to Buddhism. While studying the Sanskrit language, Xuanzang noticed that Chinese writings on Buddhism contained many teachings that were confusing or even contradictory to those of Indian Buddhist texts. He decided to travel to India, visit the holy sites of Buddhism, and study with the most knowledgeable Buddhist teachers and sages to learn about his faith from the purest sources.

Xuanzang could not have imagined the difficulties he would face. Immediately after his departure from China, his guide abandoned him in the Gobi desert. After losing his water bag and collapsing in the heat, Xuanzang made his way to the oasis town of Turpan on the silk roads. The Buddhist ruler of Turpan provided the devout pilgrim with travel supplies and rich gifts to support his mission. Among the presents were twenty-four letters of introduction to rulers of lands on the way to India, each one attached to a bolt of silk, five hundred additional bolts of silk and two carts of fruit for the most important ruler, thirty horses, twenty-five laborers, and five hundred bolts of silk along with gold, silver, and silk clothes for Xuanzang to use as travel funds. After departing from Turpan, Xuanzang crossed three of the world's highest mountain ranges—the Tian Shan, Hindu Kush, and Pamir ranges—and lost one-third of his party to exposure and starvation in the Tian Shan. He crossed yawning gorges thousands of meters deep on foot bridges fashioned from rope or chains, and he faced numerous attacks by bandits, as well as confrontations with demons, dragons, and evil spirits.

Yet Xuanzang persisted and arrived in India in 630. He lived there for more than twelve years, visiting the holy sites of Buddhism and devoting himself to the study of languages and Buddhist doctrine, especially at Nalanda, the center of advanced Buddhist education in India. He also amassed a huge collection of relics and images, as

The features of the emperor Tang Taizong reflect his Turkish and Chinese ancestry. • Emperor T'ai-tsung of T'ang Leaf J of *Portraits of Emperors of Successive Dynasties* by Yao Wen-han. 1788. The Metropolitan Museum of Art. Gift of Mrs. Edward S. Harkness, 1947 (47.81.1). Photograph © 1955. The Metropolitan Museum of Art.

well as some 657 books, all of which he packed into 527 crates and transported back to China in order to advance the understanding of Buddhism in his native land.

By the time of his return in 645, Xuanzang had logged more than sixteen thousand kilometers (ten thousand miles) on the road. News of the holy monk's efforts had reached the imperial court, and even though Xuanzang had violated the ban on travel, he received a hero's welcome and an audience with the emperor. Until his death in 664, Xuanzang spent his remaining years translating Buddhist treatises into Chinese and promoting his faith. His efforts helped to popularize Buddhism and bring about nearly universal adoption of the faith throughout China.

Xuanzang undertook his journey at a propitious time. For more than 350 years after the fall of the Han dynasty, war, invasion, conquest, and foreign rule disrupted Chinese society. Toward the end of the sixth century, however, centralized imperial rule returned to China. The Sui and Tang dynasties restored order and presided over an era of rapid economic growth in China. Agricultural yields rose dramatically, and technological innovations boosted the production of manufactured goods. China stood alongside the Byzantine and Abbasid empires as a political and economic anchor of the postclassical world.

For China the postclassical era was an age of intense interaction with other peoples. Chinese merchants participated in trade networks that linked most regions of the eastern hemisphere. Buddhism spread beyond its homeland of India, attracted a large popular following in China, and even influenced the thought of Confucian scholars. A resurgent China made its influence felt throughout east Asia: diplomats and armed forces introduced Chinese ways into Korea and Vietnam, and rulers of the Japanese islands looked to China for guidance in matters of political organization. Korea, Vietnam, and Japan retained their distinctiveness, but all three lands drew deep inspiration from China and participated in a larger east Asian society centered on China.

THE RESTORATION OF CENTRALIZED IMPERIAL RULE IN CHINA

During the centuries following the Han dynasty, several regional kingdoms made bids to assert their authority over all of China, but none possessed the resources to dominate its rivals over the long term. In the late sixth century, however, Yang Jian, an ambitious ruler in northern China, embarked on a series of military campaigns that brought all of China once again under centralized imperial rule. Yang Jian's Sui dynasty survived less than thirty years, but the tradition of centralized rule outlived his house. The Tang dynasty replaced the Sui, and the Song succeeded the Tang. The Tang and Song dynasties organized Chinese society so efficiently that China became a center of exceptional agricultural and industrial production. Indeed, much of the eastern hemisphere felt the effects of the powerful Chinese economy of the Tang and Song dynasties.

The Sui Dynasty

Establishment of the Dynasty Like Qin Shihuangdi some eight centuries years earlier, Yang Jian imposed tight political discipline on his own state and then extended his rule to the rest of China. Yang Jian began his rise to power when a Mongolian ruler appointed him duke of Sui in northern China. In 580 the Mongolian ruler died, leaving a seven-year-old

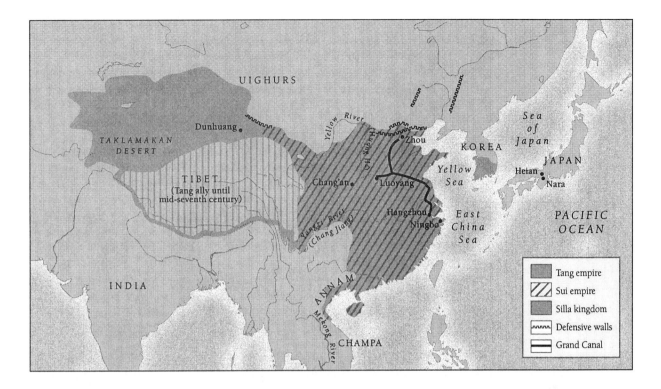

MAP [14.1]
The Sui and Tang
dynasties.

son as his heir. Yang Jian installed the boy as ruler, but forced his abdication one
year later, claiming the throne and the Mandate of Heaven for himself. During the
next decade Yang Jian sent military expeditions into central Asia and southern
China. By 589 the house of Sui ruled all of China.

Like the rulers of the Qin dynasty, the emperors of the Sui dynasty (589–618 C.E.)
placed enormous demands on their subjects in the course of building a strong, centralized government. The Sui emperors ordered the construction of palaces and granaries,
carried out extensive repairs on defensive walls, dispatched military forces to central
Asia and Korea, levied high taxes, and demanded compulsory labor services.

The most elaborate project undertaken during the Sui dynasty was the construction of the Grand Canal, which was one of the world's largest waterworks projects
before modern times. The second emperor, Sui Yangdi (reigned 604–618 C.E.),
began work on the canal to facilitate trade between northern and southern China,
particularly to make the abundant supplies of rice and other food crops from the
Yangzi River valley available to residents of northern regions. The only practical and
economical way to transport food crops in large quantities was by water. But since
Chinese rivers generally flow from west to east, only an artificial waterway could support a large volume of trade between north and south.

The Grand Canal was really a series of artificial waterways that ultimately reached
from Hangzhou in the south to the imperial capital of Chang'an in the west to the
city of Zhuo (near modern Beijing) in the north. Sui Yangdi used canals dug as early
as the Zhou dynasty, but he linked them into a network that served much of China.
When completed, the Grand Canal extended almost 2,000 kilometers (1,240 miles)
and reportedly was forty paces wide, with roads running parallel to the waterway on
either side.

The Grand Canal

Though expensive to construct, Sui Yangdi's investment in the Grand Canal paid dividends for more than a thousand years. It integrated the economies of northern and southern China, thereby establishing an economic foundation for political and cultural unity. Until the arrival of railroads in the twentieth century, the Grand Canal served as the principal conduit for internal trade. Indeed, the canal continues to function even today, although mechanical transport has diminished its significance as a trade route.

Sui Yangdi's construction projects served China well over a long term, but their dependence on high taxes and forced labor generated hostility toward his rule. The Grand Canal alone required the services of conscripted laborers by the millions. Military reverses in Korea prompted discontented subjects to revolt against Sui rule. During the late 610s rebellions broke out in northern China when Sui Yangdi sought additional resources for his Korean campaign. In 618 a disgruntled minister assassinated the emperor and brought the dynasty to a sudden end.

The Tang Dynasty

Soon after Sui Yangdi's death, a rebel leader seized Chang'an and proclaimed himself emperor of a new dynasty that he named Tang after his ancestral lands. The dynasty survived for almost three hundred years (618–907 C.E.), and Tang rulers organized China into a powerful, productive, and prosperous society.

Tang Taizong   Much of the Tang's success was due to the energy, ability, and policies of the dynasty's second emperor, Tang Taizong (reigned 627–649 C.E.). Taizong was both ambitious and ruthless: in making his way to the imperial throne, he murdered his two brothers and pushed his father aside. Once on the throne, however, he displayed a high sense of duty and strove conscientiously to provide effective, stable government. He built a splendid capital at Chang'an, and he saw himself as a Confucian ruler who heeded the interests of his subjects. Contemporaries reported that banditry ended during his reign, that the price of rice remained low, and that taxes levied on peasants amounted to only one-fortieth of the annual harvest—a 2.5 percent tax rate—although required rent payments and compulsory labor services meant that the effective rate of taxation was somewhat higher. These reports suggest that China enjoyed an era of unusual stability and prosperity during the reign of Tang Taizong.

Three policies in particular help to explain the success of the early Tang dynasty: maintenance of a well-articulated transportation and communications network, distribution of land according to the principles of the equal-field system, and reliance on a bureaucracy based on merit. All three policies originated in

Horses were crucial for communications, transportation, and military affairs in Tang China, and the animals became favorite subjects of artists. Many Tang tombs contain finely produced ceramic horses like this handsome steed decorated with buff, brown, and green glazes from the early eighth century. • Victoria & Albert Museum, London/Art Resource, NY

the Sui dynasty, but Tang rulers applied them more systematically and effectively than their predecessors had.

Apart from the Grand Canal, which served as the principal route for long-distance transportation within China, Tang rulers maintained an extensive communications network based on roads, horses, and sometimes human runners. Along the main routes Tang officials maintained inns, postal stations, and stables, which provided rest and refreshment for travelers, couriers, and their mounts. Using couriers traveling by horse, the Tang court could communicate with the most distant cities in the empire in about eight days. Even human runners provided impressively speedy services: relay teams of some 9,600 runners supplied the Tang court at Chang'an with seafood delivered fresh from Ningbo, more than 1,000 kilometers (620 miles) away!

Transportation and Communications

The equal-field system governed the allocation of agricultural land. Its purpose was to ensure an equitable distribution of land and to avoid the concentration of landed property that had caused social problems during the Han dynasty. The system allotted land to individuals and their families according to the land's fertility and the recipients' needs. About one-fifth of the land became the hereditary possession of the recipients, while the rest remained available for redistribution when the original recipients' needs and circumstances changed.

The Equal-Field System

For about a century administrators were able to apply the principles of the equal-field system relatively consistently. By the early eighth century, however, the system showed signs of strain. A rapidly rising population placed pressure on the land available for distribution. Meanwhile, through favors, bribery, or intimidation of administrators, influential families found ways to retain land scheduled for redistribution. Furthermore, large parcels of land fell out of the system altogether when Buddhist monasteries acquired them. Nevertheless, during the first half of the Tang dynasty, the system provided a foundation for stability and prosperity in the Chinese countryside.

Ceramic statuette of a Confucian official wearing his distinctive scholar's hat and wide-sleeved cloak with decorated borders. Note his air of formality, quiet dignity, and self-confidence. • Cultural Relics Publishing House, Beijing

The Tang dynasty also relied heavily on a bureaucracy based on merit, as reflected by performance on imperial civil service examinations. Following the example of the Han dynasty, Sui and Tang rulers recruited government officials from the ranks of candidates who had progressed through the Confucian educational system and had mastered a sophisticated curriculum concentrating on the classic works of Chinese literature and philosophy.

Bureaucracy of Merit

Although powerful families used their influence to place relatives in positions of authority, most office holders won their posts because of intellectual ability. Members of this talented class were generally loyal to the dynasty, and they worked to preserve and strengthen the state. The Confucian educational system and the related civil service served Chinese governments so well that with modifications and an occasional interruption, they survived for thirteen centuries, disappearing only after the collapse of the Qing dynasty in the early twentieth century.

Soon after its foundation, the powerful and dynamic Tang state began to flex its military muscles. In the north Tang forces brought Manchuria under imperial authority and forced the Silla kingdom in Korea to acknowledge the Tang emperor as overlord. To the south Tang armies conquered the northern part of Vietnam. To the west they extended Tang authority as far as the Aral Sea and brought much of the high plateau of Tibet under Tang control. Territorially, the Tang empire ranks among the largest in Chinese history.

Tang Foreign Relations   In an effort to fashion a stable diplomatic order, the Tang emperors revived the Han dynasty's practice of maintaining tributary relationships between China and neighboring lands. According to Chinese political theory, China was the Middle Kingdom, a powerful realm with the responsibility to bring order to subordinate lands through a system of tributary relationships. Neighboring lands and peoples would recognize Chinese emperors as their overlords. As tokens of their subordinate status, envoys from these states would regularly deliver gifts to the court of the Middle Kingdom and would perform the kowtow—a ritual prostration during which subordinates knelt before the emperor and touched their foreheads to the ground. In return, tributary states received confirmation of their authority as well as lavish gifts. Because Chinese authorities often had little real influence in these supposedly subordinate lands, there was always something of a fictional quality to the system. Nevertheless, it was extremely important throughout east Asia and central Asia because it institutionalized relations between China and neighboring lands, fostering trade and cultural exchanges as well as diplomatic contacts.

Tang Decline   Under able rulers such as Taizong, the Tang dynasty flourished. During the mid-eighth century, however, casual and careless leadership brought the dynasty to a crisis from which it never fully recovered. In 755, while the emperor neglected public affairs in favor of music and his mistress, An Lushan, one of the dynasty's foremost military commanders, mounted a rebellion and captured the capital at Chang'an, as well as the secondary capital at Luoyang. His revolt was short-lived: by 757 Tang forces had suppressed An Lushan's army and recovered their capitals. But the rebellion left the dynasty in a gravely weakened state. Tang commanders had to invite a nomadic Turkish people, the Uighurs, to bring an army into China to oust An Lushan from the imperial capitals. In return for their services, the Uighurs demanded the right to sack Chang'an and Luoyang after the expulsion of the rebels. Indeed, for several decades the Uighurs were de facto rulers of the imperial capitals.

The Tang imperial house never regained control of affairs after this crisis. The equal-field system deteriorated, and dwindling tax receipts failed to meet dynastic needs. Imperial armies were unable to resist the encroachments of Turkish peoples in the late eighth century. During the ninth century a series of rebellions devastated the Chinese countryside. One uprising led by the military commander Huang Chao embroiled much of eastern China for almost a decade from 875 to 884. Huang Chao's revolt reflected and fueled popular discontent: he routinely pillaged the wealthy and distributed a portion of his plunder among the poor. In an effort to

In this wall painting from the tomb of a Tang prince, three Chinese officials (at left) receive envoys from foreign lands who pay their respects to representatives of the Middle Kingdom. The envoys probably come from the Byzantine empire, Korea, and Siberia. • Cultural Relics Publishing House, Beijing

control the rebels, the Tang emperors granted progressively greater power and authority to regional military commanders, who gradually became the effective rulers of China. In 907 the last Tang emperor abdicated his throne, and the dynasty came to an end.

The Song Dynasty

Following the Tang collapse, warlords ruled China until the Song dynasty reimposed centralized imperial rule in the late tenth century. Though it survived for more than three centuries, the Song dynasty (960–1279 C.E.) never built a very powerful state. It was among the least militarized of all the Chinese dynasties, placing much more emphasis on civil administration, industry, education, and the arts than on military affairs.

The first Song emperor, Song Taizu (reigned 960–976 C.E.), himself inaugurated this policy. Song Taizu began his career as a junior military officer serving one of the most powerful warlords in northern China. He had a reputation for honesty and effectiveness, and in 960 his troops proclaimed him emperor. During the next several years, he and his army subjected the warlords to their authority and consolidated Song control throughout China. He then persuaded his generals to retire honorably to a life of leisure so that they would not seek to displace him, and he set about organizing a centralized administration that placed military forces under tight supervision.

Song Taizu

MAP [14.2]

The Song dynasty.

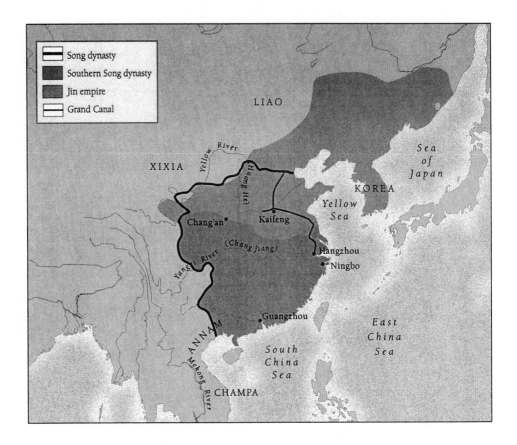

Song Taizu regarded all state officials, even minor functionaries in distant provinces, as servants of the imperial government. In exchange for their loyalty, Song rulers rewarded these officials handsomely. They vastly expanded the bureaucracy based on merit by creating more opportunities for individuals to seek a Confucian education and take civil service examinations. They accepted many more candidates into the bureaucracy than their Sui and Tang predecessors, and they provided generous salaries for those who qualified for government appointments. They even placed civil bureaucrats in charge of military forces.

Song Weaknesses   The Song approach to administration resulted in a more centralized imperial government than earlier Chinese dynasties had enjoyed. But it caused two big problems that weakened the dynasty and eventually brought about its fall. The first problem was financial: the enormous Song bureaucracy devoured China's surplus production. As the number of bureaucrats and the size of their rewards grew, the imperial treasury came under tremendous pressure. Efforts to raise taxes aggravated the peasants, who mounted two major rebellions in the early twelfth century. By that time, however, bureaucrats dominated the Song administration to the point that it was impossible to reform the system.

The second problem was military. Scholar bureaucrats generally had little military education and little talent for military affairs, yet they led Song armies in the field and made military decisions. It was no coincidence that nomadic peoples flourished along China's northern border throughout the Song dynasty. From the early tenth through the early twelfth century, the Khitan, a seminomadic people from Manchuria, ruled a vast empire stretching from northern Korea to Mongolia. Dur-

ing the first half of the Song dynasty, the Khitan demanded and received large tribute payments of silk and silver from the Song state to the south. In the early twelfth
century, the nomadic Jurchen conquered the Khitan, overran northern China, and
captured the Song capital. Thereafter the Song dynasty survived only in southern
China, sharing a border with the Jurchen state about midway between the Yellow
River and the Yangzi River until 1279, when Mongol forces incorporated all of
China in their empire and ended the dynasty.

THE ECONOMIC DEVELOPMENT
OF TANG AND SONG CHINA

Although the Song dynasty did not develop a particularly strong military capacity,
it benefitted from a remarkable series of agricultural, technological, industrial, and
commercial developments that transformed China into the economic powerhouse
of Eurasia. This economic development originated in the Tang dynasty, but its results became most clear during the Song, which presided over a land of enormous
prosperity. The economic surge of Tang and Song times had implications that
went well beyond China, since it stimulated trade and production throughout
much of the eastern hemisphere for more than half a millennium, from about 600
to 1300 C.E.

Agricultural Development

The foundation of economic development in Tang and Song China was a surge in   *Fast-Ripening Rice*
agricultural production. Sui and Tang armies prepared the way for increased agricultural productivity when they imposed their control over southern China and ventured into Vietnam. In Vietnam they encountered new strains of fast-ripening rice
that enabled cultivators to harvest two crops per year. When introduced to the fertile
fields of southern China, fast-ripening rice quickly resulted in an expanded supply of
food. As in the case of the *dar al-Islam,* Tang and Song China benefitted enormously from the introduction of new food crops.

Chinese cultivators also increased their productivity by adopting improved agri-   *New Agricultural*
cultural techniques. They made increased use of heavy iron plows, and they har-   *Techniques*
nessed oxen (in the north) and water buffaloes (in the south) to help prepare land for
cultivation. They enriched the soil with manure and composted organic matter. They
also organized extensive irrigation systems. These included not only reservoirs, dikes,
dams, and canals but also pumps and water wheels, powered by both animal and
human energy, that moved water into irrigation systems. Artificial irrigation made it
possible to extend cultivation to new lands, including terraced mountainsides—a development that vastly expanded China's agricultural potential.

Increased agricultural production had dramatic results. One was a rapid expan-   *Population Growth*
sion of the Chinese population. After the fall of the Han dynasty, the population of
China reached a low point at about 45 million people in 600 C.E. By 800 it had rebounded to 50 million people, and two centuries later to 60 million. By 1127, when
the Jurchen conquered the northern half of the Song state, the Chinese population
had passed the 100 million mark, and by 1200 it stood at about 115 million. This
rapid population growth reflected both the productivity of the agricultural economy
and the well-organized distribution of food through transportation networks built
during Sui and Tang times.

A wall painting in a Buddhist cave depicts a peasant plowing his field in the rain with the aid of an ox and a heavy plow. Other peasants have found shelter from the rain and consume a midday meal brought to them by their wives. • Cultural Relics Publishing House, Beijing

Urbanization   Increased food supplies encouraged the growth of cities. During the Tang dynasty the imperial capital of Chang'an was the world's most populous city with perhaps as many as two million residents. During the Song dynasty China was the most urbanized land in the world. In the late thirteenth century, Hangzhou, capital of the later Song dynasty, had more than one million residents. They supported hundreds of restaurants, taverns, teahouses, brothels, music halls, theaters, club houses, gardens, markets, craft shops, and specialty stores dealing in silk, gems, porcelain, lacquerware, and other goods. As in any city, residents observed peculiar local customs. Taverns often had several floors, for example, and patrons gravitated to higher or lower stories according to their plans: those desiring only a cup or two of wine sat at street level, whereas those planning an extended evening of revelry sought tables on the higher floors. As a capital, Hangzhou was something of a special case among cities, but during the Tang and Song eras, scores of Chinese cities boasted populations of one hundred thousand or more.

Another result of increased food production was the emergence of a commercialized agricultural economy. Because fast-ripening rice yielded bountiful harvests, many cultivators could purchase inexpensive rice and raise vegetables and fruits for sale on the commercial market. Cultivators specialized in crops that grew well in their own regions, and they often exported their harvests to distant regions. By the twelfth century, for example, the wealthy southern province of Fujian imported rice and devoted its land to the production of lychees, oranges, and sugarcane, which fetched high prices in northern markets. Indeed, market-oriented cultivation went so far that authorities tried—with only limited success—to require Fujianese to grow rice so as to avoid excessive dependence on imports.

Alongside increasing wealth and agricultural productivity, Tang and especially Song China experienced a tightening of patriarchal social structures, which perhaps represented an effort to preserve family fortunes through enhanced family solidarity. During the Song dynasty the veneration of family ancestors became much more elaborate than before. Instead of simply remembering ancestors and invoking their aid in rituals performed at home, descendants diligently sought the graves of their earliest traceable forefathers and then arranged elaborate graveside rituals in their honor. Whole extended families often traveled great distances to attend annual rituals venerating deceased ancestors—a practice that strengthened the sense of family identity and cohesiveness.

Patriarchal Social Structures

Strengthened patriarchal authority also helps to explain the popularity of foot binding, which spread among privileged classes during the Song era. Foot binding involved the tight wrapping of young girls' feet with strips of cloth that prevented natural growth of the bones and resulted in tiny, malformed, curved feet. Women with bound feet could not walk easily or naturally. Usually they needed canes to walk by themselves, and sometimes they depended on servants to carry them around in litters. Foot binding never became universal in China—it was impractical for peasants or lower-class working women in the cities—but wealthy families often bound the feet of their daughters to enhance their attractiveness, display their high social standing, and gain increased control over the girls' behavior. Like the practice of veiling women in the Islamic world, foot binding placed women of privileged classes under tight supervision of their husbands or other male guardians, who then managed the women's affairs in the interests of the larger family.

Foot Binding

Technological and Industrial Development

Abundant supplies of food enabled many people to pursue technological and industrial interests. During the Tang and Song dynasties, Chinese craftsmen generated a remarkable range of technological innovations. During Tang times they discovered techniques of producing high-quality porcelain, which was lighter, thinner, and adaptable to more uses than earlier pottery. When fired with glazes, porcelain could also become an aesthetically appealing utensil and even a work of art. Porcelain technology gradually diffused to other societies, and Abbasid craftsmen in particular produced porcelain in large quantities. Yet demand for Chinese porcelain remained high, and the Chinese exported vast quantities of porcelain during the Tang and Song dynasties. Archaeologists have turned up Tang and Song porcelain at sites all along the trade networks of the postclassical era: Chinese porcelain graced the tables of wealthy and refined households in southeast Asia, India, Persia, and the port cities of east Africa. Tang and Song products gained such a reputation that fine porcelain has come to be known generally as *chinaware*.

Porcelain

Tang and Song craftsmen also improved metallurgical technologies. Production of iron and steel surged during this era, due partly to techniques that resulted in stronger and more useful metals. Chinese craftsmen discovered that they could use coke instead of coal in their furnaces and produce superior grades of metal. Between the early ninth and the early twelfth century, iron production increased almost tenfold according to official records, which understate total production. Most of the increased supply of

Metallurgy

iron and steel went into weaponry and agricultural tools: during the early Song dynasty, imperial armaments manufacturers produced 16.5 million iron arrowheads per year. Iron and steel also went into construction projects involving large structures such as bridges and pagodas. As in the case of porcelain technology, metallurgical techniques soon diffused to lands beyond China. Indeed, Song military difficulties stemmed partly from the fact that nomadic peoples quickly learned Chinese techniques and fashioned their own iron weapons for use in campaigns against China.

Gunpowder   Quite apart from improving existing technologies, Tang and Song craftsmen also invented entirely new products, tools, and techniques, most notably gunpowder, printing, and naval technologies. Daoist alchemists discovered how to make gunpowder during the Tang dynasty, as they tested the properties of various experimental concoctions while seeking elixirs to prolong life. They soon learned that it was unwise to mix charcoal, saltpeter, sulphur, and arsenic, because the volatile compound often resulted in singed beards and destroyed buildings. Military officials, however, recognized opportunity in the explosive mixture. By the mid-tenth century they were using gunpowder in bamboo "fire lances," a kind of flame thrower, and by the eleventh century they had fashioned primitive bombs.

The earliest gunpowder weapons had limited military effectiveness: they probably caused more confusion because of noise and smoke than damage because of their destructive potential. Over time, however, refinements enhanced their effectiveness. Knowledge of gunpowder chemistry quickly diffused through Eurasia, and by the late thirteenth century peoples of southwest Asia and Europe were experimenting with metal-barreled cannons.

Printing   The precise origins of printing lie obscured in the mists of time. Although some form of printing may have predated the Sui dynasty, only during the Tang era did printing become common. The earliest printers employed block-printing techniques: they carved a reverse image of an entire page into a wooden block, inked the block, and then pressed a sheet of paper on top. By the mid-eleventh century printers had begun to experiment with reusable, movable type: instead of carving images into blocks, they fashioned dies in the shape of ideographs, arranged them in a frame, inked them, and pressed the frame over paper sheets.

The technology of movable type not only speeded up the process of composing text for printing but also enabled printers to make revisions and corrections. Printing made it possible to produce texts quickly, cheaply, and in huge quantities. By the late ninth century, printed copies of Buddhist texts, Confucian works, calendars, agricultural treatises, and popular works appeared in large quantities, particularly in southwestern China (modern Sichuan province). Song dynasty officials disseminated printed works broadly by visiting the countryside with pamphlets that outlined effective agricultural techniques.

Naval Technology   Chinese inventiveness extended also to naval technology. Before Tang times Chinese mariners did not venture very far from land. They traveled the sea-lanes to Korea, Japan, and the Ryukyu islands but relied on Persian, Arab, Indian, and Malay mariners for long-distance maritime trade. During the Tang dynasty, however, Chinese consumers developed a taste for the spices and exotic products of southeast Asian islands, and Chinese mariners increasingly visited those lands in their own ships. By the time of the Song dynasty, Chinese seafarers sailed ships fastened with iron nails, waterproofed with oils, furnished with watertight bulkheads, driven by canvas and bamboo sails, steered by rudders, and navigated with the aid of the "south-pointing needle"—the magnetic compass. Larger ships sometimes even had small rockets powered by gunpowder. Chinese ships mostly plied the waters between Japan and the

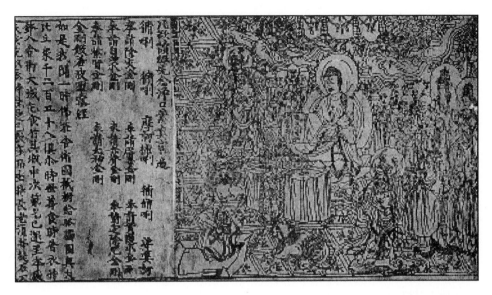

A printed book from the twelfth century presents a Chinese translation of a Buddhist text, along with a block-printed illustration of the Buddha addressing his followers. • © The British Library

Malay peninsula, but some of them ventured into the Indian Ocean and called at ports in India, Ceylon, Persia, and east Africa. These long-distance travels helped to diffuse elements of Chinese naval technology, particularly the compass, which soon became the common property of mariners throughout the Indian Ocean basin.

The Emergence of a Market Economy

Increased agricultural production, improved transportation systems, population growth, urbanization, and industrial production combined to stimulate the Chinese economy. China's various regions increasingly specialized in the cultivation of particular food crops or the production of particular manufactured goods, trading their own products for imports from other regions. The market was not the only influence on the Chinese economy: government bureaucracies played a large role in the distribution of staple foods such as rice, wheat, and millet, and dynastic authorities closely watched militarily sensitive enterprises such as the iron industry. Nevertheless, millions of cultivators produced fruits and vegetables for sale on the open market, and manufacturers of silk, porcelain, and other goods supplied both domestic and foreign markets. The Chinese economy became more tightly integrated than ever before, and foreign demand for Chinese products fueled rapid economic expansion.

Indeed, trade grew so rapidly during Tang and Song times that China experienced a shortage of the copper coins that served as money for most transactions. To alleviate the shortage, Chinese merchants developed alternatives to cash that resulted in even more economic growth. Letters of credit came into common use during the early Tang dynasty. Known as "flying cash," they enabled merchants to deposit goods or cash at one location and draw the equivalent in cash or merchandise elsewhere in China. Later developments included the use of promissory notes, which pledged payment of a given sum of money at a later date, and checks, which entitled the bearer to draw funds against cash deposited with bankers.

Financial Instruments

Paper Money   The search for alternatives to cash also led to the invention of paper money. Wealthy merchants pioneered the use of printed paper money during the late ninth century. In return for cash deposits from their clients, they issued printed notes that the clients could redeem for merchandise. In a society short of cash, these notes greatly facilitated commercial transactions. Occasionally, however, because of temporary economic reverses or poor management, merchants were not able to honor their notes. The resulting discontent among creditors often led to disorder and sometimes even to riots.

By the eleventh century, however, the Chinese economy had become so dependent on alternatives to cash that it was impractical to banish paper money altogether. To preserve its convenience while forestalling public disorder, governmental authorities forbade private parties from issuing paper money and reserved that right for the state. The first paper money printed under government auspices appeared in 1024 in Sichuan province, the most active center of early printing. By the end of the century, government authorities throughout most of China issued printed paper money—complete with serial numbers and dire warnings against the printing of counterfeit notes. Rulers of nomadic peoples in central Asia soon began to adopt the practice in their own states.

Printed paper money caused serious problems for several centuries after its appearance. Quite apart from contamination of the money supply by counterfeit notes, government authorities frequently printed currency representing more value than they actually possessed in cash reserves—a practice not unknown in more recent times. The result was a partial loss of public confidence in paper money. By the late eleventh century, some notes of paper money would fetch only 95 percent of their face value in cash. Not until the Qing dynasty (1644–1911 C.E.) did Chinese authorities place the issuance of printed money under tight fiscal controls. In spite of abuses, however, printed paper money provided a powerful stimulus to the Chinese economy.

A Cosmopolitan Society   Trade and urbanization transformed Tang and Song China into a prosperous, cosmopolitan society. Merchants from India, Persia, and central Asia congregated in large trading cities like Chang'an and Luoyang, and Arab, Persian, and Malay seafarers established communities especially in bustling southern Chinese port cities like Guangzhou and Quanzhou. Contemporary reports said that the rebel general Huang Chao massacred 120,000 foreigners when he sacked Guangzhou and subjected it to a reign of terror in 879.

China and the Hemispheric Economy   Indeed, high productivity and trade brought the Tang and Song economy a dynamism that China's borders could not restrain. Chinese consumers developed a taste for exotic goods that stimulated trade throughout much of the eastern hemisphere. Spices from the islands of southeast Asia made their way to China, along with products as diverse as kingfisher feathers and tortoise shell from Vietnam, pearls and incense from India, and horses and melons from central Asia. These items became symbols of a refined, elegant lifestyle—in many cases because of attractive qualities inherent in the commodities themselves but sometimes simply because of their scarcity and foreign provenance. In exchange for such exotic items, Chinese sent abroad vast quantities of silk, porcelain, and laquerware. In central Asia, southeast Asia, India, Persia, and the port cities of east Africa, wealthy merchants and rulers wore Chinese silk and set their tables with Chinese porcelain. China's economic surge during the Tang and Song dynasties thus promoted trade and economic growth throughout much of the eastern hemisphere.

THE ARAB MERCHANT SULEIMAN ON BUSINESS PRACTICES IN TANG CHINA

. . .

The Arab merchant Suleiman made several commercial ventures by ship to India and China during the early ninth century C.E. In 851 he wrote an account of his travels, describing India and China for Muslim readers in southwest Asia. His report throws particularly interesting light on the economic conditions and business practices of Tang China.

Young and old Chinese all wear silk clothes in both winter and summer, but silk of the best quality is reserved for the kings. . . . During the winter, the men wear two, three, four, five pairs of pants, and even more, according to their means. This practice has the goal of protecting the lower body from the high humidity of the land, which they fear. During the summer, they wear a single shirt of silk or some similar material. They do not wear turbans. . . .

In China, commercial transactions are carried out with the aid of copper coins. The Chinese royal treasury is identical to that of other kings, but only the king of China has a treasury that uses copper coins as a standard. These copper coins serve as the money of the land. The Chinese have gold, silver, fine pearls, fancy silk textiles, raw silk, and all this in large quantities, but they are considered commodities, and only copper coins serve as money.

Imports into China include ivory, incense, copper ingots, shells of sea turtles, and rhinoceros horn, with which the Chinese make ornaments. . . .

The Chinese conduct commercial transactions and business affairs with equity. When someone lends money to another person, he writes up a note documenting the loan. The borrower writes up another note on which he affixes an imprint of his index finger and middle finger together. Then they put the two notes together, roll them up, and write a formula at the point where one touches the other [so that part of the written formula appears on each note]. Next, they separate the notes and entrust to the lender the one on which the borrower recognizes his debt. If the borrower denies his debt later on, they say to him, "Present the note that the lender gave to you." If the borrower maintains that he has no such note from the lender, and denies that he ever agreed to the note with his fingerprints on it, and if the lender's note has disappeared, they say to him, "Declare in writing that you have not contracted this debt, but if later the lender brings forth proof that you have contracted this debt that you deny, you will receive twenty blows of the cane on the back and you will be ordered to pay a penalty of twenty million copper coins." This sum is equal to about 2,000 dinars [gold coins used in the Abbasid empire]. Twenty blows of the cane brings on death. Thus no one in China dares to make such a declaration for fear of losing at the same time both life and fortune. We have seen no one who has agreed when invited to make such a declaration. The Chinese are thus equitable to each other. No one in China is treated unjustly.

SOURCE: Gabriel Ferrand, tr. *Voyage du marchand arabe Sulayman en Inde et en Chine.* Paris, 1922, pp. 45, 53–54, 60–61. (Translated into English by Jerry H. Bentley.)

CULTURAL CHANGE IN TANG AND SONG CHINA

Interactions with peoples of other societies encouraged cultural change in postclassical China. The Confucian and Daoist traditions did not disappear. But they made way for a foreign religious faith—Mahayana Buddhism—and they developed along new lines that reflected the conditions of Tang and Song society.

The Establishment of Buddhism

Buddhist merchants traveling the ancient silk roads visited China as early as the second century B.C.E. During the Han dynasty their faith attracted little interest there: Confucianism, Daoism, and cults that honored family ancestors were the most popular cultural alternatives. After the fall of the Han, however, the Confucian tradition suffered a loss of credibility. The purpose and rationale of Confucianism was to maintain public order and provide honest, effective government. But in an age of warlords and nomadic invasions, it seemed that the Confucian tradition had simply failed. Confucian educational and civil service systems fell into disuse, and rulers openly scorned Confucian values.

Foreign Religions in China

During the unsettled centuries following the fall of the Han dynasty, several foreign religions established communities in China. Nestorian Christians and Manichaeans settled in China alongside Zoroastrians fleeing the Islamic conquerors of Persia. Nestorians established communities in China by the late sixth century. The emperor Tang Taizong himself issued a proclamation praising their doctrine, and he allowed them to open monasteries in Chang'an and other cities. By the mid-seventh century Arab and Persian merchants had also established Muslim communities in the port cities of south China. Indeed, legend holds that an uncle of Muhammad himself built a small red mosque in the port city of Guangzhou. These religions of salvation mostly served the needs of foreign merchants trading in China and converts from nomadic societies. Sophisticated residents of Chinese cities appreciated foreign music and dance, as well as foreign foods and trade goods, but foreign religious faiths attracted little interest.

Dunhuang

Yet Mahayana Buddhism gradually found a popular following in Tang and Song China. Buddhism came to China over the silk roads. Residents of oasis cities in central Asia had converted to Buddhism as early as the first or second century B.C.E., and the oases became sites of Buddhist missionary efforts. By the fourth century C.E., a sizeable Buddhist community had emerged at Dunhuang in western China (modern Gansu province). Between about 600 and 1000 C.E., Buddhists built hundreds of cave temples in the vicinity of Dunhuang and decorated them with murals depicting events in the lives of the Buddha and the *boddhisatvas* who played prominent roles in Mahayana Buddhism. They also assembled libraries of religious literature and operated scriptoria to produce Buddhist texts. Missions supported by establishments such as those at Dunhuang helped Buddhism to establish a foothold in China.

Buddhism in China

Buddhism attracted Chinese interest partly because of its high standards of morality, its intellectual sophistication, and its promise of salvation. Practical concerns also help to account for its appeal. Buddhists established monastic communities in China and accumulated sizable estates donated by wealthy converts. They cultivated these lands intensively and stored a portion of their harvests for distribution among local residents during times of drought, famine, or other hardship. Buddhist monasteries thus became important elements in the local economies of Chinese communities.

In some ways Buddhism posed a challenge to Chinese cultural and social traditions. Buddhist theologians typically took written texts as points of departure for elaborate, speculative investigations into metaphysical themes such as the nature of the soul. Among Chinese intellectuals, however, only the Confucians placed great emphasis on written texts, and they devoted their energies mostly to practical issues. Buddhist morality called for individuals to strive for perfection by observing an as-

Ceramic model depicting a wine merchant from southwest Asia marketing his product. Foreign merchants were familiar figures in all the major cities of Tang China. • Royal Ontario Museum. George Crofts Collection.

Foreign music and dance were very popular in the large cities of Tang China. This ceramic model depicts a troupe of musicians from southwest Asia performing on a platform mounted on a camel. Many such models survive from Tang times. • Cultural Relics Publishing House, Beijing

cetic ideal, and it encouraged serious Buddhists to follow a celibate, monastic lifestyle. By contrast, Chinese morality centered on the family unit and the obligations of filial piety, and it strongly encouraged procreation so that generations of offspring would be available to venerate family ancestors. Some Chinese held that Buddhist monasteries were economically harmful, since they paid no taxes, whereas others scorned Buddhism as an inferior creed because of its foreign origins.

Because of these differences and concerns, Buddhist missionaries sought to tailor their message to Chinese audiences. They explained Buddhist concepts in vocabulary borrowed from Chinese cultural traditions, particularly Daoism. They translated the Indian term *dharma* (the basic Buddhist doctrine) as *dao* ("the way" in the Daoist sense of the term), and they translated the Indian term *nirvana* (personal salvation that comes after an individual soul escapes from the cycle of incarnation) as *wuwei* (the Daoist ethic of noncompetition). While encouraging the establishment of monasteries and the observance of celibacy, they also recognized the validity of

Buddhism and Daoism

This painting on a silk scroll depicts the return of the monk Xuanzang to China. His baggage included 657 books, mostly Buddhist treatises but also a few works on grammar and logic, as well as hundreds of relics and images. • Fujita Art Museum, Osaka

family life and offered Buddhism as a faith that would benefit the extended Chinese family: one son in the monastery, they taught, would bring salvation for ten generations of his kin.

Chan Buddhism   The result was a syncretic faith, a Buddhism with Chinese characteristics. The most popular school of Buddhism in China, for example, was the Chan (also known by its Japanese name, Zen). Chan Buddhists had little interest in written texts, but instead emphasized intuition and sudden flashes of insight in their search for spiritual enlightenment. In this respect they resembled Daoists as much as they did Buddhists.

During the Tang and Song dynasties, this syncretic Buddhism became an immensely popular and influential faith in China. Monasteries appeared in all the major cities, and stupas dotted the Chinese landscape. The monk Xuanzang (602–664) was only one of many devout pilgrims who traveled to India to visit holy sites and learn about Buddhism in its homeland. Many of these pilgrims returned with copies of treatises that deepened the understanding of Buddhism in China. Xuanzang and other pilgrims played roles of enormous significance in establishing Buddhism as a popular faith in China.

Hostility to Buddhism   In spite of its popularity, Buddhism met determined resistance from Daoists and Confucians. Daoists resented the popular following that Buddhists attracted, which resulted in diminished resources available for their own tradition. Confucians despised Buddhists' exaltation of celibacy, and they denounced the faith as an alien superstition. They also condemned Buddhist monasteries as wasteful, unproductive burdens on society.

Persecution   During the late Tang dynasty, Daoist and Confucian critics of Buddhism found allies in the imperial court. Beginning in the 840s the Tang emperors ordered the closure of monasteries and the expulsion of Buddhists, as well as Zoroastrians, Nestorian Christians, and Manichaeans. Motivated largely by a desire to seize property belonging to foreign religious establishments, the Tang rulers did not implement their policy in a thorough way. While it discouraged further expansion, Tang policy did not eradicate foreign faiths from China. Buddhism in particular enjoyed popular support that enabled it to survive. Indeed, it even influenced the development of the Confucian tradition during the Song dynasty.

Neo-Confucianism

The Song emperors did not persecute Buddhists, but they actively supported native Chinese cultural traditions in hopes of limiting the influence of foreign religions. They contributed particularly generously to the Confucian tradition. They sponsored the studies of Confucian scholars, for example, and subsidized the printing and dissemination of Confucian writings.

Yet the Confucian tradition of the Song dynasty differed from that of earlier times. The earliest Confucians had concentrated resolutely on practical issues of politics and morality, since they took the organization of a stable social order as their principal concern. Confucians of the Song dynasty studied the classic works of their tradition, but they also became familiar with the writings of Buddhists. They found much to admire in Buddhist thought. Buddhism not only offered a tradition of logical thought and argumentation but also dealt with issues, such as the nature of the soul and the individual's relationship with the cosmos, not systematically explored by Confucian thinkers. Thus Confucians of the Song dynasty drew a great deal of inspiration from Buddhism. Because their thought reflected the influence of Buddhism as well as original Confucian values, it has come to be known as neo-Confucianism.

Confucians and Buddhism

The most important representative of Song neo-Confucianism was the philosopher Zhu Xi (1130–1200 C.E.). A prolific writer, Zhu Xi maintained a deep commitment to Confucian values emphasizing proper personal behavior and social harmony. Among his writings was an influential treatise entitled *Family Rituals* that provided detailed instructions for weddings, funerals, veneration of ancestors, and other family ceremonies. As a good Confucian, Zhu Xi considered it a matter of the highest importance that individuals play their proper roles both in their family and in the larger society.

Zhu Xi

Yet Zhu Xi became fascinated with the philosophical and speculative features of Buddhist thought. He argued in good Confucian fashion for the observance of high moral standards, and he believed that academic and philosophical investigations were important for practical affairs. But he concentrated his own efforts on abstract and abstruse issues of more theoretical than practical significance. He wrote extensively on metaphysical themes such as the nature of reality. He argued in a manner reminiscent of Plato that two elements accounted for all physical being: *li,* a principle somewhat similar to Plato's Forms or Ideas that defines the essence of the being, and *qi,* its material form.

Neo-Confucianism ranks as an important cultural development for two reasons. First, it illustrates the deep influence of Buddhism in Chinese society. Even though the neo-Confucians rejected Buddhism as a faith, their writings adapted Buddhist themes and reasoning to Confucian interests and values. Second, neo-Confucianism influenced east Asian thought over a very long term. Except for the century when nomadic Mongols dominated China (1279–1368 C.E.), neo-Confucianism enjoyed the status of an officially recognized creed from the Song dynasty until the early twentieth century. Not only in China but also in lands that fell within China's cultural orbit—particularly Korea, Vietnam, and Japan—neo-Confucianism shaped philosophical, political, and moral thought for half a millennium and more.

Neo-Confucian Influence

CHINA IN EAST ASIA

As in the cases of Byzantium and the *dar al-Islam*, Chinese society influenced the development of neighboring lands during postclassical times. Chinese armies periodically invaded Korea and Vietnam, and Chinese merchants established commercial relations with Japan as well as with Korea and Vietnam. Chinese techniques of government and administration helped shape public life in Korea, Vietnam, and Japan, and Chinese values and cultural traditions won a prominent place alongside native traditions. By no means did these lands become absorbed into China: all maintained distinctive identities and cultural traditions. Yet they also drew deep inspiration from Chinese examples and built societies that reflected their participation in a larger east Asian society revolving around China.

Korea and Vietnam

Chinese armies ventured into Korea and Vietnam on campaigns of imperial expansion as early as the Qin and Han dynasties. As the Han dynasty weakened, however, local aristocrats organized movements that ousted Chinese forces from both lands. Only during the powerful Tang dynasty did Chinese resources once again enable military authorities to mount large-scale campaigns. Although the two lands responded differently to Chinese imperial expansion, both borrowed Chinese political and cultural traditions and used them in their own societies.

The Silla Dynasty   During the seventh century Tang armies conquered much of Korea before the native Silla dynasty rallied to prevent Chinese domination of the peninsula. Both Tang and Silla authorities preferred to avoid a long and costly conflict, so they agreed to a political compromise: Chinese forces withdrew from Korea, and the Silla king recognized the Tang emperor as his overlord. In theory, Korea was a vassal state in a vast Chinese empire. In practice, however, Korea was in most respects an independent kingdom, although the ruling dynasty prudently maintained cordial relations with its powerful neighbor.

Thus Korea entered into a tributary relationship with China. Envoys of the Silla kings regularly delivered gifts to Chinese emperors and performed the kowtow, but these concessions brought considerable benefits to the Koreans. In return for their recognition of Chinese supremacy, they received gifts more valuable than the tribute they delivered to China. Moreover, the tributary relationship opened the doors for Korean merchants to trade in China.

Chinese Influence in Korea   Meanwhile, the tributary relationship facilitated the spread of Chinese political and cultural influences to Korea. Embassies delivering tribute to China included Korean royal officials who observed the workings of the Chinese court and bureaucracy and then organized the Korean court on similar lines. The Silla kings even built a new capital at Kumsong modeled on the Tang capital at Chang'an. Alongside royal officials, tribute embassies included scholars who studied Chinese thought and literature and who took copies of Chinese writings back to Korea. Their efforts helped to build Korean interest in the Confucian tradition, particularly among educated aristocrats. While Korean elite classes turned to Confucius, Chinese schools of Buddhism attracted widespread popular interest. Chan Buddhism, which promised individual salvation, won the allegiance of peasants and commoners.

China and Korea differed in many respects. Most notably, perhaps, aristocrats and royal houses dominated Korean society much more than was the case in China. Although the Korean monarchy sponsored Chinese schools and a Confucian examination system, Korea never established a bureaucracy based on merit such as that of Tang and Song China. Political initiative remained firmly in the hands of the ruling classes. Nevertheless, extensive dealings with its powerful neighbor ensured that Korea reflected the influence of Chinese political and cultural traditions.

Chinese relations with Vietnam were far more tense than with Korea. When *China and Vietnam* Tang armies ventured into the land that Chinese called Nam Viet, they encountered spirited resistance on the part of the Viet people, who had settled in the region around the Red River. Tang forces soon won control of Viet towns and cities, and they launched efforts to absorb the Viets into Chinese society, just as their predecessors had absorbed the indigenous peoples of the Yangzi River valley. The Viets readily adopted Chinese agricultural methods and irrigation systems, as well as Chinese schools and administrative techniques. Like their Korean counterparts, Viet elites studied Confucian texts and took examinations based on a Chinese-style education, and Viet traders marketed their wares in China. Vietnamese authorities even entered into tributary relationships with the Chinese court. Yet the Viets resented Chinese efforts to dominate the southern land, and they mounted a series of revolts against Tang authorities. As the Tang dynasty fell during the early tenth century, the Viets won their independence and successfully resisted later Chinese efforts at imperial expansion to the south.

Like Korea, Vietnam differed from China in many ways. Many Vietnamese retained their indigenous religions in preference to Chinese cultural traditions. Women played a much more prominent role in Vietnamese society and economy than did their Chinese counterparts. Southeast Asian women had dominated local and regional markets for centuries, and they participated actively in business ventures closed to women in the more rigidly patriarchal society of China.

Tang dynasty pottery figure of a Vietnamese dancer. Commercial and tributary relationships introduced southeast Asian performers to China, where sophisticated urban communities appreciated their exotic entertainment. • Courtesy of the Trustees of the V & A. Photograph courtesy of the V & A Picture Library

Nevertheless, Chinese traditions found a place in the southern land. Vietnamese authorities established an administrative system and bureaucracy modeled on that of China, and Viet ruling classes prepared for their careers by pursuing a Confucian education. Furthermore, Buddhism came to Vietnam from China as well as India and won a large popular following. Thus, like Korea, Vietnam *Chinese Influence* absorbed political and cultural influence from China and reflected the development *in Vietnam* of a larger east Asian society centered on China.

Early Japan

Chinese armies never invaded Japan, but Chinese traditions deeply influenced Japanese political and cultural development. The earliest inhabitants of Japan were nomadic peoples from northeast Asia. They migrated to Japan, perhaps across land bridges that formed during an ice age, about two hundred thousand years ago. Their language, material culture, and religion derived from their parent society in northeast Asia. As the population of the islands grew and built a settled agricultural society, small states dominated by aristocratic clans emerged. By the middle of the first millennium C.E., several dozen states ruled small regions.

Nara Japan   The establishment of the powerful Sui and Tang dynasties in China had repercussions in Japan, where they suggested the value of centralized imperial government. One of the aristocratic clans in Japan insisted on its precedence over the others, although in fact it had never wielded effective authority outside its own territory in central Japan. Inspired by the Tang example, this clan claimed imperial authority and introduced a series of reforms designed to centralize Japanese politics. The imperial house established a court modeled on that of the Tang, instituted a Chinese-style bureaucracy, implemented an equal-field system, provided official support for Confucianism and Buddhism, and in the year 710 moved to a new capital city at Nara (near modern Kyoto) that was a replica of the Tang capital at Chang'an. Never was Chinese influence more prominent in Japan than during the Nara period (710–794 C.E.).

Yet Japan did not lose its distinctive characteristics or become simply a smaller model of Chinese society. While adopting Confucian and Buddhist traditions from China, for example, the Japanese continued to observe the rites of Shinto, their indigenous religion, which revolved around the veneration of ancestors and a host of nature spirits and deities. Japanese society reflected the influence of Chinese traditions but still developed along its own lines.

The experiences of the Heian, Kamakura, and Muromachi periods clearly illustrate this point. In 794 the emperor of Japan transferred his court from Nara to a newly constructed capital at nearby Heian (modern Kyoto). During the next four centuries, Heian became the seat of a refined and sophisticated society that drew inspiration from China but also elaborated distinctively Japanese political and cultural traditions.

Heian Japan   During the Heian period (794–1185 C.E.), local rulers on the island of Honshu mostly recognized the emperor as Japan's supreme political authority. Unlike their Chinese counterparts, however, Japanese emperors rarely ruled, but rather served as ceremonial figureheads and symbols of authority. Effective power lay in the hands of the Fujiwara family, an aristocratic clan that controlled affairs from behind the throne through its influence over the imperial house and manipulation of its members.

Since the ninth century the Japanese political order has almost continuously featured a split between a publicly recognized imperial authority and a separate agent of effective rule. This pattern helps to account for the remarkable longevity of the Japanese imperial house. Because emperors have not ruled, they have not been subject to deposition during times of turmoil: ruling parties and factions have come and gone, but the imperial house has survived.

The cultural development of Heian Japan also reflected both the influence of Chinese traditions and the elaboration of peculiarly Japanese ways. Most literature imitated Chinese models and indeed was written in the Chinese language. Boys and young men who received a formal education in Heian Japan learned Chinese, read the classic works of China, and wrote in the foreign tongue. Officials at court conducted business and kept records in Chinese, and literary figures wrote histories and treatises in the style popular in China. Even Japanese writing reflected Chinese influence, since scholars borrowed many Chinese characters and used them to represent Japanese words. They also adapted some Chinese characters into a Japanese syllabic script, in which symbols represent whole syllables rather than a single sound, as in an alphabetic script.

The Tale of Genji

Because Japanese women rarely received a formal Chinese-style education, in Heian times aristocratic women made the most notable contributions to literature in the Japanese language. Of the many literary works that have survived from this era, none reflects Heian court life better than *The Tale of Genji*. Composed by Murasaki Shikibu, a lady-in-waiting at the Heian court who wrote in syllabic script rather than Chinese characters, this sophisticated work relates the experiences of a fictitious imperial prince named Genji. Living amid gardens and palaces, Genji and his friends devoted themselves to the cultivation of an ultrarefined lifestyle; and they became adept at mixing subtle perfumes, composing splendid verses in fine calligraphic hand, and wooing sophisticated women.

The Tale of Genji also offers a meditation on the passing of time and the sorrows that time brings to sensitive human beings. As Genji and his friends age, they reflect on past joys and relationships no longer recoverable. Their thoughts suffuse *The Tale of Genji* with a melancholy spirit that presents a subtle contrast to the elegant atmosphere of their surroundings at the Heian court. Due to her limited command of Chinese, Lady Murasaki created one of the most remarkable literary works in the Japanese language.

Decline of Heian Japan

As the charmed circle of aristocrats and courtiers led elegant lives at the imperial capital, the Japanese countryside underwent fundamental changes that brought an end to the Heian court and its refined society. The equal-field system gradually fell into disuse in Japan as it had in China, and aristocratic clans accumulated most of the islands' lands into vast estates. By the late eleventh century, two clans in particular—the Taira and the Minamoto—overshadowed the others. During the mid-twelfth century the two engaged in outright war, and in 1185 the Minamoto emerged victorious. The Minamoto did not seek to abolish imperial authority in Japan, but rather claimed to rule the land in the name of the emperor. They installed the clan leader as *shogun*—a military governor who ruled in place of the emperor—and established the seat of their government at Kamakura, near modern Tokyo, while the imperial court remained at Kyoto. For most of the next four centuries, one branch or another of the Minamoto clan dominated political life in Japan.

Medieval Japan

Historians refer to the Kamakura and Muromachi periods as Japan's medieval period—a middle era falling between the age of Chinese influence and court domination of political life in Japan, as represented by the Nara and Heian periods, and the modern age, inaugurated by the Tokugawa dynasty in the sixteenth century, when a centralized government unified and ruled all of Japan. During this middle era Japanese society and culture took on increasingly distinctive characteristics.

Japanese Feudalism

In the Kamakura (1185–1333 C.E.) and Muromachi (1336–1573 C.E.) periods, Japan developed a feudal political order in which provincial lords wielded effective power and authority in local regions where they controlled land and economic affairs. As these lords and their clans vied for power and authority in the countryside,

Samurai flee a burning castle in this scroll painting from the late thirteenth century. The armor, weaponry, and mounts of the samurai bespeak the militarism of the Kamakura era. • Scroll with Depictions of the Night Attack on the Sanjo Palace. Japan, Kamakura period, second half of the 13th century. Fenollosa-Weld Collection. Courtesy Museum of Fine Arts, Boston

they found little use for the Chinese-style bureaucracy that Nara and Heian rulers had instituted in Japan and still less use for the elaborate protocol and refined conduct that prevailed at the courts. In place of etiquette and courtesy, they valued military talent and discipline. The mounted warrior, the *samurai,* thus played the most distinctive role in Japanese political and military affairs.

The Samurai   The samurai were professional warriors, specialists in the use of force and the arts of fighting. They served the provincial lords of Japan, who relied on the samurai both to enforce their authority in their own territories and to extend their claims to other lands. In return for these police and military services, the lords supported the samurai from the agricultural surplus and labor services of peasants working under their jurisdiction. Freed of obligations to feed, clothe, and house themselves and their families, samurai devoted themselves to hunting, riding, archery, and martial arts. They lived by an informal but widely observed code known as *bushido* ("the way of the warrior"), which emphasized above all other virtues the importance of absolute loyalty to one's lord. While esteeming traits such as strength, courage, and a spirit of aggression, bushido insisted that samurai place the interests of their lords even above their own lives. To avoid dishonor and humiliation, samurai who failed their masters commonly ended their own lives by *seppuku*—ritual suicide by disembowelment, sometimes referred to by the cruder term *hara-kiri* ("belly slicing").

Thus although it had taken its original inspiration from the Tang empire in China, the Japanese political order developed along lines different from those of the Middle Kingdom. Yet Japan clearly had a place in the larger east Asian society centered on China. Japan borrowed from China, among other things, Confucian values, Buddhist religion, a system of writing, and the ideal of centralized imperial rule. Though somewhat suppressed during the Kamakura and Muromachi periods, these elements of Chinese society not only survived in Japan but also decisively influenced Japanese development during later periods.

The revival of centralized imperial rule in China had profound implications for all of east Asia and indeed for most of the eastern hemisphere. When the Sui and Tang dynasties imposed their authority throughout China, they established a powerful state that guided political affairs throughout east Asia. Tang armies extended Chinese influence to Korea, Vietnam, and central Asia. They did not invade Japan, but the impressive political organization of China prompted the islands' rulers to imitate Tang examples. Moreover, the Sui and Tang dynasties laid a strong political foundation for rapid economic development. Chinese society prospered throughout the postclassical era, partly because of technological and industrial innovation. Tang and Song prosperity touched all of China's neighbors, since it encouraged surging commerce in east Asia. Chinese silk, porcelain, and lacquerware were prized commodities among trading peoples from southeast Asia to east Africa. Chinese inventions such as paper, printing, gunpowder, and the magnetic compass found a place in societies throughout the eastern hemisphere as they diffused across the silk roads and sea-lanes. The postclassical era was an age of religious as well as commercial and technological exchanges: Nestorian Christians, Zoroastrians, Manichaeans, and Muslims all maintained communities in Tang China, and Buddhism became the most popular religious faith in all of east Asia. During the postclassical era Chinese social organization and economic dynamism helped to sustain interactions between the peoples of the eastern hemisphere on an unprecedented scale.

CHRONOLOGY

589–618	Sui dynasty (China)
602–664	Life of Xuanzang
604–618	Reign of Sui Yangdi
618–907	Tang dynasty (China)
627–649	Reign of Tang Taizong
669–935	Silla dynasty (Korea)
710–794	Nara period (Japan)
755–757	An Lushan's rebellion
794–1185	Heian period (Japan)
875–884	Huang Chao's rebellion
960–1279	Song dynasty (China)
960–976	Reign of Song Taizu
1024	First issuance of Government-sponsored paper money
1130–1200	Life of Zhu Xi
1185–1333	Kamakura period (Japan)
1336–1573	Muromachi period (Japan)

FOR FURTHER READING

Kenneth Ch'en. *Buddhism in China: A Historical Survey.* Princeton, 1964. A clear and detailed account by an eminent scholar.

Hugh R. Clark. *Community, Trade, and Networks: Southern Fujian Province from the Third to the Thirteenth Century.* Cambridge, 1991. Excellent scholarly study exploring the transformation of a region by trade and market forces.

Peter Duus. *Feudalism in Japan.* 2nd ed. New York, 1976. A brief survey of early Japanese political history, concentrating on the Kamakura and Muromachi periods.

Mark Elvin. *The Pattern of the Chinese Past.* Stanford, 1973. A brilliant analysis of Chinese history, concentrating particularly on economic, social, and technological themes.

Jacques Gernet. *Buddhism in Chinese Society: An Economic History from the Fifth to the Tenth Century.* Trans. by F. Verellen. New York, 1995. An important study emphasizing the economic and social significance of Buddhist monasteries in the Chinese countryside.

———. *Daily Life in China on the Eve of the Mongol Invasion, 1250–1276.* Trans. by H. M. Wright. New York, 1962. Rich portrait of late Song China, emphasizing social history.

Ivan Morris. *The World of the Shining Prince: Court Life in Ancient Japan.* Harmondsworth, 1964. Vividly reconstructs the court life of Heian Japan.

Murasaki Shikibu. *The Tale of Genji.* 2 vols. Trans. by E. Seidensticker. New York, 1976. Fresh and readable translation of Lady Murasaki's classic work.

Joseph Needham. *Science in Traditional China.* Cambridge, Mass., 1981. Essays presenting the results of recent research on the history of Chinese science and technology.

Edward H. Schafer. *The Golden Peaches of Samarkand: A Study of T'ang Exotics.* Berkeley, 1963. Deals with relations between China and central Asian lands during the Tang dynasty.

———. *The Vermilion Bird: T'ang Images of the South.* Berkeley, 1967. Evocative study of relations between China and Vietnam during the Tang dynasty.

H. Paul Varley. *Japanese Culture.* 3rd ed. Honolulu, 1984. An authoritative analysis of Japanese cultural development from early times to the present.

Sally Hovey Wriggins. *Xuanzang: A Buddhist Pilgrim on the Silk Road.* Boulder, 1996. A fascinating and well-illustrated account of Xuanzang's journey to India and his influence on the development of Buddhism in China.

Arthur F. Wright. *Buddhism in Chinese History.* Stanford, 1959. A brief and incisive study of Buddhism in China by an eminent scholar.

———. *The Sui Dynasty: The Unification of China,* A.D. 581–617. New York, 1978. A useful survey that places the Sui dynasty in its larger historical context.

Zhu Xi. *Chu Hsi's "Family Rituals": A Twelfth-Century Chinese Manual for the Performance of Cappings, Weddings, Funerals, and Ancestral Rites.* Trans. by Patricia Buckley Ebrey. Princeton, 1991. Provides a translation of Zhu Xi's influential book on *Family Rituals* along with an illuminating introduction.

CHAPTER 15

INDIA AND THE INDIAN OCEAN BASIN

· · ·

Buzurg ibn Shahriyar was a tenth-century shipmaster from Siraf, a prosperous and bustling port city on the Persian Gulf coast. He probably sailed frequently to Arabia and India, and he may have ventured also to Malaya, the islands of southeast Asia, China, and east Africa. Like all sailors, he heard stories about the distant lands that mariners had visited, the different customs they observed, and the adventures that befell them during their travels. About 953 C.E. he compiled 136 such stories in his *Book of the Wonders of India.*

Buzurg's collection included a generous proportion of tall tales. He told of a giant lobster that seized a ship's anchor and dragged the vessel through the water, of mermaids and sea dragons, of creatures born from human fathers and fish mothers who lived in human society but had flippers that enabled them to swim through the water like fish, of serpents that ate cattle and elephants, of birds so large that they crushed houses, of a monkey that seduced a sailor, and of a talking lizard. Yet alongside the tall tales, many of Buzurg's stories accurately reflected the conditions of his time. One recounted the story of a king from northern India who converted to Islam and requested translations of Islamic law. Others reported on Hindu customs, shipwrecks, encounters with pirates, and slave trading.

Several of Buzurg's stories tempted readers with visions of vast wealth attainable through maritime trade. Buzurg mentioned fine diamonds from Kashmir, pearls from Ceylon, and a Jewish merchant who left Persia penniless and returned from India and China with a shipload of priceless merchandise. Despite their embellishments and exaggerations, his stories reflected the trade networks that linked the lands surrounding the Indian Ocean in the tenth century. While Buzurg clearly thought of India as a distinct land with its own customs, he also recognized a larger world of trade and communication that extended from east Africa to southeast Asia and beyond to China.

Just as China served as the principal inspiration of a larger east Asian society in the postclassical era, India influenced the development of a larger cultural zone in south and southeast Asia. Yet China and India played different roles in their respective spheres of influence. In east Asia China was the dominant power, even if it did not always exercise authority directly over its neighbors. In south and southeast Asia, however, there emerged no centralized imperial authority like the Tang dynasty in China. Indeed, although several states organized large regional kingdoms, no single

Kabir, the blind guru, weaves cloth while discussing religious matters with disciples. • © The British Museum

state was able to extend its authority to all parts of the Indian subcontinent, much less to the mainland and islands of southeast Asia.

Though politically disunited, India remained a coherent and distinct society as a result of powerful social and cultural traditions: the caste system and the Hindu religion shaped human experiences and values throughout the subcontinent during the postclassical era. Beginning in the seventh century Islam also began to attract a popular following in India, and after the eleventh century Islam deeply influenced Indian society alongside the caste system and Hinduism.

Beyond the subcontinent Indian traditions helped to shape a larger cultural zone extending to the mainland and islands of southeast Asia. Throughout most of the region, ruling classes adopted Indian forms of political organization and Indian techniques of statecraft. Indian merchants took their Hindu and Buddhist faiths to southeast Asia, where they first attracted the interest of political elites and then of the popular masses. Somewhat later, Indian merchants also helped introduce Islam to southeast Asia.

While Indian traditions influenced the political and cultural development of southeast Asia, the entire Indian Ocean basin began to move toward economic integration during the postclassical era, as Buzurg ibn Shahriyar's stories suggest. Lands on the rim of the Indian Ocean retained distinctive political and cultural traditions inherited from times past. Yet innovations in maritime technology, development of a well-articulated network of sea-lanes, and the building of port cities and entrepôts enabled peoples living around the Indian Ocean to trade and communicate more actively than ever before. As a result, peoples from east Africa to southeast Asia and China increasingly participated in the larger economic, commercial, and cultural life of the Indian Ocean basin.

 ## ISLAMIC AND HINDU KINGDOMS

Like the Han and Roman empires, the Gupta dynasty came under severe pressure from nomadic invaders. From the mid-fourth to the mid-fifth century C.E., Gupta rulers resisted the pressures and preserved order throughout much of the Indian subcontinent. Beginning in 451 C.E., however, White Huns from central Asia invaded India and disrupted the Gupta administration. By the mid-sixth century the Gupta state had collapsed, and effective political authority quickly devolved to invaders, local allies of the Guptas, and independent regional power brokers. From the end of the Gupta dynasty until the sixteenth century, when a Turkish people known as the Mughals extended their authority and their empire to most of the subcontinent, India remained a politically divided land.

The Quest for Centralized Imperial Rule

Northern and southern India followed different political trajectories after the fall of the Gupta empire. In the north politics became turbulent and almost chaotic. Local states contested for power and territory, and northern India became a region of continuous tension and intermittent war. Nomadic Turkish-speaking peoples from central Asia frequently took advantage of this unsettled state of affairs to cross the Khyber Pass and force their way into India. They eventually found niches for themselves in the caste system and became completely absorbed into Indian society. Until processes of social absorption worked themselves out, however, the arrival of nomadic peoples caused additional disruption in northern India.

Even after the collapse of the Gupta dynasty, the ideal of centralized imperial rule did not entirely disappear. During the first half of the seventh century, King Harsha (reigned 606–648 C.E.) temporarily restored unified rule in most of northern India and sought to revive imperial authority. Harsha came to the throne of his kingdom in the lower Ganges valley at the age of sixteen. Full of energy and ambition, he led his army throughout northern India. His forces included twenty thousand cavalry, fifty thousand infantry, and five thousand war elephants, and by about 612 he had subdued those who refused to recognize his authority.

Harsha

Harsha enjoyed a reputation for piety, liberality, and even scholarship. He was himself a Buddhist, but he looked kindly on other faiths as well. He built hospitals and provided free medical care for his subjects. The Chinese pilgrim Xuanzang lived in northern India during his reign and reported that Harsha liberally distributed wealth to his subjects. On one occasion, Xuanzang said, the king and his aides doled out resources continuously for seventy-five days, making gifts to half a million people. Harsha also generously patronized scholars and even wrote three plays.

Despite his energy and his favorable reputation,

MAP [15.1]

Major states of postclassical India.

Harsha was unable to restore permanent centralized rule. Since the fall of the Gupta dynasty, local rulers had established their authority too securely in India's regions for Harsha to overcome them. Harsha spent much of his reign on horseback traveling throughout his realm to solidify alliances with local rulers, who were virtually kings in their own lands. He managed to hold his loose empire together mainly by the force of his personality and his constant attention to political affairs. Ultimately, however, he fell victim to an assassin and left no heir to maintain his realm. His empire immediately disintegrated, and local rulers once again turned northern India into a battleground as they sought to enlarge their realms at the expense of their neighbors.

Collapse of Harsha's Kingdom

The Introduction of Islam to Northern India

Amid nomadic incursions and contests for power, northern India also experienced the arrival of Islam and the establishment of Islamic states. Islam reached India by several routes. One was military: Arab forces entered India as early as the mid-seventh

The Conquest of Sind

century, even before the establishment of the Umayyad caliphate, although their first expeditions were exploratory ventures rather than campaigns of conquest. In 711, however, a well-organized expedition conquered Sind, the Indus River valley in northwestern India, and incorporated it as a province of the expanding Umayyad empire. At mid-century, along with most of the rest of the *dar al-Islam,* Sind passed into the hands of the Abbasid caliphs.

Sind stood on the fringe of the Islamic world, well beyond the effective authority of the Abbasid caliphs. Much of its population remained Hindu, Buddhist, or Parsee, and it also sheltered a series of unorthodox Islamic movements. Infighting between Arab administrators eventually offered opportunities for local political elites to reassert Hindu authority over much of Sind. Yet the region remained nominally under the jurisdiction of the caliphs until the collapse of the Abbasid dynasty in 1258.

Merchants and Islam

While conquerors brought Islam to Sind, Muslim merchants took their faith to coastal regions in both northern and southern India. Arab and Persian mariners had visited Indian ports for centuries before Muhammad, and their Muslim descendants dominated trade and transportation networks between India and western lands from the seventh through the fifteenth centuries. Muslim merchants formed small communities in all the major cities of coastal India, where they played a prominent role in Indian business and commercial life. They frequently married local women, and in many cases they also found places for themselves in Indian society. Thus Islam entered India's port cities in a more gradual but no less effective way than was the case in Sind. Well before the year 1000, for example, the Gujarat region housed a large Muslim population. Muslim merchants congregated there because of the port city of Cambay, the most important trading center in India throughout the millennium from 500 to 1500 C.E.

Turkish Migrants and Islam

Islam also entered India by a third route: the migrations and invasions of Turkish-speaking peoples from central Asia. During the tenth century several Turkish groups had become acquainted with Islam through their dealings with the Abbasid caliphate and had converted to the faith. Some of these Muslim Turks entered the Abbasid realm as mercenary soldiers or migrated into Byzantine Anatolia, while others moved into Afghanistan, where they established an Islamic state.

Mahmud of Ghazni

Mahmud of Ghazni, leader of the Turks in Afghanistan, soon turned his attention to the rich land to the south. Between 1001 and 1027 he mounted seventeen raiding expeditions into India. Taking advantage of infighting between local rulers, he annexed several states in northwestern India and the Punjab. For the most part, however, Mahmud had less interest in conquering and ruling India than in plundering the wealth stored in its many well-endowed temples. Mahmud and his forces demolished hundreds of sites associated with Hindu or Buddhist faiths, and their campaigns hastened the decline of Buddhism in the land of its birth. They frequently established mosques or Islamic shrines on the sites of Hindu and Buddhist structures that they destroyed. Not surprisingly, however, Mahmud's raids did not encourage Indians to turn to Islam.

The Sultanate of Delhi

During the late twelfth century, Mahmud's successors mounted a more systematic campaign to conquer northern India and place it under Islamic rule. By the early thirteenth century, they had conquered most of the Hindu kingdoms in northern India and established an Islamic state known as the sultanate of Delhi. The sultans established their capital at Delhi, a strategic site controlling access from the Punjab to the Ganges valley, and they ruled northern India at least in name for more than three centuries, from 1206 to 1526.

During the fourteenth century the sultans of Delhi commanded an army of three hundred thousand, and their state ranked among the most powerful in the Islamic world. Yet for the most part, the authority of the sultans did not extend far beyond Delhi. They often conducted raids in the Deccan region of southern India, but they never overcame Hindu resistance there. They had no permanent bureaucracy or administrative apparatus. Even in northern India, they imposed a thin veneer of Islamic political and military authority on a land populated mostly by Hindus, and they depended on the goodwill of Hindu kings to carry out their policies and advance their interests in local regions. Indeed, they did not even enjoy comfortable control of their own court: of the thirty-five sultans of Delhi, nineteen perished at the hands of assassins. Nevertheless, the sultans prominently sponsored Islam and helped to establish a secure place for their faith in the cultural landscape of India.

Invasion and war have destroyed most early Islamic architecture in India. One monument that survives, however, is the Qutb Minar, a splendid and intricately decorated minaret 73 meters (240 feet) tall, built in the early thirteenth century by the sultans of Delhi. • Giraudon/Art Resource, NY

The Hindu Kingdoms of Southern India

Although it too remained politically divided, the southern part of the Indian subcontinent largely escaped the invasions, chronic war, and turmoil that troubled the north. Most Hindu rulers in the south presided over small, loosely administered states. Competition between states sometimes resulted in regional wars, but southern conflicts were less frequent, less intense, and less damaging than those that plagued the north.

While many regional states organized affairs in local jurisdictions, two kingdoms expanded enough to exercise at least nominal rule over much of southern India. The first was the Chola kingdom, situated in the deep south, which ruled the Coromandel coast for more than four centuries, from 850 to 1267 C.E. At its high point, during the eleventh century, Chola forces conquered Ceylon and parts of southeast Asia. Financed by the profits of trade, the Chola navy dominated the waters from the South China Sea to the Arabian Sea.

The Chola Kingdom

Chola rulers did not build a tightly centralized state: they allowed considerable autonomy for local and village institutions as long as they maintained order and delivered tax revenues on time. By the twelfth century, however, the Chola state was in decline. Native Sinhalese forces expelled Chola officials from Ceylon, and revolts erupted within southern India. The Chola realm did not entirely collapse, but by the

The kings of Vijayanagar endowed their capital with splendid buildings and even provided these handsome domed stables for their elephants. • DPA/NMK/ The Image Works

The Kingdom of Vijayanagar

early thirteenth century, much reduced in size and power, it had reverted to the status of one regional kingdom among many others in southern India.

The second state that dominated much of southern India was the kingdom of Vijayanagar, based in the northern Deccan. The kingdom owed its origin to efforts by the sultans of Delhi to extend their authority to southern India. Exploratory forays by Turkish forces provoked a defensive reaction in the south. Officials in Delhi dispatched two brothers, Harihara and Bukka, to represent the sultan and implement court policies in the south. Although they had converted from their native Hinduism to Islam, Harihara and Bukka recognized an opportunity to establish themselves as independent rulers. In 1336 they renounced Islam, returned to their original Hindu faith, and proclaimed the establishment of an independent empire of Vijayanagar (meaning "city of victory"). Their unusual coup did not lead to hostilities between Muslims and Hindus: Muslim merchants continued to trade unmolested in the ports of southern India, as they had for more than half a millennium. But the Hindu kingdom of Vijayanagar was the dominant state in southern India from the mid-fourteenth century until 1565 when it fell to Mughal conquerors from the north.

As in the north, then, political division and conflict between states characterized the political history of southern India in postclassical times. India did not generate the sort of large-scale, centralized, imperial state that guided the fortunes of postclassical societies in the eastern Mediterranean, southwest Asia, or China. States like the sultanate of Delhi in northern India and the kingdoms of Chola and Vijayanagar in the south were not powerful enough to organize political life throughout the subcontinent. Nevertheless, on the basis of trade, common social structures, and inherited cultural traditions, a coherent and distinctive society flourished in postclassical India.

PRODUCTION AND TRADE IN THE INDIAN OCEAN BASIN

As in Mediterranean, southwest Asian, and Chinese societies, agricultural yields increased significantly in postclassical India, enabling large numbers of people to devote themselves to trade and manufacturing rather than the production of food.

Trade forged links between the various regions of the subcontinent and fostered economic development in southern India. Trade also created links between India and distant lands, as merchants and manufacturers transformed the Indian Ocean basin into a vast zone of communication and exchange. The increasing prominence of trade and industry brought change to Indian society, as merchant and artisan guilds became stronger and more influential than before. Yet caste identities and loyalties also remained strong, and the caste system continued to serve as the most powerful organizing feature of Indian society.

Agriculture in the Monsoon World

Because of the rhythms of the monsoons, irrigation was essential for the mainte- *The Monsoons* nance of a large, densely populated, agricultural society. During the spring and summer, warm, moisture-laden winds from the southwest bring most of India's rainfall. During the autumn and winter, cool and very dry winds blow from the northeast. To achieve their agricultural potential, Indian lands required a good watering by the southern monsoon, supplemented by irrigation during the dry months. Light rain during the spring and summer months or short supplies of water for irrigation commonly led to drought, reduced harvests, and widespread famine.

In northern India irrigation had been a fixture of the countryside since Harappan *Irrigation Systems* times, when cultivators tapped the waters of the Indus River. Later, as Aryans migrated into the Ganges River valley, they found plentiful surface water and abundant opportunities to build irrigation systems. For the most part, however, southern India is an arid land without rivers like the Indus or Ganges that can serve as sources for large-scale irrigation. Thus as southern India became more densely populated, irrigation systems became crucial, and a great deal of energy and effort went into the construction of waterworks. Dams, reservoirs, canals, wells, and tunnels appeared in large numbers. Particularly impressive were monumental reservoirs lined with brick or stone that captured the rains of the spring and summer months and held them until the dry season, when canals carried them to thirsty fields. One such reservoir—actually an artificial lake constructed near Bhopal during the eleventh century—covered some 650 square kilometers (250 square miles). Projects of this size required enormous investments of human energy, both for their original construction and for continuing maintenance, but they led to significant increases in agricultural productivity.

As a result of this increased productivity, India's population grew steadily *Population Growth* throughout the postclassical era. In 600 C.E., shortly after the fall of the Gupta dynasty, the subcontinent's population stood at about 53 million. By 800 it had increased almost 20 percent to 64 million, and by 1000 it had grown by almost another 25 percent to 79 million. During the following centuries the rate of growth slowed, as Indian numbers increased by 4 to 5 million individuals per century. Toward 1500, however, the rate of growth increased again, and by 1500 the subcontinent's population had reached 105 million.

This demographic surge encouraged the concentration of people in cities. Dur- *Urbanization* ing the fourteenth century, the high point of the sultanate of Delhi, the capital city had a population of about four hundred thousand, which made it second only to Cairo among Muslim cities. Many other cities—particularly ports and trading centers like Cambay, Surat, Calicut, Quilon, and Masulipatam—had populations well over one hundred thousand. Cities in southern India grew especially fast, partly as a result of increasing agricultural productivity in the region.

COSMAS INDICOPLEUSTES ON TRADE IN SOUTHERN INDIA

· · ·

Cosmas Indicopleustes was a Christian monk from Egypt who lived during the sixth century c.e. *and traveled widely throughout north Africa and southwest Asia. On one of his trips, he ventured as far as India and Ceylon, which he described at some length in a work entitled* The Christian Topography. *Cosmas's account clearly shows that sixth-century India and Ceylon played prominent roles in the larger economy of the Indian Ocean basin.*

Ceylon lies on the other side of the pepper country [southern India]. Around it are numerous small islands all having fresh water and coconut trees. They nearly all have deep water close up to their shores. . . . Ceylon is a great market for the people in those parts. The island also has a church of Persian Christians who have settled there, and a priest who is appointed from Persia, and a deacon and a complete ecclesiastical ritual. But the natives and their kings are heathens. . . .

Since the island of Ceylon is in a central position, it is much frequented by ships from all parts of India and from Persia and Ethiopia, and it likewise sends out many of its own. And from the remotest countries—I mean China and other trading places—it receives silk, aloes, cloves, sandalwood, and other products, and these again are passed on to markets on this side, such as Male [the western coast of southern India], where pepper grows, and to Calliana [a port city near modern Bombay], which exports copper and sesame logs and cloth for making dresses, for it also is a great place of business. And also to Sind [Gujarat], where musk and

castor and spice are procured, and to Persia and the Homerite country [Anatolia], and to Adule [in Ethiopia]. And this island [Ceylon] receives imports from all these markets that we have mentioned and passes them on to the remoter ports, while at the same time exporting its own produce in both directions. . . .

The kings of various places in India keep elephants. . . . They may have six hundred each, or five hundred, some more, some fewer. Now the king of Ceylon gives a good price both for the elephants and for the horses that he has. The elephants he pays for by the cubit [a unit of measurement equivalent to about half a meter or eighteen inches]. For the height is measured from the ground, and the price is reckoned at so many gold coins for each cubit—fifty [coins] it may be, or a hundred, or even more. Horses they bring to him from Persia, and he buys them, exempting the importers of them from paying custom duties. The kings of the Indian subcontinent tame their elephants, which are caught wild, and employ them in war.

SOURCE: Cosmas Indicopleustes. *The Christian Topography of Cosmas, an Egyptian Monk*. Trans. by J. W. McCrindle. London: Hakluyt Society, 1897, pp. 364–72. (Translation slightly modified.)

Trade and the Economic Development of Southern India

Political fragmentation of the subcontinent did not prevent robust trade between the different states and regions of India. As the population grew, opportunities for specialized work became more numerous. Increased trade was a natural result of this process.

Internal Trade   Most regions of the Indian subcontinent were self-sufficient in staple foods such as rice, wheat, barley, and millet. The case was different, however, with iron, copper, salt, pepper, spices, condiments, and specialized crops that grew well only in certain regions. Iron came mostly from the Ganges River valley near Bengal, copper mostly from the Deccan, salt mostly from coastal regions, and pepper from southern India. These and other commodities sometimes traveled long distances to consumers in remote parts of the subcontinent. Pepper, saffron, and sugar were popular commodi-

One of the oldest surviving Hindu temples is the seaside temple at Mahabalipuram, south of Madras, which dates from the eighth century. • © Ric L. Ergenbright

ties in subcontinental trade, and even rice sometimes traveled as a trade item to northern and mountainous regions where it did not grow well.

Southern India and Ceylon benefitted especially handsomely from this trade. As invasions and conflicts disrupted northern India, southern regions experienced rapid economic development. The Chola kingdom provided relative stability in the south, and Chola expansion in southeast Asia opened markets for Indian merchants and producers. Coastal towns like Calicut and Quilon flourished, and they attracted increasing numbers of residents.

The Chola rulers allowed considerable autonomy to their subjects, and the *Temples* towns and villages of southern India largely organized their own affairs. Public life *and Society* revolved around Hindu temples that served as economic and social centers. Southern Indians used their growing wealth to build hundreds of elaborate Hindu temples, which organized agricultural activities, coordinated work on irrigation systems, and maintained reserves of surplus production for use in times of need. These temples also provided basic schooling for boys in the community, and larger temples offered advanced instruction as well. Temples often possessed large tracts of agricultural land, and they sometimes employed hundreds of people, including brahmins, attendants, musicians, servants, and slaves. To meet their financial obligations to employees, temple administrators collected a portion of the agricultural yield from lands subject to temple authority. Administrators were also responsible for keeping order in their communities and delivering tax receipts to the Cholas and other political authorities.

Temple authorities also served as bankers, made loans, and invested in commercial and business ventures. As a result, temples promoted the economic development of southern India by encouraging production and trade. Temple authorities cooperated closely with the leaders of merchant guilds in seeking commercial opportunities to exploit. The guilds often made gifts of land or money to temples by way of consolidating their relationship with the powerful economic institutions. Temples thus grew prosperous and became crucial to the economic health of southern India.

Maritime trade flourished in postclassical times. This ninth-century relief carving from the Buddhist temple at Borobodur in Java depicts a typical southeast Asian ship. • Ralph Agence/Liaison International

Cross-Cultural Trade in the Indian Ocean Basin

Indian prosperity sprang partly from the productivity of Indian society, but it depended also on the vast wealth that circulated in the commercial world of the Indian Ocean basin. Trade in the Indian Ocean was not new in postclassical times: Indian merchants had already ventured to southeast Asia during the classical era, and they dealt regularly with mariners from the Roman empire who traveled to India in search of pepper. During the postclassical era, however, larger ships and improved commercial organization supported a dramatic surge in the volume and value of trade in the Indian Ocean basin.

Dhows and Junks   The earliest voyaging in the Indian Ocean followed the coastlines, but already in classical times mariners recognized the rhythms of the monsoons. Over time they built larger ships, which enabled them to leave the coasts behind and ply the blue waters of the Indian Ocean: the dhows favored by Indian, Persian, and Arab sailors averaged about one hundred tons burden in 1000 and four hundred tons in 1500. After the naval and commercial expansion of the Song dynasty, large Chinese and southeast Asian junks also sailed the Indian Ocean: some of them could carry one thousand tons of cargo.

As large, stable ships came into use, mariners increasingly entrusted their crafts and cargoes to the reasonably predictable monsoons and sailed directly across the Arabian Sea and the Bay of Bengal. In the age of sail, it was impossible to make a round trip across the entire Indian Ocean without spending months at distant ports waiting for the winds to change, so merchants usually conducted their trade in stages.

Emporia   Because India stood in the middle of the Indian Ocean basin, it was a natural site for emporia and warehouses. Merchants coming from east Africa or Persia exchanged their cargoes at Cambay, Calicut, or Quilon for goods to take back west with the winter monsoon. Mariners from China or southeast Asia called at Indian ports and traded their cargoes for goods to ship east with the summer monsoon.

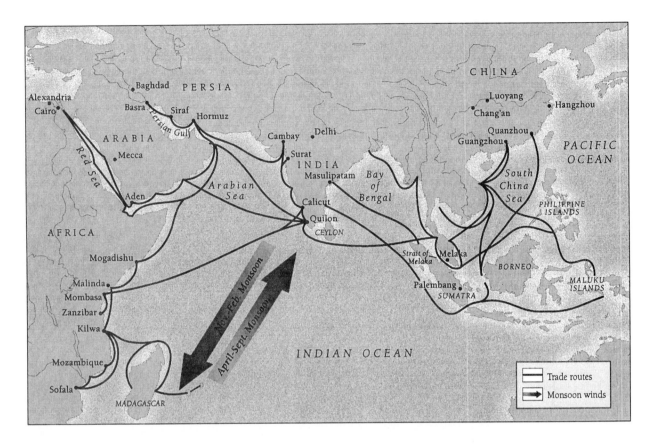

MAP [15.2]

The trading world of the Indian Ocean basin.

Merchants also built emporia outside India: the storytelling mariner Buzurg ibn Shahriyar came from the emporium of Siraf on the Persian Gulf, a port city surrounded by desert that nevertheless enjoyed fabulous wealth because of its trade with China, India, and east Africa. Because of their central location, however, Indian ports became the principal clearinghouses of trade in the Indian Ocean basin, and they became remarkably cosmopolitan centers. Hindus, Buddhists, Muslims, Jews, and others who inhabited the Indian port cities did business with counterparts from all over the eastern hemisphere and swapped stories like those recounted by Buzurg ibn Shahriyar.

Trade Goods

Particularly after the establishment of the Umayyad and Abbasid dynasties in southwest Asia and the Tang and Song dynasties in China, trade in the Indian Ocean surged. Prosperity in those lands created enormous demand for silk and porcelain from China, spices from southeast Asia, pepper, gems, pearls, and cotton from India, incense and horses from Arabia and southwest Asia, and gold, ivory, and slaves from east Africa. Indian merchants and mariners sometimes traveled to distant lands in search of these goods, but the carrying trade between India and points west fell mostly into Arab and Persian hands. During the Song dynasty Chinese junks also ventured into the western Indian Ocean and called at ports as far away as east Africa. In the Bay of Bengal and the China seas, Malay and Chinese vessels were most prominent.

Specialized Production

As the volume of trade in the Indian Ocean basin increased, lands around the ocean began to engage in specialized production of commodities for the commercial market. For centuries Indian artisans had enjoyed a reputation for the manufacture of fine cotton textiles, which they produced in small quantities for wealthy consumers.

Mealtime for a Persian merchant and his two companions served by three women attendants in this ceiling decoration from the Ajanta caves.   •   © The British Library

In postclassical times these wares came into high demand throughout the trading world of the Indian Ocean basin. In response to that demand, Indian artisans built thriving local industries around the production of high-quality cotton textiles. These industries influenced the structure of the Indian economy: they created a demand for specific agricultural products, provided a livelihood for thousands of artisans, and enabled consumers to import different goods from regions that specialized in the production of other commodities.

Alongside textiles other specialized industries that emerged in postclassical India included sugar refining, leather tanning, stone carving, and carpet weaving. Iron and steel production also emerged as prominent industries. Indian artisans became well known especially for the production of high-carbon steel that held a lethal cutting edge and that consequently came into high demand for use in knives and swords. Other lands concentrated on the production of different manufactured goods and agricultural commodities: China produced silk, porcelain, and lacquerware, southeast Asian lands provided fine spices, while incense, horses, and dates came from southwest Asia, and east Africa contributed gold, ivory, and slaves. Thus trade encouraged specialized production and economic development in all lands participating in the trade networks of the Indian Ocean basin: cross-cultural trade in postclassical times influenced the structure of economies and societies throughout much of the eastern hemisphere.

Caste and Society

The political, economic, and social changes of the postclassical era brought a series of challenges for India's caste system. Yet the system adapted to new circumstances and survived. Indeed, it became more complex and extended its geographical reach.

The caste system closely reflected changes in Indian society. It adapted to the arrival of migrants, for example, and helped to integrate them into Indian society. As Turkish peoples or Muslim merchants pursued opportunities in India, they gained recognition as distinct groups under the umbrella of the caste system. They established codes of conduct both for the regulation of behavior within their own groups and for guidance in dealing with members of other castes. Within a few generations their descendants had become absorbed into Indian society.

Caste and Migration

The caste system also accommodated the social changes brought about by trade and economic development. As merchants and manufacturers became increasingly important in the larger economy, they organized powerful guilds to represent their interests. Merchant guilds in particular wielded political and economic influence, since their members enjoyed access to considerable wealth and contributed in large measure to the economic health of their states. Guild members forged group identities by working within the caste system. Merchants specializing in particular types of commerce, such as the silk, cotton, or spice trade, established themselves as distinct subcastes, as did artisans working in particular industries, such as the iron, steel, or leather business.

Caste and Social Change

Besides becoming more complex, the caste system also extended its geographical reach. Caste distinctions first became prominent in northern India following Aryan migrations into the subcontinent. During the postclassical era, the caste system became securely established in southern India as well. Economic development aided this process by encouraging commercial relationships between southern merchants and their caste-conscious counterparts in the north. The emergence of merchant and craft guilds in southern regions strengthened the caste system, since guild members usually organized as a subcaste. Powerful temples also fostered caste distinctions. Caste-conscious brahmins who supervised the temples were particularly effective promotors of the system, since temples provided the only formal education available in most regions and also served as centers of local social life. By about the eleventh century C.E., caste had become the principal basis of social organization in southern India.

Expansion of the Caste System

THE MEETING OF HINDU
AND ISLAMIC TRADITIONS

The Indian cultural landscape underwent a thorough transformation during the postclassical era. Jainism and Buddhism lost much of their popular following. Neither faith completely disappeared from India, and indeed, a small community continues to observe each faith there even today. After 1000 C.E., however, Hindu and Islamic traditions increasingly dominated the cultural and religious life of India.

Hinduism and Islam differed profoundly as religious faiths. The Hindu pantheon made places for numerous gods and spirits, for example, whereas Islamic theology stood on the foundation of a firm and uncompromising monotheism. Yet both faiths attracted large popular followings throughout the subcontinent, with Hinduism predominating in southern India and Islam in the north.

Southern Indian artists often portrayed Shiva in bronze sculptures as a four-armed lord of dancers. In this figure from the Chola dynasty, Shira crushes a dwarf demon symbolizing ignorance with his foot. One hand holds a bell to awaken his devotees, another bears the fire used by Shiva as creator and destroyer of the world, and a third gestures Shiva's benevolence toward his followers.

• Giraudon/Art Resource, NY

The Development of Hinduism

Toward the end of the first millennium C.E., Buddhism flourished in east Asia, central Asia, and parts of southeast Asia but came under great pressure in India. Like Mahayana Buddhism, both Hinduism and Islam promised salvation to devout individuals, and they gradually attracted Buddhists to their own communities. Invasions of India by Turkish peoples hastened the decline of Buddhism because the invaders looted and destroyed Buddhist stupas and shrines. In 1196 Muslim forces overran the city of Nalanda and ravaged the schools where Xuanzang and other foreign pilgrims had studied with the world's leading Buddhist philosophers and theologians. The conquerors torched Buddhist libraries and either killed or exiled thousands of monks living at Nalanda. Buddhism soon became a minor faith in the land of its birth.

Vishnu and Shiva   Hinduism benefitted from the decline of Buddhism. One reason for the increasing popularity of Hinduism was the remarkable growth of devotional cults, particularly those dedicated to Vishnu and Shiva, two of the most important deities in the Hindu pantheon. Vishnu was the preserver of the world, a god who observed the universe from the heavens and who occasionally entered the world in human form in order to resist evil or communicate his teachings. By contrast, Shiva was both a god of fertility and a destructive deity: he brought life but also took it away when its season had passed. Hindus associated many gods and goddesses with Vishnu and Shiva, and they recognized other cults that were altogether independent of these two. But the most popular devotional cults focused on veneration of Vishnu or Shiva.

Devotional Cults   Hindus embraced the new cults warmly because they promised salvation. Devotional cults became especially popular in southern India, where individuals or family groups went to great lengths to honor their chosen deities. By venerating images of Vishnu or Shiva, offering them food and drink, and meditating on the deities and their qualities, Hindus hoped to achieve a mystic union with the gods that would bring grace and salvation. As the cults proliferated, temples and shrines dotted the landscape of southern India. Veneration of Vishnu and Shiva gradually became popular among Hindus in northern as well as southern India.

The significance of Hinduism extended well beyond popular religion: it also influenced philosophy. Brahmin philosophers such as Shankara and Ramanuja took the Upanishads as a point of departure for subtle reasoning and sophisticated metaphysics. Shankara, a southern Indian devotee of Shiva who was active during the early

Elaborate temple compounds featuring individual temples and shrines devoted to Shiva, Vishnu, and other deities promoted the spread of devotional Hinduism. Carved reliefs from the seventh century at the temple at Mamallapuram, depicted here, celebrate the Ganges River as a gift from Shiva and other gods. • New York Public Library

ninth century C.E., took it upon himself to digest all sacred Hindu writings and harmonize their sometimes contradictory teachings into a single, consistent system of thought. In a manner reminiscent of Plato, Shankara held that the physical world was illusion—a figment of the imagination—and that ultimate reality lay beyond the physical senses. Although he was a worshiper of Shiva, Shankara mistrusted emotional services and ceremonies, insisting that only by disciplined logical reasoning could human beings understand the ultimate reality of Brahman, the impersonal world-soul of the Upanishads. Only then could they appreciate the fundamental unity of the world, which Shankara considered a perfectly understandable expression of ultimate reality, even though to human physical senses that same world appears chaotic and incomprehensible. *Shankara*

Ramanuja, a devotee of Vishnu who was active during the eleventh and early twelfth centuries C.E., challenged Shankara's uncompromising insistence on logic. Also a brahmin philosopher from southern India, Ramanuja's thought reflected the deep influence of devotional cults. According to Ramanuja, intellectual understanding of ultimate reality was less important than personal union with the deity. Ramanuja granted that intellectual efforts could lead to comprehension of reality, but he held that genuine bliss came from salvation and identification of individuals with their gods. He followed the *Bhagavad Gita* in recommending intense devotion to Vishnu, and he taught that by placing themselves in the hands of Vishnu, devotees would win the god's grace and live forever in his presence. Thus in contrast to Shankara's consistent, intellectual system of thought, Ramanuja's philosophy pointed toward a Hindu theology of salvation. Indeed, his thought inspired the development of devotional cults throughout India, and it serves even today as a philosophical foundation for Hindu popular religion. *Ramanuja*

Islam and Its Appeal

The Islamic faith did not attract much immediate interest among Indians when it arrived in the subcontinent. It won gradual acceptance in merchant communities where foreign Muslim traders took local spouses and found a place in Indian society. Elsewhere, however, circumstances did not favor its adoption, since it often arrived in the cultural baggage of conquering peoples. Muslim conquerors generally reserved important political and military positions for their Arab, Persian, and Turkish companions. Only rarely did they allow Indians—even those who had converted to Islam—to hold sensitive posts. Thus quite apart from the fact that they introduced a foreign faith radically different from those of the subcontinent, conquerors offered little incentive for Indians to convert to Islam.

Conversion to Islam   Gradually, however, many Indians converted to Islam. By 1500 c.e. Indian Muslims numbered perhaps twenty-five million—about one-quarter of the subcontinent's population. Some Indians adopted Islam in hope of improving their positions in society: Hindus of lower castes, for example, hoped to escape discrimination by converting to a faith that recognized the equality of all believers. In fact, Hindus rarely improved their social standing by conversion. Often members of an entire caste or subcaste adopted Islam en masse, and after conversion they continued to play the same social and economic roles that they had before.

Sufis   In India as elsewhere, the most effective agents of conversion to Islam were Sufi mystics. Sufis encouraged a personal, emotional, devotional approach to Islam. They did not insist on fine points of doctrine, and they sometimes even permitted their followers to observe rituals or venerate spirits not recognized by the Islamic faith. Because of their piety and sincerity, however, Sufi missionaries attracted individuals searching for a faith that could provide comfort and meaning for their personal lives. Thus, like Hinduism, Indian Islam emphasized piety and devotion. Even though Hinduism and Islam were profoundly different faiths, they encouraged the cultivation of similar spiritual values that transcended the social and cultural boundary lines of postclassical India.

The Bhakti Movement   In some ways the gap between Hinduism and Islam narrowed in postclassical India because both faiths drew on long-established and long-observed cultural traditions. Sufis, for example, often attracted schools of followers in the manner of Indian gurus, spiritual leaders who taught Hindu values to disciples who congregated around them. Even more important was the development of the *bhakti* movement, a cult of love and devotion that ultimately sought to erase the distinction between Hinduism and Islam. The bhakti movement emerged in southern India during the twelfth century, and it originally encouraged a traditional piety and devotion to Hindu values. As the movement spread to the north, bhakti leaders increasingly encountered Muslims and became deeply attracted to certain Islamic values, especially monotheism and the notion of spiritual equality of all believers.

Guru Kabir   The bhakti movement gradually rejected the exclusive features of both Hinduism and Islam. Thus guru Kabir (1440–1518), a blind weaver who was one of the most famous bhakti teachers, went so far as to teach that Shiva, Vishnu, and Allah were all manifestations of a single, universal deity, whom all devout believers could find within their own hearts. The bhakti movement did not succeed in harmonizing Hinduism and Islam. Nevertheless, like the Sufis, bhakti teachers promoted values that helped to build bridges between India's social and cultural communities.

THE INFLUENCE OF INDIAN SOCIETY IN SOUTHEAST ASIA

Just as China stood at the center of a larger east Asian society, India served as the principal source of political and cultural traditions widely observed throughout south and southeast Asia. Indeed, during classical and postclassical times, Indian influences on the mainland and in the islands of southeast Asia were so strong that historians often speak of the "Indianized states" of southeast Asia. For a millennium and more, southeast Asian peoples adapted Indian political structures and religions to local needs and interests. Although Indian armed forces rarely ventured into the region, southeast Asian lands reflected the influence of Indian society, as merchants introduced Hinduism, Buddhism, Sanskrit writings, and Indian forms of political organization. Beginning about the twelfth century, Islam also found solid footing in southeast Asia, as Muslim merchants, many of them Indians, established trading communities in the important port cities of the region. During the next five hundred years, Islam attracted a sizable following and became a permanent feature in much of southeast Asia.

The Indianized States of Southeast Asia

Indian merchants visited the islands and mainland of southeast Asia from an early date, perhaps as early as 500 B.C.E. By the early centuries C.E., they had become familiar figures throughout southeast Asia, and their presence brought opportunities for the native ruling elites of the region. In exchange for spices and exotic products such as pearls, aromatics, and animal skins, Indian merchants brought textiles, beads, gold, silver, manufactured metal goods, and objects used in political or religious rituals. Southeast Asian rulers used the profits from this trade to consolidate their political control.

Indian Influence in Southeast Asia

Meanwhile, southeast Asian ruling elites became acquainted with Indian political and cultural traditions. Without necessarily giving up their own traditions, they borrowed Indian forms of political organization and accepted Indian religious faiths. On the model of Indian states, for example, they adopted kingship as the principal form of political authority. Regional kings in southeast Asia surrounded themselves with courts featuring administrators and rituals similar to those found in India.

Ruling elites also sponsored the introduction of Hinduism or Buddhism—sometimes both—into their courts. They embraced Indian literature like the *Ramayana* and the *Mahabharata,* which promoted Hindu values, as well as treatises that explained Buddhist views on the world. They did not show much enthusiasm for the Indian caste system and continued to acknowledge the deities and nature spirits that southeast Asian peoples had venerated for centuries. But ruling elites readily accepted Hinduism and Buddhism, which they found attractive because the Indian faiths reinforced the principle of monarchical rule.

The first state known to have become Indianized in this fashion was Funan, which dominated the lower reaches of the Mekong River (including parts of modern Cambodia and Vietnam) between the first and the sixth century C.E. The rulers of Funan consolidated their grip on the Mekong valley and built a capital city at the port of Oc Eo. Funan grew wealthy because it dominated the Isthmus of Kra, the narrow portion of the Malay peninsula, where merchants transported trade goods between

Funan

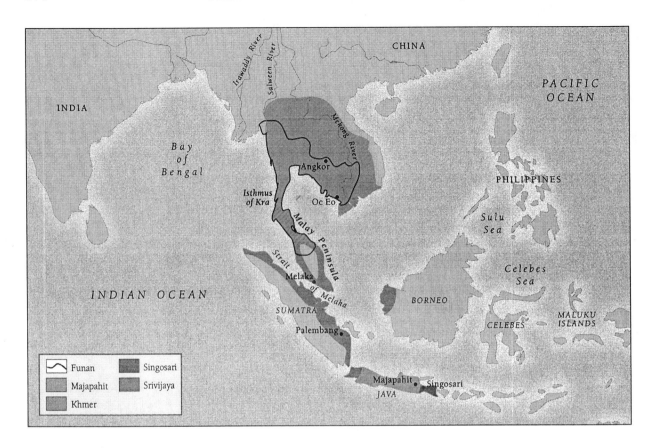

MAP [15.3]

Early states of southeast Asia.

China and India. (The short portage enabled them to avoid a long voyage around the Malay peninsula.) The rulers of Funan drew enormous wealth by controlling trade between China and India. They used their profits to construct an elaborate system of water storage and irrigation—so extensive that aerial photography still reveals its lines—that served a productive agricultural economy in the Mekong delta.

As trade with India became an increasingly important part of Funan's economy, the ruling classes adopted Indian political, cultural, and religious traditions. They took the term *raja* ("king") for themselves and claimed divine sanction for their rule in the manner of Hindu rulers in India. They established positions for administrators and bureaucrats such as those found at Indian courts and conducted official business in Sanskrit. They introduced Indian ceremonies and rituals and worshiped Vishnu, Shiva, and other Hindu deities. They continued to honor local deities, particularly water spirits venerated widely throughout southeast Asia, but they eagerly welcomed Hinduism, which offered additional recognition and divine legitimacy for their rule. At first Indian cultural and religious traditions were most prominent and most often observed at ruling courts. Over the longer term, however, these traditions extended well beyond ruling elites and won a secure place in southeast Asian society.

During the sixth century C.E., a bitter power struggle weakened Funan internally. Peoples from the north took advantage of this weakness, migrated to the lower Mekong valley in large numbers, and overwhelmed Funan. Chams settled in the southern portion of modern Vietnam, and Khmers dominated in the region occupied by modern Cambodia. By the late sixth century, Funan's intricate irrigation system had fallen into ruins, and Funan itself soon passed into oblivion.

After the fall of Funan, political leadership in southeast Asia passed to the king- *Srivijaya*
dom of Srivijaya (670–1025 C.E.) based on the island of Sumatra. The kings of Srivijaya built a powerful navy and controlled commerce in southeast Asian waters. They
compelled port cities in southeast Asia to recognize their authority, and they financed their navy and bureaucracy from taxes levied on ships passing through the
region. They maintained an all-sea trade route between China and India, eliminating
the need for the portage of trade goods across the Isthmus of Kra. As the volume of
shipping increased in the postclassical era, the Srivijaya kingdom prospered until the
expansive Chola kingdom of southern India eclipsed it in the eleventh century.

With the decline of Srivijaya, the kingdoms of Angkor (889–1431 C.E.), Singosari (1222–1292 C.E.), and Majapahit (1293–1520 C.E.) dominated affairs in
southeast Asia. Many differences characterized the Indianized states. Funan had its
base of operations in the Mekong valley, Srivijaya at Palembang in southern Sumatra, Angkor in Cambodia, and Singosari and Majapahit on the island of Java. Funan
and Angkor were land-based states that derived most of their wealth from productive agricultural economies, whereas Srivijaya, Singosari, and Majapahit were island-
based states that prospered because they controlled maritime trade. Funan and Majapahit were largely Hindu states, but the kings of Srivijaya and Angkor made deep
commitments to Buddhism. Native southeast Asian traditions survived in all the Indianized states, and at the court of Singosari, religious authorities fashioned a cultural blend of Hindu, Buddhist, and indigenous values. Sculptures at the Singosari
court depicted Hindu and Buddhist personalities, for example, but used them to
honor local deities and natural spirits rather than Indian deities.

The magnificent monuments of Angkor testify eloquently to the influence of In- *Angkor*
dian traditions in southeast Asia. Beginning in the ninth century, kings of the
Khmers began to build a capital city at Angkor Thom. With the aid of brahmin advisors from India, the kings designed the city as a microcosmic reflection of the Hindu
world order. At the center they built a temple representing the Himalayan Mount
Meru, the sacred abode of Shiva, and surrounded it with numerous smaller temples
representing other parts of the Hindu universe.

As the Khmers turned to Buddhism during the twelfth and thirteenth centuries,
they added Buddhist temples to the complex, though without removing the earlier
structures inspired by Hinduism. The entire complex formed a square with sides of
about three kilometers (two miles), surrounded by a moat filled from the Mekong
River. During the twelfth century the Khmer kings constructed a smaller but even
more elaborate temple center at Angkor Wat, about one kilometer (just over half a
mile) from Angkor Thom.

The Khmers abandoned Angkor in 1431 after Thai peoples invaded the capital
and left much of it in ruins. Soon the jungle reclaimed both Angkor Thom and
Angkor Wat, which remained largely forgotten until French missionaries and explorers rediscovered the sites in the mid-nineteenth century. Rescued from the jungle,
the temple complexes of Angkor stand today as vivid reminders of the influence of
Indian political, cultural, and religious traditions in southeast Asia.

The Arrival of Islam

Muslim merchants had ventured into southeast Asia by the eighth century, but only
during the tenth century did they become prominent in the region. Some came
from southern Arabia or Persia, but many were Indians from Gujarat or the port
cities of southern India. Thus Indian influence helped to establish Islam as well as
Hinduism and Buddhism in southeast Asia.

General view of the temple complex dedicated to Vishnu at Angkor Wat.   •   Alain Evrard/Photo Researchers, Inc.

Conversion to Islam   For several centuries Islam maintained a quiet presence in southeast Asia. Small communities of foreign merchants observed their faith in the port cities of the region but attracted little interest on the part of the native inhabitants. Gradually, however, ruling elites, traders, and others who had regular dealings with foreign Muslims became interested in the faith. During the late thirteenth century, the Venetian traveler Marco Polo visited the island of Sumatra and noted that many residents of the towns and cities had converted to Islam, while those living in the countryside and the hills retained their inherited traditions.

As in the cases of Hinduism and Buddhism, Islam did not enter southeast Asia as an exclusive faith. Ruling elites who converted to Islam often continued to honor Hindu, Buddhist, or native southeast Asian traditions. They adopted Islam less as an exclusive and absolute creed than as a faith that facilitated their dealings with foreign Muslims and provided additional divine sanction for their rule. Rarely did they push their subjects to convert to Islam, although they allowed Sufi mystics to preach their faith before popular audiences. As in India, Sufis appealed to a large public because of their reputation for sincerity and holiness. They allowed converts to retain inherited customs while adapting the message of Islam to local needs and interests.

Melaka   During the fifteenth century the spread of Islam gained momentum in southeast Asia, largely because the powerful state of Melaka sponsored the faith throughout the region. Founded during the late fourteenth century by Paramesvara, a rebellious prince from Sumatra, Melaka took advantage of its strategic location in the Strait of Melaka, near modern Singapore, and soon became prominent in the trading world of southeast Asia. During its earliest days Melaka was more a lair of pirates than a legitimate state. By the mid-fifteenth century, however, Melaka had built a substantial navy that patrolled the waters of southeast Asia and protected the region's sea-lanes. Melakan fleets compelled ships to call at the port of Melaka, where ruling authorities levied taxes on the value of their cargoes. Thus like the Indianized states of earlier centuries, Melaka became a powerful state through the control of maritime trade.

In one respect, though, Melaka differed significantly from the earlier Indianized states. Although it began as a Hindu state, Melaka soon became predominantly Islamic. About the mid-fifteenth century the Melakan ruling class converted to Islam. It welcomed theologians, Sufis, and other Islamic authorities to Melaka and sponsored missionary campaigns to spread Islam throughout southeast Asia. By the end of the fifteenth century, mosques had begun to define the urban landscapes of Java, Sumatra, and the Malay peninsula, and Islam had made its first appearance in the spice-bearing islands of Maluku and in the southern islands of the Philippine archipelago.

Thus within several centuries of its arrival, Islam was a prominent feature in the cultural landscape of southeast Asia. Along with Hinduism and Buddhism, Islam helped link southeast Asian lands to the larger cultural world of India and to the larger commercial world of the Indian Ocean basin.

With respect to political organization, India differed from postclassical societies in China, southwest Asia, and the eastern Mediterranean basin: India did not experience a return of centralized imperial rule such as that provided by the Tang and Song dynasties, the Umayyad and Abbasid dynasties, and the Byzantine empire. In other respects, however, India's development was similar to that of other postclassical societies. Increased agricultural production fueled population growth and urbanization while trade encouraged specialized industrial production and rapid economic growth. The vigorous and voluminous commerce of the Indian Ocean basin influenced the structure of economies and societies from east Asia to east Africa. It brought prosperity especially to India, which not only contributed cotton, pepper, sugar, iron, steel, and other products to the larger hemispheric economy but also served as a major clearinghouse of trade. Like contemporary societies, postclassical India experienced cultural change, and Indian traditions deeply influenced the cultural development of other lands. Hinduism and Islam emerged as the two most popular religious faiths within the subcontinent, while Indian merchants helped to establish Hinduism, Buddhism, and Islam in southeast Asian lands. Throughout the postclassical era India participated fully in the larger hemispheric zone of cross-cultural communication and exchange.

CHRONOLOGY

1st to 6th century	Kingdom of Funan
606–648	Reign of Harsha
670–1025	Kingdom of Srivijaya
711	Conquest of Sind by Umayyad forces
early 9th century	Life of Shankara
850–1267	Chola kingdom
889–1431	Kingdom of Angkor
1001–1027	Raids on India by Mahmud of Ghazni
11th to 12th century	Life of Ramanuja
12th century	Beginning of the bhakti movement
1206–1526	Sultanate of Delhi
1336–1565	Kingdom of Vijayanagar
1440–1518	Life of guru Kabir

FOR FURTHER READING

Aziz Ahmad. *Studies in Islamic Culture in the Indian Environment*. Oxford, 1964. A scholarly analysis of the arrival of Islam and its effects in India.

A. L. Basham. *The Wonder That Was India*. New York, 1954. A popular survey by a leading scholar of ancient India.

Al-Biruni. *Alberuni's India*. 2 vols. Trans. by E. Sachau. London, 1910. English translation of al-Biruni's eleventh-century description of Indian customs, religion, philosophy, geography, and astronomy.

Buzurg ibn Shahriyar. *The Book of the Wonders of India: Mainland, Sea and Islands*. Trans. by G. S. P. Freeman-Grenville. London, 1981. Stories and tall tales of a tenth-century mariner who sailed frequently between Persia and India.

K. N. Chaudhuri. *Asia before Europe: Economy and Civilisation of the Indian Ocean from the Rise of Islam to 1750*. Cambridge, 1990. Controversial and penetrating analysis of economic, social, and cultural structures shaping societies of the Indian Ocean basin.

————. *Trade and Civilisation in the Indian Ocean: An Economic History from the Rise of Islam to 1750*. Cambridge, 1985. Brilliant analysis of the commercial life of the Indian Ocean basin by a prominent scholar.

Georges Coedès. *The Indianized States of Southeast Asia*. Trans. by S. B. Cowing. Honolulu, 1968. A careful survey that is still useful, though somewhat dated.

William Theodore de Bary et al., eds. *Sources of Indian Tradition*. 2 vols. New York, 1958. An important collection of primary sources in English translation.

Bernard Groslier and Jacques Arthaud. *Angkor: Art and Civilization*. Rev. ed. Trans. by E. E. Smith. New York, 1966. Well-illustrated summary, concentrating on the magnificent temple complexes at Angkor.

Kenneth R. Hall. *Maritime Trade and State Development in Early Southeast Asia*. Honolulu, 1985. Examines the link between long-distance trade and state building in southeast Asia.

S. M. Ikram. *Muslim Civilization in India*. Ed. by A. T. Embree. New York, 1964. Important survey of Islam and its impact in India.

Eleanor Mannikka. *Angkor Wat: Time, Space, and Kingship*. Honolulu, 1996. A detailed analysis of the magnificent Cambodian temple complex from an architectural point of view.

Patricia Risso. *Merchants and Faith: Muslim Commerce and Culture in the Indian Ocean*. Boulder, 1995. Draws on recent scholarship in surveying the activities of Muslim merchants in the Indian Ocean basin from the seventh to the nineteenth centuries.

Kernial Singh Sandhu. *Early Malaysia*. Singapore, 1973. Survey concentrating on the periods of Indian and Islamic influence in southeast Asia.

Burton Stein. *Vijayanagara*. Cambridge, 1989. A recent study of the southern Hindu kingdom concentrating on political and economic history.

Romila Thapar. *A History of India*. Harmondsworth, 1966. A sound, popular survey by one of the world's leading students of early Indian history.

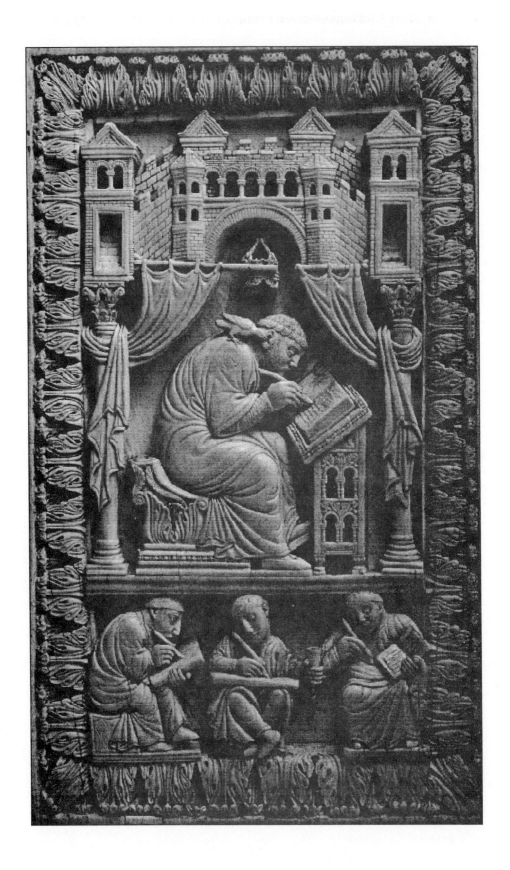

THE FOUNDATIONS
OF CHRISTIAN SOCIETY
IN WESTERN EUROPE

• • • •

*I*n 802 C.E. a most unusual traveler made his way from Baghdad to Aachen (in modern Germany), capital of the western European empire ruled by Charlemagne. The traveler was an albino elephant, a diplomatic gift from the Abbasid caliph Harun al-Rashid to Charlemagne. The elephant—whom Harun named Abu al-Abbas, in honor of the Abbasid dynasty's founder—was born in India and went to Baghdad as a present from an Indian king. From Baghdad the animal accompanied an embassy overland to Syria, then traveled by ship from Beirut to Malta and Rome, and finally went overland north to Charlemagne's court. Abu al-Abbas must have shivered through the cold, damp winters of western Europe, yet he overawed and amazed all who beheld him until his death in 810.

Charlemagne dispatched at least three embassies to Baghdad and received three in return. The embassies dealt with several issues: the safety of Christian pilgrims and merchants traveling in Abbasid-controlled Syria and Palestine, relations between Charlemagne's realm and neighboring Muslim Spain, and policy toward the Byzantine empire, which stood between western Europe and the Abbasid caliphate. Charlemagne's realm was weak and poor compared to the Abbasid empire, and by the mid-ninth century it was well on the way to dissolution. For about half a century, however, it seemed that Charlemagne and his successors might be able to establish a centralized imperial state in western Europe. His dealings with Harun al-Rashid— and the unusual odyssey of the elephant Abu al-Abbas—indicated that Charlemagne had the potential and the ambition to establish a western European empire similar to the Byzantine and Abbasid realms.

Historians refer to the era from about 500 to 1500 C.E. as the medieval period of European history—the "middle ages" falling between the classical era and modern times. During the early medieval period, from about 500 to 1000 C.E., European peoples recovered from the invasions that brought the Roman empire to an end and laid the political, economic, and cultural foundations for a new society. Europeans did not rebuild a powerful society as quickly as did the Abbasids in southwest Asia or the Tang and Song emperors of China: like India during the postclassical era, early medieval Europe was a politically disunited and disorganized region. Unlike

An ivory book cover carved in the tenth century depicts Pope Gregory I at his writing desk. • Erich Lessing/Art Resource, NY

India, though, Europe mostly disengaged from hemispheric communication and exchange. Only about the tenth century, after the establishment of effective political authority and a productive agricultural economy, were western European peoples able to reenter the larger trading world of the eastern hemisphere.

Three developments of the early medieval era served as foundations for the development of the powerful European society that emerged in the high middle ages. First, following the disruption caused by invasions and depopulation, the peoples of western Europe restored political order. Unlike their counterparts in southwest Asia and China, they did not return to centralized imperial rule, but instead resorted to a decentralized, feudal political order that vested public authority mostly in local and regional rulers. Second, European peoples began a process of economic recovery. They did not build large cities or generate a powerful industrial economy like those of the Byzantine, Abbasid, Tang, and Song empires. But they boosted agricultural production by increasing the amount of land under cultivation and introducing new tools and techniques, thus laying an agricultural foundation for trade and rapid economic development after the tenth century. Third, European peoples built an institutional framework that enabled the Christian church based in Rome to provide religious leadership and maintain cultural unity throughout western Europe. Thus, just as Confucianism, Buddhism, Hinduism, Islam, and eastern Christianity shaped cultural values in other lands, western Christianity emerged as the principal source of cultural authority in western Europe.

THE QUEST FOR POLITICAL ORDER

After toppling Rome's authority in the late fifth century C.E., Germanic invaders established successor states throughout the western Roman empire. From the fifth through the eighth century, continuing invasions and conflicts among the invaders themselves left western Europe in shambles. For a brief moment during the late eighth and early ninth centuries, it looked as though one group of Germanic invaders, the Franks, might reestablish imperial authority in western Europe. If they had succeeded, they might have played a role similar to that of the Sui and Tang dynasties in China by reviving centralized imperial rule after a hiatus of several centuries. By the late ninth century, however, the Frankish empire had fallen victim to internal power struggles and a fresh series of invasions by Muslims, Hungarian Magyars, and Vikings. Political authority in early medieval Europe then devolved to local and regional jurisdictions, and Europeans adopted a decentralized, feudal type of political organization.

Germanic Successor States

In 476 C.E. the Germanic general Odoacer deposed the last of the western Roman emperors, but the administrative apparatus of the Roman empire did not immediately disappear. Provincial governors continued to rule in their territories, aided by Roman bureaucrats and tax collectors, and Roman generals continued to field armies throughout the crumbling empire. Cities of the western Roman empire, however, lost population during the fifth century, as invasions and contests for power disrupted trade and manufacturing. This decay of Roman cities hastened imperial decline. Deprived of legitimacy and resources supplied from Rome and the other major cities of the empire, imperial institutions progressively weakened.

By the late fifth century, the invaders had organized a series of Germanic king- *Germanic* doms as successor states in place of the Roman empire. Visigoths conquered Spain *Kingdoms* during the 470s, for example, and established a kingdom there that survived until the Muslim invasions of the early eighth century. Ostrogoths dominated Italy from the fifth century until Justinian's forces reasserted imperial authority there during the 530s. The departure of Byzantine armies from Italy created a power vacuum, which the Lombard people quickly moved to fill. Although they did not establish a tightly centralized monarchy, the Lombards maintained their hegemony throughout most of Italy from the mid-sixth until the mid-eighth century. Meanwhile, begin-ning about the mid-fifth century, Gaul fell under the control of other Germanic peoples, including the Burgundians, who settled in the southern and eastern re-gions, and the Franks, who brought the more northerly and westerly regions under their control. Angles, Saxons, and other Germanic peoples from Germany and Den-mark crossed the English Channel and established regional kingdoms in Britain.

Thus throughout the western portion of the Roman empire, Germanic peoples gradually displaced the authority and institutions of Rome. None of these peoples possessed the economic and military resources—much less the political and social organization—to dominate all the others and establish their hegemony throughout western Europe. Nevertheless, the Franks built an impressive imperial state that or-ganized, at least temporarily, about half of the territories formerly embraced by the western Roman empire.

Even though their empire survived for only a short time, the Franks profoundly *The Franks* influenced the political, social, and cultural development of western Europe. Rather than participate actively in the commercial world of the Mediterranean basin, the Franks constructed a society that drew on the agricultural resources of continental Europe. As a result, the center of gravity in western Europe shifted from Italy to the northern lands of France, Germany, and the Low Countries. Furthermore, the Franks oversaw the development of feudal institutions, which influenced European politics and society for a millennium and more. Finally, they made a firm alliance with the western Christian church and helped Roman Christianity maintain its cul-tural and religious primacy in western Europe.

The Franks and the Temporary Revival of Empire

As Roman authority crumbled during the late fifth century, the Franks appeared un-likely to play a prominent role in European affairs. They had little experience in gov-ernment and little exposure to Roman society. Some of their ancestors had lived within Roman boundaries since about the third century, and a few had probably converted to Christianity. But the Franks had developed a group identity only dur-ing the third century C.E., much later than the other Germanic peoples. Not until the fifth century did a strong military and political leader emerge from their midst. That leader was Clovis, who ruled the Franks from 481 until his death in 511.

Under Clovis the Franks became the preeminent military and political power in *Clovis* western Europe. In 486 Clovis led Frankish forces on a campaign that wiped out the last vestiges of Roman authority in Gaul. Then he imposed his authority on the Franks themselves. Finally, he organized campaigns against other Germanic peoples whose states bordered the Frankish realm in Gaul. By the time of his death, Clovis had thoroughly transformed the Franks. No longer were they just one among many Germanic peoples inhabiting a crumbling Roman empire. Instead, they ranked as the most powerful and dynamic of the peoples building new states in western Europe.

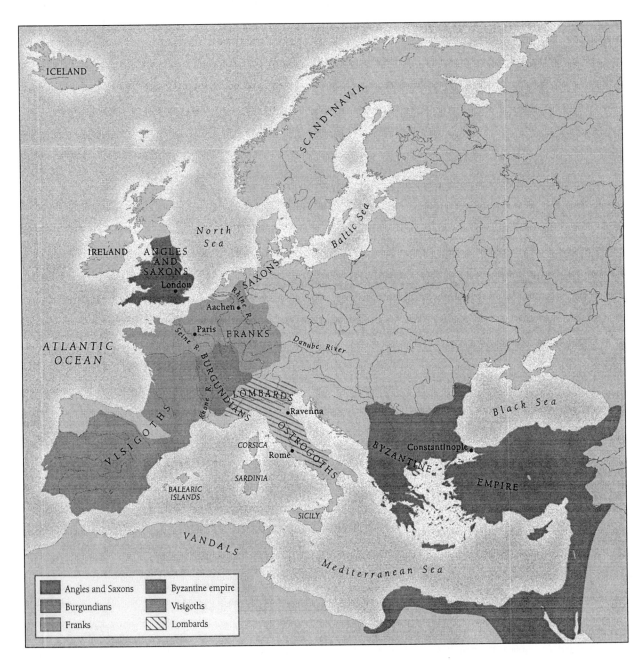

MAP [16.1]

Successor states to the Roman empire.

Clovis's Conversion   One reason for the Franks' rapid rise had to do with religion. Originally, all the Germanic invaders of the Roman empire were polytheists who honored a pantheon of warlike gods and other deities representing elements of nature such as the sun, moon, and wind. As they settled in and around the Roman empire, many Germanic peoples converted to Christianity. Most of them accepted Arian Christianity, which was popular in much of the eastern Roman empire. In both Rome and Constantinople, however, church authorities followed the decisions of church councils at Nicaea and Chalcedon and condemned Arian views as heretical. Unlike other Germanic peoples, the Franks remained mostly pagan until the time of Clovis, who converted to Roman rather than to Arian Christianity along with his army. Clovis's conversion probably reflected the influence of his wife Clotilda, a devout Christian who had long urged her husband to adopt her faith.

Manuscript illustration of the baptism of Clovis, witnessed by church officials on the left and Frankish nobles on the right. The dove represents the presence and approval of God at the ceremony. • Giraudon/Art Resource, NY

The Franks' conversion had large political implications. By adopting Roman rather than Arian Christianity, the Franks attracted the allegiance of the Christian population of the former Roman empire, as well as recognition and support from the pope and the hierarchy of the western Christian church. Alliance with the church of Rome greatly strengthened the Franks, who became the most powerful of the Germanic peoples between the fifth and ninth centuries.

The Carolingians

After Clovis's death the Frankish kings lost much of their authority, as aristocratic warriors seized effective control of affairs in their own regions. Nevertheless, Clovis's successors ruled the Frankish kingdom until the early eighth century, when the aristocratic clan of the Carolingians displaced the line of Clovis and asserted the authority of the central government. The Carolingian dynasty takes its name from its founder Charles (*Carolus* in Latin)—known as Charles Martel ("Charles the Hammer") because of his military prowess. Charles Martel himself did not rule as king of the Franks but served as deputy to the last of Clovis's descendants. In 751, however, Charles's son claimed the throne for himself.

Charlemagne

The Frankish realm reached its high point under Charles Martel's grandson Charlemagne ("Charles the Great"), who reigned from 768 to 814. Like King Harsha in India, Charlemagne temporarily reestablished centralized imperial rule in a society disrupted by invasion and contests for power between ambitious local rulers. Like Harsha again, Charlemagne possessed enormous energy, and the building of the Carolingian empire was in large measure his personal accomplishment. Although barely literate, Charlemagne was extremely intelligent. He spoke Latin, understood some Greek, and regularly conversed with theologians and other learned men. He maintained diplomatic relations with the Byzantine empire and the Abbasid caliphate. The gift of the white elephant Abu al-Abbas symbolized relations between the Carolingian and Abbasid empires, and the animal accompanied Charlemagne on many of his travels until its death.

GREGORY OF TOURS ON THE CONVERSION OF CLOVIS

• • •

St. Gregory (538–594 C.E.) was bishop of Tours in central Gaul for the last twenty-one years of his life. During this period he composed a History of the Franks, *which is the chief source of information about the early Franks. Gregory clearly embellished the story of Clovis's conversion to Christianity, but his account indicates the significance of the event both for Clovis and for the Roman church.*

The queen [Clotilda] did not cease to urge him [Clovis] to recognize the true God and cease worshiping idols. But he could not be influenced in any way to this belief, until at last a war arose with the Alamanni, in which he was driven by necessity to confess what before he had of his free will denied. It came about that as the two armies were fighting fiercely, there was much slaughter, and Clovis's army began to be in danger of destruction. He saw it and raised his eyes to heaven, and with remorse in his heart he burst into tears and cried: "Jesus Christ, whom Clotilda asserts to be the son of the living God, who art said to give aid to those in distress and to bestow victory on those who hope in thee, I beseech the glory of thy aid, with the vow that if thou wilt grant me victory over these enemies, and I shall know that power which she says that people dedicated in thy name have had from thee, I will believe in thee and be baptized in thy name. For I have invoked my own gods, but, as I see, they have withdrawn from aiding me; and therefore I believe that they possess no power, since they do not help those who obey them. I now call upon thee, I desire to believe thee, only let me be rescued from my adversaries." And when he said this, the Alamanni turned their backs, and began to disperse in flight. And when they saw that their king was killed, they submitted to the dominion of Clovis, saying: "Let not the people perish further, we pray; we are

yours now." And he stopped the fighting, and after encouraging his men retired in peace and told the queen how he had had merit to win the victory by calling on the name of Christ. . . .

Then the queen asked saint Remi, bishop of Rheims, to summon Clovis secretly, urging him to introduce the king to the word of salvation. And the bishop sent for him secretly and began to urge him to believe in the true God, maker of heaven and earth, and to cease worshiping idols, which could help neither themselves nor any one else. But the king said: "I gladly hear you, most holy father; but there remains one thing: the people who follow me cannot endure to abandon their gods; but I shall go and speak to them according to your words." He met with his followers, but before he could speak, the power of God anticipated him, and all the people cried out together: "O pious king, we reject our mortal gods, and we are ready to follow the immortal God whom Remi preaches." This was reported to the bishop, who was greatly rejoiced, and bade them get ready the baptismal font. . . . And the king was the first to ask to be baptized by the bishop. . . . And so the king confessed all-powerful God in the Trinity and was baptized in the name of the Father, Son, and Holy Spirit, and was anointed with the holy ointment with the sign of the cross of Christ. And of his army more than 3,000 were baptized.

SOURCE: Gregory of Tours. *History of the Franks.* Trans. by E. Brehaut New York: Columbia University Press, 1916, pp. 39–41. (Translation slightly modified.)

When Charlemagne inherited the Frankish throne, his realm included most of modern France as well as the lands that now form Belgium, the Netherlands, and southwestern Germany. Charlemagne was a conqueror in the mold of the Germanic peoples who invaded the Roman empire. By the time of his death in 814, Charlemagne had extended his authority to northeastern Spain, Bavaria, and Italy as far south as Rome. He campaigned for thirty-two years to impose his rule on the Saxons of northern Germany and repress their rebellions. Beyond the Carolingian empire proper, rulers in eastern Europe and southern Italy paid tribute to Charlemagne as imperial overlord.

Charlemagne established a court and capital at Aachen (in modern Germany), but like Harsha in India, he spent most of his reign traveling throughout his realm in order to maintain his authority. Such constant travel was necessary because Charlemagne did not have the financial resources to maintain an elaborate bureaucracy or an administrative apparatus that could implement his policies. Instead, Charlemagne relied on aristocratic deputies, known as counts, who held political, military, and legal authority in local jurisdictions.

Charlemagne's Administration

As represented in this bronze statue, Charlemagne spent much of his adult life on horseback. • Erich Lessing/Art Resource, NY

The counts often had their own political ambitions, and they sometimes pursued policies contrary to the interests of the central government. In an effort to bring the counts under tighter control, Charlemagne instituted a new group of imperial officials known as *missi dominici* ("envoys of the lord ruler"), who traveled every year to all local jurisdictions and reviewed the accounts of local authorities.

Charlemagne built the Frankish kingdom into an empire on the basis of military expeditions and began to outfit it with some centralized institutions. Yet he hesitated to call himself emperor because the imperial title would constitute a direct challenge to the authority of the Byzantine emperors, who regarded themselves as the sole and legitimate successors of the Roman emperors.

Only in the year 800 did Charlemagne accept the title of emperor. While campaigning in Italy Charlemagne attended religious services on Christmas Day conducted by Pope Leo III. During the services, the pope proclaimed Charlemagne emperor and placed an imperial crown on his head. It is not certain, but it is at least possible that Charlemagne did not know of the pope's plan and that Leo surprised him with an impromptu coronation: Charlemagne had no desire for strained relations with Byzantine emperors, who deeply resented the use of the imperial title in western Europe as a pretentious affront to their own dignity and authority. In any case Charlemagne had already built an imperial state, and his coronation constituted public recognition of his accomplishments.

Charlemagne as Emperor

Decline and Dissolution of the Carolingian Empire

If Charlemagne's empire had endured, Carolingian rulers might well have built a bureaucracy, used the *missi dominici* to enhance the authority of the central government, and permanently reestablished centralized imperial rule in western Europe. As it happened, however, internal disunity and external invasions brought the Carolingian empire to an early end.

MAP [16.2]

The Carolingian empire.

Louis the Pious   Charlemagne's only surviving son, Louis the Pious (reigned 814–840), succeeded his father and kept the Carolingian empire together. Lacking Charlemagne's
strong will and military skills, however, Louis lost control of the counts and other
local authorities, who increasingly pursued their own interests and ignored the central government. Moreover, even before Louis's death his three sons disputed the
inheritance of the empire and waged bitter wars against each other. In 843 they
agreed to divide the empire into three roughly equal portions, and each of them
took one portion to rule as king. Thus less than a century after its creation, the Carolingian empire dissolved.

Pope Leo III crowns Charlemagne emperor in a manuscript illustration. The coronation symbolized the firm alliance between the Franks and the Western Christian church. • Giraudon/Art Resource, NY

Invasions

Even if internal disunity had not resulted in the dismemberment of the Carolingian empire, external pressures might well have brought it down. Beginning in the early ninth century, three groups of invaders pillaged the Frankish realm in search of wealth stored in towns and monasteries. From the south came Muslims, who raided towns, villages, churches, and monasteries in Mediterranean Europe from the mid-ninth to the late tenth century. Muslim invaders also seized Sicily as well as several territories in southern Italy and southern France. From the east came the Magyars, descendants of nomadic peoples from central Asia who had settled in Hungary. Expert horsemen, the Magyars raided settlements in Germany, Italy, and southern France from the late ninth to the mid-tenth century. From the north came the Vikings, most feared of all the invaders, who began mounting raids in northern

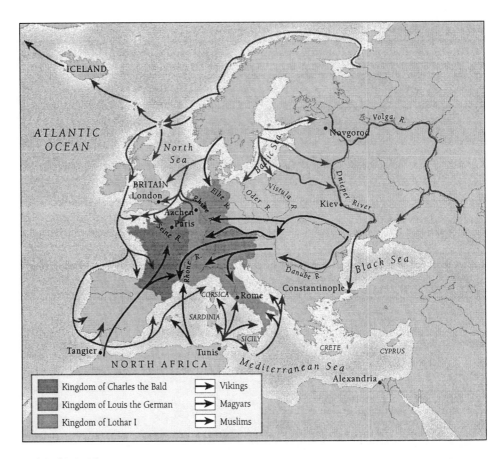

MAP [16.3]

The dissolution of the Carolingian empire and the invasions of early medieval Europe.

France even during Charlemagne's reign. The Vikings ventured across the seas from their Scandinavian homelands of Norway, Denmark, and Sweden and mounted raids in Russia, Germany, England, Ireland, France, Spain, and the Balearic Islands in the Mediterranean. By following the Russian river system to the Black Sea, they even made their way to Constantinople, which they raided at least three times during the ninth and tenth centuries. In the mid-ninth century the Vikings began to establish settlements in the lands they attacked, and from these bases they mounted methodical campaigns of conquest.

The Vikings   The Vikings were outstanding seafarers: during the ninth century some of them colonized Iceland and Greenland, and about the year 1000 a small group even established a colony in Newfoundland in modern Canada. The North American colony survived only for a few decades, and the Vikings did not create a permanent link between the world's eastern and western hemispheres. Nevertheless, the colony in North America clearly demonstrated the Vikings' ability to make their influence felt over long distances.

The Vikings sailed shallow-draft boats that could survive heavy seas but could also navigate the many rivers offering access to interior regions of Europe. Viking sailors carefully coordinated their ships' movements and timed their attacks to take advantage of the tides. Fleets of Viking boats with ferocious dragon heads mounted on their prows could arrive suddenly at a town, village, or monastery far from the sea and then spill out crews of warriors who conducted lightning raids on unprepared victims. In 844 more than 150 Viking ships sailed up the Garonne River in France, and in 845 a menacing fleet of some 800 vessels appeared without warning before the city of Hamburg. In 885 a Viking force consisting of at least 700 ships besieged Paris, and in 994 an armada of about 100 ships mounted a raid on London.

The Oseberg ship, pictured here, is the best-preserved Viking vessel from the early middle ages. Built around 800 C.E., it served as a royal tomb until its discovery in 1903. A ship this size would accomodate about forty men. • Werner Forman/Art Resource, NY

The Establishment of Regional Authorities

The Carolingians had no navy, no means to protect vulnerable sites, and no way to predict the movements of Viking raiders. Defense against the Magyars and Muslims as well as the Vikings rested principally with local forces that could respond rapidly to invasions. Because imperial authorities were unable to defend their territory, the Carolingian empire became the chief casualty of the invasions. After the ninth century, political and military initiative in western Europe passed increasingly to regional and local authorities.

Responses to ninth-century invasions took different forms in different lands. In England, which bore the brunt of the earliest Scandinavian raids, invasions prompted the series of small kingdoms established earlier by Angles, Saxons, and other Germanic peoples to merge into a single larger realm. The leader of this effort was King Alfred (reigned 871–899), who expanded from his base in southern England to territories further north held by Danish invaders. Alfred built a navy to challenge the Vikings at sea and constructed fortresses on land to secure areas that he conquered from the invaders. Danish settlers continued to occupy agricultural lands, but by the mid-tenth century Alfred's successors had established themselves as kings of all England. *England*

In Germany the response to invasion brought the end of Carolingian rule and the formation of a more effective state under a new dynasty. When Carolingian authorities were unable to prevent invasions by the Magyars, local lords took matters into their own hands. The most successful of them was King Otto I of Saxony (reigned 936–973). In 955 he faced a large Magyar army at Lechfeld on the Rhine River and inflicted a crushing defeat that effectively ended the Magyar threat. Otto *Germany* also imposed his authority throughout Germany, and twice he led armies into Italy to support the papacy against Lombard magnates. On his second venture there in 962, the pope proclaimed him emperor and bestowed an imperial crown upon him. Otto's realm was really a German kingdom rather than an empire, but the imperial title survived until the nineteenth century, and later rulers of the Holy Roman Empire dated the foundation of their state to Otto's coronation in 962. As in England, then, response to ninth-century invasions led to the organization of an effective regional state in Germany.

France   In France the end of Carolingian rule led to the proliferation of local authorities. Counts and other subordinates of the Carolingians withdrew allegiance from the central government, ruled their territories in their own interests, and usurped royal rights and prerogatives for themselves. They collected taxes, organized armed forces, built castles, and provided justice without reference to the Carolingians or other central authorities. Meanwhile, Vikings established many settlements in northern France, where they carved out small, independent states. The devolution of political and military responsibility to local authorities in tenth-century France encouraged the development of a decentralized, feudal political order.

The emergence of effective regional kingdoms and local authorities prevented the return of centralized imperial rule like that of the Carolingians or postclassical societies in China, southwest Asia, and the eastern Mediterranean region. Like postclassical India, medieval Europe became a society of competing regional states. By putting an end to the ninth-century invasions and establishing a stable political order, these states laid a foundation for social, economic, and cultural development.

FEUDAL SOCIETY

The term *feudalism* refers to the political and social order of societies that decentralize public authority and responsibility rather than vest them in a central government. Like Japan in postclassical times, medieval Europe produced one of the most elaborate feudal societies in world history. After the dissolution of the Carolingian empire, local authorities such as the counts took responsibility for maintaining order in their territories. The counts owed at least nominal allegiance to a higher authority, most often a Carolingian king descended from Louis the Pious. In fact, though, the counts acted with growing independence: they collected taxes, administered local affairs, mobilized armed forces, decided legal disputes, and sought to enhance their own authority at the expense of their superiors. In organizing public life in their territories, they elaborated a set of feudal institutions that influenced European society over the long term.

The Feudal System

Lords and Vassals   European nobles built a decentralized, feudal society as they sought to protect their lands and maintain public order during a period of weak central authority and invasions. Not surprisingly, then, the feudal system revolved around political and military relationships. The most important of these was the relationship between lord and vassal. The lord provided the vassal with a grant known as a benefice with which the vassal supported himself and his family. Benefices usually were grants of land, often called fiefs, but they sometimes took other forms, such as the right to income

In this manuscript illustration a lord (right) places his hands around the clasped hands of his vassal, symbolizing his power and authority over the vassal. With phantom arms, the vassal points toward the lands that he receives from the relationship. • Universitätsbibliothek, Heidelberg

generated by a mill, the right to receive rents or payments from a village, or even a grant of money. The benefice enabled the vassal to devote his time and energy to the service of his lord rather than the domestic tasks of cultivating food and providing for a family. A benefice also provided resources the vassal needed to maintain horses and to outfit himself with expensive military equipment such as armor and weapons. In exchange for a benefice, the vassal owed his lord loyalty, obedience, respect, counsel, and military service. When the lord did not need his services, the vassal supervised his own affairs and maintained order on the lands that made up his benefice. The vassal also spent a good deal of time learning and practicing horsemanship and the military arts.

This relationship between lord and vassal was not an entirely new creation: it had roots in the military recruitment practices of late Roman and early Frankish times. When political authorities needed bodyguards or military talent, they mobilized small private armies by attracting armed retainers into their service with grants of land or money. During the ninth and tenth centuries, however, the lord-vassal relationship became far more important than in earlier times. It became more stable because lords increasingly recognized the right of vassals to pass their benefices along to their heirs. It became more important for social order because vassals increasingly received political and legal rights over their benefices. Vassals became responsible for the organization of local public works projects, the resolution of legal disputes, and the administration of justice and thus became a hereditary class of political authorities as well as military specialists.

This feudal political order developed into a complicated and multitiered network of lord-vassal relationships. A lord with several vassals might himself be vassal to a higher lord, who might be one of several vassals to yet a greater lord in a

Feudal Politics

line of relationships extending from local communities to a king. In some ways dependence on the personal relationship between lord and vassal introduced an element of instability into the political order, since vassals—particularly those with many vassals of their own—sometimes decided unpredictably to pursue their own interests rather than those of their lords. Unless lords could discipline and control their vassals, feudalism had strong potential to lead to political chaos, as in post-Carolingian France, where ambitious local authorities largely ignored central authorities and pursued their own interests.

Yet it was also possible for high-ranking lords to build powerful states on the foundation of lord-vassal relationships. The tenth-century rulers of England and Germany closely monitored their vassals and prevented them from becoming too independent. During the high middle ages the kingdoms of both England and France depended on feudal relationships in building powerful, centralized monarchies.

Serfs and Manors in Feudal Europe

Feudalism had to do with military, political, and legal affairs and thus was the business of a tiny administrative elite composed of lords and vassals. But feudalism had important implications for the lives of all classes of people. Benefices held by feudal elites consisted most often of land cultivated by peasants who lived on the land and delivered a portion of their production to their superiors. Only by tapping this surplus agricultural production could lords and vassals maintain the feudal system.

Serfs   The development of a feudal political order accompanied fundamental changes in European society, particularly for slaves and free peasants. Both Roman and Germanic societies had recognized enslaved and free classes, and for several centuries after the fall of the western Roman empire the population of western Europe consisted mostly of slaves and free peasants. As European society regained stability following the collapse of the Roman empire and the Germanic invasions, these slaves and free peasants worked at the same kinds of agricultural tasks and frequently intermarried. Free peasants often sought protection from a lord and pledged their labor and obedience in exchange for security and land to cultivate. Beginning about the mid-seventh century, rulers and administrators recognized intermediate categories of individuals neither fully slave nor fully free. Though not chattel slaves subject to sale or a master's whim, these semifree individuals, known as *serfs*, owed obligations to the lords whose lands they cultivated.

Serfs' Obligations   Serfs usually had the right to work certain lands and to pass rights to those lands along to their heirs, so long as they observed their obligations to landlords. These obligations included both labor services and payments of rents in kind, such as a portion of a serf's own harvest, a chicken, or a dozen eggs, at specified times during the year. Male serfs typically worked three days a week in the fields of their lords and provided additional labor services during planting and harvesting seasons, while women churned butter, made cheese, brewed beer, spun thread, wove cloth, or sewed clothes for the lords and their families. Some women also kept sheep and cattle, and their obligations to lords included products from their herds. Because landlords provided them with land to cultivate, and sometimes with tools and animals as well, serfs had little opportunity to move to different lands. Indeed, they were able to do so only with the permission of their lord. They even had to pay fines for the right to marry a serf who worked for a different lord.

Manors   During the early middle ages, the institution of serfdom encouraged the development of the manor as the principal form of agricultural organization in western

Europe. A manor was a large estate consisting of fields, meadows, forests, agricultural tools, domestic animals, and sometimes lakes or rivers, as well as serfs bound to the land. The lord of the manor was usually a prominent political or military figure who had a place in the feudal hierarchy. He and his deputies provided government, administration, police services, and justice for the manor. If a dispute arose between serfs, for example, the lord and his deputies restored order, conducted an investigation, and determined how to resolve the conflict. Many lords had the authority to execute serfs for serious misconduct such as murder or other violent crimes.

By the Carolingian era manors dominated rural regions in much of France, western Germany, and the Low Countries, as well as southern England and northern Italy. In the absence of thriving cities, manors became largely self-sufficient communities. Lords of the manors maintained mills, bakeries, breweries, and wineries, and serfs produced most of the iron tools, leather goods, domestic utensils, and textiles that the manorial community needed. Small local markets, often organized near monasteries, supplied the products that residents of manors could not conveniently manufacture for themselves. During the high middle ages, craft skills developed on manors would help fuel an impressive round of economic development in western Europe.

The Economy of Feudal Europe

During the early middle ages, economic activity in western Europe was considerably slower than in China, India, southwest Asia, and the eastern Mediterranean region. Agricultural production suffered from repeated invasions by Germanic peoples, Magyars, Muslims, and Vikings, which seriously disrupted European economy and society. The decay of urban centers resulted in diminished industrial production and trade. By the tenth century, however, political stability served as a foundation for economic recovery, and western Europeans began to participate indirectly in the larger trading world of the eastern hemisphere.

Agriculture

With the establishment of the Frankish kingdom and the Carolingian empire, the European center of gravity shifted from the Mediterranean to more northern lands, particularly France. But the agricultural tools and techniques inherited from the classical Mediterranean world did not transfer very well. In light, well-drained Mediterranean soils, cultivators used small wooden plows that basically broke the surface of the soil, created a furrow, and disrupted weeds. This type of plow made little headway in the heavy, moist soils of the north.

Heavy Plows

About the sixth century a more serviceable plow became available: a heavy tool equipped with iron tips that dug into the earth and a mould-board that turned the soil so as to aerate it thoroughly and break up the root networks of weeds. The northern plow was more expensive than the light Mediterranean plow, and it required cultivators to harness much more energy to pull it through heavy soils. As a result, it was slow to come into wide use. Beginning about the eighth century, however, the heavy northern plow contributed to increased agricultural production.

As the heavy plow spread throughout western Europe during the ninth and tenth centuries, cultivators took several additional steps that increased agricultural production. Under the direction of the lords, serfs cleared new lands for cultivation. They constructed watermills, which enabled them to take advantage of a ready and renewable source of inanimate energy, thus freeing human and animal energy for other work. They also experimented with new methods of rotating crops that enabled them to cultivate land more intensively than before.

In this twelfth-century manuscript illustration, a peasant guides a heavy, wheeled plow while his wife prods the oxen that pull the plow. • Bibleoteca Meicea Laurenziana, Florence, Photo: Pineider/Index

A Rural Society   The agricultural surplus of early medieval Europe was sufficient to sustain feudal lords and their vassals, but not substantial enough to support cities with large populations of artisans, craftsmen, merchants, and professionals. Whereas cities had thrived and trade had linked all regions of the Roman empire, early medieval Europe was almost entirely a rural society that engaged in little commerce. Manors and local communities produced most of the manufactured goods that they needed, including textiles and heavy tools, and they provided both the materials and the labor for construction and other large-scale projects. Towns were few and sparsely populated, and they served as economic hubs for the areas immediately surrounding them rather than as vibrant centers integrating the economic activities of distant regions.

Trade   By the tenth century, however, political stability and increased agricultural production had begun to stimulate trade and the development of urban settlements in western Europe. This revived trade took place in the Mediterranean, the North Sea, and the Baltic Sea. Merchants from the coastal cities of Italy regularly traded across religious boundary lines with Muslims in Sicily and Tunisia, who linked Europe indirectly with the larger Islamic world of communication and exchange. Even more prominent was trade in the North Sea and Baltic Sea, where Scandinavian seafarers played the role of trader as well as raider. Their vessels called at ports from Ireland to Russia, carrying cargoes of fish and furs from Scandinavia, honey from Poland, wheat from England, wine from France, beer from the Low Countries, and swords from Germany. Because they traveled down the Russian rivers and traded actively with the Byzantine and Abbasid empires, Scandinavian merchants also traded in products from the eastern Mediterranean and the Islamic world. Most important of them was Abbasid silver, which was one of the major sources of coinage in early medieval Europe.

Population   By 900 the results of political stability and agricultural innovation were clearly evident in population figures as well as trade. In 200 C.E., before the Roman empire began to experience serious difficulties, the European population stood at about thirty-six million. It fell sharply over the next four centuries, to thirty-one million in 400 and twenty-six million in 600—a decline that reflected both the ravages of epidemic diseases and the unsettled conditions of the early middle ages. Then, gradually, the population recovered, edging up to twenty-nine million in 800 and thirty-two million in 900. By 1000 European population once again amounted to thirty-six million—the level it had reached some eight centuries earlier. By the end of the early middle ages, western Europe was poised to experience remarkable economic and demographic expansion that vastly increased European influence in the eastern hemisphere.

THE FORMATION OF CHRISTIAN EUROPE

By the time the Roman empire collapsed, Christianity was the principal source of religious, moral, and cultural authority throughout the Mediterranean basin. In the northern lands of Gaul, Germany, the British isles, and Scandinavia, however, Christianity had attracted few converts. Germanic invaders of the Roman empire sometimes embraced Arian Christianity, but not until the conversion of Clovis and the Franks did Roman Christianity enjoy a powerful and energetic sponsor in lands beyond the Mediterranean rim. One of the most important developments of the early middle ages was the conversion of western Europe to Roman Christianity. The Franks, the popes, and the monasteries played important roles in bringing about this conversion. The adoption of Roman Christianity ensured that medieval Europe would inherit crucial cultural elements from classical Roman society, including the Latin language and the institutional Roman church.

The Politics of Conversion

Clovis and the Franks won the support of the church hierarchy, as well as the Christian population of the former Roman empire, when they converted to the Roman faith. Their alliance with the Roman church also provided them with access to educated and literate individuals who could provide important political services. Scribes, secretaries, and record keepers for the Frankish kingdom came largely from the ranks of churchmen—priests, monks, bishops, and abbots—since very few others received a formal education during the early middle ages.

A deep commitment to Roman Christianity became a hallmark of Frankish policy. Clovis, his successors, and the Carolingians viewed themselves as protectors of the papacy. Charlemagne mounted a military campaign that destroyed the power of the Lombards, who had threatened the popes and the city of Rome since the sixth century, and brought most of central and northern Italy into the expanding Carolingian empire. In exchange for this military and political support, the Carolingians received recognition and backing from the popes, including the award of Charlemagne's imperial crown at the hands of Pope Leo III.

The Franks and the Church

Charlemagne not only supported the church in Italy but also worked to spread Christianity in northern lands. He maintained a school at his court in Aachen where he assembled the most prominent scholars from all parts of his empire. They corrected texts, made careful copies of the Bible and classical Latin literature, and taught Christian doctrine to men preparing for careers as priests or church officials. Charlemagne ordered monasteries throughout his empire to establish elementary schools, and he even tried to persuade village priests to provide free instruction in reading and writing. These efforts had limited success, but they certainly increased literacy in the Latin language as well as popular understanding of basic Christian doctrine.

The Spread of Christianity   Charlemagne sometimes promoted the spread of Christianity by military force. Between 772 and 804 he waged a bitter campaign against the Saxons, a pagan people inhabiting northern Germany. Alongside his claim to political hegemony, he insisted that the Saxons adopt Roman Christianity. The Saxons violently resisted both the political and the religious dimensions of Charlemagne's campaign. In the end, though, Charlemagne prevailed: the Saxons not only acknowledged Charlemagne as their political lord but also replaced their pagan traditions with Christianity.

Pagan ways did not immediately disappear from western Europe. Even within the Carolingian empire, pockets of paganism survived for several centuries after the arrival of Christianity, particularly in out-of-the-way areas that did not attract the immediate attention of conquerors or missionaries. Moreover, beyond the Carolingian empire were the Scandinavian lands, whose peoples resisted Christianity until the end of the millennium. By the year 1000, however, Christianity had won the allegiance of most people throughout western Europe and even in the Nordic lands. By sponsoring the Roman church and its missionaries, Charlemagne helped establish Christianity as the dominant religious and cultural tradition in western Europe.

The Papacy

Apart from the political support it received from the Franks, the Roman church benefitted from strong papal leadership. When the western Roman empire collapsed, the papacy survived and claimed spiritual authority over all the lands formerly embraced by the empire. For a century after the dissolution of the western Roman empire, the popes cooperated closely with the Byzantine emperors, who seemed to be the natural heirs to the emperors of Rome. Beginning in the late sixth century, however, the popes acted more independently and devoted their efforts to strengthening the western Christian church based at Rome and clearly distinguishing it from the eastern Christian church based at Constantinople. The two churches differed on many issues by the eleventh century, and in 1054 the pope and patriarch mutually excommunicated each other. After the eleventh century the two branches of Christianity formed distinct identities as the Roman Catholic and Eastern Orthodox churches.

Pope Gregory I   The individual most important for providing the Roman church with its sense of direction was Pope Gregory I (590–604 C.E.), also known as Gregory the Great. As pope, Gregory faced an array of difficult challenges. During the late sixth century the Lombards consolidated their hold on the Italian peninsula, menacing Rome and the Roman church in the process. Gregory ensured the survival of both the city and the church by mobilizing local resources and organizing the defense of Rome. He also faced difficulties within the church, since bishops frequently acted independently of the pope, as though they were supreme ecclesiastical authorities within their own dioceses. To regain the initiative, Gregory reasserted papal primacy—the claim that the bishop of Rome was the ultimate authority in the Christian church. Gregory also made contributions as a theologian: he strongly emphasized the sacrament of penance, which required individuals to confess their sins to their priests and then to atone for their sins by penitential acts prescribed by the priests—a practice that enhanced the influence of the Roman church in the lives of individuals.

Gregory strengthened the Roman church further by extending its appeal and winning new converts in western Europe. The most important of his many missionary campaigns was one directed at England, recently conquered by Angles, Saxons, and other Germanic peoples. He aimed his efforts at the kings who ruled the various regions of England, hoping that their conversion would induce their subjects to adopt Christianity. This tactic largely succeeded: by the early seventh century Christianity had established a stable foothold in England, and by 800 England was securely within the fold of the Roman church.

The Conversion of England

A fourteenth-century manuscript illustration shows St. Benedict presenting his rule to a group of nuns. • Biblioteca Seminario Vescovile, Florence, Photo: P. Tosi/Index

Gregory's successors continued his policy of expanding the Roman church through missionary activity. France and Germany offered plentiful opportunities to win converts, particularly as the Frankish kingdom and the Carolingians brought those lands under their control. Some of the popes' most effective missionaries were monks. Pope Gregory himself was a monk, and he relied heavily on the energies of his fellow monks in seeking converts in England and elsewhere.

Monasticism

Christian monasticism had its origin in Egypt. During the second and third centuries, many devout Christians sought to lead ascetic and holy lives in the deserts of Egypt. Some lived alone as hermits, and others formed communes where they devoted themselves to the pursuit of holiness rather than worldly success. When Christianity became legal during the fourth century, the monastic lifestyle became an increasingly popular alternative throughout the Roman empire. Monastic communities cropped up in Italy, Spain, Gaul, and the British isles, as well as in the eastern Mediterranean region.

During the early days of monasticism, each community developed its own rules, procedures, and priorities. Some communities demanded that their inhabitants follow extremely austere lifestyles that sapped the energy of the monks. Others did not establish any clear expectations of their recruits, with the result that monks frittered away their time or wandered aimlessly from one monastic house to another. These haphazard conditions prevented monasteries from mounting effective Christian missions.

Monastic Rules

St. Benedict of Nursia (480–547 C.E.) strengthened the early monastic movement by providing it with discipline and a sense of purpose. In 529 St. Benedict prepared a

St. Benedict

set of regulations known as Benedict's *Rule* for the monastic community that he had founded at Monte Cassino, near Rome. The *Rule* did not permit extreme asceticism, but it required monks to take vows to live communal, celibate lives under the absolute direction of the abbot who supervised the monastery: poverty, chastity, and obedience became the prime virtues for Benedictine monks. The *Rule* also called for monks to spend their time in prayer, meditation, and work. At certain hours monks came together for religious services and prayer, and they divided the remainder of the day into periods for study, reflection, and manual labor.

St. Scholastica   Monasteries throughout Europe began to adopt Benedict's *Rule* as the standard for their own houses. Through the influence of St. Benedict's sister, the nun St. Scholastica (482–543), an adaptation of the *Rule* soon provided guidance for the religious life of women living in convents. Within a century most European monasteries and convents observed the Benedictine *Rule*. During the following centuries the Roman church generated many alternatives to Benedictine monasticism. Yet even today most Roman Catholic monasteries observe rules that reflect the influence of the Benedictine tradition.

Strengthened by the discipline that the Benedictine *Rule* introduced, monasteries became a dominant feature in the social and cultural life of western Europe throughout the middle ages. Monasteries helped to provide order in the countryside, for example, and to expand agricultural production. Monasteries accumulated large landholdings—as well as authority over serfs working their lands—from the bequests of wealthy individuals seeking to contribute to the church's work and thereby to merit salvation. Particularly in France and Germany, abbots of monasteries dispatched teams of monks and serfs to clear forests, drain swamps, and prepare lands for cultivation. Indeed, monasteries organized much of the labor that brought about the expansion of agricultural production in early medieval Europe.

Monasticism and Society   As more and more monasteries appeared in Europe, they provided a variety of social services. They served as inns for travelers and places of refuge for individuals suffering from natural or other calamities. They served as orphanages and provided medical treatment for the ill and injured. They often set up schools and offered at least some rudimentary educational services for local regions, and large monasteries provided more advanced instruction for those preparing for the priesthood or high ecclesiastical positions. Some monasteries maintained

Monastic libraries were the principal centers of literacy in western Europe during the early middle ages. Monastic scribes produced many handsome copies of classical literary works as well as biblical texts. This illustration shows the opening lines of the Book of Genesis from a Bible prepared for the Carolingian king Charles the Bald in the ninth century. • Bibliothèque Nationale de France

libraries and scriptoria, where monks copied works of classical literature and philosophy as well as the scriptures and other Christian writings. Almost all works of Latin literature that have come down to the present survive because of copies made by medieval monks. Finally, monasteries served as a source of literate, educated, and talented individuals, whose secretarial and administrative services were crucial to the survival of feudal government in early medieval Europe.

Because of the various roles they played in the larger society, monasteries were particularly effective agents in the spread of Christianity. While they organized life in the countryside and provided social services, monks also zealously preached Christianity and tended to the spiritual needs of rural populations. For many people a neighboring monastery was the only source of instruction in Christian doctrine, and a local monastic church offered the only practical opportunity for them to take part in religious services. Monks patiently and persistently served the needs of rural populations, and over the decades and centuries they helped to instill Christian values in countless generations of European peasants.

Like societies in China, India, southwest Asia, and the eastern Mediterranean region, western Europe experienced massive change during the postclassical era. In some ways western Europe had the most difficult experience of all the postclassical societies. In China, southwest Asia, and the eastern Mediterranean, societies were able to preserve or reestablish centralized imperial rule that maintained order and stability while also facilitating trade and encouraging economic development. India did not generate an imperial form of government, but because of the subcontinent's geographical location and productive capacity, India participated actively in the larger economic and commercial life of the eastern hemisphere. In contrast to other postclassical societies, rulers of early medieval Europe did not reinstate an imperial form of government—except for the short-lived Carolingian empire—and western Europeans did not participate actively in the larger trading world of the eastern hemisphere. The standards of material life in early medieval Europe—as measured by agricultural and industrial production, volume of trade, and the extent of urban settlement—stood well below those of other postclassical societies.

Yet just as postclassical developments deeply influenced the evolution of societies in other lands, the early medieval era was a crucial period for the development of western Europe. In the absence of a durable centralized empire, western Europeans found ways to maintain relative order and stability by decentralizing political responsibilities and relying on local authorities for political organization. Over the longer term the feudal political order of medieval Europe discouraged the revival of empire and encouraged the emergence of regional states that organized their communities into powerful societies. During the early middle ages, western Europeans did not benefit from the commercial and biological exchanges that boosted economies in other postclassical lands, but they experimented with agricultural techniques that enabled them to expand production dramatically, conduct increased trade, and rebuild urban centers. Finally, western Christianity preserved elements of classical Roman society and established a foundation for cultural unity in western Europe, just as Buddhism, Hinduism, Islam, and eastern Christianity served as sources of cultural authority in other societies.

CHRONOLOGY

476	Fall of the western Roman empire
480–547	Life of St. Benedict of Nursia
482–543	Life of St. Scholastica
481–511	Reign of Clovis
590–604	Reign of Pope Gregory I
768–814	Reign of Charlemagne
800	Coronation of Charlemagne as emperor
814–840	Reign of Louis the Pious
843	Dissolution of the Carolingian empire
871–899	Reign of King Alfred
936–973	Reign of King Otto I of Saxony
955	Battle of Lechfeld
962	Coronation of Otto I

FOR FURTHER READING

Geoffrey Barraclough. *The Crucible of Europe.* Berkeley, 1976. A brilliant, brief analysis of early medieval Europe concentrating on the Carolingian era and its aftermath.

Robert-Henri Bautier. *The Economic Development of Medieval Europe.* New York, 1971. An excellent and well-illustrated survey, which examines the economic and social history of western Europe in the context of the larger Mediterranean basin.

Marc Bloch. *Feudal Society.* 2 vols. Trans. by L.A. Manyon. Chicago, 1961. A classic interpretation concentrating on social and economic history that has decisively influenced the way historians think about medieval Europe.

Einhard and Notker the Stammerer. *Two Lives of Charlemagne.* Ed. and trans. by Lewis Thorpe. New York, 1969. Excellent translations of two early biographies of Charlemagne.

F. L. Ganshof. *Feudalism.* Trans. by P. Grierson. New York, 1964. Provides the clearest description of feudalism as a political and military system.

———. *Frankish Institutions under Charlemagne.* Trans. by B. and M. Lyon. New York, 1970. Concise synthesis of research on Charlemagne's government.

Patrick J. Geary. *Before France and Germany: The Creation and Transformation of the Merovingian World.* New York, 1988. Draws usefully on recent research in reconstructing early medieval Europe.

———, ed. *Readings in Medieval History.* Lewiston, N.Y., 1989. Offers substantial English translations of primary sources.

Louis Halphen. *Charlemagne and the Carolingian Empire.* Trans. by G. de Nie. Amsterdam, 1977. Thorough discussion of Charlemagne's imperial creation and its larger importance in European history.

David Herlihy. *Opera Muliebra: Women and Work in Medieval Europe.* New York, 1990. Examines women's roles both in their own households and in the larger society of medieval Europe.

Richard Hodges and David Whitehouse. *Mohammed, Charlemagne and the Origins of Europe: Archaeology and the Pirenne Thesis.* Ithaca, 1983. Draws on recent archaeological discoveries in placing the early medieval European economy in hemispheric context.

Edward James. *The Franks.* Oxford, 1988. Up-to-date study based on recent scholarship.

Gwyn Jones. *A History of the Vikings.* Rev. ed. Oxford, 1984. The best general work on Viking society and Viking expansion.

Archibald Lewis. *Knights and Samurai: Feudalism in Northern France and Japan.* London, 1974. A brief and insightful work comparing the origins, development, and significance of feudalism in Europe and Japan.

Ferdinand Lot. *The End of the Ancient World and the Beginnings of the Middle Ages.* Trans. by P. and M. Leon. New York, 1961. A masterful survey of the Germanic invasions and their results for western Europe.

Rosamond McKitterick. *The Frankish Kingdoms under the Carolingians, 751–987.* New York, 1983. Comprehensive survey of the Carolingian dynasty with special attention to political, cultural, and religious developments.

J. M. Wallace-Hadrill. *The Barbarian West: The Early Middle Ages,* A.D. 400–1000. New York, 1962. A powerful and insightful synthesis by a leading scholar.

PART IV

ॐ

AN AGE OF CROSS-CULTURAL INTERACTION, 1000 TO 1500 C.E.

. . .

The half millennium from 1000 to 1500 C.E. differed markedly from early eras. During classical and post-classical times, large, regional societies situated in China, India, southwest Asia, and the Mediterranean basin dominated the eastern hemisphere. Peoples of these lands built extensive networks of trade and communication that spanned the eastern hemisphere and influenced the development of all its societies. From 1000 to 1500 C.E., however, nomadic Turkish and Mongol peoples overran settled societies and established vast transregional empires from China to eastern Europe.

Nomadic peoples toppled several postclassical states, most notably the Song empire in China and the Abbasid realm in southwest Asia. By building empires that transcended the boundaries of postclassical states, however, nomadic Turks and Mongols laid a political foundation for sharply increased trade and communication between peoples of different societies and cultural regions. Indeed, their empires prompted the peoples of the eastern hemisphere to forge closer links than ever before in history. By the mid-fourteenth century, merchants, diplomats, and missionaries traveled frequently between lands as far removed as Italy and China.

Increased trade in the Indian Ocean basin also promoted more intense cross-cultural communications. Maritime trade built on the political stability, economic expansion, and demographic growth of the postclassical era. By the fourteenth century mariners called at ports throughout the Indian Ocean basin from southeast Asia to India, Ceylon, Arabia, and east Africa, while sea-lanes through the South China Sea offered access to ports in the islands of southeast Asia, China, Japan, and Korea. Luxury goods traveled over the Indian Ocean in larger quantities than ever before. From the eleventh century forward, cargoes increasingly consisted of bulky commodities like timber, coral, steel, building materials, grains, dates, and other foodstuffs. This trade in bulk goods indicated a movement toward economic integration as societies of the Indian Ocean basin concentrated increasingly on cultivating crops or producing goods for export while importing foods or goods that they could not produce very well themselves.

Demographic growth, increased agricultural production, and economic expansion helped to underwrite rapid political development in sub-Saharan Africa and western Europe. Powerful regional states and centralized empires emerged in west Africa and central Africa while a series of wealthy city-states dominated the east African coast. In western Europe the decentralized feudal states of the early middle ages evolved into more tightly centralized regional states. Most of these regional states continued to rely on feudal principles of political organization, but they used feudal relationships between lords and vassals to enhance the power of central rulers over local challengers. Increasing volumes of trade favored this movement toward centralization in sub-Saharan Africa and western Europe, since taxes levied on trade helped to finance the professional bureaucrats and armed forces that centralized states required.

Although they did not participate in the demographic and economic expansion of the eastern hemisphere, the indigenous peoples of the Americas and Oceania also built larger and more centralized societies from 1000 to 1500 C.E. Centralized empires appeared in Mesoamerica and Andean South America while agricultural societies emerged in several regions of North America. Even in the absence of large domesticated animals, trade networks linked peoples as far distant as Mexico and the Great Lakes region. Pacific island societies also moved toward tighter political organization. Because they lived on small land bases distributed irregularly throughout a vast ocean, Pacific islanders had no realistic possibility of building large imperial states. Within their own agricultural and fishing societies, however, they established tightly centralized kingdoms that organized public affairs and sponsored distinctive cultural traditions.

During the fourteenth and fifteenth centuries C.E., western European peoples unwittingly laid the foundations of a new era in world history. While searching for sea routes to Asian markets, European mariners happened upon the continents of North and South America. They soon ventured into the Pacific Ocean, where they encountered Australia and the Pacific islands. Their voyages brought the world's various peoples for the first time into permanent and sustained communication with one another, and their interactions triggered a series of consequences that profoundly influenced modern world history. The European voyages that gave rise to this interdependent and interconnected world took place precisely because of the movement toward increasing interaction in the eastern hemisphere during the centuries following 1000 C.E. The period from 1000 to 1500 C.E. set the stage for the modern era of world history.

ASIA	AFRICA	EUROPE	AMERICAS AND OCEANIA
900	900	900	900
	Kings of Ghana convert to Islam (10th century)	Otto of Saxony crowned by Pope John XII (962) Foundation of Holy Roman Empire Hugh Capet (987)	Collapse of Teotihuacan Kingdom of Chimu in South America Cahokia mound in North America (900–1250) Toltecs in Mesoamerica (950–1150)
1000	1000	1000	1000
Saljuq Turk leader Tughril Beg recognized as sultan Battle of Manzikert (1071)	Swahili city-states dominate east African coastal trade	Leif Ericsson reached Newfoundland (1000) William of Normandy conquers England (1066) Conflict between Pope Gregory VII and Holy Roman Emperor Henry IV (1077) First Crusade (1096–1099)	Owasco tribes in North America
1100	1100	1100	1100
Jurchen conquer northern China	Construction of Great Zimbabwe Revival of Christian Axum kingdom Kingdom of Ghana	Eleanor of Aquitaine (1122–1204) St. Dominic and St. Francis	Kingdom of Chucuito in South America Trade between Hawai`i and Tahiti
1200	1200	1200	1200
Delhi sultanate (1206–1524) Chinggis Khan (1167–1227) Mongols conquer northern China and Persia (1215–1219) Hülegü conquers Abbasid empire (1258) Ilkhan dynasty in Persia (1258–1335) Golden horde invade Russia (1237–1241) Khanate of Chaghatai in central Asia Khubilai Khan (1264–1294) Yuan dynasty (1279–1368) Marco Polo Conversion of Ilkhan Ghazan to Islam (1295) Osman and foundation of Ottoman state (1299)	Sundiata (1230–1255) Mali empire (13th–15th centuries)	Fourth Crusade (1202–1204) St. Thomas Aquinas (1224–1274) Travels of Marco Polo (1271–1295)	Mexica migrate into central Mexico

ASIA	AFRICA	EUROPE	AMERICAS AND OCEANIA
1300	**1300**	**1300**	**1300**
Bubonic plague in China (1331) Emperor Hongwu (1368–1398) Ming dynasty (1368–1644) Tamerlane (1336–1405)	Kingdom of Kongo Kilwa city-state Mansa Musa (1312–1337) Pilgrimage to Mecca (1324–1325) Travels of Ibn Battuta	Francesco Petrarca (1304–1374) Bubonic plague in Europe (1348) Hundred Years' War (1337–1453)	Foundation of Tenochtitlan Construction of elaborate fishponds in Hawai`i
1400	**1400**	**1400**	**1400**
Emperor Yongle (1403–1424) *Yongle Encyclopedia* Voyages of Zheng He (1405–1433) Ottoman Turkish sultan Mehmed II captures Constantinople (1453)	Songhay empire overruns Mali	Prince Henrique of Portugal (1415) Fernando of Aragon and Isabel of Castile (1469) Christopher Columbus sails to San Salvador (1492) Vasco de Gama sails to India (1497) Reconquista of Spain complete (1492) Donatello (1386–1466), Leonardo da Vinci (1452–1519), Michelangelo (1472–1564) Desiderius Erasmus (1466–1536)	Iroquois nations in North America Mohawk, Oneida, Onondaga, Cayuga Seneca Aztec King Itzcoatl (1428–1440) Aztec King Motecuzoma I (1440–1469) Inca Emperor Pachacuti (1438–1471)

CHAPTER 17

NOMADIC EMPIRES
AND EURASIAN
INTEGRATION

• • •

uillaume Boucher was a goldsmith who lived during the early and middle decades of the thirteenth century. At some point, perhaps during the 1230s, he left his native Paris and went to Budapest, which was then a part of the kingdom of Hungary. There he was captured by Mongol warriors campaigning in Hungary. The Mongols noticed and appreciated Boucher's talents, and when they left Hungary in 1242, they took him along with other skilled captives to their central Asian homeland.

For at least the next fifteen years, Boucher lived at the Mongol capital at Karakorum. Though technically a slave, he enjoyed some prestige. He supervised fifty assistants in a workshop that produced decorative objects of gold and silver for the Mongol court. His most ingenious creation was a spectacular silver fountain in the form of a tree. Four pipes, concealed by the tree's trunk, carried wines and other intoxicating drinks to the top of the tree and then dispensed them into silver bowls from which courtiers and guests filled their cups. Apart from his famous fountain, Boucher also produced statues in gold and silver, built carriages, designed buildings, and even sewed ritual garments for Roman Catholic priests who conducted services for Christians living at Karakorum and sought converts in the Mongol empire.

Boucher was by no means the only European living at the Mongol court. His wife was a woman of French ancestry whom Boucher had met and married in Hungary. The Flemish missionary William of Rubruck visited Karakorum in 1254, and during his sojourn there he encountered a French woman named Paquette who was an attendant to a Mongol princess, an artisan from Russia (Paquette's husband), an unnamed nephew of a French bishop, a Greek soldier, and an Englishman named Basil. Other European visitors found Germans, Slavs, and Hungarians at the Mongol court, as well as Chinese, Koreans, Turks, Persians, and Armenians, among others. Many thirteenth-century roads led to Karakorum.

Nomadic peoples had made their influence felt throughout much of Eurasia as early as classical times. The Xiongnu confederation dominated central Asia and

Chabi, a Nestorian Christian and the favorite wife of Khubilai Khan, wearing the distinctive headgear reserved for Mongol women of the ruling class. • National Palace Museum Taipei, Taiwan, Republic of China

411

posed a formidable threat to the Han dynasty in China from the third to the first century B.C.E. During the second and third centuries C.E., the Huns and other nomadic peoples from central Asia launched the migrations that helped bring down the western Roman empire, and later migrations of the White Huns destroyed the Gupta state in India. Turkish peoples ruled a large central Asian empire from the sixth through the ninth centuries, and the Uighur Turks even seized the capital cities of the Tang dynasty in the mid-seventh century.

Between the eleventh and fifteenth centuries, nomadic peoples became more prominent than ever before in Eurasian affairs. Turkish peoples migrated to Persia, Anatolia, and India, where they overcame existing authorities and established new states. During the thirteenth and fourteenth centuries, the Mongols established themselves as the most powerful people of the central Asian steppes and then turned on settled societies in China, Persia, Russia, and eastern Europe. By the early fourteenth century, the Mongols had built the largest empire the world has ever seen, stretching from Korea and China in the east to Russia and Hungary in the west.

Most of the Mongol states collapsed during the late fourteenth and fifteenth centuries, but the decline of the Mongols did not signal the end of nomadic peoples' influence on Eurasian affairs. Although a native Chinese dynasty replaced the Mongol state in China, the possibility of a Mongol revival forced the new dynasty to focus attention and resources on its central Asian frontier. Moreover, from the fourteenth through the seventeenth centuries, Turkish peoples embarked on new campaigns of expansion that eventually brought most of India, much of central Asia, all of Anatolia, and a good portion of eastern Europe under their domination.

Between the eleventh and fifteenth centuries, the imperial campaigns of Turkish and Mongol peoples forged closer links than ever before between Eurasian lands. By fostering cross-cultural communication and exchange on an unprecedented scale, the nomadic empires integrated the lives of peoples and the experiences of societies throughout much of the eastern hemisphere.

 ## TURKISH MIGRATIONS AND IMPERIAL EXPANSION

Turkish peoples never formed a single, homogeneous group, but rather organized themselves into clans and tribes that often fought bitterly with one another. Turkish clans and identities probably emerged after the Xiongnu confederation broke apart in the first and second centuries C.E. All Turkish peoples spoke related languages, and all were nomads or descendants of nomads. From modest beginnings they expanded their influence until they dominated not only the steppes of central Asia but also settled societies in Persia, Anatolia, and India.

Nomadic Economy and Society

Nomadic societies in central Asia developed by adapting to the ecological conditions of arid lands. Central Asia does not receive enough rain to support large-scale agriculture. Oases permit intense cultivation of limited regions, but for the most part only grasses and shrubs grow on the central Asian steppelands, and there are no large rivers or other sources of water to support sizable irrigation systems. Humans cannot survive on grasses and shrubs, but grazing animals thrive on them. To take advantage of the vast open spaces of central Asia, nomads herded grazing animals, especially sheep and horses, but also cattle, goats, and camels.

Nomadic peoples drove their herds and flocks to lands with abundant grass and then moved them along as the animals thinned the vegetation. They did not wander aimlessly through the steppes, but rather followed migratory cycles that took account of the seasons and local climatic conditions. They lived mostly off the meat, milk, and hides of their animals. They used animal bones for tools and animal dung as fuel for fires. They made shoes and clothes out of wool from their sheep and skins from their other animals. Wool was also the source of the felt that they used to fashion large tents called *yurts* in which they lived. They even prepared an alcoholic drink from animal products by fermenting mare's milk into a potent concoction known as *kumiss*.

Nomadic Peoples and Their Animals

The aridity of the climate and the nomadic lifestyle limited the development of human societies in central Asia. Only at oases did agriculture make it possible for dense populations to congregate. Settlements were few and small—and often temporary as well, since nomads carried their collapsible felt yurts with them as they drove their herds. Nomads often engaged in small-scale cultivation of millet or vegetables when they found sources of water, but the harvests were sufficient only to supplement animal products, not to sustain whole societies. Nomads also produced limited amounts of pottery, leather goods, and iron weapons and tools. Given their migratory habits, however, both intensive agriculture and large-scale craft production were practical impossibilities.

Thus nomads avidly sought opportunities to trade with settled peoples, and as early as the classical era brisk trade linked nomadic and settled societies. Much of this commerce took place on a small scale as nomads sought agricultural products and manufactured goods to satisfy their immediate needs. Often, however, nomads also participated in long-distance trade networks. Because of their mobility and their familiarity with large regions of central Asia, nomadic peoples were ideally suited to organize and lead the caravans that crossed central Asia and linked settled societies from China to the Mediterranean basin. During the postclassical era and later, Turkish peoples were especially prominent on the caravan routes of central Asia.

Nomadic and Settled Peoples

Nomadic society generated two social classes: nobles and commoners. Charismatic leaders won recognition as nobles and thereby acquired the prestige needed to organize clans and tribes into alliances. Normally, nobles did little governing, since clans and tribes looked after their own affairs and resented interference. During times of war, however, nobles wielded absolute authority over their forces, and they dealt swiftly and summarily with those who did not obey orders.

Nomadic Society

The nobility was a fluid class. Leaders passed noble status along to their heirs, but the heirs could lose their status if they did not continue to provide appropriate leadership for their clans and tribes. Over the course of a few generations, nobles could return to the status of commoners who tended their own herds and followed new leaders. Meanwhile, commoners could win recognition as nobles by outstanding conduct, particularly by courageous behavior during war. Then, if they were clever diplomats, they could arrange alliances between clans and tribes and gain enough support to displace established leaders.

A wall painting from a cave at Dunhuang, a major oasis on the silk road, depicts a band of sword-wielding thieves (left) holding up a party of Turkish merchants (right). According to convention, the artist represented the Turks with pale skins, long noses, and deep-set eyes. • Cultural Relics Publishing House, Beijing

Nomadic Religion   The earliest religion of the Turkish peoples revolved around shamans—religious specialists who possessed supernatural powers, communicated with the gods and nature spirits, invoked divine aid on behalf of their communities, and informed their companions of the gods' will. Yet many Turkish peoples became attracted to the religious and cultural traditions they encountered when trading with peoples of settled societies. They did not abandon their inherited beliefs or their shamans, but by the sixth century C.E. many Turks had converted to Buddhism, Nestorian Christianity, or Manichaeism. Partly because of their newly adopted religious and cultural traditions and partly because of their prominence in Eurasian trade networks, Turkish peoples also developed a written script.

In the tenth century Turks living near the Abbasid empire began to turn to Islam. Their conversion had great significance. When Turkish peoples began to migrate into settled societies in large numbers, they helped spread Islam to new lands, particularly Anatolia and northern India. The boundaries of the Islamic world thus expanded along with the political and military influence of Turkish peoples.

Military   This expansion took place when nomadic leaders organized vast confederations
Organization   of peoples all subject, at least nominally, to a *khan* ("ruler"). In fact, khans rarely ruled directly, but rather through the leaders of allied tribes. Yet when organized on a large scale, nomadic peoples wielded massive military power due mostly to their

outstanding cavalry forces. Nomadic warriors learned to ride horses as children, and they had superior equestrian skills. Their arrows flew with deadly accuracy even when launched from the backs of galloping horses. Moreover, units of warriors coordinated their movements to outmaneuver and overwhelm their opponents.

Few armies were able to resist the mobility and discipline of well-organized nomadic warriors. When they found themselves at a disadvantage, they often were able to beat a hasty retreat and escape from their less speedy adversaries. With this military background several groups of Turkish nomads began in the tenth century C.E. to seize the wealth of settled societies and build imperial states in the regions surrounding central Asia.

Turkish Empires in Persia, Anatolia, and India

Turkish peoples entered Persia, Anatolia, and India at different times and for different purposes. They approached Abbasid Persia much as Germanic peoples had earlier approached the Roman empire. From about the mid-eighth to the mid-tenth century, Turkish peoples lived mostly on the borders of the Abbasid realm, which offered abundant opportunities for trade. By the mid- to late tenth century, large numbers of

Head of a Turkish noble from a grave monument of about the seventh century C.E. The carving bears an inscription on the neck, but scholars have not been able to decipher it. • The State Hermitage Museum, St. Petersburg

Saljuq Turks served in Abbasid armies and lived in the Abbasid realm itself. By the mid-eleventh century the Saljuqs overshadowed the Abbasid caliphs. Indeed, in 1055 the caliph recognized the Saljuq leader Tughril Beg as *sultan* ("chieftain"). Tughril first consolidated his hold on the Abbasid capital at Baghdad, then he and his successors extended Turkish rule to Syria, Palestine, and other parts of the realm. For the last two centuries of the Abbasid state, the caliphs served as figureheads of authority while actual governance lay in the hands of the Turkish sultans.

Saljuq Turks and the Abbasid Empire

While some Turkish peoples established themselves in Abbasid Persia, others turned their attention to the rich land of Anatolia, breadbasket of the Byzantine empire. Led by the Saljuqs, Turkish peoples began migrating into Anatolia in large numbers in the early eleventh century. In 1071 Saljuq forces inflicted a devastating defeat on the Byzantine army at Manzikert in eastern Anatolia and even took the Byzantine emperor captive. Following this victory Saljuqs and other Turkish groups entered Anatolia almost at will. The peasants of Anatolia, who mostly resented their Byzantine overlords, looked upon the Saljuqs as liberators rather than conquerors.

Saljuq Turks and the Byzantine Empire

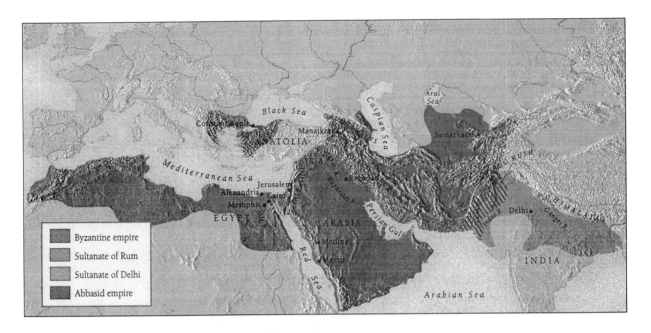

MAP [17.1]

Turkish empires.

The migrants thoroughly transformed Anatolia. Turkish groups displaced Byzantine authorities and set up their own political and social institutions. They levied taxes on the Byzantine church, restricted its activities, and sometimes confiscated church property. Meanwhile, they welcomed converts to Islam and made political, social, and economic opportunities available to them. By 1453, when Ottoman Turks captured the Byzantine capital at Constantinople, Byzantine and Christian Anatolia had become largely a Turkish and Islamic land.

Ghaznavid Turks and Northern India

While the Saljuqs spearheaded Turkish migrations in Abbasid Persia and Byzantine Anatolia, Mahmud of Ghazni led the Turkish Ghaznavids of Afghanistan in raids on lucrative sites in northern India. When the Ghaznavids began their campaigns in the early eleventh century, their principal goal was plunder. Gradually, though, they became more interested in permanent rule. They asserted their authority first over the Punjab and then over Gujarat and Bengal. By the late twelfth century, the Turkish sultanate of Delhi claimed authority over all of northern India, although its effective power did not extend much beyond the capital of Delhi.

As in Anatolia, Turkish rule had great social and cultural implications in India. Mahmud of Ghazni was a zealous foe of Buddhism and Hinduism alike, and he launched frequent raids on shrines, temples, and monasteries. His forces stripped Buddhist and Hindu establishments of their wealth, destroyed their buildings, and often slaughtered their residents and attendants as well. As Turkish invaders repressed Buddhism and Hinduism, they encouraged conversion to Islam and enabled their faith to establish a secure presence in northern India.

Though undertaken by different groups, for different reasons, and by different means, the Turkish conquests of Persia, Anatolia, and India represented part of a larger expansive movement by nomadic peoples. In all three cases the formidable military prowess of Turkish peoples enabled them to move beyond the steppelands of central Asia and dominate settled societies. By the thirteenth century, the influence of nomadic peoples was greater than ever before in Eurasian history. Yet the Turkish conquests represented only a prelude to an astonishing round of empire building launched by the Mongols during the thirteenth and fourteenth centuries.

THE MONGOL EMPIRES

For most of history the nomadic Mongols lived on the high steppelands of eastern central Asia. Like other nomadic peoples, they displayed deep loyalty to kin groups organized into families, clans, and tribes. They frequently allied with Turkish peoples who built empires on the steppes, but they rarely played a leading role in the organization of states before the thirteenth century. Strong loyalties to kinship groups made it difficult for the Mongols to organize a stable society on a large scale. During the early thirteenth century, however, Chinggis Khan forged the various Mongol tribes into a powerful alliance that built the largest empire that the world has ever seen. Although the vast Mongol realm soon dissolved into a series of smaller empires—most of which disappeared within a century—the Mongols' imperial venture brought the societies of Eurasia into closer contact than ever before.

Chinggis Khan and the Making of the Mongol Empire

The unifier of the Mongols was Temüjin, born about 1167 into a noble family. His father was a prominent warrior who forged an alliance between several Mongol clans and seemed likely to become a powerful leader. When Temüjin was about ten years old, however, rivals poisoned his father and destroyed the alliance. Abandoned by his father's allies, Temüjin led a precarious existence for some years. He lived in poverty, since rivals seized the family's animals, and several times eluded enemies seeking to eliminate him as a potential threat to their own ambitions. A rival once captured him and imprisoned him in a wooden cage, but Temüjin made a daring midnight escape and regained his freedom.

During the late twelfth century, Temüjin made an alliance with a prominent Mongol clan leader. He also mastered the art of steppe diplomacy, which called for displays of personal courage in battle, combined with intense loyalty to allies—as well as a willingness to betray allies or superiors to improve one's position—and the ability to entice previously unaffiliated tribes into cooperative relationships. Temüjin gradually strengthened his position, sometimes by forging useful alliances, often by conquering rival contenders for power, and occasionally by turning suddenly against a troublesome ally. He eventually brought all the Mongol tribes into a

Chinggis Khan's Rise to Power

This painting by a Chinese artist depicts Chinggis Khan at age of about sixty. Though his conquests were behind him, Chinggis Khan's focus and determination are readily apparent in this portrait.
• National Palace Museum Taipei, Taiwan, Republic of China

single confederation, and in 1206 an assembly of Mongol leaders recognized Temüjin's supremacy by proclaiming him Chinggis Khan ("universal ruler").

Mongol Political Organization   Chinggis Khan's policies greatly strengthened the Mongol people. Earlier nomadic state builders had ruled largely through the leaders of allied tribes. Because of his personal experiences, however, Chinggis Khan mistrusted the Mongols' tribal organization. He broke up the tribes and forced men of fighting age to join new military units with no tribal affiliations. He chose high military and political officials not on the basis of kinship or tribal status, but rather because of their talents or their loyalty to him. Although he spent most of his life on horseback, Chinggis Khan also established a capital at Karakorum—present-day Har Horin, located about 300 kilometers (186 miles) west of the modern Mongolian capital of Ulaanbaatar—where he built a luxurious palace. As command center of Chinggis Khan's empire, Karakorum symbolized a source of Mongol authority superior to the clan or tribe. Chinggis Khan's policies created a Mongol state that was not only much stronger than any earlier nomadic confederation but also less troubled by conflicts between clans and tribes.

The most important institution of the Mongol state was the army, which magnified the power of the small population. In the thirteenth century the Mongol population stood at about one million people—less than 1 percent of China's numbers. During Chinggis Khan's life, his army numbered only 100,000 to 125,000 Mongols, although allied peoples also contributed forces. How was it possible for so few people to conquer the better part of Eurasia?

Mongol Arms   Like earlier nomadic armies, Mongol forces relied on outstanding horsemanship. Mongols grew up riding horses, and they honed their equestrian skills by hunting and playing competitive games on horseback. Their bows, short enough for archers to use while riding, were also stiff, firing arrows that could fell enemies at 200 meters (656 feet). Mongol horsemen were among the most mobile forces of the premodern world, sometimes traveling more than one hundred kilometers (sixty-two miles) per day to surprise an enemy. Furthermore, the Mongols understood the psychological dimensions of warfare and used them to their advantage. If enemies surrendered without resistance, the Mongols usually spared their lives, and they provided generous treatment for artisans, craftsmen, and those with military skills. In the event of resistance, however, they ruthlessly slaughtered whole populations, sparing only a few, whom they sometimes drove before their armies as human shields during future conflicts.

A Persian manuscript illustration depicts Chinggis Khan and his cavalry in hot pursuit of retreating forces. • Bibilothèque Nationale de France

Once he had united the Mongols, Chinggis Khan turned his army and his attention to other parts of central Asia and particularly to nearby settled societies. He attacked the various Turkish peoples ruling in Tibet, northern China, Persia, and the central Asian steppes. His conquests in central Asia were important because they protected him against the possibility that other nomadic leaders might chal-

MARCO POLO ON MONGOL MILITARY TACTICS

• • •

The Venetian Marco Polo traveled extensively through central Asia and China in the late thirteenth century, when Mongol empires dominated Asia. His book of travel writings is an especially valuable source of information about the Mongol age. Among other things, he described the Mongol way of making war.

Their arms are bows and arrows, sword and mace; but above all the bow, for they are capital archers, indeed the best that are known. . . .

When a Mongol prince goes forth to war, he takes with him, say, 100,000 horse. Well, he appoints an officer to every ten men, one to every hundred, one to every thousand, and one to every ten thousand, so that his own orders have to be given to ten persons only, and each of these ten persons has to pass the orders only to another ten, and so on, no one having to give orders to more than ten. And every one in turn is responsible only to the officer immediately over him; and the discipline and order that comes of this method is marvellous, for they are a people very obedient to their chiefs. . . .

When they are going on a distant expedition they take no gear with them except two leather bottles for milk, a little earthenware pot to cook their meat in, and a little tent to shelter them from rain. And in case of great urgency they will ride ten days on end without lighting a fire or taking a meal. On such an occasion they will sustain themselves on the blood of their horses, opening a vein and letting the blood jet into their mouths, drinking till they have had enough, and then staunching it. . . .

When they come to an engagement with the enemy, they will gain the victory in this fashion. They never let themselves get into a regular medley, but keep perpetually riding round and shooting into the enemy. And as they do not count it any shame to run away in battle, they will sometimes pretend to do so, and in running away they turn in the saddle and shoot hard and strong at the foe, and in this way make great havoc. Their horses are trained so perfectly that they will double hither and thither, just like a dog, in a way that is quite astonishing. Thus they fight to as good purpose in running away as if they stood and faced the enemy because of the vast volleys of arrows that they shoot in this way, turning round upon their pursuers, who are fancying that they have won the battle. But when the Mongols see that they have killed and wounded a good many horses and men, they wheel round bodily and return to the charge in perfect order and with loud cries, and in a very short time the enemy are routed. In truth they are stout and valiant solders, and inured to war. And you perceive that it is just when the enemy sees them run, and imagines that he has gained the battle, that he has in reality lost it, for the Mongols wheel round in a moment when they judge the right time has come. And after this fashion they have won many a fight.

SOURCE: Marco Polo. *The Book of Ser Marco Polo,* 3rd ed. Trans. and ed. by Henry Yule and
Henri Cordier. London: John Murray, 1921, pp. 260–63. (Translation slightly modified.)

lenge his rule. But the Mongol campaigns in China and Persia had especially far-reaching consequences.

Chinggis Khan himself extended Mongol rule to northern China, dominated since 1127 C.E. by the nomadic Jurchen people, while the Song dynasty continued to rule in southern China. The conquest of China began in 1211 C.E. when Mongol raiding parties invaded the Jurchen realm. Raids quickly became more frequent and intense, and soon they developed into a campaign of conquest. By 1215 the Mongols had captured the Jurchen capital near modern Beijing, which under the new name of Khanbaliq ("city of the khan") served also as the Mongol capital in China. Fighting between Mongols and Jurchen continued until 1234, but by 1220 the Mongols had largely established control over northern China.

*Mongol Conquest
of Northern China*

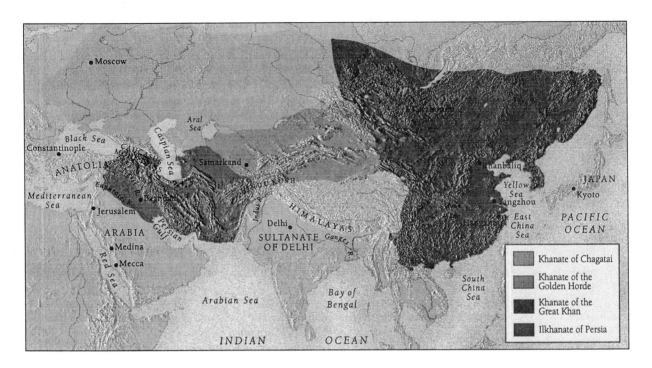

Moscow

Aral Sea

Black Sea
Constantinople

Caspian Sea

ANATOLIA

Samarkand

Mediterranean Sea

Jerusalem

HINDU KUSH

HIMALAYAS

Indus R.

Ganges

Delhi

SULTANATE OF DELHI

ARABIA

Medina

Mecca

Red Sea

Persian Gulf

Euphrates R.

Arabian Sea

Bay of Bengal

INDIAN   OCEAN

hanbaliq

Yellow Sea
angzhou

East China Sea

South China Sea

JAPAN
Kyoto

PACIFIC OCEAN

	Khanate of Chagatai
	Khanate of the Golden Horde
	Khanate of the Great Khan
	Ilkhanate of Persia

MAP [17.2]

The Mongol empires.

Mongol Conquest
of Persia

While part of his army consolidated the Mongol hold on northern China, Chinggis Khan led another force to Afghanistan and Persia, ruled at that time by a successor to the Saljuqs known as the Khwarazm shah. In 1218 Chinggis Khan sought to open trade and diplomatic relations with the Khwarazm shah. The shah despised the Mongols, however, and he ordered his officials to murder Chinggis Khan's envoys and the merchants accompanying them. The following year Chinggis Khan took his army west to seek revenge. Mongol forces pursued the Khwarazm shah to an island in the Caspian Sea where he died. Meanwhile, they shattered the shah's army and seized control of his realm.

To forestall any possibility that the shah's state might survive and constitute a challenge to his own empire, Chinggis Khan wreaked destruction on the conquered land. The Mongols ravaged one city after another, demolishing buildings and massacring hundreds of thousands of people. Some cities never recovered. The Mongols also destroyed the delicate *qanat* irrigation systems that sustained agriculture in the arid region, resulting in severely reduced agricultural production. For centuries after the Mongol conquest, Persian chroniclers cursed the invaders and the devastation they visited upon the land.

By the time of his death in 1227, Chinggis Khan had laid the foundation of a vast and mighty empire. He had united the Mongols, established Mongol supremacy in central Asia, and extended Mongol control to northern China in the east and Persia in the west. Chinggis Khan was a conqueror, however, not an administrator. He ruled the Mongols themselves through his control over the army, but he did not establish a central government for the lands that he conquered. Instead, he assigned Mongol overlords to supervise local administrators and to extract a generous tribute for the Mongols' own uses. Chinggis Khan's heirs continued his conquests, but they also undertook the task of designing a more permanent administration to guide the fortunes of the Mongol empire.

The Mongol Empires after Chinggis Khan

Chinggis Khan's death touched off a struggle for power among his sons and grandsons, several of whom had ambitions to succeed the great khan. Eventually, his heirs divided Chinggis Khan's vast realm into four regional empires. The great khans ruled China, the wealthiest of Mongol lands. Descendants of Chaghatai, one of Chinggis Khan's sons, ruled the khanate of Chaghatai in central Asia. Persia fell under the authority of rulers known as the ilkhans, and the khans of the Golden Horde dominated Russia. The great khans were nominally superior to the others, but they were rarely able to enforce their claims to authority. In fact, for as long as the Mongol empires survived, ambition fueled constant tension and occasional conflict among the four khans.

The consolidation of Mongol rule in China came during the reign of Khubilai, one of Chinggis Khan's grandsons. Khubilai was perhaps the most talented of the great conqueror's descendants. He unleashed ruthless attacks against his enemies, but he also took an interest in cultural matters and worked to improve the welfare of his subjects. He actively promoted Buddhism, and he provided support also for Daoists, Muslims, and Christians in his realm. The famous Venetian traveler Marco Polo, who lived almost two decades at Khubilai's court, praised him for his generosity toward the poor and his efforts to build roads. Though named great khan in 1260, Khubilai spent four years fighting off contenders. From 1264 until his death in 1294, Khubilai Khan presided over the Mongol empire at its height.

Khubilai Khan

Khubilai extended Mongol rule to all of China. From his base at Khanbaliq, he relentlessly attacked the Song dynasty in southern China. The Song capital at Hangzhou fell to Mongol forces in 1276, and within three years Khubilai had eliminated resistance throughout China. In 1279 he proclaimed himself emperor and established the Yuan dynasty, which ruled China until its collapse in 1368.

Mongol Conquest of Southern China

Beyond China, Khubilai had little success as a conqueror. During the 1270s and 1280s, he launched several invasions of Vietnam, Cambodia, and Burma, as well as a naval expedition against Java involving five hundred to one thousand ships and twenty thousand troops. But Mongol forces did not adapt well to the humid, tropical jungles of southeast Asia. Pasture lands

This portrait by a Chinese artist depicts a genial Khubilai Khan who has become well acquainted with Chinese ways. • National Palace Museum Taipei, Taiwan, Republic of China

were inadequate for their horses, and the fearsome Mongol horsemen were unable to cope with the guerrilla tactics employed by the defenders. In 1274 and again in 1281, Khubilai also attempted seaborne invasions of Japan, but on both occasions typhoons thwarted his plans. The storm of 1281 was especially vicious: it destroyed about 4,500 Mongol vessels carrying more than one hundred thousand armed troops—the largest seaborne expedition before World War II. Japanese defenders attributed their continued independence to the *kamikaze* ("divine winds").

The Golden Horde   As Khubilai consolidated his hold on east Asia, his cousins and brothers tightened Mongol control on lands to the west. Mongols of the group known as the Golden Horde overran Russia between 1237 and 1241 and then mounted exploratory expeditions into Poland, Hungary, and eastern Germany in 1241 and 1242. Mongols of the Golden Horde prized the steppes north of the Black Sea as prime pastureland for their horses. They maintained a large army on the steppes from which they mounted raids into Russia. They did not occupy Russia, which they regarded as an unattractive land of forests, but they extracted tribute from the Russian cities and agricultural provinces. The Golden Horde maintained its hegemony in Russia until the mid-fifteenth century, when the princes of Moscow rejected its authority while building a powerful Russian state. By the mid-sixteenth century Russian conquerors had extended their control to the steppes, but Mongol khans descended from the Golden Horde continued to rule the Crimea until the late eighteenth century.

The Ilkhanate   While the Golden Horde established its authority in Russia, Khubilai's brother
of Persia   Hülegü toppled the Abbasid empire and established the Mongol ilkhanate in Persia. In 1258 he captured the Abbasid capital of Baghdad after a brief siege. His troops looted the city, executed the caliph, and massacred more than two hundred thousand residents by Hülegü's own estimate. From Persia, Hülegü's army ventured into Syria, but Muslim forces from Egypt soon expelled them and placed a limit on Mongol expansion to the southwest.

When the Mongols crushed ruling regimes in settled societies, particularly in China and Persia, they discovered that they needed to become governors as well as conquerors. The Mongols had no experience administering complex societies, where successful governance required talents beyond the equestrian and military skills esteemed on the steppes. They had a difficult time adjusting to their role as administrators. Indeed, they never became entirely comfortable in the role, and most of their conquests fell out of their hands within a century.

Mongol Rule in   The Mongols adopted different tactics in the different lands that they ruled. In
Persia   Persia they made important concessions to local interests. Although Mongols and their allies occupied the highest administrative positions, Persians served as ministers, provincial governors, and state officials at all lower levels. The Mongols basically allowed the Persians to administer the ilkhanate as long as they delivered tax receipts and maintained order.

Over time, the Mongols even assimilated to Persian cultural traditions. The early Mongol rulers of Persia mostly observed their native shamanism, but they tolerated all faiths—including Islam, Nestorian Christianity, Buddhism, and Judaism—and they ended the privileges given Muslims during the Abbasid caliphate. Gradually, however, the Mongols themselves gravitated toward Islam. In 1295 Ilkhan Ghazan publicly converted to Islam, and most of the Mongols in Persia followed his example. Ghazan's conversion sparked large-scale massacres of Christians and Jews, and it signaled the return of Islam to a privileged position in Persian society. It also indicated the absorption of the Mongols into Muslim Persian society.

Mongol Rule   In China, by contrast, the Mongol overlords stood aloof from their subjects,
in China   whom they scorned as mere cultivators. They outlawed intermarriage between Mongols and Chinese and forbade the Chinese from learning the Mongol language. Soon after their conquest some of the victors went so far as to suggest that the Mongols

The siege of Baghdad: a Persian manuscript illustration depicts Mongol forces camped outside the city walls while residents huddle within. • Bibilothèque Nationale de France

exterminate the Chinese people and convert China itself into pastureland for their horses. Cooler heads eventually prevailed, and the Mongols decided simply to extract as much revenue as possible from their Chinese subjects. In doing so, however, they did not make as much use of native administrative talent as did their counterparts in Persia. Instead, they brought foreign administrators into China and placed them in charge. Along with their nomadic allies, the Mongols' administrative staff included Arabs, Persians, and perhaps even Europeans: Marco Polo may have served as an administrator in the city of Yangzhou during the reign of Khubilai Khan.

The Mongols also resisted assimilation to Chinese cultural traditions. They ended the privileges enjoyed by the Confucian scholars, and they dismantled the Confucian educational and examination system, which had produced untold generations of civil servants for the Chinese bureaucracy. They did not persecute Confucians, but they allowed the Confucian tradition to wither in the absence of official support. Meanwhile, to remain on good terms with subjects of different faiths, the Mongols allowed the construction of churches, temples, and shrines, and they even subsidized some religious establishments. They tolerated all cultural and religious traditions in China, including Confucianism, Daoism, Buddhism, and Nestorian Christianity. Of Khubilai Khan's four wives, his favorite was Chabi, a Nestorian Christian.

For their part the Mongols mostly continued to follow their native shamanist cults, although many of the ruling elite became enchanted with the Lamaist school of Buddhism that developed in Tibet. Lamaist Buddhism held several attractions for the Mongols. It made a prominent place for magic and supernatural powers, and in that respect it resembled the Mongols' shamanism. Moreover, Lamaist Buddhist leaders officially recognized the Mongols as legitimate rulers and went out of their way to court the Mongols' favor. They numbered the Mongols in the ranks of universal

The Mongols and Buddhism

Buddhist rulers and even recognized the Mongol khans as incarnations of the Buddha himself. Thus it is not surprising that the Mongol ruling elites would find Lamaist Buddhism attractive.

The Mongols and Eurasian Integration

The Mongols and Trade

In building their vast empire, the Mongols sponsored interaction among peoples of different societies and linked the lands of the Eurasian landmass more directly than ever before. Several specific policies of the Mongols encouraged this increasing integration of Eurasian lands and peoples. One had to do with trade. As a nomadic people dependent on commerce with settled agricultural societies, the Mongols worked to secure trade routes and ensure the safety of merchants passing through their territories. The Mongol khans frequently fought among themselves, but they maintained reasonably good order within their realms and allowed merchants, ambassadors, and missionaries to travel unmolested through their empires. As a result, long-distance travel and trade became much less risky than in earlier times. Merchants increased their commercial investments, and the volume of long-distance trade across central Asia dwarfed that of earlier eras. Lands as distant as China and western Europe became directly linked for the first time because of the ability of individuals to travel across the entire Eurasian landmass.

Diplomatic Missions

Like trade, diplomatic communication was essential to the Mongols, and their protection of roads and travelers benefited ambassadors as well as merchants. Chinggis Khan destroyed the Khwarazm shah in Persia because the shah unwisely murdered the Mongol envoys Chinggis Khan dispatched in hopes of opening diplomatic and commercial relations. Throughout the Mongol era the great khans in China, the ilkhans in Persia, and the other khans maintained close communications by means of diplomatic embassies. They also had diplomatic dealings with rulers in Korea, Vietnam, India, western Europe, and other lands as well.

Resettlement

Another Mongol policy that encouraged Eurasian integration was the practice of resettling peoples in new lands. As a nomadic people, the Mongols had limited numbers of skilled artisans and educated individuals, but the more their empire expanded, the more they needed the services of specialized craftsmen and literate administrators. Mongol overlords recruited the talent they needed largely from the ranks of their allies and the peoples they conquered, and they often moved people far from their homelands to sites where they could best make use of their services. Among the most important of the Mongols' allies were the Uighur Turks, who lived mostly in oasis cities along the silk roads. The Uighurs were literate and often highly educated, and they provided many of the clerks, secretaries, and administrators who ran the Mongol empires, as well as units of soldiers who bolstered Mongol garrisons. Arab and Persian Muslims were also prominent among those who administered the Mongols' affairs far from their homelands.

Conquered peoples also supplied the Mongols with talent. When they overcame a city, Mongol forces routinely surveyed the captured population, separated out those with specialized skills, and sent them to the capital at Karakorum or some other place where there was demand for their services. From the ranks of conquered peoples came soldiers, bodyguards, administrators, secretaries, translators, physicians, armor makers, metalsmiths, miners, carpenters, masons, textile workers, musicians, and jewelers. After the 1230s the Mongols often took censuses of lands they conquered, partly to levy taxes and conscript military forces and partly to locate talented individuals. The Parisian goldsmith Guillaume Boucher was only one among thousands of foreign-born individuals who became permanent residents of the Mongol capital at Karakorum because of their special talents. Like their protection of trade and diplomacy, the Mongols' policy of resettling allies and conquered peoples promoted Eurasian integration by increasing communication and exchange between peoples of different societies.

Decline of the Mongols in Persia and China

Soon after the long and prosperous reign of Khubilai Khan, the Mongols encountered serious difficulties governing Persia and China. In Persia excessive spending strained the treasury, and overexploitation of the peasantry led to reduced revenues. In the early 1290s the ilkhan tried to resolve his financial difficulties by introducing paper money and ordering all subjects to accept it for payment of all debts. The purpose of this measure was to drive precious metals into the hands of the government, but the policy was a miserable failure: rather than accept paper that they regarded as worthless, merchants simply closed their shops. Commerce ground to a halt until the ilkhan rescinded his order. Meanwhile, factional struggles plagued the Mongol leadership. The regime went into steep decline after the death of Ilkhan Ghazan in 1304. When the last of the Mongol rulers died without an heir in 1335, the ilkhanate itself simply collapsed. Government in Persia devolved to local levels until late in the fourteenth century when Turkish peoples reintroduced effective central government.

Collapse of the Ilkhanate

Mongol decline in China was a more complicated affair. As in Persia, it had an economic dimension. The Mongols continued to use the paper money that Chinese had introduced during the Tang and Song dynasties, but they did not maintain adequate reserves of the bullion that backed up paper notes. The general population soon lost confidence in paper money, and prices rose sharply as a reflection of its diminished value. As in Persia, too, factions and infighting hastened Mongol decline in China. As the richest of the Mongol empires, China attracted the attention of ambitious warriors. Beginning in the 1320s power struggles, imperial assassinations, and civil war convulsed the Mongol regime in China.

Decline of the Yuan Dynasty

Apart from financial difficulties and factional divisions, the Mongol rulers of China also faced an onslaught of epidemic disease. By facilitating trade and communications throughout Eurasia, the Mongols unwittingly expedited the spread of bubonic plague (discussed in chapter 21). During the 1330s plague erupted in southwestern China. From there it spread throughout China and central Asia, and by the late 1340s it had reached southwest Asia and Europe, where it became known as the Black Death. Bubonic plague sometimes killed half or more of an exposed population, particularly during the furious initial years of the epidemic, and it seriously disrupted economies and societies throughout much of Eurasia. In China depopulation and labor shortages that followed on the heels of epidemic plague weakened the Mongol regime. (Plague would also have caused serious problems for the Mongol rulers of Persia had the ilkhanate not collapsed before its arrival.)

Bubonic Plague

The Mongols also faced a rebellious subject population in China. The Mongols stood apart from their Chinese subjects, who returned the contempt of their conquerors. Beginning in the 1340s southern China became a hotbed of peasant rebellion and banditry, which the Mongols could not control. In 1368 rebel forces captured Khanbaliq, and the Mongols departed China en masse and returned to the steppes.

Despite the collapse of the Mongol regimes in Persia and China, Mongol states did not completely disappear. The khanate of Chaghatai continued to prevail in central Asia, and Mongols posed a threat to the northwestern borders of China until the

Surviving Mongol Khanates

eighteenth century. Meanwhile, the khanate of the Golden Horde continued to dominate the Caucasus and the steppelands north of the Black Sea and Caspian Sea until the mid-sixteenth century when a resurgent Russian state brought the Golden Horde down. As in the case of China, however, Mongols continued to threaten Russia until the eighteenth century, and Mongols who had settled in the Crimean peninsula retained their identity until Josef Stalin forcibly moved them to other parts of the Soviet Union in the mid-twentieth century.

 AFTER THE MONGOLS

By no means did the decline of the Mongols signal the end of nomadic peoples' influence in Eurasia. As Mongol strength waned, Turkish peoples resumed the expansive campaigns that the Mongols had interrupted. During the late fourteenth and early fifteenth centuries, the Turkish conqueror Tamerlane built a central Asian empire rivaling that of Chinggis Khan himself. Although Tamerlane's empire foundered soon after his death, it deeply influenced three surviving Turkish Muslim states—the Mughal empire in India, the Safavid empire in Persia, and the Ottoman empire based in Anatolia—and also embraced much of southwest Asia, southeastern Europe, and north Africa.

Tamerlane the Whirlwind

The Lame Conqueror   The rapid collapse of the Mongol states left gaping power vacuums in China and Persia. While the native Ming dynasty filled the vacuum in China, a self-made Turkish conqueror named Timur moved on Persia. Because he walked with a limp, contemporaries referred to him as Timur-i lang—"Timur the Lame," an appellation that made its way into English as Tamerlane.

Born about 1336 near Samarkand, Tamerlane took Chinggis Khan as his model. Like Chinggis Khan, Tamerlane came from a family of the minor nobility and had to make his own way to power. Like Chinggis Khan, too, he was a charismatic leader and a courageous warrior, and he attracted a band of loyal followers. During the 1360s he eliminated rivals to power, either by persuading them to join him as allies or by defeating their armies on the battlefield, and he won recognition as leader of his own tribe. By 1370 he had extended his authority throughout the khanate of Chaghatai and begun to build a magnificent imperial capital in Samarkand.

Tamerlane's Conquests   For the rest of his life, Tamerlane led his armies on campaigns of conquest. He turned first to the region between Persia and Afghanistan, and he took special care to establish his authority in the rich cities so that he could levy taxes on trade and agricultural production. Next he attacked the Golden Horde in the Caucasus region and Russia, and by the mid-1390s he had severely weakened it. During the last years of the century, he invaded India and subjected Delhi to a ferocious sack: contemporary chroniclers reported, with some exaggeration, that for a period of two months after the attack not even birds visited the devastated city. Later Tamerlane campaigned along the Ganges, although he never attempted to incorporate India into his empire. He opened the new century with campaigns in southwest Asia and Anatolia. In 1404 he began preparations for an invasion of China, and he was leading his army east when he fell ill and died in 1405.

Like his model Chinggis Khan, Tamerlane was a conqueror, not a governor. He spent almost his entire adult life planning and fighting military campaigns: he even

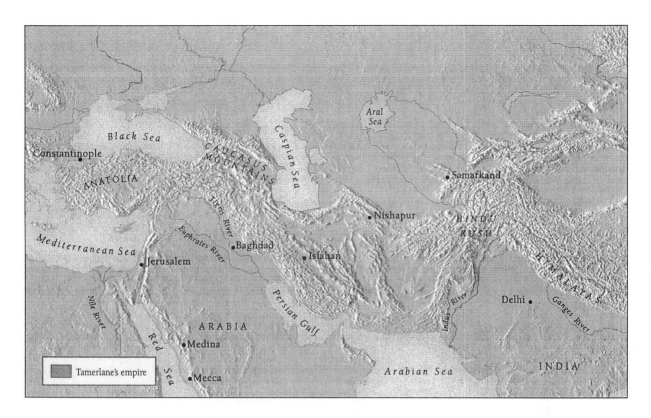

MAP [17.3]
Tamerlane's empire.

had himself carried around on a litter during his final illness, as he prepared to invade China. He did not create an imperial administration, but rather ruled through tribal leaders who were his allies. He appointed overlords in the territories he conquered, but they relied on existing bureaucratic structures and simply received taxes and tributes on his behalf.

Given its loose organization, it is not surprising that Tamerlane's empire experienced stresses and strains after the conqueror's death. Tamerlane's sons and grandsons engaged in a long series of bitter conflicts that resulted in the contraction of his empire and its

Spoils from Tamerlane's campaigns and raids enriched the conqueror's capital at Samarkand. Among other buildings, they financed the magnificent tomb where Tamerlane's remains still rest. • Art Resource, NY

Tamerlane's Heirs

division into four main regions. For a century after Tamerlane's death, however, they maintained control over the region from Persia to Afghanistan. When the last vestiges of Tamerlane's imperial creation disappeared, in the early sixteenth century, the Mughal, Safavid, and Ottoman empires that replaced it all clearly reflected the Turkish Muslim legacy of the lame conqueror.

The Foundation of the Ottoman Empire

Chapter 27 will discuss the Mughal empire in India and the Safavid empire in Persia, both of which emerged during the early sixteenth century as Tamerlane's empire finally dissolved. The early stages of Ottoman expansion predated Tamerlane, however, and the foundation of the Ottoman empire throws additional light on the influence of nomadic peoples during the period 1000 to 1500 C.E.

Osman   After the Mongol conquest of Persia, large numbers of nomadic Turks migrated from central Asia to the ilkhanate and beyond to the territories in Anatolia that the Saljuq Turks had seized from the Byzantine empire. There they followed charismatic leaders who organized further campaigns of conquest. Among these leaders was Osman, who during the late thirteenth and early fourteenth centuries carved a small state for himself in northwestern Anatolia. In 1299 Osman declared independence from the Saljuq sultan and launched a campaign to build a state at the expense of the Byzantine empire. After every successful operation Osman attracted more and more followers, who came to be known as Osmanlis or Ottomans.

Ottoman Conquests   During the 1350s, the Ottomans gained a considerable advantage over their Turkish rivals when they established a foothold across the Dardanelles at Gallipoli in the Balkan peninsula. The Ottomans quickly moved to expand the boundaries of their Balkan holdings. Byzantine forces resisted Ottoman incursions, but because of political fragmentation, ineffective government, and exploitation of the peasantry, the Ottomans found abundant local support. By the 1380s the Ottomans had become by far the most powerful people in the Balkan peninsula, and by the end of the century they were poised to capture Constantinople and take over the Byzantine empire.

Tamerlane temporarily delayed Ottoman expansion in the Byzantine realm. In 1402 Tamerlane's forces crushed the Ottoman army, captured the sultan, and subjected the Ottoman state to the conqueror's authority. After Tamerlane's death Ottoman leaders had to reestablish their rule in their own realm. This undertaking involved both the repression of ambitious local princes who sought to build power bases at Ottoman expense and the defense of Ottoman territories against Byzantine, Venetian, and other Christian forces that sought to turn back the advance of the Turkish Muslims. By the 1440s the Ottomans had recovered their balance and begun again to expand in the Byzantine empire.

The Capture   The campaign culminated in 1453 when Sultan Mehmed II, known as Mehmed *of Constantinople*   the Conqueror, captured the Byzantine capital of Constantinople. After subjecting it to a sack, he made the city his own capital under the Turkish name of Istanbul. With Istanbul as a base, the Ottomans quickly absorbed the remainder of the Byzantine empire. By 1480 they controlled all of Greece and the Balkan region. They continued to expand throughout most of the sixteenth century as well, extending their rule to southwest Asia, southeastern Europe, Egypt, and north Africa. Once again, then, a nomadic people asserted control over a long-settled society and quickly built a vast empire.

Although besieged by Ottoman forces, Constantinople received
supplies from the sea for almost two months before Ottomans
destroyed the city walls and completed their conquest of the
Byzantine empire. • Bibilothèque Nationale de France

During the half millennium from 1000 to 1500 C.E., nomadic peoples of central Asia played a larger role than ever before in world history. As early as the second millennium B.C.E., they had periodically threatened states from China to the eastern Mediterranean region, and from classical times they had traded regularly and actively with peoples of settled societies. From 1000 to 1500 their relations with neighboring peoples changed, as they dominated affairs in most of Eurasia through their conquests and their construction of vast transregional empires. Turkish peoples built the most durable of the nomadic empires, but the spectacular conquests of the Mongols most clearly demonstrated the potential of nomadic peoples to project their formidable military power to settled agricultural societies. By establishing connections

that spanned the Eurasian landmass, the nomadic empires laid the foundation for increasing communication, exchange, and interaction among peoples of different societies and thereby fostered the integration of the eastern hemisphere. The age of nomadic empires from 1000 to 1500 C.E. foreshadowed the integrated world of
modern times.

CHRONOLOGY

1055	Tughril Beg named sultan
1071	Battle of Manzikert
1206–1227	Reign of Chinggis Khan
1211–1234	Mongol conquest of northern China
1219–1221	Mongol conquest of Persia
1237–1241	Mongol conquest of Russia
1258	Mongol capture of Baghdad
1264–1279	Mongol conquest of southern China
1264–1294	Reign of Khubilai Khan
1279–1368	Yuan dynasty
1295	Conversion of Ilkhan Ghazan to Islam
1336–1405	Life of Tamerlane
1453	Ottoman capture of Constantinople

FOR FURTHER READING

S. A. M. Adshead. *Central Asia in World History*. New York, 1993. A provocative essay on central Asia
     and its place in the larger world.
Thomas T. Allsen. *Mongol Imperialism: The Policies of the Grand Qan Möngke in China, Russia, and the
     Islamic Lands, 1251–1259*. Berkeley, 1987. Scholarly analysis of Mongol empire building by Chinggis
     Khan's successors.
Thomas J. Barfield. *The Nomadic Alternative*. Englewood Cliffs, N.J., 1993. A sensitive study of nomadic
     societies in Africa and Eurasia by a leading anthropologist.
———. *The Perilous Frontier: Nomadic Empires and China*. Cambridge, Mass., 1989. Scholarly examina-
     tion of the relationship between nomadic empires and Chinese society.
Vladimir N. Basilov, ed. *Nomads of Eurasia*. Trans. by M. F. Zirin. Los Angeles, 1989. Lavishly illus-
     trated volume that presents translations of essays by Russian scholars on nomadic societies.
René Grousset. *Conqueror of the World: The Life of Chingis-khan*. Trans. by M. McKellar and D. Sinor.
     New York, 1966. Lively account of Chinggis Khan's life and career.
———. *The Empire of the Steppes: A History of Central Asia*. Trans. by N. Walford. New Brunswick,
     1970. A popular account, still useful though somewhat dated, of nomadic empires in central Asia.
Charles J. Halperin. *Russia and the Golden Horde: The Mongol Impact on Medieval Russian History*.
     Bloomington, 1985. An insightful study of the Golden Horde and its influence on Russian society.
Halil Inalcik. *The Ottoman Empire: The Classical Age, 1300–1600*. Trans. by N. Itzkowitz and C. Imber.
     New York, 1973. The best short introduction to early Ottoman history.
Paul Kahn, ed. *The Secret History of the Mongols: The Origin of Chingis Khan*. Adapted from the transla-
     tion of F.W. Cleaves. San Francisco, 1984. A translation of the Mongols' history of their own society,
     adapted for modern readers.
Adam T. Kessler. *Empires beyond the Great Wall: The Heritage of Genghis Khan*. Los Angeles, 1993. Well-
     illustrated survey of nomadic states in central Asia from the Xiongnu to the Mongols.

Beatrice Forbes Manz. *The Rise and Rule of Tamerlane*. Cambridge, 1989. Scholarly analysis of Tamerlane's career and his empire.

David Morgan. *Medieval Persia, 1040–1797*. London, 1988. A brief and insightful survey concentrating on the eras of Turkish and Mongol dominance in Persia.

———. *The Mongols*. Oxford, 1986. Lucid and witty study that makes use of recent scholarship: the best short work on the Mongols.

Michael Prawdin. *The Mongol Empire: Its Rise and Legacy*. 2nd ed. Trans. by E. and C. Paul. New York, 1961. A vivid and detailed study examining Mongol history from Chinggis Khan to Tamerlane.

Tamara Talbot Rice. *The Seljuks in Asia Minor*. London, 1961. Well-illustrated survey of Saljuq history and society, concentrating on the Saljuqs in Anatolia.

Morris Rossabi. *Khubilai Khan: His Life and Times*. Berkeley, 1988. Excellent scholarly study of the greatest of the great khans.

Arthur Waldron. *The Great Wall of China: From History to Myth*. Cambridge, 1989. Examines the role of defensive walls, including the Great Wall, in Chinese efforts to forestall raids by nomadic peoples of central Asia.

CHAPTER 18

STATES AND SOCIETIES
OF SUB-SAHARAN AFRICA

· · ·

A remarkable oral tradition preserves the story of the lion prince Sundiata, thirteenth-century founder of the Mali empire in west Africa. Oral traditions include stories, histories, epics, and other accounts transmitted by professional singers and storytellers known in Africa as griots. Until scholars began to collect and publish African oral traditions about the middle of the twentieth century, the story of Sundiata was available only when a griot recited it.

According to the oral tradition, Sundiata's father ruled a small west African kingdom in the northeastern part of what is now Guinea. Despite his royal parentage, Sundiata had a difficult childhood, since a congenitally defective leg left him partially crippled. When the old king died, his enemies invaded the kingdom and killed the royal offspring, sparing the child Sundiata because they thought his physical condition would prevent him from posing a threat to their ambitions. But Sundiata overcame his injury, learned to use the bow and arrow, and strengthened himself by hunting in the forest. As he grew stronger, Sundiata's enemies began to fear him, and they forced him to seek refuge in a neighboring kingdom. While in exile, Sundiata distinguished himself as a warrior and assembled a powerful cavalry force staffed by loyal followers and allies.

About 1235 Sundiata returned to his homeland and claimed the throne. His cavalry slashed through the countryside, defeating his enemies almost at will. Within a few years he had overcome resistance, established the Mali empire, and consolidated his rule throughout the valley of the Niger River. Although he respected traditional religious beliefs and magical powers, Sundiata was also a Muslim, and he welcomed Muslim merchants from north Africa into his realm. He built a capital city at Niani, which soon became a thriving commercial center. Indeed, as a result of its control of the gold trade—and the political stability provided by Sundiata—the Mali empire became probably the wealthiest land in sub-Saharan Africa. For two centuries after Sundiata's death about 1260, the lion prince's legacy shaped the lives of west African peoples and linked west Africa with north Africa and the Mediterranean basin.

From the classical era forward, peoples from east Asia to the Mediterranean basin established extensive networks of trade and communication. African peoples living south of the Sahara desert participated in the larger economy of the eastern

A bronze plaque from the kingdom of Benin depicts a local chief flanked by warriors and attendants.

• Warrior Chief, Warriors and Attendants. Court of Benin. 16–17th century. The Metropolitan Museum of Art. Gift of Mr. and Mrs. Klaus G. Perls, 1990. (1990.332). Photograph © 1991 The Metropolitan Museum of Art.

hemisphere, though not so fully as their counterparts in north Africa, who from ancient times were prominent in the trading world of the Mediterranean basin. Geographical conditions help to explain why trade and communication networks did not embrace sub-Saharan Africa as readily as they did other regions: the Sahara desert poses a formidable challenge to overland travelers from the north, the African coastlines offer few good natural harbors, and cataracts complicate travel up the continent's major rivers.

Yet like their Eurasian and north African counterparts, peoples of sub-Saharan Africa organized productive societies and built powerful states. Beginning in the second millennium B.C.E., Bantu-speaking peoples migrated from their west African homeland and established societies throughout most of the continent south of the Sahara. The Bantu migrations spread political, social, economic, and cultural influences that shaped African societies over the long term. During the eighth century C.E., Muslim merchants introduced their Islamic faith to sub-Saharan Africa and linked the region to the larger trading world of the eastern hemisphere. The interaction between Bantu and Islamic traditions profoundly influenced the development of African societies.

THE BANTU MIGRATIONS

The long-term process known as the Bantu migrations might have begun as early as 2000 B.C.E. The Bantu, who all spoke tongues belonging to the Bantu family of languages, most likely originated in the region around modern Nigeria. Gradually, they spread south and east, absorbing local populations of hunting, gathering, and fishing peoples into their own agricultural societies. Over the centuries, as some groups of Bantu settled and others moved on, their languages differentiated into upwards of five hundred distinct but related tongues. By 1000 C.E. Bantu peoples occupied most of sub-Saharan Africa, excepting only small pockets populated by hunting and gathering peoples, and they began to establish large states that mediated connections between sub-Saharan Africa and other regions of the eastern hemisphere.

The Dynamics of Bantu Expansion

Bantu Agriculture   The precise motives of the early Bantu migrants remain shrouded in the mists of time, but it seems likely that population pressures drove the migrations. The earliest migrants relied on an agricultural rather than a hunting-and-gathering economy. Their staple foods were yams, millet, and sorghum, supplemented by vegetables and occasionally by meat. Agriculture enabled the Bantu population to increase more rapidly than the populations of their hunting and gathering neighbors. When the increasing numbers of individual Bantu settlements began to put pressure on the available resources, groups of Bantu left their parent societies and moved to new territories. In the new agricultural societies, this process repeated itself.

The expansion of agricultural peoples into lands inhabited by hunting and gathering peoples led to sharp conflicts over land use. Oral traditions that preserve memories of the migrations from Bantu viewpoints often depict hunting and gathering peoples such as the pygmies of the rain forests as inferior and even subhuman. Yet oral traditions also suggest that relations between Bantu and indigenous peoples were not always hostile. Many stories relate that hunting, gathering, and fishing peoples helped Bantu migrants learn how to cope with new environments. It is clear, too, that Bantu absorbed other peoples into their own society. Many peoples found agriculture an attractive alternative to their hunting and gathering economies, since it provided increased supplies of food and supported larger populations. As a result, they often intermarried with Bantu peoples, adopted Bantu languages, and joined Bantu society.

For the most part the Bantu migrations proceeded slowly, since it might take a generation or more for a group to experience population pressure and divide. At several junctures, however, the pace of the migrations quickened. By the middle of the first millennium B.C.E., for example, Bantu peoples had begun to produce iron. It is not certain how they acquired the technology of iron production. Some scholars believe that merchants from north Africa introduced iron metallurgy south of the Sahara, whereas others argue that Bantu peoples independently discovered how to smelt iron. In either case iron production appeared early among the Bantu: archaeologists have uncovered evidence of ironworking in both Nigeria and the Great Lakes region of east Africa by the seventh and sixth centuries B.C.E., and possibly as early as the ninth century B.C.E. Iron tools enabled the Bantu to clear land and expand the zone of agriculture more efficiently than before, which in turn brought population growth and increased momentum to the Bantu migrations.

Iron Metallurgy

The introduction of bananas to Africa caused another migratory surge. First domesticated in southeast Asia, bananas entered Africa by way of sea-lanes across the Indian Ocean. During the late centuries B.C.E., Malay seafarers from the islands that make up modern Indonesia sailed west beyond India, and by the early centuries C.E. they were exploring the east African coasts. Between about 300 and 500 C.E., they colonized the island of Madagascar and established banana cultivation there. (Apart from bananas, they also brought southeast Asian cultural traditions. Malagasy, the language spoken on Madagascar even today, belongs to the Austronesian family of languages.) From Madagascar bananas easily made the jump to the east African mainland. By 500 C.E. several varieties of bananas had become well established in Africa. They provided a nutritious supplement to Bantu diets and enabled the Bantu to expand into heavily forested regions where yams and millet did not grow well. Thus cultivation of bananas increased the supply of food available to the Bantu, enriched their diets, and allowed them to expand more rapidly than before.

Bananas

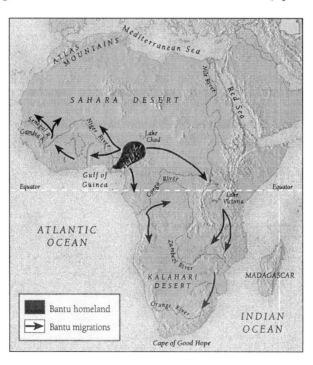

MAP [18.1]

The Bantu migrations.

Population Growth

The population history of sub-Saharan Africa clearly reflects the significance of iron metallurgy and bananas. In 400 B.C.E., before ironworking had deeply influenced the continent's societies, the population of sub-Saharan Africa stood at about 3.5 million. By the turn of the millennium, human numbers exceeded 11 million. By 800 C.E., after banana cultivation had spread throughout the continent, the sub-Saharan population had climbed to 17 million. And by 1000, when the Bantu migrations had introduced agriculture and iron metallurgy to most regions of sub-Saharan Africa, the population had passed 22 million.

Bantu Political Organization

By 1000 C.E., after more than two millennia of migrations, the Bantu had approached the limits of their expansion. Their migrations did not completely end at that point: some Bantu peoples continued their movements as late as the nineteenth century. Since agricultural peoples already occupied most of the continent, however, migrating into new territories and forming new settlements was much more difficult than in previous centuries. Instead of migrating in search of new lands to cultivate, then, the Bantu developed increasingly complex forms of government that enabled them to organize their existing societies more efficiently.

"Stateless Society"

Scholars often use the term *stateless society* to refer to one form of social organization widely prevalent in Africa during and after the Bantu migrations. Although somewhat misleading, since it seems to imply that Bantu societies had little or no government, the term accurately reflects the fact that early Bantu societies did not depend on an elaborate hierarchy of officials or a bureaucratic apparatus to administer their affairs. Instead, Bantu peoples governed themselves mostly through family and kinship groups.

Bantu peoples usually settled in villages with populations averaging about one hundred people. Male heads of families constituted a village's ruling council, which decided the public affairs for the entire group. The most prominent of the family heads presided over the village as a chief and represented the settlement when it dealt with neighboring peoples. A group of villages constituted a district, which became the principal focus of ethnic loyalties. Usually there was no chief or larger government for the district. Instead, village chiefs negotiated on matters concerning two or more villages. Meanwhile, within individual villages, family and kinship groups disciplined their own members as necessary.

This type of organization lends itself particularly well to small-scale communities, but stateless societies often grew to large proportions. Some networks of villages and districts organized the public affairs of several hundred thousand people. By the nineteenth century, for example, the Tiv people of Nigeria, numbering almost one million, conducted their affairs in a stateless society built on a foundation of family and kinship groups.

Chiefdoms

After about 1000 C.E., however, stateless societies faced difficult challenges. Population growth strained resources, but few lands were available for migrants to settle. Conflicts between villages and districts became more frequent and more intense. Increased conflict encouraged Bantu communities to organize military forces for both offensive and defensive purposes, and military organization in turn encouraged the development of more formal structures of government. Many districts fell under the leadership of powerful chiefs, who overrode kinship networks and imposed their own authority on their territories. Some of these chiefs conquered their neighbors and consolidated their lands into small kingdoms such as those of Ife and Benin in western Nigeria.

In a few cases dynamic kingdoms emerged and organized the public affairs of large territories. One was the kingdom of Kongo. About 1000 C.E. population pressure and military challenge encouraged the formation of small states embracing a few villages each in the valley of the Congo River (also known as the Zaire River). By 1200 conflict between these small states had resulted in the emergence of larger, regional principalities. During the fourteenth century one of these principalities overcame its neighbors and built the kingdom of Kongo, which embraced much of modern-day Republic of Congo and Angola.

The central government of Kongo included the king and officials who oversaw military, judicial,

Kingdom of Kongo

According to legend, this handsome terra-cotta head represents an ambitious warrior who usurped power in the small state of Ife (in modern Nigeria). Produced shortly after 1000 C.E., it testifies to the increasing tensions in sub-Saharan politics after the turn of the millennium. • Ife Museum © Dirk Bakker, 1978

and financial affairs. Beneath the central government were six provinces administered by governors, each of whom supervised several districts administered by subordinate officials. Within the districts, villages ruled by chiefs provided local government. Though not the only kingdom in sub-Saharan Africa, Kongo was perhaps the most tightly centralized of the early Bantu kingdoms. In most cases the king or other central administrators could appoint or replace local officials at will, and the central government maintained a royal currency system based on cowries, sea shells that came from the Indian Ocean. The kingdom of Kongo provided effective organization from the fourteenth until the mid-seventeenth century when Portuguese slave traders undermined the authority of the kings and the central government.

Stateless societies did not disappear with the emergence of formal states. To the contrary, they survived into the nineteenth century in much of sub-Saharan Africa. Yet regional states and large kingdoms became increasingly prominent during the centuries after 1000 C.E. as Bantu peoples responded to population pressures and military challenges facing their societies.

ISLAMIC KINGDOMS AND EMPIRES

While Bantu peoples organized societies on the basis of African traditions, merchants from north Africa and southwest Asia introduced their Islamic faith to sub-Saharan Africa. Islam arrived by two routes: it went to west Africa overland by trans-Saharan camel caravans, and it traveled to coastal east Africa over the sea-lanes of the Indian Ocean in the vessels of merchant mariners. After the eighth century C.E., Islam profoundly influenced the political, social, and economic development of sub-Saharan Africa, as well as its cultural and religious development.

Trans-Saharan Trade and Islamic States in West Africa

The Sahara desert has never served as an absolute barrier to communication between human societies. Small numbers of nomadic peoples have lived in the desert itself ever since a process of desiccation created the Sahara beginning about 5000 B.C.E. These nomads migrated around the desert and had dealings with other peoples settled on its fringes. Even in ancient and classical times, merchants occasionally organized commercial expeditions across the desert, although the value and volume of trade in the Mediterranean basin greatly exceeded that crossing the Sahara.

Camels   The arrival of the camel quickened the pace of communication and transportation across the Sahara. Camels came to north Africa from Arabia, by way of Egypt and the Sudan, about the seventh century B.C.E. During the late centuries B.C.E., a special camel saddle, which took advantage of the animals' distinctive physical structure, also made its way to north Africa. Because a caravan took seventy to ninety days to cross the Sahara and because camels could travel long distances before needing water, they proved to be useful beasts of burden in an arid region. After about 500 C.E. camels increasingly replaced horses and donkeys as the preferred transport animals throughout the Sahara, as well as in the deserts of central Asia.

In this engraving by a German artist of the mid-nineteenth century, a small caravan approaches Timbuktu. Camels and donkeys serve as beasts of burden, and horse-mounted escorts accompany the party. • New York Public Library. General Research Division. Astor, Lenox and Tilden Foundations

When Arab conquerors established their Islamic faith in north Africa during the seventh and eighth centuries, they also integrated the region into a rapidly expanding zone of commerce and communication. Thus it was natural for Muslims in north Africa to explore the potential of trade across the Sahara. By the late eighth century, Islamic merchants had trekked across the desert and established commercial relations with societies in sub-Saharan west Africa.

The principal state of west Africa at the time of the Muslims' arrival there was the kingdom of Ghana (not related to the modern state of Ghana), situated between the Senegal and Niger Rivers in a region straddling the border between the modern states of Mali and Mauritania. Ghana emerged as a kingdom at an uncertain but early date: according to legends preserved by Arab travelers, as many as twenty-two kings ruled in Ghana before Muhammad and his companions embarked on the *hijra*. Ghana probably developed as a state during the fifth or sixth century C.E. when settled, agricultural peoples sought to protect their societies from the raids of camel-riding nomads who increasingly came out of the Sahara. When Muslims arrived in west Africa, the kingdom of Ghana was a regional state much like Ife, Benin, and others that Bantu peoples had already established or would soon build in other parts of sub-Saharan Africa.

The Kingdom of Ghana

As trade and traffic across the desert increased, Ghana underwent a dramatic transformation. It became the most important commercial site in west Africa because it became the center for trade in gold. Ghana itself did not produce gold, but the kings procured nuggets from lands to the south—probably from the region around the headwaters of the Niger, Gambia, and Senegal Rivers, which enjoyed the world's largest supply of gold available at the time. By controlling and taxing trade in the precious metal, the kings both enriched and strengthened their realm. Apart from gold, merchants from Ghana also provided ivory and slaves for traders from north Africa. In exchange, they received horses, cloth, small manufactured wares, and salt—a crucial commodity in the tropics, but one that local sources could not supply in large quantities.

Integration into trans-Saharan trade networks brought enormous wealth and considerable power to Ghana. The kingdom's capital and principal trading site stood at Koumbi-Saleh, a small town today, but a thriving commercial center with a population of some fifteen thousand to twenty thousand people when the kingdom was at its height, from the eleventh to the early thirteenth century. Al-Bakri, a Spanish Muslim traveler of the mid-eleventh century, described Koumbi-Saleh as a flourishing site with buildings of stone and more than a dozen mosques. Koumbi-Saleh's wealth also supported a large number of *qadi* and Muslim scholars. From taxes levied on trade passing through Ghana, the kings financed a large army—al-Bakri reported that they could field two hundred thousand warriors—that protected the sources of gold, maintained order in the kingdom, kept allied and tributary states in line, and defended Ghana against nomadic incursions from the Sahara.

Koumbi-Saleh

By about the tenth century, the kings of Ghana had converted to Islam. Their conversion led to improved relations with Muslim merchants from north Africa as well as Muslim nomads from the desert who transported trade goods across the Sahara. It also brought them recognition and support from Muslim states in north Africa. The kings of Ghana made no attempt to impose Islam forcibly on their society—unlike the neighboring kings of Takrur, who zealously campaigned for the conversion of their entire kingdom—nor did they accept Islam exclusively even for their own purposes. Instead, they continued to observe traditional religious customs: al-Bakri mentioned, for example, that native religious specialists practiced magic and kept idols in the woods surrounding the royal palace at Koumbi-Saleh.

Islam in West Africa

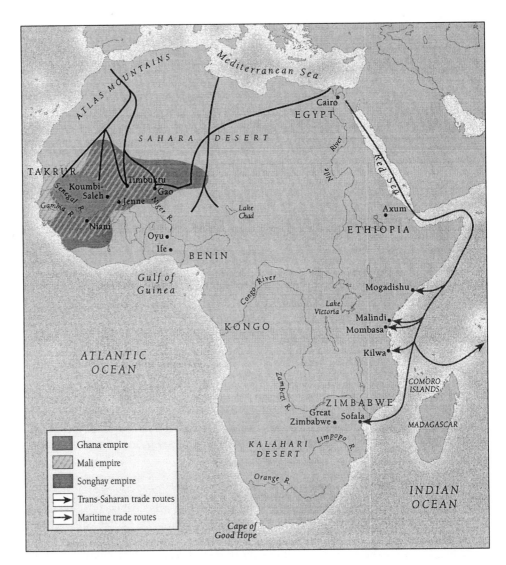

MAP [18.2]

Kingdoms and empires of sub-Saharan Africa.

Even in the absence of efforts to impose Islam on Ghana, however, the faith attracted converts, particularly among those engaged in trade with Muslim merchants from the north.

As the kingdom expanded to the north, it became vulnerable to attacks by nomadic peoples from the Sahara who sought to seize some of the kingdom's wealth. During the early thirteenth century, raids from the desert weakened the kingdom, and it soon collapsed. Several successor states took over portions of Ghana's territory, but political leadership in west Africa fell to the powerful Mali empire, which emerged just as the kingdom of Ghana dissolved.

Sundiata   The lion prince Sundiata (reigned 1230–1255) built the Mali empire during the first half of the thirteenth century after his return from exile. While away from home, he made astute alliances with local rulers, gained a reputation for courage in

battle, and assembled a large army dominated by cavalry. By about 1235 he had
consolidated his hold on the Mali empire, which embraced Ghana as well as
other, neighboring kingdoms in the regions surrounding the Senegal and
Niger Rivers. The empire included most
of the modern state of Mali and extended also to lands now known as
Mauritania, Senegal, Gambia, Guinea-
Bissau, Guinea, and Sierra Leone.

Mali benefitted from trans-Saharan
trade on an even larger scale than Ghana.
From the thirteenth until the late fifteenth century, Mali controlled and
taxed almost all trade passing through
west Africa. Enormous caravans with as
many as twenty-five thousand camels
linked Mali to north Africa. The capital
city of Niani attracted merchants seeking
to enter the gold trade, and market cities
on the caravan routes like Timbuktu,
Gao, and Jenne became prosperous centers featuring buildings of brick and

*The Mali Empire
and Trade*

This terra-cotta sculpture from the thirteenth or
fourteenth century depicts a helmeted and armored
warrior astride a horse with elaborate harness and
head protection. • Werner Forman/Art
Resource, NY

stone. Like the kings of Ghana, the rulers of Mali honored Islam and provided protection, lodging, and comforts for Muslim merchants from the north. Although they
did not force Islam on their realm, they encouraged its spread on a voluntary basis.

The significance of trade and Islam for west Africa became clearest during the   *Mansa Musa*
reign of Sundiata's grand-nephew Mansa Musa, who ruled Mali from 1312 to 1337,
during the high point of the empire. Mansa Musa observed Islamic tradition by
making his pilgrimage to Mecca in 1324–1325. His party formed a gargantuan caravan that included thousands of soldiers, attendants, subjects, and slaves, as well as a
hundred camels carrying satchels of gold. Mansa Musa bestowed lavish gifts on
those who hosted him along the way, and during his three-month visit to Cairo, he
distributed so much gold that the metal's value declined by as much as 25 percent
on local markets.

Mansa Musa drew great inspiration from his pilgrimage to Mecca, and upon re-   *Mansa Musa*
turn to Mali he took his religion even more seriously than before. He built mosques,   *and Islam*
particularly in the trading cities frequented by Muslim merchants, and he sent
promising students to study with distinguished Islamic scholars in north Africa. He
also established religious schools and brought in Arabian and north African teachers,
including four descendants of Muhammad himself, to make Islam better known in
Mali.

Within a century of Mansa Musa's reign, Mali would be in serious decline: factions crippled the central government, provinces seceded from the empire, and military pressures came both from neighboring kingdoms and from desert nomads. By
the late fifteenth century, the Songhay empire had completely overcome Mali. Yet
Mansa Musa and other Mali rulers had established a tradition of centralized government that the Songhay realm itself would continue, and they had ensured that Islam
would have a prominent place in west African society over the long term.

Mansa Musa enjoyed a widespread reputation as the wealthiest king in the world. On this map, prepared in 1375 by a cartographer from the Mediterranean island of Majorca, Mansa Musa holds a gold nugget about the size of a grapefruit. • Bibliothèque Nationale de France

The Indian Ocean Trade and Islamic States in East Africa

While trans-Saharan caravan traffic linked west Africa to the larger trading world of the eastern hemisphere, merchant mariners sailing the sea-lanes of the Indian Ocean performed a similar service for coastal east Africa. Indian and Persian sailors had visited the east African coasts after about 500 B.C.E., and Hellenistic and Roman mariners sailed through the Red Sea en route to the same coasts. After the late centuries B.C.E., Malay seafarers also ventured into the western Indian Ocean from their island homelands in southeast Asia, and by the fourth and fifth centuries C.E. they had established colonies on the island of Madagascar. These early visitors had limited opportunities to trade, however, since east African populations consisted mostly of hunting, gathering, and fishing peoples.

By the second century C.E., Bantu peoples had populated much of east Africa. They introduced agriculture, cattle herding, and iron metallurgy to the region, and as elsewhere in sub-Saharan Africa, they founded complex societies governed by small, local states. As their population increased, Bantu peoples founded settlements on the coasts and offshore islands as well as the interior regions of east Africa. These coast dwellers supplemented their agricultural production with ocean fishing and maritime trade. They were the builders of Swahili society.

The Swahili   *Swahili* is an Arabic term meaning "coasters," referring to those who engaged in trade along the east African coast. The Swahili dominated the east African coast from Mogadishu in the north to Kilwa, the Comoro Islands, and Sofala in the south. They spoke Swahili, a Bantu language supplemented with words and ideas borrowed from Arabic. Swahili peoples developed different dialects, but they communicated readily among themselves because individuals frequently visited other Swahili communities in their ocean-going craft. Indeed, all along the east African coast, Swahili society underwent similar patterns of development with respect to language, religion, architecture, and technology.

By the tenth century Swahili society attracted increasing attention from Islamic merchants. From the interior regions of east Africa, the Swahili obtained gold, slaves, ivory, and exotic local products such as tortoise shells and leopard skins, which they traded for pottery, glass, and textiles that Muslim merchants brought from Persia, India, and China. As in west Africa, the rapidly increasing volume and value of trade had large repercussions for Swahili states and societies.

The Swahili City-States

By the eleventh and twelfth centuries, trade had brought tremendous wealth to coastal east Africa. By controlling and taxing trade within their jurisdictions, local chiefs strengthened their own authority and increased the influence of their communities. Gradually, trade concentrated at several coastal and island port cities that enjoyed sheltered or especially convenient locations: Mogadishu, Lamu, Malindi, Mombasa, Zanzibar, Kilwa, Mozambique, and Sofala. Each of these sites developed into a powerful city-state governed by a king who supervised trade and organized public life in the region.

The cities themselves underwent an impressive transformation. Villages in the interior regions of east Africa had buildings made of wood and dried mud, the principal materials used even for prominent structures like mosques. By about the twelfth century, however, Swahili peoples began to construct much larger buildings of coral, and by the fifteenth century the main Swahili towns boasted handsome stone mosques and public buildings. Meanwhile, the ruling elites and wealthy merchants of Swahili trading cities dressed in silk and fine cotton clothes, and they set their tables with porcelain imported from China.

This fine piece of Chinese porcelain, probably produced in the fifteenth century, found its way into a Swahili tomb in modern Dar es Salaam, Tanzania. • Werner Forman/Art Resource, NY

Travelers' reports and recent archaeological discoveries have thrown especially clear light on the development of Kilwa, one of the busiest city-states on the east African coast. The earliest Bantu inhabitants of Kilwa relied mostly on fishing and engaged in a limited amount of trade between about 800 and 1000 C.E. During the next two centuries, they imported pottery and stoneware from other regions in east Africa and began to rely more on agriculture to support their growing numbers. By the early thirteenth century, Kilwans were prosperous enough to erect multistory stone buildings, and they used copper coins to facilitate economic transactions. Between 1300 and 1505, when Portuguese mariners subjected the city to a devastating sack, Kilwa enjoyed tremendous prosperity. The Moroccan traveler Ibn Battuta visited the city in 1331 and reported that Muslim scholars from Arabia and Persia lived at Kilwa and consulted regularly with the local ruler.

Kilwa

Ruins of Kilwa's Great Mosque, built during the thirteenth century, testify to the wealth that Indian Ocean trade brought to the city. • Werner Forman/Art Resource, NY

With a population of about twelve thousand, Kilwa was a thriving city with many stone buildings and mosques. Residents imported cotton and silk textiles, as well as perfumes and pearls from India, and archaeologists have unearthed a staggering amount of Chinese porcelain. Merchants of Kilwa imported these products in exchange for gold, slaves, and ivory obtained from interior regions. By the late fifteenth century, Kilwa exported about a ton of gold per year. Participation in Indian Ocean trade networks brought similar experiences to the other major Swahili cities.

In fact, the influence of long-distance trade passed well beyond the coasts to the interior regions of east Africa. Villagers in the interior did not enjoy the sumptuous lifestyles of the Swahili elites, but trade and the wealth that it brought underwrote the establishment of large and powerful kingdoms in east and central Africa.

Zimbabwe   The best known of these kingdoms was Zimbabwe. The term *zimbabwe* refers simply to the dwelling of a chief. As early as the fifth and sixth centuries C.E., the region occupied by the modern states of Zimbabwe and Mozambique featured many wooden residences known throughout the land as *zimbabwe*. By the ninth century chiefs had begun to build their *zimbabwe* of stone—indicating an increasingly complex and well-organized society that could invest resources in expensive construction projects. About the early twelfth century, a magnificent stone complex known as Great Zimbabwe appeared near Nyanda in the modern state of Zimbabwe. Within stone walls five meters (sixteen feet) thick and ten meters (thirty-two feet) tall, Great Zimbabwe was a city of stone towers, palaces, and public buildings that served as the capital of a large kingdom situated between the Zambesi and the Limpopo Rivers. At the time of its greatest extent, during the late fifteenth century, up to eighteen thousand people may have lived within the walls of Great Zimbabwe, and the kingdom stretched from the outskirts of the Swahili city of Sofala deep into the interior of south-central Africa.

Kings residing at Great Zimbabwe controlled and taxed the trade between the interior and coastal regions. They organized the flow of gold, ivory, slaves, and local products from sources of supply to the coast. Their control over these products enabled them to forge alliances with local leaders and to profit handsomely from commercial transactions. Just as the trans-Saharan trade encouraged the building of states and empires in west Africa, the Indian Ocean trade generated wealth that financed the organization of city-states on the coast and large kingdoms in the interior regions of east and central Africa.

JOÃO DE BARROS ON KILWA

• • •

João de Barros was a Portuguese historian of the early sixteenth century. For many years he maintained the official records of Portuguese navigators who sailed through the Indian Ocean to the markets of Asia, and on the basis of their reports he compiled a work entitled Asia, *a massive account of the lands visited by Portuguese mariners. When describing Kilwa, de Barros supplemented navigators' reports with a locally produced chronicle outlining Kilwa's history.*

The first foreign people whom the fame of gold attracted to settle in the land of Zanzibar was a tribe of Arabs—as Arabia is very close—banished from their country after receiving the creed of Muhammad. This tribe was called Zaidites, as we have learned from a chronicle of the kings of Kilwa. . . . The cause of their exile was because they followed the [Shiite] doctrine of a Muslim named Zaid, who was grandson of al-Hasan, son of Ali the nephew of Muhammad and husband of his daughter Aisha. This Zaid held various opinions contrary to the Quran, and all those who followed his doctrine the Muslims called Zaidites, . . . and they look upon them as heretics. As these were the first people to come from outside to inhabit this land, they did not found any celebrated towns, but only collected in places where they could live in security from the Kaffirs [indigenous inhabitants]. . . .

This town of Kilwa, although situated in Zanzibar, on the coast of the mainland, is surrounded by the sea, which forms a strait that makes Kilwa an island. It is very fertile in palms and all kinds of thorny fruit trees, and in the vegetables that we have in Portugal. It has some cattle of different kinds and a large number of hens, pigeons, turtle doves, and other kinds of birds unknown to us. The ordinary food of the people is millet, rice, different kinds of cultivated roots, and a large quantity of wild fruit, with which the poor maintain themselves. The water is obtained principally from wells, and is not very healthy, as the land is marshy and the town situated on the coast of the strait, where it encroaches on the shore and forms a kind of bay.

The greater number of the houses are built of stone and mortar, with flat roofs, and at the back there are orchards planted with fruit trees and palms to give shade and please the sight as well as for their fruit. The streets are narrow as these orchards are large, this being the custom among the Muslims, that they may be better able to defend themselves. Here the streets are so narrow that one can jump from one roof to the other on the opposite side. At one part of the town the king had his palace, built in the style of a fortress, with towers and turrets and every kind of defense, with a door opening to the quay to allow entrance from the sea, and another large door on the side of the fortress that opened on the town. Facing it was a large open space where they hauled the vessels up, in front of which our ships had anchored.

SOURCE: George McCall Theal. *Records of South-Eastern Africa,* 9 vols. London: William Clowes and Sons, 1898–1903, 6:233–35. (Translation slightly modified.)

Islam in East Africa

Again as in the case of west Africa, trade brought cultural as well as political changes to east Africa. Like their counterparts in west Africa, the ruling elites and the wealthy merchants of east Africa converted to the Islamic faith. They did not necessarily give up their religious and cultural traditions, but rather continued to observe them for purposes of providing cultural leadership in their societies. By adopting Islam, however, they laid a cultural foundation for close cooperation with Muslim merchants trading in the Indian Ocean basin. Moreover, Islam served as a fresh source of legitimacy for their rule, since they gained recognition from Islamic states in southwest Asia, and their conversion opened the door to political alliances with Muslim rulers in other lands. Even though the conversion of elite classes did not bring about the immediate spread of Islam throughout their societies, it enabled Islam to establish a presence in east Africa under the sponsorship of some particularly influential patrons. The faith eventually attracted interest in larger circles and became one of the principal cultural and religious traditions of east Africa.

BANTU SOCIETY AND CULTURAL DEVELOPMENT

By the eleventh century C.E., Africa was a land of enormous diversity. The peoples of sub-Saharan Africa spoke some eight hundred different languages, and the continent supported a wide variety of societies and economies: mobile bands of hunting and gathering peoples, fishing peoples who lived alongside the continent's lakes and coasts, nomadic herders, subsistence farmers who migrated periodically to fresh lands, settled cultivators, and city-based societies that drew their livelihoods from mining, manufacturing, and trade. Although this diversity makes it difficult to speak of African society and cultural development in general terms, certain social forms and cultural patterns appeared widely throughout sub-Saharan Africa.

Social Classes

In kingdoms, empires, and city-states, such as Kongo, Mali, and Kilwa, African peoples developed complex societies with clearly defined classes: ruling elites, military nobles, administrative officials, religious authorities, wealthy merchants, business entrepreneurs, common people, peasants, and slaves. These societies more or less resembled those found in other settled, agricultural lands of Eurasia organized by powerful states.

In the small states and stateless societies of sub-Saharan Africa, however, social structures were different. Small states often generated an aristocratic or ruling elite, and they always recognized a class of religious authorities. Generally speaking, however, outside the larger states and empires, kinship, sex and gender expectations, and age groupings were the principal considerations that determined social position in sub-Saharan Africa.

Kinship Groups   Extended families and clans served as the main foundation of social and economic organization in small-scale agricultural societies. Unlike most societies in north Africa and Eurasia, the institution of privately owned property did not exist in sub-Saharan Africa. Instead, communities claimed rights to land and used it in common. The villages of sub-Saharan Africa, where most of the population lived, generally consisted of several extended family groups. Male heads of families jointly governed the village and organized the work of their own groups. They allocated portions of the communal lands for their relatives to cultivate and were responsible for distributing harvests equitably among all members of their groups. Thus most villagers functioned in society first as members of a family or clan.

Sex and Gender   Sex and gender relations also influenced the roles individuals played in society.
Relations   Sex largely determined work roles. Men usually undertook the heavy labor of clearing land and preparing it for cultivation. Both men and women participated in the planting and harvesting of crops, and women also tended to domestic chores and took primary responsibility for child rearing.

In this cave painting women and children tend to domestic chores near their huts (represented by white ovals on the left) while men herd cattle. • Erich Lessing/Art Resource, NY

Women's Roles

As in other societies, men largely monopolized public authority. Yet women in sub-Saharan Africa generally had more opportunities open to them than their counterparts in other lands. Women enjoyed high honor as the sources of life. On at least a few occasions, women made their ways to positions of power, and aristocratic women often influenced public affairs by virtue of their prominence within their own families. Women merchants commonly traded at markets, and they participated actively in both local and long-distance trade in Africa. Sometimes women even engaged in combat and organized all-female military units.

The arrival of Islam did not change the status of women in sub-Saharan Africa as dramatically as it did in Arabia and southwest Asia. South of the Sahara early converts to Islam came mostly from the ranks of the ruling elites and the merchant classes. Because it did not become a popular faith for several centuries after its introduction, Islam did not deeply influence the customs of most Africans. Even at royal courts where Islam attracted eager converts, Muslims of sub-Saharan Africa simply did not honor the same social codes as their counterparts in Arabia, southwest Asia, and north Africa. In a few societies upper-class Muslim women wore veils and led secluded lives. For the most part, however, Muslim women in sub-Saharan Africa socialized freely with men outside their immediate families, and they continued to appear and work openly in society in ways not permitted to women in other Islamic lands. Thus Islam did relatively little to curtail the opportunities available to women or to compromise their status in sub-Saharan Africa.

Age Grades

Apart from kinship and sex and gender expectations, African society also made a place for age groups. Throughout much of sub-Saharan Africa, individuals born within a few years of one another constituted publicly recognized groups known as "age grades" or "age sets." As the years passed, members of age grades jointly assumed responsibility for tasks appropriate to their levels of strength, energy, maturity, and experience. During their early years, for example, members of an age grade performed light public chores. At a later age they provided military service and still later military or political leadership. Thus age grades helped to integrate societies founded principally on the basis of kinship.

Slavery   One class of individuals stood apart from the other social groups: slaves. As in other lands, the institution of slavery had a place in Africa since remote antiquity. Most slaves were captives of war. Others came from the ranks of debtors, suspected witches, and criminals. Within Africa most slaves probably worked as agricultural laborers, although many also worked as construction laborers, miners, or porters.

Slaves were an important form of personal wealth in sub-Saharan Africa. Although the absence of private property prevented people from becoming wealthy through the accumulation of landholdings, the accumulation of slaves enabled individuals or families to increase their agricultural production and also to enhance their positions in society. Thus slave trading and slave holding were prominent features of sub-Saharan African society.

Slave Trading   After about the eleventh century C.E., the expansion of the trans-Saharan and Indian Ocean trade networks stimulated increased traffic in African slaves. Muslim merchants provided access to markets in India, Persia, southwest Asia, and the Mediterranean basin where the demand for slaves outstripped the supply available from eastern Europe, previously the main source of slaves. As a result, merchants from northern lands traded in sub-Saharan Africa not only for gold, ivory, and exotic local products but also for slaves.

In response to this demand, slave raiding became an increasingly prominent activity within Africa itself. Rulers of large-scale states and empires began to make war on smaller states and stateless societies, which could not defend themselves effectively against better organized neighbors, in search of captives destined for northern slave markets. In some years ten thousand to twenty thousand Africans left their homes as slaves. During the mid-fourteenth century, the Moroccan traveler Ibn Battuta crossed the Sahara desert in a caravan that included six hundred slaves bound for north Africa and the Mediterranean basin. Mansa Musa of Mali set out on his pilgrimage to Mecca with five hundred slaves, many of whom he distributed along the way as gifts to his hosts. Other slaves departed from the coastal cities of east Africa for destinations in Persia and India.

Though smaller than the Atlantic slave trade of modern times, the Islamic slave trade was a sizable affair: between 750 and 1500 C.E. the number of African slaves transported to northern destinations may have exceeded ten million. The high demand led to the creation of networks within Africa that supplied slaves and served as a foundation for the Atlantic slave trade in later centuries.

African Religion

Most peoples of sub-Saharan Africa descended from Bantu stock, but they developed a wide range of languages, societies, and cultural traditions. Religious beliefs and practices in premodern Africa took many forms. The continent's peoples referred to their deities by different names, told different stories about them, and honored them with different rituals. Yet certain features were common to most religions of sub-Saharan Africa. In combination, these features offer considerable insight into the cultural and religious climate of sub-Saharan Africa in premodern times.

Creator God   All African peoples, with few if any exceptions, recognized a single, superior, male creator god called by many different names. Some considered this god all-powerful, others regarded him as all-knowing, and many considered him both omnipotent and omniscient. All agreed that this superior deity had created the earth and humankind and that he was the source of order in the world. Most African peoples believed that the creator god did not intervene or participate directly in the day-to-day affairs of the world, but they believed that in fashioning the world he had established the principles that governed its development.

Apart from the superior creator god, Africans recognized many lesser gods and spirits often associated with the sun, wind, rain, trees, rivers, and other natural features. Unlike the creator god, these lesser deities participated actively in the workings of the world. They could confer or withhold benefits and bring favor or injury to humans. Similarly, most Africans believed that the souls of departed ancestors had the power to intervene in the lives and experiences of their descendants: the departed could shape events to the advantage of descendants who behaved properly and honored their ancestors and bring misfortune as punishment for evil behavior and neglect of their ancestors' memory. Much of the ritual of African religions focused on honoring of deities, spirits, or ancestors' souls to win their favor or regain their goodwill. The rituals included prayers, animal sacrifices, and ceremonies marking important stages of life—such as birth, circumcision, marriage, and death.

Like other peoples of the world, Africans recognized classes of religious specialists—individuals who by virtue of their innate abilities or extensive training had the power to mediate between humanity and supernatural beings. Often referred to as diviners, they were intelligent people, usually men, though sometimes women as well, who understood clearly the networks of political, social, economic, and psychological relationships within their communities. When afflicted by illness, sterility, crop failure, or some other disaster, individuals or groups consulted diviners to learn the cause of their misfortune. Diviners then consulted oracles, identified the causes of the trouble, and prescribed medicine, rituals, or sacrifices designed to eliminate the problem and bring about a return to normality.

Lesser Gods and Spirits

Diviners

For the most part African religion did not concern itself with matters of theology, but rather with the more practical business of explaining, predicting, and controlling the experiences of individuals and groups in the world. Thus African religion strongly emphasized morality and proper behavior as essential to the maintenance of an orderly world. Failure to observe high moral standards would lead to disorder, which would displease deities, spirits, and departed ancestors and ensure that misfortune befell the negligent parties. Because proper moral behavior was

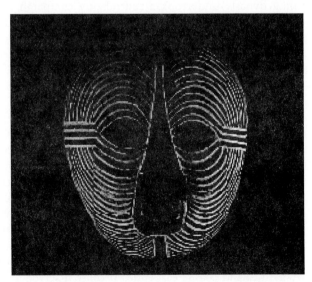

Entrancing and enthralling masks like this one from Congo were essential to the proper observance of religious rituals, which often involved communicating with natural or animal spirits. Masks transformed diviners and provided them with powers not accessible to normal humans. • Marc and Evelyne Bernheim/Woodfin Camp & Associates

so important to their fortunes, family and kinship groups took responsibility for policing their members and disciplining those who fell short of expected standards.

The Arrival of Christianity and Islam

Alongside religions that concentrated on the practical matter of maintaining an orderly world, two religions of salvation won converts in sub-Saharan Africa—Christianity and Islam. Both arrived in Africa as foreign faiths introduced by foreign peoples, and in time the sub-Saharan adherents adapted both faiths to the needs and interests of their societies.

Early Christianity in North Africa

Christianity reached Egypt and north Africa during the first century C.E., soon after the faith's appearance, as it attracted converts throughout the Mediterranean basin. Alexandria in Egypt became one of the most prominent centers of early Christian thought, and north Africa was the home of St. Augustine, among many other leaders of the fledgling church. Yet for several centuries Christianity remained a Mediterranean faith whose appeal did not reach sub-Saharan Africa.

The Christian Kingdom of Axum

About the middle of the fourth century C.E., Christianity established a foothold in the kingdom of Axum, located in the highlands of modern Ethiopia. The ruling elites of Axum converted to Christianity on their own initiative, possibly in hopes of improving relations with their powerful neighbors to the north in Christian Egypt. Their conversion introduced Christianity to Africa south of the Sahara.

The fortunes of Christianity in Ethiopia reflected the larger political experience of the region. In the sixth century C.E., the ruling house of Axum fell into decline, and during the next several centuries the expansion of Islam left an isolated island of Christianity in the Ethiopian highlands. During the twelfth century, however, a new ruling dynasty undertook a centralizing campaign and enthusiastically promoted Christianity as a faith that could provide cultural unity for the land. From the twelfth through the sixteenth century, Christianity enjoyed particular favor in Ethiopia, whose rulers encouraged monasticism and carved eleven massive churches right into hillsides. Indeed, Christianity retained its privileged status in Ethiopia until it fell out of favor following the socialist revolution of 1974.

Ethiopian Christianity

During the centuries after the Islamic conquests of Egypt, the Sudan, and northern Africa, Ethiopian Christians had little contact with Christians in other lands. As a result, although Ethiopian Christianity retained basic Christian theology and rituals, it increasingly reflected the interests of its African devotees. Ethiopian Christians believed that a large host of evil spirits populated the world, for example, and carried amulets or charms for protection against these menacing spirits. Not until the sixteenth century, when Portuguese mariners began to visit Ethiopia en route to India, did Ethiopians reestablish relations with Christians from other lands. By that time the Portuguese had introduced their Roman Catholic faith to the kingdom of Kongo, and Christianity began to win a place for itself elsewhere in sub-Saharan Africa.

Meanwhile, Islam appealed strongly to ruling elites and merchants in sub-Saharan west Africa and coastal east Africa because it served as a cultural foundation for their business relationships with Muslim merchants from north Africa and southwest Asia. Nonetheless African ruling elites and merchants did not convert to Islam purely for mercenary reasons. To the contrary, the converts often took their new faith seriously. They built mosques, founded religious schools, invited experts in Islamic law into their lands, and displayed real enthusiasm for their adopted faith. Mansa Musa's pilgrimage to Mecca and his support of Islam in Mali represented a devotion to Islam shared by untold numbers of sub-Saharan Muslims.

The church of St. George at Lalibela, Ethiopia, a massive structure in the form of a cross constructed by excavating the earth and rock surrounding the church itself.   •   Chester Higgins, Jr./Photo Researchers, Inc.

Constructed during the fourteenth century, the Great Mosque at Jenne served as a principal center of Islamic education and scholarship in the Mali empire.   •   Charles Lenars/The Stock Market

African Islam

As in the case of Christianity, Islam in sub-Saharan Africa reflected the interests of local converts. Thus as in India, southeast Asia, and other lands, Islam made a place for the inherited traditions and beliefs of sub-Saharan Muslims. Africans who converted to Islam continued to take protective measures against the workings of evil spirits and witches, for example, and to participate in rituals designed to please nature deities and the spirits of departed ancestors.

Islam and African Society

Islam also had to accommodate African notions of proper relations between the sexes. When Ibn Battuta visited Mali in the mid-fourteenth century, he took deep offense at casual conversations that women had with men other than their husbands, and he became especially incensed when he observed women going about in public, even at the imperial court, dressed only in loincloths. Yet his hosts, even those who considered themselves pious Muslims, paid no heed to his railings and the lectures he delivered about the proper behavior and dress of women in Islamic society.

Indeed, during the early centuries after its introduction to the region, Islam supplemented rather than replaced the traditional religions of sub-Saharan Africa. West African merchants sometimes adopted Islam when they engaged actively in trade, since a common faith facilitated their dealings with Muslim merchants from other lands, but returned to their inherited traditions when they turned from mercantile to other pursuits. And ruling elites routinely continued to honor inherited religious traditions, which provided powerful sanctions for their rule, long after adopting Islam for the various advantages that it made available to them.

*S*tates and societies of sub-Saharan Africa differed considerably from those in other parts of the eastern hemisphere. The foundations of most sub-Saharan societies were the agricultural economy and iron-working skills that Bantu-speaking peoples spread throughout most of the African continent. As Bantu peoples migrated to new regions and established new communities, they usually based their societies on kin groups rather than state structures that predominated elsewhere in the eastern hemisphere. When Bantu societies came into conflict with one another, however, they increasingly established formal political authorities to guide their affairs. Bantu peoples organized states of various sizes, some very small and others quite large. When they entered into commercial relationships with Muslim peoples in southwest Asia and north Africa, they also built formidable imperial states in west Africa and bustling city-states in coastal east Africa. These states had far-reaching implications for sub-Saharan societies because they depended on a regular and reliable flow of trade goods—particularly gold, ivory, and slaves—and they encouraged African peoples to organize themselves politically and economically to satisfy the demands of foreign Muslim merchants. Trade also had cultural implications because it facilitated the introduction of Islam, which together with Bantu traditions profoundly influenced the development of sub-Saharan societies. After the eighth century ruling elites in both west Africa and coastal east Africa mostly accepted Islam and strengthened its position in their societies by building mosques, consulting Muslim advisors, and supporting Islamic schools. By 1500 C.E. Bantu traditions and Islamic influences had combined to fashion a series of powerful, productive, and distinctive societies in sub-Saharan Africa.

CHRONOLOGY

2000 B.C.E.–1000 C.E.	Bantu migrations
4th century C.E.	Introduction of bananas to Africa
11th to 13th century	Kingdom of Ghana
11th to 15th century	Swahili cities
12th to 15th century	Kingdom of Great Zimbabwe
12th to 16th century	Christian kingdom of Axum
13th to 15th century	Mali empire
1230–1255	Reign of Sundiata
14th to 17th century	Kingdom of Kongo
1312–1337	Reign of Mansa Musa
1324–1325	Mansa Musa's pilgrimage to Mecca

FOR FURTHER READING

Ibn Battuta. *Ibn Battuta in Black Africa*. Ed. and trans. by Said Hamdun and Noel King. London, 1975. Translations of travel accounts of visits to coastal east Africa and the empire of Mali by a famous fourteenth-century Moroccan traveler.

Paul Bohannan and Philip D. Curtin. *Africa and Africans*. 3rd ed. Prospect Heights, Ill., 1988. Exploration of themes in African history, society, and culture by an anthropologist and a historian.

E. W. Bovill. *The Golden Trade of the Moors*. 2nd ed. London, 1968. Popular history of west Africa concentrating on the trans-Saharan caravan trade.

Basil Davidson. *A History of East and Central Africa to the Late Nineteenth Century*. Garden City, N.Y., 1969. Brief survey by a leading popular historian of sub-Saharan Africa.

———. *The Lost Cities of Africa*. Rev. ed. Boston, 1987. Excellent popular account that examines cities of sub-Saharan Africa in the light of recent archaeological discoveries.

G. S. P. Freeman-Grenville, ed. *The East African Coast: Select Documents from the First to the Nineteenth Century*. Oxford, 1962. Translations of documents illustrating the history of trade and political development in coastal east Africa.

E. Bolaji Idowu. *African Traditional Religion: A Definition*. Maryknoll, N.Y., 1973. Brief survey of traditional African religious beliefs from an African perspective.

Robert W. July. *Precolonial Africa: An Economic and Social History*. New York, 1975. Excellent short analysis of African social and economic history.

Nehemia Levtzion. *Ancient Ghana and Mali*. London, 1973. Concentrates on the political, social, and cultural history of west African kingdoms and empires.

Ali A. Mazrui. *The Africans: A Triple Heritage*. Boston, 1986. Emphasizes the legacies of indigenous, Islamic, and western influences on African history.

John S. Mbiti. *African Religions and Philosophy*. 2nd ed. London, 1990. A thorough and systematic study of traditional African religions in their cultural context.

John Middleton. *The World of the Swahili: An African Mercantile Civilization*. New Haven, 1992. Rich scholarly analysis that places modern Swahili society and culture in its historical context.

D. T. Niane, ed. *Sundiata: An Epic of Old Mali*. Trans. by G.D. Pickett. London, 1965. Translation of the story of Sundiata, founder of the Mali empire, as preserved in African oral tradition.

Derek Nurse and Thomas Spear. *The Swahili: Reconstructing the History and Language of an African Society, 800–1500*. Philadelphia, 1985. A short but solid and insightful survey of Swahili history.

Roland Oliver and J. D. Fage. *A Short History of Africa*. 6th ed. London, 1988. Brief survey from paleolithic times to the present.

Jan Vansina. *Paths in the Rainforests: Toward a History of Political Tradition in Equatorial Africa*. Madison, 1990. A brilliant synthesis of early African history by one of the world's foremost historians of Africa.

WESTERN EUROPE DURING THE HIGH MIDDLE AGES

• • • •

*I*n 1260 C.E. two brothers, Niccolò and Maffeo Polo, traveled from their native Venice to Constantinople. The Polo brothers were jewel merchants, and while in Constantinople, they decided to pursue opportunities further east. They went first to Soldaia (modern Sudak), near Caffa on the Black Sea, and then to the trading cities of Sarai and Bulghar on the Volga River. At that point they might have returned home except that a war broke out behind them and prevented them from retracing their steps, so they joined a caravan and continued east. They spent three years in the great central Asian trading city of Bokhara, where they received an invitation to join a diplomatic embassy going to the court of Khubilai Khan. They readily agreed and traveled by caravan to the Mongol court, where the great khan received them and inquired about their land, rulers, and religion.

Khubilai was especially interested in learning more about Roman Catholic Christianity, most likely because he ruled a multicultural empire and wished to maintain harmony among the cultural and religious groups inhabiting his realm. Thus he asked the Polo brothers to return to Europe and request the pope to send learned theologians who could serve as authoritative sources of information on Christian doctrine. They accepted the mission and returned to Italy in 1269 as envoys of the great khan.

The Polo brothers were not able to satisfy the great khan's desire for expertise in Christian doctrine. The pope designated two missionaries to accompany the Polos, and the party set out in 1271, together with Niccolò's seventeen-year-old son Marco Polo. Soon, however, the missionaries became alarmed at fighting along the route, and they decided to abandon the embassy and return to Europe. Thus only the Polos completed the journey, arriving at the Mongol court of Shangdu in 1274. Although they presented Khubilai with presents and letters from the pope rather than the requested missionaries, the great khan received them warmly and welcomed them to his court. In fact, they remained in China in the service of the great khan for the next seventeen years. Their mission gave rise to Marco Polo's celebrated account of his travels, and it signaled the reintegration of Europe into the political and economic affairs of the larger eastern hemisphere.

Cloth merchants cut and sew woolen fabrics in a town market while customers shop and a man receives a shave. • Bibliothèque Nationale de France

During the early middle ages, western Europe was a violent and disorderly land. The collapse of the western Roman empire and invasions by migratory peoples wrecked European society and economy. The Carolingian empire provided order only for a short time before a new series of invasions brought it down. As a result of the turmoil and disarray that plagued Europe during the half millennium from 500 to 1000 C.E., western Europeans played little role in the development of a hemispheric economy during the era dominated by the Tang, Song, Abbasid, and Byzantine empires.

During the early middle ages, however, Europeans laid the foundations of a more dynamic society. The feudal system became the basis for a stable political order. New tools and technologies led to increased agricultural production and economic growth. The missionary efforts of the western Christian church brought cultural and religious unity to most of Europe. During the "high middle ages" of European history—the period from about 1000 to 1300 C.E.—European peoples built a vibrant and powerful society on the political, economic, and cultural foundations laid during the early middle ages.

Although the idea of empire continued to fascinate political thinkers and leaders, empire builders of the high middle ages did not manage to bring all of Europe under their control. Instead, local rulers organized powerful regional states based on the principles of feudalism. Increased agricultural production fueled rapid population growth. Economic expansion led to increased long-distance trade, enriched cities, and supported the establishment of new towns. Cultural and religious affairs also reflected the dynamism of the high middle ages, as European philosophers and theologians reconsidered traditional doctrines in light of fresh knowledge.

Political organization, demographic increase, and economic growth pushed Europeans once again into the larger world. European merchants began to participate directly in the commercial economy of the eastern hemisphere, sometimes traveling as far as China in search of luxury goods. Ambitious military and political leaders expanded the boundaries of Christendom by seizing Muslim-held territories in Spain and the Mediterranean islands. European forces even mounted a series of military crusades that sought to bring Islamic lands of the eastern Mediterranean basin under Christian control. They ultimately failed, but the crusades clearly demonstrated that Europeans were beginning to play a much larger role in the world than they had for the previous half millennium.

 ## THE ESTABLISHMENT OF REGIONAL STATES

Long after its disappearance the Roman empire inspired European philosophers, theologians, and rulers, who dreamed of a centralized political structure embracing all of Christian Europe. Beginning in the late tenth century, German princes formed the so-called Holy Roman Empire, which they viewed as a Christian revival of the earlier Roman empire. In fact, however, the Roman empire returned only in name. Whenever the medieval emperors attempted to extend their influence beyond Germany, they faced stiff resistance from the popes and the princes of other European lands. Meanwhile, independent feudal monarchies emerged in France and England, and other authorities ruled in the various regions of Italy and Spain. Thus medieval Europe was a political mosaic of independent and competing regional states. These states frequently clashed with one another, and they all faced perennial challenges from within. Yet they also organized their own territories efficiently, and they laid the political foundations for the emergence of powerful national states in a later era.

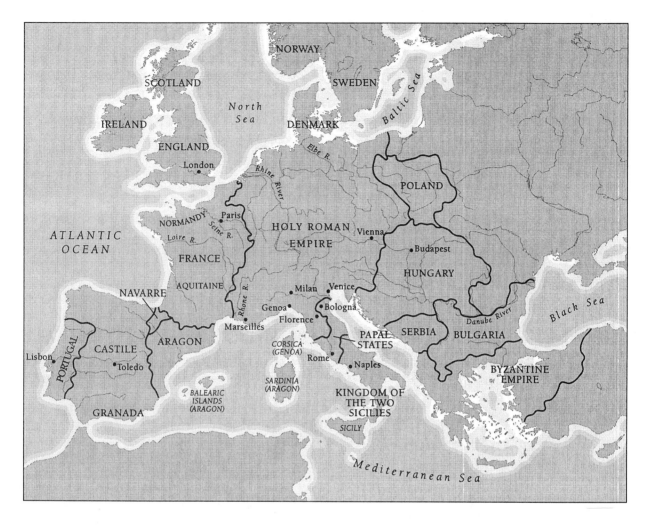

MAP [19.1]
The regional states of medieval Europe.

The Holy Roman Empire

As the Carolingian empire faded during the ninth century, counts, dukes, and other local authorities took responsibility for providing order in their own regions. Gradually, some of them extended their influence beyond their own jurisdictions and built larger states. Otto of Saxony was particularly aggressive. By the mid-tenth century, he had established himself as king in northern Germany. He campaigned east of the Elbe and Danube Rivers in lands populated by Slavic peoples (in what is now eastern Germany, western Poland, and the Czech Republic), and twice he ventured into Italy to quell political disturbances, protect the church, and seek opportunities in the south. In appreciation for his aid to the church, Pope John XII proclaimed Otto emperor in 962 C.E. Thus was born the Holy Roman Empire.

Otto I

The imperial title had considerable cachet, and on several occasions energetic emperors almost transformed the Holy Roman Empire into a hegemonic state that might have reintroduced imperial unity to Europe. Conflict with the papacy, however, prevented the emperors from building a strong and dynamic state. Although the popes crowned the medieval emperors, their relations were usually tense, since both popes and emperors made large claims to authority in Christian Europe. Relations became especially strained when emperors sought to influence the selection of church officials, which the popes regarded as their own prerogative, or when emperors sought to extend their authority into Italy, where the popes had long provided political leadership.

Investiture Contest

Neither the popes nor the emperors were strong enough to dominate the other, but the popes were able to prevent the emperors from building a powerful imperial state that would threaten the papacy as Europe's principal spiritual authority. The capacity of the papacy to weaken the empire became apparent during the Investiture Contest, a controversy over the appointment of church officials in the late eleventh and early twelfth centuries. From the earliest days of the Holy Roman Empire, imperial authorities had named important church officials to their positions, since the higher clergy provided political as well as religious services. In an effort to regain control of the clergy and ensure that church officials met appropriate spiritual criteria, Pope Gregory VII (1073–1085 C.E.) ordered an end to the practice of lay investiture—the selection and installation of church officials by lay rulers such as the emperors. When Emperor Henry IV (1056–1106 C.E.) challenged the pope's policy, Gregory excommunicated him and released his subjects from their duty to obey him. The German princes then took the opportunity to rebel against the emperor. Henry eventually regained control of the empire but only after beseeching Gregory's mercy while standing barefoot in the snow. Because of the pope's intervention in imperial affairs, however, the German princes won concessions that enhanced their independence and diminished the emperor's authority.

Frederick Barbarossa

Popes and emperors clashed over their conflicting interests in Italy as well as the appointment of church officials. Among the most vigorous of the medieval emperors was Frederick I, known as Frederick Barbarossa—"the red beard"—a vigorous and gallant man who reigned from 1152 to 1190 C.E. Working from his ancestral lands in southern Germany, Barbarossa sought to absorb the wealthy and increasingly urban region of Lombardy in northern Italy. Integration of Lombardy with his German holdings would have provided Barbarossa with the resources to control the German princes, build a powerful state, and dominate much of Europe. This prospect did not appeal to the popes, who marshaled support from other European states on behalf of the Italian cities. By the end of Barbarossa's reign, the papal coalition had forced the emperor to relinquish his rights in Lombardy. Once again, papal policies forestalled the transformation of the Holy Roman Empire into a powerful state.

Voltaire, the eighteenth-century French writer, once quipped that the Holy Roman Empire was "neither holy, nor Roman, nor an empire." Indeed, the Holy Roman Empire was an empire principally in name. In reality, it was a regional state ruling Germany, though it also wielded influence intermittently in eastern Europe and Italy. In no sense, however, did the Holy Roman Empire restore imperial unity to western Europe.

Feudal Monarchies in France and England

In the absence of an effective imperial power, regional states emerged throughout medieval Europe. In France and England princes established regional monarchies on the basis of the feudal system.

Capetian France

The feudal monarchy of France grew slowly from humble beginnings. When the last of the Carolingians died, in 987 C.E., the feudal lords of France elected a minor noble named Hugh Capet to serve as king. Capet held only a small territory around Paris, and he was in no position to challenge his vassals, some of whom were far more powerful than the king himself. During the next three centuries, however, his

King Louis IX (reigned 1226–1270 C.E.), also known as St. Louis, helped to consolidate the Capetian hold on the French monarchy. In this fourteenth-century manuscript illustration, he hears the petitions of humble subjects (right), while hanged criminals (left) serve as a reminder of felony's results. • New York Public Library

descendants, known as the Capetian kings, gradually added to their resources and expanded their political influence. Relying on feudal principles governing the relationship between lord and vassal, they absorbed the territories of vassals who died without heirs and established the right to administer justice throughout the realm. By the early fourteenth century, the Capetian Kings had gradually centralized power and authority in France.

The Normans

The feudal monarchy of England developed quite differently. The founders of the English monarchy were Normans—descendants of Vikings who carved out a state on the peninsula of Normandy in France during the ninth century. Though nominally subject to Carolingian and later to Capetian rulers, the dukes of Normandy in fact pursued their own interests with little regard for their feudal lords. Within Normandy the dukes built a tightly centralized state in which all authority stemmed from the dukes themselves. The dukes also retained title to all land in Normandy, and in an effort to forestall conflicts of interest they strictly limited the right of vassals to grant land to subvassals.

Norman England

In 1066 Duke William of Normandy invaded England, then ruled by descendants of the Angles, Saxons, and other Germanic peoples who had migrated there during the fifth and sixth centuries. Following a speedy military victory, the duke, now known as William the Conqueror, introduced Norman-style feudalism to England. While retaining many institutions of their Anglo-Saxon predecessors, the Norman kings of England ruled over a much more tightly centralized realm than did the Capetian kings of France.

Both the Capetians and the Normans faced challenges from vassals seeking to pursue independent policies or enlarge their powers at the expense of the monarchs. Both dynasties also faced external challenges: indeed, they often battled each other, since

The Bayeux tapestry, a magnificent mural of woven linen about 70 meters (230 feet) long, depicts the Norman invasion and conquest of England in 1066. In this section Norman warriors sail across the English Channel and disembark in southern England.

● Erich Lessing/Art Resource, NY

the Normans periodically sought to expand their possessions in France. On the basis of relationships between lords and vassals, however, both the Capetians and the Normans managed to organize feudal monarchies that maintained order and provided reasonably good government.

Regional States in Italy and Iberia

Regional states emerged also in other lands of medieval Europe, though not on such a large scale as the feudal monarchies of France and England. In Italy, for example, no single regime controlled the entire peninsula. Rather a series of ecclesiastical states, city-states, and principalities competed for power and position. In central Italy the popes had provided political leadership since the Carolingian era. Indeed, although the papacy was a spiritual rather than a political post, the popes ruled a good-sized territory in central Italy known as the Papal State. In northern Italy, too, the church influenced political affairs, since bishops of the major cities took much of the initiative in organizing public life in their regions. During the high middle ages, however, as the cities grew wealthy from trade and manufacturing, lay classes challenged the bishops and eventually displaced them as ruling authorities.

Church Influence in Italy

By about the twelfth century, a series of prosperous city-states—including Florence, Bologna, Genoa, Milan, and Venice—dominated not only their own urban districts but also the surrounding hinterlands. Meanwhile, in southern Italy, Norman adventurers—cousins of those who conquered Anglo-Saxon England—invaded territories still claimed by the Byzantine empire and various Muslim states. With papal approval and support, they overcame Byzantine and Muslim authorities, brought southern Italy into the orbit of Roman Catholic Christianity, and laid the foundations for the emergence of the powerful kingdom of Naples.

Italian States

As in Italy, a series of regional states competed for power in the Iberian peninsula. From the eighth to the eleventh centuries, Muslim conquerors ruled most of the peninsula. Only in northern Spain did small Christian states survive the Muslim conquest. Beginning in the mid-eleventh century, though, Christian adventurers from these states began to attack Muslim territories and enlarge their own domains. By the late thirteenth century, the Christian kingdoms of Castile, Aragon, and Portugal controlled most of the Iberian peninsula, leaving only the small kingdom of Granada in Muslim hands.

Christian and Muslim States in Iberia

With its Holy Roman Empire, feudal monarchies, ecclesiastical principalities, city-states, and new states founded on conquest, medieval Europe might seem to present a chaotic and confusing political spectacle, particularly when compared to a land such as China, reunified by centralized imperial rule. Moreover, European rulers rarely sought to maintain the current state of affairs, but rather campaigned constantly to enlarge their holdings at the expense of their neighbors. As a result, the political history of medieval Europe was a complicated affair. Yet the regional states of the high middle ages effectively tended to public affairs in limited regions. In doing so, they fashioned alternatives to a centralized empire as a form of political organization.

ECONOMIC GROWTH AND SOCIAL DEVELOPMENT

As regional states provided increasingly effective political organization, medieval Europe experienced dramatic economic growth and social development. The economic revival closely resembled the processes that in an earlier era had strengthened China, India, and the Islamic world. Increased agricultural production, urbanization, manufacturing, and trade transformed Europe into a powerful society and drew it once again into commercial relationships with distant lands.

The Palazzo Vecchio, originally constructed in the thirteenth century, served as governmental headquarters for the city-state of Florence. The structure reflects the growing independence and self-confidence of medieval Italian cities. • Marco Cristofori/The Stock Market

Growth of the Agricultural Economy

As in China, India, and the Islamic world during the early postclassical era, a dramatic increase in agricultural yields was the foundation of economic growth and social development in medieval Europe. Several developments help to account for this increased agricultural production: the opening of new lands to cultivation, improved agricultural techniques, the use of new tools and technologies, and the introduction of new crops.

Beginning in the late tenth century, as feudal lords pacified their territories and put an end to invasions, Europe began to experience population pressure. In response serfs and monks cleared forests, drained swamps, and increased the amount of land devoted to agriculture. At first feudal lords opposed these efforts, since they reduced the amount of land available for game preserves, where nobles enjoyed hunting wild animals. Gradually, however, the lords realized that expanding agricultural production would yield higher taxes and increase their own wealth. By the early twelfth century, lords were encouraging the expansion of cultivation, and the process gathered momentum.

Expansion of Arable Land

Meanwhile, reliance on improved methods of cultivation and better agricultural technology led to significantly higher productivity. During the high middle ages, European cultivators refined and improved their techniques in the interests of larger yields. They experimented with new crops and with different cycles of crop rotation to ensure the most abundant harvests possible without compromising the fertility of

Improved Agricultural Techniques

the soil. They increased cultivation especially of beans, which not only provided dietary protein but also enriched the land because of their property of fixing nitrogen in the soils where they grow. They kept more domestic animals, which not only served as beasts of burden and sources of food but also enriched fields with their droppings. By the thirteenth century observation and experimentation had vastly increased understanding of agricultural affairs. News of these discoveries circulated widely throughout Europe in books and treatises on household economics and agricultural methods. Written in vernacular languages for lay readers, these works helped to publicize innovations, which in turn led to increased agricultural productivity.

New Tools and Technologies   During the high middle ages, European peoples expanded their use of watermills and heavy plows, which had appeared during the early middle ages, and also introduced new tools and technologies. Two simple items in particular—the horseshoe and the horse collar—made it possible to increase sharply the amount of land that cultivators could work. Horseshoes helped to prevent softened and split hooves on horses that tramped through moist European soils. Horse collars placed the burden of a heavy load on an animal's chest and shoulders rather than its neck and enabled horses to pull heavy plows without choking. Thus Europeans could hitch their plows to horses rather than to slower oxen and bring more land under the plow.

New Crops   Expansion of land under cultivation, improved methods of cultivation, and the use of new tools and technologies combined to increase both the quantity and the quality of food supplies. During the early middle ages, the European diet consisted almost entirely of grains and grain products such as gruel and bread. During the centuries from 1000 to 1300, meat, dairy products, fish, vegetables, and legumes such as beans and peas became much more prominent in the European diet, though without displacing grains as staple foods.

Population Growth   As in other lands, increased agricultural productivity supported rapid population growth in medieval Europe. In 800 C.E., during the Carolingian era, European population stood at about twenty-nine million. By 1000, when regional states had ended invasions and restored order, it had edged up to thirty-six million. During the next few centuries, as the agricultural economy expanded, population burgeoned. By 1100 it had reached forty-four million; by 1200 it had risen to fifty-eight million, an increase of more than 30 percent within one century; and by 1300 it had grown an additional 36 percent to seventy-nine million. During the fourteenth century, epidemic plague severely reduced populations and disrupted economies in Europe as well as Asia and north Africa—a development discussed in chapter 21. Between 1000 and 1300, however, rapid demographic growth helped stimulate a vigorous revival of towns and trade in medieval Europe.

The Revival of Towns and Trade

Urbanization   With abundant supplies of food, European society was able to support large numbers of urban residents—artisans, craftsmen, merchants, and professionals. Attracted by urban opportunities, peasants and serfs from the countryside flocked to established cities and founded new towns at strategically located sites. Cities founded during Roman times, such as Paris, London, and Toledo, became thriving centers of government and business, and new urban centers emerged from Venice in northern Italy to Bergen on the west coast of Norway. Northern Italy and Flanders (the northwestern part of modern Belgium) experienced especially strong urbanization. For the first time since the fall of the western Roman empire, cities began to play a major role in European economic and social development.

Venice, home of Marco Polo and a legion of merchants, drew enormous prosperity from trade. Street vendors, shopkeepers, and merchant ships figure prominently in this illumination from a fourteenth-century manuscript. • The Bodleian Library, University of Oxford, Ms. Bodl. 264, fol. 218r

The growth of towns and cities brought about increasing specialization of labor, which in turn resulted in dramatic expansion of manufacturing and trade. Manufacturing concentrated especially on the production of wool textiles. The cities of Italy and Flanders in particular became lively centers for the spinning, weaving, and dying of wool. Trade in wool products helped to fuel economic development throughout Europe. By the twelfth century the counts of Champagne in northern France sponsored fairs that operated almost year-round and that served as vast marketplaces where merchants from all parts of Europe compared and exchanged goods.

Textile Production

The revival of urban society was most pronounced in Italy, which was geographically well situated to participate in the trade networks of the Mediterranean basin. During the tenth century the cities of Amalfi and Venice served as ports for merchants engaged in trade with Byzantine and Muslim partners in the eastern Mediterranean. During the next century the commercial networks of the Mediterranean widened to embrace Genoa, Pisa, Naples, and other Italian cities. Italian merchants exchanged salt, olive oil, wine, wool fabrics, leather products, and glass for luxury goods such as gems, spices, silk, and other goods from India, southeast Asia, and China that Muslim merchants brought to eastern Mediterranean markets.

Mediterranean Trade

As trade expanded, Italian merchants established colonies in the major ports and commercial centers of the Mediterranean and the Black Sea. By the thirteenth century Venetian and Genoese merchants maintained large communities in Constantinople,

FRANCESCO BALDUCCI PEGOLOTTI ON TRADE BETWEEN EUROPE AND CHINA

• • •

Francesco Balducci Pegolotti was an employee of a Florentine banking company. He traveled as far as London and Cyprus on bank business. Although he probably did not travel to Asia, Pegolotti learned about conditions that long-distance traders faced from many merchants who ventured far from home. About 1340 Pegolotti compiled their reports into a book of information and advice for merchants traveling between the port of Tana (modern Rostov) on the Sea of Azov and China.

In the first place, you must let your beard grow long and not shave. And at Tana you should furnish yourself with a dragoman [guide and interpreter]. And you must not try to save money in the matter of dragomen by taking a bad one instead of a good one. For the additional wages of the good one will not cost you so much as you will save by having him. And besides the dragoman it will be well to take at least two good men servants who are acquainted with the [Turkish] Cumanian tongue. . . .

The road you travel from Tana to Cathay [China] is perfectly safe, whether by day or by night, according to what the merchants say who have used it. Only if the merchant, in going or coming, should die upon the road, everything belonging to him will become the perquisite of the lord of the country in which he dies, and the officers of the lord will take possession of all. And in like manner if he die in Cathay. But if his brother be with him, or an intimate friend and comrade calling himself his brother, then to him they will surrender the property of the deceased, and so it will be rescued. . . .

Cathay is a province which contains a multitude of cities and towns. Among others there is one in particular, that is to say the capital city, to which is great resort of merchants, and in which there is a vast amount of trade; and this city is called Khanbaliq. And the said city hath a circuit of one hundred miles, and is all full of people and houses and of dwellers in the said city.

You may calculate that a merchant with a dragoman and two men servants and with goods to the value of twenty-five thousand golden florins should spend on his way to Cathay from sixty to eighty ingots of silver, and not more if he manages well; and for all the road back again from Cathay to Tana, including the expenses of living and the pay of servants, and all other charges, the cost will be about five ingots per head of pack animals, or something less. And you may reckon the ingot to be worth five golden florins. . . .

Anyone from Genoa or Venice wishing to go to the places above named and to make the journey to Cathay should carry linens with him, and if he visits Urgench [in modern Uzbekistan] he will dispose of these well. In Urgench he should purchase ingots of silver, and with these he should proceed without making any further investment, unless it be some bales of the very finest stuffs which go in small bulk, and cost no more for carriage than coarser stuffs would do.

Whatever silver the merchants may carry with them as far as Cathay the lord of Cathay will take from them and put into his treasury. And to merchants who thus bring silver they give that paper money of theirs in exchange . . . and with this money you can readily buy silk and all other merchandise that you have a desire to buy. And all the people of the country are bound to receive it. And yet you shall not pay a higher price for your goods because your money is of paper.

SOURCE: Henry Yule and Henri Cordier, eds. *Cathay and the Way Thither,* 2nd ed., 4 vols. London: Hakluyt Society, 1913–16, 3:151–55. (Translation slightly modified.)

Alexandria, Cairo, Damascus, and the Black Sea ports of Tana, Caffa, and Trebizond. Caffa was the first destination of the Venetian brothers Niccoló and Maffeo Polo when they embarked on their commercial venture of 1260. These trading posts enabled them to deal with Muslim merchants engaged in the Indian Ocean and overland trade with India, southeast Asia, and China. By the mid-thirteenth century the Polos and a few other Italian merchants were beginning to venture beyond the eastern Mediterranean region to central Asia, India, and China in search of commercial opportunities.

Although medieval trade was most active in the Mediterranean basin, a lively commerce grew up also in the northern seas. The Baltic Sea and the North Sea were sites of a particularly well-developed trade network known as the Hanseatic League, or more simply as the Hansa—an association of trading cities stretching from Novgorod to London and embracing all the significant commercial centers of Poland, northern Germany, and Scandinavia. The Hansa dominated trade in grain, fish, furs, timber, and pitch from northern Europe. The fairs of Champagne and the Rhine, Danube, and other major European rivers linked the Hansa trade network with that of the Mediterranean. *The Hanseatic League*

As in postclassical China and the Islamic world, a rapidly increasing volume of trade encouraged the development of credit, banking, and new forms of business organization in Europe. Bankers issued letters of credit to merchants traveling to distant *Improved Business Techniques*

markets, thus freeing them from the risk and inconvenience of carrying cash or bullion. Having arrived at their destinations, merchants exchanged their letters of credit for merchandise or cash in the local currency. In the absence of credit and banking, it would have been impossible for merchants to trade on a large scale.

Meanwhile, merchants devised new ways of spreading and pooling the risks of commercial investments. They entered into partnerships with other merchants, and they limited the liability of partners to the extent of their individual investments. The limitation on individual liability encouraged the formation of commercial partnerships, thus further stimulating the European economy.

Social Change

Medieval social commentators frequently held that European society embraced three estates or classes: "those who pray, those who fight, and those who work." Those who prayed were

Genoese bankers change money and check the accounts of their clients in this fourteenth-century manuscript illumination.
• © The British Library

The Three Estates

clergy of the Roman Catholic church. From lowly parish priests to bishops, cardinals, and popes, the clergy constituted a spiritual estate owing its loyalty to the church rather than secular rulers. The fighters came from the ranks of feudal nobles. They inherited their positions in society and received an education that concentrated on equestrian skills and military arts. Finally, there were those who worked—the vast majority of the population—who mostly cultivated land as peasants dependent for protection on their lords, those who fought.

The formula dividing society neatly into three classes captures some important truths about medieval Europe. It clearly reflects a society marked by political, social, and economic inequality: although they did not necessarily lead lives of luxury, those who prayed and those who fought enjoyed rights and honors denied to those who worked. Though bound by secular law, for example, clerics were members of an international spiritual society before they were subjects of a lord, and if they became involved in legal difficulties, they normally faced courts of law administered by the church rather than secular rulers. For their part the nobles mostly lived off the surplus production of dependent peasants and serfs.

Chivalry

Yet while expressing some truths, the formula overlooks processes that brought considerable change to medieval European society. Within the ranks of the feudal nobles, for example, an emphasis on chivalry and courtly behavior gradually introduced expectations of high ethical standards and refined manners that encouraged warriors to become cultivated leaders of society. Chivalry was an informal but widely recognized code of ethics and behavior considered appropriate for feudal nobles. Church officials originally promoted the chivalric code in an effort to curb fighting within Christendom. By the twelfth century the ritual by which a young man became initiated into the feudal nobility as a knight commonly called for the candidate to place his sword upon a church altar and pledge his service to God. Thus rather than seeking wealth and power, the noble who observed the chivalric code would devote himself to the causes of order, piety, and the Christian faith.

Troubadours

Aristocratic women found the chivalric code much to their liking, and they went to some lengths to spread its values. Instead of emphasizing the code's religious dimensions, however, they promoted refined behavior and tender, respectful relations between the sexes. Reflections of their interests survive in the songs and poems of the troubadours, a class of traveling poets, minstrels, and entertainers whom aristocratic women enthusiastically patronized. The troubadours, who were most active in southern France and northern Italy, drew inspiration from a long tradition of love poetry produced in nearby Muslim Spain. Many troubadours visited the expanding Christian kingdoms of Spain, where they heard love poems and songs from servants, slaves, and musicians of Muslim ancestry. Enchanted by this refined literature, they began to produce similar verses for their own aristocratic patrons.

Eleanor of Aquitaine

During the late twelfth and thirteenth centuries, troubadours traveled from one aristocratic court to another, where noblewomen rewarded them for singing songs and reciting verses that celebrated passionate love between a man and a woman. Troubadours flocked especially to Poitiers where Eleanor of Aquitaine (1122–1204) liberally supported romantic poets and entertainers. Eleanor was the most celebrated woman of her day, and she used her influence to encourage the cultivation of good manners, refinement, and romantic love. The troubadours' performances did not instantly transform rough warriors into polished courtiers. Over a long term, however, the code of chivalry and the romantic poetry and song presented at aristocratic courts gradually softened the manners of the feudal nobility.

Social change also touched those who worked. By the twelfth century the ranks of workers included not only peasants but also increasing numbers of merchants, artisans, craftsmen, and professionals such as physicians and lawyers who filled the growing towns of medieval Europe. The expansion of the urban working population promoted the development of towns and cities as jurisdictions that fit awkwardly in the framework of a feudal political order. Because of their military power, feudal lords could dominate small towns and tax their wealth. As towns grew larger, however, urban populations were increasingly able to resist the demands of feudal nobles and guide their own affairs. By the late eleventh century, inhabitants of prosperous towns were demanding that local feudal lords grant them charters of incorporation that exempted them from feudal regulation, allowed them to manage their own affairs, and abolished taxes and tolls on commerce within the urban district. Sometimes groups of cities organized leagues to advance their commercial interests, as in the case of the Hansa, or to protect themselves against the encroachments of political authorities.

Independent Cities

The cities of medieval Europe were by no means egalitarian societies: cities attracted noble migrants as well as peasants and serfs, and urban nobles often dominated city affairs. Yet medieval towns and cities also reflected the interests and contributions of the working classes. Merchants and workers in all the arts, crafts, and trades organized guilds that regulated the production and sale of goods within their jurisdictions. By the thirteenth century the guilds had come to control much of the urban economy of medieval Europe. They established standards of quality for manufactured goods, sometimes even requiring members to adopt specific techniques of production, and they determined the prices at which members had to sell their products. In an effort to maintain a balance between supply and demand—and to protect their members' interests—they also regulated the entry of new workers into their groups.

Guilds

Women who lived in the countryside continued to perform the same kinds of tasks that their ancestors tended to in the early middle ages: household chores, weaving, and the care of domestic animals. But medieval towns and cities offered fresh opportunities for women as well as for men. In the patriarchal society of medieval Europe, few routes to public authority were open to women, but in the larger towns and cities women worked alongside men as butchers, brewers, bakers, candlemakers, fishmongers, shoemakers, gemsmiths, innkeepers, launderers,

Urban Women

Women were prominent in the markets of medieval Europe and sometimes worked as bankers or tailors, as in this manuscript illustration. • Bibliothèque Nationale de France

money changers, merchants, and occasionally as physicians and pharmacists. Women dominated some occupations, particularly those involving textiles and decorative arts, such as sewing, spinning, weaving, and the making of hats, wigs, and fur garments.

Most guilds admitted women into their ranks, and some guilds had exclusively female memberships. In thirteenth-century Paris, for example, there were approximately one hundred guilds. Six of them admitted only women, but another eighty included women as well as men among their members. The increasing prominence of women in European society illustrates the significance of towns and cities as agents of social change in medieval Europe.

EUROPEAN CHRISTIANITY DURING THE HIGH MIDDLE AGES

Roman Catholic Christianity guided European thought on religious, moral, and ethical matters. Representatives of the Roman church administered the rituals associated with birth, marriage, and death. Most of the art, literature, and music of the high middle ages drew inspiration from Christian doctrines and stories. Just as mosques and minarets defined the skylines of Muslim cities, the spires of churches and cathedrals dominated the landscape of medieval Europe, testifying visually to the importance of religion and the pervasive presence of the Roman Catholic church.

Western Christianity changed in several ways between 1000 and 1300. As the Roman Catholic church developed an identity distinct from the Eastern Orthodox church, western theologians became reacquainted with the works of Aristotle—mostly unknown to European scholars of the early middle ages—and they produced an impressive synthesis of Aristotelian philosophy and Christian values. Meanwhile, lay classes elaborated a rich tradition of popular religion. Some popular religious movements posed challenges to Roman Catholicism by advocating theological and institutional changes that would have thoroughly transformed the established church. For the most part, however, popular religion remained within the bounds of Roman Catholic orthodoxy and represented an effort to express Christianity in terms meaningful to the laity of medieval Europe.

Schools, Universities, and Scholastic Theology

During the early middle ages, European society was not stable and wealthy enough to support institutions of advanced education. Monasteries sometimes maintained schools that provided a rudimentary education, and political leaders occasionally supported scholars who lived at their courts, but very few schools offered formal education beyond an elementary level. In the absence of a widely observed curriculum or course of study, early medieval scholars drew their inspiration from the Bible and from major spokesmen of the early Christian church such as St. Augustine of Hippo.

Cathedral Schools   During the high middle ages, economic development sharply increased the wealth of Europe and made more resources available for education. Meanwhile, an increasingly complex society created a demand for educated individuals who could deal with complicated political, legal, and theological issues. Beginning in the early eleventh century, bishops and archbishops in France and northern Italy organized schools in their cathedrals and invited well-known scholars to serve as master teachers. Schools in the cathedrals of Paris, Chartres, and Bologna in particular attracted students from all parts of Europe.

By the twelfth century the cathedral schools had established formal curricula based on writings in Latin, the official language of the Roman Catholic church. Instruction concentrated on the liberal arts, especially literature and philosophy. Students read the Bible and the church fathers, such as St. Augustine, St. Jerome, and St. Ambrose, as well as classical Latin literature and the few works of Plato and Aristotle that were available in Latin translation. Some cathedral schools also offered advanced instruction in law, medicine, and theology.

Universities

About the mid-twelfth century students and teachers organized academic guilds and persuaded political authorities to grant charters guaranteeing their rights. Student guilds demanded fair treatment for students from townspeople, who sometimes charged excessive rates for room and board, and called on their teachers to provide rigorous, high-quality instruction. Faculty guilds sought to vest teachers with the right to bestow academic degrees, which served as licenses to teach in other cities, and to control the curriculum in their own institutions. These guilds had the effect of transforming cathedral schools into universities. The first universities were those of Bologna, Paris, and Salerno—noted for instruction in law, theology, and medicine, respectively—but by the late thirteenth century, universities had appeared also in Rome, Naples, Seville, Salamanca, Oxford, Cambridge, and other cities throughout Europe.

The Influence of Aristotle

The evolution of the university coincided with the rediscovery of the works of Aristotle. European scholars of the early middle ages knew only a few of Aristotle's minor works that were available in Latin translation. Byzantine scholars knew Aristotle in the original Greek, but they rarely had any dealings with their Roman Catholic counterparts. During the high middle ages, as commerce and communication increased between Byzantine Orthodox and Roman Catholic Christians, western Europeans learned about Artistotle's thought and obtained Latin translations from Byzantine philosophers. Western European scholars learned about Aristotle also through Muslim philosophers who appreciated the power of his thought and had most of his works translated into Arabic. Christian and Jewish scholars in Sicily and Spain became aware of these Arabic translations, which they retranslated into Latin. Although the resulting works had their flaws—since they filtered Aristotle's original Greek through both Arabic and Latin—they made Aristotle's thought accessible to European Christian scholars.

Scholasticism: St. Thomas Aquinas

During the thirteenth century understanding of Aristotle's thought and Latin translations of his works spread throughout Europe, and they profoundly influenced almost all branches of thought. The most notable result was the emergence of scholastic theology, which sought to synthesize the beliefs and values of Christianity with the logical rigor of Greek philosophy. The most famous of the scholastic theologians was St. Thomas Aquinas (1225–1274), who spent most of his career teaching at the University of Paris. While holding fervently to his Christian convictions, St. Thomas believed that Aristotle had understood and explained the workings of the world better than any other thinker of any era. St. Thomas saw no contradiction between Aristotle and Christian revelation, but rather viewed them as complementary authorities: Aristotle provided the most powerful analysis of the world according to human reason while Christianity explained the world and human life as the results of a divine plan. By combining Aristotle's rational power with the teachings of Christianity, St. Thomas expected to formulate the most truthful and persuasive system of thought possible.

In St. Thomas's view, for example, belief in the existence of God did not depend exclusively upon an individual's faith. By drawing upon Aristotle, St. Thomas believed, it was possible to prove rationally that God exists. Aristotle himself never recognized a personal deity such as the Jewish and Christian God, but he argued that a conscious agent had set the world in motion. St. Thomas borrowed Aristotle's arguments and identified the conscious agent with the Jewish and Christian God, who outlined his plan for the world in the Hebrew scriptures and the Christian New Testament. Thus as expressed in the thought of St. Thomas Aquinas, scholastic theology represented the harmonization of Aristotle with Christianity and the synthesis of reason and faith. Like the neo-Confucianism of Zhu Xi or the Islamic philosophy of Ibn Rushd, scholastic theology reinterpreted inherited beliefs in light of the most advanced knowledge of the time.

Popular Religion

St. Thomas and the other scholastic theologians addressed a sophisticated, intellectual elite, not the common people of medieval Europe. The popular masses neither knew nor cared much about Aristotle. For their purposes Christianity was important primarily as a set of beliefs and rituals that gave meaning to individual lives and that bound them together into coherent communities. Thus formal doctrine and theology did not appeal to popular audiences as much as the ceremonies and observances that involved individuals in the life of a larger community.

Sacraments   Popular piety generally entailed observance of the sacraments and devotion to the saints recognized by the Roman Catholic church. Sacraments are holy rituals that bring spiritual blessings on the observants. The church recognized seven sacraments, including baptism, matrimony, penance, and the Eucharist. By far the most popular was the Eucharist, during which priests offered a ritual meal commemorating Jesus' last meal with his disciples before his trial and execution by Roman authorities. Because the sacrament kept individuals in good standing with the church, conscientious believers observed it weekly, and the especially devout on a daily basis. In addition to preparing individuals for salvation and symbolizing their membership in a holy community, the Eucharist had more mundane uses: popular beliefs held that the sacrament would protect individuals from sudden death and advance their worldly interests.

Devotion to Saints   Popular religion also took the form of devotion to the saints. According to church teachings, saints were human beings who had led such exemplary lives that God held them in special esteem. As a result, they enjoyed special influence with heavenly authorities and were able to intervene on behalf of individuals living in the world. Medieval Europeans constantly prayed for saints to look after their spiritual interests and to ensure them of admission to heaven. Often they also invoked the aid of saints who had reputations for helping living people as well as souls of the dead. Tradition held that certain saints could cure diseases, relieve toothaches, and guide sailors through storms to a port.

The Virgin Mary   During the high middle ages, the most popular saint was always the Virgin Mary, mother of Jesus, who personified the Christian ideal of womanhood, love, and sympathy, and who reportedly lavished aid on her devotees. According to a widely circulated story, the Virgin once even spared a criminal from hanging when he called upon her name. During the twelfth and thirteenth centuries, Europeans dedicated hundreds of churches and cathedrals to the Virgin, among them the splendid cathedral of Notre Dame ("Our Lady") of Paris.

Saints' Relics   Medieval Europeans went to great lengths to express their adoration of the Virgin and other saints through veneration of their relics and physical remains, widely believed to retain the powers associated with the holy individuals themselves. Churches assembled vast collections of relics, such as clothes, locks of hair, teeth,

Architects and laborers sometimes worked more than a century to construct the massive gothic cathedrals of medieval Europe. Built during the twelfth and thirteenth centuries, the magnificent cathedral of Notre Dame in Paris honors the Virgin Mary • Scala/Art Resource, NY

and bones of famous saints. Especially esteemed were relics associated with Jesus or the Virgin, such as the crown of thorns that Jesus reportedly wore during his crucifixion or drops of the Virgin's milk miraculously preserved in a vial. The practice of assembling relics clearly opened the door to fraud, but medieval Europeans avidly continued to admire and venerate saints' relics.

Some collections of relics became famous well beyond their own regions. Like Muslims making the hajj, pilgrims trekked long distances to honor the saints the relics represented. Throughout the high middle ages, streams of pilgrims visited two European cities in particular—Rome in Italy and Compostela in Spain—and some ventured even farther to Jerusalem and the holy land of Christian origins. Rome was the spiritual center of western Christian society: apart from the popes and the central administration of the Roman Catholic church, the relics of St. Peter and St. Paul, the two most prominent apostles of early Christianity, rested in the churches of Rome. Compostela stood on the very periphery of Christian society, in a remote corner of northwestern Spain. Yet the relics of St. James preserved in the cathedral of Santiago de Compostela exercised a powerful attraction for the pious, who made Compostela the second-most popular pilgrimage destination of medieval Europe. Some devoted pilgrims also visited Jerusalem and the sites associated with the origins of Christianity: spiritual as well as commercial interests called Europeans into the larger world.

Pilgrimage

The making of pilgrimages became so common during the high middle ages that a travel industry emerged to serve the needs of pilgrims. Inns dotted the routes leading to popular churches and shrines, and guides shepherded groups of pilgrims to religious sites and explained their significance. There were even guide books that pointed out the major attractions along pilgrims' routes and warned them of difficult terrain and unscrupulous scoundrels who took advantage of visitors.

Reform Movements and Popular Heresies

Although veneration of the saints and the making of pilgrimages indicated a deep reservoir of piety, popular religion also reflected the social and economic development of medieval Europe. As Europe's wealth increased, several groups of particularly devout individuals feared that European society was becoming excessively materialistic. Even the Roman Catholic church seemed tainted by materialism. Benedictine monasteries, in which monks originally observed the virtues of poverty, chastity, and obedience, had in many cases become comfortable retreats where privileged individuals led leisurely lives. Meanwhile, the central administration of the Roman church expanded dramatically as lawyers and bureaucrats ran the church's affairs and sought ways to swell its treasury.

Dominicans and Franciscans   The devout responded to this state of affairs in several ways. Working within the Roman church, some individuals organized movements designed to champion spiritual over materialistic values. Most prominent of them were St. Dominic (1170–1221) and St. Francis (1182–1226). During the thirteenth century St. Dominic and St. Francis founded orders of mendicants ("beggars"), known as the Dominican and Franciscan friars, who would have no personal possessions and would have to beg their food and other needs from audiences to whom they preached. Mendicants were especially active in towns and cities, where they addressed throngs of recently arrived migrants whose numbers were so large that existing urban churches and clergy could not serve them well. The Dominicans and Franciscans also worked zealously to combat heterodox movements and to persuade heretics to return to the Roman Catholic church.

Popular Heresy   Whereas the Dominicans and Franciscans worked within the church, others rejected the Roman Catholic church altogether and organized alternative religious movements. During the twelfth and thirteenth centuries in particular, several popular movements protested the increasing materialism of European society. The Waldensians, who were most active in southern France and northern Italy, despised the Roman Catholic clergy as immoral and corrupt, and they advocated modest and simple lives. They asserted the right of the laity to preach and administer sacraments—functions that the church reserved exclusively for priests—and they did not hesitate to criticize the church on the basis of biblical teachings. Although church authorities declared them heretical, the Waldensians continued to attract enthusiastic participants: a few Waldensians survive even today.

The Cathars   The Cathars, sometimes called Albigensians, went even further than the Waldensians. As Europeans participated more actively in long-distance trade networks, they encountered ideas popular in the Byzantine empire and elsewhere in the Mediterranean basin. Most active in southern France and northern Italy, the Cathars adopted the teachings of heretical groups in eastern Europe who viewed the world as the site of an unrelenting, cosmic struggle between the forces of good and evil. They considered the material world evil and advocated an ascetic, pure, spiritual existence. Those who sought spiritual perfection renounced wealth and marriage and adopted a strict vegetarian diet. They also rejected the Roman Catholic church, which they considered hopelessly corrupt, along with its priests and sacraments.

St. Francis of Assisi was the son of a wealthy merchant in central Italy,
but he abandoned the comforts that he inherited and pledged himself to
a life of poverty and preaching. Stories represented in this fresco from the
basilica of St. Francis at Assisi report that he preached to the birds and
encouraged them to sing in praise of God. • Scala/Art Resource, NY

Their teachings and rapidly growing numbers posed such a direct challenge to
the Roman church that Pope Innocent III called for a military campaign to destroy
the Cathars. During the early thirteenth century, feudal warriors from northern
France undertook the so-called Albigensian crusade, which ruthlessly crushed Cathar
communities in southern France. Although a few Cathars survived in remote regions, by the fifteenth century they had almost entirely disappeared.

THE MEDIEVAL EXPANSION OF EUROPE

During the high middle ages, the relationship between western European peoples
and their neighbors underwent dramatic change. Powerful states, economic expansion, and demographic growth all strengthened European society while church officials encouraged the colonization of pagan and Muslim lands as a way to extend
the influence of Roman Catholic Christianity. Beginning about the mid-eleventh

century Europeans embarked upon expansive ventures on several fronts: Atlantic, Baltic, and Mediterranean. Scandinavian seafarers ventured into the Atlantic Ocean, establishing colonies in Iceland, Greenland, and even for a short time in North America. In the Baltic region Europeans conquered and introduced Christianity to Prussia, Livonia, Lithuania, and Finland. In the Mediterranean basin Europeans recaptured Spain and the Mediterranean islands that Muslims had conquered between the eighth and tenth centuries. Finally, knights from all over Europe mounted enormous campaigns designed to seize the holy land of Palestine from Muslims and place it under Christian authority. As military ventures, the crusades achieved limited success, since they brought the holy land into Christian hands only temporarily. Nevertheless, the crusades signaled clearly that Europeans were beginning to play a much larger role in the affairs of the eastern hemisphere than they had during the early middle ages.

Atlantic and Baltic Colonization

Vinland   When feudal states began to emerge and protect western Europe from Viking raids during the ninth and tenth centuries, Scandinavian seafarers turned their attention to the islands of the North Atlantic Ocean. They occupied Iceland beginning in the late ninth century, and at the end of the tenth century a party led by Eric the Red discovered Greenland and established a small colony there. About 1000 C.E. his son Leif Ericsson led another exploratory party south and west of Greenland, arriving eventually at modern Newfoundland in Canada. There the party found plentiful supplies of fish and timber. Because of the wild grapes growing in the region, Leif called it Vinland. During the years following Leif's voyage, Greenlanders made several efforts to establish permanent colonies in Vinland.

Since the 1960s, archaeologists in northern Newfoundland have uncovered Scandinavian tools and building foundations dating to the early eleventh century. From this evidence and the stories of maritime ventures preserved in Scandinavian sagas, it is clear that the Greenlanders founded a colony in Newfoundland and maintained it for several decades. Ultimately they left Vinland—or died there—since they did not have the resources to sustain a settlement over the stormy seas of the North Atlantic Ocean. Nonetheless, the establishment of even a short-lived colony indicated a growing capacity of Europeans to venture into the larger world.

Christianity in Scandinavia   While Scandinavians explored the North Atlantic, the Roman Catholic church drew Scandinavia itself into the community of Christian Europe. The kings of Denmark and Norway converted to Christianity in the tenth century. Conversion of their subjects came gradually and with considerable resistance, since most held tightly to their inherited traditions. Yet royal support for the Roman Catholic church ensured that Christianity would have a place in Danish and Norwegian societies. In 999 or 1000 the Norwegian colony in Iceland also formally adopted Christianity. Between the twelfth and fourteenth centuries, Sweden and Finland followed their neighbors into the Christian faith.

Crusading Orders and Baltic Expansion   In the Baltic lands of Prussia, Livonia, and Lithuania, Christian authority arrived in the wake of military conquest. During the era of crusades, zealous Christians formed a series of hybrid, military-religious orders. The most prominent were the Templars, Hospitallers, and Teutonic Knights, who not only took religious vows as monks but also pledged to devote their lives and efforts to the struggle against Muslims and pagans. The Teutonic Knights were most active in the Baltic region,

CHAPTER 19 WESTERN EUROPE DURING THE HIGH MIDDLE AGES

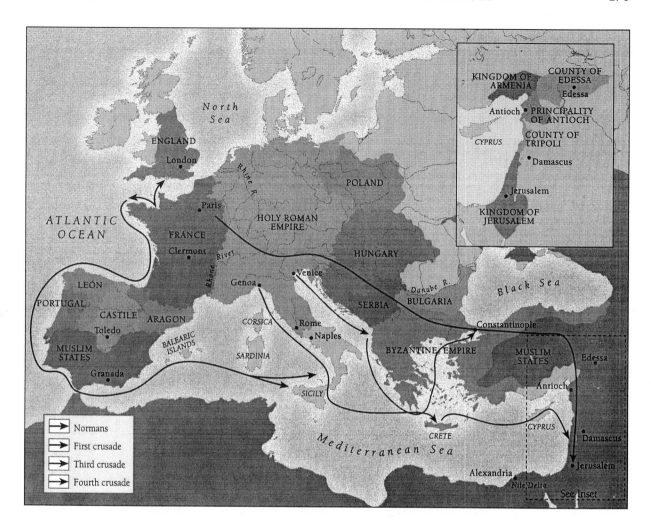

MAP [19.2]

The medieval expansion of Europe.

where they waged military campaigns against the pagan Slavic peoples during the twelfth and thirteenth centuries. Aided by German missionaries, the Knights founded churches and monasteries in the territories they subdued. By the late thirteenth century, the Roman Catholic church had established its presence throughout the Baltic region, which progressively became absorbed into the larger society of Christian Europe.

The Reconquest of Sicily and Spain

The boundaries of Christian Europe also expanded in the Mediterranean basin. There Europeans came into conflict with Muslims, whose ancestors had conquered the major Mediterranean islands and most of the Iberian peninsula between the eighth and tenth centuries. As their society became stronger, Europeans undertook to reconquer those territories and reintegrate them into Christian society.

Most important of the islands was Sicily, which Muslims had conquered in the ninth century. During the eleventh century Norman warriors returned Sicily to Christian hands. The Norman adventurer Robert Guiscard carved out a state for

The Reconquest of Sicily

himself in southern Italy while his brother Roger undertook the conquest of Sicily. By 1090 after almost twenty years of conflict, Roger had established his authority throughout the island. Missionaries and clergy soon appeared and reintroduced Roman Catholic Christianity to Sicily. Islam did not disappear immediately: Muslims continued to practice their faith privately, and Muslim scholars in Sicily introduced their Christian counterparts to the Arabic translations of Aristotle that inspired the scholastic philosophers. Over the longer term, however, as Muslims either left Sicily or converted to Christianity, Islam gradually disappeared from the island.

The Reconquista *of Spain*

The reconquest of Spain—known as the *reconquista*—took a much longer time than did the recapture of Sicily. Following the Muslim invasion and conquest of the early eighth century, the caliphate of Córdoba ruled almost all of the Iberian peninsula. A small Christian state survived in Catalonia in the far northeast, and the kingdom of León resisted Muslim advances in the far northwest. The process of *reconquista* began in the 1060s from these Christian toeholds. By 1085 Christian forces had pushed as far south as Toledo, and by 1150 they had recaptured Lisbon and es-

The Alhambra Palace in Granada was seat of the last Islamic state in southern Spain. Kept cool by running water, the Alhambra was an elegant and luxurious home for its refined residents.

• J. Messerschmidt/The Stock Market

tablished their authority over half of the peninsula. Their successes lured reinforcements from France and England, and in the first half of the thirteenth century a new round of campaigns brought most of Iberia as well as the Balearic Islands into Christian hands. Only the kingdom of Granada in the far south of the peninsula remained Muslim. It survived as an outpost of Islam until 1492, when Christian forces mounted a campaign that conquered Granada and completed the *reconquista*.

The political, economic, and demographic strength of Christian Europe helps to explain the reconquests of Sicily and Spain as military ventures. Especially in the case of Spain, however, it is clear that religious concerns also helped to drive the *reconquista*. The popes and other leading clergy of the Roman Catholic church regarded Islam as an affront to Christianity, and they enthusiastically encouraged campaigns against the Muslims. When reconquered territories fell into Christian hands, church officials immediately established bishoprics and asserted Christian authority. They also organized campaigns to convert local populations. Dominican friars were especially active in Spain. They appealed to learned audiences by explaining Christianity in the terms of scholastic theology and arguments derived from Aristotle, whom Muslim intellectuals held in high esteem. When addressing popular audiences, they simply outlined the basic teachings of Christianity and urged their listeners to convert. With the establishment of Christian rule, the Roman Catholic church began to displace Islam in conquered Spain.

The Crusades

The term *crusade* refers to a holy war. It derives from the Latin word *crux,* meaning "cross," the device on which Roman authorities had executed Jesus. When a pope declared a crusade, warriors would "take up the cross" as a symbol of their faith, sew strips of cloth in the form of a cross on the backs of their garments, and venture forth to fight on behalf of Christianity. The wars that Christians fought against pagans in the Baltic and Muslims in the Mediterranean were crusades in this sense of the term, as was the campaign waged by Roman Catholic Christians against Cathar heretics in southern France. In popular usage, though, the crusades generally refer to the massive expeditions that Roman Catholic Christians mounted in an effort to recapture Palestine, the land of Christian origins, and the holy city of Jerusalem from Muslim authorities.

Pope Urban II launched the crusades in 1095. While meeting with bishops at the Council of Clermont, he called for Christian knights to take up arms and seize the holy land, promising salvation for those who fell during the campaign. The response to Urban's appeal was immediate and enthusiastic. A zealous preacher named Peter the Hermit traveled throughout France, Germany, and the Low Countries whipping up support among popular audiences. Within a year of Pope Urban's call, the Hermit had organized a ragtag army of poor knights and enthusiastic peasants—including women as well as men—and set out for Palestine without proper training, discipline, weapons, supplies, or plans. Not surprisingly, the campaign was a disaster: participants fought not only with Greeks and Turks they met on the road to Palestine but also among themselves. Many members of Peter's band died in these conflicts, and Turkish forces captured others and forced them into slavery. Few made it beyond Anatolia or back to Europe. Yet the campaign indicated the high level of interest that the crusading idea generated among the European public. *Urban II*

Shortly after Peter's ill-fated venture, French and Norman nobles organized a more respectable military expedition to the holy land. In late 1096 the crusading armies began the long trek to Palestine. In 1097 and 1098 they captured Edessa, Antioch, and other strategic sites. In 1099 Jerusalem itself fell to the crusaders, who then proceeded to extend their conquests and carve conquered territories into feudal states. *The First Crusade*

Although the crusaders did not realize it, hindsight shows that their quick victories came largely because of division and disarray in the ranks of their Muslim foes. The crusaders' successes, however, encouraged Turks, Egyptians, and other Muslims to settle their differences, at least temporarily, in the interests of expelling European Christians from the eastern Mediterranean. By the mid-twelfth century the crusader communities had come under tremendous pressure. The crusader state of Edessa fell to Turks in 1147, and the Muslim leader Salah al-Din, known to Europeans as Saladin, recaptured Jerusalem in 1187. Crusaders maintained several of their enclaves for another century, but Saladin's victories sealed the fate of Christian forces in the eastern Mediterranean.

Europeans did not immediately concede Palestine to the Muslims. By the mid-thirteenth century they had launched five major crusades, but none of the later ventures succeeded in reestablishing a Christian presence in Palestine. The fourth crusade (1202–1204) went badly astray when the crusaders conquered Constantinople, subjected the city to a ruthless sack, and installed a Roman Catholic regime that survived until 1261. The Byzantine empire never fully recovered from this blow and *Later Crusades* lumbered along in serious decline until Ottoman Turks toppled it in 1453. Even though the later crusades failed in their principal objective, the crusading idea inspired European dreams of conquest in the eastern Mediterranean until the late sixteenth century.

Economic Consequences of the Crusades

As holy wars intended to reestablish Roman Catholic Christianity in the eastern Mediterranean basin, the crusades were wars of European expansion. Yet in the long run, the crusades were much more important for their economic and commercial consequences. Even as Europeans built crusader states in the eastern Mediterranean, they traded eagerly with Muslim merchants of the region. In exchange for woolen textiles, furs, and timber, Europeans obtained silk and cotton textiles, spices, and sugar. During the crusading era demand for these commodities increased throughout Europe, as large numbers of people developed a taste for goods previously available only to a wealthy few. Seeking to meet the rising demand for luxury goods, Italian merchants increasingly frequented the commercial centers and port cities of Constantinople, Alexandria, Cairo, Damascus, Tana, Caffa, and Trebizond. By the twelfth and thirteenth centuries, Italian merchants had begun to travel well beyond Egypt, Palestine, and Syria to avoid Muslim middlemen and deal directly with the ultimate producers of silks and spices in India, southeast Asia, and China. Thus although the crusades largely failed as military ventures, they encouraged the reintegration of Europe into the larger economy of the eastern hemisphere.

From 1000 to 1300 western Europe underwent thorough political and economic reorganization. Building on foundations laid during the early middle ages, political leaders founded a series of independent regional states based on feudal relations between lords and vassals. Despite the establishment of the Holy Roman Empire, they did not revive central imperial authority in western Europe. Regional states maintained good order and fostered rapid economic growth. Agricultural improvements brought increased food supplies, which encouraged urbanization, manufacturing, and trade. By the thirteenth century European peoples traded actively throughout the Mediterranean, Baltic, and North Sea regions, and a few plucky merchants even ventured as far away as China in search of commercial opportunities. As in the early middle ages, Roman Catholic Christianity was the cultural foundation of European society. The church prospered during the high middle ages, and advanced educational institutions like cathedral schools and universities reinforced the influence of Roman Catholic Christianity throughout Europe. Christianity even played a role in European political and military expansion, since church officials encouraged crusaders to conquer pagan and Muslim peoples in Baltic and Mediterranean lands. Thus between 1000 and 1300, western European peoples strengthened their own society and began in various ways to interact regularly with their counterparts in other regions of the eastern hemisphere.

CHRONOLOGY

962	Coronation of Otto I as Holy Roman Emperor
1056–1106	Reign of Emperor Henry IV
1066	Norman invasion of England
1073–1085	Reign of Pope Gregory VII
1096–1099	First crusade
1122–1204	Life of Eleanor of Aquitaine
1152–1190	Reign of Emperor Frederick Barbarossa
1170–1221	Life of St. Dominic
1182–1226	Life of St. Francis
1202–1204	Fourth crusade
1225–1274	Life of St. Thomas Aquinas
1271–1295	Marco Polo's trip to China

FOR FURTHER READING

Robert Bartlett. *The Making of Europe: Conquest, Colonization and Cultural Change, 950–1350.* Princeton, 1993. A well-documented examination of European expansion from a cultural point of view.

Robert-Henri Bautier. *The Economic Development of Medieval Europe.* New York, 1971. An excellent and well-illustrated survey that puts the economic and social history of western Europe in the context of the larger Mediterranean basin.

Marc Bloch. *Feudal Society.* 2 vols. Trans. by L. A. Manyon. Chicago, 1961. A classic interpretation concentrating on social and economic history that has decisively influenced the way historians think about medieval Europe.

Rosalind Brooke and Christopher Brooke. *Popular Religion in the Middle Ages: Western Europe, 1000–1300.* London, 1984. Well-illustrated essays on the faith of the masses.

Georges Duby. *Rural Economy and Country Life in the Medieval West.* Trans. by C. Postan. Columbia, S.C., 1968. Authoritative and well-documented study of the medieval agrarian world by a distinguished scholar.

Patrick J. Geary, ed. *Readings in Medieval History.* Lewiston, N.Y., 1989. Offers substantial English translations of primary sources.

Jean Gimpel. *The Medieval Machine: The Industrial Revolution of the Middle Ages.* New York, 1976. Explores the role of science and technology in the economy and society of medieval Europe.

David Herlihy. *Opera Muliebra: Women and Work in Medieval Europe.* New York, 1990. Examines women's roles both in their own households and in the larger society of medieval Europe.

Archibald Lewis. *Knights and Samurai: Feudalism in Northern France and Japan.* London, 1974. A brief and insightful work comparing the origins, development, and significance of feudalism in Europe and Japan.

Robert S. Lopez. *The Commercial Revolution of the Middle Ages, 950–1350.* Englewood Cliffs, N.J., 1971. A succinct account of economic development during the high middle ages.

Robert S. Lopez and I. W. Raymond, eds. *Medieval Trade in the Mediterranean World.* New York, 1955. Offers translations of documents illustrating patterns and problems of trade in the medieval Mediterranean.

Hans Eberhard Mayer. *The Crusades.* 2nd ed. Oxford, 1988. Perhaps the best short history of the crusades.

J. R. S. Phillips. *The Medieval Expansion of Europe.* Oxford, 1988. Excellent survey of European ventures in the larger world during the high and late middle ages.

Jonathan Riley-Smith. *The Crusades: A Short History.* New Haven, 1987. Synthesizes a great deal of recent scholarship on the crusades.

Armando Sapori. *The Italian Merchant in the Middle Ages.* Trans. by P. A. Kennen. New York, 1970. Spirited account of medieval Italian merchants and their activities.

Shulamith Shahar. *The Fourth Estate: A History of Women in the Middle Ages.* Trans. by C. Galai. London, 1983. Well-documented study of women and their status in medieval society.

Lynn White, Jr. *Medieval Technology and Social Change.* Oxford, 1962. Pioneering study of technological diffusion and the role of technology in European economy and society.

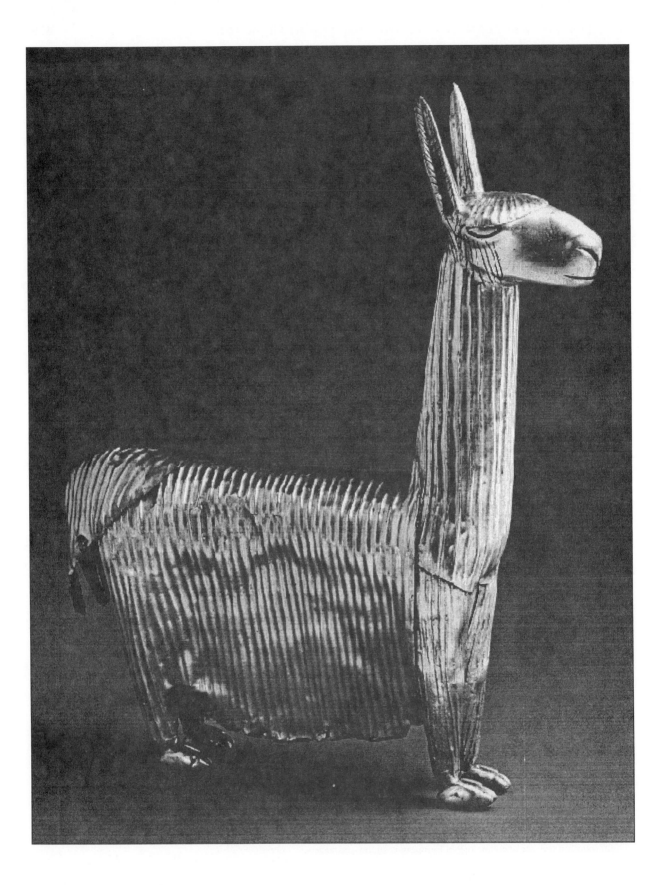

WORLDS APART: THE AMERICAS AND OCEANIA

• • •

In November 1519 a small Spanish army entered Tenochtitlan, capital city of the Aztec empire. The Spanish forces came in search of gold, and they had heard many reports about the wealth of the Aztec empire. Yet none of these reports prepared them adequately for what they saw.

Years after the conquest of the Aztec empire, Bernal Díaz del Castillo, an officer in the Spanish army, described Tenochtitlan at its high point. The city itself sat in the water of Lake Texcoco, connected to the surrounding land by three broad causeways, and as in Venice, canals allowed canoes to navigate to all parts of the city. The imperial palace included many large rooms and apartments. Its armory, well stocked with swords, lances, knives, bows, arrows, slings, armor, and shields, attracted Bernal Díaz's professional attention. The aviary of Tenochtitlan included eagles, hawks, parrots, and smaller birds in its collection, and jaguars, mountain lions, wolves, foxes, and rattlesnakes were noteworthy residents of the zoo.

To Bernal Díaz the two most impressive sights were the markets and temples of Tenochtitlan. The markets astonished him because of their size, the variety of goods they offered, and the order that prevailed there. In the principal market at Tlatelolco, a district of Tenochtitlan, Bernal Díaz found gold and silver jewelry, gems, feathers, embroidery, slaves, cotton, cacao, animal skins, maize, beans, vegetables, fruits, poultry, meat, fish, salt, paper, and tools. It would take more than two days, he said, to walk around the market and investigate all the goods offered for sale. His well-traveled companions-in-arms compared the market of Tlatelolco favorably to those of Rome and Constantinople.

The temples also struck Bernal Díaz, though in a different way. Aztec temples were the principal sites of rituals involving human sacrifice. Bernal Díaz described his ascent to the top of the main pyramidal temple in Tenochtitlan, where fresh blood lay pooled around the stone that served as a sacrificial altar. He described priests with hair entangled and matted with blood. Interior rooms of the temple were so encrusted with blood, Bernal Díaz reported, that their walls and floors had turned black, and the stench overcame even professional Spanish soldiers. Some of the interior rooms held the dismembered limbs of sacrificial victims, while others were resting places for thousands of human skulls and bones.

The contrast between Tenochtitlan's markets and temples challenged Bernal Díaz and his fellow soldiers. In the markets they witnessed peaceful and orderly exchange of

A handsome llama fashioned from silver sheet from Inca Peru. • Courtesy Dept. of Library Services, American Museum of Natural History, New York/Photo: John Bigelow Taylor. 5004(2)

the kind that took place all over the world. In the temples, however, they saw signs of human sacrifice on a scale rarely matched, if ever, anywhere in the world. Yet by the cultural standards of the Aztec empire, there was no difficulty reconciling the commercial activity of the marketplaces with the human sacrifice of the temples. Both had a place in the maintenance of the world: trade enabled a complex society to function while sacrificial rituals pleased the gods and persuaded them to keep the world going.

Although the peoples of Africa, Asia, and Europe interacted regularly before modern times, the indigenous peoples of the Americas had only sporadic dealings with their contemporaries across the oceans. Scandinavian seafarers established a short-lived colony in Newfoundland, and occasional ships from Europe and west Africa may have made their way to the western hemisphere. Before 1492, however, interaction between peoples of the eastern and western hemispheres was fleeting and random rather than a sustained and regular affair. During the period from 1000 to 1500 C.E., however, like their counterparts in the eastern hemisphere, the peoples of North and South America organized large empires with distinctive cultural and religious traditions, and they created elaborate trade networks touching most regions of the American continents.

The indigenous peoples of Australia and the Pacific islands led their lives in even more isolation than did the inhabitants of the Americas. Asian trade networks extended to the Philippines, the islands of Indonesia, and New Guinea, but they touched only a few regions of northern Australia, and they did not reach the more distant island societies of the Pacific Ocean. Pacific islanders themselves often sailed over the open ocean, creating and sustaining links between the societies of various island groups, but they did not venture to Australia or the Asian and American continents bordering the Pacific Ocean. Even though they had extremely limited amounts of land and other natural resources to work with, by the thirteenth century C.E. they had established well-organized agricultural societies and chiefly states throughout the Pacific islands.

STATES AND EMPIRES IN MESOAMERICA AND NORTH AMERICA

Mesoamerica entered an era of war and conquest in the eighth century C.E. Great stores of wealth had accumulated in Teotihuacan, the largest early city in Mesoamerica. When Teotihuacan declined, it became a target for less-prosperous but well-organized forces from the countryside and northern Mexico. Attacks on Teotihuacan opened a long era of militarization and empire building in Mesoamerica that lasted until Spanish forces conquered the region in the sixteenth century. Most prominent of the peoples contesting for power in Mesoamerica were the Mexica, the architects of the Aztec empire.

The Toltecs and the Mexica

During the ninth and early tenth centuries, after the collapse of Teotihuacan, several regional states dominated portions of the high central valley of Mexico, the area surrounding Mexico City where agricultural societies had flourished since the late centuries B.C.E. Although these successor states and their societies shared the religious and cultural traditions of Teotihuacan, they fought relentlessly among themselves. Their capital cities all stood on well-defended hill sites, and warriors figured prominently in their works of art.

With the emergence of the Toltecs and later the Mexica, central Mexico again came under unified rule. The Toltecs began to migrate into the area about the eighth century. They came from the arid land of northwestern Mexico, and they settled mostly at Tula, about fifty kilometers (thirty-one miles) northwest of modern Mexico City. Though situated in a corner of the valley of Mexico that possesses thin soil and receives little rainfall, the Toltecs tapped the waters of the nearby River Tula to irrigate crops of maize, beans, peppers, tomatoes, chiles, and cotton. At its high point, from about 950 to 1150 C.E., Tula supported an urban population that might have reached sixty thousand people. Another sixty thousand lived in the surrounding region. *Toltecs*

The Toltecs maintained a large and powerful army that campaigned periodically throughout central Mexico. They built a compact regional empire and maintained fortresses far to the northwest to protect their state from invasion by nomadic peoples. From the mid-tenth through the mid-twelfth centuries they exacted tribute from subject peoples and transformed their capital into a wealthy city. Residents lived in spacious houses made of stone, adobe, or mud and sometimes covered their packed-earth floors with plaster.

The city of Tula became an important center of weaving, pottery, and obsidian work, and residents imported large quantities of jade, turquoise, animal skins, exotic bird feathers, and other luxury goods from elsewhere in Mesoamerica. The Toltecs maintained close relations with societies on the Gulf coast as well as with the Maya of Yucatan. Indeed, Tula shared numerous architectural designs and art motifs with the Maya city of Chichén Itzá some 1,500 kilometers (932 miles) to the east. *Tula*

Beginning about 1125 C.E. the Toltec empire faced serious difficulties as conflicts between the different ethnic groups living at Tula led to civil strife. By the mid-twelfth century large numbers of migrants—mostly nomadic peoples from northwestern Mexico—had entered Tula and settled in the surrounding area. By 1175 the combination of civil conflict and nomadic incursion had destroyed the Toltec state. Archaeological evidence suggests that fire destroyed much of Tula about the same time. Large numbers of people continued to inhabit the region around Tula, but by the end of the twelfth century the Toltecs no longer dominated Mesoamerica.

Among the migrants drawn to central Mexico from northwestern regions was a people who called themselves the Mexica, often referred to as Aztecs because they dominated the alliance that built the Aztec empire in the fifteenth century. (The term *Aztec* derives from *Aztlán,* "the place of the seven legendary caves," which the Mexica remembered as the home of their ancestors.) The Mexica arrived in central Mexico about the middle of the thirteenth century. They had a reputation for making trouble by kidnapping women from nearby communities and seizing land already cultivated by others. On several occasions their neighbors became tired of their disorderly behavior and forced them to move. For a century they migrated around central Mexico, jostling and fighting with other peoples and sometimes surviving only by eating fly eggs and snakes. *The Mexica*

About 1345 the Mexica settled on an island in a marshy region of Lake Texcoco and founded the city that would become their capital—Tenochtitlan, on top of which Spanish conquerors later built Mexico City. Though inconvenient at first, the site offered several advantages. The lake harbored plentiful supplies of fish, frogs, and waterfowl. Moreover, the lake enabled the Mexica to develop the *chinampa* system of agriculture. The Mexica dredged a rich and fertile muck from the lake's bottom and built it up into small plots of land known as *chinampas*. During the dry season cultivators tapped water from canals leading from the lake to their plots, and in the temperate climate they grew crops of maize, beans, squashes, tomatoes, peppers, *Tenochtitlan*

Although the lakes of central Mexico have largely disappeared, a few *chinampas* survive, such as this one in Xochimilco, near modern Mexico City. • Robert Frerck/Woodfin Camp

and chiles year-round. Finally, the lake served as a natural defense: waters protected Tenochtitlan on all sides, and Mexica warriors patrolled the three causeways that eventually linked their capital to the surrounding mainland.

By the early fifteenth century, the Mexica were powerful enough to overcome their immediate neighbors and demand tribute from their new subjects. During the middle decades of the century, prodded by the military elite that ruled

The Aztec Empire   Tenochtitlan, the Mexica launched ambitious campaigns of imperial expansion. Under the rule of "the Obsidian Serpent" Itzcóatl (1428–1440) and Motecuzoma I (1440–1469), also known as Moctezuma or Montezuma, they advanced first against Oaxaca in southwestern Mexico. After conquering the city and slaying many of its inhabitants, they populated Oaxaca with colonists, and the city became a bulwark for the emerging Mexica empire.

The Mexica next turned their attention to the Gulf coast, whose tropical products made welcome tribute items in Tenochtitlan. Finally, they conquered the cities of the high plateaus between Tenochtitlan and the Gulf coast. About the mid-fifteenth century the Mexica joined forces with two neighboring cities, Texcoco and Tlacopan (modern Tacuba), to create a triple alliance that guided the Aztec empire. Dominated by the Mexica and Tenochtitlan, the allies imposed their rule on about twenty-one million people and most of Mesoamerica, excluding only the arid northern and western regions and a few small pockets where independent states resisted the expanding empire.

Tribute and Trade   The main objective of the triple alliance was to exact tribute from subject peoples. From nearby peoples the Mexica and their allies received food crops and manufactured items such as textiles, rabbit-fur blankets, embroidered clothes, jewelry, and obsidian knives. Tribute obligations were sometimes very oppressive for subject peoples. The annual tribute owed by the state of Tochtepec on the Gulf coast, for example, included 9,600 cloaks, 1,600 women's garments, two hundred loads of cacao, and sixteen thousand rubber balls, among other items. Ruling elites entrusted some of these tribute items to Mexica merchants, who took them to distant lands and exchanged them for local products. These included luxury items such as translucent jade, emeralds, tortoise shells, jaguar skins, parrot feathers, sea shells, and game animals. The tropical lowlands also supplied vanilla beans and cacao—the source of cocoa and chocolate—from which Mexica elites prepared tasty beverages.

Unlike imperial states in the eastern hemisphere, the Aztec empire had no elaborate bureaucracy or administration. The Mexica and their allies simply conquered their subjects and assessed tribute, leaving local governance and the collection of tribute in the hands of the conquered peoples themselves. The allies did not even maintain military garrisons throughout their empire. Nor did they keep a perma-

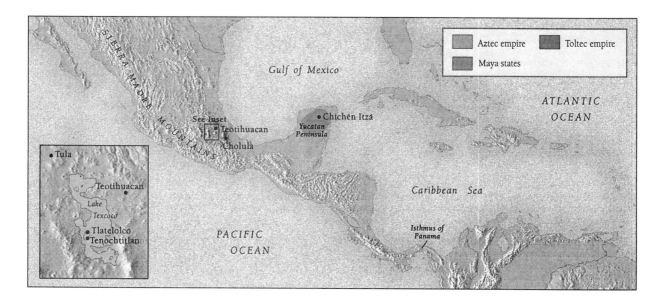

MAP [20.1]

The Toltec and Aztec empires.

nent, standing army. They simply assembled forces as needed when they launched campaigns of expansion or mounted punitive expeditions against insubordinate subjects. Nevertheless, the Mexica in particular had a reputation for military prowess, and fear of reprisal kept most subject peoples in line.

At the high point of the Aztec empire in the early sixteenth century, tribute from some 489 subject territories flowed into Tenochtitlan, which was an enormously wealthy city. The Mexica capital had a population of about two hundred thousand people, and another three hundred thousand lived in nearby towns and suburban areas. The principal market had separate sections for merchants dealing in gold, silver, slaves, henequen and cotton cloth, shoes, animal skins, turkeys, dogs, wild game, maize, beans, peppers, cacao, and fruits.

Bernal Díaz del Castillo marveled at the sight before him when he first laid eyes on Tenochtitlan:

> And when we saw so many cities and villages built in the water and other great towns on dry land and that straight and level causeway going towards Mexico [Tenochtitlan], we were amazed . . . on account of the great towers and [temples] and buildings rising from the water, and all built of masonry. And some of our soldiers even asked whether the things that we saw were not a dream? It is not to be wondered at that I here write it down in this manner, for there is so much to think over that I do not know how to describe it, seeing things as we did that had never been heard of or seen before, not even dreamed about.

Mexica Society

More information survives about the Mexica than about any other people of the pre-Columbian Americas. A few Mexica books survived the Spanish conquest of the Aztec empire, and they offer direct testimony about the Mexica way of life. Moreover, a great deal of information survives from lengthy interviews conducted by Spanish missionaries with priests, elders, and other leaders of the Mexica during the mid-sixteenth century. Their reports fill many thick volumes and shed considerable light on Mexica society.

Social Structure

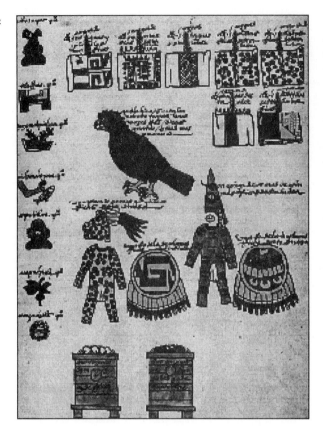

A Spanish copy of a Mexica list records tribute owed by six northwestern towns to the ruler Motecuzoma II. Each two years the towns delivered, among other items, women's skirts and blouses, men's shirts, warriors' armor and shields, an eagle, and various quantities of maize, beans, and other foods. • The Bodleian Library, University of Oxford. Ms. Arch. Selden. A.1 fol 3lr

Mexica society was rigidly hierarchical, with public honors and rewards going mostly to the military elite. The Mexica looked upon all males as potential warriors, and individuals of common birth could distinguish themselves on the battlefield and thereby improve their social standing. For the most part, however, the military elite came from the Mexica aristocracy. Men of noble birth received the most careful instruction and intense training in military affairs, and they enjoyed the best opportunities to display their talents on the battlefield.

The Mexica showered wealth and honors on the military elite. Accomplished warriors received extensive land grants as well as tribute from commoners for their support. The most successful warriors formed a council whose members selected the ruler, discussed public issues, and filled government positions. They ate the best foods—turkey, pheasant, duck, deer, boar,

Warriors

and rabbit—and they consumed most of the luxury items like vanilla and cacao that came into Mexica society by way of trade or tribute. Even dress reflected social status in Mexica society. Sumptuary laws required commoners to wear coarse, burlap-like garments made of henequen but permitted aristocrats to drape themselves in cotton. Warriors enjoyed the right to don brightly colored capes and adorn themselves with lipplugs and eagle feathers after they captured enemies on the battlefield and brought them back to Tenochtitlan.

Mexica Women

Women played almost no public role in a society so dominated by military values, but they wielded influence within their families and enjoyed high honor as mothers of warriors. Mexica women did not inherit property or hold official positions, and the law subjected them to the strict authority of their fathers and husbands. Women were prominent in the marketplaces, as well as in crafts involving embroidery and needlework. Yet Mexica society prodded them toward motherhood and homemaking.

With the exception of a few who dedicated themselves to the service of a temple, all Mexica women married. Mexica values taught that their principal function was to bear children, especially males who might become distinguished warriors, and society recognized the bearing of children as equal to a warrior's capture of enemy in battle. Indeed, women who died in childbirth won the same fame as warriors who died valiantly on the battlefield. Even among the elite classes, Mexica women had the responsibilities of raising young children and preparing food for their families.

Alongside the military aristocracy, a priestly class also ranked among the Mexica elite. Priests received a special education in calendrical and ritual lore, and they presided over religious ceremonies that the Mexica viewed as crucial to the continuation of the world. Priests read omens and ex-

A Mexica manuscript known as the Codex Borgia depicts Quetzalcóatl (left) as the lord of life and Tezcatlipoca (right) as the god of death. • Biblioteca Apostolica Vaticana/Index

plained the forces that drove the world, thereby wielding considerable influence as advisers to Mexica rulers. On a few occasions priests even became supreme rulers of the Aztec empire: the ill-fated Motecuzoma II (reigned 1502–1520), ruler of the Aztec empire when Spanish invaders appeared in 1519, was a priest of the most popular Mexica cult.

Priests

The bulk of the Mexica population lived in hamlets and cultivated *chinampas* and fields allocated to their clans. They also worked on lands awarded to aristocrats and prominent warriors and contributed labor services to public works projects involving the construction of palaces, temples, roads, and irrigation systems. Cultivators delivered periodic tribute payments to state agents, who distributed a portion of what they collected to the elite classes and stored the remainder in state granaries and warehouses. In addition to these cultivators of common birth, Mexica society included a large number of slaves, who usually worked as domestic servants. Most slaves were not foreigners, but Mexica. Families sometimes sold younger members into servitude out of financial distress, while other Mexica were forced into slavery because of criminal behavior.

Cultivators and Slaves

Skilled craftsmen, particularly those who worked with gold, silver, cotton textiles, tropical bird feathers, and other items destined for consumption by the elite, enjoyed considerable prestige in Mexica society. Merchants specializing in long-distance trade occupied an important but somewhat more tenuous position in Mexica society. Merchants supplied the exotic products such as gems, animal skins, and tropical bird feathers consumed by the elites and provided political and military intelligence about the lands they visited. Yet they often fell under suspicion as greedy profiteers, and aristocratic warriors frequently extorted wealth and goods from merchants who lacked powerful patrons or protectors.

Craftsmen and Merchants

MEXICA EXPECTATIONS OF BOYS AND GIRLS

• • •

Bernardino de Sahagún was a Franciscan missionary who worked to convert the Mexica to Christianity in the mid-sixteenth century. He interviewed Mexica elders and assembled a vast amount of information about their society before the arrival of Europeans. His records include the speeches made by midwives as they delivered infants to aristocratic families. The speeches indicate clearly the roles men and women were expected to play in Mexica society.

[To a newborn boy the midwife said:] "Heed, hearken: thy home is not here, for thou art an eagle, thou art an ocelot; thou art a roseate spoonbill, thou art a troupial. Thou art the serpent, the bird of the lord of the near, of the nigh. Here is only the place of thy nest. Thou hast only been hatched here; thou hast only come, arrived. Thou art only come forth on earth here. Here dost thou bud, blossom, germinate. Here thou becomest the chip, the fragment [of thy mother]. Here are only the cradle, thy cradle blanket, the resting place of thy head: only thy place of arrival. Thou belongest out there; out there thou hast been consecrated. Thou hast been sent into warfare. War is thy desert, thy task. Thou shalt give drink, nourishment, food to the sun, the lord of the earth. Thy real home, thy property, thy lot is the home of the sun there in the heavens. . . . Perhaps thou wilt receive the gift, perhaps thou wilt merit death [in battle] by the obsidian knife, the flowered death by the obsidian knife. . . ."

And if it were a female, the midwife said to her when she cut her umbilical cord: "My beloved maiden, my beloved noblewoman, thou has endured fatigue! Our lord, the lord of the near, of the nigh, hath sent thee. Thou hast come to arrive at a place of weariness, a place of anguish, a place of fatigue where there is cold, there is wind. . . . Thou wilt be in the heart of the home, thou wilt go nowhere, thou wilt nowhere become a wanderer, thou becomest the banked fire, the hearth stones. Here our lord planteth thee, burieth thee. And thou wilt become fatigued, thou wilt become tired; thou art to provide water, to grind maize, to drudge; thou art to sweat by the ashes, by the hearth."

Then the midwife buried the umbilical cord of the noblewoman by the hearth. It was said that by this she signified that the little woman would nowhere wander. Her dwelling place was only within the house; her home was only within the house; it was not necessary for her to go anywhere. And it meant that her very duty was drink, food. She was to prepare drink, to prepare food, to grind, to spin, to weave.

SOURCE: Bernardino de Sahagún. *Florentine Codex: General History of the Things of New Spain,* 13 vols. Trans. by Charles E. Dibble and Arthur J. O. Anderson. Salt Lake City: University of Utah Press, 1950–82, 7:171–73 (book 6, chapter 31).

Mexica Religion

When they migrated to central Mexico, the Mexica already spoke the Nahuatl language, which had been the prevalent tongue in the region since the time of the Toltecs. The Mexica soon adopted other cultural and religious traditions, some of which dated from the time of the Olmecs, shared by all the peoples of Mesoamerica. Most Mesoamerican peoples played a ball game in formal courts, for example, and maintained a complicated calendar based on a solar year of 365 days and a ritual year of 260 days. The Mexica enthusiastically adopted the ball game, and they kept a sophisticated calendar, although it was not as elaborate as the Maya calendar.

Mexica Gods   The Mexica also absorbed the religious beliefs common to Mesoamerica. Two of their principal gods—Tezcatlipoca, "the Smoking Mirror," and Quetzalcóatl, "the Feathered Serpent"—had figured in Mesoamerican pantheons at least since

In this manuscript illustration an aide stretches a victim over a sacrificial altar while a priest opens his chest, removes the still-beating heart, and offers it to Huitzilopochtli. At the bottom of the structure, attendants remove the body of an earlier victim. • Bibloteca Nazionale Centrale, Florence. Photo: Pineider/Index

the time of Teotihuacan, although different peoples knew them by various names. Tezcatlipoca was a powerful figure, the giver and taker of life and the patron deity of warriors, whereas Quetzalcóatl had a reputation for supporting arts, crafts, and agriculture.

Ritual Bloodletting

Like their predecessors, the Mexica believed that their gods had set the world in motion through acts of individual sacrifice. By letting their blood flow, the gods had given the earth the moisture it needed to bear maize and other crops. To propitiate the gods and ensure the continuation of the world, the Mexica honored their deities through sacrificial bloodletting. Mexica priests regularly performed acts of self-sacrifice, piercing their earlobes or penises with cactus spines in honor of the primeval acts of their gods. The religious beliefs and bloodletting rituals clearly reflected the desire of the Mexica to keep their agricultural society going.

Huitzilopochtli

Mexica priests also presided over the sacrificial killing of human victims. From the time of the Olmecs, and possibly even earlier, Mesoamerican peoples had regarded the ritual sacrifice of human beings as essential to the world's survival. The Mexica, however, placed much more emphasis on human sacrifice than their predecessors. To a large extent the Mexica enthusiasm for human sacrifice followed from their devotion to the god Huitzilopochtli. Mexica warriors took Huitzilopochtli as their patron deity in the early years of the fourteenth century as they subjected neighboring peoples to their rule. Military success persuaded them that Huitzilopochtli especially favored the Mexica, and as military successes mounted, the priests of Huitzilopochtli's cult demanded sacrificial victims to keep the war god appeased.

The Mexica honored Huitzilopochtli with a large temple at the center of Tenochtitlan. They expanded the temple on several occasions and celebrated each time with rounds of sacrifice. When dedicating the temple after its final expansion in 1487, priests reportedly sacrificed eighty thousand victims to the war god. Although this figure may be exaggerated, there is no doubt that during the fifteenth and early sixteenth centuries constant streams of victims fed Huitzilopochtli's appetite for blood. Spanish conquerors found racks holding the skulls of hundreds of thousands of sacrificial victims in temples dedicated to Huitzilopochtli throughout the Aztec empire.

Some of the victims were Mexica criminals, while others came as tribute from neighboring peoples or from the ranks of warriors captured on the battlefield during the many conflicts between the Mexica and their neighbors. In all cases the Mexica viewed human sacrifice not as a gruesome form of entertainment, but as a ritual essential to the world's survival. They believed that the blood of sacrificial victims sustained the sun and secured a continuing supply of moisture for the earth, thus ensuring that human communities would be able to cultivate their crops and perpetuate their societies.

Peoples and Societies of the North

Beyond Mexico the peoples of North America developed a rich variety of political, social, and cultural traditions. Many North American peoples depended on hunting, fishing, and collecting edible plants. In the arctic and subarctic regions, for example, diets included sea mammals like whale, seal, and walrus supplemented by land mammals like moose and caribou. Peoples in coastal regions consumed fish, but in interior regions such as the North American plains, they hunted large animals like bison and deer. Throughout the continent nuts, berries, roots, and grasses such as wild rice supplemented the meat provided by hunters and fishermen. Like their counterparts elsewhere, hunting, fishing, and foraging peoples of North America built societies on a relatively small scale, since food resources in the wild would not support dense populations.

Pueblo and Navajo Societies

In several regions of North America, agricultural economies enabled peoples to maintain settled societies with large populations. In what is now the American southwest, for example, Pueblo and Navajo peoples tapped river waters to irrigate crops of maize, which constituted as much as 80 percent of their diets. They also cultivated beans, squashes, and sunflowers, and they supplemented their crops with wild plants and small game such as rabbit. The hot and dry environment periodically brought drought and famine. Nevertheless, by about 700 C.E. they began to construct permanent stone and adobe buildings. Archaeologists have discovered about 125 sites where agricultural peoples built such communities.

Iroquois Peoples

Large-scale agricultural societies emerged also in the woodlands east of the Mississippi River. Woodlands peoples began to cultivate maize and beans during the early centuries C.E., and after about 800 these cultivated foods made up the bulk of their diets. They lived in settled communities, and they often surrounded their larger settlements with wooden palisades, which served as defensive walls. By 1000, for example, the Owasco people had established a distinct society in what is now upstate New York, and by about 1400 the five Iroquois nations (Mohawk, Oneida, Onondaga, Cayuga, and Seneca) had emerged from Owasco society. Women were in charge of Iroquois villages and longhouses, in which several related families lived together, and supervised cultivation of fields surrounding their settlements. Men took responsibility for affairs beyond the village—hunting, fishing, and war.

The most impressive structures of the woodlands were the enormous earthen mounds that dotted the countryside throughout the eastern half of North America. Woodlands peoples used these mounds sometimes as stages for ceremonies and rituals, often as platforms for dwellings, and occasionally as burial sites. Modern agriculture, road building, and real estate development have destroyed most of these mounds, but several surviving examples demonstrate that they sometimes reached gigantic proportions.

Mound-Building Peoples

The largest surviving structure is a mound at Cahokia near East St. Louis, Illinois. More than 30 meters (100 feet) high, 300 meters (1,000 feet) long, and 200 meters (650 feet) wide, it was the third-largest structure in the western hemisphere before the arrival of Europeans. Only the temple of the sun in Teotihuacan and the temple of Quetzalcóatl in Cholula were larger. When the Cahokia society was at its height, from approximately 900 to 1250 C.E., more than one hundred smaller mounds stood within a few kilometers of the highest and most massive mound. Cahokia society probably owed its large size to its location—near the junction of the Missouri and Mississippi Rivers—astride trade routes running

Cahokia

The central mound at Cahokia, sometimes called Monk's Mound.

● Cahokia Mounds State Historic Site

north, south, east, and west. Scholars have estimated that during the twelfth century, fifteen thousand to thirty-eight thousand people lived in the vicinity of the Cahokia mounds.

Since peoples north of Mexico had no writing, information about their societies comes almost exclusively from archaeological discoveries. Burial sites reveal that mound-building peoples recognized various social classes, since they bestowed grave goods of differing quality and quantities on their departed kin. Archaeologists have shown, too, that trade linked widely separated regions and peoples of North America. An elaborate network of rivers—notably the Mississippi, Missouri, Ohio, and Tennessee Rivers, along with their many tributaries—facilitated travel and trade by canoe in the eastern half of North America. Throughout the eastern woodlands, archaeologists have turned up stones with sharp cutting edges from the Rocky Mountains, copper from the Great Lakes region, seashells from Florida, minerals from the upper reaches of the Mississippi River, and mica from the southern Appalachian mountains.

Detailed understanding of early North America is probably lost forever: archaeology sheds limited light on political history, social organization, or religious beliefs. Yet it is clear that some early American peoples built settled, agricultural societies that regularly interacted with each other. Their efforts testify to the human impulse to establish densely populated societies and to enter into commercial relationships with others.

ᘛ STATES AND EMPIRES IN SOUTH AMERICA

South American peoples had no script and no tradition of writing before the arrival of Spanish invaders in the early sixteenth century. As a result, the experiences of early South American societies are much more difficult to recover than those of Mesoamerica, where writing had been in use since the fifth century B.C.E. Yet from archaeological evidence and information recorded by Spanish conquerors, it is possible to reconstruct much of the historical experience of Andean South America, which had been the site of complex societies since the first millennium B.C.E. As in Mesoamerica, cities and secular government began to overshadow ceremonial centers and priestly regimes during the centuries from 1000 to 1500 C.E. Toward the end of the period, like the Mexica in Mesoamerica, the Incas built a powerful state, extended their authority over a vast region, and established the largest empire South America had ever seen.

The Coming of the Incas

After the disappearance of the Chavín and Moche societies, a series of autonomous regional states organized public affairs in Andean South America. The states frequently clashed, but rarely did one of them gain a long-term advantage over the others. For the most part they controlled areas either in the mountainous highlands or in the valleys and coastal plains.

Chucuito
After the twelfth century, for example, the kingdom of Chucuito dominated the highlands region around Lake Titicaca, which straddles the border between modern Peru and Bolivia at about four thousand meters (thirteen thousand feet) of elevation. Chucuito depended on the cultivation of potatoes and the herding of llamas and alpacas—camel-like beasts that were the only large domesticated animals anywhere in the Americas before the sixteenth century. In elaborately terraced fields built with stone retaining walls, cultivators harvested potatoes of many different colors, sizes, and tastes. Like maize in Mesoamerica, potatoes served as the staple of the highlanders' diet, which revolved around a potato-based stew enlivened by maize, tomatoes, green vegetables, peppers, chiles, and meat from llamas, alpacas, or tender, domesticated guinea pigs.

Apart from meat, llamas and alpacas provided the highlanders with wool, hides, and dung, widely used as fuel in a land with few trees. In exchange for potatoes and woolen textiles, the highlanders obtained maize and coca leaves from societies in lower valleys. They used maize to enhance their diet and to brew a beerlike beverage, and they chewed the coca leaves, which worked as a mild stimulant and enhanced stamina in the thin air of the high Andes. (When processed, coca leaves yield a much more powerful stimulant with addictive properties—cocaine.)

Chimu
In the lowlands the powerful kingdom of Chimu (sometimes referred to as Chimor) emerged in the tenth century and expanded to dominate some 900 kilometers (560 miles) of the Peruvian coast for about a century before the arrival of the Incas in the mid-fifteenth century. Chimu governed a large and thriving society. Irrigation networks tapped the rivers and streams flowing from the Andes mountains, watered fields in the lowlands, and helped to generate abundant yields of maize and sweet potatoes. Judging from goods excavated at grave sites, Chimu society enjoyed considerable wealth and recognized clear distinctions between social classes.

Chimu's capital city, Chanchan, whose ruins lie close to the modern city of Trujillo, had a population that exceeded fifty thousand and may have approached one hundred thousand. Chanchan featured massive brick buildings, which indicated a capacity for mobilizing large numbers of people and resources for public purposes. The city's geography itself reflected a well-defined social order: each block belonged to an individual clan that supervised the affairs of its own members and coordinated their efforts with those of other clans.

For several centuries regional states like Chucuito and Chimu maintained order in Andean South America. Yet within a period of about thirty years, these and other regional states fell under the domination of the dynamic and expansive society of the Incas. The word *Inca* originally was the title of the rulers of a small kingdom in the valley of Cuzco, but in modern usage the term refers more broadly to those who spoke the Incas' Quechua language, or even to all subjects of the Inca empire.

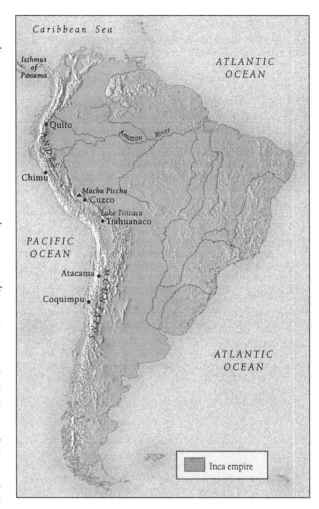

MAP [20.2]

The Inca empire.

After a long period of migration in the highlands, the Incas settled in the region around Lake Titicaca about the mid-thirteenth century. At first they lived as one among many peoples inhabiting the region. About 1438, however, the Inca ruler Pachacuti (reigned 1438–1471) launched a series of military campaigns that vastly expanded the Incas' authority. Pachacuti first extended Inca control over the southern and northern highlands and then turned his forces on the coastal kingdom of Chimu. Though well defended, Chimu had to submit to the Incas when Pachacuti gained control of the waters that supplied Chimu's irrigation system.

By the late fifteenth century, the Incas had built a huge empire stretching more than 4,000 kilometers (2,500 miles) from modern Quito to Santiago. It embraced almost all of modern Peru, most of Ecuador, much of Bolivia, and parts of Chile and Argentina as well. Only the tropical rain forests of the Amazon and other river valleys

The Inca Empire

set a limit to Inca expansion to the east, and the Pacific Ocean defined its western boundary. With a population of about 11.5 million people, the Inca empire easily ranked as the largest state ever built in South America.

The Incas ruled as a military and administrative elite. They led armies composed mostly of conquered peoples, and they staffed the bureaucracy that managed the empire's political affairs. But the Incas themselves were not numerous enough to overwhelm their subjects. They routinely sought to encourage obedience among subject peoples by taking hostages from their ruling classes and forcing them to live at the Inca capital. When conquered peoples became restive or uncooperative, the Incas sent loyal subjects as colonists, provided them with choice land and economic benefits, and established them in garrisons to maintain order. When conquered peoples rebelled, Inca armies forced them to leave their homes and resettle in distant parts of the empire.

Quipu and Inca Administration

Administration of the Inca empire rested with a large class of bureaucrats. In the absence of a script, bureaucrats relied on a mnemonic aid known as *quipu* to keep track of their responsibilities. Quipu consisted of an array of small cords of various colors and lengths, all suspended from one large, thick cord. Experts tied a series of knots in the small cords, which sometimes numbered a hundred or more, to help them remember certain kinds of information. Most quipu recorded statistical information having to do with population, state property, taxes, and labor services that communities owed to the central government. Occasionally, though, quipu also helped experts to remember historical information having to do with the establishment of the Inca empire, the Inca rulers, and their deeds. Although much more unwieldy and less flexible than writing, quipu enabled Inca bureaucrats to keep track of information well enough to run an orderly empire.

The different colors of quipu threads designated the different items recorded: population, animals, textiles, weapons, and perhaps even rulers and notable events of their reigns. People needed an advanced education to record and "read" information by quipu. • Courtesy Dept. of Library Services, American Museum of Natural History. Photo: Perkins/Becket. 3614(2)

Cuzco

The Inca capital at Cuzco served as the administrative, religious, and ceremonial center of the empire. Cuzco's population exceeded one hundred thousand and may have reached three hundred thousand at the high point of the Inca empire in the late fifteenth century. Most prominent of the residents were the Inca rulers and high nobility, the high priests of the various religious cults, and the hostages of conquered peoples who lived with their families under the watchful eyes of Inca guardians. Cuzco had many handsome buildings of red stone, and the most important temples and palaces sported gold facings.

A magnificent and extensive road system enabled the central government at *Inca Roads*
Cuzco to communicate with all parts of the far-flung Inca empire and to dispatch
large military forces rapidly to distant trouble spots. Two roads linked the Inca realm
from north to south—one passing through the mountains, the other running along
the coast. Scholars have estimated the combined length of these roads at 16,000
kilometers (9,944 miles). During the early sixteenth century, Spanish conquerors
marveled at the roads—paved with stone, shaded by trees, and wide enough to accommodate eight horsemen riding abreast. A corps of official runners carried messages along the roads so that news and information could travel between Cuzco and
the most distant parts of the empire within a few days. When the Inca rulers desired
a meal of fresh fish, they dispatched runners from Cuzco to the coast more than 320
kilometers (200 miles) away and had their catch within two days. As in the cases of
empires in other parts of the world, the Incas' roads favored their efforts at centralization. Their roads even facilitated the spread of the Quechua language and their
religious cult focusing on the sun, both of which became established throughout
their empire.

Inca Society and Religion

Despite these splendid roads, Inca society did not generate large classes of mer- *Trade*
chants and skilled craftsmen. On the local level the Incas and their subjects bartered
surplus agricultural production and handcrafted goods among themselves. Long-
distance trade, however, fell under the supervision of the central government. Administrators organized exchanges of agricultural products, textiles, pottery, jewelry,
and craft goods, but the Inca state did not permit individuals to become independent merchants. In the absence of a market economy, there was no opportunity for
a large class of professional, skilled craftsmen to emerge. Many individuals produced
pottery, textiles, and tools for local consumption, and a few produced especially fine
goods for the ruling, priestly, and aristocratic classes. But skilled craftsmen were
much less prominent among the Incas than among the Mexica and the peoples of
the eastern hemisphere.

The main classes in Inca society were the rulers, aristocrats, priests, and peasant *Ruling Elites*
cultivators of common birth. The Incas considered their chief ruler a deity descended
from the sun. In theory, this god-king owned all land, livestock, and property in the
Inca realm, which he governed as an absolute and infallible ruler. Inca rulers retained
their prestige even after death. Their descendants mummified the royal remains and
regarded departed kings as intermediaries with the gods. Succeeding rulers often de-
liberated state policy in the presence of royal mummies so as to benefit from their
counsel. Through their bureaucracy, staffed mostly by aristocrats, Inca god-kings allocated land to their subjects, who cultivated it on behalf of the state.

Like the ruling elites, Inca aristocrats and priests led privileged lives. Aristocrats *Aristocrats*
consumed fine foods and dressed in embroidered clothes provided by common sub- *and Priests*
jects. Aristocrats also had the right to wear large ear spools that distended their lobes
so much that Spanish conquerors referred to them as "big ears." Priests often came
from royal and aristocratic families. They led celibate and ascetic lives, but they
deeply influenced Inca society because of their education and their responsibility for
overseeing religious rituals. The major temples supported hundreds of priests, along
with attendants and virgin women devoted to divine service who prepared ceremonial meals and wove fine ritual garments for the priestly staff.

Descendants prepare a ritual meal for a mummified Inca ruler (depicted in the background). • Det Kongelige Bibliotek, Copenhagen

Fulfilling her tribute duty, an Inca woman weaves woolen fabric on a loom attached to a tree. • Det Kongelige Bibliotek, Copenhagen

Peasants   The cultivators were mostly peasants of common birth who worked the lands allocated to them and delivered substantial portions of their production to the bureaucrats. Much of this surplus production went to support the ruling, aristocratic, and priestly classes. The rest went into state storehouses for public relief in times of famine and for the support of widows, orphans, and others unable to cultivate land for themselves. Apart from a portion of their agricultural production, commoners also owed compulsory labor services to the Inca state. Men provided the heavy labor required for the construction, maintenance, and repair of roads, buildings, and irrigation systems. Women delivered tribute in the form of textiles, pottery, and jewelry. With the aid of quipu, Inca bureaucrats kept track of the labor service and tribute owed by local communities.

Inca Gods:
Inti and Viracocha   Members of the Inca ruling class venerated the sun as a god and as their major deity, whom they called Inti. They also recognized the moon, stars, planets, rain, and other natural forces as divine. Some Incas, including the energetic ruler Pachacuti, also showed special favor to the god Viracocha, creator of the world, humankind, and all else in the universe. The cult of the sun, however, outshone all the others. In Cuzco alone some four thousand priests, attendants, and virgin devotees served Inti, whose temple attracted pilgrims from all parts of the Inca empire. Priests of all cults honored their deities with sacrifices, which in Inca society usually took the form of agricultural produce or animals such as llamas and guinea pigs rather than humans.

Moral Thought   Alongside sacrifices and ritual ceremonies, Inca religion had a strong moral dimension. The Incas taught a concept of sin as a violation of the established social or natural order, and they believed in a life beyond death during which individuals would receive rewards or punishments based on the quality of their earthly lives. Sin, they believed, would bring divine disaster both for individuals and for their larger communities. The Incas also observed rituals of confession and penance by which priests absolved individuals of their sins and returned them to the good graces of the gods.

THE SOCIETIES OF OCEANIA

Like the peoples of the Americas, the inhabitants of Oceania built and maintained societies with little outside influence. The aboriginal peoples of Australia ventured over vast stretches of their continent and created networks of trade and exchange between hunting and gathering societies. Only in the far north, however, did they deal with peoples beyond Australia as they traded sporadically with merchants from New Guinea and the islands of southeast Asia. Meanwhile, throughout the Pacific Ocean, islanders built complex agricultural societies. By the time European mariners sailed into the Pacific Ocean in the sixteenth century, the larger island groups had sizable populations, hierarchical social orders, and hereditary chiefly rulers. In the central and western Pacific, mariners also sailed regularly between island groups and established elaborate trade networks.

The Nomadic Foragers of Australia

After the aboriginal peoples of Australia learned how to exploit the resources of the continent's varied regions, they led lives that in some ways changed little over the centuries. Unlike their neighbors to the north, they did not turn to agriculture. The inhabitants of New Guinea began to herd swine and cultivate root crops about 5000 B.C.E., and the inhabitants of islands in the Torres Strait (which separates Australia from New Guinea) took up gardening soon thereafter. Although aboriginal peoples of northern Australia must have known about foods cultivated in neighboring lands, they maintained nomadic, foraging societies until European peoples migrated to Australia in large numbers during the nineteenth and twentieth centuries.

As a result of their mobile and nomadic way of life, aboriginal Australians frequently met and interacted with peoples of neighboring societies. Because Australia is a continent of enormous climatic and ecological diversity, different peoples enjoyed access to food and other resources unknown to others they encountered during their seasonal migrations. Even though as nomads they did not accumulate large quantities of material goods, groups regularly exchanged surplus food and small items when they met.

Trade

This sort of small-scale exchange eventually enabled trade goods to spread throughout most of Australia. Individuals did not travel along all the trade routes. Instead, trade goods passed from one aboriginal community to another until they came to rest in regions often distant from their origins. Pearly oyster shells were among the most popular trade items. Archaeologists have turned up many of these shells fashioned into jewelry more than 1,600 kilometers (1,000 miles) from the waters where the oysters bred. From interior regions came stone axe heads, spears, boomerangs, furs, skins, and fibers.

Aboriginal peoples occasionally traded foodstuffs, but with the exception of some root vegetables, these items were generally too perishable for exchange. Peoples on the north coast also engaged in a limited amount of trade with mariners from New Guinea and the islands of southeast Asia. Australian spears and highly

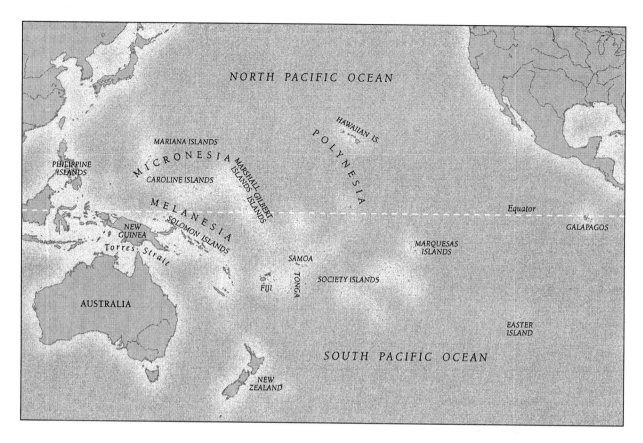

MAP [20.3]

The societies of Oceania.

*Cultural and
Religious Traditions*

prized pearly shells went north in exchange for exotic items like the striking flowers of the bird-of-paradise plant, stone clubs, decorative trinkets—and occasionally iron axes, much coveted by aboriginal peoples who had no tradition of metallurgy.

In spite of seasonal migrations, frequent encounters with peoples from other aboriginal societies, and trade over long distances, the cultural traditions of Australian peoples mostly did not diffuse much beyond the regions inhabited by individual societies. Aboriginal peoples paid close attention to the prominent geographical features of the lands around them. Rocks, mountains, forests, mineral deposits, and bodies of water were crucial for their survival, and they related stories and myths about these and other geographical features. Often they conducted religious observances designed to ensure continuing supplies of animals, plant life, and water. Given the intense concern of aboriginal peoples with their immediate environments, their cultural and religious traditions focused on local matters and did not appeal to peoples from other regions.

The Development of Pacific Island Societies

By the early centuries C.E., human migrants had established agricultural societies in almost all the island groups of the Pacific Ocean. About the middle of the first millennium C.E., they ventured to the large islands of New Zealand—the last large, habitable region of the earth to receive members of the human species. After 1000 C.E. Polynesians inhabiting the larger Pacific islands grew much more numerous than their distant cousins in Micronesia and Melanesia, and their surging population prompted remarkable social and political development.

A fishpond still existing on the Hawaiian island of Molokai required massive amounts of labor for its construction. • Bishop Museum, Honolulu

Trade between Island Groups

In the central and western regions of the Pacific, where several clusters of islands are relatively close to each other, mariners linked island societies. Regional trade networks facilitated exchanges of useful goods like axes and pottery, exotic items like shells and decorative ornaments, and sometimes even foodstuffs like yams. Regional trade within individual island groups served social and political as well as economic functions, since it helped ruling elites establish and maintain harmonious relations with each other. In some cases trade crossed longer distances and linked different island groups. Inhabitants of the Tonga, Samoa, and Fiji islands traded mats and canoes, for example, and also intermarried, thus creating political and social relationships.

Elsewhere in Polynesia, however, vast stretches of deep blue water discouraged travel between different island groups and prevented the organization of trade networks. Inhabitants of the Hawaiian islands or New Zealand exchanged goods among themselves, but they did not trade or communicate regularly with their contemporaries in Tahiti, Samoa, or Tonga. Two-way voyaging probably linked Hawai`i with Tahiti and the Marquesas islands during the twelfth and thirteenth centuries. For the most part, however, after the voyages that took human migrants to Hawai`i, Easter Island, and New Zealand, those remote islands—all situated thousands of kilometers from the nearest inhabited lands—had little or no contact with peoples of other societies until European mariners ventured into the Pacific Ocean.

Population Growth

Thus Polynesians of the eastern Pacific and New Zealand built their societies largely in isolation. They cultivated taro, yams, sweet potatoes, bananas, breadfruit, and coconuts, and they kept domesticated pigs and dogs. They also fed on abundant supplies of fish, which they caught by spear, net, and hook. After about the fourteenth century, as their population increased, the inhabitants of Hawai`i built ingenious fishponds that allowed small fry to swim from the ocean through narrow gates into rock-enclosed spaces but prevented larger fish from escaping. Fishponds enabled Hawaiians to harvest large quantities of mature fish with relative ease and thus contributed to the islanders' food supplies. The establishment of agricultural and fishing societies led to rapid population growth in all the larger Pacific island groups—Samoa, Tonga, the Society Islands (including Tahiti), and Hawai`i. In Hawai`i, the most heavily populated of the Polynesian island groups, the human population may have exceeded five hundred thousand when European mariners arrived in the late eighteenth century.

The Development of Social Classes

Beginning about the thirteenth century C.E., expanding populations prompted Pacific islanders to develop increasingly complex social and political structures. Especially on the larger islands, workers became more specialized: some concentrated on cultivating certain crops while others devoted their efforts to fishing, producing axes, or constructing large, sea-going canoes. Distinct classes emerged as aristocratic and ruling elites decided the course of public affairs in their societies and extracted surplus agricultural production from those of common birth. The islands of Tonga, Tahiti, and Hawai`i had especially stratified societies with sharp distinctions between various classes of high chiefs, lesser chiefs, and commoners. Hawaiian society also recognized distinct classes of priests and skilled craftsmen, such as adze makers and canoe builders, ranking between the chiefly and common classes.

The Formation of Chiefly States

In addition to distinct social classes, island societies generated strong political leadership. Ruling chiefs generally oversaw public affairs in portions of an island, sometimes in an entire island, and occasionally in several islands situated close to each other. In Tonga and Hawai`i high chiefs frequently launched campaigns to bring additional islands under their control and create large centralized states. Rarely, however, were these militant chiefs able to overcome geographical and logistical difficulties and realize their expansionist ambitions before the nineteenth century.

Nevertheless, high chiefs guided the affairs of complex societies throughout Polynesia. They allocated lands to families, mobilized labor for construction projects, and organized men into military forces. They commanded enormous respect within their societies. In Hawai`i, for example, the classes of high chiefs known as *ali`i nui* intermarried, ate the best fish and other foods that were *kapu* ("taboo") to commoners, and had the right to wear magnificent cloaks adorned with thousands of bright red and yellow bird feathers. Indeed, a *kapu* forbade commoners from approaching or even casting a shadow on the *ali`i nui*.

Polynesian Religion

High chiefs worked closely with priests, who served as intermediaries between human communities and the gods. Gods of war and agriculture were common throughout the Pacific islands, but individual islands and island groups recognized deities particular to their own regions and interests. The most distinctive architecture of early Pacific societies was the ceremonial precinct and temple structure known as *marae* (or *heiau* in Hawaiian). *Marae* often had several terraced floors with a rock or coral wall designating the boundaries of the sacred space. In Tonga and Samoa, temples made of timber and thatched roofs served as places of worship, sacrifice, and communication between priests and the gods, whereas in eastern Polynesia religious ceremonies took place on platforms in open-air courtyards. The largest of these structures, the *marae* Mahaiatea on Tahiti, took the form of a step pyramid about 15 meters (49 feet) high with a base measuring 81 by 22 meters (266 by 72 feet).

Pacific island societies, among the most isolated on earth before European mariners ventured into the Pacific Ocean, did not enjoy access to the range of technologies developed by continental peoples until the sixteenth and later centuries. Yet Pacific islanders cleverly exploited their environments, established productive agricultural economies, built elaborate, well-organized societies, and reached out when possible to engage in trade with their neighbors. Their achievements testify anew to the human impulses toward densely populated communities and interaction with other societies.

The Tahitian *marae* Mahaitea does not survive, but a drawing based on a sketch by an eighteenth-century English artist clearly shows that the temple was a massive structure that required considerable organization of labor by the chiefly and priestly classes. • New York Public Library, General Research Division, Astor, Lenox and Tilden Foundations

The original inhabitants of the Americas and Oceania lived in societies that were considerably smaller than those of the eastern hemisphere. They did not possess the metallurgical technologies that enabled their counterparts to exploit the natural environment, nor did they possess the transportation technologies based on wheeled vehicles and domesticated animals that facilitated trade and communication among peoples of the eastern hemisphere. Nevertheless, long before they entered into sustained interaction with European and other peoples, they built complex societies and developed sophisticated cultural and religious traditions. Indigenous peoples established foraging, fishing, and agricultural societies throughout the Americas, and they fashioned tools from wood, stone, and bone that enabled them to produce enough food to support sizable communities. In Mesoamerica and Andean South America, they also built large imperial states that organized public affairs on a large scale. The cultural and religious traditions of these imperial societies reflected their concern for agricultural production and the maintenance of complex social structures.

The original inhabitants of Australia and the Pacific islands built societies on a smaller scale than did the peoples of the Americas, but they too devised effective means of exploiting the natural environment and organizing flourishing communities. Australia was a continent of foraging nomadic peoples, whereas the Pacific islands supported densely populated agricultural societies. Although they had no communication with peoples of the Americas or the eastern hemisphere, the peoples of Oceania traded and interacted regularly with their neighbors and inhabitants of the Pacific islands sometimes undertook lengthy voyages to trade with distant island groups.

CHRONOLOGY

AMERICAS

950–1150	High point of the Toltec empire
1175	Collapse of the Toltec empire
1250	Inca settlement near Cuzco
1345	Foundation of Tenochtitlan by the Mexica
1400	Emergence of the five Iroquois nations
1428–1440	Reign of the Aztec ruler Itzcóatl
1438–1471	Reign of the Inca ruler Pachacuti
1440–1469	Reign of the Aztec ruler Motecuzoma I
1502–1520	Reign of the Aztec ruler Motecuzoma II
1519	Arrival of Spanish conquerors in Mexico

OCEANIA

Eleventh century	Beginning of population growth in Pacific islands
Twelfth century	Beginning of two-way voyages between Hawai`i and Tahiti and the Marquesas islands
Thirteenth century	Emergence of distinct social classes and chiefly states
Fourteenth century	Construction of fishponds in Hawai`i

FOR FURTHER READING

Peter Bellwood. *The Polynesians: Prehistory of an Island People.* Rev. ed. London, 1987. Well-illustrated popular account emphasizing the origins and early development of Polynesian societies.

Geoffrey Blainey. *Triumph of the Nomads: A History of Aboriginal Australia.* Melbourne, 1975. A sympathetic account of Australia before European arrival, well informed by recent archaeological discoveries.

Inga Clendinnen. *Aztecs: An Interpretation.* Cambridge, 1991. A brilliant recreation of the Mexica world, concentrating on cultural and social themes.

George A. Collier, Renato I. Rosaldo, and John D. Wirth, eds. *The Inca and Aztec States, 1400–1800: Anthropology and History.* New York, 1982. Seventeen well-focused essays represent approaches that scholars have recently taken to the Inca and Aztec empires.

Nigel Davies. *The Ancient Kingdoms of Mexico.* Harmondsworth, 1983. Popular account that reflects recent research.

Hans Dietrich Disselhoff. *Daily Life in Ancient Peru.* Trans. by A. Jaffa. New York, 1967. A well-illustrated volume concentrating on social history that places Inca society in larger historical context.

Ben Finney. *Voyage of Rediscovery: A Cultural Odyssey through Polynesia.* Berkeley, 1994. Fascinating account of efforts to understand ancient Polynesian techniques of seafaring and to chart the courses of Polynesian migrations.

Jesse D. Jennings, ed. *The Prehistory of Polynesia.* Cambridge, Mass., 1979. Brings together essays by prominent scholars on Polynesia before the arrival of Europeans in the Pacific Ocean.

Friedrich Katz. *The Ancient American Civilizations.* Trans. by K. M. L. Simpson. New York, 1972. Detailed survey that compares the experiences of Mesoamerica and Andean South America.

Patrick V. Kirch. *The Evolution of the Polynesian Chiefdoms.* Cambridge, 1984. Examines the development of Polynesian societies in light of recent archaeological discoveries.

Miguel León-Portilla. *The Aztec Image of Self and Society: An Introduction to Nahua Culture.* Salt Lake City, 1992. An excellent guide to Mexica social and cultural history by the foremost student of the Mexica.

David Lewis. *We, the Navigators: The Ancient Art of Landfinding in the Pacific.* Honolulu, 1973. Fascinating reconstruction of traditional methods of noninstrumental navigation used by seafaring peoples of the Pacific islands.

Alfred Métraux. *The History of the Incas.* Trans. by G. Ordish. New York, 1969. A well-illustrated and well-informed popular account.

Lynda Norene Shaffer. *Native Americans before 1492: The Moundbuilding Centers of the Eastern Woodlands.* Armonk, N.Y., 1992. Draws on recent research in placing the societies of mound-building peoples in larger historical context.

Muriel Porter Weaver. *The Aztecs, Maya, and Their Predecessors: Archaeology of Mesoamerica.* 3rd ed. New York, 1993. An up-to-date survey based on recent historical and archaeological research.

Eric Wolf. *Sons of the Shaking Earth.* Chicago, 1959. Thoughtful analysis of Mesoamerican history by a leading anthropologist and historian.

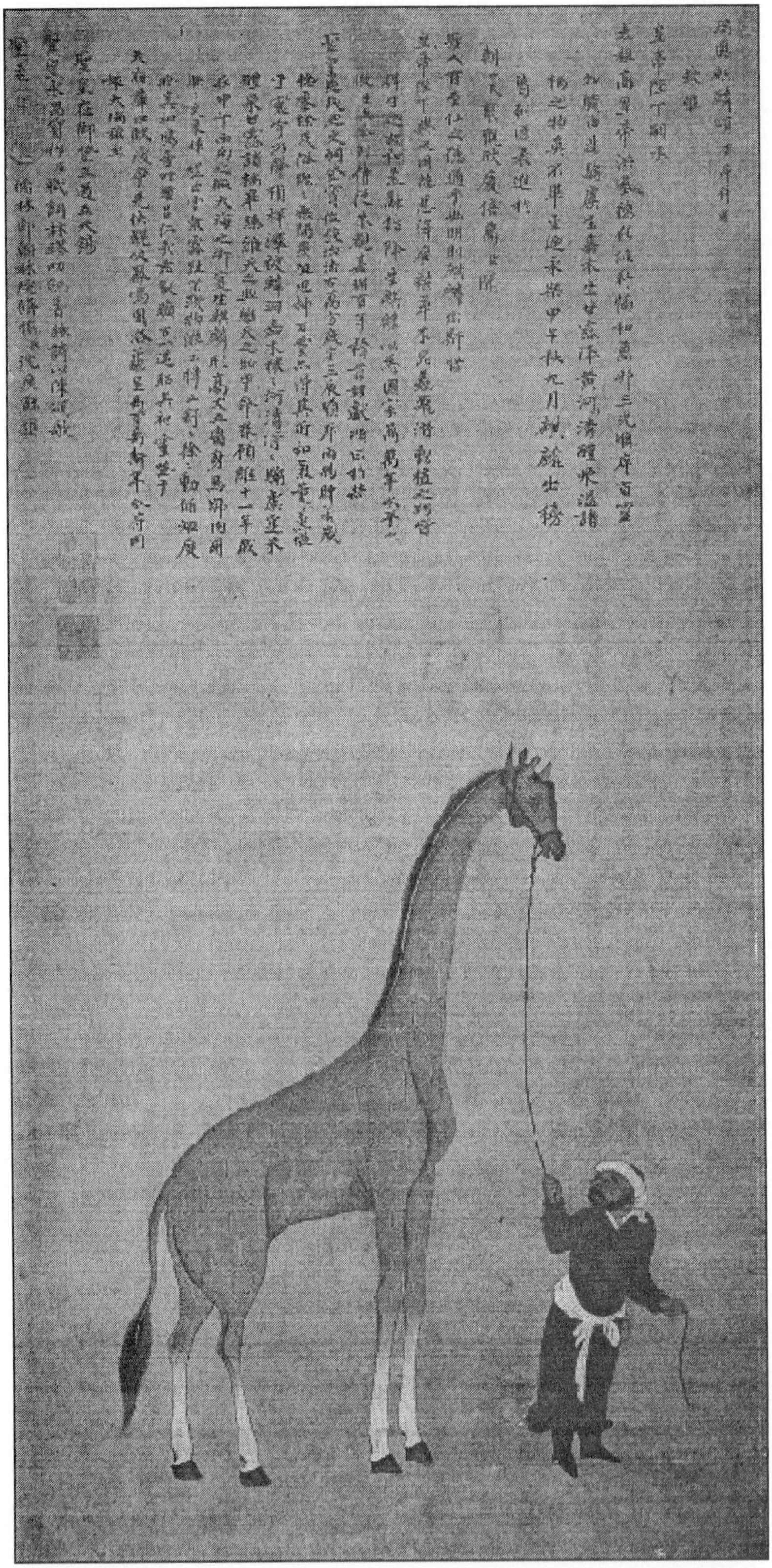

REACHING OUT: CROSS-CULTURAL INTERACTIONS

. . .

One of the great world travelers of all time was the Morrocan legal scholar Ibn Battuta. Born in 1304 at Tangier, Ibn Battuta followed family tradition and studied Islamic law. In 1325 he left Morocco, perhaps for the first time, to make a pilgrimage to Mecca. He traveled by caravan across north Africa and through Egypt, Palestine, and Syria, arriving at Mecca in 1326. After completing his hajj Ibn Battuta did not head for home, but spent a year visiting Mesopotamia and Persia; then he traveled by ship through the Red Sea and down the east African coast as far south as Kilwa. By 1330 he had returned to Mecca, but he did not stay there long. When he learned that the sultan of Delhi offered handsome rewards to foreign legal scholars, he set off for India. Instead of traveling there directly by sailing across the Arabian Sea, however, he followed a long and circuitous land route that took him through Egypt, Syria, Anatolia, Constantinople, the Black Sea, and the great trading cities of central Asia, Bokhara and Samarkand. Only in 1333 did he arrive in Delhi from the north.

For the next eight years, Ibn Battuta remained in India, serving mostly as a *qadi* (judge) in the government of Muhammad ibn Tughluq, the sultan of Delhi. In 1341 Muhammad appointed him to head an enormous embassy to China, but a violent storm destroyed the party's ships as they prepared to depart Calicut for the sea voyage to China. All personal goods and diplomatic presents sank with the ships, and many of the passengers drowned. (Ibn Battuta survived because he was on shore attending Friday prayers at the mosque when the storm struck.) For the next several years, Ibn Battuta made his way around southern India, Ceylon, and the Maldive Islands, where he served as a *qadi* for the recently founded Islamic sultanate, before continuing to China on his own about 1345. He visited the bustling southern Chinese port cities of Quanzhou and Guangzhou, where he found large communities of Muslim merchants, before returning to Morocco in 1349 by way of southern India, the Persian Gulf, Syria, Egypt, and Mecca.

Still Ibn Battuta's travels were not complete. In 1350 he made a short trip to the kingdom of Granada in southern Spain, and in 1353 he joined a camel caravan across the Sahara desert to visit the Mali empire, returning to Morocco in 1355.

A giraffe from east Africa sent as a present to China in 1414 and painted by a Chinese artist at the Ming zoo. • National Palace Museum, Taipei, Taiwan, Republic of China

During his travels Ibn Battuta visited the equivalent of forty-four modern countries and logged more than 117,000 kilometers (73,000 miles). His account of his adventures stands with Marco Polo's book among the classic works of travel literature.

Between 1000 and 1500 C.E., the peoples of the eastern hemisphere traveled, traded, communicated, and interacted more regularly and intensively than ever before. The large empires of the Mongols and other nomadic peoples provided a political foundation for this cross-cultural interaction. When they conquered and pacified vast regions, nomadic peoples provided safe roads for merchants, diplomats, missionaries, and other travelers. Quite apart from the nomadic empires, improvements in maritime technology led to increased traffic in the sea-lanes of the Indian Ocean and the South China Sea. As a result, long-distance travel became much more common than in earlier eras, and individual travelers like Ibn Battuta and Marco Polo sometimes ventured throughout much of the eastern hemisphere.

Merchants and travelers exchanged more than trade goods. They diffused technologies and spread religious faiths. They also exchanged diseases and facilitated the spread of pathogens that caused massive and deadly epidemics. During the middle decades of the fourteenth century, bubonic plague traveled the trade routes from western China to central Asia, southwest Asia, north Africa, and Europe. During its initial, furious onslaught, bubonic plague ravaged societies wherever it struck, and it continued to cause epidemics for three centuries and more.

Gradually, however, societies recovered from the plague. By the early fifteenth century, Chinese and western European peoples in particular had restabilized their societies and begun to renew cross-cultural contacts. In the European case, this effort had profound consequences for modern world history. As they sought entry to the markets of Asia, European mariners not only established direct connections with African and Asian peoples but also sailed to the western hemisphere and the Pacific Ocean. Their voyages established permanent, sustained contact between the indigenous peoples of the Americas and the Pacific islands and the peoples of the eastern hemisphere. Thus cross-cultural interactions of the period 1000 to 1500 pointed toward global interdependence, a principal characteristic of modern world history.

LONG-DISTANCE TRADE AND TRAVEL

Travelers embarked on long-distance journeys for a variety of reasons. Nomadic peoples ranged widely in the course of migrations and campaigns of conquest. East European and African slaves traveled involuntarily to the Mediterranean basin, southwest Asia, India, and sometimes even southern China. Buddhist, Christian, and Muslim pilgrims undertook extraordinary journeys to visit holy shrines. Three of the more important motives for long-distance travel between 1000 and 1500 C.E. were trade, diplomacy, and missionary activity. The cross-cultural interactions that resulted helped spread technological innovations throughout the eastern hemisphere.

Patterns of Long-Distance Trade

Merchants engaged in long-distance trade relied on two principal networks of trade routes. Luxury goods of high value relative to their weight, such as silk textiles and precious stones, often traveled overland on the silk roads used since classical times. Bulkier commodities, such as steel, stone, coral, and building materials, traveled the sea-lanes of the Indian Ocean, since it would have been unprofitable to transport them overland. The silk roads linked all of the Eurasian landmass, and trans-Saharan caravan routes drew west Africa into the larger economy of the eastern hemisphere. The sea-lanes of the Indian Ocean served ports in southeast Asia, India, Arabia, and east Africa, while also offering access via the South China Sea to ports in China, Japan, Korea, and the spice-bearing islands of southeast Asia. Thus, in combination, land and sea routes touched almost every corner of the eastern hemisphere.

The magnificent twelfth-century caravenserai at Tercan in eastern Anatolia provided food, lodging, and protection for merchants traveling with camels, donkeys, and horses. The Saljuqs built caravanserais throughout Anatolia. • Josephine Powell

Trading Cities

As the volume of trade increased, the major trading cities and ports grew rapidly, attracting buyers, sellers, brokers, and bankers from parts near and far. Khanbaliq (modern Beijing), Hangzhou, Quanzhou, Melaka, Cambay, Samarkand, Hormuz, Baghdad, Caffa, Cairo, Alexandria, Kilwa, Constantinople, Venice, Timbuktu, and many other cities had large quarters occupied by communities of foreign merchants. When a trading or port city enjoyed a strategic location, maintained good order, and resisted the temptation to levy excessive customs fees, it had the potential to become a major emporium serving long-distance trade networks. A case in point is Melaka (in modern Malaysia). Founded in the 1390s, within a few decades Melaka became the principal clearinghouse of trade in the eastern Indian Ocean. The city's authorities policed the strategic Strait of Melaka and maintained a safe market that welcomed all merchants and levied reasonable fees on goods exchanged there. By the end of the fifteenth century, Melaka had a population of some fifty thousand people, and in the early sixteenth century the Portuguese merchant Tomé Pires reported that more than eighty languages could be heard in the city's streets.

During the early and middle decades of the thirteenth century, the Mongols' campaigns caused economic disruption throughout much of Eurasia—particularly in China and southwest Asia, where Mongol forces toppled the Song and Abbasid dynasties. Mongol conquests inaugurated a long period of economic decline in southwest Asia where the conquerors destroyed cities and allowed irrigation systems to fall into disrepair. As the Mongols consolidated their hold on conquered lands, however, they laid the political foundation for a surge in long-distance trade along the silk roads. Merchants traveling the silk roads faced less risk of banditry or political turbulence than in previous times. Meanwhile, strong economies in China, India, and western Europe fueled demand for foreign commodities. Many merchants traveled the whole distance from Europe to China in pursuit of profit.

Marco Polo

The best-known long-distance traveler of Mongol times was the Venetian Marco Polo (1253–1324). Marco's father Niccoló and uncle Maffeo were among the first European merchants to visit China; between 1260 and 1269 they traveled and traded throughout Mongol lands, and they met Khubilai Khan as he was consolidating his hold on China. When they returned to China in 1271, seventeen-year-old

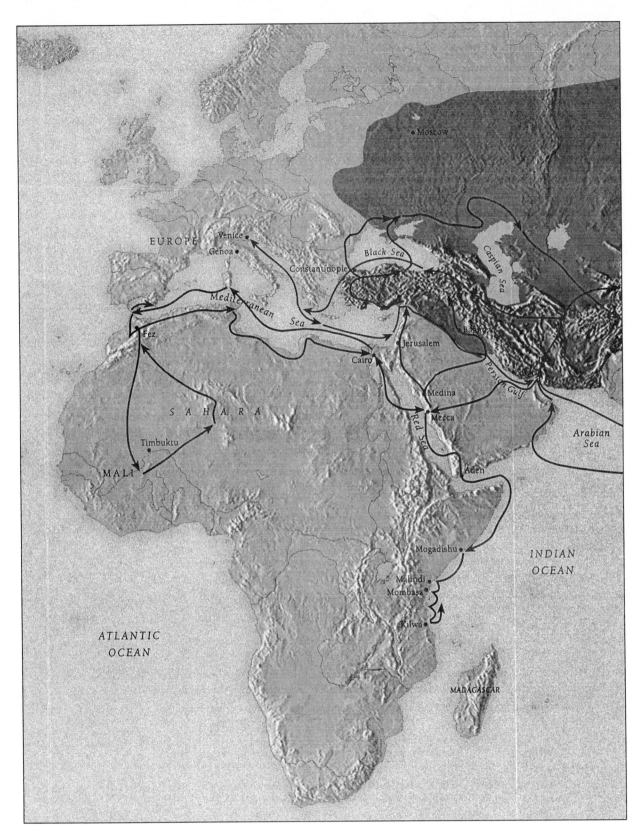

MAP [21.1]

Trade and travel during the Mongol era.

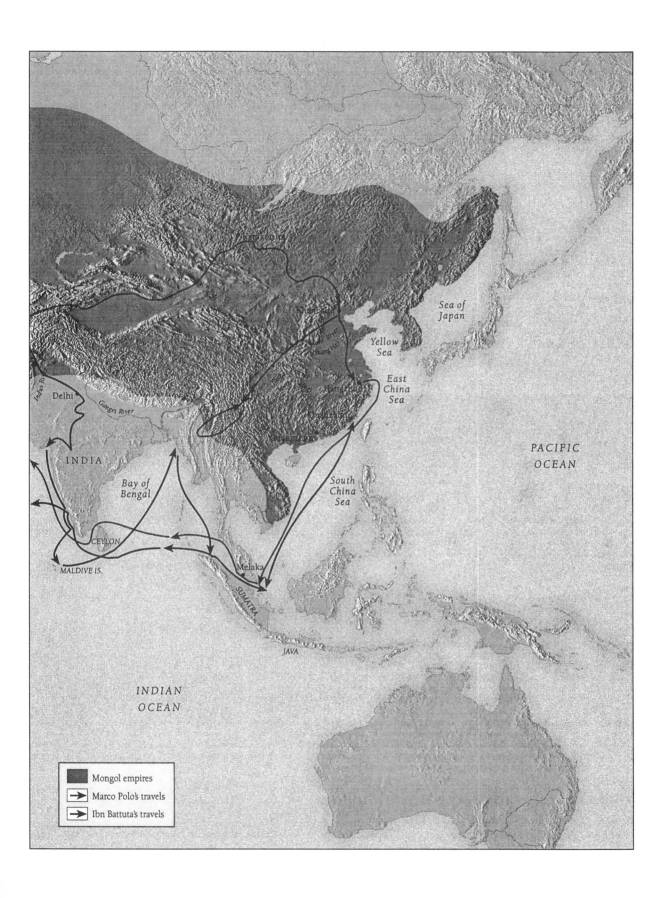

▨	Mongol empires
⬛➤	Marco Polo's travels
⬛➤	Ibn Battuta's travels

Delhi

INDIA

Indus R.

Ganges River

Bay of
Bengal

CEYLON

MALDIVE IS.

SUMATRA

Melaka

JAVA

INDIAN
OCEAN

Yellow
Sea

Sea of
Japan

East
China
Sea

South
China
Sea

PACIFIC
OCEAN

River
(Yang He)

An illumination from a fourteenth-century French manuscript depicts Marco Polo picking pepper with inhabitants in southern India. • Bibliothèque Nationale de France

Marco Polo accompanied them. The great khan took a special liking to Marco, who was a marvelous conversationalist and storyteller. Khubilai allowed Marco to pursue his mercantile interests in China and also sent him on numerous diplomatic missions, partly because Marco regaled him with stories about the distant parts of his realm. After seventeen years in China, the Polos decided to return to Venice, and Khubilai granted them permission to leave. They went back on the sea route by way of Sumatra, Ceylon, India, and Arabia, arriving in Venice in 1295.

A historical accident has preserved the story of Marco Polo's travels. After his return from China, Marco was captured and made a prisoner of war during a conflict between his native Venice and its commercial rival Genoa. While imprisoned, Marco related tales of his travels to his fellow prisoners. One of them was a writer of romances, and he compiled the stories into a large volume that circulated rapidly throughout Europe.

In spite of occasional exaggerations and tall tales, Marco's stories deeply influenced European readers. Marco always mentioned the textiles, spices, gems, and other goods he observed during his travels, and European merchants took note, eager to participate in the lucrative trade networks of Eurasia. The Polos were among the first Europeans to visit China, but they were not the last. In their wake came hundreds of others, mostly Italians. In most cases their stories do not survive, but their travels helped to increase European participation in the larger economy of the eastern hemisphere.

Political and Diplomatic Travel

Marco Polo came from a family of merchants, and merchants were among the most avid readers of his stories. Marco himself most likely collaborated closely with Italian merchants during his years in China. Yet his experiences also throw light on long-distance travel undertaken for political and diplomatic purposes. Khubilai Khan and the other Mongol rulers of China did not entirely trust their Chinese subjects and regularly appointed foreigners to administrative posts. In his account of his travels, Marco reported that Khubilai appointed him governor of the large trading city of Yangzhou. There is no independent evidence to confirm this claim, but Marco may well have filled some sort of administrative position. In addition, he represented Khubilai Khan's interests on diplomatic missions. To support himself in China, then, Marco supplemented his mercantile ventures with various official duties assigned to him by his patron, the great khan.

The emergence of elaborate trading networks and the establishment of vast imperial states created great demand for political and diplomatic representation during the centuries after 1000 C.E. The thirteenth century was a time of especially active diplomacy involving parties as distant as the Mongols and western Europeans, both of whom considered a military alliance against their common Muslim foes. As European Christians sought to revive the crusading movement and recapture Jerusalem from Muslim forces, the Mongols were attacking the Abbasid empire from the east. During the 1240s and 1250s, Pope Innocent IV dispatched a series of envoys who invited the Mongol khans to convert to Christianity and join Europeans in an alliance against the Muslims. The khans declined the invitation, proposing in reply that the pope and European Christians submit to Mongol rule or face destruction.

Mongol-Christian Diplomacy

Although the early round of Mongol-European diplomacy offered little promise of cooperation, the Mongols later initiated another effort. In 1287 the Mongol ilkhan of Persia planned to invade the Muslim-held lands of southwest Asia, capture Jerusalem, and crush Islam as a political force in the region. In hopes of attracting support for the project, he dispatched Rabban Sauma, a Nestorian Christian priest of Turkish ancestry, as an envoy to the pope and European political leaders.

Rabban Sauma

Rabban Sauma met with the kings of France and England, the pope, and other high officials of the Roman Catholic church. He enjoyed a fine reception, but he did not succeed in attracting European support for the ilkhan. Only a few years later, in 1295, Ghazan, the new ilkhan of Persia, converted to Islam, thus precluding any further possibility of an alliance·between the Mongols of Persia and European Christians. Nevertheless, the flurry of diplomatic activity illustrates the complexity of political affairs in the eastern hemisphere and the need for diplomatic consultation over long distances.

The expansion of Islamic influence in the eastern hemisphere encouraged a different kind of politically motivated travel. Legal scholars and judges played a crucial role in Islamic societies, since the *sharia* prescribed religious observances and social relationships based on the Quran. Conversions to Islam and the establishment of Islamic states in India, southeast Asia, and sub-Saharan Africa created a demand for Muslims educated in Islamic law. After about the eleventh century, educated Muslims from southwest Asia and north Africa regularly traveled to recently converted lands to help instill Islamic values.

Best known of the Muslim travelers was Ibn Battuta (1304–1369). Islamic rulers governed most of the lands Ibn Battuta visited—including India, the Maldive Islands, the Swahili city-states of east Africa, and the Mali empire—but very few Muslims educated in the law were available in those lands. With his legal credentials Ibn Battuta had little difficulty finding government positions. As *qadi* and advisor to the sultan of Delhi, he supervised the affairs of a wealthy mosque and heard cases at law, which he strictly enforced according to Islamic standards of justice. On one occasion Ibn Buttuta sentenced a man to receive eighty lashes because he had drunk wine eight years earlier.

Ibn Battuta

After leaving northern India, Ibn Battuta obtained a post as *qadi* in the Maldive Islands. There he heard cases at law and worked zealously to promote proper observance of Islam. He ordered lashings for men who did not attend Friday prayers, and he once sentenced a thief to lose his right hand in accordance with punishment prescribed by the *sharia*. He also attempted, unsuccessfully, to persuade island women to meet the standards of modesty observed in other Islamic lands by covering their breasts. In both east and west Africa, Ibn Battuta consulted with Muslim rulers and offered advice about government, women's dress, and proper relationships between the sexes. Like many other legal scholars whose stories went unrecorded, Ibn Battuta provided guidance in the ways of Islam in societies recently converted to the faith.

Missionary Campaigns

Sufi Missionaries

Islamic values spread not only through the efforts of legal scholars, but also through the missionary activities of Sufi mystics. As in the early days of Islam, Sufis ventured to recently conquered or converted lands and sought to win a popular following for the faith in India, southeast Asia, and sub-Saharan Africa. Sufis did not insist on a strict, doctrinally correct understanding of Islam, but rather emphasized piety and devotion to Allah. They even tolerated continuing reverence of traditional deities, whom the Sufis treated as manifestations of Allah and his powers. By taking a flexible approach to their missions, the Sufis spread Islamic values without facing the resistance that unyielding and doctrinaire campaigns would likely have provoked.

Christian Missionaries

The Mongols in China

Latin tombstone (1342) of Catherine Vilioni, Yang-chou

Caterina Vilioni, daughter of the Venetian merchant Domenico Vilioni, died in the Chinese trading city of Yangzhou in 1342. Her tombstone, which shows she was part of the Roman Catholic community in Yangzhou, came to light during a construction project in 1951. • Private Collection

Meanwhile, Roman Catholic missionaries also traveled long distances in the interests of spreading Christianity. Missionaries accompanied the crusaders and other forces to all the lands where Europeans extended their influence after the year 1000. In lands where European conquerors maintained a long-term presence—such as the Baltic lands, the Balkan region, Sicily, and Spain—missionaries attracted converts in large numbers, and Roman Catholic Christianity became securely established. In the eastern Mediterranean region, however, where crusaders were unable to hold their conquests permanently, Christianity remained a minority faith.

The most ambitious missions sought to convert Mongols and Chinese to Roman Catholic Christianity. Until the arrival of European merchants and diplomats in the thirteenth century, probably no Roman Catholic had ever ventured as far east as China. As more Europeans traveled to China, their expatriate communities created a demand for Roman Catholic services. Many of the

Roman Catholic priests who traveled to China probably intended to serve the needs of these communities, but some of them also sought to attract converts.

Most active of the Roman Catholic missionaries in China was John of Montecorvino, an Italian Franciscan who went to China in 1291, became the first archbishop of Khanbaliq in 1307, and died there in 1328. While serving the community of Roman Catholic expatriates in China, John worked energetically to establish Christianity in the host society. He translated the New Testament and the Book of Psalms into Turkish, a language commonly used at the Mongol court, and he built several churches in China. He took in young boys from Mongol and Chinese families, baptized them, and taught them Latin and Roman Catholic rituals. By 1305 he claimed to have baptized six thousand individuals, and he invited the great khan himself to convert to Christianity. Although popular and widely respected among Europeans, Chinese, and Mongols alike, John attracted few Asian peoples to Christianity.

John of Montecorvino

Roman Catholic authorities in Europe dispatched many other priests and missionaries to China during the early fourteenth century, but like John of Montecorvino, they won few converts. Missions successfully established Christian communities in Scandinavia, eastern Europe, Spain, and the Mediterranean islands that European armies recaptured from Muslims during the centuries after 1000 C.E., but east Asia was too distant for the resources available to the Roman church. Nevertheless, missions to China continued until the mid-fourteenth century, when the collapse of the Mongol's Yuan dynasty and the eruption of epidemic disease temporarily disrupted long-distance travel across Eurasia.

Agricultural and Technological Diffusion

Large numbers of long-distance travelers facilitated agricultural and technological diffusion during the period from 1000 to 1500. Indeed, technological diffusion sometimes facilitated long-distance travel itself. The magnetic compass, for example, invented in China during the Tang or Song dynasty, spread throughout the Indian Ocean basin during the eleventh century, and by the mid-twelfth century European mariners used compasses in the Mediterranean and the Atlantic Ocean. Diffusion of the compass was a boon to maritime trade, since it allowed mariners to sail over long stretches of deep water with confidence in their ability to find their destinations and return home safely.

Long-distance journeys enabled Muslim travelers to introduce new food and commercial crops to sub-Saharan Africa. Food crops included citrus fruits and Asian strains of rice, which enriched diets in west Africa after the eleventh century. Muslims also introduced cotton to west Africa, and by 1100 cotton fabrics had become popular with the ruling elites and wealthy merchants of the west African kingdoms. Cotton grew well in the savannas, and by 1500 it was the principal textile produced in sub-Saharan Africa.

Spread of Crops

Muslims were also instrumental in the continuing diffusion of sugarcane. Muslim merchants and other travelers had begun large-scale cultivation of sugarcane in southwest Asia and north Africa during the Abbasid caliphate. They experimented with the plant in west Africa but had limited success because of adverse environmental conditions.

Sugarcane

After the twelfth century, however, Muslims facilitated the westward spread of sugarcane by acquainting European crusaders with crystallized sugar refined from cane. Up to that time Europeans had little access to refined sugar, and they relied on honey and fruits as sweeteners. They immediately appreciated the convenience

JOHN OF MONTECORVINO ON HIS MISSION IN CHINA

• • •

The Franciscan John of Montecorvino (1247–1328) served as a Roman Catholic missionary in Armenia, Persia, and India before going to China in 1291. There he served as priest to expatriate European Christians, and he sought to attract converts to Christianity from the Mongol and Chinese communities. In a letter of 8 January 1305 asking for support from his fellow Franciscans in Italy, John outlined some of his activities during the previous thirteen years.

[After spending thirteen months in India] I proceeded on my further journey and made my way to China, the realm of the emperor of the Mongols who is called the great khan. To him I presented the letter of our lord the pope and invited him to adopt the Catholic faith of our Lord Jesus Christ, but he had grown too old in idolatry. However, he bestows many kindnesses upon the Christians, and these two years past I have gotten along well with him. . . .

I have built a church in the city of Khanbaliq, in which the king has his chief residence. This I completed six years ago; and I have built a bell tower to it and put three bells in it. I have baptized there, as well as I can estimate, up to this time some 6,000 persons. . . . And I am often still engaged in baptizing.

Also I have gradually bought one hundred and fifty boys, the children of pagan parents and of ages varying from seven to eleven, who had never learned any religion. These boys I have baptized, and I have taught them Greek and Latin after our manner. Also I have written out Psalters for them, with thirty hymnals and breviaries [prayer books]. By help of these, eleven of the boys already know our service and form a choir and take their weekly turn of duty as they do in convents,

whether I am there or not. Many of the boys are also employed in writing out Psalters and other suitable things. His Majesty the Emperor moreover delights much to hear them chanting. I have the bells rung at all the canonical hours, and with my congregation of babes and sucklings I perform divine service, and the chanting we do by ear because I have no service book with the notes. . . .

Indeed if I had but two or three comrades to aid me, it is possible that the emperor khan himself would have been baptized by this time! I ask then for such brethren to come, if any are willing to come, such I mean as will make it their great business to lead exemplary lives. . . .

I have myself grown old and grey, more with toil and trouble than with years, for I am not more than fifty-eight. I have got a competent knowledge of the language and script which is most generally used by the Tartars. And I have already translated into that language and script the New Testament and the Psalter and have caused them to be written out in the fairest penmanship they have, and so by writing, reading, and preaching, I bear open and public testimony to the law of Christ.

SOURCE: Henry Yule and Henri Cordier, eds. *Cathay and the Way Thither,* 4 vols. London: Hakluyt, 1913–16, 3:45–50. (Translation slightly modified.)

of refined sugar. Italian entrepreneurs began to organize sugarcane plantations on Mediterranean islands such as Sicily, Cyprus, Crete, and Rhodes. Rapidly increasing demand for refined sugar encouraged investors to seek suitable locations throughout the Mediterranean basin. The cultivation of sugarcane had deep social and economic implications. Besides influencing local economic development in lands where it spread, it touched distant societies as well. Like their Muslim predecessors, European sugar producers often staffed their plantations with slave laborers, and the growth of plantations fueled an increasing demand for Muslim war captives and black Africans who could supply labor services.

English forces besiege a French citadel during the Hundred Years' War (1337–1453). Note that the besiegers on the left side of this manuscript illustration employ cannons and smaller firearms that launch gunpowder bombs. • © The British Library

Gunpowder Technologies

Although Muslim merchants and travelers were especially prominent agents of diffusion, Mongols also contributed to the process, notably by helping to spread gunpowder technologies west from China. Mongol invaders learned about gunpowder from Chinese military engineers in the early thirteenth century and soon incorporated gunpowder-based weapons into their arsenal: as early as 1214 Chinggis Khan's armies included an artillery unit. During the 1250s, as they campaigned in Persia and southwest Asia, the Mongols used catapults and trebuchets to lob gunpowder bombs into cities under siege. Muslim armies soon developed similar weapons in response.

By 1258 gunpowder had reached Europe—possibly by way of Mongol-ruled Russia—and Europeans had begun to experiment with gunpowder-fueled rockets. By the early fourteenth century, armies from China to Europe possessed primitive cannons. Although not especially accurate, the weapons were powerful enough to blow holes in the defensive walls of cities under siege. Thus with the assistance of Mongol warriors, gunpowder technology rapidly spread from its homeland in China across the entire Eurasian landmass.

Agricultural and technological diffusions of the era 1000 to 1500 were by no means unique processes in world history. For millennia agricultural crops and technological skills had spread widely whenever peoples of different societies interacted with one another. Because of the particularly intense interactions of the period from 1000 to 1500, however, agricultural and technological diffusion profoundly influenced the lives of peoples throughout the eastern hemisphere. The spread of food crops enriched diets and supported increasing populations while the spread of industrial crops like cotton promoted economic development. The diffusion of the magnetic compass enabled mariners to sail the seas more safely and effectively, and the spread of gunpowder technology changed forever the nature of war.

 ## CRISIS AND RECOVERY

As Eurasian peoples traveled over long distances, they not only exchanged trade goods, agricultural crops, and technological expertise, but also unwittingly helped disease pathogens to spread. When diseases broke out among previously unexposed populations, they often caused massive epidemics that severely disrupted whole societies. During the fourteenth century bubonic plague erupted in epidemics that ravaged societies throughout most of Asia, Europe, and north Africa. Epidemic plague struck intermittently until the seventeenth century, but by the fifteenth century Chinese and western European societies had begun to recover from its effects and wield their influence in the larger world.

Bubonic Plague

Bubonic plague spread from the Yunnan region of southwestern China where it probably had been endemic for centuries. The plague bacillus infects rodents such as rats, squirrels, and prairie dogs, and fleas transmit the pathogen from one rodent to another. If rodent populations decline, fleas seek other hosts and sometimes spread the disease to human victims. In the early fourteenth century, Mongol military campaigns helped plague spread from Yunnan to China's interior: an epidemic of 1331 reportedly killed 90 percent of the population in Hebei province in northeastern China, near modern Beijing. During the 1350s epidemics broke out in widely scattered regions of China, and contemporaries reported that plague carried away two-thirds of the population in some afflicted areas.

Spread of Plague   During the 1340s Mongols, merchants, and other travelers helped to spread the disease along trade routes to points west of China. It thrived in the oases and trading cities of central Asia where domestic animals and rodents provided abundant breeding grounds for fleas and the plague bacillus. By 1346 it had reached the Black Sea ports of Caffa and Tana. In 1347 Italian merchants fled plague-infected Black Sea ports and unwittingly spread the disease throughout the Mediterranean basin. By 1348, following the trade routes, plague had sparked epidemics in most of western Europe.

Wherever it appeared, bubonic plague struck with frightful effects. Victims developed inflamed lymph nodes particularly in the neck, armpit, and groin areas, and most died within a few days after the onset of symptoms. Internal hemorrhaging often discolored the inflammations known as buboes—which gave rise to the term *bubonic* plague—and because of the black or purple swellings, Europeans referred to plague as the "Black Death." Bubonic plague typically killed 60 to 70 percent of its human victims and had the potential to ravage a society within a few months. In some small villages and towns, disease wiped out the entire population. A spate of new births generally followed outbreaks of plague as societies tried to replenish their numbers, but plague also returned and claimed new victims. In Europe plague erupted intermittently from the 1340s until the late seventeenth century.

Some parts of the eastern hemisphere did not suffer directly from plague epidemics. Scandinavia and India seem to have escaped the plague's worst effects. In fact, Indian population grew from 91 million in the year 1300 to 97 million a century later and 105 million in 1500. Epidemics also largely bypassed sub-Saharan Africa, even though plague had long been endemic in the Great Lakes region of east Africa.

In this painting survivors tend to plague victims in medieval Europe, as a new victim with swollen lymph glands on his neck collapses from the disease's effects. • The Walters Art Gallery, Baltimore

Population Decline

In lands hard hit by plague, however, it took a century and more to begin recovery from the demographic consequences of epidemic disease. In 1300 China's population, already reduced by conflicts with the Mongols since the early thirteenth century, stood at eighty-five million. In 1400, after about seventy years of epidemic plague, Chinese numbers amounted to only seventy-five million. A century later demographic recovery was underway, and China's population rebounded to one hundred million. European society also reeled from the effects of bubonic plague. From seventy-nine million in 1300, European population dropped by almost 25 percent to sixty million in 1400. As in China, demographic recovery was underway in 1500 when European population climbed to eighty-one million. Islamic societies in southwest Asia, Egypt, and north Africa also suffered devastating population losses, and demographic recovery took much longer there than in China and Europe. In Egypt human population probably did not reach preplague levels until the nineteenth century.

Social and Economic Effects

Because of the heavy demographic toll that it levied, bubonic plague disrupted societies and economies throughout Eurasia and north Africa. Epidemics killed the young, the weak, and the old in especially high numbers, but they spared no group. Peasants and laborers, artisans and craftsmen, merchants and bankers, priests and nuns, rulers and bureaucrats all fell before the plague's onslaught. The disease caused massive labor shortages, which in turn generated social unrest. In western Europe, for example, workers demanded higher wages, and many left their homes in search of better working conditions. Political authorities responded by freezing wages and forbidding workers to leave their homes. The result was a series of rebellions in both rural and urban settings by disgruntled workers. Authorities eventually extinguished the revolts but only after considerable social disruption and loss of life.

By the seventeenth century the plague had lost much of its ferocity. Epidemics occurred more sporadically, and they did not seriously diminish human populations. Since the 1940s antibiotic drugs have brought the disease largely under control among human populations, although it survives in rodent communities throughout much of the world.

Recovery in China: The Ming Dynasty

In 1368, as bubonic plague raged in China, the Mongols' Yuan dynasty collapsed, leaving China in a state of both demographic and political turmoil. An increasing birthrate soon helped to replenish human numbers. Political recovery accompanied the demographic rebound.

Hongwu

When the Yuan dynasty fell, the Mongols left China and returned to the steppes, leaving the governance of the land once again in Chinese hands. The new emperor came from a family so poor that he spent much of his youth as a beggar. Orphaned, he entered a Buddhist monastery to assure himself of food, clothing, and shelter. Because of his size and strength, he came to the notice of military commanders, and he made his way through the ranks to lead the rebellious forces that toppled the Yuan dynasty. In 1368 he became Emperor Hongwu, and he proclaimed the establishment of the Ming ("brilliant") dynasty, which lasted until 1644.

Ming Centralization

Hongwu immediately set about eliminating all traces of Mongol rule and establishing a government on the model of traditional Chinese dynasties. Like the founders of several earlier Chinese dynasties, Hongwu had little interest in scholarly matters, but he reestablished the Confucian educational and civil service systems to ensure a supply of talented officials and bureaucrats. At the same time he moved to centralize authority more tightly than ever before in Chinese history. In 1380, when he suspected his chief minister of involvement in a treasonous plot, Hongwu executed the minister and his bureaucratic allies and also abolished the minister's position altogether. From that time forward the Ming emperors ruled directly, without the aid of chief ministers, and they closely supervised imperial affairs.

The Ming emperors insisted on absolute obedience to the policies and initiatives of the central government. They relied heavily on the mandarins, a special class of powerful officials sent out as emissaries of the central government to ensure that local officials implemented imperial policy. The Ming emperors also turned to eunuchs for governmental services. Earlier Chinese emperors, as well as rulers of other lands, had long relied on eunuchs, since they could not generate families and build power bases that might challenge ruling houses. In keeping with their centralizing policy, however, the Ming emperors employed eunuchs much more extensively than any of their predecessors, in the expectation that servants whose fortunes depended exclusively on the emperors' favor would work especially diligently to advance the emperors' interests.

Mandarins and Eunuchs

The employment of mandarins and eunuchs enhanced the authority of the central government. The tightly centralized administration instituted by the early Ming emperors lasted more than five hundred years. Although the dynasty fell in 1644 to Manchu invaders, who founded the Qing dynasty, the Manchus retained the administrative framework of the Ming state, which largely survived until the collapse of the Qing dynasty in 1911.

While building a centralized administration, the Ming emperors also worked toward economic recovery from nomadic rule and epidemic disease. The new rulers conscripted laborers to rebuild irrigation systems that had fallen into disrepair during the previous century, and agricultural production surged as a result. At the same time they promoted the manufacture of porcelain, lacquerware, and fine silk and cotton textiles. They did not actively promote trade with other lands, but private Chinese merchants eagerly sought commercial opportunities and conducted a thriving business marketing Chinese products in ports and trading cities from Japan to the islands of southeast Asia. Meanwhile, domestic trade surged within China, reflecting increasing productivity and prosperity.

Economic Recovery

Alongside political and economic recovery, the Ming dynasty also sponsored a kind of cultural revival in China. Emperor Hongwu tried to eradicate all signs of the recent nomadic occupation by discouraging the use

Cultural Revival

Ming craftsmen won worldwide fame for their blue-and-white porcelain, which inspired the founders of the Delft porcelain factory in the Netherlands. This covered jar dates from the early fifteenth century. • Photograph courtesy of the Royal Ontario Museum © ROM

of Mongol names and the wearing of Mongol dress. Ming emperors actively promoted Chinese cultural traditions, particularly the Confucian and neo-Confucian schools. Hongwu's successor Yongle organized the preparation of a vast encyclopedia that compiled all significant works of Chinese history, philosophy, and literature. This *Yongle Encyclopedia* ran to almost twenty-three thousand manuscript rolls, each equivalent to a medium-size book. The government originally planned to issue a printed edition of the encyclopedia, but abandoned the project because of its enormous expense. Nevertheless, the *Yongle Encyclopedia* was a remarkable anthology, and it signaled the Ming rulers' interest in supporting native Chinese cultural traditions.

Recovery in Western Europe: State Building

Demographic recovery strengthened states in western Europe as it did in China. In Europe, however, political authority rested with a series of regional states rather than a centralized empire. By the late fifteenth century, states in Italy, Spain, France, and England had devised techniques of government that vastly enhanced their power.

During the later middle ages (1300–1500), internal problems as well as bubonic plague complicated European political affairs. The Holy Roman Empire survived in name, but after the mid-thirteenth century effective authority lay with the German princes and the Italian city-states rather than the emperor. In Spain descendants of Muslim conquerors held the kingdom of Granada in the southern portion of the Iberian peninsula. The kings of France and England sparred constantly over lands claimed by both. Their hostilities eventually resulted in the Hundred Years' War (1337–1453), a protracted series of intermittent campaigns in which the warring factions sought control of lands in France.

Taxes and Armies   By the late fifteenth century, however, regional states in western Europe had greatly strengthened their societies, and some had also laid the foundations for the emergence of powerful monarchies. The state-building efforts of the later middle ages involved two especially important elements. The first was the development of fresh sources of finance, usually through new taxes levied directly on citizens and subjects, which supplemented the income that rulers received from their feudal subordinates. The second was the maintenance of large standing armies, often composed of mercenary forces and equipped with gunpowder weapons, supported by state funds.

Italian States   The state-building process began in Italy, where profits from industrial production and trade enriched the major cities. The principal Italian states—the city-states of Milan, Venice, and Florence, the papal state based in Rome, and the kingdom of Naples—needed large numbers of officials to administer their complex affairs. They also needed ready access to military forces that could protect their interests. Beginning as early as the thirteenth century, the Italian city-states financed these needs by levying direct taxes and issuing long-term bonds that they repaid from treasury receipts. With fresh sources of finance, the principal Italian states strengthened their authority within their own boundaries and between them controlled public affairs in most of the Italian peninsula.

France and England   During the fourteenth and fifteenth centuries, Italian administrative methods made their way beyond the Alps. Partly because of the enormous expenses they incurred during the Hundred Years' War, the kings of France and England began to levy direct taxes and assemble powerful armies. The French kings taxed sales, hearths, and salt; their English counterparts instituted annual taxes on hearths, individuals, and plow teams. Rulers in both lands asserted the authority of the central government over the feudal nobility. The English kings did not establish a standing army, but they were able to raise powerful forces when rebellion threatened public order. In France, however, King Louis XI (reigned 1461–1483) maintained a permanent army of about fifteen thousand troops, many of them professional mercenary soldiers equipped with firearms. Because the high expense of maintaining such forces was beyond the means of the nobility, Louis and his successors enjoyed a decisive edge over ambitious feudal subordinates seeking to challenge royal authority or build local power bases.

The process of state building was most dramatic in Spain where the marriage in 1469 of Fernando of Aragon and Isabel of Castile united the two wealthiest and most important Iberian realms. Receipts from the sales tax, the primary source of royal income, supported a powerful standing army. Under Fernando and Isabel, popularly known as the Catholic Kings, Christian forces completed the *reconquista* by conquering the kingdom of Granada and absorbing it into their state. The Catholic Kings also projected their authority beyond Iberia. When a French army threatened the kingdom of Naples in 1494, they seized southern Italy, and by 1559 Spanish forces had established their hegemony throughout most of the Italian peninsula. Fernando and Isabel also sought to make a place for Spain in the markets of Asia by sponsoring Christopher Columbus's quest for a western route to China.

Spain

Competition between European states intensified as they tightened their authority in their territories. This competition led to frequent small-scale wars between European states, and it encouraged the rapid development of military and naval technology. As states sought technological advantages over their neighbors, they encouraged the refinement and improvement of weapons, ships, and sails. When one state acquired powerful weapons—such as personal firearms or ships equipped with cannons—neighboring states sought more advanced devices in the interests of security. Thus technological innovations vastly strengthened European armies just as they began to venture again into the larger world.

Recovery in Western Europe: The Renaissance

Demographic recovery and state-building efforts in western Europe coincided with a remarkable cultural flowering known as the Renaissance. The French word *renaissance* means "rebirth," and it refers to a revival of interest in the arts and learning that took place from the fourteenth to the sixteenth century and that reflected the continuing development of a sophisticated urban society in western Europe. Painters, sculptors, and architects of the Renaissance era drew inspiration from classical Greek and Roman artists rather than from their medieval predecessors. They admired the convincing realism of classical sculpture and the stately simplicity of classical architecture. In their efforts to revive classical aesthetic standards, they transformed European art. Meanwhile, Renaissance scholars known as humanists looked to classical rather than medieval literary models, and they sought to update medieval moral thought and adapt it to the needs of a bustling urban society.

Just as they pioneered new techniques of statecraft, the Italian city-states also sponsored Renaissance innovations in art and architecture. In search of realistic depictions, Italian artists studied the human form and represented the emotions of their subjects. Italian painters like Masaccio (1401–1428) and Leonardo da Vinci

Italian Renaissance Art

The Last Supper, a fresco painted by Leonardo da Vinci in the dining hall of a monastery in Milan about 1495, depicts Jesus' last meal with his disciples before Roman authorities executed him by crucifixion. The receding walls and ceiling in the banquet scene illustrate Leonardo's reliance on the technique of linear perspective in designing this painting. • Scala/Art Resource, NY

(1452–1519) relied on the technique of linear perspective to represent the three dimensions of real life on flat, two-dimensional surfaces. Sculptors like Donatello (1386–1466) and Michelangelo Buonarotti (1475–1564) sought to depict their subjects in natural poses that reflected the actual workings of human muscles rather than in the awkward and rigid postures often found in earlier sculptures.

Renaissance Architecture   Renaissance architects designed buildings in the simple, elegant style preferred by their classical Greek and Roman predecessors. Their most impressive achievement was the construction of domed buildings—awesome structures that enclosed large spaces but kept them open and airy under massive domes. Roman architects had built domes, but their technology and engineering did not survive the collapse of the Roman empire. Inspired by the Pantheon, a handsome Roman temple constructed in the second century C.E., the Florentine architect Filippo Brunelleschi (1377–1446) reinvented equipment and designs for a large dome. During the 1420s and 1430s, he oversaw the construction of a magnificent dome on the cathedral of Florence. Residents of Florence took Brunelleschi's dome as a symbol of the city's wealth and its leadership in artistic and cultural affairs.

Like Renaissance artists and architects, scholars and literary figures known as humanists also drew inspiration from classical models. The term *humanist* referred to scholars interested in the humanities—literature, history, and moral philosophy. They had nothing to do with the secular and often antireligious interests of movements that go under the name humanism today: to the contrary, Renaissance humanists were deeply committed to Christianity. Several humanists worked diligently to prepare accurate texts and translations of the New Testament and other important Christian writings. Most notable of them was Desiderius Erasmus of Rotterdam (1466–1536), who in 1516 published the first edition of the Greek New Testament along with a revised Latin translation and copious annotations. Other humanists drew inspiration from the intense spirituality and high moral standards of early Christianity and promoted those values in their own society.

Brunelleschi's magnificent dome on the cathedral of Florence dominates the city's skyline even today. • Sylvain Grandadam/Photo Researchers, Inc.

The Humanists

Humanists scorned the dense and often convoluted writing style of the scholastic theologians. Instead they preferred the elegant and polished language of classical Greek and Roman authors and the early church fathers, whose works they considered more engaging and more persuasive than the weighty tomes of medieval philosophers and theologians. Thus humanists such as the Florentine Francesco Petrarca (1304–1374) traveled throughout Europe searching for manuscripts of classical works. In the monastic libraries of Italy, Switzerland, and southern France, they found hundreds of Latin writings that medieval scholars had overlooked. During the fifteenth century Italian humanists became acquainted with Byzantine scholars and enlarged the body of classical Greek as well as Latin works available to scholars.

Humanist Moral Thought

Classical Greek and Latin values encouraged the humanists to reconsider medieval ethical teachings. Medieval moral philosophers had taught that the most honorable calling was that of monks and nuns who withdrew from the world and dedicated their lives to prayer, contemplation, and the glorification of God, but the humanists drew inspiration from classical authors like Cicero, who demonstrated that it was possible to lead a morally virtuous life while participating actively in the affairs of the world. Renaissance humanists argued that it was perfectly honorable for Christians to enter into marriage, business relationships, and public affairs, and they offered a spirited defense for those who rejected the cloister in favor of an active life in society. Humanist moral thought thus represented an effort to reconcile Christian values and ethics with the increasingly urban and commercial society of Renaissance Europe.

EXPLORATION AND COLONIZATION

As peoples of the eastern hemisphere recovered from demographic collapse and restored order to their societies, they also sought to revive the networks of long-distance trade and communication that epidemic plague had disrupted. Most active in this effort were China and western Europe—the two societies that recovered most rapidly from the disasters of the fourteenth century. During the early Ming dynasty, Chinese ports accommodated foreign traders, and mariners mounted a series of enormous naval expeditions that visited almost all parts of the Indian Ocean basin. Meanwhile, Europeans ventured from the Mediterranean into the Atlantic Ocean, which served as a highway to sub-Saharan Africa and the Indian Ocean basin. By the end of the fifteenth century, Europeans not only had established sea-lanes to India but also had made several return voyages to the American continents, thus inaugurating a process that brought all the world's peoples into permanent and sustained interaction.

The Chinese Reconnaissance of the Indian Ocean Basin

Having ousted the Mongols, the early Ming emperors were not eager to have large numbers of foreigners residing in China. Yet the emperors permitted foreign merchants to trade in the closely supervised ports of Quanzhou and Guangzhou, where they obtained Chinese silk, porcelain, and manufactured goods in exchange for pearls, gems, spices, cotton fabrics, and exotic products like tortoise shells and animal skins. The early Ming emperors also refurbished the large Chinese navy built during the Song dynasty, and they allowed Chinese merchants to participate in overseas trading ventures in Japan and southeast Asia.

Zheng He's Expeditions   Moreover, for almost thirty years, the Ming government sponsored a series of seven massive naval expeditions designed to establish a Chinese presence in the Indian Ocean basin. Emperor Yongle organized the expeditions for two main purposes: to impose imperial control over foreign trade with China and to impress foreign peoples with the power and might that the Ming dynasty had restored to China. Indeed, he might well have hoped to extend the tributary system, by which Chinese dynasties traditionally recognized foreign peoples, to lands in the Indian Ocean basin.

The expeditions took place between 1405 and 1433. Leading them was the eunuch admiral Zheng He, a Muslim from Yunnan in southwestern China who rose through the ranks of eunuch administrators to become a trusted advisor of Yongle. Zheng He embarked on each voyage with an awesome fleet of vessels complemented by armed forces large enough to overcome resistance at any port where the expedition called. On the first voyage, for example, Zheng He's fleet consisted of 317 ships accompanied by almost twenty-eight thousand armed troops. Many of these vessels were mammoth, nine-masted "treasure ships" with four decks capable of accommodating five hundred or more passengers, as well as massive stores of cargo. Measuring up to 124 meters (408 feet) long and 51 meters (166 feet) wide, these treasure ships were by far the largest marine craft the world had ever seen.

On the first three voyages, Zheng He took his fleet to southeast Asia, India, and Ceylon. The fourth expedition went to the Persian Gulf and Arabia, and later expeditions ventured down the east African coast, calling at ports as far south as Malindi in modern Kenya. Throughout his travels Zheng He liberally dispensed gifts of Chinese silk, porcelain, and other goods. In return he received rich and unusual presents from his hosts, including African zebras and giraffes that ended their days in the Ming imperial zoo. Zheng He and his companions paid respect to the local deities and customs they encountered, and in Ceylon they erected a monument honoring Buddha, Allah, and Vishnu.

Zheng He generally sought to attain his goals through diplomacy. For the most part his large contingents of armed troops overawed his hosts, and he had little need to engage in hostilities. But a contemporary reported that Zheng He walked like a tiger, and he did not shrink from violence when he considered it necessary to impress foreign peoples with China's military might. He ruthlessly suppressed pirates who had long plagued Chinese and southeast Asian waters. He also intervened in a civil disturbance in order to establish his authority in Ceylon, and he made displays of military force when local officials threatened his fleet in Arabia and east Africa. The seven expeditions established a Chinese presence and reputation in the Indian Ocean basin. Returning from his fourth voyage, Zheng He brought envoys from thirty states who traveled to China and paid their respects at the Ming court.

Chinese Naval Power

Yet suddenly, in the mid-1430s, the Ming emperors decided to end the expeditions. Confucian ministers, who mistrusted Zheng He and the eunuchs who supported the voyages, argued that resources committed to the expensive expeditions would go to better uses if devoted to agriculture. Moreover, during the 1420s and 1430s the Mongols mounted a new military threat from the northwest, and land forces urgently needed financial support.

End of the Voyages

Thus in 1433, after Zheng He's seventh voyage, the expeditions ended. Chinese merchants continued to trade in Japan and southeast Asia, but imperial officials destroyed most of the nautical charts that Zheng He had carefully prepared and gave up any plans to maintain a Chinese presence in the Indian Ocean. The decommissioned treasure ships sat in harbors until they rotted away, and Chinese craftsmen forgot the technology of building such large vessels. Yet Zheng He's voyages demonstrated clearly that China could exercise military, political, and economic influence throughout the Indian Ocean basin.

European Exploration in the Atlantic and Indian Oceans

As Chinese fleets reconnoitered the Indian Ocean, European mariners were preparing to enter both the Atlantic and the Indian Ocean basins. Unlike Zheng He and his companions, Europeans did not venture onto the seas in the interests of diplomacy or in hopes of establishing a political and military reputation in foreign lands. Instead, they acted on two different but complementary motives: the desire to expand the boundaries of Roman Catholic Christianity and the desire to profit from commercial opportunities.

The experience of Portugal illustrates this mixture of motives. Though Portuguese merchants were not especially prominent in trading circles, Portuguese fishermen had a long tradition of seafaring in the stormy Atlantic Ocean. Building on this experience, Portuguese mariners emerged as the early leaders in both Atlantic exploration and the search for a sea route to Asian markets through the Indian Ocean. During the fifteenth century Prince Henrique of Portugal, often called Prince Henry the Navigator, embarked on an ambitious campaign to spread

Portuguese Exploration

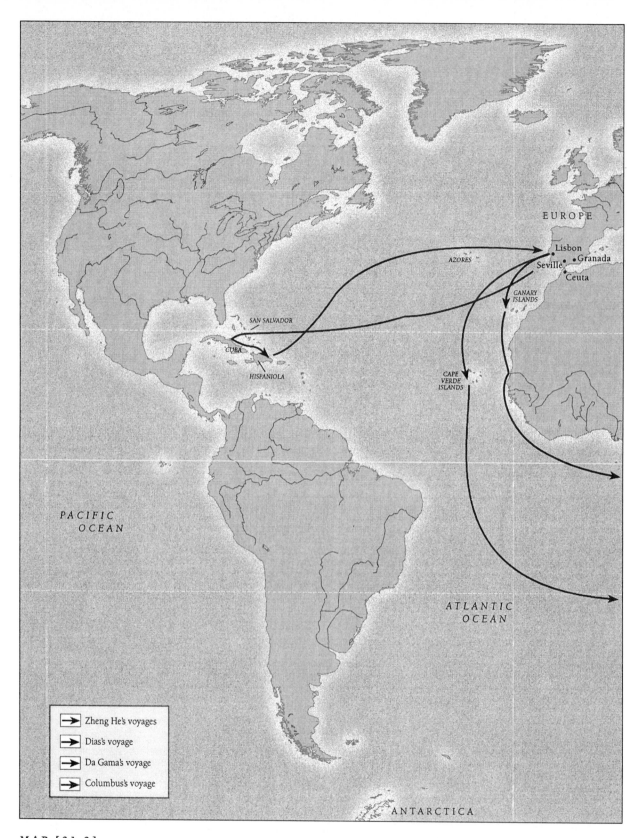

MAP [21.2]

Chinese and European voyages of exploration.

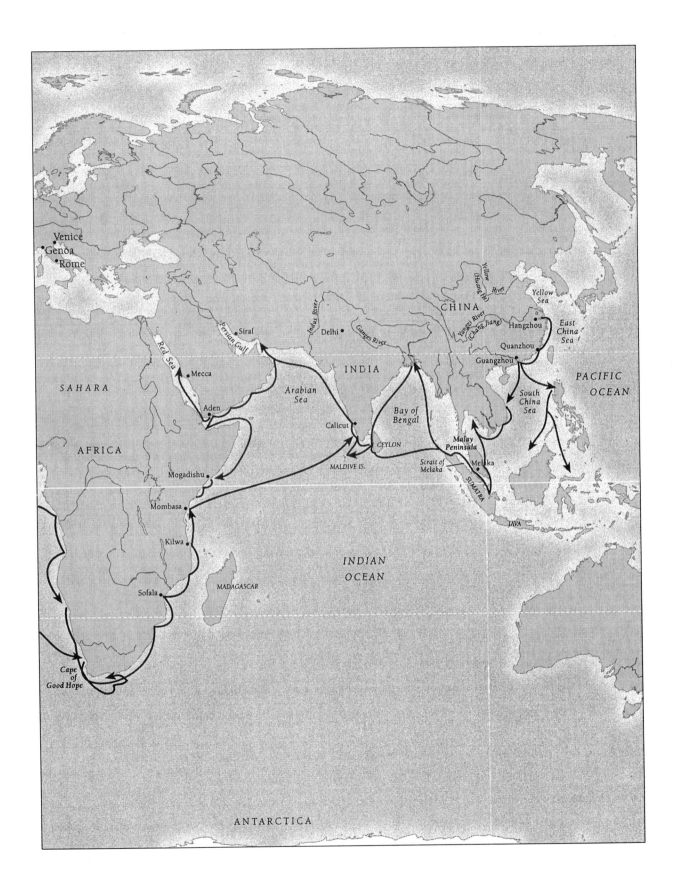

Christianity and increase Portuguese influence on the seas. In 1415 he seized the Moroccan city of Ceuta, which guarded the Strait of Gibraltar from the south. He regarded his victory both as a blow against Islam and as a strategic move enabling Christian vessels to move freely between the Mediterranean and the Atlantic.

Colonization of the Atlantic Islands

Following the capture of Ceuta, Henrique encouraged Portuguese mariners to venture into the Atlantic. During their voyages they discovered the Madeiras and Azores Islands, all uninhabited, which they soon colonized. They also made an unsuccessful effort to occupy the Canary Islands, inhabited by indigenous peoples but claimed since the early fifteenth century by the kingdom of Castile. Later discoveries included the Cape Verde islands, Fernando Po, São Tomé, and Principe off the west African coast. Since these Atlantic islands enjoyed fertile soils and a Mediterranean climate, Portuguese entrepreneurs soon began to cultivate sugarcane there, often in collaboration with Italian investors. Italians had financed sugar plantations in the Mediterranean islands since the twelfth century, and their commercial networks provided a ready means to distribute sugar to Europeans who were rapidly developing a taste for sweets.

Slave Trade

During the middle decades of the fifteenth century, a series of Portuguese fleets also explored the west African coast, each expedition proceeding a bit further than its predecessor. Originally, the Portuguese traded guns, textiles, and other manufactured items for African gold and slaves. Portuguese traders took full advantage of the long-established African commerce in slaves, but they also changed the nature of the slave trade by dramatically increasing its volume and by sending slaves to new destinations. By the mid-fifteenth century the Portuguese dispatched thousands of slaves annually from their forts on the African coast and offshore islands. They delivered most of their human cargo to recently founded plantations in the Atlantic islands, where the slaves worked as laborers, although some worked as domestic servants in Europe. The use of African slaves to perform heavy labor on commercial plantations soon became common practice, and it fueled the development of a huge, Atlantic-wide trade that delivered as many as twelve million enslaved Africans to destinations in North America, South America, and the Caribbean region.

Indian Ocean Trade

While some Portuguese mariners traded profitably in west Africa, others sought to enter the lucrative trade in Asian silk and spices. A sea route to Asian markets would enable Portuguese merchants to avoid Muslim and Italian middlemen, through whom almost all Asian luxury goods reached European markets, and participate directly in the flourishing commercial world of the Indian Ocean basin. Toward the end of the fifteenth century, Portuguese mariners began to search seriously for a sea-lane from Europe around Africa and into the Indian Ocean. By 1488 Bartolomeu Dias had sailed around the Cape of Good Hope and entered the Indian Ocean. Restless because of the long journey and distance from home, the crew forced Dias to return immediately to Portugal, but his voyage proved that it was possible to sail from Europe to the Indian Ocean. In 1497 Vasco da Gama departed Portugal with the intention of sailing to India. After rounding the Cape of Good Hope, he cruised up the east African coast and found a Muslim pilot who showed him how to take advantage of the seasonal monsoon winds to sail across the Arabian Sea to India. In 1498 he arrived at Calicut, and by 1499 he had returned to Lisbon with a hugely profitable cargo of pepper and spices.

For most of the following century, Portuguese merchants and mariners dominated trade between Europe and Asia. Indeed, they attempted to control all shipping in the Indian Ocean. Their ships, armed with cannons, were able to overpower the vessels of Arabs, Persians, Indians, southeast Asians, and others who sailed the Indian Ocean. They did not have enough ships to oversee all trade in the region,

Although Christopher Columbus believed that he had sailed into Asian waters, later mariners soon realized that the Americas were continents unknown to geographers of the eastern hemisphere. This map, prepared in 1532 by the German cartographer Sebastian Münster, shows that by the early sixteenth century European geographers had acquired a rough but accurate understanding of South America but had reconnoitered only the Atlantic coastline of North America • Photo courtesy of the Royal Ontario Museum © ROM

but the entry of Portuguese mariners into the Indian Ocean signaled the beginning of European imperialism in Asia.

Christopher Columbus

While Portuguese seafarers sought a sea route around Africa to India, the Genoese mariner Cristóforo Colombo, known in English as Christopher Columbus, conceived the idea of sailing west to reach Asian markets. Because geographers in the eastern hemisphere knew nothing of the Americas, Columbus's notion made a certain amount of good sense, although many doubted that his plan could lead to profitable trade because of the long distances involved. After the king of Portugal declined to sponsor an expedition to test Columbus's plan, the Catholic Kings, Fernando and Isabel of Spain, agreed to underwrite a voyage. In 1492 Columbus set sail. After a stop in the Canary Islands to take on supplies and make repairs, his fleet of three ships crossed the Atlantic Ocean, reaching land at San Salvador (Watling Island) in the Bahamas.

Columbus returned to Spain without the gold, silk, and spices that he had expected to find, but he persistently held that he had reached islands near the Asian mainland and the markets of China and Japan. Although he made three more voyages to the Caribbean region, Columbus never acknowledged that his expeditions had not reached Asia. News of his voyages spread rapidly, however, and by the end of the fifteenth century other mariners had explored the Caribbean and the American continents enough to realize that the western hemisphere constituted a world apart from Europe, Asia, and Africa.

As European mariners ventured into the Indian and Atlantic Ocean basins, they unwittingly inaugurated a new era in world history. For millennia peoples of different societies had traded, communicated, and interacted. As technologies of transportation improved, they dealt with peoples at increasingly greater distances. By 1500 the Indian Ocean served as a highway linking peoples from China to east Africa, and overland traffic kept the silk roads busy from China to the Mediterranean Sea. Trade goods, diplomatic missions, religious faiths, technological skills, agricultural crops, and disease pathogens all moved readily over the sea-lanes and the silk roads, and they profoundly influenced the development of societies throughout the eastern hemisphere. In the western hemisphere trading networks linked lands as distant as Mexico and the Great Lakes region while Pacific islanders regularly traveled and traded between island groups.

Never before, however, had peoples of the eastern hemisphere, the western hemisphere, and Oceania dealt with each other on a regular and systematic basis. The voyages of European mariners during the fifteenth and following centuries initiated a long-term process—one that continues in the present day—that brought all regions and peoples of planet earth into permanent and sustained interaction. The formation and reconfiguration of global networks of power, communication, and exchange that followed from these interactions rank among the most prominent themes of modern world history.

CHRONOLOGY

1214	Creation of a Mongol artillery unit
1253–1324	Life of Marco Polo
1287–1288	Rabban Sauma's embassy to Europe
1291–1328	John of Montecorvino's mission to China
1304–1369	Life of Ibn Battuta
1304–1374	Life of Francesco Petrarca
1330s	First outbreaks of bubonic plague in China
1347	Arrival of bubonic plague in the Mediterranean basin
1337–1453	Hundred Years' War
1368–1644	Ming dynasty
1405–1433	Zheng He's expeditions in the Indian Ocean
1466–1536	Life of Desiderius Erasmus of Rotterdam

FOR FURTHER READING

Janet L. Abu-Lughod. *Before European Hegemony: The World System, A.D. 1250–1350.* New York, 1989. An important study of long-distance trade networks during the Mongol era.

Jerry H. Bentley. *Humanists and Holy Writ: New Testament Scholarship in the Renaissance.* Princeton, 1983. Examines Renaissance humanists' efforts to prepare accurate texts, translations, and commentaries on the New Testament.

———. *Old World Encounters: Cross-Cultural Contacts and Exchanges in Pre-Modern Times.* New York, 1993. Studies cultural and religious exchanges in the eastern hemisphere before 1500 C.E.

Luce Boulnois. *The Silk Road*. Trans. by D. Chamberlain. New York, 1966. Popular account of trade and travel over the silk roads.

K. N. Chaudhuri. *Asia before Europe: Economy and Civilisation of the Indian Ocean from the Rise of Islam to 1750*. Cambridge, 1990. Controversial and penetrating analysis of economic, social, and cultural structures shaping societies of the Indian Ocean basin.

———. *Trade and Civilisation in the Indian Ocean: An Economic History from the Rise of Islam to 1750*. Cambridge, 1985. Brilliant analysis of the commercial life of the Indian Ocean basin by a prominent scholar.

Philip D. Curtin. *Cross-Cultural Trade in World History*. Cambridge, 1984. Ground-breaking analysis of patterns of long-distance trade concentrating on merchant communities in foreign lands.

Christopher Dawson, ed. *Mission to Asia*. Toronto, 1980. Translations of travel accounts and letters by European missionaries in central Asia and China during the Mongol era.

Michael W. Dols. *The Black Death in the Middle East*. Princeton, 1977. Careful, scholarly investigation of bubonic plague and its effects in southwest Asia.

Ross E. Dunn. *The Adventures of Ibn Battuta: A Muslim Traveler of the 14th Century*. Berkeley, 1986. Fascinating reconstruction of Ibn Battuta's travels and experiences.

Mark Elvin. *The Pattern of the Chinese Past*. Stanford, 1973. Brilliant analysis of Chinese history concentrating on social and economic developments.

Felipe Fernández-Armesto. *Before Columbus: Exploration and Colonisation from the Mediterranean to the Atlantic, 1229–1492*. London, 1987. Scholarly survey of early European ventures in the Atlantic Ocean.

Robert S. Gottfried. *The Black Death: Natural and Human Disaster in Medieval Europe*. New York, 1983. The best general study of bubonic plague and its effects in Europe.

Margaret L. King. *Women of the Renaissance*. Chicago, 1991. A lively and imaginative discussion of women's roles and experiences in Renaissance Europe.

Louise L. Levathes. *When China Ruled the Seas: The Treasure Fleet of the Dragon Throne, 1405–1433*. New York, 1994. Excellent popular account of Zheng He's voyages.

William H. McNeill. *Plagues and Peoples*. Garden City, N.Y., 1976. A pioneering study of infectious and contagious diseases and their effects in world history.

Lauro Martines. *Power and Imagination: City States in Renaissance Italy*. New York, 1979. An attractive and thoughtful analysis of the Italian Renaissance.

Arnold Pacey. *Technology in World Civilization: A Thousand-Year History*. Oxford, 1990. A brief and insightful study that concentrates on processes of technological diffusion.

J. R. S. Phillips. *The Medieval Expansion of Europe*. Oxford, 1988. Surveys European ventures into the larger world during the high and late middle ages.

William D. Phillips, Jr. and Carla Rahn Phillips. *The Worlds of Christopher Columbus*. New York, 1992. The best general work on Christopher Columbus.

Marco Polo. *The Travels*. Trans. by R. Latham. Harmondsworth, 1958. An accurate translation of Marco Polo's work based on reliable scholarship.

CREDITS

...

TEXT

Chapter 1

From: Richard E. Leakey, *The Making of Mankind,* pp 18, 20. Copyright 1981, Rainbird Publishing Group.

Chapter 2

From: James Pritchard, *Ancient Near Eastern Texts Relating to the Old Testament.* Copyright 1955 by Princeton University Press. Reprinted by permission of Princeton University Press.

Chapter 3

Ralph T. Griffith, trans. *The Hymns of the Rigveda,* 4 vols. 2/e (Benares: E.J. Lazarus, 1889–92), 4:289–93. F. Max Muler, trans., *The Upanishads,* 2 vols. (London: Oxford University Press, 1900), 1:101, 104–105.

Chapter 4

James Legge, trans. *The Chinese Classics,* 5 vols. (London: Henry Frowde, 1893), 4:12–13.; James Legge, trans. *The Chinese Classics,* 5 vols. (London: Henry Frowde, 1893), 4:171–72; James Legge, trans. *The Chinese Classics,* 5 vols. (London: Henry Frowde, 1893). 4:250–53.

Chapter 5

Reprinted with the permission of Simon & Schuster from *POPOL VUH* by Dennis Tedlock. Copyright (c) 1985 by Dennis Tedlock.

Chapter 6

D.J. Irani, *The Divine Songs of Zarathushtra.* London: George Allen & Unwin, 1924.

Chapter 7

James Legge, trans., *The Chinese Classics,* 7 vols. (Oxford: Clarendon Press, 1893): 1:45, 146, 152, 254, 258–59, 266. Lionel Giles, trans., *The Sayings of Lao Tzu* (London: John Murray, 1905), pp 26, 29–30, 41, 50.

Chapter 8

The Bhagavad Gita, trans., by Kashinalh Tnimbak Telang, in F. Max Muller, ed., *The Sacred Books of the East,* vol. 8 (Oxford: Clarendon Press, 1908), p 45–48.

Chapter 9

F.J. Church, trans., *The Trial and Death of Socrates,* 2/e London: Macmillan, 1886), p 76–78.

Chapter 10

Matthew 5:3–13, 5:38–45, 6:7–12 (Authorized version).

Chapter 11

Wilhelm von Hartel, ed. S. *Thasci Cecili Cypriani Opera Omnia in Corpus Scriptorum Ecclesiasticorum Latinorum* (Vienna, 1868), vol. 3, p 305–306. Translation by Jerry Bentley.

Chapter 12

Benjamin of Trudela, *The Itinerary of Benjamin of Trudela,* trans. by M.N. Adler (London: H. Frowde, 1907).

Chapter 13

The Qur'an. 2 vols. Trans. by E.H. Palmer. Oxford: Clarendon Press, 1880, 2:328–29, 2:341, 2:80–81. Benjamin of Trudela, *The Itinerary of Benjamin of Trudela,* trans. by M.N. Adler (London: H. Frowde, 1907), p. 35–42.

Chapter 14

Gabriel Ferrand, trans. *Voyage du Merchand Arabe Sulayman en Inde et en Chine.* Paris, 1922, p 45, 53–54, 60–61. Translated into English by Jerry Bentley.

Chapter 15

Cosmas Indicopleustes, *The Christian Topography of Cosmas, an Egyptian Monk.* Trans. by J.W. McCrindle, (London: Hakluyt Society, 1897), p 364–72.

Chapter 16

Gregory of Tours, *History of the Franks,* trans. by E. Biehaut (New York: Columbia University Press, 1916), p 39–41.

Chapter 17

Marco Polo, *The Book of Ser Marco Polo,* 3/e. trans. and ed/by Henry Yule and Henri Cordier (London: John Murray, 1921), p 260–63.

Chapter 18

George McCall Theal, *Records of South-Eastern Africa,* 9 vols. (London: William Clowes and Sons, 1989–1903), 6:233–35.

Chapter 19

Henry Yule and Henri Cordier, eds. *Cathay and the Way Thither,* 2/e, 4 vols., (London: Hakluyt Society, 1913–1916), 3:151–55.

Chapter 20

Bernal Diaz del Castillo, *The True History of the Conquest of New Spain,* 5 vols., trans. by A.P. Maudslay (London: Hakluyt Society, 1910), 2:37; *Bernardino de Sahagun,* Florentine Codex: General History of the Things of New Spain, 13 vols., trans. by Charles E. Dibble and Arthur J.O. Anderson. Copyright 1982. Reprinted by permission of the University of Utah Press and the School of American Research.

Chapter 21

Henry Yule and Henri Cordier, eds. *Cathay and the Way Thither,* 2/e, 4 vols., (London: Hakluyt Society, 1913–1916), 3:45–50.